The
Chinese
Market
Economy

The Chinese Market Economy

1000–1500

William Guanglin Liu

SUNY
PRESS

Cover image is from Wikimedia Commons and is a detail of the Chinese cityscape handscroll *Along the River During Qingming Festival*, ink and colors on silk, 25.5 × 525 cm.

Published by State University of New York Press, Albany

© 2015 State University of New York

For information, contact State University of New York Press, Albany, NY
www.sunypress.edu

Production, Diane Ganeles
Marketing, Fran Keneston

Library of Congress Cataloging-in-Publication Data

Liu, William Guanglin.
    The Chinese market economy, 1000–1500 / William Guanglin Liu.
        pages cm
    Includes bibliographical references and index.
    ISBN 978-1-4384-5567-9 (hardcover : alk. paper)
    ISBN 978-1-4384-5568-6 (paperback : alk. paper)
    ISBN 978-1-4384-5569-3 (e-book)
    1. China—Economic conditions—To 1644.   2. China—Economic policy—To 1644.   3. China—Commerce—History—To 1500.   I. Title.
    HC427.6.L5828 2015
    330.951'02—dc23   2014017092

10 9 8 7 6 5 4 3 2 1

Contents

Illustrations

Maps

Figures

Tables

Acknowledgments

This book is dedicated to Professor Dwight H. Perkins. Although I alone am responsible for the analysis in the text, I could not have undertaken this study without his mentorship at Harvard. Dwight encouraged and supervised my Ph.D. thesis writing when I attempted to exploit certain historical data I found from the extant sources. Needless to say, his research on Chinese economic history, especially his work on Chinese agricultural development from 1368 on, laid the very foundation of my current project.

I benefited from the help of many individuals and institutes and it is a pleasure to have this opportunity to express my appreciation. My gratitude first goes to Professor Peter K. Bol, who is the most inspiring teacher I have met, and Professors Philip Kuhn, Jeffrey Williamson and other faculty members at Harvard graduate school. I am also grateful to the Harvard-Yenching Institute for supporting my graduate study, and to the Harvard-Yenching Library for allowing me a wonderful research experience. In preparing this book, I have benefited throughout these years from discussions and associations with many teachers, friends, and colleagues. I cannot adequately acknowledge the valuable suggestions and comments on my written work and presentations that have been given so generously by so many scholars over the past decade. In particular I would like to thank Professor Peter Lindert, Philip Hoffman, Patrick K. O'Brien, Kevin O'Rouke, Charles Hartman, Peter Perdue, Kenneth Pomeranz, Richard von Glahn, Ma Keyao, Cao Shuji, Wu Songdi, Liang Keng-yao, Bozhong Li, James C. Lee, James Kung. The National Science Foundation and NBER provided a grant for the collection of raw data that was crucial in developing this project. I shall thank the HKUST, my home institute, and the Research Grant Committee of Hong Kong for their generous support that allowed me to spend time in Boston conducting research to finalize my manuscript. I am also indebted to Chen Zhang and Anne NG, who patiently read through the manuscript to give invaluable editing advices. Nancy Ellegate and Diane Ganeles at the SUNY Press guided me through the whole review, editorial and publication process.

Finally, my deepest debt of thanks goes to my wife Hanrui Wang. This book could not have been conceived or completed without her constant loving support.

W. G. L.

Dynasties, Events, and Equivalents

I. Dynasties and Events

The Chinese Dynasties

Tang (618–907)
Song (960–1279):
    Northern Song (960–1127)
    Southern Song (1127–1279)
Yuan, the rule of Mongols in China (1271–1368)
Ming (1368–1644)
Early Ming (1368–1450)
Qing (1644–1911)

The An-Lushan Rebellion (755–763)
The Mongol Conquest of China (1211–1276)

II. Weights and Capacity

Weights: picul (*dan* 担) is a unit of weight equal to 100 catties (*jin* 斤) or 50 kg.

1 picul (*dan*) = 100 catties (*jin*) = 50 kg
1 catty (*jin*) = 16 taels (*liang* 兩) = 500 g = 1.1 pounds
20 picul (*dan*) = 1 metric ton
2,000 catties = 1 metric ton

1 Tang *jin* = 670 g
1 Song *jin* = 640 g
1 Yuan *jin* = 620 g
1 Ming *jin* = 590 g
1 Qing *jin* = 590 g

1 tael (*liang* 兩) = 10 *qian* (錢) = 100 *fen* (分) = 37.3 g

1 Song tael = 40 g
1 Ming tael = 36.9 g
1 Qing tael = 37.3 g

Volumes:

Grain

Shi (石) is the basic unit of traditional Chinese volume measurement for grain: 1 *shi* equals 100 liters; 1 *shi* of husked rice usually weighs 150 catties (*jin* 斤), 75 kg., or 1.5 piculs; 1 *shi* of wheat equals 140 catties (*jin*) or 70 kg.

1 *shi* (石) = 100 liters = 22 English gallons
1 *shi* (石) = 10 *dou* (斗) = 100 *sheng* (升)
1 *sheng* = 1 liter

1 Song *shi* = 0.67 *shi* = 67 liters
1 Yuan *shi* = 0.95 *shi* = 95 liters
1 Ming *shi* = 1.0 *shi* = 100 liters
1 Qing *shi* = 1.0 *shi* = 100 liters

Textiles: for handmade cotton cloth, 1 bolt (*pi* 匹) is the basic unit.

1 bolt = 3.63 square yards
1 bolt of cotton cloth weights 0.375 pounds

Li (里) is the basic unit of traditional Chinese measurement for distance.

1 *li* = 0.3107 mile
1 Sui *li* = 415 meters
1 Tang *li* = 450 meters
1 Song *li* = 465 meters
1 Ming *li* = 510 meters
1 Qing *li* = 510 meters

Mu (畝) is the basic unit of traditional Chinese land measurement.

1 *mu* = 0.1647 acre
1 *qing* (頃) = 100 *mu* = 16.4737 acres

1 Song *mu* = 0.1399 acre
1 Yuan *mu* = 0.1399 acre
1 Ming *mu* = 0.1434 acre
1 Qing *mu* = 0.1518 acre

III. Units of Currencies

Silver:

Tael (*liang* 兩) is the basic unit of traditional Chinese silver measurement: 1 tael of silver is about 37.68 g of silver.

1 tael of silver = 37.68 g of silver
1 metric ton of silver = 26,000 taels of silver
100,000 taels of silver = 3.846 metric ton of silver
1 Song tael of silver = 40 g
1 Ming tael of silver = 36.9 g

Coin:

Wen (文) is the smallest unit of traditional Chinese coins: Usually 1 bronze coin is worth 1 *wen*; 1,000 *wen* equals 1 string of cash (1 貫 or 1 緡). In the Song, 1 string of cash often contained fewer coins but was rated as equivalent to a full string of 1,000 coins due to severe shortages of coin. The Song government established the official "short string" (*shengbo* 省陌) at 770 coins per string of cash.

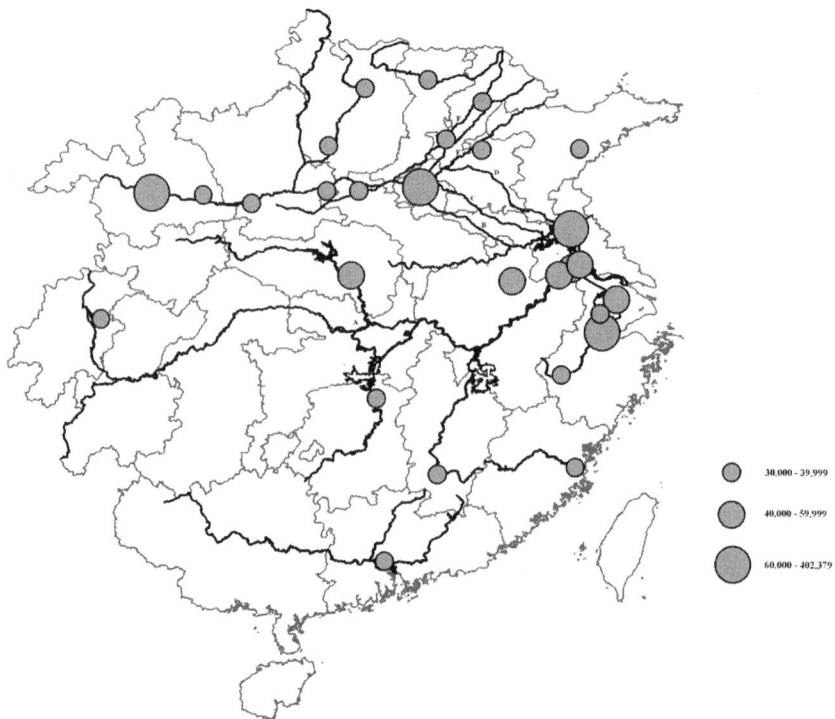

Map 1. Water routes and long-distance trade in Song China, ca. 1077 AD

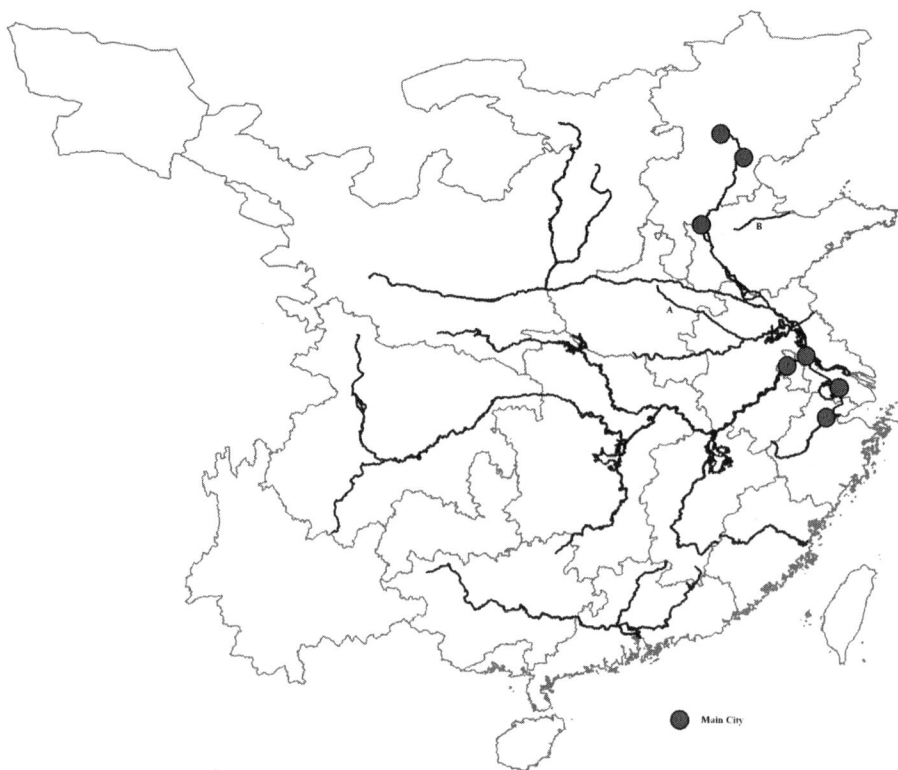

Map 2. Water routes and long-distance trade in late sixteenth-century China

Introduction

After the Chinese government adopted economic policies toward an open market in the 1980s, this country has maintained a spectacular record in both market expansion and economic growth over the past thirty years. China is expected to be the largest market economy in the world in two decades. For the social scientist, this is an astonishingly successful story of development in our world. But viewed from a historical perspective, China is only regaining her leading position in the world economy that she had achieved a millennium ago. China's unusual market development challenges any historical theorization that presumes a linear economic progression. Hence, the historical account of the drastic rise and fall of her market economy from 1000 to 1500 becomes an essential chapter in world history.

Market expansion after 750 AD significantly transformed the Chinese economy and society. Toward the end of the eleventh century, China reached an unprecedented high level of commercial and income development under a state that relied on market forces in key areas of its governance. The Mongol conquest of China (1206–1279) and the subsequent rise of an autocratic regime in early Ming China from 1368 onward were the most devastating events that led to the lasting deterioration of her market economy until the mid-1500s. Consequently, the estimated living standards of the prosperous Lower Yangtze region dropped at least 50 percent between 1080 and 1400.

The economy of imperial China was a complicated system for its massive territory and population. Although the territory controlled by the Song dynasty was the smallest in comparison to any other major unifying dynastic regimes over the past two millennia, it is a magnificent political economy entity when measured by European standards. The estimated size is about 2.6 million square kilometers, as large as nearly five times that of modern France, the latter being the largest country in Western Europe.[1] The population in Song China already reached 100 million at the dawn of the twelfth century. By the modern standard achieved in industrialized civilization, the technology exploited in the handcrafts industries, the commercialization of agriculture, and the integration in the traditional Chinese economy were at a primary stage of development. Nonetheless, people were not always living self-sufficient lives isolated from each other. By the eleventh century, Chinese society was rather mobile and its economy much integrated. One can name a few contributing factors: Woodblock printing made it much easier for the spread of knowledge and technology, the economy was substantially monetized with sufficient supply of bronze coins, water transportation developed due to the building of canals and the application of technical innovations to the ship industry, among other advances; the market was thus expanding rapidly. Nonetheless, it is difficult for a contemporary reader to imagine a market economy that flourished a millennium ago. To help the reader appreciate the markets of traditional China, I begin with a visual tour of a temporarily and spatially distanced urban center.

The first scene for our trip is the scroll of *Qingming shanghe tu* ("Upper river during the Qingming festival," abbreviated hereafter as the Qingming scroll), a panoramic painting by Song dynasty artist Zhang Zeduan (1085–1145).[2] It is the single most widely known work in China and an iconic painting in the world. Despite its well-known reputation as China's *Mona Lisa*,[3] the Qingming scroll presents an image of commoners in an urban scene rather than a portrait of a single individual. The scroll depicts a total of 814 people, 28 boats, 60 draft animals, 30 buildings, 20 vehicles, 9 sedan chairs, and 170 trees. People from all professions are represented: peddlers, jugglers, actors, beggars, alms-seeking monks, fortune tellers and seers, waiters, doctors, innkeepers, bookkeepers and pawnbrokers, millers, metalworkers, carpenters, masons, teachers and scholars, and a few officials.

The scroll captures rich and firsthand information of urban life in preindustrial China: We can see on the street loads of coal moving by pack animals such as donkeys and mules that were necessary supplies for over a million residents in the winter; restaurants, wine bars, and inns of all kinds; and wheeled wagons and sedan chairs. Just at the corner of the city gate, a tax officer guarded the entrance into the courtyard while another staff, holding a list of reported articles, checked the goods neatly packaged on the ground with the merchants surrounding. The central focus of the scroll is a large arched bridge stretched across the canal. A large boat approaches at an awkward angle with its mast not completely lowered, threatening to crash into the bridge. The crowds on the bridge and along the riverside are shouting and gesturing toward the boat. Someone near the apex of the bridge lowers a rope to the outstretched arms of the crew below . . .

The Qingming scroll depicted "an unprecedented development of commerce and urban culture" in Song China.[4] Why a seemingly ordinary mid-spring day when numerous people came to watch these boats going upstream and approaching the city gate of the capital was chosen by Zhang as the major theme for this painting is not mysterious at all. Kaifeng, the model of the city in this painting, was the capital of the Song dynasty until 1127 and the hub of national transportation and communication. For historians, the Qingming scroll is an encyclopedia for urban commerce and long-distance trade in eleventh-century China, a period of market expansion. Both for the Song empire and for the capital, the Bian Canal as presented in the scroll was the main artery of the economy. The estimated urban population of Kaifeng reached 1.2 to 1.4 million, about 1 to 2 percent of the national total, a marvelous achievement in urbanization in the preindustrial world. To supply food for urban residents, annually over 6 million Song *shi* of grain were shipped to the capital along four waterways, among which the shipments along the Bian Canal reached around 4 million.[5]

As the canal fostered commerce, it also brought fortune to the state treasury. The Song state levied a transition tax against all goods at the rate of 2 percent and an additional sale tax at the rate of 3 percent. While the eighteen harbor cities along the Bian Canal and the Sishui Canal produced 0.7 million strings of commercial taxes in 1077, the capital district contributed 388,313 strings of cash, about 5 percent of the total. The tax office within the capital city, known as the municipal tax bureau, alone contributed 235,612 strings.[6] The Song state gained power from taxing an expanding economy, and the majority of its tax revenues came from the nation's commercial wealth. Tax officers and their routine duties were vividly recorded here by the painter.

We can explain the importance of trade and commercial taxes by making another calculation. Researchers have pointed out that most of the subjects in the scroll were daily wage-earners and lived a poor life.[7] Taking the soldier as an example, an ordinary soldier of the central armies stationed at the capital received annual salaries that varied between 50 to 70 strings of cash. This payment can be converted as 170 *wen* a day for 365 working days or 200 *wen* for 300 working days or so. For an ordinary soldier in local armies, the yearly pay was around 40 strings. The daily wage can be computed accordingly as 130 *wen* for 300 working days. Therefore, the annual tax income of 235,612 strings collected by the Kaifeng municipal tax office could be used to support nearly 4,000 soldiers to guard the capital or nearly 6,000 soldiers at a local place. Hired physical laborers in transportation might earn a similar rate in daily wages. Yet many urban poor earned even less than soldiers. The daily workers depicted on the scroll such as street vendors and hawkers selling goods they carried on their shoulders, performers, artisans, and waiters, earned just 100 *wen* or below. The capital population comprised 0.30 to 0.7 million military residents (soldiers and their family members) and 0.7 million civil residents, who were mostly classified as low-income households. Therefore, although the market expanded rapidly in eleventh-century China, the majority living at the largest city in the world then lived a hard life. As I demonstrate in this book, growth likely took place in Song China due to market expansion, and in this book I address inequality as part of my examination of this unique case of preindustrial growth.

The next scene on our visual trip is depicted by accounts of Zheng He (1371–1433), the famous eunuch admiral, and the grand Chinese fleets under his command. Zheng He's seven voyages from 1405 to 1433 best illustrate the height of the early Ming's military might and the influence of Beijing-centered hegemony. For the first voyage in 1405 to 1407, the fleet was comprised of 317 junks, and the total crew amounted to 27,000 men, an unmatched size for an oceangoing expedition in the early modern world. Although Louise Levathes lamented in *When China Ruled the Sea*, a popular narrative about these expeditions in the early fifteenth century, that the abrupt withdrawal of the fleets led to China's loss of colonial power over the China Sea and Indian Ocean, she nevertheless inadvertently identified the planned nature of Zheng He's seven voyages: The court mobilized resources and staff across half of the empire's territory to accomplish this urgent objective. To produce these seagoing treasure boats, corvée laborers and craftsmen were summoned to work in state shipyards that were located along the lower Yangtze River and the coastline of Southeast China; the shipped products such as porcelain and silk textiles were made in government-owned workshops. In 1433, just three years after Zheng He started the seventh voyage, the court ordered 443,500 ceramic objects from the imperial workshop administered by the eunuch at Jingdezhen. This workshop was also responsible for supplying porcelain to Zheng He's fleets. The twenty-nine textile workshops constituted the largest sector of the early Ming state-administered industries, and the majority was distributed at the prefectural seats across the Mid- and Lower Yangtze. The Nanjing Palace Bureau for Textile Products (*Nanjing neizhiran ju*) was the biggest textile workshop and directly managed by the eunuch. The annual quota for all imperial workshops was 35,436 bolts, and this Nanjing royal workshop alone contributed

5,000 bolts.[8] The gigantic crews of Zheng He's fleets were drafted from soldiers. For the fourth voyage, according to contemporary writing, 26,800 out of the total 28,568 were soldiers and another 338 people were military commanders.[9] Every aspect of the voyages had little to do with the market.

It is also noteworthy that money played a very little role in carrying out such a grand scheme. The early Ming state issued a huge amount of *baochao* for the operation of a command system, especially for paying salaries to soldiers and officials. As discussed later, it was not real money but a means to replace hard currencies and regulate the prices. After Zheng He's fleet return to the harbor in the Lower Yangtze, the court rewarded all crews with *baochao*—a kind of paper bills—the estimated total is close to 40,000 *ding*. On most occasions of trading with foreigners, Chinese envoys provided porcelain, textiles, metal works, and other handicrafts in exchange for rhinoceros tusks, elephant ivory, gemstones, coral, tortoise shells, sappan wood, pepper, cloves, and other species; all were offered as tribute to the emperor. When the supply of species and sappan wood, for instance, far exceeded the needs of the court, the excess was not sold at the market but distributed to soldiers and military commanders as a substantial part of their monthly salaries. Of course the exchange rate was officially regulated through *baochao* under such circumstances.

The early Ming rulers who dispatched Zheng He and his fleets pursued a political and social order by installing an anti-market mechanism. Comparing the Qingming scroll with Zheng He's voyages, we must ask how and why the role of the market in preindustrial China could have changed so fundamentally. I further argue that this radical change caused a shift from a market-based economic system in the Song era to a command economy system that prevailed in the first century of the Ming dynasty (1368–1450). As Zheng He's seven voyages have shown, a command economy was a state initiative. For scholars who are familiar with Chinese history, the early Ming is a period of imperial expansion that went far beyond what the central power of the Song dynasty could imagine. Although the population in 1393 was just over half of that in the 1120s, the territory of the early Ming empire was nearly doubled that of the Song in the early twelfth century. The court launched many national projects, such as the building of three capital cities, including Nanjing, Fengyang, and Beijing; the construction of the Grand Canal; and the invasion into Mongolia and Vietnam, all of which proved the state's capacity in mobilizing manpower and resources. Yet this system was mostly operated by an anti-market mechanism at the cost of freedom and welfare of the Ming populace.

Just before and after Zheng He's voyage, the early Ming emperors repeatedly issued the ban against overseas trade by private merchants. The prohibition of private business was not contradictory to the rulers since it demonstrated the power of the state in monopolizing communication and trade with foreigners. Yet this policy to ban maritime trade imposed severe hardships on coastal communities. Ganpu, a township in Zhejiang, became an important harbor for maritime trade in the Song era. The town households numbered as many as 5,000. In 1236, Zhang Enqi, the local commissioner of maritime revenues, gladly wrote in a stone inscription that the number of town residents was growing, soldiers and people lived together happily, and the merchants were satisfied with their business; all were looking toward a very promising future. When it came to the mid-sixteenth century, the compiler of the new gazetteer lamented the town's declining economy due to the over-two-centuries ban on maritime trade:

The times have changed and human circumstance altered, so as to be totally different from how they were in the past. Ever since the prohibition of maritime trade, walls were built where the official troops stand guard, sources of profit are cut off, and all traces of the past [prosperity] have disappeared. People see nothing out of the ordinary, nor do they admire foreign objects. Their only occupations were farming, fishing, and woodcutting, and for women, nothing more than domestic chores. Up to the Chenghua and the Hongzhi eras, less than a hundred and fifty years have passed, and we may be alienated and excluded by our neighbors for being poor, but in fact, we with our simple ways have built a [home] land of happiness.[10]

This brief description points to the lasting impacts of the early Ming policies on the economy in coastal regions. Not only was the local community deprived of access to trade and commerce and forced to feed themselves by farming, the military forces were also disconnected from the market. The early Ming court stationed 2,240 soldiers at Ganpu for defense against pirates. From this number, 112 soldiers were assigned to cultivate the land. But the majority relied on the grain taxes paid by the farmers of nearby counties. The early Ming military system, especially the military farm, reinforced the demonetization of the economy.

Although the original thought of a command mechanism based on direct control of population can be traced back to the Legalist theory that prevailed in the Warring States period (475 BC–221 BC),[11] the rise of a command economy in fourteenth-century China was chiefly attributed to the changing mode of state power to wage wars after the Mongol conquest. Inspired by the nomadic military mode, the Ming dynasty that immediately followed the fall of Mongolian rule in China deliberately and systematically attempted to mobilize resources and manpower in a command mechanism as an alternative to relying on a market mechanism. Consequently, this tightly controlled economic system substantially changed the conventional way of living by violence and horror. To explore this important change and the subsequent results, I propose to use the concept of a command economy that is modified to fit the context of preindustrial China, which is different from that used in prevailing economic theories.[12]

A command economy, by definition, means top-down authority, rather than a market mechanism, governs the allocation of resources.[13] The command economy in early Ming China presents a radical kind of state intervention that aimed to produce a self-sufficient mode of human society via coercive means and by minimizing the influence of the market in the distribution of production resources. The central question remaining here is how could early Ming emperors exert power over society so successfully to change the way ordinary people lived for centuries? Precisely because a normal pattern of state power in a traditional economy lacked the necessary techniques and institutions to penetrate society until the Industrial Revolution, most social scientists think that the rise of a command economy system is a very recent phenomenon in history. The fact that the early Ming state employed a huge amount of corvée laborers in construction, industries, and public services, though helpful in demonstrating the intimidating power of the Ming state, is not sufficient to prove that the operation of this system deprived the right of common people and hence caused a great loss in their welfare. Therefore, changes in the daily life of coastal communities such as Ganpu can serve as important evidence.

Moreover, strong evidence for a planned economy in the early Ming comes from agriculture. The majority of the Chinese population farmed in inland areas. A compelling argument for the anti-market nature of the early Ming regime must explain state control of agriculture—the main sector of the economy in both Song and Ming eras—in depth. To provide a solid argument, I define the operation of the early Ming command economy in the following ways: First, depriving the mobility of members of society by restricting their freedom of migration, travel, and employment; second, regulating prices by issuing paper notes and prohibiting precious metals from circulation; third, demonetizing the economy by promoting payment in kind and labor services in public finance and other service and industrial sectors; and fourth, attempting to control agricultural production through expropriation of private landholdings in Jiangnan and implementing massive involuntary migration and military farms in North and Central China.

These are the four aspects in which the early Ming state system operated as a command economy, and I illustrate each one with quantitative information and detailed examples. I then compare the early Ming command system with the Song market-based system point by point based on quantitative evidence. Most historians of China are familiar with the generally accepted view of two economic booms in the Song and mid-Ming and the depressing downturn during the interim period. Lacking a solid economic explanation for the Song-Yuan-Ming transition, quantitative analysis helps to clarify historical assumptions and highlights certain data sources that may lead to the reinterpretation and reexamination of events that had hitherto found support only in anecdotal accounts.

The preindustrial economic and demographic data that a historian is able to obtain could hardly satisfy social scientists studying the modern world. All estimates made in this book are, of course, no more than approximations. Yet a demonstration of the consistent conclusions derived independently from different data sources is a major step toward establishing a new mode of persuasive explanation. This consistency check also includes an examination of the compatibility between what these data present and their particular historical contexts.

By adopting a macroeconomic approach, I am able to connect data analysis with historical inquiry. To observe the performance of the market economy in preindustrial China, I have focused my research on five major aspects: the degree of commercialization, population growth, GDP per capita, real wages, and agricultural productivity. For each aspect, I examine the directions, trends, and patterns in economic terms as depicted by available data and present these findings against their respective institutional backgrounds as well as important events in each period.

As an analytical framework, the macroeconomic approach covers changes on both the supply and the demand side. The common obstacle shared by Chinese economic historians, namely, insufficient information, would place inevitable limitations on an evaluation of long-term changes in Chinese market economy. My research is further complicated by the fact that few predecessors have paid sufficient attention to the demand side of economic changes. I take the first step to analyze these demand-based data (wages, prices, money stocks, consumption, and so on) to indicate long-term trends and structural linkages in the Chinese preindustrial economy. Such findings help to verify observations on economic changes made from the commonly used supply perspective, such as the relationship between population growth, the acreage of the cultivated land, and farm yields per acre.

Eight appendices and additional discussion in the individual chapters of this book deal with the quality and consistency of Chinese historical data. The major data sources used in this study to support the comparison of the market economy in the Song and Ming eras concentrate on two periods: the eleventh century and the first hundred years of the Ming dynasty. Fortunately, for these two periods, we can find the richest and most reliable data among all the extant data sources.

A unique contribution this book makes is the exploitation of the Song economic data in a rudimentary yet systematic way. Although the extant Song data is probably one-fifth or one-tenth of the Ming data, the quality of the former far surpasses that of the latter. Most of the Song data come from *Song huiyao jigao*, a most important collection of Song official documents and financial data. Next to the *Song huiyao jigao* are *Wenxian tongkao* and *Xu zizhi tongjian changbian*, which were both compiled based on primary sources and official archives. The nature of the Song data is closely related to the capacity of the state to tax the market. As I discuss in chapter 2, the Song state differs from other Chinese regimes in that indirect taxation, as opposed to land taxes, was the major source of state revenues. For this reason, household registration in the Song era allowed free migration and placed no direct tax burden on a household when it registered. This policy greatly reduced the extent of the taxpayers' incentives to underreport the population during official registration. Therefore, most of the extant records of Song aggregate households were consistent with each other. The land data, on the other hand, were liable to be attacked as problems of underreporting immediately upon registration of any land, the landowner would be held responsible for a tax duty. In the view of Song officials and literati underreporting produced the unfiar distribution of land taxes.

The most important source of quantitative information for the study of the eleventh-century economy is the annual financial and administrative report prepared by the central fiscal administration. This report included not only information on aggregate households, land acreage, tax revenues, and state budgets but also the breakdowns at either the circuit or prefecture level. None of the Song annual budget report is extant. But fortunately, for the year 1077, most of the categories in public finance are preserved in the *Song huiyao jigao* and *Wenxian tongkao*. Modern researchers have speculated that this unique case of data preservation was largely due to the publication and circulation of a book titled *Zhongshu beidui*, which was a collection of the official documents and financial reports prepared by Bi Zhongyan in 1080. This single source, which concentrates on a short interval of two to three years, provides the rare chance for modern scholars to obtain a snapshot of the Chinese economy in the eleventh century. Furthermore, the data far surpass our expectations because they often cover all the prefectures in the empire, sometimes even down to the county level. In the case of commercial tax collection, the range of the localities even goes down to the township level.

Early Ming data are relatively rich and largely preserved in the *Mingshilu* (*Veritable Records of the Ming*), the imperial annals that recorded the day-to-day events important for the Ming dynasty. In the first century of the Ming dynasty, early Ming emperors turned the entire empire into a command economy. All the people, regardless of their circumstances, were organized into a *lijia* system and needed to report to the government routinely. Firsthand information provided in the *Mingshilu* and other primary sources, such as the *Zhusi zhizhang* and *Ming huidian*, have now become invaluable evidence for studying the Chinese economy in the late fourteenth and early fifteenth centuries.

The value of the early Ming data has already been widely recognized largely due to the important work carried out by Ho Ping-ti and Dwight Perkins. Ho's work (1959) points out the high quality of the 1393 census data but discredits all the population returns in the succeeding centuries because they were more like changes in fiscal units rather than reports on real population. Based on this research, Perkins further examined the key economic data in the early Ming period (Perkins 1969). He used a wide range of primary and secondary sources and made great efforts to reconstruct the Ming acreage and population information at both the national and provincial levels. Through their research, Ho and Perkins have proven the economic data on the early Ming command economy to be reliable. Following up on their work, I have presented some new relevant information on military farms, forced migration, and the barter economy during this period that will enhance our understanding of the early Mind economic system.

Quantitative analysis clearly indicates that China was significantly transformed by market development during the eleventh century. Each kind of data from this period reflects rapid development in related but different economic aspects, and together they point to the rising trend in the overall economy. The population data show a swift growth in the number of households across the country. The 1077 commercial tax data proves that rapid progress achieved in the Song waterway system should be understood in the context of the transformation of the economy and political power during the centuries after the An Lushan Rebellion. Water transport undoubtedly played a vital role in the eleventh century beyond facilitating economic growth: The efficient transportation system was essential in sustaining the Song mercantile state. Other market-based data, such as the reconstruction of the size of the domestic market in 1077, the estimated money stock for the Northern Song period, and the estimated volumes of major commodities in eleventh-century trade, all demonstrate that the performance of the market economy in the eleventh century reached an unprecedentedly high level.

This book elaborates on China's intriguing retreat from a prosperous market economy to a stifling command economy in the century between 1368 and 1450. This retreat is the most drastic change during the last millennium of imperial China. The rich collection of early Ming data provides a rare opportunity to scrutinize different aspects of the largest command economy that the preindustrial world had ever seen. Based on the data on the *lijia* system, forced migration, and the military farm system, we can easily pinpoint the working foundation of the early Ming court's coercive power. A command economy by definition rests on strict control of the population and allows no space for free migration. Various policies designed to strengthen the court's absolute power, such as in-kind payments, forced migrations, mandatory duties, and the employment of corvée laborers in public projects, severely constrained economic development. These anti-market policies were enforced to remove the market mechanism that had once advanced China's market economy. The diminishing volume of commercial transactions in the early Ming period dragged prices down to an extremely low level for almost a century, which was a clear manifestation of the deterioration of the market economy. By the late fourteenth century, prices had almost regressed to the original low level in the mid-tenth century before the founding of the Song.

Other market-related figures further demonstrate the regress in economic development in the Ming. The Ming land tax data show the demonetization in the economy and especially in public finance. Payment in kind prevailed until 1500 in both payment to the state and in business transactions. The early Ming state registered only 10.6 million households, barely two-thirds of the Song population in 1078. The difference in the size of domestic markets between 1077 and 1381 was even greater than that of aggregate households. In monetary terms, trade volume per household in the mid-eleventh century was about seven to ten times that of the 1380s. Contrary to their predecessors, early Ming farmers lived in a world without any need for the market or for money. While the early Ming anti-market policies eventually failed to sustain a viable command economy, it succeeded in demolishing trade and shrinking domestic markets.

One key argument in this study reveals the costly economic consequences caused by early Ming autocratic rule. The comparison between the Song economy in the late eleventh century and the early Ming economic system around 1400 strongly suggests that the market could play an important role in fostering economic development in preindustrial China. It could also significantly benefit the majority of the population by sustaining a higher standard of living. The demolishing of the market conversely could reduce the commoners' freedom to pursue economic opportunities and trigger a substantial decline in their income. More importantly, my examination of the different attitudes of the Chinese regimes toward trade and industry, including their tax and monetization policies and efforts to maintain a market-friendly infrastructure and promote agricultural improvements, serves to remind political economists that any state's market policies should be held accountable for their contemporary as well as long-term economic consequences. By focusing on how market developments impacted economic history, this study challenges historians to scrutinize various assumptions embedded in general historiographical theories and paradigms.

Structure of the Book

This book is the result of finding, examining, and analyzing various kinds of raw data obtained from primary and secondary sources. Although my exploration is a first attempt to examine market expansion and contraction based on economic data and as such introduce numerous debates on methodology and the nature of resources, it challenges the prevailing assumptions on the dynamics and structure of the market economy over the last millennium of Chinese history and refutes the Ricardo-Malthusian explanation by pointing to a declining living standard in the first century of the Ming dynasty.

This book comprises four parts, eight chapters, and eight appendices. Part 1 includes chapter 1, and chapter 2, and discusses the methodological and data issues that are necessary to conduct a comparison of the market performance between the Song and Ming. Part 2, including chapters 3, 4, and 5, aims to measure the size and structure of the market economy in Song China from different perspectives. Part 3, including chapters 6, 7, and 8, describes the market disintegration after the Mongol conquest of China and examines the effects on growth and welfare that were brought on by the shift from a market-based system in the eleventh century to the command system that prevailed around 1400. The eight appendices present all economic data for further reference. In the following, I briefly lay out the major points of each chapter.

Chapter 2 is chiefly devoted to a discussion on the nature of the Chinese historical data. I provide a brief general survey of three different types of Chinese tax data, chronologically the poll tax data, the indirect taxation data, and the land tax data, each reflective of their respective institutional backgrounds. An important conclusion one can draw from this comparison is that extant data for the six centuries from 900 to 1500 are the most reliable resources for quantitative analysis of the Chinese economy prior to 1800. Other observations include the fact that the Song economic data, especially the indirect taxation data, highlight the performance and structure of a vibrant market economy. In contrast, the early Ming data demonstrate clearly the rise of a strictly controlled command economy.

In chapters 3 and 4, I investigate how the Chinese market performed. Chapter 3 studies the size of the Chinese market economy based on two independent approaches. I first compare the money stock at aggregate and per capita levels over the two periods of transformation. Then, I reconstruct the size of the domestic market in 1077 and 1381 based on commercial tax data. Evidence derived from both approaches indicates that the end of the eleventh century marked the peak of market development during the the six centuries in discussion.

Chapter 4 describes the emergence of a nationwide market based on the Kaifeng-centered waterway network in the eleventh century. I use the detailed 1077 commercial tax data to argue that rapid progress achieved in the Song waterway system should be understood in the context of economic and political changes during the Tang-Song transformation. The vital role water transport played in the eleventh century was far beyond economic growth, for a mercantile state such as the Song dynasty could not live without an efficient transportation system.

Chapter 5 focuses on ecological, demographic, and economic changes between 1271 and 1450, namely, the interim between the Tang-Song transformation and the Ming-Qing transformation. This has been the least studied period in Chinese economic history due to a variety of reasons, including the scant amount of historical information in comparison to the rich records about the Song dynasty. Luckily one can find important population and taxation data that reveal how the population and the market economy decline radically in the two centuries from 1200 to 1400. Moreover, while the fact that Yuan state revenues were highly monetized may suggest a dynamic market at the turn of the fourteenth century, further analyses expose how highly volatile the Yuan market was due to structural weakness in its economic system. The decline in North China's trade after 1125, as I further argue, came as a result of the disintegration of its water transportation. Ecological changes, warfare, and dysfunctional governments all contributed to the permanent loss of inland waterway networks. This backwardness in water transportation entails a slow recovery of long-distance trade until the 1550s when infrastructure over water regained prominence.

In chapter 6, I make a tentative estimation of the national income and real wages in the Ming era and compare it to that of 1080 and 1880. Dramatic changes in prices were the most important signs of a market cycle. The standard index of rice price based on silver value clearly indicates a cyclical upswing between 960 and 1279. During the Ming period, prices moved in the opposite direction. By the late fourteenth century, it had almost returned to the original low level of the mid-tenth century. This chapter also attempts to compare living standards by reporting long-term changes in soldiers' real wages. The wage data show that Song soldiers were paid much more than their Ming counterparts. The low-level of soldiers' wages persisted throughout much of the

Ming dynasty. Only after 1550 did the wages of Ming soldiers begin to rise to a level comparable to the thirteenth century.

I take the wages of soldiers as the foundation to estimate national income and real income per capita in the Song and Ming eras. Three benchmark years are chosen for the estimation: 1080, 1400, and 1580. The comparison immediately points to the unusually low level of real income per capita in the early Ming, which was only half of the early twelfth century. Meanwhile, I try to extract historical implications from the interesting fact that the proportion of tax revenues to the national income in the early Ming doubled that of the eleventh century.

In chapter 7 I use the Jiangnan region as an example to test my living standard argument. Supported by detailed documentation, I demonstrate a severe decline in household income in Jiangnan immediately after the first Ming emperor enforced his land policies. The decline in rural household income is of extreme importance because Jiangnan was not only the most agriculturally advanced area in thirteenth- and fourteenth-century China but was also the economic foundation for early Ming state power. However, I find the decline in the living standard of Jiangnan did not necessarily reflect a fall in farm outputs per acre. This decline was rather caused by an enormous increase in land taxes that seriously overburdened local farmers.

In chapter 8, I caution that one should not overestimate the importance of the Jiangnan case study, since the land acreage of Jiangnan accounted for only a minor percentage of the national total. For both the government-compiled records in 1080 and the adjusted land acreage in 1393, the land acreage north of the Yangtze River accounted for two-thirds of the total land under cultivation in China. To present a more balanced perspective, chapter 8 examines agricultural development across the whole empire while focusing on North China and the way agriculture integrated with the market economy. Agriculture was the main sector in a traditional economy and yet the most difficult to be commercialized. Building on earlier chapters that focused mostly on the money economy, here I show how growth in the agricultural sector could be accounted for by market integration achieved during the Tang-Song transformation. Because the Tang-Song and the Ming-Qing transformation paradigms are founded largely on a market-expansion theory in Chinese economic history, I provide a survey of long-term changes in China's agriculture from 980 to 1580 to highlight the relationship between market trends and agricultural productivity.

My study of long-term agricultural changes shows two patterns that prevailed in more than half of the territory before and after the Mongol conquest: intensive farming and extensive farming. The majority of cultivated acreage reported in 1400 was concentrated in depopulated areas in North, Central, and East China. Zhu Yuanzhang's anti-market policies set the path toward extensive agriculture. As most farmers were commanded to cultivate nearly 100 *mu* (about 16 acres) per household with poor facilities, a meager return that barely supported the farmer and his family members was an unavoidable outcome. Consequently, an unusually low national average in farm yields per acre occurred as the early Ming policies generated a regression toward extensive agriculture.

In summary, I aim to explore the relationship between welfare and the market in preindustrial China. I first investigate the role that the market played in the economy during the Song and Ming eras. As market expansion in the eleventh century is placed side by side with the regression caused by early Ming command economy around 1400, farmers' living standards in two opposite economic systems are brought into sharp contrast. The development of the eleventh-century domestic market is the only example of market expansion in premodern China that can be proven by quantitative evidence in a systematic way. In light of this market development, evidence from the agricultural sector suggests that rural households enjoyed a relatively high living standard. The rise of intensive farming laid a solid foundation for the increase of aggregate grain outputs during the Song dynasty. By portraying China's intriguing retreat from a prosperous market economy to a stifling command economy between 1368 and 1450, I offer an analytical explanation for this well-known but ill-explored period of recession. I argue that farmers suffered substantially from the lack of a free market to stimulate production. Furthermore, involuntary migration and the lack of capital and drafting animals led to the return of extensive farming. Thus, the living standard declined severely even when the man to land ratio reached a climax in late imperial China.

My research demonstrates a complicated relationship between changes in population, the market, and welfare. The market played an important role in increasing productivity and promoting people's welfare in a traditional economy on both the macro and micro levels. At the macro level, the economic stability in a monetized economy is necessarily supported by a sufficient money supply, development in water transportation, and organizational innovations that come together to reduce the transaction costs and increase market integration. This is the key step toward achieving a maximum level of specialization in production across regions and sectors. At the micro level, market expansion transformed both urban and rural communities. A farmer was provided with the protection of private ownership and enjoyed the freedom to migrate and choose his career. The lucrative gains offered by a vibrant market provided the economic incentive to exploit advanced farming technologies. By arguing that market expansion as a complicated mechanism was the major source for preindustrial growth, my research challenges the prevailing theories such as the Skinnerian model and agricultural fundamentalism (such as the Ricardo-Malthusian theory) that fail to take the market mechanism seriously for a variety of reasons. The Skinnerian model views market expansion as a function of increase in population density. The Ricardo-Malthusian model explicitly puts changes in population at the center and holds a negative view on the relationship between agricultural productivity and population growth. These theories assume the market can at best perform a minor role in moderating the painfully depressed economic conditions already determined by the declining marginal return of labor inputs. Only a quantitative evidence–based measurement of market performance can provide a comprehensive assessment of the role of the market in welfare and development.

Part I

The Market Economy
in Late Imperial China

Chapter 1

Issues and Approaches

This book examines the expansion and contraction of the market in China's preindustrial economy and their impact on living standards and social welfare. It focuses on two interrelated theoretical issues: the relationship between the market and growth in a traditional economy—namely, increases in agricultural productivity—and the importance of the market in maintaining a higher living standard. In other words, the question raised here is whether there was an alternative mechanism in a preindustrial society other than the market that could either increase the efficiency of production or promote the economic welfare of the commoners.

Underlying this inquiry is the relationship between freedom and welfare in a traditional economy. The rise of a market economy in an agrarian society is usually associated with a shift from a prevailing self-sufficient mode in agricultural production to a market-driven production mode in which commercialization stimulates farmers' efforts to combine land, labor, and capital to maximize productivity. Such progress could not happen until farmers—the majority of the population—gained freedom to migrate and choose their careers, secured private property rights, and gained easy access to information about the market. It is safe to assume that only when an individual is legally or customarily entitled to exercise his negotiating rights at the marketplace would he have strong incentives to produce for the market. In short, market expansion is closely linked to institutional changes that would allow an ordinary farmer to possess more freedom and have access to move up the social status hierarchy. Yet, this institutional linkage in a traditional economy may be strong or weak in different cultural and social contexts. On the other hand, the fact that inequality always coexists with market expansion even in a preindustrial economy leads to a moral issue: Did the few benefit at the expense of the majority? Is it possible for the majority of the peasants, who lived a life much less monetized and distanced from the market mechanism in comparison to a modern individual, to advance their social and economic status through an alternative path based on a self-sufficient mode?

This study aims to demonstrate the role a market plays in economic development and social welfare through a comparison between the market-driven case and the alternative case—a command economy system. The expansion and contraction of the Chinese market economy in the five centuries between 1000 and 1500 offer historians a rare chance to compare two opposite modes of preindustrial economic systems—a market-driven mode in the Song era and the anti-market, self-sufficient mode in the early Ming era—and their greatly different impacts on productivity and living standards per se. Employing the latter as a counterfactual model, a preliminary claim on the important role of the market expansion in preindustrial China's development can be firmly established.

Until very recently, most scholars would have considered such a question impracticable. Economists typically differentiate between economic expansion due to population growth, which implies no increase in living standards and economic growth due to technical innovations, which is often associated with increases in outputs per capita. Due to the lack of technical innovations and capital investments, the preindustrial economy, which is by and large an agrarian economy, is typically characterized either by stagnation or a decline in living standards, and therefore there was no substantial difference in the performance of the economies across the countries until the Industrial Revolution.

Yet empirical studies of economic development in late medieval and early modern Europe raise serious doubts about this Malthusian view. Scholars now argue for premodern economic growth, also known as Smithian growth, which is believed to have occurred due to increased specialization that could be further attributed to market expansion.[1] The recent debate on the divergence between China and Europe, especially on the different living standards during the eighteenth century between Jiangnan, the core area of the Lower Yangtze, and Britain highlights the important role of the market in driving growth in preindustrial societies of both ends of the Eurasian continent.[2] The Californian School, a group of revisionists in eighteenth-century Chinese economic history, use Jiangnan as an example to prove that the market did play a similar role in China as in preindustrial Western Europe in raising the living standards of rural households. Despite fragmentary quantitative evidence and certain conflicting arguments, most scholars in the China-Europe divergence debate assert that in seventeenth- and eighteenth-century China, "property rights were as secure as those in Europe and markets as efficient," a prerequisite to preindustrial growth, and come to agree that growth did happen across the countries at the two ends of the Eurasian continent.[3] The reconstruction of Chinese rural household income and farm productivity based on the information from agricultural treatises further leads to a tentative yet important conclusion that Jiangnan's living standards were no lower than those in England, with the latter showing the highest level in early modern Europe.[4] However, this East-West comparison has to face challenges not only from difficulties in measuring the standard of living in the past but also from the great divergence among different regions within a country such as China. It rather reveals "the highly complex and diverse pattern of the standard of living in the pre-industrial period" and therefore calls for much more empirical research on areas of growth in China's traditional economies.[5]

The complexity of this debate is compounded by the fact that during this period, China's domestic economy developed unevenly both spatially and temporally, and yet at the same time China was the largest market economy in the world from the eleventh century to the early eighteenth century. China contributed roughly one-sixth to one-third of the estimated total products to the world economy.[6] And yet, surprisingly, this once leading market economy did not pioneer the transformation into an industrial economy. Instead, it soon lagged behind and became backward as the European powers industrialized, a process that rapidly widened the GDP per capita gap between Western

Europe and the rest of the world. China's early yet ephemeral economic success and the late yet rapid rise of the West concern many scholars who are keen to identify the foundation and sources of economic growth in traditional societies.

The central piece of the great divergence debate is preindustrial growth driven by market expansion. Preindustrial growth in Chinese history often refers to technical innovations and economic growth in two particular periods. The first occurred in Song China, or the *medieval* economic revolution, as Elvin proposes in his qualitative study of Chinese economic history, which manifested itself in innovations and growth in farming, water transportation, money and credit, market structure and urbanization, and finally science and technology.[7] The second occurred as the market economy revived after 1500 and led to the subsequent development in urbanization and agricultural productivity.

The preindustrial growth theory refers to two lines of reasoning: market expansion and the consequential development in various sectors of the economy that raised productivity and promoted the standard of living. For both lines of reasoning, economic data is crucial for researchers to gauge the mechanism and size of the market, which is necessary to further assess the influence of market expansion on welfare. Without quantitative evidence, economic historians would likely make an assertion rather than a sound argument. Unfortunately, as my review shows, there is little quantitative evidence available to buttress such empirical research when researchers focus on post-1500s China alone. This is a long-standing obstacle in understanding China's historical economy.

In the succeeding sections, I follow two lines of reasoning, namely, market expansion and agricultural productivity, to review relevant studies in the current literature. At the end of this chapter, I put forward a coherent framework to study the role of the market in preindustrial China by comparing the two economic systems in Song (960–1275) and early Ming eras. I aim to explore the role of the market in sustaining growth and promoting welfare in the five centuries that precede the great divergence. It compares the market expansion in the eleventh century with the rise of a command economy in the first century of the Ming dynasty. A comprehensive framework is thus needed to define and observe the efficiency of the specific economic system in the market versus command economy comparison. Furthermore, in the former case, despite economic development, inequality became a serious issue that attracted attention from the government and Confucian literati. In a striking contrast, China became an egalitarian society in the early Ming era because Zhu Yuanzhang, the founder of the Ming dynasty, purged the big landowners and merchants in the Lower Yangtze and confiscated their property and estates. The comparison also considers the farmer in a market society with his counterpart in an egalitarian society: Did the market increase household income for an ordinary farmer or even help to reduce the extent of inequality in rural areas? Did the members of the rural community, now being significantly disconnected from the market, benefit from the egalitarian society scheme enforced by the early Ming court? All these important questions are explored in this book. Fortunately, I have found rich and reliable data for most of this period. Based on this advantage, this comparative study thoroughly investigates three fundamental areas: changes in the size and structure of domestic markets, changes in China's agricultural productivity, and changes in real income (real wages, household incomes, etc.).

Depicting Market Expansion in Preindustrial China

A historical inquiry into preindustrial economic growth driven by market expansion should consider many institutional and technical factors, such as water transportation, money stocks, and taxation. Without these supporting factors, the market could hardly perform an important role in integrating an originally isolated agrarian economy and becoming a strong incentive for farmers to improve technologies and increase investments to achieve greater output. The rise of a market economy is also dependent on institutional innovations, which would lead to reduced transaction costs and make trade feasible for the population. A market-friendly government is a prerequisite to transform a traditional economy by protecting private property rights, permitting commoners to migrate, offering free choice of careers, providing sufficient money supply, and investing in transportation projects to ensure the free flow of labor, capital, and goods within the country.

In reality, progress was always complicated by the very slow and often conflicting evolution of the market economy in the two millennia of imperial China. Although the existence of the market in China can be traced back to the Warring States period, the role of the market had been greatly constrained by all kinds of social and economic factors, such as the prohibition of free migration, slavery and indentured laborers, and the aristocratic landownership. Moreover, a barter economy dominated, and silk textiles were identified as the main medium of exchange over many centuries until the An Lushan Rebellion (755–763 AD; the Rebellion hereafter).

The central question for the study of Chinese economic history is to trace when and how the market first transformed the Chinese economy and society. This must be a point in Chinese history when the market gained overwhelming influence in society by expelling barter exchanges from many important economic activities and by linking local markets into an integrated system through interregional trade. Also, at this point the market economy became self-sustainable in the long run and could not be arbitrarily averted by internal challenges, such as institutional irregularities, and external shocks, such as nomadic invasions as well as natural disasters.

For almost a century, scholars have been divided into two camps: proponents of the Tang-Song transformation favor a major turning point around 1100, while proponents of the Ming-Qing transformation argue for 1550 as the major turning point.[8] As early as the 1910s, Japanese scholars, especially those of the Kyoto School, had already argued that the Tang-Song transformation made China a "modern" civilization centuries before Europe by emancipating bondsmen to become free farmers and accelerating market development. This "early modern (*kinsei*) China" paradigm, also called the Naito-Miyazaki hypothesis of the Tang-Song transformation, was a watershed in twentieth-century Chinese historiography. These Kyoto scholars launched a severe attack on the Eurocentric paradigm by arguing explicitly for a "Song Renaissance," an all-embracing transformation in almost every economic, social, and political field that occurred three centuries earlier than the European Renaissance.

Other scholars have argued that transformation of such magnitude only occurred at a national level four centuries later in the sixteenth century; some even contended its late arrival in the eighteenth century. Soon after the end of the Second World War, Fu Yiling (1956, 1957), for instance, called attention to the transformative role of market forces—the concurrence of markets, urbanizations, and the rise of merchant groups—

in mid- and late Ming China. Fu's work influenced Chinese historians so profoundly that market towns and merchants subsequently became the central foci of Ming-Qing economic history.[9]

For historians of the People's Republic of China and younger generations of historians in Japan who were inspired by popular Marxist theories and approaches, the emergence of a market economy in the sixteenth century marked a new era in Chinese history, which they named the "sprouts of Chinese capitalism (*ziben zhuyi mengya*)." This approach recognized China's preindustrial market development, but it still showed that it followed closely behind the rise of a market economy in Western Europe. For these scholars, adapting the Tang-Song transformation paradigm would contradict the linear development theory assumed by many Marxist historians: If China was the first country transformed by the market, why did industrial capitalism fail to follow? Although both paradigms aim to reject the stagnant image of China described by Western historians ever since the Enlightenment, they differ substantially from each other. How to reconcile these two paradigms has subsequently become one of the major issues for the study of Chinese economic history.

G. William Skinner's model of a macro-regional marketing system integrated the two transformations into a story of continuous development of rural markets. Skinner proposed that China was "more of division than of unity," and that to explain "the complexity of pre-industrial China's structure," one should focus on rural markets as the basic unit of traditional Chinese society. He further argued that commercialization in agriculture was driven by ever-intensifying rural marketing networks because the market made it convenient for peasants to exchange goods and services. In his ideal pattern, the location of a central place in a market network is determined by topography and to some extent the demand density (the distribution of demand and purchasing power, and equal transportation facility in all directions). Assuming all other variables are equal, the demand density is finally determined by population density, a major dynamic source for the making of a market network.[10]

The two major concepts of Skinner's model, the hierarchical structure of Chinese society and bureaucratic administration, and the distinction between "core" and "periphery" in a macro region,[11] have gained tremendous acceptance throughout the field as they undermined the myth of China as a unified and homogeneous empire and encouraged the boom of regional studies.[12] Despite the success of the Skinner model in defining the spatial and social context of economic growth in preindustrial China, the concept of rural markets lacks the support of quantitative evidence necessary to accurately define, not to mention truly explain, the sources of preindustrial economic growth. Unlike other studies that followed the neoclassical economic models, such macroeconomic indicators as prices, trade and transportation, wages and incomes, and taxation were entirely absent from the Skinnerian model. When applied to long-term changes in the economy at the aggregate level, especially changes in the structure of the market economy, the explanatory power of Skinner's model is severely challenged. All of his principal concepts, such as autonomous macro regions, the proposed relation between the cores and peripheries, and the formation of rural markets, can hardly be validated by empirical data.[13]

Skinner was keen to identify developments in commerce and urbanization during both the Tang-Song and the Ming-Qing transformations, two economic cycles he named "the medieval urban revolution" and the "late imperial urban development," respectively.

Yet his interpretation of the relationship between these two cycles is ambiguous and even paradoxical. On the one hand, he suggested that the burgeoning of market towns during the Tang-Song transformation period was confined to the Lower Yangtze region and that this phenomenon extended to the entire country during the Ming-Qing periods. Therefore, urban development at the latter stage was "more mature" and "more integrated."[14] However, this suggestion was not supported by any quantitative evidence. On the other hand, by comparing the rate of urbanization in the eleventh century with that of the mid-nineteenth century, he concluded that the level of urbanization achieved in the most advanced regions, probably in many other regions, too, were higher in the medieval era than in late imperial times.[15] The rate of urbanization in traditional societies is important as it indicates the ratio between the nonagricultural and agricultural sectors and speaks directly to preindustrial growth. This is certainly a paradox when he claims that more mature and integrated urbanization only occurred after the Song dynasty when the estimated rate of urbanization during that era was lower.[16]

The paradox in Skinner's account of the two transformations and their relationship can be traced back to a problematic interpretation of the market structure in imperial China. The markets in a traditional economy, as indicated by some empirical research, showed a complicated structure: The large numbers of towns and rural markets lay at the bottom of the market hierarchy, followed by intraregional trade and small city–based commerce, and, finally, long-distance trade and urban consumption at large cities were at the top of the hierarchy.[17] The importance of these markets follows a descending order in this hierarchy, and most standard textbooks focus on long-distance trade and large cities.

However, for Skinner, the study of trade means the study of rural markets. The number of markets and towns is generally assumed to be either equivalent to or as important as the size of trade itself. Following this logic, much effort was spent extracting records preserved in gazetteers to prove an increasing number of rural markets in China from 1550 to the twentieth century: Rural markets were recorded in the late Ming as numbering 6,674, and the figure continued to climb until it reached 18,645 in the eighteenth century, a nearly threefold increase within a span of two hundred years.[18] Such a phenomenal increase is often cited as strong evidence to demonstrate the unprecedented development of the market economy.

In reality, comparing the number of rural markets at the national level between Song and Ming eras merely documents the increase in the number of rural marketplaces. According to state registrations in the Song period, the number of rural markets in the eleventh century already amounted to 20,606,[19] but it would be absurd to conclude that trade volume in the Song period was three times larger than the late sixteenth century. The number of markets alone cannot determine the actual volume of goods traded. The only conclusion one can derive from this comparison is that trade in both the eleventh and eighteenth century benefited immensely from the increased number of rural markets.[20] A survey measuring long-term changes in the size of long-distance trade during the Song and Ming eras, which is much more important to understanding economic history, is completely missing from these studies.[21]

It is not surprising that scholars have for decades felt the need to develop a comprehensive framework to link and explain the two transformations, the Tang-Song transformation and the Ming-Qing transformation, in late imperial China. Both Elvin and Skinner raised such questions as continuity and/or difference between these two eras.

The Skinner model is by nature a social history approach and cannot exactly predict long-term changes in the size and structure of the market economy. Nor is it able to demonstrate key indicators of a rapidly expanding market economy such as specialization in production and the decline in transaction costs. These tantalizing gaps in current research call for an economic approach to study the expansion and contraction of the market in late imperial China. Building on previously documented development of market towns, this economic study focuses on changes in the volume of major goods traded in domestic markets, development in water transport, and the fluctuation of money stocks at the aggregate and per capita levels.

The path-breaking yet lamentably unfinished work of Robert Hartwell, a grand survey of the full cycle of macro-regional changes in China from 750 to 1550, also alerted researchers to long-term changes in the Chinese economy in the Song-Yuan-Ming eras.[22] Although this analytical framework appears promising, Hartwell's survey is largely an unfinished project because he, like Skinner, offers few thoughts on how the market mechanism affected the structural transformation of the economy and society at the macro level, especially how the market was at work via prices and wages.[23] He identifies demographic changes, for instance, as the only key variable for the pattern of regional development and even for the making of the Tang-Song and Ming-Qing transformations in general. In his explanation, population is treated as both a cause for and an outcome of long-term changes in the macro-regional economies over centuries.[24] To avoid this tautology, a complete picture of the pre-1500 Chinese market economy must be reconstructed to help the reader identify major trends in the Chinese economy by providing a nationwide survey of long-term changes both in the market and in living standards.

Measuring Agricultural Productivity

The exploration of the relationship between the market and welfare inevitably leads us to the assessment of the performance of the market economy. All this is related to the living standard issue. Narrowly defined, a better-off economic situation often refers to both a rising trend in income and real wages and a more equal distribution of wealth. From a broadly defined perspective, it includes a wider range of improvements such as longer life expectancy, easy access to medical care, and increased rates of urbanization and literacy.[25] Furthermore, if there is a positive relationship between improved welfare and freedom in a preindustrial economy, the market would play a decisive role in promoting the well-being of farmers.

In empirical research, the gauging of welfare has been often replaced with improvements in productivity. Given the absence of direct and systematic evidence on Chinese living standards in the past and the predominantly rural nature of the Chinese economy and society, most historians have used changes in agricultural productivity as a proxy for measuring living standards. Presumably, preindustrial growth caused by market expansion would raise per capita outputs and, by implication, a higher living standard. The primary concern is whether the marginal product of labor input in agriculture would exceed the substance cost. This concern remains a core issue in our exploration, and we must question whether the total cultivated acreage or farm yield per acre was growing proportionately to population growth in imperial China.[26]

Perkins proposed three key variables to account for agricultural development: per capita output, population, and cultivated acreage. His overall conclusion was that per capita output in China, and therefore Chinese living standards, remained roughly stable over the six centuries from 1368 to 1968. Expansion of aggregate acreage and the increase in farm yields per acre, in other words, was able to sustain a tenfold increase in population from 65 million to 647 million.[27] Nonetheless, Perkins frankly acknowledges that his observation was limited by the lack of quantitative evidence available for the centuries between 1450 and 1850. His work chiefly reinforced and exemplified the influential theory by Ester Boserup on the relationship between population growth and economic development.[28] Like Boserup, Perkins assumes that for many centuries of Chinese history, demands from increases in population determined the aggregate output and methods of agricultural productions. Yet Perkins's trajectory is flawed by his assumption of constant per head grain consumption. Some scholars are beginning to draw opposite observations based on their studies of the same region, Jiangnan.[29]

It is necessary to summarize the agricultural productivity research achieved over the past half century. First, there is a departure from supply fundamentalism, which not only uses cereal outputs per unit of land as the key criterion for agricultural development but also presumes the increase in farm yields per acre was the single cause for other important changes in the economy and society, to eco-agricultural history. Second, the lack of data on population and land acreage for most periods of late imperial China greatly weakened the explanatory power of these research studies. In the following, I will first review supply fundamentalism. My review concentrates on two lines of argument, Marxist productivity determinism and the Ricardo-Malthusian model; both present a linear explanation by focusing exclusively on technical innovations as the basis of explanation. Finally, I will evaluate the contributions and weaknesses of an eco-agricultural history approach that has been widely adopted by revisionists in the studies of the Lower Yangtze's economic development after 1980. These studies highlight the important role of the market in the rise of intensive farming and greatly advance our understanding of the complicated relationship between population growth, market expansion, and the spread of technical innovations.

Supply fundamentalism—agricultural fundamentalism in particular—views preindustrial economic growth more or less as progress determined only by supply, especially by the increase in farm yield per acre or per capita. Although this type of agricultural fundamentalism can be found in the studies of European economic history, scholars in China originally borrowed the theory from a Marx-Malthusian framework. The fundamental principle of Marxism believes that the relations of production must depend on and be decided by the forces of production, especially productivity represented in technological equipment and knowledge. The Malthusian narrative shares a common view that, due to the diminishing return on the increases of labor inputs and the stagnation of technology, accelerated population growth would inevitably obstruct growth in a traditional economy and lead wages even below the level of subsistence wage. In these productivity- and technology-oriented studies, a reader often finds the role of the market is missing from the discussion—only progress in technology productivity is assumed to be the driving force for human development and a worthy subject for research.

In the People's Republic of China, many pro-Marxist scholars view agricultural productivity as the only causative factor that contributed to population growth, development in trade and the handicraft industry, and even structural change in state tax revenue. In his all-inclusive hypothesis of preindustrial China's social, financial, and cultural changes, the historian Meng Wentong argued that there is a linear relationship between the production capacities of a farmer (as represented by farm yields per acre) and the rates of land tax. The long-term changes in farm yields per acre also determined the pattern of tax mechanism and military establishment for each period of Chinese history.[30]

The weakness in Meng's theory—and many similar explanations—lies in its purely mechanical causal understanding of agricultural productivity.[31] While it is inevitable for researchers to depend on widely scattered statistical evidence on agricultural productivity in preindustrial China, it is crucial that scholars remember that such evidence is highly localized and varied greatly within China's heterogeneous economic systems. In reality, there were great discrepancies in farm yields not only across regions but also within a region due to varying capital investment, quality of seeds and tools, weather conditions, access to the market, among other factors. Given the great ecological diversity within China's continental empire, the idea of a uniform standard in per acre farm yields, as suggested for agriculture in China century by century, is unacceptable to a modern researcher. With great diversity in mind, it is impossible to determine any definitive corresponding relationship between productivity and institutional changes in a single direction.

Those scholars who attempt to provide a nationwide average of per acre farm yields also face enormous difficulties caused by the poor quality of empirical data. Among the three key criteria, namely, population growth, cultivated acreage, and per capita/per acre farm yields, data on Chinese population is relatively rich in information but also laden with obvious errors. Official Ming national demographic figures after 1393, for example, show abnormally slight changes and only accounted for a minor portion of the entire population. The number of the officially registered aggregate population, for instance, declined slightly from 60 million in 1393 to 56 million in 1602. Given nearly three centuries of unification and peace, it is hard to believe such population stagnation really occurred.

Marxist historians also fail to recognize the importance of promarket institutions, be they property rights to land, money supply, or the role of the state, for preindustrial growth. Anti-market policies implemented by Zhu Yuanzhang, for instance, are interpreted as a necessary step that effectively led to economic recovery decades later. Despite the fact that the early Ming emperors not only disfavored local elite (often the literati and wealthy) but also put restrictions on the work and life of commoners, scholars still tend to believe that any policy enforced by Zhu Yuanzhang was aimed to recover the economy by protecting farmers and encouraging agricultural production.[32] In their narratives, they applaud the adoption of the *lijia*, the self-sufficient mode exerted by Zhu Yuanzhang to replace the government as the basic social and economic unit, cheer the military farm and involuntary migration, and remain indifferent to those anti-market measures. Yet for the first half of the fifteenth century, the economy was still in decline. It was around 1500 that the economy eventually came out of crisis and the market resurged. It took more than a century for the economic revival to take place, a period much longer than expected. One may doubt whether these anti-market measures could really benefit an ordinary farmer. In a command economy system, the central power is able to purge the elite group and deprive the important right of commoners at the same time. An expansion in the economy beyond agriculture such as urban industries and consumption or an increase in the wealth other than land, though hated by Zhu Yuanzhang, is not necessarily bad to agricultural development. As a farmer gains an important part of his income from producing for the market, he likely concentrates production resources such as capital and materials on a specific product. Both the individual farmer and the economy benefit from such development. The anti-market measures will simply prevent a farmer from doing so by blocking the channel between agriculture and commerce.

The prevailing Ricardo-Malthusian explanation constitutes another line of agricultural fundamentalism in the current literature on Chinese economic history. Population growth would necessarily raise aggregate demand for food. The increase of cereal production could be met by either the expansion of land under cultivation or the increase in per acre farm yields, or both. The key proposition of the Ricardo-Malthusian theory is that population growth would inevitably exceed the expansion of acreage and improvements in farming practices that are needed to increase farm yields per acre. Taking a pessimistic view of technical innovations and capital inputs in preindustrial society, these scholars assert that a decline in marginal return of labor input is unavoidable in the long run, when the opening up of new land stops and surplus labor was exploited on a limited amount of farmland, disproportionate to inputs of capital. Consequently, living standards would stagnate or even decline due to the decline in agricultural productivity. In his seminal research on economic growth and technical innovations during the Tang-Song transformation, Mark Elvin applies the Ricardo-Malthusian model to explain why China, after advancing ahead in commercialization, which he terms the "medieval commercial revolution," failed to industrialized in the succeeding centuries. Elvin first identifies the occurrence of the *medieval* economic revolution (economic growth and invention of new techniques of production) and attributes it to the opening of the frontier in the south along with migration and technology transfer between the eighth and the twelfth centuries.[33] As land became scanty, agriculture, once the leading sector, could not sustain technology-based progress. From the fourteenth century on, the entire economic system was reoriented to maximize cereal products, often by raising farm yields per acre through extra labor that caused a sharp diminishing returns to inputs of labor. The high-level equilibrium trap, he argues, occurred in China's economy because agricultural development, which was by and large aimed to meet the needs of the ever-expanding population at a subsistence level, had no space for technical advancement.[34]

Elvin's macro-narrative is descriptive and lacks the support of quantitative evidence. Kang Chao's work on preindustrial China's agriculture aims to fill this gap by adapting a quantitative approach that is also explicitly based on the Ricardo-Malthusian model. In his exploration of long-term changes in the labor to land ratio in China over a period of three thousand years, Kang Chao made unrelenting efforts to identify average farm yields per acre for each period. Reporting 501 catties for per capita grain output in the first century, 735 catties in the eleventh century, and 309 in 1952, Chao observed a long trend of decline over the last millennium. He further provided an index of real wages over two millennia: 150 in the first century, 195 in the eleventh century, 45 in the twelfth century, and 40 in the eighteenth century.[35] Chao concluded that a decline in per capita grain output and real wages occurred apparently after AD 1100 due to the lack of technical innovations.[36] Chao's research thus reaffirmed the already widely held Malthusian theory that overpopulation impeded the labor-efficient technical innovations that are the prerequisite of intensive farming. Ultimately, it was the immense rural population that impoverished China.

However, the validity of this broad statement is questionable. There are a few important flaws in Chao's assumption and the data series on which his assumption depended. First, Chao assumed that a well-performing market economy, including free migration, private landownership, social division of labor, and the pricing mechanism in exchange of goods and charge of services, already existed in China no later than 300 BC.[37] This assertion contradicts an important fact that slaves and corvée labor, tribute and customary gifts, the rigid control of land allocation and household registration, and the barter economy prevailed in China for many centuries until the eve of the Rebellion in the mid-eighth century. Only then did free migration and private landownership become popular. Second, Chao assumes that the government in preindustrial China produced reliable reports on changes in the size of cultivated land. Similarly, he gave no particular explanation of how the Chinese government could have managed such enormous reporting projects at a plausible social and economic cost. He also failed to acknowledge the fact that if demographic data were proven untrustworthy for many centuries of Chinese history, data on cultivated land and per acre farm yields fared even worse. In fact, Chao relied on disparate evidence to construct a countrywide average farm yield per acre. His argument is supported only by a dozen anecdotal examples instead of reconstructed patterns of continuous farm yields and real wages based on actual quantitative data.

This weakness in evidence inevitably leads to controversies with Chao's major findings. Chao assumed that per head farm yields would decline substantially in late imperial China because steady population growth led to a less optimal man to land ratio. Yet, this assumption lacks support for the entire post-Song period. According to Perkins's research, as the Chinese population increased 300 percent from 1393 to 1776, its cultivated acreage also expanded 250 percent.[38] In other words, the man to land ratio declined only moderately during the three and a half centuries from 1400 to 1770 and the expansion of cultivated acreage contributed to more than half of the increase in grain output.[39] Fragmentary evidence also leads to further inconsistency in an effort to pinpoint when the Malthusian trap supposedly took place. While Elvin chose the fourteenth century as the turning point, Chao argued for the twelfth century largely based on the sharp decline in real wages, even though he was only able to find six records and decided to settle on the lowest value.[40] Interestingly, according to Chao's index of per capita grain output, the date for a substantial decline was 1952, which would offer us a third time frame benchmarking the anticipated Malthusian decline.

As I discuss in chapter 2, the early Ming population and land acreage data are the only reliable quantitative evidence one can find during the Ming dynasty. China's aggregate households in 1397 was only two-thirds of that around 1120, indicating that the population shrank to the smallest size in the last millennium of imperial China, and that the man to land ratio was consequently optimized. If we follow the Ricardo-Malthusian theory to its logical conclusion, China would avoid the high equilibrium trap and move on to modern economic growth. It is also reasonable to assume that early Ming farmers were better off than their ancestors in the twelfth century, since wages must have risen as the land supply increased and the labor supply became relatively scanty. Yet, none of these occurred in the early Ming period. On the contrary, the early Ming economy, as I argue later in this book, deteriorated severely. This paradox constitutes a major challenge to the Ricardo-Malthusian explanation advocated by Elvin and Chao.

The linear explanation advocated by both the Marxist productivity determinism or the Ricardo-Malthusian model isolated agricultural development from changes in the nonagricultural sector and paid little attention to its interdependence with the market economy. Agriculture, or more narrowly defined as cereal production, is rightly viewed as the foundation of a preindustrial society. However, one can by no means take this *foundation* as a direct and single *cause* of important changes in a preindustrial economy.[41] For instance, growth in agricultural productivity also depends on the costs of transportation and access to large trading networks. These linear explanations also fail to provide a cohesive account that addresses explicitly the influence of market expansion.

The rise of eco-agricultural history in the 1980s represented a departure from the more traditional studies of farm yields per acre or "agricultural fundamentalism" and significantly reshaped our understanding of agricultural development in the Jiangnan region. Japanese scholars, such as Yoshikazu Takaya and Tadayo Watabe, conducted comparative studies of the historical development of rice farming in Asia and the rest of the world. These scholars followed Boserup's theory to explain that such technical innovations as seeding, fertilizing, and irrigation are products of population growth, especially increases in population density, and recognized the latter as the foundation of agricultural development. They further introduced an intensive farming model to account for the evolution of grain production. Contrary to the agricultural fundamentalist model, this model associates the emergence of intensive farming in Jiangnan with the opening of an external market for grain, increases in capital input and technical innovations, and the inflow of immigrants.[42]

Y. Shiba's work illustrates the importance of the eco-agricultural approach and overturns the overpopulation explanations that previously dominated the field. In his groundbreaking work on agricultural development in the Lower Yangtze region, Shiba adopted this approach to trace the course of development in intensive farming. His research points to rapid increases in agricultural productivity from 1030 through 1206. However, the Lower Yangtze region in the thirteenth century only marked the initial stage of intensive farming. It took a couple of centuries of development before the region fully enjoyed its benefits. Building on Shiba's and other Japanese scholarship, Li Bozhong elaborated on the concept that a higher living standard was based on intensive farming, and he provided a comprehensive survey of farming practice in Jiangnan from 600 to 1800. Contrary to Chao's pessimistic view of intensive farming, Li emphasized that technical breakthroughs, especially the application of a trinity model of intensive farming,[43] led to a rise in peasant family household income along with a rise in labor productivity. Li's model presents an optimum pattern of the peasant family economy that allowed peasants to maximize their labor productivity. Therefore, at least in the Jiangnan area, "there is no reason to believe that early and mid-Qing agriculture stagnated; on the contrary, it grew."[44]

As Li demonstrates in his analysis of the peasant family economy in Jiangnan, especially in his carefully chosen case of the Songjiang area, major breakthroughs in agriculture did not occur prior to 1600. The fertilizer revolution, which entailed one of the most significant improvements in agricultural productivity by applying supplementary fertilizer during the growth stage of crops, only took place "in the early and mid-Qing."[45] Li explains that although its coverage was far from complete at the time, new approaches that advanced double-cropping systems in paddy lands, for instance, "spread to a dominant position in the mid-seventeenth century."[46] Advances of double-cropping systems in mulberry groves and cotton fields appeared as late as the eighteenth and mid-nineteenth centuries.[47] In fact, Li's empirical research shows that improvements in agricultural productivity through applications of these technical innovations started in the seventeenth century and matured during the eighteenth and nineteenth centuries.[48]

Li's observation undermines the prevailing argument that agricultural productivity in the sixteenth century reached an extremely high level. In other words, during the entire Ming-Qing transformation period, development in the first two centuries from 1500 to 1700 could only be considered a preliminary stage. Li's estimates of long-term changes in per *mu* yields place the Song period at a very low position if not the lowest. As reproduced in table 1-1, the Late Song era performed most poorly in the increases in agricultural productivity over the millennium in Jiangnan.

Li not only openly doubted the Song agricultural revolution thesis but also offered a series of estimates on farm yields from the sixteenth to the nineteenth century to support his revisionist paradigm, (see table 1-1), which strongly disagrees with the "Song economic revolution" thesis.[49] In strong opposition to Song experts, such as Qi Xia, Min Zongdian, and Liang Keng-yao, who espouse the progress in Song's agricultural output and farming technology achieved in the Lower Yangtze region, Li denounced these arguments as severely biased due to the selective use of evidence.[50] However, Li was also criticized for his own selective use of evidence in estimating average farm yields per *mu* and for his misunderstanding of the double-cropping system.[51] The dispute between Li and his opponents over the dissemination of important farming technologies over Jiangnan in the eleventh century, such as the planting of early-ripening rice seeds, still needs to be resolved.

Most studies of agricultural development in China fail to acknowledge changes in prices and aggregate demand, such as consumption goods and services in the private sector, when they assumed that the peasant family economy was deeply involved in the market.[52] Consequently, they were blind to how farmers made adjustments to their family economy, say, in the allocation of labor, capital, and resources for cereal and textile production, in corresponding to changes in prices. In this case, Li's emphasis on the importance of markets in economic studies was inevitably hampered by the absence of systematic data on prices and wages in the last millennium. The increase in aggregate demand, although infrequent in a preindustrial economy, could spur changes on the supply side. For example, the high level of prices and money supply indicate that the

Table 1-1. Increases in Jiangnan's farm yields per *mu*, 300–1930 (*shi/mu*)

Period	Six Dynasties (229–589)	Tang (618–907)	Late Song (1127–1275)	Early Ming (1368–1450)	Late Ming-Qing (1550–1850)	1930
Yields	0.48	1.39	0.78–1	1.4–2.1	1.7–2.5	1.3
Index*	100	214–286	163–208	292–438	354–520	269

Sources: Li Bozhong 1998b, 38; 1998d, 125–26, 130–1.

*For index, Six Dynasties = 100.

eighteenth-century economic boom during the Qing era was driven by an expansion in aggregate demand.[53] The trinity model of the peasant family economy in Jiangnan no doubt highlights that preindustrial growth could be achieved on the basis of division of labor without dramatic changes in technology. This pattern of preindustrial growth also suggests that our previously simplistic and mechanistic understanding of why agricultural production changed needs to be modified. As Li explicitly states, changes in agriculture can be either the cause or the consequence of other social and economic changes.[54] One can find in Li's model a huge discrepancy between agricultural development as indicated by an obvious increase in the estimated farm yields per acre in the Lower Yangtze and the expansion of the market economy as indicated by changes in money stocks and prices. The Chinese economy was highly demonetized both in the seventh and early fifteenth centuries, yet according to Li, average farm yields per *mu* achieved unprecedented increases during these times. In contrast, average farm yields per *mu* of the Lower Yangtze region either stagnated or slumped in the twelfth and twentieth centuries, which happened to be periods of rapid commercialization and urbanization.

Although Li's overall image of agricultural development in Jiangnan from 600 to 1800 is much more persuasive than Chao's, the descending stages of farming productivity during the Ming dynasty would raise more question on the dynamics and trajectory of preindustrial growth in China if it is proven to be true. Using the connection between market expansion at the aggregate level and improvements in agricultural productivity at a specific region, I have reviewed the debate on Jiangnan's agricultural development in the last millennium.[55] Despite the various views represented in current literature, my research demonstrates that intensive farming in twelfth-century Jiangnan was, as in many other regions during the Tang-Song transformation, obviously on the rising tide and probably continued to rise into the thirteenth and early fourteenth centuries.

In contrast, a political economy study of Jiangnan in early Ming, especially the increase in taxation via a severe extirpation of private landownership, suggests a sharp decline in the living standard of the rural households. Most importantly, one must go beyond Jiangnan to obtain a comprehensive picture of agricultural development throughout China during these five centuries. Although Jiangnan became the most economically advanced region in China after the Tang-Song transformation, it only constitutes a small portion of the Lower Yangtze region, which in turn is only one of the nine major macro regions in preindustrial China.[56] Jiangnan was the only region that maintained moderate growth in local population between 1200 and 1400. For many other regions, such as North China, Sichuan, and the Mid-Yangtze, depopulation and de-urbanization prevailed along with the rise of a command economy after the Mongol conquest of China. Most farmers who tilled the land were either soldiers or involuntary migrants, and a market mechanism was largely absent in the reclamation of wasteland. Poor farming equipment, the lack of draft animals, and no access to the market were major challenges to these farmers. Average family farm size expanded as the land supply increased significantly. However, one may doubt whether this increasing trend of per capita farmland would, as the Ricardo-Malthusian model suggests, lead to an increase in per capita agricultural outputs. It has become necessary for current scholarship to collect all available information and reconstruct the cereal production in these regions with regard to the changes in both population density and the expansion and contraction of the market.

The Macroeconomic Approach: A Coherent Framework to Measure the Impact of Market Expansion on Welfare

Despite many efforts made by researchers, we are still far from gaining a comprehensive understanding of the role of market forces in China's preindustrial growth. The review of the current scholarship in preceding sections reveals certain urgent problems that we must resolve, namely, the lack of a coherent framework, quantitative evidence, and a political economy perspective. In the following, I first raise the major questions that we need to address with regard to the study of the Chinese market economy. Following a brief comment on each question, I provide my solution, one that attempts to incorporate framework, perspective, and evidence into a coherent argument.

The debate between the Tang-Song transformation and the Ming-Qing transformation paradigm encourages researchers to comprehensively survey long-term changes in the performance of the market economy. Yet the lack of a comprehensive framework based on quantitative evidence leads to a wide gap separating the market-based approach and the production-based approach in empirical researches. I have reviewed in the previous pages various empirical studies that aimed to establish a clear picture of major changes in the Chinese market economy over the last millennium. These studies are roughly divided into two camps: one focusing on market expansion, and the other following the line of agricultural productivity. My review reveals a clear disconnection between the two camps: namely, the missing linkage between the working of the market mechanism through prices and wages on the one hand and increases in farming production on the other hand. Although in a coherent framework changes on one side are important to the other side, due to differences in their methodology and insufficient quantitative evidence, the current studies produced some uncertainties and even controversies for a reader. Most of all, as this book aims to study the relationship between freedom and welfare in late imperial China, the inquiry necessarily follows a causative line to explore market expansion and its impacts on living standards and agricultural productivity.

I thus propose a macroeconomic approach to integrate these empirical studies into a coherent framework that enables us to assess market performance. This approach is based on the premise that the market is the endogenous variable that contributes to preindustrial growth and to improvements in the living standard. Under this framework, a comprehensive assessment of market performance is conducted according to the following criteria:

a. Population growth;

b. Degree of commercialization, such as the size of the domestic market, share of urban population in the national total, and the size of money supply;

c. The size and sophistication of state power measured through

   (i) tax collected per capita

   (ii) structure of taxes, assuming that sophistication means a move along the Schumpeterian trajectory toward a tax state;

d. GDP per capita and real wages, especially the real wage of laborers;

e. Agricultural productivity, such as farm yields per acre or per household.

Here I explain briefly why these criteria are indispensable in observing the performance of the market economy. A comprehensive performance assessment includes, first, an investigation of how the market expanded and contracted as measured by criteria a, b, and c; and second, an evaluation of how the expansion and contraction produced different results on standard of living as measured by criteria d and e. The investigation starts with a survey of population growth because it is the chief factor in influencing changes in both supply and demand of a preindustrial economy. Technically, the comparison of market performance in the Song and Ming eras must be conducted with an accurate calculation at the per capita level. Thus, no meaningful comparison can be achieved without reliable population data.

Beyond changes in population, one needs to consider how to measure the size and structure of a market economy in imperial China. I have listed three criteria earlier: the size of domestic markets, share of urban population in the national total, and the size of money supply. Evidence for a preindustrial market is usually imperfect. Yet a coherent framework allows a researcher to find the increasing connection among the related sectors in the economy. When the market expands, for instance, one can expect the development of long-distance trade facilitated by water transport. It also requires a sufficient money supply and the necessary infrastructure that the state would help to make available. Rising transportation costs and diminishing money stock during a period of a market boom are unlikely—even if these occur, they cannot be sustained long. As we study the performance of the market economy over time, methodically, this interconnectedness in the expansion and contraction of the market economy provides an important chance for us to assess the quality of the data and further analyze them on a macro-economic ground. Similarly, the rise of a command economy means a contraction in the market. One can use the extent of demonetization to measure the power of a command system in a preindustrial world. Payment in kind and labor service replaced money in state finance. Money and pricing were not to have important impacts on the allocation of goods or services. Private initiatives in mining, commerce, and industries were discouraged or even banned. The economy disintegrates greatly along with the market contraction. Most of all, one identifies a key criterion of how the economy was planned in a preindustrial world—legally and essentially in reality how people lost freedom in choosing profession and residential place. Involuntary migration and military farms of massive size are important to indicate the operation of the command mechanism in agricultural production. In researching them, quantitative evidence from different aspects come together to prove how the command system was operated as an alternative to the market mechanism—the command power would not sustain its operation if there was a major controversy within the system, say, if people were allowed to migrate freely to make a better living or soldiers began to receive cash payments and gave up military farms.

Next, I follow the framework to examine the impact of market expansion and contraction on standard of living. If the market performs an important role in promoting welfare, as the preindustrial growth theory suggests, one can find a corresponding rise in living standards as agricultural productivity increases. Luckily, we have the early Ming case, an economic system that succeeded the Song pattern of the market economy. The rise of a command economy system as an alternative to the market mechanism provides an extremely rare chance to draw a comparison of household income and agricultural productivity. Taking this command economy as a counterfactual model for comparison, a reader can clearly make sense of the central issue in discussion. The major challenge I face here, however, is the relatively poor quality of income and production data. To make a meaningful comparison, therefore, I attempt to address a broad range of estimated outputs made by different scholars to counterweight the influence of any estimation that was derived based on only a handful of samples. More importantly, the key to overcoming entrenched biases is to employ different approaches to reach various tentative conclusions. If they all point to the same direction, then we can be confident of having come to a valid conclusion.

I first choose real wages as the basis to reconstruct national incomes in Song and Ming China, with a specific focus on military wages. Then I choose rural household incomes to develop a cross-dynastic comparison at the macro-regional level. In the study of national income, both household income and wage belong to the demand-based perspective. The scanty information on real wages in preindustrial China forces me to adopt the military wage as the foundation for comparison. The comparison of household income is also confined to Jiangnan. Finally, to provide a comprehensive understanding, I turn to the supply side and choose agricultural productivity to test the validity of my conclusion. This supply-centered perspective helps to triangulate the observation made on welfare based on a demand-centered perspective. Rather than simply producing an average estimate based on comprehensive data collected across the country, I select important local cases from different macro regions to build up an index representative of regional variations.

As the comparative framework is well defined, two other major problems remain to be resolved: the lack of quantitative evidence and the lack of a political economy perspective. The introduction of a political economy perspective directly addresses the shift from a market-based economic system to a command economy system after the Mongol conquest and highlights the importance of the political economy of early Ming China. This often glossed-over transitional period deserves ample attention because it provides a crucial linkage between the Tang-Song transformation and the Ming-Qing transformation.[57] A thorough examination of this interim period is necessary if we are to obtain a comprehensive understanding of the two transformations.

This interim period starts from the collapse of Northern Song in 1127. By 1120, the market has expanded to an unprecedented level and population reached about 100 million. A Kaifeng-centered market system functioned as the engine for the long eleventh-century economic expansion until it was crushed by the Jurchen invasion in 1125. Jurchen nomadic power gained firm control of North China, and the defeated Song court moved from Kaifeng to Hangzhou, a city in the Lower Yangtze, where it continued to govern the south until the Mongols destroyed the Song dynasty and unified China in 1279. The rise of the Mongol empire put an end to the over-five-centuries-long multi-state system in China and East Asia. However, after only eighty years, this giant Eurasian empire fell apart. Zhu Yuanzhang, one of the leaders of many rebellions throughout the late Yuan, overthrew the Mongols and founded the Ming dynasty (1368–1644).

The market expansion and population growth in the eleventh century was associated with the formation of a Kaifeng-centered military-fiscal power. Many Song historians have acknowledged that this new type of state power relied on an intense inland waterway network with Kaifeng at its center. The essential connection between the Song state and market expansion is demonstrated in three areas: the majority of state revenues were collected from long-distance trade and urban consumption, the structure of state finance was highly monetized, and the soldiers were all recruited from the volunteers who were attracted by pay and other benefits. This practice was particularly true for the military recruitment in times of famine.[58] Therefore, the Song state gained a lot from market expansion and thus became supportive to trade. In the Skinnerian paradigm, the Song-Yuan-Ming transition is described as a Kaifeng-centered economic cycle being replaced by a Beijing-centered one, both being macro-regional cycles. As Skinner and later Hartwell argue, this replacement is indicated mostly by demographic changes. In doing so, they regrettably fail to recognize the rise of a command economy along with the formation of Beijing-centered political power.[59]

A command economy is an administrative system alternative to the market mechanism. It is difficult to tell how early an exact idea of a demonetized administration came to mind for the Chinese political elite,[60] but the Mongol conquest was certainly a key step in the formation of a command system. Although Mongolian nobilities developed a much more friendly relationship with merchants, such as the moneylenders from Central Asia known as *semu*, the origin of their dynastic rule in China was institutionally based on pastoralism, the structure of which was hierarchical and patriarchal.[61] The nomadic conquest significantly influenced the evolution of Chinese society and greatly changed the relationship between the state and the market. The revival of poll taxes and corvée labor, the creation of hereditary military services that isolated the recruitment of military staff from the process of employment, the spread of military farms, and most of all, the making of Beijing as the capital all significantly reduced the central power's reliance on the market mechanism and thereby moved the state system away from the primary path that was oriented during the Tang-Song transformation. It is also worth noting that the Mongol rule is a combination of many different and even opposite kinds of policies and practices. The Lower Yangtze, the heartland of the Chinese market economy, remained prosperous and engaged more actively in international trade. In North and Northwest China, the economy was plagued by the huge loss of population caused by wars and natural disasters. As the size of the Chinese empire greatly expanded after the Mongol conquest, her economy became much less integrated and became unstable due to the weakness in its structure.

A command economy is a state initiative that is intended to replace the role of market forces with a command system. Either labor service or payment in kind that worked to support a barter economy in earlier times was insufficient to be called a command economy. It must be a planned system rather than a gradual evolution. Therefore, the formation of a command economy system did not come into view until Zhu Yuanzhang deliberately enforced anti-market policies nationwide. To reorganize society into a command system, he employed three key institutes/methods: *lijia*, military farm and involuntary migration, and *baochao*. Designed to be self-sufficient and mutually supervised units, *lijia* served to control the population everywhere. Military households were forbidden to migrate because the government thought any moving of those households from the current location would lead to their escape from the obligations of providing soldiers. Farmers and artisans were also confined to their registered places and organized into the *lijia* system.[62] Military farms distanced the military provision, the largest category in state expenditure, from the market, and involuntary migration was planned to reopen the vast expanses of wasteland. *Baochao* was a paper bill issued by the court to take the place of hard currencies such as coins and silver at the market; the latter was forbidden and must be sold to the state at the official rate.

This research is essentially concerned with a comparison of the market-based system with a command economy, and it is necessary to find an ending date. Although this command system lasted no more than a century, it is not easy to pin down an exact time in history for its collapse. With the sudden death of Zhu Di in 1424, the emperor who dispatched Zheng He and decided to move the capital to Beijing, the pace of imperial expansion also stopped like a sailing ship without wind. But the collapse of such a giant organization was not designed but pushed by the accumulation of controversies and conflicts within it. This process was uneven and sometimes reversed. To take *baochao* as an example of a radical change in policy: Soon after the *baochao* was formally issued in 1375, the court issued these bills without restraint, which not surprisingly resulted in a severe depreciation. According to the original regulation, 1 *guan* of *baochao* was equivalent of 1 tael of silver. By 1426, 100 *guan* was worth 1 tael.[63] People rejected *baochao* and turned back to silver. After a few fruitless efforts, in 1436, only ten years after Zhu Di's death, the court decided to accept silver as a means of payment. This change in policy marked a turning point in the monetary history of the Ming dynasty: State power succumbed to the power of a market it had made every effort to destroy sixty years before. In other cases, the collapse of the command system came out decades later. The ban on free migration generally applied to any registered household. The land-tax system, a tributary way of collecting and moving grain taxes, demanded that a farmer perform his duty at a specific spot as registered in the *lijia* system. A peasant family, if migrating to a settlement rather than their registered place, would be forced to return to their original *lijia* unit. In imperial edicts, the court repeatedly warned such vagrant peasants to return to their early settlements. In 1430, Zhang Ben, the acting minister of the Revenue Ministry, warned that illegal migrants who failed to then return home would be drafted for military services, and anyone who helped to shelter these migrants or failed to report them to the administration would receive the same punishment. An migrant could apply for the legal status of alien residents, according to this rule, only when he succeeded in performing his tax duties and labor services at his home settlement, no matter how far away he had already migrated.[64] One can imagine how much of a strain it would be for a migrating peasant family if they wanted to be recognized as legal migrants—they had to pay taxes in two different places.

An overwhelming majority of Ming migrants would have failed to meet this requirement, since the total number of registered households showed no sign of increase after 1400 and even declined substantially after 1450, although the real population in the fifteenth century must have far exceeded the population in 1393.[65] Massive resistance against such coercive control should be the principal reason for the collapse of early Ming despotism. Yet, early in the dynasty, the government stiffened its laws by prosecuting such violations. Even when it came to the Zhengtong reign (1436–49), one can still find some records about using Ming troops to pacify the remote mountain areas where illegal migrants moved in for mining or farming.[66] Two rebellions in mid-fifteenth-century China were also closely related to migrants: One is the Deng Maoqi Rebellion (1448–1449) in the center part of Fujian, a case of miner bandits as recorded in contemporary writings; the other is the revolt in the western mountain and highland areas in Hubei, which involved about 1 million illegal migrants.[67] After pacifying the rebellion in West Hubei, in 1476 the Ming court established a new prefecture in the rebellion area and recognized the rights of migrants to stay permanently and cultivate the free land in their new homes. This event marks an important change in the state policy on migration. Suffice it to say the command system collapsed rapidly toward the end of the fifteenth century. But as an important exception to this general trend in Ming China's politics, the policy on maritime trade remained unchanged. Only when it came to the Longqing reign (1567–1572) did the court lift the ban by allowing Chinese merchants from Fujian to use a small sea harbor for shipping abroad. Largely for convenience, this exploration chose 1500 as the ending year for the early Ming command system. The comparison between Song and early Ming is a hitherto unexplored perspective and highlights the differences between the market mechanism and the command system in a traditional economy. In contrast, the revival of the market economy in the sixteenth century is a well-known story and is considered as a secondary concern in this book.

Chapter 2

The Nature of Song
and Ming Economic Data

Since the Warring States period, Chinese states were interested in population registration for the purpose of military mobilization and taxation.[1] From the onset of state formation in ancient time, theorists had emphasized the importance of direct state control over resources and the populace. They also embraced the principle of state power based on law and institutions, particularly on the military meritocracy in which conscripted soldiers were granted landholdings in accordance to their military achievements.[2] "A strong country must know thirteen figures," suggested the Lord of Shang (390–338 BC), the most influential Legalist in the Warring States period, to the king of Qin, "the number of granaries within its borders, the number of able-bodied men and women, the number of old and of weak people, the number of officials and officers, the number of those making a livelihood by talking, the number of useful people, the number of horses and oxen, the quantity of fodder and straw."[3] Hence, most Chinese historical economic data were made available because of tax collection and military mobilization.

Demographic changes are of extreme importance to indicate and explain long-term changes in the traditional economy. From an incomparably early time, Chinese governments already attempted to undertake censuses and left us with the richest population information among preindustrial countries. According to the earliest extant record, the Chinese population reached 12,233,062 households and 59,594,978 individuals in 2 AD. Studies of household registration at the micro-level also reveal the local government made great efforts to investigate and report a full coverage of household members, male and female, young and old, even including female servants.[4] Yet evidence from the micro-level research cannot lead to a conclusion that the macro-level aggregate data preserved in historical documents are trustworthy for studying the main trend of long-term demographic changes. In his general survey of the population figures reported on twenty-nine years of the period from AD 2 to 742, Hans Bielenstein finds only those of the years AD 2, 156, 609, and 742 are more or less the results of the real census.[5] When one conjectures the population development during this period based on these four censuses, however, "the population curve is actually very even."[6] The number of aggregate population might fluctuate in the periods between these benchmark years, but the Chinese population in 742 AD just remained at the same level as it was seven centuries ago.[7] But this is not the most extreme case. For the Ming dynasty, the highest population figure was that obtained from the early Ming censuses between 1381 and 1393. Through the succeeding nearly three hundred years, the reported numbers remained constant or even lower. It is useless to reconstruct the population history of Ming China based on these totals.

This book aims to provide a comprehensive description of the expansion and contraction of the Chinese market economy during the Song and Ming eras in four areas: population growth, urbanization, and land acreages; trade, water transports, and the money supply; taxation; and prices, real wages, and household income. Before advancing the comparison of the two dynastic periods, it is necessary to verify all data discussed here are relevant and reliable. In the two millennia prior to 1800, the Chinese bureaucracy produced a huge amount of economic data, including comprehensive coverage of Chinese population, land acreage, and taxation. Yet, as shown in the appendices, the quality of these data is far from satisfactory, and the distribution of reliable data was extremely uneven across the last millennium of imperial Chinese history. It is not the case that the later the period, the better the data quality. Surprisingly, the data from the five centuries prior to 1400 are much more reliable. Most noticeable is the fact that the quality of economic data concentrating around 1080 and 1393 AD come close to modern surveys and provide trustworthy information on the main trend of long-term changes in the Chinese economy and population. In this chapter, I explain why the series of reliable data on preindustrial China are only found in the five centuries between 980 and 1500.

The Ho Puzzle and the Reliability of Chinese Population Data

Though one is expected to find richer and more detailed statistical materials in a later period, it is rather against common sense that most of the macro-level economic data produced in the centuries after 1500 are untrustworthy. Yet this judgment is a major finding in the economic history of late imperial China. Over the five hundred years after 1400, the recorded totals of population and land acreage, which comprised the major body of Chinese economic data sources, either stagnated or showed inadequately slow change—clearly, such data does not reflect actual historical conditions. Taking the Ming population data as an example, the 1400s mark an end to trustworthy official records. The reliable records of household registration are those made in 1381, 1391, and 1393.[8] The quality of the cultivated land acreage data is even worse, and the relatively reliable records are those of 1502.[9] During the years from 1398 to 1867, Ho remarks, "with the exception of the 1602 return, there was no consistent change in the reported area."[10]

Largely owing to Ho Ping-ti's study, we come to know how the reporting procedure of population and land changed significantly over the course of the Ming dynasty. Ho persuasively argues that the population returns in the Hongwu reign (1368–1398) were conducted in association with the establishment of the *lijia* system throughout rural communities. The system must be as precise as was practicable because the collection of land taxes and assignment of labor services were made possible only through a strict control of the population and landholdings. Thus, the rise of a command economy laid a firm foundation for the initial success, although it inadvertently led to the ultimate failure of the Ming population registration system. Despite that the first two or three population returns were "by definition and in practice very close to modern registrations," the Ming population registration system became more reflective of taxation and labor services quotas than real changes in the population.[11] Chinese population data remained unreliable until 1775, when the Qing emperor ordered a new report on local population for famine relief preparation. For the first time in the past four centuries, reporting population to the government was not directly for taxation purposes. Local people were thus encouraged to self-report truthfully, and the information collected at the local level was relatively trustworthy. By this time, the reported Chinese population had reached 268 million and the estimated total would have been 311 million.[12] Based on these figures, within four hundred years from 1393 to 1776, the Chinese population leaped from 60 million to over 300 million. Extant records offer few clues as to where, when, and how this drastic increase occurred. Thus, for any study of the Ming-Qing economy, the lack of accurate information on aggregate population remains an unresolved challenge.

Ho's study helps to establish justification for a reliable set of quantitative data. Ho uncovered an unwritten principle that guided the report of Chinese aggregate population, which I named the "Ho puzzle." It refers to an underreporting pattern in population registration due to the prevailing concerns of tax collection. In this sense, the rise of a command economy may have laid a firm foundation for the initial success, but it also led to the ultimate failure of the Ming population registration system. The Ho puzzle can be applied to many periods of Chinese population history when the control of the populace was the basis of tax collection. In table 2-1, I take the population registration in the Sui (581–618 AD) and Tang (608–907 AD) dynasties as an example to demonstrate the corresponding relationship between the fluctuation of household numeration and the effectiveness of governmental control. The population of dynastic China during this period is represented by entries for twenty-four dates that cover about 230 years from 606 AD through 835 AD.

A steady and thus plausible growth in aggregate households occurred only to the half century between 705 and 754. Registered households peaked in 754 by arriving at

Table 2-1. Changes in registered Chinese population, 606–844 AD

Year	Persons	Households	Year	Persons	Households
606	46,019,956	8,907,536	757	—	8,018,710
627	—	3,000,000	760	16,900,386	2,933,174
639	12,000,000	2,992,779	764	16,900,000	2,900,000
650	—	3,800,000	766–779	—	1,200,000
652	—	3,850,000	780	—	3,805,076
705	37,140,000	6,156,141	806–820	—	2,473,963
726	41,419,712	7,069,565	812	—	2,440,254
732	45,431,265	7,861,236	812–824	—	3,944,959
734	46,285,161	8,018,710	825–826	—	3,978,982
740	48,143,609	8,412,871	827–835	—	4,357,575
742	48,909,800	8,525,763	839	—	4,996,752
754	52,880,488	9,069,154	841	—	2,114,960
755	52,919,309	8,914,709	844	—	4,955,151
756	—	8,018,710			

Source: Durand 1960, 223.

9.07 million. At the same time the average household size slightly declined from 5.89 to 5.72 people but bounced back to 5.83 people in 754. As the population grew, both the economy and the empire expanded significantly during the first half of the eighth century.[13] Nonetheless, this growth would be invisible without an effective administration of the household registration during this period. From 703 AD on, the court routinely dispatched censors to examine the underreporting problems caused chiefly by migration of farmers. Emperor Xuanzong (712–756 AD) launched a national scale campaign in the years between 721 and 725 to register unreported households nationwide. More than 0.8 million households were added to the state register, about 10 percent of the national total.[14] Except for the recorded populations between 705 and 755, the figures recorded in table 2-1 display such radical changes that they prompt one to doubt whether population returns conducted during the Sui-Tang eras consistently covered the entire population. Although the decline between 760 and 845 AD can be partly attributed to depopulation caused by wars, it is still difficult to believe that in just five years the Chinese aggregate population could have been reduced by two-thirds between 755 and 760. Most scholars tend to accept that such a huge loss was largely due to the court's weakening power after the mid-Tang An Lushan Rebellion to enforce population registration. As Bielenstein notes, this sudden reduction reveals the simple fact that immediately after the Rebellion the disorganization made it impossible for a "complete registration" of the total.[15] The situation was believed to be especially true due to the independence of local warlords who refused to send tribute grain to the capital.[16]

For the Tang dynasty, the population return was the first and most important step to fighting for the control of resources as the majority of state revenues were collected through poll tax. Consequently, the court forbade free migration for fear of losing tax incomes and potential supply to fund the militia.[17] There was constant struggle between the various regulations issued by the court to control the populace and the farmers' endless attempts at tax evasion. For the first half century, the numbers of registered households remained below four million. Even for the recorded populations of the years between 705 and 755, which seem relatively reliable, underreporting was still unavoidable. The sharp decline in registered population after 755 signaled the end of this poll tax–based system. Officials attempted to generate new revenue by taxing commerce and developing state monopolies over salt and alcohol immediately after the Rebellion. Changes in the reported aggregate population in Tang and Ming eras testify to the limit of states' capacity to run a command economy by coercively administering the populace and landholdings. In any case, the tax-burdened population records guaranteed that such figures had little to do with real demographic change as the state lost strict control over rural communities. In the Ming dynasty, Zhu Yuanzhang built up the *lijia* system for control of population. The household registration directly served to provide economic resources to the state including grain taxes and labor services. After 1393, the population return was no longer able to report real changes in the economy. Following the same line of reasoning, one can take the year of 1500—for population data it is 1400—as the ending date for reliable quantitative evidence.

An inquiry into the upper time limit of reliable economic data brings us to the Song dynasty, which presents a different case from the Ho puzzle. The most salient characteristic of Song state finance was the dominant position of indirect taxation. The poll taxes played a tiny role in Song taxation. And hence, the state capacity was no longer relying on direct control of the populace. The Song central government taxed trade—particularly consumption goods—to finance the civil and military apparatus and to pay for important strategic and logistic needs. This was especially true for the New Policies era (1068–1120). As I will discuss in chapter 2, under such circumstances, the populations reported from household registrations were trustworthy as they did not serve the purpose of taxation.

This major finding rather supports and further develops the Ho puzzle, a well-known thesis on the quality and nature of the population data in late imperial China. In his pathbreaking study of the population and land acreages preserved in official reports, Ho Ping-ti found that the population figures presented by the imperial surveys in 1393 are trustworthy and credited this to the efficiency of the early Ming administration. However, ever since then, underreporting prevailed across the country owing to both a decline in state capacity and a growing tendency in peoples to avoid taxation and labor service.[18] I have extended the survey on economic data into the four centuries that preceded the founding of the Ming dynasty in 1368 AD. Though produced in different historical contexts than that of the early Ming, they are similar to the 1393 data set in being trustworthy.

A crucial step to understanding the nature of Chinese economic data and the uneven distribution of reliable data over the last millennia calls for a clear definition of the Ho puzzle. Specifically, the Ho puzzle arises from the controversial nature inherent in the population data produced by the Ming administration. In general, economic data in imperial China was gathered primarily for taxation purposes. The state mechanism in the first century of the Ming dynasty can be broadly characterized as a command economy system with such characteristics as the imposition of poll taxes, labor services, and tax payment in kind. Hence, most of the government-generated economic data are irrelevant to changes in the economy and are particularly inappropriate for the study of market development. In fact, over the debate on the nature of these data, some scholars openly doubt whether it is possible to reconstruct the size and structure of the Chinese economy based on such historical data.[19]

A comprehensive view of the data generation enables us to choose qualified evidence for economic analysis. As the state power in the Song dynasty was based on the market, a major portion of its total state revenue was drawn from indirect taxation, which meant that the state could afford to give up control of the populace and land resources as a means of extracting revenue. As a result, population registration did not necessarily produce the tax burden at the first instance. Take the assessment and collection of land taxes as an example. Rural households no longer paid taxes or provided labor to the state based upon age or gender. The landless, who roughly accounted for more than one-third of the population, were exempted first.[20] The taxes were largely distributed among landowners in correspondence to the level of household wealth. Following this principle, more than half of the landowners in Song China had a family farm of medium size or below and paid a moderate amount of taxes. Although household registration provided important information that the collection of land taxes necessarily needed, the majority of rural populations did not feel the immediate threat of being overtaxed. After all, it was the wealthiest that paid the most.[21] As rapid growth in wealth rather than increase of population became the major source for tax revenues, the state allowed freedom of migration and protected the right of private property. To maximize the taxes against urban consumption, the Song state even encouraged migrants to move into cities and towns. In short, reliable market information came possible only when state power in imperial China was both able and willing to tap the market for taxation purposes. Neither an autocratic state based on a command economy such as the early Ming court nor an agrarian regime based on land taxes such as the Chinese state after 1500 was interested in or capable of performing such a task as the Song state undertook.

If my interpretation of the Ho puzzle and the nature of Chinese economic data is correct, we come to the astonishing conclusion that for only five centuries out of the two millennia of Chinese history can one find reliable quantitative evidence for the study of the Chinese economy at the national level. To fully prove this point, nothing less is required than conducting empirical analysis on the state-produced economic information in historical contexts. In the remaining sections of this chapter, I offer a brief description of the patterns and structures of taxation, such as poll taxes, land taxes, and indirect taxes, with regard to the specific state system that produced such data. Although the description focuses on the comparison between Song and Ming, it also covers the financial system of Han and Tang dynasties, which predominantly relied on poll taxes and corvée labor. The core argument is how the economic data generation was interrelated to the evolution of the tax mechanism. Through a comparison on the different kinds of economic data produced by Chinese bureaucracy in the two millennia, one can tell it was the difference in interests, perspective, and capacity of state power that produced different natures of economic information. A modern researcher may tell, just as Ho and Perkins did, how that information was reliable or faulty, yet that scholar cannot reconstruct the size and structure of the economy based on economic data that were originally irrelevant to real changes.

The Poll Tax Era: 220 BC to 755 AD

The first millennium of imperial China can be characterized as governed by poll tax regimes. This characterization is particularly revealing in the population data produced in this era, which constituted the most important and richest part of Chinese historical data. A few scholars have argued the military reforms, especially the conscription of soldiers at a national scale, greatly pushed the development of household registrations in the sixth century BC, the earliest extant record of official population registrations provided by archaeologists date back to the decades around 221 BC.[22] The studies of these records reveal that the collection of poll tax necessitates a thorough control of the population. A family would be registered in official records and then assigned a landholding for making a living.[23] In return, they would pay taxes in grain, cash, and textiles to the state. Military services and corvée services are the most important duties that the registered household had to fulfill. To provide accurate information for these services, household members must be identified by gender and age. Family-owned servants and slaves were also required to serve. Exercising strict control over the population was the key solution to strengthening state power. Whenever the state lost control, its revenues declined, and the pool for the supply of military staff dwindled. Both the allotment of household landholdings and the distribution of tax quotas were calculated exactly by the production potential of the local population, that is, by using the size of a family at the very basic level. This relationship between the poll tax and household registration in imperial China demonstrates that it was the interests of the state, especially the modes of taxation and military mobilization that determined the nature of the economic data.[24]

Yet here comes a major difference in the means of tax payment that leads us to distinguish a monetized pattern from a demonetized pattern. At an early stage, the unified Chinese empire preferred money in poll taxes. In the Han dynasty (206 BC–220 AD), for instance, all men and women between the ages of fifteen and fifty-six needed to pay eighty bronze coins a head per year, a tax known as *suanfu*. A child between the ages of three and fourteen paid twenty coins per year, known as *koufu* (see table 2-2). The numbers of registered aggregate population ranged between 48 to 56 million in the second century; the taxes collected via *suanfu* and *koufu* alone probably amounted to 3.8 to 4.5 billion coins, which was sufficient to maintain the annual state budget.[25]

Except for the head taxes directly levied from family members, an adult male at the age of twenty-three or above had to provide military service at the frontier for three days each year. An estimated 120,000 to 150,000 people were required to fulfill their duty each year. Alternatively, he could pay a sum of three hundred coins to remit such labor duty—a fee known as *gengfu*. This levy is similar to the poll tax in that it was required of all males regardless of wealth and social status. The fact that Han poll tax was collected via money indicates that the peasantry of those days was substantially involved in a money economy, though the extent and real cause are subject to suspicion. Nishijima also mentioned that the imperial minting output reached a yearly average of 0.22 million of strings during the years from 113 BC to the dawn of the first century AD. However, he remarked further that "the large circulation of money during the Han period was the medium through which the state exerted its control over the people by means of the tax system" rather than "the natural result of a fully developed monetary economy."[26] Since the poll tax was indiscriminately distributed among adult males and females at a fixed quota, it neither reflected economic changes at the macro level nor portrayed an image of social structure and wealth distribution.

Given the need to collect the poll taxes and assign labor and military services, it is without dispute in theory and many times evident in practice that the household registration established in the Han dynasty includes all members of a family. Therefore, both the average family size and the ratio between the males and females drawn from the totals can be used to test the credibility of the population figures. The regional distribution of the reported totals can be further used to detect the variances among different macro-regions in imperial China. Thanks to the well-planned and strictly enforced mechanism in enumerating population nationwide, we know China's aggregate population reached nearly 60 million at 2 AD, a first trustworthy figure on China's aggregate population. Persons per family amounted to 4.9.[27] The regional distribution of registered households demonstrates the dominance of the northern population in China in the first century. To be more specific, nearly two-thirds of the national total were living in the Mid- and Lower-Yellow River regions. For all the newly conquered territories in Northwest and Southwest China such as Dunhuang, Zhangye, and Jiaozhi, the density of population was as low as below 2 people per square kilometer.[28] All this testifies to the ability of the imperial administration in acquiring economic information that was necessary for maintaining taxation. The efficiency of the Han dynasty administration can, however, not be overrated. The quality of the extant figures varied greatly. From a statistical perspective, the inconsistency between the reported totals is the crucial weakness in the household enumeration. The total reported in AD 2, for instance, was the highest among all eleven aggregate figures of the Han dynasty that covered the period from 2 AD to 156 AD. The lack of reasonable changes in aggregate figures makes them suspicious. In the first century after 2 AD, the totals show abrupt changes by a decrease from one-half to one-third of the population. In the half century from 105 AD to 146 AD the totals remained nearly unchangeable.[29] A modern researcher thus finds it is impossible to conjecture the trend in long-term changes of the real populations of the time in discussion.[30]

The household registration also comprised the information of landholdings that were owned by each household. The Han dynasty reported land acreage, but these scanty records were even more problematic. Land taxes were levied at the rate of one-thirtieth of farm yield across the Han empire. The size of registered land under cultivation in 145 AD was reported to be 695, 767, 620 Han *mu*. Therefore, the land taxes would amount to 20.9 million Han *shi* if one assumes the farm yield per *mu* was 1 Han *shi* at a tax rate of 0.03 Han *shi* per *mu*. In monetary terms, the total of estimated land taxes probably equaled 3.1 billion coins, less than that of the poll taxes and *gengfu* added together.[31]

The collapse of the Han empire in the second century gave way to an aristocratic world based on a barter economy. While textile and grain replaced coins as the method of tax payment, the poll tax remained the dominant mode of taxation in the financial system. Furthermore, largely due to the establishment of the nomadic regimes in North China and depopulation caused by wars and epidemics, the collection of poll tax became closely associated with the establishment of the militia and the equal-field system, a state-planned land tenure institution. This system continued into the Tang dynasty, when shortly after its reunification of China, the early Tang court issued a code in 624 AD that regulated both land allotment and the collection of poll taxes (see table 2-2).

On the surface, the Tang tax mechanism was simple enough to allow no place for money payment. The poll taxes chiefly targeted male adults between the ages of twenty-one and fifty-nine. They were allotted 100 *mu* of land to farm and in return paid 2 *shi* of millet known as *zu* and 20 feet of textile known as *diao* to the state. In addition, they also needed to work twenty days at a state-assigned post each year. Yet these three tax components were convertible. According to the code, for those who liked to be exempted from labor services, each day of work may be paid in kind by 3 feet of textile, a fee known

Table 2-2. Tang land allotment and taxation statutes, 582 AD

Recipient	Commute land	Hereditary land	Textile payment	Grain payment	Labor service
Teenage (4–15)	—	—	Not eligible	Not eligible	Not eligible
Adolescent (16–20)	80 Tang *mu*	20 Tang *mu*	Not eligible	Not eligible	Not eligible
Male adult/ couple (21–59)	80 Tang *mu*	20 Tang *mu*	20 feet	2 *shi* of millet	20 days
Widow (21–59)	30 Tang *mu*	—	Not eligible	Not eligible	Not eligible
Senior (60 and above)	40 Tang *mu*	—	Not eligible	Not eligible	Not eligible
Handicapped			Not eligible	Not eligible	Not eligible

Source: *Tongdian, juan 2, juan 6.* Also see Twitchett 1970, 124–53. For discussion on minor changes in the regulations over the centuries from 485 to 755 AD, see Yang 2003, 31–40, 61–106; Wu 1992, 64–122.

as *yong*. Thus, to be exempt from the twenty days of service would cost an individual 60 feet of textiles. Meanwhile, a man who is retained for additional services owed no *diao* payment after the completion of fifteen days of work. If he were to complete thirty days of work, both his *diao* and *zu* payments would be remitted. The exchange rate between *zu*, *diao*, and *yong* in this case was 1 (15):1 (15):1.3 (20).[32]

From the state's perspective, however tax payers converted their payment, the taxation amounted to the summation of all three sources. Whether paid in *zu*, *diao*, or *yong*, total payment would add up to 2 *shi* of grain and 80 feet of textile per household or per adult male. Once the proportion of the taxable people was decided, the state could automatically estimate its annual budgetary income. In real terms, 10 feet of textile equaled 1.5 to 2.7 *shi* of millet. Textiles such as silk fabrics and hemp cloth constituted the overwhelmingly dominant share of the poll taxes.

Although simply designed, the Tang code regarding land allotment, tax payment, and labor service required the firm control of rural households. First of all, all households must be reregistered. Migration was allowed only when the government felt the necessity to organize labor for land cultivation in depopulated areas. In the code, a densely populated area known as *zhaixiang* was differentiated from sparsely populated areas known as *kuanxiang*. While the allotted land in the former can be reduced to half of the standard allotment, it could double in the latter. Hence, a merchant could acquire 50 Tang *mu* of the landholding in a relatively sparsely populated place but was denied such rights in densely populated areas. The most important distinction made in household registration was between tax-exempted people and taxable people, the latter legally referred to adult males aged between twenty-one and fifty-nine and without physical disability.[33] In the household register, each family must report the number of family members, servants and slaves, all with clear information about their age, physical capacity and social or marital status, which were used to determine their tax duty. A household with one or more taxable individual would be classified as a taxable household.[34] Documenting this information in detail laid a solid foundation for the collection of poll taxes.

In the household register, each family must report the number of family members, servants and slaves, all with clear information about their age, physical capacity, and social or marital status, which were used to determine their tax duty. A household with one or more taxable individual would be classified as a taxable household. Documenting this information in detail laid a solid foundation for the collection of poll taxes. In table 2-3, I present an example of the household registration in a sub-county in Turfan. For an estimated population as small as 2,500, the households/people were classified into nineteen categories. Every year, the lower-level administrations would report to the higher level the exact changes in the number of taxable households along with tax-exempt ones. According to the code, people who were on labor service duty received no pay from the government. Therefore, the assignment of labor service, especially the fulfillment of military service, urged the government to take household registration seriously.

Given the registered population of 60 million during the High Tang period, this must have been an arduous task for local administrative staff. To maintain this pro-command economy required the state to limit the mobility of the population, and free migration was viewed particularly as a threat. The taxable populations accounted for a relatively small percentage of the total. In this sub-county, only 273 adult males were on duty, while the tax-exempted population totaled 1,447 individuals. During the Tianbao reign (742–56 AD), the court claimed a total population of 52,919,309, among which

Table 2-3. The taxable and tax-exempted individuals in a sub-county in Turfan, 651 AD

A. Estimated Total: 500 x 5 = 2,500 individuals
B. Estimated adult males: 500 individuals
C. Reported adult males on tax duty: 273 individuals
D. Tax-exempted people: 1,447 individuals; this category includes the following:
    I. Male
        a. Teenage (4–15): 270 individuals
        b. Children (below 4): 30
        c. Senior: 77
        d. Handicapped: 2+
        e. Tax free for merit: 49
    II. Female
        a. Senior widow: 106
        b. Widow: ?*
        c. Handicapped: 2
        d. Others: 13
        e. Teenage: 279
        f. Children: 37
        g. Married women: ?
    II. Bondsmen and Servants
        a. Slave: 152
        b. Maid: 182
        c. Serf: 3
        d. Dependent female: ?

Source: Tang 1983. There were nineteen categories in Item D. I have reorganized and combined them into sixteen categories.

*Question marks indicate unavailable information.

44,700,988 were tax-exempted and 8,208,321 were taxable people.[35] The ratio between the taxable and the tax-exempt was 1:5.4.

Such blatant attempts to expand state power across the vast number of local communities via coercive means were often undermined by the challenges from both within and outside the state apparatus. Even for the recorded populations of the years between 705 and 755, which seem relatively reliable, underreporting was still unavoidable. In 723 AD, the court appointed Yuwen Rong on a mission to examine the unreported migrants and their landholdings across the country. In the following year, about 0.8 million households were added to the population registration.[36] The Rebellion and the subsequent turmoil irreversibly undermined state power. The number of registered households in 780 was 3.09 million, only one-third of that in 754 (see table 2-1). Officials attempted to generate new revenue by taxing commerce and developing state monopolies over salt and alcohol immediately after the Rebellion. The huge loss of registered households caused by free migration and local independence finally undermined the poll tax system. In 779, the Tang court formally abolished the *zu-yong-diao* system, reassigned tax duty based on farm size, and collected in the spring and autumn of the year a reform known as the two-tax system. For the succeeding six centuries before the establishment of the Ming dynasty in 1368, the poll tax no longer constituted a major tax form in China.

The poll tax data, especially the Tang equitable-land data and the *zu-yong-diao* system, bear no informative data on market development. The Tang court cared little beyond population control in terms of fiscal administration. Even the size of aggregate landholdings in official records was not the real acreage of cultivated land but estimation based on the regulation of the equitable-land system.[37] The collapse of this system was a result of an evolution from a barter economy into a money economy. The economic data produced after the Rebellion not only far exceeded that of preceding periods in the absolute amount but also demonstrated a different nature of the information that was closely related to a genuine market economy.

The Indirect Taxation Era:
The Song Fiscal State and the Birth of Market-Based Data

The early Tang court (618–712) was the last state in imperial China to adopt "a rigid system of state-controlled land tenure" by allocating a fixed amount of land to each married couple. The collapse of the command economy immediately after the Rebellion gave rise to mercantile powers. In the ensuing centuries preceding China's reunification in 979, commercialized warfare, especially the recruitment of a large number of soldiers for standing armies, forced the government to resort to unprecedented methods to secure money. The Song state was the first unified state power—probably the only one before 1800, as I will demonstrate in the following pages—that gradually came to know how to tax the market effectively. Hereafter, it shall be referred to as a "tax state" for its ability to extract a large amount of tax revenue from nonagricultural sectors.[38]

When the Chinese economy evolved from a barter economy into a money economy during the Tang-Song transformation, its financial structure did indeed undergo a revolution as Twitchett suggested. Before the Rebellion, the poll tax was the most important source for state revenues. Twenty-seven million bolts and hanks of textiles were collected from the poll tax (see table 2-4). As textiles were broadly used in tax payment and in

Table 2-4. Comparison of taxation in Tang and Song eras

Year	Population (000 households)	Aggregate acreage: (000 million shi mu)	Direct taxes in grain (000 shi)	Direct taxes textile (000 bolts)	Direct taxes in cash (000 strings)	Indirect taxes (000 strings)
740s	8,200	664	25,000	27,000	2,000	0
1077	14,245	462–666	22,710	2,175	4,650	11,677

Sources: Twitchett 1970, 153–56; Bao 2001, 318; Chao, 89; Wu Songdi 2000, 347.

1. The Tang court relied on its control of population to secure resources and labor services. Therefore no record of the size of the cultivated land was made. Du You, a high official, reported 8.2 million registered households in the Tianbao period (742–756) and estimated 70 *mu* of landholdings per household (Twitchett, 153). This means 620 million *mu* (8,200,000 x 70). However, this figure is based on Du's rough estimate and the size of the *mu* is also subject to question. For convenience of comparison, I follow Wu Hui and Chao to assume that the estimated 70 *mu* allotment was measured in Han *mu*, thus equivalent to 100 Tang *mu*, or 81 *shi mu*. It is apparent that this approach probably overestimates China's aggregate acreage in the eighth century. The Song figure was based on a land survey in 1072, which originally recorded 462 million *mu*. Chao adjusts the figure to be 666 million *mu* (Chao, 79–80, 87).

2. In the 740s, grain revenue amounted to 25 million Tang *shi*. In addition, the Tang court also collected textiles from registered households, which amounted to 27 million bolts and hanks. In addition, on average, each household was estimated to pay 250 *wen* of cash, and the total was about 2 million strings. For the tax revenues collected in 1077, see Bao 2001, 318.

public expenditure, it gained the status as a medium of exchange throughout the empire. Cash payment already appeared in state revenues in the 740s. This was an important development in comparison with the earlier periods of the medieval economy. However, this cash revenue had little to do with the *zu-yong-diao* system. It was obtained from household tax (*hushui*), a surcharge added to the poll tax in the first half of the eighth century. The average amount collected from each household was estimated to be 250 *wen* of cash, and the total was about 2 million strings in the 740s (see table 2-4). This small amount was already the peak record of cash revenues that the aristocratic Chinese state could acquire for many centuries before the Rebellion.[39]

Cash revenues took a great leap forward during the centuries after the Rebellion. In 1077, the cash revenue increased to 16 million strings, about eight times that of the 740s. The two major sources that contributed to the cash collected by the Song state were land taxes and indirect taxes, with the latter contributing the larger portion. The poll tax never played an important role in the Song tax regime. Consequently, the Song tax administration needed to target taxpayers in a way compatible with market development and free migration.

What made the Song tax regime unusual among the Chinese dynasties was that it no longer relied on land taxes to keep up its revenues. Analyses of tax revenue collected in 1077 obviously indicate that an indirect tax–based regime was in the making (see table 2-5). Excise, or taxes and profits from state monopolies of tea, salt, and liquor, constituted the largest source of state revenues. By the 1070s the Song dynasty had become a strong tax state that managed to tax trade, especially the trading of consumption goods.

Excise was the cornerstone of indirect taxes, and its origin could be traced back to the various methods used by the Tang court to raise revenues in the anti-Rebellion period. Tea and salt were produced in places distant from consumers and would be taxed along trade routes. Liquor production and consumption were very narrowly confined to a local area. The alcohol monopoly was mostly enforced in urban communities, while rural households were allowed to only produce enough for private consumption. The government would either strictly control the production and sale of these commodities or farm out the business to agents. In the latter case, officials granted a short-term franchise to the highest bidder. In the late Tang, revenues from state monopolies normally amounted

Table 2-5. Components of Song revenues in 1077

Taxes	Amount (in 000 string)	Percentage
Land taxes	20,213	32.9
Excise	21,924	35.7
Commercial taxes	8,680	14.1
Tax farming (wine monopoly, transportation, and other services)	6,027	10.0
Customs	540	1.0
Mining	3,973	6.5
Total	62,697	100.0

Source: Bao 2001, 318.

to less than 6 million strings. The salt monopoly was the single largest source of income, with the tea and liquor monopolies generating smaller portions.[40]

As population growth and urbanization continued over the first one and a half centuries of the Song dynasty, revenues generated by state monopolies steadily increased. For instance, commercial taxes levied against tea shipments from the Lower Yangtze, Fujian, and Guangdong reached 1.25 million strings of cash in 1109, and the central government also received 0.6 million from selling permits to tea merchants. In addition, the tea monopoly in Sichuan alone contributed 1 million strings of iron coins.[41] The annual output of tea in the eleventh century was estimated to be 90 to 100 million Song *jin*, of which 37 million *jin* were distributed to the northern provinces through long-distance trade routes.[42] Revenues from the salt monopoly likewise increased from 3 million in 997 to 12 million strings in 1077.[43] The alcohol monopoly in 1077 was estimated to generate 7.9 million strings.[44] In total, state monopoly revenues expanded from 5 to 6 million strings in the mid-eighth century to about 22 million strings in the late eleventh century.

The Land Taxes Era: An Inefficient Mode of Taxation

The two-tax system reform in 780 was aimed to reconstruct the basis of state finance by consolidating the role of agricultural taxes. Yet what happened during the succeeding years, to the dismay of the Tang court, proved that the state could not get rid of its reliance on monopolies.[45] Nonetheless, the collection of land taxes shifted the state's focus from the strict control of household registration to land registration. The court viewed land taxes as the major tax levied in the countryside and attempted to combine all the other kinds of levies into it.[46] The reform had a far-reaching effect on the relationship between Chinese bureaucratic administration and local communities. As Yang Yan, the chief minister who initiated the reform, addressed clearly in his memorial, "Households should be registered according to their actual residence, with no distinction whether they are local families or immigrants. Persons should be distinguished according to whether they are rich or poor, not differentiated as 'adults' or 'adolescents.'"[47] Hence, the government recognized the right of free migration and protected the private ownership of landholdings in order to make possible the assessment of land taxes across the countryside.[48] The introduction of the land taxes occurred at a time when the central authority at Chang'an was weakened. The court could control only part of the empire. For nearly three hundred prefectures, warlords controlled seventy-one prefectures and refused to report registration of households. The central authority received annual tax revenues from only forty-nine prefectures, most of which were located in the south.[49] China was soon divided, and one could hardly expect the effective operation of the land taxes until the Song court reunited the whole country in 980 AD. It was first represented in household registration. According to *Taiping huanyu ji*, the national geography published shortly after the reunification, the registered aggregate households reached 5,859,551. For the first time in Chinese history, we find the division between the landless and landlords: 3,443,843 for the total number of landlords (*zhuhu*) and 2,415,708 for the landless (*kehu*).[50] What is more important, the compiler also clearly recorded the subtotals of the landless and landlords for most prefectures. In the new regulation issued in 1033, the Song state ordered local officials, for purposes of taxation, to rank all landowners into five levels in correspondence to their wealth. This policy distinguished the class of landowners from that of the tenants, who were exempted from paying taxes.[51] All this made the Song legislation the first in Chinese history to interfere minimally over the distribution of landholdings.

Yet in reality, the collection of land taxes was much more problematic than it appeared, and the share of the land taxes in the state tax revenues continued to decline throughout the three hundred years from 960 to 1127. For a rural community, either land surveying or self-reporting of landownership, including the grading of land fertility, had to be done before the quotas were settled with varying tax rates.[52] To secure tax revenues from a multitude of agricultural sources, the administration must tax agricultural outputs rather than singularly using grain as the only unit of payment. Mulberry, hemp, and sericulture also became the target.[53] Land taxes also targeted nonagricultural incomes such as the leasing of storage houses, vehicles, and interests of loans. In many areas of South China the poll tax was still exploited as supplementary sources until the Renzong reign (1022–1063), and adult males were required to pay a sum of cash each year. Toward the mid-eleventh century, the court ordered the local officials of all prefectures to follow the same guide in compiling the household-income register (*wudeng dingchanbu*). All landowners should be ranked into five classes in descending order of wealth. It should identify two major criteria for the tax assessment in rural communities: the productivity of farmland as presented in land prices, or the monetized index of farm outputs per acre and the amount of household income gained from other facilities and capital. In spite of this general guideline, land assessment was still carried out at the county level and tax rates varied in correspondence to local situations.[54]

Due to the efforts of Song local officials information such as the total acreage under cultivation in the eleventh century, among other invaluable data, became available to modern researchers that one cannot expect for the preceding dynasties. Yet the collection of land taxes was inefficient from the very beginning. Land taxes alone comprised only a minor portion of the Song state's budgetary revenues and an even slighter portion of cash revenues. In 1077, Song China likely had a population of over 80 million, three-fourths of whom belonged to the agricultural sector. However, the share of land taxes declined from 67 percent in 997 to 32 percent in 1077 (see table 2-6). In the late thirteenth century, the share of land tax in Song tax revenue further declined to about 15–20 percent, while the monetized share in land taxes was much higher than one century before.[55]

Table 2-6. Changes of the tax structure, 997–1077
(in 0,000 *strings*)

Time	Land taxes	Percentage	Indirect taxes	Percentage
997	24,081	67.3	11,677	32.7
1021	26,412	49.7	26,700	50.3
1077	20,213	32.2	42,484	67.7

Source: Bao 2001, 316–19.

This declining trend can be chiefly attributed to two factors: the low and almost fixed tax rate adopted by the Song administration and the underreporting of farmlands by private owners. The Song court had to compromise on a very low rate because of all kinds of technical difficulties it encountered in the collection of land taxes. As Song population more than tripled in the eleventh century, the reported acreage increased only by 50 percent. Underreporting as a means of tax evasion was a well-known fact to Song contemporaries. Many estimated that at least half of the cultivated land across the country was missing from the tax accounts. Even for the reported acreage, the tax rate was not high. The grain revenues collected in 1077, for instance, amounted to 17,887, 257 Song *shi*, only 1.6 Song *shi* per landowning household or 0.04 Song *shi* per *mu*.[56]

The conservatism in the collection of land taxes is also well known to the students of Ming-Qing history. This origin should be traced back to the Song land tax administration. Other than the two factors discussed previously that resulted in the state's declining capacity to collect agricultural taxes, one should also pay attention to the inflation factor. As tax payments were often converted into money, a fixed quota of land taxes could easily cause a substantial decline in real tax revenues over a long period. However, one major difference between the Song fiscal state and the land-tax-based financial regime in Ming and Qing eras led to opposite economic development. For the Song fiscal state, substantial tax income from nonagricultural sectors, especially from consumption and trade, could increase along with market expansion and population growth and thus maintain real state revenues at a stable level, an achievement that later dynasties failed to follow.

The Heyday of a Command Economy Era and the Early Ming Data

The collapse of the Southern Song in 1279 signaled an end to the indirect taxation era. Regimes primarily based on land-taxes prevailed in China after Zhu Yuanzhang established the Ming dynasty in 1368. Researchers have elaborated on the unusual scale of government-organized migration in the late fourteenth century to demonstrate the strict control the Ming government exercised over the populace. The Ming government in its first century succeeded in forcing people to move from rich, densely settled areas to devastated areas in northern and southwestern China. The total number of migrants, according to Cao Shuji, may have reached 11 million, over one-sixth of the early Ming population.[57]

In other important fields, the early Ming regime also produced rich firsthand information documenting the largest command economy in the preindustrial world. The Ming government enforced strict control over the people in their occupations and residences through a thorough household registration system. All the households under a certain jurisdiction were identified by profession (peasants, artisans, soldiers, and so on) and organized into the *lijia* system. Ten households formed one *jia*, and eleven *jia* constituted one *li*. Those who were registered could not freely change their professions or move to another location other than the registered one.[58] The comprehensive occupational categories covered all kinds of professional workers, including military and administrative service, such as soldiers, mining laborers, and artisans, as well as nonprofessionals, such as sedan carriers, trumpeters, and graveyard keepers. The majority of households in the registration system were farmers, who were summoned for three months of mandatory service once every three years to work for the state. Ming labor services included essential state projects, such as building city walls or conveying grain taxes to the capital.

The ideology of the early Ming government was that the people, under the Ming emperor's direct leadership, would organize themselves both to serve the state and to maintain the harmony of local society. Neither the market nor the bureaucracy was favored as the means for state building because both were believed to nurture corruption at the governmental and local community level. Thus, the early Ming state relied solely upon its direct control over individuals and resources.

The most reliable economic data come from the military farm. The early Ming military organization comprised 2.76 million soldiers, and if we take into account their immediate families, their extended families in their hometowns, and the personnel in reserves, the number of households involved in military services would amount to 2.19 million, about 20 percent of the total households registered.[59] Yet the early Ming state spent very little to sustain such a large number of soldiers and staff. The troops, for instance, whether stationed in the hinterland or the frontier, had to expend more than half of their manpower to cultivate and farm in order to sustain themselves. In 1403, the grain output from military farms was reported to be 23 million *shi*, which was close to the amount of land taxes the Ming government could collect yearly from rural households.[60] Extant records not only report the rise and decline of military farms in nearly two centuries but also tell many details about the daily life of ordinary soldiers and farming practice, such as the lack of farming tools and draft animals, the ratio between seeds and harvested outputs at each farm, and so on. In that sense, the military history provides invaluable sources for modern researchers to analyze the operation of a preindustrial command economy and its impact on local societies in Ming China.[61]

People were required to provide services according to status, which the state assigned to them, and their duties would be transferred to the succeeding generation when the seniors passed away. Soldiers in the military, for instance, were enrolled in the registration system as "military households." Once a family was chosen to be a military household, it was obliged to remain as such over generations. A person needed to request permission from the government if he wish to migrate, change professions, or travel.[62]

The Hongwu reign was exceptional for its effective management of the population and land distribution through the *lijia* system. Nominally, the early Ming policies lasted for one and a half centuries, but in reality, government control loosened as the recovery of the market economy and the prosperity of local society in many parts of Ming China, especially in the Lower Yangtze region, began as early as the late fifteenth century. Many scholars have described the Ming economy at that time as so vibrant that it was entering an economic and cultural boom that were to last well into the eighteenth century.

However, after 1400, as Ho Ping-ti demonstrated, the recorded figures of the Ming population increasingly resembled mere fiscal data and became less reflective of the real changes in the population. Moreover, the collapse of the early Ming system also terminated any effective state intervention into the private economy so that the sixteenth-century economic boom made no significant contribution to Ming state revenues.[63] One is left with little information in official documents regarding the wealth of trade and population changes. Therefore, estimates of growth in sixteenth- and seventeenth-century China's economy and population should be made with great caution.

The Debate over Song Population Data

How to interpret data collected from the Song population registration is a major problem that concerns modern researchers in the field. Except for the influence of Marxist historiography, which is skeptical of any attempts to identify an important case of market development that occurred earlier in a place other than early modern Europe, researchers are left with few analytic models to explain the Song China scenario. While the unit of a household in early Ming and other Chinese dynastic population data was usually reported to have four to six members, known as *kou*, the same term in the Song records often referred to about two members (see table 2-7). Based on this departure from the norm, some scholars thus discredit all Song population data and deemed such information unreliable.

If we focus on aggregate households rather than on the total number of registered individuals per household, the Song data are surprisingly excellent. Liang Fangzhong presented a comprehensive collection of Chinese registered population records from 2 AD down to 1911. One can immediately discern that most of these figures were *not* real population figures. For instance, while the number of registered households reached 12, 233, 062 in 2 AD, it drastically declined to only 1,473,423 in the 260s and jumped up to 2,459,840 in 280. Although military conflicts ravaged China during the Three Kingdom period (220–280 AD), it is very unlikely that Chinese aggregate population could dwindle to one-sixth of the size from two centuries ago and then skyrocket in just two decades. A more plausible explanation is that the weakening central power, when facing challenges from warlords and magnates, gradually lost control of its resources and population. A large number of households and a vast amount of land were controlled directly by magnates that became hidden from the census.[64]

In contrast, all the extant Song aggregate population figures appear consistent. As shown in table 2-8, the aggregate households tripled over the course of the eleventh century. The figures presented here indicate decennial growth at a reasonable rate without the drastic fluctuation found in earlier data.

The distrust of the Song population data is due to a major misunderstanding of the nature of the Song population registration system. One can use Dwight Perkins's

Table 2-7. Average size of Chinese families, AD 2–1626

Dynasties	Persons per household
Western Han (AD 2)	4.9
Eastern Han (AD 57–156)	4.9–5.8
Sui (AD 606)	5.2
Tang (AD 705–755)	5.7–6.0
Song (AD 1006–1223)	1.4–2.6
Jin (AD 1187–1207)	6.4–6.7
Yuan (AD 1290–1292)	4.5–4.6
Ming (AD 1381–1626)	4.8–7.1

Source: Durand 1960, 212.

Table 2-8. Decennial report of Song population, 1003–1100

Year	Aggregate households	Total numbers	Numbers per household
1003	6,864,160	14,278,040	2.08
1014	9,055,729	21,996,965	2.43
1023	9,898,121	25,455,859	2.57
1034	10,296,565	26,205,441	2.55
1045	10,682,947	21,654,163	2.03
1053	10,792,705	22,292,861	2.07
1063	12,462,317	26,421,651	2.12
1072	15,091,560	21,867,852	1.45
1083	17,211,713	24,969,300	1.45
1094	19,120,921	42,566,243	2.23
1103	20,524,065	45,981,845	2.24
1110	20,882,258	46,734,784	2.24

Source: Table A-1 in appendix A in this volume.

method to test whether or not Chinese historical data can be treated as valid quantitative evidence. In this regard, the Chinese historical data in the centuries from 900 to 1500 are, contrary to some scholars' assumptions, reliable. A full discussion is presented in appendix A in the present volume. Here I focus on the context of the Song household registration system.

The major factor that distinguishes the Song population registration is that, as many Song history researchers have already pointed out, it included adult males only.[65] The total members of a household, hence the average family size, did not exceed three persons; this is a strong indication of the accuracy of the Song household registration system. In 963, the court issued an edict requiring all prefectures to report their populations. The family members per household reported in the tax account only referred to males aged between twenty and fifty-nine. All females were excluded.[66]

As Wu Songdi clearly explains, the Song court (usually the *sansi* administration) required local officials to collect information only on property, land, and male members of each household in their routine report. No imperial edict requiring the registration of female population was ever found in Song documents. Usually, it was during a famine relief that we find the local administration reporting the full number of household members. Obviously, the officials believed the distribution of food necessitated genuine head counts. On such occasions, the reported family members per household often exceeded five or six persons.

Although Wu's argument is supported by solid reasoning, the question still remains why so many demographic historians tend to dispute the reliability of Song population data. If Wu's explanation is valid, the real question underlying the current debate is why censuses conducted by other dynastic regimes needed to, in principle, report all members of a family while the Song administration alone considered this unnecessary.

In this book, I argue that it is the market-based financial institution that made the Song case different from all other dynasties in China. The Song household registration can be taken impartially because it was not directly related to the purpose of taxation, not to mention the state's noninterventionist policies over residential registration and physical mobility. An institutional analysis of the Song dynasty will readily demonstrate contrasting characteristics between Song and early Ming population administration and migration policies. The growth of the population in Song times accompanied the rise of a market economy and urbanization. The literature on Song institutional and legal history points to the fact that laborers migrated from the countryside to the cities or changed from one profession to another by choice, usually driven by opportunities provided by the market economy. To maintain its capacity to negotiate with local communities in a market economy, the Song government was consistently sensitive to information regarding changes in the labor forces and wealth. The official registration of local households was carried out once every three years with particular emphases on revaluating property and recording the number of male adults.[67] Thus, the most distinctive feature we find in Song official records of the population and households is a clear division between the treatment of taxable and nontaxable people, the so-called *zhuhu* and *kehu*, respectively.[68] For those falling into the former category, all of his and his family's mobile and immobile properties (cash, estate, farm, incomes, etc.) were meticulously assessed.[69]

This vision of wealth enabled Song officials to tax people in accordance with the total amount of family property and income, regardless of where they lived (urban or rural), the size of their families, or how they earned their income (farmers, merchants, owners of transport vehicles, or landlords). For this reason, the Song state showed no interest in tracking migration, conducting precise head counts, or controlling labor distribution. However, there was no national standard for assessing property gradations. Local officials graded all taxable farming families (*xiangcunzhuhu*) invariably into five income levels from high to low and urban residents (*fangguohu*) into ten income levels. On the contrary, *kehu*, such as tenants on a farm or urban laborers, were defined as employed laborers without any other major taxable income.[70] In the 1260s, the urban *kehu* population at Fuzhou, a middle-level city in the mid-Yangtze region, was about 65,000, nearly one-half of the registered urban population.[71]

Conclusion

Ho's study on the population and land acreage in Ming China reveals a corresponding relationship between the quality of economic data and the way in which they were generated. In this chapter, I follow such an institutional perspective to provide a general survey of Chinese historical data with their dynastic contexts. I extend the survey many centuries before the founding of the Ming dynasty in 1368, and my survey refers to three major types of officially generated data sources. The first and oldest type of Chinese historical data was generated for the collection of poll taxes. The Chinese state drew the majority of its revenues via poll tax until the outburst of the Rebellion in 755 AD. The second type of data came from the rise of a new kind of fiscal administration during the centuries after the Rebellion, a professional service that drew most of its revenues from consumption taxes while relying minimally on labor services. Under such circumstances the government also allowed freedom of migration and protected private property ownership. The third type of data came from a conservative administration whose major income was based on land taxes and preferred to use fixed quotas known as financial conservatism, a term well known in the study of Ming-Qing eras. Although

Ho points to the first and the third type that prevailed in Ming China, he largely fails to address the second type that is most important for the study of market expansion in the eleventh century.

Song economic data, the data source Ho has ignored, can be credited for the valuable information they provide for in-depth market analysis. This is largely due to a new mechanism in reporting population that was devised by the central administration in Song China. Any increase in population, when discovered and reported by local officials in household registration, did not result in an increase in taxation. On the other hand, the Song central administration was keen to demographic changes and viewed population growth as a sign of economic development. A local administrator would be promoted after the reported increase in households was proven true. Unlike the command economy–based fiscal administration, the Song fiscal state was the only indirect taxation regime in pre-1800s imperial China that drew the majority of its tax revenues from taxing the market. It was unnecessary for the Song statesmen to count heads in tax assessment. This new finding rather supports and further develops the Ho puzzle. The underreporting of Chinese population in official records, as Ho clearly demonstrates, was owing to the purpose of taxation evasion, an inevitable consequence of the poll tax–based financial system. Presumably, if the taxation bears little relation to household registration and at the same time if the administration would make serious efforts to collect updated information on demographic changes, the Ho puzzle could be avoided. The population reported from the local administration was trustworthy, as they did not directly serve the purpose of taxation.

For a modern researcher, what the Song statesmen did provides important information about changes in the structure of income and consumption in world history as early as the eleventh century. An important conclusion we can draw from the preceding discussion is that the extant data for the six centuries between 900 and 1500 are the most reliable, if not the only set of reliable data, for quantitative analysis of the Chinese economy prior to 1800. The Song economic data, especially data relating to indirect taxation, highlight the performance and structure of an expanding market economy. In contrast, the early Ming data demonstrate clearly the rise of a command economy.

Due to the influence of Marxist ideology, Chinese historians have paid much attention to changes in the sixteenth-century economy and sought empirical evidence documenting market development. Unfortunately, most of the evidence they have found is no more than personal accounts, isolated cases, and descriptive stories.[72] The Ho puzzle clearly points to the invalidity of records created after 1400 that document the Chinese population and cultivated land. Yet, what should really interest economic historians is to move away from the Ming-Qing transformation and asks instead how the rich amount of pre-1368 data on the Chinese economy and population can help us understand premodern economic development.

Part II

The Song Era

Chapter 3

How Large Was the Money Economy?

The first major characteristic observed from long-term economic changes in China is the existence of two contrasting economic cycles during the six intervening centuries between 900 and 1500. During the Song era from 960 to 1120, population growth and market development engineered economic expansion to an unprecedented level. This expansive cycle, however, halted after 1200. The Mongol conquest in the thirteenth century caused a radical decline in the Chinese aggregate population and devastated the economy in North and Central China. The retreating cycle worsened during the succeeding two centuries by the establishment of a command economy and by all kinds of anti-market policies that the early Ming court implemented.

The fourteenth-century turning point thesis held by Elvin, Skinner, and Hartwell explicitly takes demographic change as the major cause for the making of these two cycles and assumes the economy would have recovered to the same level when the population reached the same size.[1] This assumption is highly problematic and rather misleading when applied to the performance of the early Ming economy. Despite the close connection between population decline and the major trend in price movements, a shrinking in the size of the market economy was even more dramatic than the decline in the population. The following three chapters are aimed to provide a comprehensive survey of the two cycles based upon quantitative evidence. Chapter 4 focuses on the expansion of the Kaifeng-centered waterway transportation network in the eleventh century, and this investigation strongly supports the Song commercial revolution thesis. Chapter 5 depicts the disintegration of the Chinese market economy after the Mongol conquest. This chapter outlines an overview by examining these two contrasting cycles from a market perspective, in particular changes in prices, per capita money stock, and the reconstruction of domestic markets.

In the first section in this chapter, I provide a brief comparison of demographic and price changes during the Song and Ming eras. This comparison suggests a severe contraction in the market economy during the fourteenth and fifteenth centuries. To test this proposition, I further use the commercial tax data from 1077 and 1381 to establish that domestic markets were much larger in the Song than in early Ming China. In the second section, I argue that the rise of a command economy in the early Ming, which promoted the prevalence of payment in kind and labor services and severely undermined the needs for hard currencies, is the real cause of very low prices in the early Ming era. In the third section, I compare the money stock in the eleventh and sixteenth centuries to highlight the underdevelopment of the market economy in the Ming era in contrast to the Song. A shocking decline in the money supply at both the aggregate level and per capita level in the Song-Yuan-Ming transitional period significantly contributed to the price divergence between Song and Ming. Yet the principal forces that drove Ming prices down were anti-market policies implemented by the early Ming court.

Divergence in the Song and Ming Economies: Population and Price

Changes in population and in prices are extremely important in defining long-term trends in any economy. As this book focuses on market development, the core question underlying the six-century population and price changes is what happened to the market? Did the market expand and shrink at the same pace as changes in the population? Or, was demarketization the major cause of the downward movement in prices during the fifteenth century? These questions lead to an investigation of the correlation between demographic change and movement in prices during the five centuries.

Fortunately, extant records from the Song dynasty offer a uniquely comprehensive view of population development in the pre-Mongol conquest period. For instance, we have at least one reliable record for every two or three years to estimate aggregate population from 980 to 1109 and from 1149 to 1223, respectively. In the first phase, Song China achieved an annual rate of population growth of 0.92 percent.[2] Therefore, it is beyond doubt that the Song population in the 1120s had already reached 110 million. Population growth and commercialization together laid a solid foundation for the expansion of the Chinese economy in the long eleventh century.

The population-centered narratives identified the Mongol conquest as a crucial point that linked the two economic cycles. The Mongol conquest of North China inflicted a fatal blow to the economy and the population of the region. The national censuses conducted by the imperial administration between 980 and 1391 provide backbone information of this drastic decline.[3] The census conducted in 1270 recorded 1.9 million households, which was roughly one-fifth of the previously recorded population in North China before the conquest.[4] Such radical decline in aggregate population, especially the changes in regional distribution, is rarely seen in world demographic history and should be recognized as an indispensable factor causing economic decline. Although the Mongol conquest of the Southern Song in South China was much less destructive, the military campaigns took an unavoidably heavy toll on the upper- and mid-Yangtze regions. The prolonged military conflicts between the Mongols and the Southern Song in Sichuan lasted for over forty years, far longer than in any other provinces. From 1173 to 1270–1290, the registered households in Sichuan declined from 2.7 million to 0.9 million.[5] In contrast, the central provinces in the middle Lower Yangtze valley, including Hunan and Jiangxi, rose significantly. The population in Hunan increased ten times from 980 to 1290, which ranked first among the southern provinces for growth rates of population.[6]

Next, I turn to examine long-term changes in prices during the same period. Both Peng and Chuan Hansheng demonstrate that Ming food prices remained comparatively low when measured against preceding dynasties.[7] Yet the long-term effects of low prices have rarely been discussed in relation to the working of the Ming economy. I recomputed a number of Peng's series on grain prices and converted them into a standard index based on silver value to obtain a comprehensive view of changes in prices over the six centuries from Song to Ming China.

The history of prices shows two phases of diametrically opposite movements that further reflect changes in the market economy. As Peng's rice index shows (see table B-1 in appendix B; hereafter, I call this the Peng index), if we set the price of 961–970 at 100 points, the Song grain price gradually climbed up to 200 points over nearly a hundred years. By the beginning of the thirteenth century, it had risen to three and a half to four times that of the early Song grain price. Moreover, after 1126, the grain price in southern China increased 50 percent during the twelfth century alone. Thus, during these three centuries, the grain price continuously rose to reach a four- to fivefold increase from pre-Song times, reaching a new height of 350 to 400 points. Assuming that the grain price reflects the general change of prices, this rising trend actually can be traced to an even earlier time. Scholars working on the economic history of Tang China (618–907) have pointed out that price levels during the Tang dynasty began to rise in the late eighth century immediately after the Rebellion. According to these researchers, by the beginning of the Song dynasty, the silk price, for instance, was double that of the early eighth century.[8]

However, the upward trend in prices came to an end in the late fourteenth century. During the Ming period, prices moved in the opposite direction. The Peng index indicates that by the early Ming period they had almost returned to the original low level of the mid-tenth century. Yet this was not the lowest point to be seen. Grain prices bottomed out during the first half of the fifteenth century. Not until the mid-sixteenth century did Ming grain price reach 250 points. Furthermore, it was only in the second quarter of the eighteenth century that grain prices again attained the highest level achieved during the Song.

While the population-centered narrative points to radical demographic change during the Mongol conquest, price movement that indicates an obvious divergence, the huge difference in the market performance, took place after the establishment of the Ming dynasty—that is almost ninety years after the Mongol troops terminated the Southern Song dynasty and enjoyed sixty years of peace. The first century of the Ming dynasty was a crucial turning point between the price movement of the Tang-Song transformation era and that of the Ming-Qing transformation era. During the late fourteenth and fifteenth centuries, prices plunged dramatically to the lowest level we have seen since the tumultuous ninth century and only recovered sluggishly by 1500. A century-long deflation clearly indicates the enduring negative consequences of early Ming policies on the economy. It was not until the mid-eighteenth century that prices eventually climbed back to the high level achieved in the mid-thirteenth century. Two questions arise from the preceding comparison: Why did price levels remain so low in the early Ming period and take such a long time to bounce back to the thirteenth-century level? Second, how much can one attribute the prolonged deflation to a severe market contraction, and to what extent is the fall in production outputs associated with a decline in the living standard?

Under normal circumstances, the Fisher equation can provide a theoretical approach to explore long-term changes in prices from a monetary perspective. Presumably, the direction and degree of changes in prices (thus P) depend on changes in the other three variables: money stocks (M), velocity of money in circulation (V), and total outputs (T). The last variable can be reached by aggregate population times per capita outputs.

As one applies this model to price movements during the Song-Yuan-Ming transition, a relative decline in average food price might have resulted from any of the following: a decline in M and V and an increase in T, per capita outputs times aggregate population, or a combination of both.

Obviously demographic change cannot justify such a decline in average prices during the transitional period. The Fisher equation proposes that if per capita outputs remain stable and other variables equal, population decline would cause proportionally an increase in average price. Yet this is opposite to what really happened. First, for the first century of the Ming dynasty, average price levels were far below that of the 1110s. Second, the timing does not support the population decline as a chief cause for the price movements. Chinese households reached 21,114,000 around 1200, then declined to 14,724,000 households in 1391, and gradually recovered to 18,839,000 households in 1542.[9] However, this radical decline in aggregate population took place during the Mongol conquest, far ahead of the plunge in prices. If we focus on Jiangnan, the most advanced economic region in China, the population increased steadily from 1162 to 1391. Yet the prices then were the lowest reached during these three centuries.

One may also try to account for the sharp decline in early Ming average price levels by looking at the changes on the monetary side of the equation, especially the money stock. In theory, a decline in the money stock may result from two possible causes. The first possibility is the extraction of money in absolute amount due to exports of hard currencies and hoarding and melting for making utensils. In other words, hard currencies were in short supply. The monetarist quantity theory of money further suggests that changes in prices were essentially caused by changes in the money stock to the same extent. Logically, changes in the money stock (M) at one side of the equation would raise or lower proportionately the nominal price of outputs (thus P) on the other side of the equation yet produce few impacts on real aggregate outputs (T).[10] To apply this assumption to the early Ming economy, one will reach a conclusion that the radical decline in early Ming prices was only a monetary phenomenon that had little to do with the real economy.

Empirical evidence challenges such a monetarist explanation. Most important of all, there is a two-century time lag between the decline in supply of hard currency and the occurrence of the great deflation. While the insufficient supply of bronze coins was already strongly felt after 1127, a rising trend in the price of rice continued until a sudden reversion in 1368. Neither the destruction of the Northern Song in the north nor the Mongol conquest of China stopped the rising trend. The monetary system in the early Ming period was, in fact, quite similar to the Yuan system.[11] Yet, the prices in Song and Ming eras diverged greatly. Price levels in the 1370s were already only 75 percent of that in the 1120s, but they declined again in the first half of the fifteenth century to just 20 percent of that in the 1370s.

The price movement within the Ming period itself contradicts this monetarist explanation. Leaving aside the great gap between the Song and Ming money supply, price levels during the Ming dynasty showed a steeper decline in the first half of the fifteenth century and leveled out low for most of the remaining century. It was not until the end of the fifteenth century that price levels started to move toward a higher level again. This trend implies no corresponding relationship between price levels and the Ming money supply as there were few significant changes in the latter since the end of the fourteenth century. While most of the imperial mints were closed in the 1390s, silver output from state-controlled domestic mines did reach a relatively high level in the 1410s.[12] In other words, the money supply during the Yongle reign was actually larger than that of the periods before or after. Yet grain prices began to decline again immediately after 1400. Thus, there is no reason to believe that the money supply factor alone suffices to explain the movement of price levels during the fifteenth century.

Price changes are initially related to the amount of money in circulation. But not all price movements can be fully accounted for by the monetary theory. This is often true when the market is fragile and the need for hard currencies become unstable due to dramatic institutional changes. The rise of a command economy, for instance, would greatly restrict the extent of monetization and decrease the need for hard currencies. Both the enforcement of baochao as the only legitimate medium of exchange and the rise of a barter economy significantly undermined the market structure in the early Ming.

Although the baochao was nominally a state-sanctioned currency, it was primarily issued as a means of payment to officials and soldiers only and assumed a very minor role in meeting the monetary needs of the private sectors in the economy. Moreover, the baochao was designed for the state's fiscal (anti-market) purposes, which soon became irrelevant to metallic currencies in circulation.[13] There was a battle between the court and merchants and landlords from the Lower Yangtze region, who wielded monetary power at the market based on their wealth in gold and silver. The court aimed to undermine their power by defining paper bills as the only legitimate currency and forced the wealthy to sell precious metals in exchange for baochao.[14]

To regulate the market via baochao proved a disaster. Soon after the baochao was formally issued in 1375, the court issued this currency without restraint, which not surprisingly resulted in severe depreciation. In 1390, Zhu Yuanzhang issued as a general reward to soldiers and officials no less than 95 million guan of paper notes, which was nearly five times the annual state income recorded for those years.[15] The depreciation of baochao worsened during the Yongle reign (1403–1424): According to the regulation of the Hongwu reign, 1 guan of baochao could buy 1 shi of rice and was officially equal to 1,000 wen of bronze coins. But in 1407, 1 guan of baochao could buy only 1/30 shi of rice. In 1448, a decade later, it was only worth 2 wen even at the official rate, reflecting a five hundred times depreciation rate in comparison to its original value. However, this hyperinflation did not make the real economy inflationary; the prices measured by both bronze coins and silver remained quite low throughout the fifteenth century.[16] It rather isolated the circulation of baochao from the market: While the Ming government continuously issued and distributed baochao mostly as payment to officials and soldiers, people no longer accepted this paper bill as real money. Thus, as the baochao lost its value and failed to maintain its purchasing power at the markets due to unconstrained over-issuing, it hardly qualified as a form of credible and meaningful money. Nonetheless, this paper bill policy had been carried on during most of the early Ming period. It inevitably damaged the role of hard currencies at earlier decades when the court did not allow use of silver in trade. The negative consequence could be felt even in the latter decades. People had to look for standard currency by themselves for exchange of goods when baochao became worthless pieces of paper. All of this promoted barter at local markets and made the shrinking market even more fragile.

Payment in kind prevailed throughout the entire early Ming period. This explicitly points to the rise of a barter economy in the Lower Yangtze, the leading region in the

Chinese economy. Other regional economies were even more demonetized. Contemporary writings indicated that the circulation of coins was limited to the corridor along the Grand Canal. In 1503, the censor Zhang Wen reported to the court,

> Rice, grain, silver and cloth—but not coin—were used as money in the central provinces of Jiangxi and Huguang. Even more primitive commodity monies were employed in the less commercialized northwestern and southwestern provinces. For example, furs substituted for money in Shanxi and Shaanxi, while, as in the past, cowrie shells constituted the primary medium of exchange in Yunnan.[17]

For our purpose of measuring the amount of money in circulation during the early Ming, barter raises an unsolvable problem because technically it is impossible to convert diversified means of payment into a standard money unit. Dramatic changes in prices and population during the Song-Yuan-Ming transition period reflected tremendous fluctuation in supply and demand. The rise of a command economy would restrain the market and suppress aggregate demands. As expected, prices would fall to a surprisingly low level if commercial transactions dwindle. People naturally needed relatively less money in a barter economy. The Fisher equation, however, is not applicable to such analysis. In the following section, I address the issue of plummeting prices from a political economic perspective, namely, that prices plummeted due to the diminishing demand for hard currencies, which was in turn caused by the significant contraction of the market.

The Rise of a Command Economy in the Early Ming

The striking decline in prices from the Song to the Ming reflects an equally dramatic decline in the demand for goods and labor.[18] It was the rise of a command economy that fundamentally undermined the need for hard currencies, which further drove price levels down and kept them sluggish for such a long period. Zhu Yuanzhang's anti-market policies, especially the demonetization of the economy, should be chiefly responsible for this deflation.[19] The early Ming economy would only require a small amount of money because of the dominance of payment in kind in state finance and the sharp decline in long-distance trade. Meanwhile, the rural economy was also highly demonetized.

Several pieces of evidence from the early Ming period point out precisely the diminution of hard currency used in transactions in rural markets. In a mountain village situated in Huizhou, a region in the far western part of the Lower Yangtze, the Wang brothers, Wang Qiugan and Wang Qiuguan, left behind thirty-nine contracts for land purchases (see table 6-2). These land purchases mostly occurred in the early Ming, with the first case recorded in 1393, just seven years after the establishment of the Ming dynasty, and the last case in 1430.

The preserved contracts of land purchases at Huizhou provide invaluable evidence of what happened to rural markets in the century.[20] These data also demonstrate that from the late fourteenth century until the mid-fifteenth century, people had to use cloth, grain, and silver to complete all business transactions. From 1393 to 1430, the Wang brothers used cloth and grain twenty-two times to complete transactions, which account for 56

Table 3-1. Land purchase in Huizhou, 1393–1430*

Period	(a) Baochao	(b) Coin	(c) In kind	(d) Silver	(e) Record	(f) c/e (percentage)	(g) a/e (percentage)
1393–1398	6	—	4	—	10	40	6
1399–1402	3	—	8	5	18	44.4	16.7
1403–1413	0	0	6	0	6	100	0
1414–1424	—	—	—	—	0	0	0
1425–1430	0	0	5	0	5	100	0
Total	9	0	22	5	39	56.4	23

Source: Ming-Qing Huizhou shehui jingji ziliao congbian, vol. 1, 1–15, 24–26; vol. 2, 19–23, 28.

*The contracts of the Wang brothers are preserved at Anhui Provincial Museum and History Institute, China Academy of Social Sciences. These contracts, along with many other land documents, have been published in Ming-Qing Huizhou shehui jingji ziliao congbian, vol. 1–2, 1988, 1990.

percent of the total. At the dawn of the fifteenth century, paper bills were withdrawn from circulation. Silver was not permitted as currency in the early Ming period. However, payment in silver represented one-third of land purchases. The units and quality of payments made by silver varied tremendously and were vividly described with particular attention in the contracts. Some cases even indicated that silver came from personal ornaments.

The early Ming rulers' attempt to create the largest command economy in China left no space for commerce or a free labor market. Institutionally, the *lijia* system instated the self-sufficient model for rural communities and made the exchange of goods less necessary. Many merchants and craftsmen from the Lower Yangtze were, according to official records, deployed for administrative and military services to the capital or to frontier garrisons. More devastatingly, they were paid very low wages, if any, and had to make a living from other resources. From the Wang brothers' contracts, I found six cases of land sales compelled by the burdensome task of transporting grain taxes. In the summer of 1401, six farmers from the same locale had to sell their small plots of land to the Wangs in order to raise enough money for traveling expenses to fulfill the mandatory duty of delivering grain taxes to designated state depots.[21]

The land sale contracts from the Huizhou archives also demonstrate a decline in land prices. Most parcels of land in Huizhou were sold at low prices for urgent needs.[22] The price, if paid in grain, often doubled the annual rent of the land. Although in terms of *baochao*, the land value was inflated in the Yongle reign, the prices of Huizhou land in the early Ming period remained as low as less than 1 *tael* of silver per *mu* (1 *mu* = 0.16441 acre) until the 1440s. The price rose to about 10 taels in the Hongzhi reign (1488–1505) and even lowered somewhat in the late-sixteenth and mid-seventeenth centuries. In the late seventeenth and the first decade of the eighteenth century, it rose slowly but with increased speed in the second decade and came to a peak in the Qianlong reign (1736–1795), with the average price of over about 20 taels per *mu*.

Delivery and transportation of grain taxes were not the only burdens for most peasants in the Lower Yangtze, who had to convey on a rotating basis all grain taxes at their own expense to the state depots situated primarily in the capital. Doushan Gong, patriarch of a famous lineage in Huizhou, was from a military household. His lineage established collective property in 1399 in order to collaboratively support lineage members who had to fulfill military duties at a remote garrison in Manchuria, which was thousands of miles away from Huizhou. Both his father and his older brother died while serving at that garrison. The lineage had to keep providing a male adult to serve in the military as well as financing all his living expenses there.[23] Such mandatory duties greatly relieved the government's dependency on the market for resources and services, yet they drained private wealth and stifled commercial or industrial growth by repressing a free labor market.

In addition to grain transportation and military services, the early Ming state employed more than a hundred thousand craftsmen and laborers in construction projects; these workers were classified as artisans in the Yellow Registers (*huangce*). As mentioned earlier in the various capital building projects, in 1393, more than 230,000 artisans across the country were recorded in the Yellow Registers for the building of Nanjing's city wall alone.[24] They were called on once every three years from their rural residences and worked at the assigned posts for three months. Unfortunately for these artisans, there is no evidence indicating that they were able to conduct private business there or that a commercial network spawned along the migratory routes. Thus, despite large-scale permissive mobility among the common people, the building of early Ming cities and the Grand Canal created no positive impact on trade. Whereas urban consumption laid a solid foundation for market development in the Song era, the early Ming cities were nothing more than a military post populated by underpaid and underfed involuntary laborers.

All these anti-market policies, such as unilateral payments, forced migrations, mandatory duties, and the employment of corvée laborers in public projects, severely constrained development in business and market networks.[25] For long-distance trade, one can hardly find any preserved record. Scholars tend to misinterpret the construction of the Grand Canal as a symbolic achievement of long-distance trade under the Ming government. In fact, early cargos conveyed via the Grand Canal were state-mandated goods and services, the transportation of which contributed little to commercial development. At its inception, ships on private business did not have normal rights of use. For instance, the burdensome task of transporting grain tribute through the Grand Canal to feed officials and soldiers stationed at the capital worsened when Zhu Di, the second Ming emperor, decided to move the capital north to Beijing. These voluminous long-distance shipments stifled market development since corvée laborers and soldiers were used extensively to execute grain transportation, and the ships used in transportation were built entirely by involuntary artisans at government docks, which also added no cost to the state.[26] As late as the 1430s, Zhou Chen, a provincial governor in the Lower Yangtze delta, reported that native people would avoid taxes and labor services by fleeing the countryside to seek refuge in cities and on ferries along the Grand Canal, where they were at least able to earn extra income by conducting small-scale business.[27] From 1470 onward, each tribute junk was allowed to load just 10 *shi* of tax-free products as compensation for its sailors. Roughly a century later, compensation increased to about 50 to 60 *shi*.[28] Therefore, the construction of the Grand Canal cannot be used as evidence to indicate the existence of long-distance trading activities.

The century-long deflation reflects a sluggish economy. In extant gazetteers, scholars find a few towns and periodic markets dating back to the early Ming period, while the majority of local markets and towns only came into being in the sixteenth century.[29] One can hardly expect that rural communities would absorb a good deal of currency. The land sale contracts from the Huizhou archives also demonstrate the dominant pattern of land transactions in the early Ming: Most land parcels were sold in small sizes and at low prices.[30] The weak market demand should have been a direct cause of low-level prices in early Ming commerce. The anti-market policies of the early Ming government certainly shattered commercial centers like the Lower Yangtze's society and delayed the recovery of a market economy nationwide.

Reconstruction of Domestic Markets in 1077 AD and 1381 AD

While circumstantial evidence supports the view of the absence of a market mechanism in China after the establishment of the Ming dynasty, in this section I further substantiate this view by reconstructing China's domestic markets based on commercial tax data. My reconstruction provides future researchers with an important measurement of market development in preindustrial China. Perkins already attempted to compare the size of the domestic market based on the 1077 data and the late Qing commercial tax sources known as the *lijin* data. Based on the *lijin* data, Perkins reaches an estimate of 420 million taels in interprovince trade of domestically produced goods during the late nineteenth century.[31] With certain adjustments from the analysis of the maritime custom data and the discussion on the underestimation in the Henan, Shandong, Hunan, and Guangxi figures, Perkins accordingly proposes an increase to 600 to 700 million taels at the turn of the century.[32] The estimated interprovince trade of 420 million taels would account for 12.6 percent of the estimated national income in the 1880s.[33]

Using the same method, Perkins estimates that the domestic market size in 1077 amounted to 70 to 140 million taels based on Song commercial tax data. An adjustment can be made to Perkins's estimate on the 1077 tax figure. The aggregate figure he cites, which was 6,918,159 strings of cash, is somewhat underreported because it missed the revenues coming from Sichuan.[34] The total commercial tax revenue collected in 1077, as noted earlier, was about 7.7 million strings. Presuming a commercial tax rate of 5 to 10 percent, total trade volume amounts to 77 to 154 million strings/taels.[35] Therefore, it is safe to estimate that the extent of long-distance trade in 1077 was at least 100 million strings/taels.

Following Perkins's method, I try to compare the size of domestic markets between the mid-eleventh century and the last decades of the fourteenth century. Early Ming tax records were well preserved for the most part, making the year 1381 a suitable candidate as the third benchmark year in addition to 1077 and the 1890s for gauging market development during the last millennium of imperial China. The early Ming had no transit taxes. The commercial tax collected by the local tax administrations was sale tax mostly paid in *baochao* and was identified as the core part of an indirect tax known as *kecheng*.[36] I collected some figures on tax revenue between 1381 and 1429 from the *Mingshilu*, which are presented in table 3-2.

The 1381 *baochao*-bronze coin revenue report is an invaluable resource for the study of early Ming domestic market for two reasons. First, the court soon fixed the quota for the collection of commercial taxes.[37] Hence, the collection of commercial taxes became increasingly irrelevant to real changes in trade. Second, the severe depreciation in the value of *baochao* after 1381 also produced difficulties in converting the total of the revenue into silver-measured amounts. This makes the 1381 figure the only reliable data for the reconstruction of the early Ming market.

Table 3-2. *Kecheng* revenues, 1381–1429 (000 *ding*[a] in *baochao*)

1381	44[b]	1404	5,668
1390	4,076	1407	10,496
1391	4,053	1417	16,880
1402	4,617	1429	32,787

Source: MLJJ, 429–44.

a. *Baochao* is the paper bills issued by the Ming state. 1 *ding* = 5 *guan*.

b. The 1381 figure was reported to be 222,030 *guan*, including *baochao* and bronze coins. I convert it into *ding* in *baochao* according to the official rate. According to the official rate established during the Hongwu reign, 1 *guan* = 1 tael of silver = 1,000 *wen* of cash.

The Ming administration adopted more than one universal form of tax payment. When Zhu Yuanzhang attempted to tax merchants in early years, both hard currencies and payment in kind were allowed. As paper bills were issued in 1375, the government generally encouraged tax payment in both *baochao* and coins. For sake of comparison, all kinds of tax payments must be added up. Yet both the economic policy and the forms of tax payment varied so dramatically in this period that one can hardly find appropriate conversion rates for different forms of payment. In 1380, many tax stations reported commercial taxes levied in rice. As the commercial taxes in 1381 were reported in both *baochao* and bronze coins, a bilateral-currency one, it is possible for me to handle this issue because the conversion rate between them was relatively stable then.

The depreciation in *baochao* soon led to enormous growth in the nominal value of taxes paid by paper bills. The early Ming *kecheng* data show at least two augmentations caused by severe depreciations. First, the *kecheng* revenues for 1390, 1391, and 1402 shown in table 3-2 approximate 4 million *ding*, or 20 million *guan*, of *baochao*. The second took place after Zhu Di came to the throne in 1403. His expansive policies greatly worsened the status of paper bills, whose credibility were already in danger. As shown in the table, the *kecheng* revenues increased from 5.67 million *ding* in 1404 to 32.8 million *ding* in 1429. But in real value the *kecheng* revenues were losing quickly as the court felt no constraint to over-issue these bills. In 1375, 1 *guan* of *baochao* was worth 1 tael of silver; in 1452, even in official rates, 500 *guan* of *baochao* equaled only 1 tael of silver, indicating a rate of depreciation to one-five hundredth. In many places people rejected using *baochao* as payments.[38] All this makes the 1381 *kecheng* revenues the only available source for the reconstruction of domestic markets in the early Ming era.

My estimation suggests a radical decline in China's domestic markets during the late fourteenth century. In 1381, the amount of *baochao* revenues amounted to 222, 030 *guan*. Presuming most of the *baochao* revenues were derived from payments of commercial taxes, say, 80 percent, then commercial taxes would have amounted to roughly 17,624 *guan*.[39] The standard rate of commercial taxes in the Ming dynasty was one-thirtieth of the value of the goods. By multiplying this figure by thirty, we arrive at the gross value of the domestic market at 5,328,720 *guan*, or 5.3 million taels of silver. This figure seemed unusually small even in comparison to the value of the mid-eleventh-century Song domestic market at 100 million taels. The estimated size of trade in 1381 might increase a little if we take into account that 364 tax stations were ordered to be closed in 1380 for their insignificant contribution to the total.[40] Supposing the average tax amount for these 364 stations was 300 *shi* of rice, then, the total tax collected by these institutions can be converted to 109,200 taels of silver at the exchange rate of 1:1. After including this portion, the highest gross value of the early Ming domestic market can be projected at 8.58 million taels of silver.

The comparison drawn from my reconstruction of domestic markets in 1077 and 1381 is consistent with the conclusions drawn from other empirical data. For instance, the 10.6 million households registered by the Ming government in the 1390s equates to only two-thirds of the Song population in 1078 (16.6 million registered households). In monetary terms, trade volume per household in the mid-eleventh century was about seven to ten times that of the 1380s. Compared to preceding generations, early Ming farmers lived in a world without much access to or need for the market. The early Ming

Table 3-3. Shares of long-distance trade to national income, 1077–1880 (000,000 taels of silver)

Year	Long-distance trade in contemporary price (000,000 tael)	Long-distance trade measured in rice (000,000 shi)	National incomes measured in rice (000,000 shi)	Share of long-distance trade to national income
1077	100	100	662	15.1
1381	6.67–8.58	6.67–8.58	140–230	2.9–6.1
1880–1889	420–500	262–312	1749–2077	12.6–17.8

anti-market policies should, therefore, be primarily responsible for this unusual shrinking of domestic trade.

Long-Term Changes in the Money Supply

Long-term changes in the money stock indicate exactly the monetary needs required by market development and urbanization. The Song financial revolution story and the Ming silver economy story both depict an extraordinary expansion of money supply in the eleventh and sixteenth century, respectively. In the following section, I examine the propositions presented in these two stories by providing a general survey on long-term changes in money stocks over the ten centuries from 750 to 1750.

In the first story, the expansion in the eleventh-century domestic market was associated with a "financial revolution."[41] An unprecedented increase in the means of payment marked one of the most striking features in the economic history of this period. In addition to bronze coins and precious metals, a variety of credit tools were invented for the needs of long-distance trade and public finance. One may conduct transactions using promissory notes including *yanyin*, *jiaoyin*, *chayin*, and *huizi* that were backed by precious metals (gold and silver) and expensive goods (tea, salt, spice, and alum), all of which were widely used.[42]

In the second story, the sixteenth century is viewed as a crucial period in Chinese monetary history for the massive import of silver into China, which, in turn, caused a transition toward the dominant position of silver as the major medium of exchanges in domestic markets as well as a means of payment in public finance. The rise of the silver economy, as the argument goes, relates the Chinese economy to an emerging global trade network that intimates market demands at an unprecedented scale.[43] This argument reiterates the bullionist view that a nation's prosperity depends on the means of payment, especially the role that precious metals play in this aspect. Yet, by focusing solely on the transition in metallic currencies, such an argument has to a great extent misinterpreted the relationship between the evolution of the Chinese monetary system and market development.

From a comparative viewpoint, the story of the silver economy immediately encounters at least one major challenge: How could the late Ming economy, if it was as advanced as suggested in this theory, depend on a single medium of exchange such as silver? After all, what should concern us is not the kind of currency but the amount of money to fulfill the needs of a developing market economy. Bronze coins are not necessarily inferior to silver as long as the former is maintained in sufficient amount and is supported by other monetary means.[44] In any case, the circulation of silver was much greater in Song China than in Ming China prior to 1580. Song mercantilism encouraged silver and gold mining, which produced the largest amount of silver in imperial China prior to 1700.[45] The monetarist argument of the silver economy pays no attention to the actual size of the money stock, namely, how much money was in circulation regardless of the types of currency that included bronze coins, silver, or other negotiable instruments. Furthermore, the silver influx in sixteenth-century China undoubtedly stimulated a market economy, but the peak years of silver imports from America and Japan occurred only in the first half of the seventeenth century.[46] Thus, how did the Ming market economy sustain itself prior to that date? To solve these problems, the first step is to quantify the money stock in the Song and Ming eras.

To estimate the money stock in the Ming dynasty, I will first exclude *baochao* from being considered part of the money stock in the fifteenth and sixteen centuries. Although the *baochao* was nominally a state-sanctioned currency, I have argued before that *baochao* should be excluded for its insignificant role in the real economy. It was primarily issued as a means of payment to officials and soldiers only and assumed a very minor role to meet the monetary needs of the private sectors in the economy. Moreover, the *baochao* was designed for the state's fiscal (anti-market) purposes and soon became irrelevant to metallic currencies in circulation.[47]

It rather isolated the circulation of *baochao* from the market: While the Ming government kept issuing and distributing *baochao* mostly as payment to officials and soldiers, people no longer accepted this paper bill as real money. Thus, as the *baochao* lost its value and failed to maintain its purchasing power at the markets due to unconstrained over-issuing; it hardly qualified as a form of credible and meaningful money.

To make the Song and Ming money stocks comparable, I restrict my investigation to metallic money such as coins and silver. It is not difficult at all to obtain an accurate estimation of the total amount of Song coins in circulation. It is a well-known fact that the Song state minted the largest number of bronze coins in Chinese monetary history; most of them were made prior to 1125. Even today, what archaeologists frequently discover in hoard sites in China and Asia are mostly Song coins, a fact testifying to the broad circulation of Song coins and the important role they played in trade. For the minting of bronze coins in Song China, we have reliable records for most periods.[48] The total adds up to 193.4 million strings of bronze coins prior to the Jurchen invasion in 1125. Recently, Gao Congming has reexamined Hino's and Peng's estimates on the output of Song imperial mints and suggested that the total amount of Song coinage (excluding steel coins) prior to 1125 was around 262 million strings of coins.[49] Both his estimate and mine give weight to the New Policy period as a key moment of high coinage. However, whereas Gao is more optimistic on the later decades (1100–1125) of the New Policy, I give the former decade better assessment. Both sets of figures are estimated output, yet they indicate a spectrum in which real output could fall. Archaeologists and numismatists have noticed that most of the Song coins weighed evenly and held consistently to a standard of material-combination used in mintage.[50] These characteristics rule out the possibility of counterfeiting currency in large quantities, which allow me to calculate the real Song money stock based on products from the imperial mints only.

To estimate the amount of hard currencies that circulated in the sixteenth century is a far more difficult task. The Ming government was neither willing nor able to create large amounts of coinage. From 1368 through 1572, the Ming imperial mints produced 4 to 6 million strings of coins, a figure roughly matching the annual output of the Song mints in the 1080s.[51] However, coins, including those from previous dynasties and even counterfeit currency, were accepted by the imperial authority to be used in small transactions. Most of the Ming hard currencies were thus Song coins and silver.[52] The major question is what percentage of sixteenth-century circulating coinage were Song coins? The survival of coins is hard to gauge since even hard currencies such as bronze coins were not necessarily preserved well for circulation. Wars, floods, and epidemics often forced people to flee their residences in haste and leave their money behind. Hoarding, deterioration, and melting also caused a large amount of coins to go out of circulation. Thus, with Ming coins also sharing an indefinable percentage of the total volume of circulating money, it is hard to calculate the precise money stock circulating in Ming China.

Yet thanks to wide distribution of Chinese coins during these six centuries, we do have circumstantial evidence to estimate the ratio of circulating Song and Ming coins at certain times. Song coins were widely used as the medium of international trade before the arrival of European merchants in East Asia in the sixteenth century. Many East Asian countries even identified the Song coins as legitimate currency in their own markets. Archaeologists in China and Asia have reported a lot of findings about the hoarding of Song coins. Hoardings in Japan are particularly important because Japan began to import large amounts of coins from China between 1270 and 1550.[53] This is exactly the period we are concerned about, and the types of coins exported to Japan should be similar to those circulated in Ming China's domestic markets. The study of the Chinese coins found in Japan reveals a ratio between Song coins and Ming coins: For every eight Song coins, there is one Ming coin. Therefore, I adopt the rate of 8:1 as the standard ratio between Song and Ming coins in circulation during the Ming dynasty.[54] This rate will increase the sixteenth-century money stock to 36 to 54 million strings of coins, an amount roughly equal to only 15 to 27 percent of the Song money stock prior to 1125 but already far exceeding the estimated amount of Ming-minted bronze coins in circulation.

The recovery of the money economy in Ming China is often characterized by the use of silver. Yet, how much silver was available during the mid-Ming to stimulate this economic rebound? For domestic production of silver, Chuan notes that the Ming state lagged behind the Song in silver mining. In contrast to the average annual mining revenue of 223,850 taels of silver in the eleventh century, the Ming mining output was only 100,000 taels of silver per year (about 220,000 taels in the early fifteenth century, declining to 50,000 taels in succeeding periods).[55] The total amount from 1390 through 1520, according to Chuan, was about 11,395,775 taels.[56] Since there were no annual records reported after 1520, Wang Yuxun can only estimate Ming silver revenues based on partial evidence for the later period (1520–1664). According to Wang, the total amount in the late sixteenth and early seventeenth centuries should be 13,820,100 taels, which was even larger than that in the preceding periods.[57] The aggregate silver output from domestic mining, then, according to this optimistic view, would reach 25 million taels. A modest estimate, however, would suggest 15 to 25 million taels of silver.

The preceding estimation highlights the paucity of hard currencies in the Ming econ-omy during its second century. We need to keep in mind that, before significant imports of silver into China after 1550—quite late for Ming history—the money supply from domestic production was very limited: 15 to 25 million taels of silver plus 36 to 54 million strings of coins would add up to 46.5 to 71.5 million strings of coins in total value.[58] This figure is only half of the money stock of the Song state prior to 1043. In the decades after the New Policies, output of coinage outperformed all that had ever been achieved previously by the Song imperial mints. Atwell keenly notes the "economic retrenchment in China" during 1430–1450 by pointing out that "economic activity in the Ming Empire slowed dramatically during the mid-fourteenth century."[59] Nonetheless, he misidentifies the early years of the Ming dynasty, especially the Yongle reign, as a period of economic recovery and expansion.[60] As measured by the amount of hard currencies in circulation, Chinese money stocks declined rapidly after the Mongol conquest, and this worsening situation continued into the fifteenth century. There is no important and direct evidence, as Atwell admits, that Zheng He's fleets brought back to China a large amount of silver and gold.[61] Given such low values of the estimated money stock around 1550, it is easy to understand how people desperately looked for hard currencies when the market resurged then. Atwell acutely observes the relationship between the prevalence of counterfeiting coins in Ming China, which greatly increased costs for transactions at local markets and discouraged farm-ers to produce for the market, and the short supply of hard currencies. But he mistakenly viewed the mid-fifteenth century as a period of rampant growth in counterfeiting.[62] Many empirical researches already demonstrated that it was in the mid-sixteenth century that the prevalence of counterfeiting coins became a painfully acute problem.[63]

The import of silver in huge amounts during the years from 1550 to 1645 has been used to argue that the late Ming money economy developed to an unprecedented size bolstered by its strong connection to an emerging world economy. However, because of the lack of hard data in Chinese sources pertaining to the precise amount of imported silver in Ming China, the impact of silver imports has remained a speculation at best and has not been tested in a quantitative way. To solve the problem, one has to rely on the records documented by officials and merchants in Japan, Manila, Macao, and Europe, countries that did not necessarily distinguish their exports to China from those to other countries in East Asia and Southeast Asia. Researchers generally disagreed on the aggregate value of silver imported to China in exchange for Chinese goods, such as silk and tea, in the late Ming. The estimates, for instance, vary from 100 million to over 300 million taels for the inflow of silver by the end of the Ming dynasty (see table 3-4). What they can agree on is the trend that silver imports grew rapidly during the first half of the seventeenth century.

These estimates clearly prove the significance of silver imports to a Chinese econo-my that was under transition toward monetization. Richard von Glahn argues that "during the second half of the sixteenth century, silver imports were adding at least eight times more bullion to China's stock of money than domestic mines; in the first half of the seventeenth century, imports exceeded domestic production by perhaps twenty-fold."[64] Yet von Glahn's calculation only tells part of the story about the role of imported silver in the monetization of the economy in late sixteenth-century China. If we recall that the Ming money stock (bronze coins plus silver) before 1550 was estimated to be 40 to 63 million strings of bronze coins, it follows that the import of silver would cause

Table 3-4. Estimates of Chinese imports of silver, 1550–1645
(in millions of taels[a])

Year	Von Glahn	Wu Chengming	Yamamura and Kamiki	Chuan
1550–1600	57.7–62.5	41.27–51.77	47.4–63.5	—
1601–1645	134.2	44.4–59.4	184.9–225.1	—
Total, 1550–1645	191.9–196.7	85.7–111.2	232.4–288.9	45.8

Sources: Von Glahn 1996, 140; Wu Chengming, 2002, 170–73; Yamamura and Kamiki, 1983; Chuan, for Japan, 1984, 644; for Spain, 1957 (also see Lin 1990, 303–4).

a. I have converted the weight unit into tael: 1 ton = 27,000 taels.

the money stock to swell 100 percent around 1600 and more than 250 percent around 1650.[65] The Ming empire found no rival in the world in absorbing such a large amount of precious metals from an emerging global economy, an amount that far exceeded the size of its original money stock provided by domestic mining and the aid of bronze coins from the Song dynasty. Scholars have emphasized that the bullion flow from America into Europe after the discovery of the New World played a vital role in bringing about the collapse of the European feudal system. However, imports between 1500 and 1650 only increased Europe's stock of silver bullion by 26.7 percent. For gold, the increase was even lower, 3.6 percent.[66] In comparison, the bullion flow triggered by European colonization caused a much more profound change in the Ming market economy than it did in early modern European economies.

In sum, the size of the Ming monetary economy around 1600 could probably be as large as 174 to 200.7 million strings of bronze coins, an amount that already approximates the Song's money stock in the early eleventh century. Estimates of coins in circulation and silver imports suggest an obvious delay in the expansion of the Ming money supply prior to 1580 in proportion to monetary demands from a reemerging market economy. According to current literatures, the development of domestic markets in the sixteenth and seventeenth centuries was achieved on the basis of specialization in agriculture and handicraft industries, a specialization that led to increasing exchanges between agricultural products and nonagricultural goods across regions. This vibrant exchange of commodities in turn led to increased productivity on both sides. This pattern has been recognized as a successful way to achieve a high-level market economy and has been labeled the Jiangnan path.[67] However, such a theory reserves little space for the argument of foreign trade and silver imports as an engine for development on a national scale. Since regional specialization in agriculture and industry was a gradual process starting from the late fifteenth century, its maturity and subsequent contribution to the Ming economy should be considered independently from foreign trade, which was still negligible until the late sixteenth century. Silver imports only began to influence economic trends almost a century later. This suggests that silver import may have reinvigorated economic growth but did not spur the economic recovery from the early Ming slump. As such, one must ask how the Ming market economy could maintain expansion at the national level with such a small stock of money before 1580.[68]

Unlike early modern Europe, one cannot find a corresponding relationship between silver imports and prices in sixteenth-century China. At the end of the century, silver imports began to surpass domestic money supplies, which I estimate to be 36 to 54 million strings of coins. However, the prices still remained stable around 1600.[69] Furthermore, as I discuss later, both nominal and real wages changed little despite a drastic increase in money supply and a growing market economy. How to explain the expansion of the market economy in late Ming at an aggregate level still remains a puzzle. In sum, there is no direct evidence either to support or deny the existence of a market economy of such a large size. Neither do we have a clear idea of the exact population size around 1600.[70]

I generalize my cross-dynastic comparison of late imperial China's money stocks in table 3-5. This is the first attempt to provide the estimated quantity of hard currencies at both aggregate and per capita levels.[71] These figures are not accurate values as much as those of statistical research, but they are sound estimations that rather indicate the

Table 3-5. Money stock in China, 750–1750

	Tang (750)	Song (1120)	Ming (1550)	Ming (1600)	Qing (1750)
Bronze coin (000,000 string)	21.3–42.6[a]	193.4–262	36–54[c]	36–54	122.8–146.8
Coins per capita[d] (in strings)	0.31–0.61	1.53	0.18–0.45	0.18–0.45	0.4–0.48
Silver (in millions of taels)	—	—	15–25	125.8–130.6	317
Money stock (in millions of strings)	21.3–42.6	193.4–262[b]	46.5–71.5	124–145[e]	376–400[f]
Money stock per capita (in strings)	0.31–0.61	1.53	0.23–0.6	0.62–1.21	1.25–1.33

Sources: for Tang China in 750, see Peng 1965, 781. For an estimate of coins and silver in the Qing, see Lin Manhung, 1991.

a. Peng assumes private coins were probably not different from the total for official coins, thus doubling the amount of the officially minted coins to get this figure. I decided to use the amount of officially minted coins as a low-bound value for my estimate of the money stock in Tang China and Peng's figure as the high-bound value.

b. I include only such coinage as the Song money stock. In fact, it would be larger if we take into account precious metals (gold and silver) and commercial bills.

c. Ming official coinage accounts for only one-ninth of coins in stock. The majority are Song coins.

d. The aggregate population for each period is assumed to be: Song (1120)—126 million;

Ming (1550, 1600)—120~200 million; Qing (1750)—300 million.

e. 1 tael of silver is equal to 0.7 string of coins.

f. 1 tael of silver is equal to 0.8 string of coins.

range of possible outcomes. The estimations of Tang and late Ming are uncertain due to the poor quality of demographic and minting data. Without good demographic data, estimate of the size of the monetary economy in late Ming China will remain speculative by nature. Moreover, such speculation will only be relevant to further analysis of the late Ming case if a benchmark year with rich and high-quality data is selected.[72] I thus give an estimate of the monetary economy in 1750, a year in which the eighteenth-century economy was starting to reach prosperity.

The preceding comparison points to the two trade booms, respectively centered around 1120 AD and 1750 AD, in monetary terms. Market expansion is associated with development in urbanization and trade that would stimulate an upward movement in prices. During a market developing period, the expansion of the market also produces increasing demands for hard currencies. The money supply expanded remarkably to a total value of 400 million strings of coins around 1750, a height in Chinese monetary history. Song China, however, maintained the record of money stock per capita and is second only to the Qing in total value.

A Tentative Conclusion

The contraction of the market led to the diminishing of China's money stock. While depopulation and deurbanization after the Mongol conquest significantly weakened the structure of domestic markets, the demonetization of the Chinese economy was directly caused by the rise of a command economy after the establishment of the Ming dynasty. The early Ming economy had little use for monetary exchange as it was operated on the basis of a barter economy and "corvée services." In essence, early Ming farmers and artisans paid taxes in lieu of grain and other kinds of local products to the state and had little need for hard currencies.[73] Many projects, including grain transportation and military defense, were enforced on the basis of unilateral payments. The early Ming state's three capitals (Fengyang, Nanjing, and Beijing), for instance, were built by corvée laborers enlisted from rural communities, soldiers, and prisoners. For each project, the average number of laborers exceeded 1 million people.[74] Except for reimbursements made on rare occasions, most of these seasonal laborers working for state projects were supposed to feed themselves, while some soldiers and artisans working yearly were paid in grain, the amount of which was less than what was required to support a family. The command system in the early decades proved effective. Needless to say, the effective operation of this command system severely damaged the market mechanism and particularly constrained the role of money.

Based on commercial tax data, I reconstruct the size of domestic markets in 1077 and in 1381 with respect to downward movements in Chinese population and prices in the centuries from 1200 to 1450. The size of long-distance trade and urban markets reached 100 million taels of silver and above in 1077. In comparison, the estimated gross value of trade in 1381 plunged to 5.3 to 8.58 million taels. The early Ming state implemented demonetization and anti-trade policies to minimize the role of the market in the Chinese economy and society. My reconstruction reveals that early Ming people lived in a world with little need for the exchange of goods.

I further investigate long-term changes in money stock during the Song and Ming eras. My estimation leads to the tentative yet welcoming conclusion that the Song money supply measured in bronze coins alone (not including silver, gold, securities, and paper notes[75]) far exceeded that of the Ming, even if one includes both silver and bronze coins in the latter case. This extrapolation is strongly consistent with the conclusion drawn from the comparison based on the reconstruction of domestic markets in 1077 and 1381. Briefly speaking, over the five centuries from 1000 to 1500, the expansion and contraction of the Chinese market was obviously associated with a shift from a market-centered economic system in the Song era to a command system that prevailed in the early Ming era.

My comparison adds a bitter taste to the silver economy story. It was the rejection of *baochao* by society at large and the inability of the government to provide large amounts of coinage that gave rise to the prevalence of silver as the standard value. The distinction between precious metals and bronze coins is not a decisive factor that led to this monetary transition. It is true that bronze coins were much more convenient for small-sum trade and were welcomed by farmers and poor urban residents. Yet with the help of the newly innovated instruments of credit, Song merchants could easily save on the costs of transferring the low-value, heavy coins in long-distance trade by using bills of exchange issued or guaranteed by the imperial ministry of the treasury. According to my comparison, until 1580, thus for the greater part of the Ming era, the money supply per capita seems to have remained very low. The need for hard currencies, especially those in small denominations like bronze coins, was painfully felt when the market rose again at the dawn of the sixteenth century. A major inadequacy resulted from the insufficient supply: 1 tael of silver was the equivalent of 1,000 *wen* of bronze coins. As most transactions in rural marketplaces were worth small sums, say, a dozen *wen* in coins, silver was not convenient at all. The small denomination money was extremely important to facilitate commercialization in agriculture. The lack of a standard medium of exchange encouraged rural communities to choose local equivalents from time to time, and counterfeiting prevailed across the country after 1550. The local people adopting their own standard currency different from each other greatly increased transaction costs and obstructed market integration.

Silver imports did play a significant role in the monetization of the later Ming economy. Yet the question is whether these radical changes, such as monetization in taxation, the relaxation of population control, and the resurgence of market towns can be viewed as an unprecedented development in Chinese history? If one chooses the unique economically depressing early Ming command economy as the backdrop against which to measure the sixteenth-century blossoming market economy, then there will be no doubt about this developmental story. However, the sixteenth-century economic development loses its original qualities if viewed from a broader and more comprehensive survey of the Chinese market economy over the last millennium, especially next to the Song market economy.

My interpretation becomes more persuasive as I am able to show how the collapse of the Ming command economy coincided with the recovery of prices and the reemergence of a vibrant market. Scholars in China and Japan have exclaimed the revolutionary change in the sixteenth-century economy and public finance; meanwhile, they are also puzzled by the long-term deflation in Ming China, which lasted more than a century from 1400 down to 1580. The internal controversy of the silver economy story is directly related to the bullion famine issue associated with the prevalence of counterfeiting coins: Why did it not happen earlier, say, in the first century of the Ming dynasty? Why did people not feel the paucity of hard currencies until the end of the fifteenth century? The answer lies at hand as we turn to examine the demonetized nature of the early Ming economy and its negative impact on the need for hard currencies in sustaining a market. The monetary history of Ming China thus unfolded in a trilogy: demonetization in the first century, low-degree monetization based on partial recovery in the second century, and full development in the third century. The comparison of money stocks and market size between Song and Ming is particularly helpful to examine the expansion and contraction of the market economy during the five centuries. Only from this comparative perspective can we understand the market history of Ming China.

Chapter 4

Trade and Water Transport in the Eleventh Century

During the Tang-Song transformation period from 750 AD to 1100 AD, rapid development in both inland water transportation and maritime trade significantly reduced transportation costs. The expansion of trade networks in the eleventh century must have been accompanied by considerably improved access to waterway transport.[1] This was one of the factors that promoted commercialization and urbanization in Song China. Modern researchers have even used the term "revolution" to describe the vital role water transport played in Song China's economic growth.[2] Although we might expect technical innovations to have been the major source of economic growth, technology alone does not explain why and how such progress could occur in Song China. It is noteworthy that few attempts have been made to identify the relationship between the structure of the Song waterways and the emerging domestic market. The central issues of the water transport revolution, especially the decline in transportation costs, the extension of waterways, and how they came together to facilitate the circulation of goods, have largely remained unexplored. This will only add to our confusion about the term "revolution": Was progress in Song water transportation solely attributable to the advancement of technology, or was the outburst of technical innovations a result of the great expansion of the market in the eleventh century, which is a unique event in global history?

The Song waterway system should be understood in the context of the transformation of the economy and political power during the Tang-Song transformation. As ancient and medieval Chinese empires based their capitals at Chang'an, an inland city in the northwest lacking convenient access to navigable water routes, for many centuries China's political center relied heavily on supplies confined to the Chang'an basin. Miyazaki thus defined these empires as Chang'an-centered, self-sufficient powers. China entered the early modern (kinsei) phase when the capital moved at the dawn of the tenth century from Chang'an to Kaifeng, the hub of inland water transportation; this gave rise to a mercantile state economically based on water (canal) transportation and long-distance trade.[3]

While Miyazaki argued that cheap transportation costs not only facilitated the expansion of long-distance trade but also aided a centralized military-fiscal power that gained strength from effective control of the market, his opponents raised doubts about the sustainability of this Kaifeng-centered trade network and deny its positive impact on the Chinese economy. The lack of a comprehensive survey of the Song transportation structure has made it difficult for either side to develop its arguments. Due to the scarcity of firsthand information, our understanding of Song water transport is far from clear. Nonetheless, the progress in water transport that resulted from the thorough transformation of the preexisting system during the Tang-Song transformation should refer to concomitant changes in the following aspects:

1. Enormous increases in the capacity of the shipping industry (the total number and tonnage of ships);

2. a substantial decline in transportation costs;

3. a major increase in the total mileage of navigable channels.

None of these aspects has ever been addressed in a systematic way. This chapter aims to provide an overall assessment based on the 1077 commercial tax data. I then review the unprecedented level of development in Song water transport, especially in the application of technical innovations. The formation of an efficient waterway network in the eleventh century was an important factor in the rise of a national market centered on Kaifeng and boosted economic progress. My study also supports Miyazaki's argument that water transportation contributed to the rise of a fiscal power in many ways. Whether or not we use the term "early modern," what arose during this period was an emerging national market centered on Kaifeng that gave an important boost to economic progress across the empire. The Song transportation structure made important contributions to both intersectoral and interregional trade. This development suggests the rise of a consumer society, the members of which mostly live in urban areas and communicate via waterways.

The Structure of Song Inland Water Transport

Many of the shipping and navigational technologies used in inland water transport were invented many centuries before the Song. Archaeologists have found that the craft of shipbuilding was already advanced in the Han dynasty (202 BC–220 AD), although there is little evidence of rapid development in inland trade via rivers.[4] Because a real breakthrough in any given sector of the economy depends on the popular utilization of new strategies, in most cases the needs of the Chinese society were the forces driving popular utilization of inventions in water transport.[5] This is evident in the Tang-Song transformation period, especially during the eleventh century. In his seminal study of transformation in China's population, politics, and society from CE 750 to 1550, Robert Hartwell has in particular identified seven macro regions and distinguished interregional networks of goods, services, and land from interregional integration caused by a significant decline in transport costs.[6] On the one hand, the monumental growth in money supply, numerous technical innovations, and urbanization reinforced the development that took place in water transportation. On the other hand, as Miyazaki's canal-based transportation thesis indicates, both the state and the market probably benefited greatly from the economic integration propelled by the rapid development of inland water transportation.

This Tang-Song transformation paradigm illustrates the backdrop for major breakthroughs in water transportation. The backwardness seen in Chinese water transport for many centuries may have been caused by the slow development of the market economy until the mid-eighth century. Nonetheless, some modern researchers impressed by the reconstruction of the Grand Canal in 605–610 AD—the longest canal in Chinese history—have portrayed the rapid development of water transport as a trend that began no later than the early seventh century. For this purpose, in addition to citing the example of the Grand Canal, they also like to quote an excerpt Cui Rong wrote in 703 AD:

> Boats gather on every stream in the empire. To one side they reach into Szechwan and up the Han River valley. They point the way to Fukien and Kwangtung. Through the Seven Marshes and the Ten Swamps, the Three Rivers and the Five Lakes, they draw in the Yellow River and the Lo (River), embracing also Huai-an and Hai-chou. Great ships in thousands and tens of thousands carry goods back and forth. If they lay unused for a single moment, ten thousand merchants would be bankrupted. If these were ruined, then others would have no one on whom to depend for their livelihood.[7]

This description suggests the formation of a national trade network at the dawn of the eighth century. However, this excerpt comes from a memorial that Cui wrote to oppose a national transit tax collection plan. In his memorial, Cui overestimated in particular the number of transportation vehicles in sea routes and inland waterways. He argued that the assessment of taxable goods at checkpoints would lead to great delays in shipments and that the levying rate might be prohibitive to merchants. The memorial is too vague for one to tell precisely how many ships were routinely exploited by merchants. In fact, water transportation between the north and the south was still backward at this time. The Grand Canal is the most important channel for China's long-distance trade, and its construction dates back to the Warring States period, yet it only began to play a vital role in forming long-distance trade between the south and the north from CE 750 onward.[8] In the one thousand years between its initial construction and the collapse of the Tang dynasty in 907, it was possible to ship grain and textiles from the south to Chang'an via the canal for no more than seventy years.[9] It is safe to say for most of these centuries there was not a strong need for the shipment of goods from the south.

Even within such a short period of time, the shipment records were not entirely satisfactory. Traveling up and down the canal was fraught with difficulties. It took ten months for the Tang government to ship tributary grain from the Yangtze delta to Luoyang, a harbor city at the mid-Yellow River. More than half of this time was spent at connection points because the sail capacity varied among the water channels. The cold weather in the winter, the frequency of rainfall caused by seasonal changes, and the decrease in the depth of water along the upstream course of the river all contributed to changes in navigation condition. Transportation from Luoyang westward to Chang'an, the capital of the Tang dynasty, was extremely difficult. The court suffered severely from the inefficiency of shipments and had to move the central government to Luoyang temporarily to receive grain supplies.[10] It was only in 735 AD that sufficiently substantial improvements in canal transportation began to enable the court to ship over 2 million Tang *shi* of grain to the capital, about ten times the volume shipped in the late seventh century.[11] Cui's report, though indicative of the ongoing process of change, exaggerated the amount of shipments and cannot be taken as solid evidence.

Furthermore, the gap between the colorful description in Cui's memorial and other official documents about tributary shipments points to the need for a reappraisal of the evolution of water transport based on quantitative evidence. Empirical data can provide firsthand information on the relationship between trade and water transport, which in turn will tell us exactly how and why developments in transportation occurred. Luckily we have the official records of the 2,060 tax stations and their tax quotas in 1077. *Song huiyao jigao* (Important Documents of the Song) preserves rich information on the collection of commercial taxes. Modern researchers are fortunate to find in a particular portion—*shangshui zalu*—a complete list of the 2,060 tax stations and their tax quotas in 1077.[12]

Ikeda was the first scholar to make use of the 1077 data to demonstrate a correlation between trade and transportation. He asserted that the collection of commercial taxes was determined first by the increasing volume of goods transported over rivers and canals and, second, by the important impact of urban consumption.[13] Following the lead of Ikeda's groundbreaking work, I have tabulated the revenues collected from tax stations at the cities adjacent to inland harbors and waterways that had tax quotas of at least 1,000 strings (hereafter referred to as IHR cities).

The tabulation in table 4-1 demonstrates that Song long-distance trade was facilitated by effective inland waterway transportation. Excluding the Lower Yangtze, the 262 IHR cities produced 3.3 million strings in 1077.[14] In other words, commercial taxes collected from these cities (about 12 percent of the Chinese cities in the late eleventh century) accounted for 43 percent of the total tax revenue. If we factor in the Lower Yangtze, total commercial taxes collected from inland waterway cities amounted to nearly 4 million strings, more than half of the total recorded in the 1077 data.[15] Moreover, the 262 IHR cities were all located along eleven waterways. Table 4-1 reports the amount of tax collected from each waterway and its share of the total collected in 1077. The reported items number twelve, and each represents a major water channel that might comprise a few connected rivers and canals. For instance, the Qiantang River and the Jiangnan-Zhedong Canal were the backbone of the waterway networks in Liangzhe lu, a provincial unit largely confined to modern Zhejiang but also including Suzhou and Changshu. According to my own estimation, the river cities along the Qiantang River and the Jiangnan (linking Hangzhou to Suzhou and Zhenjiang) and Zhedong canals (linking Ningbo to Hangzhou) should have accounted for at least two-thirds of Liangzhe lu commercial taxes, hence 643,500 strings. For convenience, they were treated as one waterway in table 4-1. The Yangtze River, though displayed as two different items in table 4-1, is of course counted as a single waterway here.

My survey of the 1077 data reveals that interregional trade coexisted with intraregional networks in the eleventh century. Water transport did play a vital role in forming a burgeoning national market, though the majority of long-distance goods were shipped along only a dozen waterways, especially those that facilitated long-distance north-south trade. There were thousands of rivers in the eleventh century, whose navigable mileage far exceeded the total length of several large rivers. Most of them, however, were incapable of facilitating the transportation of goods beyond local markets.[16] Thus, shipments conducted through the eleven waterways listed in Table 4-1 accounted for more than half of the total trade volume in the Song. Among the eleven waterways, only the Pearl River and parts of the Yangtze River could sustain navigation without major investments of money and labor (such as dredging the riverbed, bank building, and lock building).[17]

Table 4-1. The major waterways in 1077

Route	Length* (mile)	Number of river cities	Amount of tax (000 strings)	Share of tax in 1077 SCT**
The entire country	136,700	2060	7,702	100
The mainstream of the Yangtze River in Sichuan	640	48	724.2	9.4
The Qiantang River and the Jiangnan-Zhedong Canal	376 + 250	—	643.5	8.4
The Yangtze River (from Kuizhou down to the sea)	1,100	28	360	4.7
The Huai River and the Bian Canal (including Kaifeng)	620 + 370	25	711.2	9.2
The Huimin Canal-Wo River	155	14	120.9	1.6
The Gan River	467	34	267.3	3.5
The Han River and the Han-Yangtze Canal	950	11	167.8	2.2
The Yongji (yuqu) Canal and the Haihe River basin	530 + 435	27 (15 + 12)	291.3 (106 + 191)	3.9
The Guangji-Qing Canal and the lower Yellow River	280 (canalized only)	31 (19 + 12)	300.1 (159.2 + 140.9)	3.8
The main body of the Wei River and the Luo and Qin rivers centered around Luoyang	500 (Wei River only)	19 (13 + 6)	212.4 (156.1 + 56.3)	2.8
The Min River	360	8	95.6	1.2
The Pearl River	325 + 290 (East and north branches only)	17	75.4	1.0
IHR cities***	7,544	262	3,975.4	51.6

Source: the 1077 data.

*The length of the natural rivers such as the Min River and the Wei River are reported on the basis of modern surveys. For the lengths of the Bian and Jiangnan canals, see the estimates (Zou 2005, 88; An, 674). The Yongji Canal was recorded at over 2,000 Sui *li*, and for the Guangji-Qing Canal and the Huimin Canal (down to Caikou-zhen), I made a rough estimate of the length using the map provide by Tan, ed., *Zhongguo lishi tuji*.

**SCT is the abbreviation for Song commercial tax data.

***This refers to cities adjacent to inland harbors and waterways that had tax quotas of no less than 1,000 strings (thus the IHR cities in the following tables).

Other waterways were either partly canalized rivers or canals.[18] Canals and artificial waterways included the Yongji (*Yuqu*), Bian, Jiangnan Canal, Zhedong, and Guangji-Qing Canals. They were built over the topographically flattest part of North and East China plain and had a combined length of 1,000 miles, longer than even the mainstream of the mid- and lower Yangtze River. Partly canalized rivers were the reworkings of lesser branches of natural rivers that flowed into trade channels. The Han River, for instance, was an important river system. Many of its tributaries stretched from the main river into the mid-Yangtze River basin (Hubei), the mid-Yellow River basin (Henan and Kaifeng), Sichuan, and Shaanxi. As early as the eighth century, officials attempted to turn the Han River into a gateway to trade because of its great strategic significance to the central government in the north. In the tenth century the Song central administration launched several ambitious projects to improve commerce, but only the construction of the Jianghan Canal succeeded in greatly reducing the shipping distance between the Yangtze and Han rivers. This success made Xiangyang the most important entrepôt in Central China.[19]

The cost to maintaining navigable rivers to connect China's many regions always consumed a portion of trade profits. This was particularly true in the construction of canals on the grand plateau of North China. As early as the third century, construction of the Baigou Canal helped to ship grain from Henan to Beijing and to the northern part of Hebei.[20] From the sixth century to the early twelfth century, canal construction became one of the priorities of the court due to military and economic concerns. The eleventh century marked a new period of massive canal construction.[21]

The number of canal projects raises an interesting question: Why did the Song administration and its predecessors launch so many transportation projects? Would it not have been better for the Song state to concentrate on improving waterway transportation in areas such as Southeast China, where an abundance of rainfall consistently enriched river runoff? From modern surveys, we know that the combination of rivers in North and Northeast China and the interior drainage basins of Northwest China accounted for only 13.8 percent of national river runoff resources. The Yellow River basin (covering 7.8 percent of the total area of China) has an annual runoff of only 2.2 percent.[22] Even though the Yellow River basin was warmer and wetter a millennium ago, the variance is not big enough to challenge this conclusion.[23] Furthermore, the unevenness of China's topography, where the west is generally at a higher altitude than the east, means that all the major rivers such as the Yellow and Yangtze rivers (the two longest rivers in China), run eastward toward the Pacific Ocean.

Although high transportation costs would certainly constrain trade volume, reduced costs cannot be the sole factor that contributed to the rise of long-distance trade.[24] The increasingly distinctive variations between regional economies played a much more significant role in shaping China's long-distance trade.[25] As one of the largest empires in Eurasia, China's territory extended thousands of miles from south to north and encompassed a great diversity of ecological zones with a broad array of natural resources. Trade between the north and the south was therefore largely determined by their comparative advantages and resource endowments (such as climatic and soil conditions and density of population). Yet this huge potential for trade was not realized until product specialization between north and south became evident during the Tang-Song transformation. While it is true that the Yellow River basin had been the leading area of trade and industry for many centuries, by the time of the Song reunification in the tenth century, the economy of the south, especially the lower Yangtze River basin, began to surpass that of the north and was able to produce some important goods such as rice, tea, and silk textiles in large quantities for the market in the north.[26]

This transformation paved the way for south-north trade in Song China.[27] In 1078, over 55 million people were living in the south, approximately the same as the European population in 1500, and over 28 million in the north, roughly the same as the European population in 1000.[28] The huge size of the two economies offered important opportunities for bilateral trade. Tea, for instance, entered Song long-distance trade because of the high consumer demand in North China and Central Asia, where no local supply of tea was available. About 20 million Song *jin* of tea was shipped annually from the Mid-, Lower-Yangtze, Zhejiang, and Fujian via waterways through the Jiangnan Canal to the north.[29]

The distribution of cities with a large amount of commercial taxes reveals that long-distance trade between the south and the north dominated water transportation. In table 4-2, Guo listed all the Song cities that collected 30,000 or more strings of commercial taxes

Table 4-2. The twenty-eight cities with the highest commercial tax quotas in 1077

Rank	Province	City	Tax amount
1	Henan	Kaifeng	402,379
2	Zhejiang	Hangzhou	82173
3	Gansu	Qinzhou	79,959
4	Jiangsu	Chuzhou	67882
5	Hubei	Xiangyang	55,467
6	Jiangsu	Zhenzhou	53,536
7	Jiangsu	Suzhou	51,035
8	Anhui	Luzhou	50,316
9	Jiangsu	Nanjing	45,059
10	Jiangsu	Yangzhou	41,849
11	Jiangxi	Ganzhou	39,888
12	Hebei	Zhending	39,590
13	Zhejiang	Quzhou	39,384
14	Zhejiang	Huzhou	39,312
15	Hebei	Daming	38,628
16	Shaanxi	Xi'an	38,446
17	Fujian	Fuzhou	38,401
18	Henan	Luoyang	37,944
19	Guangdong	Guangzhou	37,308
20	Shandong	Mizhou	36,727
21	Hunan	Changsha	33,939
22	Sichuan	Chengdu	33,754
23	Shanxi	Linfei	33,137
24	Shandong	Yunzhou	32,444
25	Shanxi	Taiyuan	30,724
26	Henan	Shanzhou	30,636
27	Shaanxi	Fengxiang	30,463
28	Shandong	Dezhou	30,429
Total			1,571,349 20% of the total commercial tax collected in 1077

Source: Guo Zhengzhong 1997a, 224–25, 233.

in 1077. These twenty-eight cities contributed 1,571,349 strings, or about 20 percent of the 1077 commercial tax revenues.[30] Only five of these cities (Chengdu, Changsha, Zhenzhou, Yangzhou, and Nanjing) were located along the mainstream of the Yangtze River, but eight or one-third of them were located along the Grand Canal. Most of the key commercial centers were, in fact, located along the Grand Canal and other north-going water routes. Ranked according to commercial tax revenues collected, the top eleven of twenty-eight cities, except for Qinzhou, which ranked third, and Nanjing, which ranked ninth, were all based along the northward or southward water routes. Kaifeng and Hangzhou, the starting and ending points of the Grand Canal in the eleventh century, ranked as the first and second largest commercial centers. The Grand Canal also linked the industrial and commercial cities in the region of Lake Tai such as Suzhou and Huzhou to the markets in the north. The rise of large cities along the Yangtze River, such as Yangzhou, Zhenzhou, Hukou, Wuweijun, Qizhou, was primarily due to their function as transfer ports for north-south trade rather than as ports on the Yangtze River trade route.

Rivers and canals running in a north-south direction served as channels that linked the Yangtze River, the Yellow River basin, and to some degree, the Pearl River basin. Together, they constituted a nationwide network that allowed trade between the south and the north to grow on an unprecedented scale.[31] These rivers and canals formed the backbone of dense trade networks. The 1077 tax data enable us to breakdown the seven important inland waterways that contributed to expansion of north-south trade:

1. The Gan River that links the Pearl River basin and the Yangtze River basin.

2. The Han River and the Jianghan Canal that link the upper and middle parts of both the Yellow River basin and the Yangtze River basin.

3. The southern and middle parts of the Grand Canal: the Jiangnan Canal (from Hangzhou to Zhenjiang) and the Sishui Canal (from Yangzhou to Chuzhou).

4. The Huai River and the Bian Canal.

5. The Yongji (*yuqu*) Canal that links Kaifeng and Hebei.

6. The Wuhu-Wuweijun-Luzhou route and the Ying-Wo-Huimin Canal.

7. The Jialing River that links the Sichuan basin and Shaanxi.

Facilitated by these seven waterways, long-distance trade between the south and the north became a reality. By the eleventh century, exported goods such as spices and ambergris were being shipped from Southeast China's sea harbor cities to inland harbor cities in the north over hundreds of miles away. One route, for instance, started from Guangzhou at the southern end of the Pearl River. Goods were then transferred to locales further north, first upstream to Ganzhou, a port city in the upper part of the Gan River in southern Jiangxi, and then via the Gan River, the Yangtze River, and the Grand Canal to Kaifeng and other cities in the north.[32] Ganzhou's position as the port center of this long-distance waterway trade route made it a high-ranking city in South China in the amount of commercial taxes it generated, as shown by table 4-2. In 1077, Ganzhou produced 39,889 strings of cash in commercial taxes, exceeding the amount generated in Guangzhou. However, the volume of trade among seaport cities such as Guangzhou and Quanzhou may have been underreported because taxes levied against exported goods by the Song maritime customs (*shibosi*) were not added to local commercial taxes.

One may even argue that, in terms of facilitating Song long-distance trade, these southward or northward branches played an even more important role than the main-stream of the Yangtze River.[33] In addition to the Gan River, the Jialing River and the Han River also became main channels in the upper- and mid-Yangtze River basins. The Jialing River, a southward branch of the Yangtze River in Sichuan, extended deep into Shaanxi and linked up with the Wei River via a short overland passage. This route rep-resented the oldest communication route between Chang'an and Chengdu and remained the most important one for long-distance trade between Sichuan, Shaanxi, and Gansu in the eleventh century.[34] In 1077, cities along this route such as Fengzhou (10,837 strings), Guzhen (24,816 strings), Jiezhou (13,172 strings), Xingzhou (16,558 strings), Sanquan (14,293 strings), and Lizhou (21,526 strings) collected large amounts of commercial tax revenue.[35]

The Han River was not only the longest branch of the Yangtze River[36] but was also the most important waterway in Central China. This gave rise to Xiangyang, which developed at an unusually fast pace and became one of the largest entrepôts of long-distance trade in the Yangtze River basin.[37] In addition to Xiangyang, harbor cities such as Yueyang, Changsha, Luzhou (Hefei), and Yunzhou all played an active part in aiding north-south trade in Central and East China. Both Yueyang and Changsha became impor-tant port cities because they linked north Guangxi and Hunan, especially the developing area around Dongting Lake, to Central and North China via the Han River.[38] The rise of Luzhou is related to an important but often ignored trade route lying between the Grand Canal and the Han River. It was a shortcut for goods shipped from Jiangxi and southern Anhui to Kaifeng and for this reason was called "shortcut-to-capital." This route crossed the mid-Yangtze River at Wuhu and Wuweijun and reached Luzhou, where shipments would take a short overland passage before moving along the Ying and Cai rivers (the Huimin Canal) to the capital. In the Northern Song period, it was viewed as the second most important link between Kaifeng and the south after the Bian Canal.[39] Luzhou became a vital center because of its role as a nexus between water transport and overland transportation.

The rise of Luzhou highlights the success of the Huai River basin in the Song mar-ket economy. In the eleventh century, the Huai River had many connecting tributaries and lakes. This created a powerful waterway network that allowed access to local and national markets (see tables A-6 and A-7). Among the many goods shipped long distance from these entrepôts, tea received special attention from the Song government. In one instance, merchants purchased 10,533,749 Song *jin* (about 6,741,599 kg) of tea from the thirteen official agencies established in the south of the Huai River and shipped it north along the Grand Canal and the tributaries of the Huai River.[40] Unfortunately, in the succeeding centuries, war and flood devastated the region, and it gradually became the most impoverished part of East China.

Following this direction further south from Luzhou, one can find Shuzhou, Liu'an, Shouzhou, Haozhou, and Wuweijun, which were also important for the transfer of goods such as tea, salt, silk textiles, and industrial products to Kaifeng and other cities in

North China. Nonetheless, these port cities along the mainstream of the Yangtze River contributed less commercial taxes than the cities located on the north-going branches or lakes. For example, Jiangling (8,468 strings) and Wuhan (14,462 strings) contributed less than Xiangyang, Changsha, and Yueyang. Hukou was the first major harbor on the lower Yangtze River, yet its commercial tax (19,838 strings) was less than half that of Ganzhou (39,887 strings).[41] Even the commercial tax in Yangzhou was less than that of Xiangyang. Furthermore, none of the top four commercial centers in eleventh-century China—Kaifeng, Hangzhou, Qinzhou, and Chuzhou—were located in the Yangtze River basin. The Grand Canal, which extended from Hangzhou to Kaifeng and linked the four major river basins in East China (the Yellow River, the Huai River, the Yangtze River, and the Qiantang River), was the most important route for north-south trade. Commercial taxes contributed by the large port cities along the Grand Canal were more than double the amount collected along the main body of the mid- and lower Yangtze River.

Growth in a traditional economy can be measured by the expansion of nonagricultural sectors, especially developments in urbanization and long-distance trade. Both are demonstrated in the commercial taxes collected in 1077. Comparatively speaking, the water transportation factor (thus long-distance trade) was more influential than urbanization (that is urban business) in promoting the volume of marketed goods. I have identified seven major inland waterways that pushed the expansion on of north-south trade in Song China. Reviewing the twenty-eight cities listed in table 4-2, one can find that the top eleven cities were major players in long-distance trade and nine facilitated north-south trade. This phenomenon once again demonstrates the important role of water transportation in the expansion of the market economy in the eleventh century. The studies of water transportation nonetheless assume market needs will lead to the innovation and eventually transform the way that technologies were exploited. In the following section, we will find how progress, chiefly the sharp decline in costs of shipment, was made available in Song China's shipping industries and navigation due to the pull from the market factor.

The Decline of Transportation Costs

Historians have acknowledged a breakthrough in Chinese transportation during the Song-Yuan period.[42] This breakthrough was achieved primarily in waterway transport and can be summarized as follows:[43]

1. A remarkable phase of development in the shipping industry spurred an increase in the labor force associated with shipping.

2. Newly developed multifaceted industrial technologies enabled the production of ships (of various kinds and sizes) adapted to different water channels.

3. There were innovations in engineering techniques for the construction of canals and locks, the dredging of rivers, and the upgrading of inland waterway channels.

4. Institutional innovations were made in business organizations such as partnerships, and investments became separated from ownership in ocean shipping.

5. Commercial bookkeeping and contracts were used in dividing profits, delivering goods, and hiring sailors and laborers.[44]

As Shiba has suggested, the Song commercial revolution was the result of a successful combination of technological innovations in the shipping industry and managerial improvements in the transportation business.[45] It is well known that Song China's nautical technologies led the world. Private-sector demands propelled technical innovations in shipbuilding and navigation. These cost-saving improvements and innovations clearly played a part in promoting trade. For the marine trade, Chinese junks gradually replaced Persian and Southeast Asian ships in the Indian Ocean and South China Sea.[46] Coastal transportation and harbor services in major coastal harbors in thirteenth-century East Zhenjiang are estimated to have employed at least 200,000 laborers.[47] Meanwhile, the volume of shipping over inland water routes was also impressive. In the late eighth century, the boats for tributary grain along the Grand Canal "carried almost a third of the total carried by the British trading fleet in the middle of the eighteenth century."[48]

It was not surprising that these technical and organizational innovations brought about an enormous decline in freight rates during the Tang-Song transformation. The Song government reported freight rates in employing private ships and carts for public services. These regulated freight rates followed market prices and thus varied from region to region. Records of these policies and regulations date back to the 1100s, though they were not preserved in an official compendium—*Laws and Regulations of the Qingyuan Period* (*Qingyuan tiaofa shilei*)—until 1202. As Kiyokoba notes, the freight rates represent all costs of shipping or transportation in the late eleventh and early twelfth centuries, or even earlier.

By the late eleventh century, water transportation costs had fallen to (in nominal terms) one-fifth of their prices in the mid-eighth century. To transport 100 *jin* of goods over 100 *li* via water route, the average rates in 738 were 150 *wen* upstream and 50 *wen* downstream. In 1202, the rates were 30 *wen* upstream and 10 *wen* downstream.[49] In one Hebei case reported in 1079, private boats were employed to transport grain in place of delivery by the military with government-owned ships. According to the official concerned, the freight rate for private shipping was about 13 to 15 *wen* per Song *shi* per 100 *li*, or 9 to 10 *wen* per 100 Song *jin*/100 *li*.[50] This figure is exactly the same as the freight rate reported in table 4-3. It is noteworthy that the grain price in the first half of the eighth century was comparatively low at about 252 *wen* per *shi*. In the eleventh century, the average price of grain was 520 *wen* per *shi*.[51] Factoring in the inflation rate, the cost fell by nearly seven-eighths. In 1167, the Song court employed merchant vessels to ship salt from Zhenzhou (a harbor city close to Yangzhou) to Wuhan, an upstream journey of 1,500 *li* (433 miles) along the Yangtze River. Freight was prepaid at the rate of 44 *wen* per 100 *jin*/100 *li*.[52] The payment, however, was slightly higher in nominal terms than the standard rate of only 30 *wen*. Yet considering that the standard rate (30 *wen* per 100 *jin*/100 *li*) was set a century ago, this 1167 price means there was actually a further decrease in water transportation costs in the twelfth century.[53]

Table 4-3. Freight rates: Tang and Song

	Type	Sub-type	Price: wen 100 jin/100 li*	Index of freight rate**
Tang (738)	Land	Horse/mule-pack	80–150	800–1,500
		Cart carriage[1]	Total: 70–240	1,700–2,400
		Cart	90	
		Labor	80–150	
	Waterway	Shipping on the Yellow River	Upstream: 160 Downstream: 60	1,600 600
		Shipping on the Yangtze River	Upstream: 150 Downstream: 40	1,500 400
		Shipping on other rivers	Upstream: 150 Downstream: 50	1,500 500
Song (1202)	Land	All inclusive	100	1,000
	Waterway		Upstream: 30 Downstream: 10	300 100

Sources: Kiyokoba 1992, 66.

1. The cart rental cost (*chezhaijiao*) was 900 *wen* per 1,000 *jin*/100 *li*. In addition to this base cost, the employer had to pay for labor for freight at a rate of 80 to 100 *wen* per 100 *jin*/100 *li* over plain roads, and for uphill at a rate of 120 to 150 *wen* per 100 *jin*/100 *li* (Kiyokoba 1991, 62–64).

*1 Tang *jin* is 670 g and 1 Song *jin* is 640 g. In the Tang dynasty, 1 *li* was about 450 meters, and in the Song dynasty, 1 *li* was 465 meters. These variations can be ignored for comparison here.

**Song waterway (downstream) price = 100.

By any measure, this astonishing decrease in shipping costs took place nationwide owing to developments in three areas: technical innovations in shipbuilding, canal construction, and improvements in navigation. For any traditional economy that relied on water routes as the main channel for transportation and communication, a sharp decline in shipping costs would greatly promote trade between the north and the south and push forward market integration. An enduring and effective waterway network undoubtedly facilitated specialization of production in different localities, which is a major source for preindustrial growth. The relationship between technical innovations, shipping costs, and the expansion of domestic markets is highly intricate and must be examined from a political economy perspective on questions such as how the unprecedented development in long-distance trade was associated with the Kaifeng-centered political regime, a promarket state power that benefited greatly from the market expansion.

Kaifeng in the Eleventh-Century National Market

For political economists and economic historians, the cornerstone of a market economy is a national market that transcends the isolation of regional economies. The formative stage of a national market is indicated by an obvious increase in market integration. One of the ways to measure that quantitatively is to check whether price changes synchronized across the country. Studies of the eighteenth-century rice market demonstrate a strong correlation between prices in urban rice markets in the Mid-Yangtze, Lower Yangtze, and the Grand Canal. This indicates that water transportation was critical to the integration of China's traditional markets.[54] Because data on grain prices were scarce in the seven centuries prior to 1700, the same test is not possible for the Song and the Ming. Nevertheless, some studies do point to an obvious difference between the two dynasties: Changes in Song grain prices in different local markets seem interrelated over the course of nearly three centuries, whereas sixteenth-century grain markets in China fell short of a coherent pattern.[55]

The Kaifeng market took the lead in the rising grain price trend of the eleventh century, followed by markets in other regions (see table 4-4). In 1086, Zhang Dun, the

Table 4-4. Variance in grain prices in eleventh-century markets (*wen* per Song *shi*)

Year	Kaifeng	Shandong	Zhejiang	Shaanxi	Shanxi
979–989	100	—	—	—	100
1008–1012	300*	300	—	—	100*
1022–1028	600*	100	700	—	—
1043–1053	—	500	700–	900	500
1063–1075	900–	400	500–800	1000	800
1080–1089	—	—	600–900	2000	300
1090–1099	—	—	700	3000	—
1100–1120	—	1,120	2,550	—	1,200

*Millet

Sources: Long, 1993; Wang Shengduo, 2004.

minister of national defense, reported to the court on the variance in grain prices between different macro regions in North China. According to Zhang, 100 Song *shi* of grain (mixed elements) could be sold at 20 strings in inland regions that have access to water transportation, at 14 to 15 strings in inland regions without access to water transportation, at about 30 strings at the frontier of Hebei, and at 40 to 50 strings in the frontier regions of Shanxi and Shaanxi.[56] This difference demonstrates the important relationship between water transportation and grain prices. North Hebei, as the data suggest, had a much closer relationship with Kaifeng's market than the frontier regions of Shanxi and Shaanxi. While the latter two regions were not effectively connected to the waterway network centered on Kaifeng, high grain prices there may be explained by the fact that, in the mid-eleventh century, the Song court sent a large number of soldiers to Shaanxi. The extra population produced higher consumption demand and drove up grain prices to a level much higher than that in Kaifeng.[57]

Market integration in the Northern Song was enhanced by two particular developments. First, the Song central government implemented mercantile policies[58]—such as ensuring sufficient money supply, private property protection and contractual enforcement, foreign trade promotion, money payments and governmental purchases, and the use of bills of exchange—all these reduced transaction costs and promoted trade. Second, the advanced waterway network greatly lowered transportation costs. For the first factor, grain provision is a good example of the Song state's positive attitude toward the market mechanism. Grain tribute collected by the Song court via land taxes reached only half the amount in the early Ming.[59] The Song administration often appealed to the markets to make provisions. From 1040 to 1043, the Song court dispensed 70 million bolts of silk cloth in purchasing 84.4 million *shi* of grain, a figure that exceeded the grain tribute collected via land taxes.[60] The Song court in the eleventh century purchased 1.3 to 2 million *shi* of grain annually in the Lower Yangtze and shipped it along the Bian Canal to Kaifeng.[61] In 1091, the Grain Transportation Institute (*fayunshi*) was not willing to use reserved funds to purchase grain from private markets in the mid-Huai River. Su Shi, then the prefect at Hangzhou, complained that officials were too lazy because grain could easily be purchased from prefectures south of the mid-Yangtze River. Their memorials compared the average rice prices among three locations during the harvest season: 670 to 700 *wen* per *shi* for the Lake Tai region, 770 *wen* for the port cities along the mid-Huai River, and 700 *wen* for Nanjing and nearby cities along the Yangtze River.[62] The fact that grain prices of the three key marketing areas were highly consistent testifies to the existence of well-developed interregional trade facilitated by water transportation.

Buoyed by these advantages, Kaifeng developed into the hub of the national market.[63] Commercial tax data available for this period covers a broad range of consumption goods shipped along water routes, and the distribution of tax amounts highlights the role of Kaifeng in the state's communication and transportation networks. From the mid-eighth century to the eleventh century, Kaifeng's population increased fifteenfold.[64] By the mid-eleventh century, it is possible that Kaifeng had more than 1 million residents. A portion of the residents belonged to the military or served as administrative staff. Yet Kaifeng's dominance was the result of long-distance trade rather than of urban consumption; the latter is heavily dependent on the size of the urban population. As one historian writes, Kaifeng was "the most important administrative, military, manufacturing, and commercial center" in China.[65]

One can test Kaifeng's vital role as the "hub of national communications" in three respects. First, in eleventh century, this city itself had a higher share of commercial taxes than any other city, a fact that indicates unusual development in long-distance trade rather urban consumption. Both long-distance trade and urban consumption contributed to the commercial taxes collected at each city. Table 4-5 illustrates the relationship between population and commercial taxes collected in five large cities in 1077. The capital city Kaifeng produced 402,379 strings of commercial tax revenue. Hangzhou, the biggest commercial city in the Lower Yangtze with a large number of urban residents, ranked second in the amount of urban commercial taxes. However, Hangzhou's tax revenue (82,173 strings) was only one-fifth that of Kaifeng. This huge gap in taxation was far greater than the gap between the sizes of their urban populations. Taking a further step to test the role of Kaifeng in long-distance trade, one may compare it with the other four cities (Hangzhou, Suzhou, Nanchang, and Daming). Kaifeng's urban population could hardly match the four cities combined. Yet the amount of commercial taxes contributed by Kaifeng far exceeded their total. Therefore, we can reasonably deduce that it was Kaifeng's strategic role in the national market and not urban consumption that explains its leading contribution to commercial taxes in 1077.

Second, let us focus on the extent of intraregional trade. If one draws a circle extending 200 kilometers (about 120 miles) out from Kaifeng, one will find an intensive trade and communication zone around the greater capital region. This enabled an easy inflow of commodities and information among hundreds of cities. For the twenty-eight cities displayed in table 4-2, even when one excludes Kaifeng, the commercial taxes collected from these cities amounted to 1,168,430, or about 15 percent of the total commercial taxes. The share was even bigger than that of any waterway listed in table 4-1. For instance, the river-port cities along the major body of the Yangtze River from Kuizhou down to the sea provided about 4.7 percent of commercial taxes. The upper Yangtze River (Sichuan) basin (9.4 percent) and the lower Yangtze (8.4 percent) ranked immediately below the greater Kaifeng region in terms of its share of commercial taxes. This triangular structure of Song intraregional trade attests to the unique balance maintained in trade and industry between the north and the south that was made possible only with the help of a sophisticated water transport network evident in eleventh-century Kaifeng.[66]

Other factors, such as a relatively balanced level of development between the north and south, no doubt contributed to Kaifeng's leading role in China's eleventh-century economy. Population density statistics from a preindustrial economy provide firsthand evidence on variations in agricultural productivity, the degree of urbanization, and devel-

Table 4-5. Estimated Song urban population and commercial taxes

	Kaifeng	Hangzhou	Suzhou	Nanchang	Daming
Commercial taxes (string)	402, 379	82,173	51,035	28,904	38,628
Urban population (000)	900–1,200	<600	500	200–300	<300

Sources: 1077 Song commercial tax data; Wu Songdi 2000, 574–73, 590, 592, 599.

opment in trade and transportation. Most prefectures in the Lower Yangtze region had a total of over 15,000 households in 1102, and in the cases of Suzhou and Hangzhou, the number was above 20,000 households. Yet it was the Chengdu plain in the upper Yangtze River that was the most densely populated region of Song China until the devastating Mongol conquest.[67] In contrast, the population in many of the northern prefectures was half that number, or in some cases, even less. However, the number of local households in a few regions such as Kaifeng, Yingtianfu, Yunzhou, Luoyang, Caizhou, Yingzhou, Daming, Bozhou, and Suzhou was 10,000 or higher in 1078. Of these regions, Kaifeng, Xingrenfu (including Jiyin), Yuzhou, Puzhou, Daming, and Bozhou had a population density close to the Lower Yangtze (see appendix C).

During the Tang-Song transformation, population density in the lower Yangtze increased greatly from 4.6 households per square kilometer in 980 to 15.4 in 1078. In contrast, the population in the north grew at a much slower pace. For example, the population in Daming *fu* increased from 9.2 to 16.9 households per square kilometer over the same period.[68] Thus, it is not surprising that Hebei's population-density ranking dropped from the first to the third during the greater part of the eleventh century. From a national perspective, economic data on commercial taxes, population density, and the distribution of industries show that the economic gap between the Lower Yangtze, the upper Yangtze River basin, and the Kaifeng-centered core regions in the north was not yet substantial. In terms of trade and industry, the core regions in the north may have taken the lead.[69] Such a balance reflects the transitional nature of the eleventh-century market economy. Moreover, it laid the very foundation of the paramount importance of Kaifeng. It was not until the collapse of the Kaifeng-centered trade network that a more substantial gap would emerge first between the north and the south and, second, between the Lower Yangtze and other regions.

Third, one may move beyond this 200-kilometer range to capture a full view of Kaifeng as a hub of waterway transportation. It becomes even more evident that a Kaifeng-centered transportation system played a vital role in forming the national market because Kaifeng's central position allowed for the integration of many inland waterways. Until the twelfth century, most cities on the grand plateau were not only located near rivers and canals, but were also linked by this intensive waterway network. Kaifeng's status as the center of grain transportation from the ninth century onward was the very reason it became the Song capital.[70]

What did Kaifeng look like as the center of the national market? One can examine major trade routes linking Kaifeng and urban markets nationwide via waterways in four directions: the Wei River and the mid-Yellow River in the west, the Yongji Canal in the north, the Guangji-Qing Canal in the east, and the Bian Canal and its tributary in the south.

To the west, the Wei River and the Yellow River allowed shipments of wood, grain, and coal from Gansu, Shaanxi, and Shanxi to reach Kaifeng via Shanzhou. This water route had been the most important passage for the Tang court in Chang'an, which could hardly survive without a large tribute of grain from the Huai and lower Yangtze River basins. In the late tenth century, the Song court established the *Sanmen-Baibofayunsi* 三門白波发運司 (Grain Transportation Institute at Sanmen and Baibo) to ship 800,000 Song *shi* (40,200 tons) of grain each year to Kaifeng via the mid-Yellow River.[71] Shanzhou, the entrepôt for interregional trade between Shaanxi and Kaifeng, contributed 30,635 strings of cash to the Song commercial tax administration. From the mid-eleventh century, the Kaifeng administration had been sending a large amount of military supplies to troops stationed in these frontier regions. However, it also attempted to open markets along the frontier for foreign trade. The best example of Kaifeng's success as a political and economic center in exploiting resources from the periphery is Qinzhou's wood exports. As a Song military stronghold in Central Asia, Qinzhou evolved into an important supplier of wood for Kaifeng's urban construction. As shown in the 1077 data, Qinzhou paid the highest amount of commercial tax (79,959 strings) among the cities in the west. It ranked third nationwide after Kaifeng and Hangzhou. In addition to Qinzhou and Shanzhou, Xi'an (38,445 strings), Fengxiang (30,642 strings), Jinzhou (33,136 strings), and Taiyuan (30,724 strings) were the leading taxpaying cities in the northwest because they were local centers of water transportation. In 1077, trade along the Wei River and its branches produced 217,190 strings of commercial taxes. This ranked the Wei River among one of the eleven most significant waterways in the eleventh century (see table 4-1).

For the northward route, the Yongji Canal, which largely followed the direction of the Baigou Canal, extended from Daming into northern Hebei. After the eighth century Daming had been the largest city in this region, the provincial capital of the eastern Hebei circuit, and a center of commerce and industry.[72] It controlled the transfer of goods to the frontier along the Yongji Canal and linked to Kaifeng via the Yellow River. In 1077, Daming alone produced 38,628 strings of commercial taxes. In 1034, 1048, 1066, and 1099, breaks in the dikes caused the Yellow River to change its course, first flowing northward to the Hai River before heading in a more southerly direction. However, these changes in course were confined to the Hebei plain, and Hebei's existing waterways were not destroyed.[73] In some periods of the eleventh century, the divided branches that resulted from the course changes could be used for transport and were easily incorporated into the existing waterway network. As we see in the 1077 data, quite a few cities in Shandong and Hebei were located along or connected to the lower Yellow River (see table C-4 in the appendices).

For the eastward route, the Guangji-Qing Canal linked Kaifeng and Shandong to form another entrepôt of north-south trade around Yunzhou. Yunzhou contributed 32,444 strings of commercial taxes in 1077, and if one takes into account the commercial taxes collected by Fujiaya, a nearby tax station, the total reaches 54,911 strings. The Guangji-Qing Canal passed through Juye Lake, the transportation center of the Yellow River plain, and became the most important waterway in Shandong. There were nineteen river-port cities along the Guangji-Qing Canal (see table C-5 in the appendices) with commercial tax quotas of more than 1,000 strings in 1077. These cities together produced 159,234 strings, accounting for 22 percent of the total commercial taxes collected in Shandong.[74] By contrast, there were twelve river-port cities on or close to the lower Yellow River (see table C-4 in the appendices). Their aggregate tax amounted to 140,907 strings, a figure that accounted for 31 percent of total commercial taxes collected in east Hebei and Shandong.[75]

Among southward routes, the Bian Canal and its tributary canal—the Huimin Canal, along with the Huai River and its multiple branches—constituted the densest network for north-south trade. The eighteen harbor cities along the Bian Canal and the Sishui Canal produced 0.7 million strings of commercial taxes in 1077 (see table C-6 in appendix C).

As Kracke writes, eleventh-century Kaifeng was a city that "evidently far outdistanced all its rivals among China's economic centers." Moreover, its role as "the hub of national communications" surely accounted for this superiority.[76] Kaifeng played an integral role in the evolution of the economy and transportation in North China over many centuries. Its rise to preeminence undoubtedly encouraged the exploitation of cost-saving innovations and made the Song state the most successful canal-building regime in Chinese history. This monumental phase of development in Song water transportation should be understood against the background of the emergence of a national market during the Tang-Song transformation, especially in the context of the key role that Kaifeng had played in the eleventh century.

Conclusion

My analysis of the 1077 data supports Miyazaki's argument about the rise of a canal-based transportation system in the eleventh century. There is a dynamic relationship between state power, market expansion, and water transportation. The balance between the north and the south during the Tang-Song transformation fueled an unprecedented period of development in Song long-distance trade. As McNeil indicated, it was the first time in global history that the state's power relied heavily on long-distance trade and water transport.[77] Song mercantile policies clearly demonstrate how the Song state managed this situation. This period (including the first two decades of the twelfth century) might be called the "canal century" because the Song government constructed and maintained the largest number of canals and partially canalized rivers in Chinese history, most of which were used to connect the extant rivers into an extensive network of inland waterways. In the north, the massive scale of canal construction placed Kaifeng at the center of national trade and communications. In addition to state security and political concerns, the pursuit of money itself—the very mercantile nature of the eleventh-century Chinese state—motivated the government to invest so heavily in these canal projects.

The Kaifeng-centered political regime benefited from developments in long-distance trade and urbanization. The Song state was the only fiscal state in China prior to 1880 to derive more than two-thirds of its tax revenues from indirect taxes. Commercial taxes collected in 1077, for instance, amounted to 7.7 million strings of cash, about one-third of the amount levied in land taxes. In the late eleventh century the Song court had to negotiate with 11.2 million rural households over the collection of land taxes, an unenviable task by any standard, while the amount of commercial taxes collected from the twelve major water routes presented in table 4.1 easily added up to one-sixth of land tax revenues. Monopoly revenues from alcohol, salt, and tea produced a larger share of Song state revenues than any other kind of tax. Yet both tea and salt were products that had to be shipped over long distances to reach consumers.[78] We can hardly imagine how the Song state could have survived had it not made tremendous efforts to facilitate the shipment of goods in return for these huge tax revenues.

Both eleventh-century trade and the Song fiscal state were sustainable largely due to the existence of a national water transportation network. The integration of the domestic market and an advanced water transport system are two sides of the same coin. The Northern Song supported, benefited from, and enabled water transport to thrive.

The 1077 data show that the most far-reaching consequence of this amalgam was the emergence of a national market for the first time in Chinese history. A systematic decline in inland water transportation occurred throughout China after the Song dynasty drew to a close in 1279. The disintegration of water transport networks in North China in the post-Song period was largely caused by warfare, ecological deterioration, and floods on the Yellow River. Until the seventeenth century, important trade routes were confined to no more than three waterways: the Grand Canal, the Gan River in Jiangxi, and the lower Yangtze River.

Part III

The Ming Er

Chapter 5

China after 1200

Crisis and Disintegration

China in the three centuries from 1200 to 1500 witnessed a shift from a Kaifeng-centered market system to a Beijing-centered command power. The Mongol conquest of China (1206–1279) and the rise of an autocratic regime in early Ming China from 1368 onward were the most important events that contributed to the downward turn in the Chinese market economy during the next three and half centuries.[1] Both census and taxation data vividly reveal how radically aggregate population and urbanization during these four centuries declined. The Mongol conquest, especially the wars between the Mongols and Jurchens from 1211 to 1234 in the north, dealt a devastating blow to the economy. The conquest of the Southern Song in South China was much less destructive, but the military campaigns took an unavoidably heavy toll on the upper- and mid-Yangtze region. In terms of interregional trade, the Kaifeng-centered water transportation regime ended in 1125 when Jurchen troops occupied North China. From then on until Zhu Yuanzhang established the Ming dynasty in 1368, China was ravaged by continuous wars and natural disasters. Consequently, early Ming aggregate households as of 1393 amounted to only 6 million, merely 29 percent of the Song registered households recorded in 1109.[2]

In this chapter I reassess the post-1200 economic crisis in a full-scale view. The story I tell about China in these centuries is far more than a demographic one. Nor is it about an economic downturn in a short period. After the Mongol conqueror unified China under the Yuan dynasty, there was an odd discord between the ever-expanding size of the empire and the integration of the national economy. In the centuries after the Mongol conquest, Chinese imperial power greatly expanded territorially and marched far into Central Asia. For the first time, Beijing, a frontier city once repeatedly subjected to nomadic conquests, became the imperial capital. However, with the sharp decline in aggregate population and anti-market policies implemented by the early Ming court, the Chinese economy greatly disintegrated. The recovery, especially the recovery of long-distance trade, was to be delayed until the 1500s, and this recovery was confined to just a few major inland waterways.[3] With the sole exception of the northern stretch of China's Grand Canal, water transports in the north fell into disarray. The full development of the domestic market did not come until the eighteenth century.

While this gloomy economic downturn has been a well-known fact, this chapter explores in great depth the key questions of when and how China plunged into such a deep recession and why the revival took such a long time to materialize. Along with the destruction of important inland waterways and depopulation in many areas, no single city in the north could play a leading role such as Kaifeng ever did in the eleventh century to boost long-distance trade. Facing those challenges, the government failed to maintain inland water transportation projects but often appealed to military farms for consolidating the supply, and many local economic units in North, Central, and Northwest China were forced to adapt to regional needs.

To gain a comprehensive understanding of the structural changes in the economy after 1200, I particularly identify in my analysis three kinds of factors—demographic, environmental, and political economical—that contributed to economic disintegration after the Mongol conquest: sharp decline in population density and urbanization, the destruction of almost all important waterways in North China, the incapability of the state to maintain the infrastructure and supply currencies, and in particular the anti-market policies such as demonetization in taxation.

A Sharp Decline in Population and Urban Consumption

The collapse of the Kaifeng-centered market meant an end to the economic expansion that had prevailed throughout the eleventh century. But this did not immediately steer the economy in the opposite direction. Although wars between the north, which was now controlled by the Jurchens, and the south, which was controlled by the Song, periodically broke out, these conflicts were often confined to specific locales and did not lead to heavy loss of lives. More importantly, trade between the two sides was maintained during peace times. Population growth, the most important factor in a preindustrial economy, also varied greatly between the north and the south. In table 5-1, I collect changes in the aggregate households of both the north and the south over the four centuries from 980 to 1398. China's aggregate households reached over 20 million in 1207 that represented an obvious increase. Nevertheless, this growth is less significant when compared to the unprecedented rate of population growth in the eleventh century (see column IV of table 5-1).

It was, however, the Mongol conquest that inflicted a fatal blow to North China's economy and population. Immediately after the Mongols conquered the entire Jurchen-held territory, they conducted the first census in 1235. The remaining households amounted to only 0.87 million, roughly 10 percent of the population in North China reported before the conquest. This figure must be slightly underreported since many families fled from their homes to avoid the brutal fighting.

This is also a period in which one can find regional prosperity in Jiangnan, and southeast coastal areas, partially supported by overseas trade, existed together with devastated inland cities of North and Northwest China. The national survey soon after the unification of China in 1279 indicated a serious imbalance between the south and the north in population density and commercialization. In table 5-2, I have reported all the *lu* (route, the local administrative unit) with a population of over thirty thousand households in 1270–1290 (table 5-2). There were twenty-one *lu*-level administrative units in the north and seventy-eight in the south. The emerging demographic gap between the north and the south as shown in table 5-2 points to the structural weakness of the economy. The population density in many northern administrative units could

Table 5-1. Changes in distribution of aggregate households in China, 980–1391

Year	I Aggregate households in the north (000)	II Index of population growth (980 = 100)	III Aggregate households in the south (000)	IV Index of population growth (980 = 100)	V III/I	VI Total households
980	2,544	100	3,874	100	1.52	6,418
1102	5,917	233	12,196	315	2.06	18,113
1207	8,413–9,879	331–388	12,669	327	1.28–1.51	21,082–22,548
1291	1,939	76	11,840	306	6.11	13,779
1391	2,280	90	8,420	217	3.69	10,680

Sources: Wu Songdi 2000, 385–36, 210, 633; Cao 2000a, 34–35.

not remotely match their southern counterparts. In addition, China's western regions (both southwest and northwest) also suffered a great loss of population. In contrast, East and Central China, especially Hunan and Jiangxi, experienced a rapid growth in population.

Over the succeeding century, the population in North China eventually doubled (see table 5-1), but this increase could not hide the fact that the proportion of the population in North China against the national total substantially declined during this interim period. In 1391, the entire population of the south was about 3.69 times that of the north. While in 1102, this ratio was 2:1. The radical decline in aggregate population, especially changes in regional distribution, is a rare case in demographic history and should be identified as the principle factor that caused the downturn of the economy. In the following pages, I provide an overall assessment of this unique depopulation and deurbanization process in North China based on various quantitative sources.

Demographic information is one excellent indicator of economic health. As the aggregate population declined, the population in the Lower Yangtze continued to grow. For the first time, the population in this region alone surpassed the entire population in the north. As a result of this reversal of regional demographic change, the prosperous Lower Yangtze region easily gained important influence during this era as it found no rival throughout the empire. Because the census survey of the Lower Yangtze was conducted soon after the Mongol conquest of the south, this growth should be treated as part of the population expansion toward the end of the Song dynasty. If we focus on *lu* with at least one hundred thousand households, the difference between the north and the south becomes even more striking. There were only three *lu* (Dadu, Zhending, and Jining) in the north that reach this figure, whereas there were twenty-one such areas in the Lower Yangtze region. Such divergence across a north-south divide clearly implies a structurally weak political and economic administration.

Like population changes, the quantity and spatial distribution of commercial taxes show a comparable major decline and geographic shift in trade between the eleventh and thirteenth centuries. In *Yuan-dian-zhang* (Statutes and Precedents of the Yuan Dynasty), one can find the names and locations of 131 local tax stations, about two-thirds to three-fourths of the total tax stations in Yuan China, along with their annual quotas recorded in 1303. At first glance, these tax quotas would suggest that cities in the north played an important role in Yuan commerce. Together, these northern cities contributed 56 percent of total commercial taxes and 33.8 percent of liquor taxes. *Fuli*, large administrative areas governed directly by the court, for instance, accounted for 32.3 percent and Henan 15.7 percent of total commercial taxes. However, this might be misleading because most reported tax stations under the control of Henan Province in the late thirteenth century were located in modern Anhui, which is viewed as part of East China today.[4] If these administratively changing units are eliminated from Henan altogether, the distribution certainly favors South China. In table 5-4, I present tax stations in accord with changes to modern administrative units. Central China and East China together, for instance, accounted for nearly 46 percent of all the tax stations across the country.

Commercial tax data also illuminate how the urban economy of northern and southwestern China was particularly devastated. The largest contributors mentioned in the *Yuan-dian-zhang*, that is, the top centers of urban consumption, were Dadu (Beijing),

Table 5-2. Demographic changes in the Yuan dynasty, 1270–1290 (*lu* with households above 30,000)

1. The north	23		

North China	21		
Regions	*Households*	*Regions*	*Households*
Dadu	147,590	Shangdu	41,062
Baoding lu	75,182	Zhending lu	134,986
Shunde lu	30,501	Guangpin lu	41,446
Daming lu	68,639	Huaiqing lu	34,933
Hejian lu	79,226	Dongping lu	44,731
Dongchang lu	33,102	Caozhou	37,153
Yidu lu	77,164	Jinan lu	63,289
Datong lu	45,945	Jining lu	75,404
Jinning lu	120,630	Daning lu	46,006
Bianlaing lu	30,018		

Northwest China	2		
Regions	*Households*	*Regions*	*Households*
Gongchangfu	45,135	Fenyuan lu	33,935

2. The South	78		

Central China	31		
Central China—Hubei: 4			
Regions	*Households*	*Regions*	*Households*
Qizhou lu	39,190	Wuchang lu	114,632
Zhongxing lu	170,682	Xiazhou lu	37,291

Central China—Hunan: 15			
Regions	*Households*	*Regions*	*Households*
Yuezhou lu	137,508	Changde lu	206,425
Fengzhou lu	209,989	Tianlin lu	603,501
Chenzhou lu	83,223	Yuanzhou lu	48,632
Xingguo lu	50,952	Henzhou lu	113,373
Yongzhou lu	55,666	Chenzhou lu	61,259
Baoqing lu	72,309	Wugang lu	77,207
Guiyang lu	65,057	Chaling lu	36,642
Daozhou lu	78,018		

Central China—Jiangxi: 12			
Regions	*Households*	*Regions*	*Households*
Longxing lu	371,436	Ji'an lu	444,083
Ruizhou lu	144,572	Yuanzhou lu	198,563
Linjiang lu	158,348	Fuzhou lu	218,455
Jiangzhou lu	83,977	Nankang lu	95,678
Ganzhou lu	71,287	Jianchang lu	92,223
Nan'an lu	50,611	Xinzhou lu	132,290

continued on next page

Table 5-2. *Continued.*

East China	33		

East China—Anhui: 8

Regions	Households	Regions	Households
Luzhou lu	31,746	Anqing lu	35,106
Taiping lu	76,202	Chizhou lu	68,547
Ningguo lu	232,538	Huizhou lu	157,471
Guangde lu	56,513	Jiande lu	103,481

East China—Jiangsu: 9

Regions	Households	Regions	Households
Huai'an lu	91,022	Gaoyoufu	50,098
Yangzhou lu	249,466	Jiangyinzhou	53,821
Pingjiang lu	466,158	Changzhou lu	209,732
Zhenjiang lu	103,315	Songjiangfu	163,931
Jiqing lu	214,538		

East China—Zhejiang: 16

Regions	Households	Regions	Households
Hangzhou lu	360,850	Huzhou lu	254,345
Jiaxing lu	426,656	Chuzhou lu	132,754
Quzhou lu	108,567	Wuzhou lu	221,118
Shaoxing lu	151,234	Wenzhou lu	187,403
Taizhou lu	196,415	Chuzhou lu	132,754
Qingyuan lu	241,457	Shaoxing lu	151,234
Quzhou lu	108,567	Taizhou lu	196,415
Wenzhou lu	187,403		

Southeast China	13		

Southeast China—Fujian: 7

Regions	Households	Regions	Households
Fuzhou lu	799,694	Jianning lu	127,254
Quanzhou lu	89,060	Xinghua lu	67,739
Shaowu lu	64,127	Yanping lu	89,825
Dingzhou lu	41,423		

Southeast China—Guangdong: 5

Regions	Households	Regions	Households
Guangzhou lu	170,216	Chaozhou lu	63,650
Zhaoqing lu	33,338	Leizhou lu	89,535
Qianning anfusi	75,837		

Southeast China—Guangxi: 1

Regions	Households
Jingjiang lu	210,852

Southwest China	1

Regions	Households
Chengdu lu	32,912

Source: Wu Songdi 2000, 334–43.

Hangzhou, and Zhenzhou, which are all located along the Grand Canal and are all either within or in close proximity to the eastern coastal regions. Conversely, commercial taxes radically declined in Shaanxi, Henan, and Sichuan. For instance, Sichuan contributed only 4.1 percent of the total tax amounts (see table 5-3) and had only three cities with tax stations (table 5-4). Moreover, there were only 32,912 households living in Sichuan (table 5-2). This decline is striking when compared to the 1077 commercial tax data that showed that Sichuan contributed a significant share to the national commercial taxes (10.8 percent) and had a population density comparable to the Lower Yangtze region.[5] In contrast, the central provinces in the middle Lower Yangtze valley, which included Hubei, Hunan, and Jiangxi, contributed a significant share of commercial taxes (14 percent), an amount almost doubling their share recorded in the 1077 tax data. In addition, there were also tax stations in thirty-seven cities, about 22.7 percent of the national total. This speculation of regional trade growth based on commercial tax data depicts exactly the same story that we have learned from observation of the Song-Yuan population data. Just as Hunan saw its population increased by 1010 percent from 980 to 1290 to rank first in the south, so did it become a major contributor of commercial taxes.[6]

Extant data, while incomplete, present a complex and unstable image of the Chinese economy under Mongol rule where a depressed national economy coexisted with localized vibrant markets, especially in the Jiangnan area. I discuss the role intensive farming development played in the context of this dynamic phenomenon during the thirteenth century in chapter 8. Rapid development of maritime trade was another obvious clue that accounted for regional prosperity.[7] But as a whole, the Mongol conquest caused a

Table 5-3. Distribution of indirect taxes and population in Yuan China, 1303

Region	Households (000)	%	Commercial tax (000 ding[1])	%	Liquor tax (000 ding)	%
Fuli[2]	148	1.5	10,306	2.6	56,243	11.5
Liaoyang	15	0.2	8,273	2.0	2,250	0.4
Henan[3]	400	4.1	147,428	36.5	75,077	15.4
Shaanxi	300	3.1	45,579	11.3	11,774	2.4
Sichuan	450	4.7	16,676	4.1	7,590	1.6
Gansu	100	1	17,361	4.3	20,078	4.1
Yunnan	—	—	—	—	—	—
Jiangzhe	2,400	24.9	26,927	6.7	196,654	40.4
Jiangxi	2,448	25.4	62,512	16.3	58,640	12.0
Huguang	3,380	35.1	68,844	17	58,848	12.1
Total	9,641	100	403,906	100	487,154	100

Source: Yuan shi, shihuo, section 2. Except for fuli, all the regions refer to the provinces (xingshen) that were governed by Branch Secretariats. The Henan Province, for instance, includes modern Henan, Anhui, and part of Hubei.

1. The unit of tax amount is ding.

2. Fuli refers to the areas governed directly by the central authority at Beijing, including Inner Mongolia, Beijing, Hebei, Shandong, and Shanxi.

3. It includes Jiangsu, Zhejiang, and Fujian.

Table 5-4. The regional distribution of tax stations, 1303

Macro region	N	NW	E	C	SE	SW	Total
Number	66	3	49	37	5	3	163
Percentage	40.5	1.8	30.1	22.7	3.1	1.8	100

Source: Table D-11.

substantial decline in aggregate population and the demise of the national market along with the collapse of an effective inland water transport network.

Disappearance of Monetized Taxation during the Late Fourteenth Century

The study of the Yuan-Ming transition reveals the rise of a demonetized financial system after the establishment of the Ming dynasty in 1368. At the same time, market development came to a complete halt in the once commercially vibrant Lower Yangtze region. In other words, it was the early Ming policies rather than the Mongol conquest that brought about the only temporary demonetized economy in China over the last millennium. Although the Yuan administration was severely weakened by decentralization, its state revenues were largely collected in cash. Mongol nobility embraced the market and were particularly friendly toward merchants and travelers from foreign countries.[8] The Yuan government was also committed to the maintenance of communication and a transportation route along a corridor between the Lower Yangtze and the capital in the north.[9]

The Yuan state concentrated fiscal extraction on commerce into one instrument, a sales tax, literally, *shangshui*, which was levied on all retail businesses. There were only 170 to 200 tax stations set up nationwide, about one-sixth of the total number of county-level administrative units.[10] Therefore, Yuan tax data more likely reflected the concentration of urban consumption rather than the constituency of internal trade network and the inflow of goods across borders. Furthermore, the collection of sales taxes at local markets was also accomplished through liturgies rather than bureaucratic administration. A large number of tax intermediaries were allowed or employed by the state to work as local agents for liturgical tax collection.[11] This is an important sign that the Yuan administration gave up its responsibility for tax collection in many areas.

Despite Yuan rulers' welcoming attitude toward commerce, the market economy under their rule was disrupted by monetary problems. State finance after the Mongol conquest was highly monetized. In 1328, the court reported 12.1 million Yuan *shi* for grain revenues that were largely collected from agriculture and 9.5 million *ding* for cash revenues that were mostly collected from the alcohol and salt monopolies (see table 5-5). The 9.5 million *ding* in cash revenues or 4.75 billion *guan*, although itself an unmatched record in monetary terms, could be converted to no more than 12 million Yuan *shi* of rice, which is quite close to the tax payment in grain.[12] In other words, agriculture and urban consumption/ long-distance trade each contributed half of the total. However, taxes from nonagricultural sectors were poorly managed. The increase in cash revenues lagged far behind the inflation

Table 5-5. Major components in Yuan tax revenue, 1328

	Land taxes in cash (ding*)	Liquor and vinegar (ding)	Salt (ding)	Commercial taxes (ding)
Amount	149,273	491,754	7,661,000	939,682
Percentage	1.6	5.2	80.6	10

Source: Chen & Shi, 511.

*The figures reported here are in the *zhongtong* bill; 1 *ding* = 50 *guan*.

caused by overexpansive monetary policies. In 1260, Kublai issued the zhongtong bill, a paper currency, as the only medium of exchange. In 1287, the central administration began to issue the *zhiyuan* bills without restraint. Toward the end of the thirteenth century, the total value of *zhiyuan* bills probably reached 2 million *ding*, an increase of roughly 20 times their value in 1273.[13] The impact of uncontrolled inflation was widely felt as one Chinese scholar-official complained that prices had risen more than tenfold.[14]

The decentralized nature of the Mongol political system made it impossible to build a powerful fiscal state similar to the Song. The Yuan tax administration was incapable of taxing movable goods. Its cash revenues mostly came from profits made from salt monopolies.[15] The latter increased from 1.7 million *ding* at the turn of the fourteenth century to 7.6 million *ding* in 1328. In consequence, cash revenues rose from below 1 million *ding* in 1284 to 9.5 million *ding* in 1328. The salt monopoly made the greatest contribution to this magnificent increase. However, salt consumption was the least elastic among consumption goods. Rather, this increase reflected the impact of inflation.[16] Liquor revenues and commercial taxes were levied upon urban consumption but formed a minor percentage of the total cash revenues. The collection of transit taxes had to be abandoned due to the difficulty in maintaining the network of inland waterways. As Dadu (Beijing), the newly built capital, was far from the Lower Yangtze region, the court had minimal control over these important economic centers.

A major change in the financial structure during the Yuan-Ming transition was brought out by demonetization. The early Ming administration promoted payment in kind in all aspects of state revenues: land taxes (*fushui* or *shuiliang*), indirect taxes (*kecheng*), and labor services. Labor services played an important role in the early Ming command economy, while land taxes remained the largest source of tax revenues and were paid in kind. Indirect taxes, including a broad range of nonagricultural sources, such as the salt and tea monopolies, commercial taxes, and taxed goods from nonagricultural households,[17] all of which were collectively called *kecheng* in the official documents, were on many occasions collected in kind rather than in cash. The *kecheng* quota was fixed for many decades without change. For these two reasons, the modern researcher will find it difficult to distinguish between income from commercial taxes and direct taxes that were recorded in the Ming gazetteers.

Except for changes in tax payments, the collection of indirect taxes in the early Ming largely followed Yuan practice. The Ming tax stations known as commercial tax offices (*shuike si* and *shuikeju*, hereafter abbreviated as CTOs) were distributed all over the country.[18] The total number of CTOs, according to the *Mingshilu*, reached 460, which only represented one-third of the total of early Ming administrative units. An alternate estimate puts the number of CTOs as high as 828, which were about two-thirds of the total administrative units.[19] Nonetheless, the scarcity of CTOs dispersed across such a vast empire indicates the slow recovery of trade.

The distribution of tax stations in the fourteenth century demonstrates a shrinking of the domestic market. The number of Ming tax stations in the 1390s, whether the number was 460 or 828, was much smaller than that in 1077, which reached 2,060. Table 5-6 shows the distribution of all the tax institutes that can be identified in the text of *MHD*. Although the early Ming tax stations outnumbered those of Yuan China, the structure of their distribution did not change much. The majority were concentrated in the Lower Yangtze, Zhejiang, Jiangxi, and Shandong. One can find the least number in Guangxi and Guangdong (five stations), Sichuan (ten stations), and Hebei (ten stations), Henan (eighteen stations). If it is assumed that the distribution of tax stations was closely associated with the volume of trade in regional markets with a certain degree of urbanization, one can conclude that these undertaxed regions had probably deurbanized by the late fourteenth century. In 1380, the Ming founder shut down 364 CTOs because their annual tax income was below 500 *shi* of rice.[20] After 1400, especially during the Zhengtong reign (1436–1449), the Ming court continued to reduce tax stations according to the decline in commercial tax revenues. By 1585, only 111 CTOs were scattered throughout the Ming empire. Commercial taxes were in fact collected through tax-farming or liturgical services and lost their influence on state revenues. By the 1570s, it is estimated that the amount of CTO revenues was between 150,000 to 200,000 taels, which was at most 5.8 percent of the non-land-tax revenues.[21] In any case, this was often submitted along with other kinds of indirect taxes without differentiation.

Another major change in the early Ming financial administration was that its concern over monetary policy far outweighed its concern over state revenues from indirect

Table 5-6. The distribution of early Ming CTOs

The South	139	The North	241
1. Nanjing	14	1. Beijing	16
2. Jiangsu	39	2. Hebei	10
3. Zhejiang	58	3. Henan	18
4. Jiangxi	31	4. Shandong	44
5. Hubei & Hunan	26	5. Shaanxi	11
6. Fujian	23	6. Shanxi	26
7. Guangdong	5	7. Anhui[a]	14
8. Guangxi	5		
9. Sichuan	10		
10. Yunnan & Guizhou	15		

Source: MHD, vol. 35. The total is 380, much less than the two reported aggregate figures mentioned earlier.

a. Includes Fengyang and Huai'an.

b. Includes Luzhou, Ningguo, Taiping, and Huizhou.

taxation. Unlike the Yuan, the market-based tax revenues such as monopolies and commercial taxes comprised a tiny share in the total tax revenues in the Ming. From such a view, market expansion was rather unwelcoming, since it might threaten the command economy by encouraging free migration and circulation of goods and knowledge across the empire and, at the same time, provide little return to the state power. In contrast, payment in kind and *baochao* consolidated the command power of the state. The tax policies thus served the monetary policy as the early Ming court issued a huge amount of paper money. These policies severely undermined the stable foundation upon which goods were normally traded. In 1375, the Ming court decided to issue paper notes and ordered that 70 percent of all indirect taxes (*kecheng*) must be paid in *baochao* and 30 percent in bronze coins. At the same time, people were forbidden to use gold or silver to make payments. The 1380 edict mentioned previously mandated commercial taxes to be levied in rice.[22] In the same year, the Ming court began to use rice as payment to all officials and soldiers. The lack of circulating money in the early Ming financial system, especially hard currencies, can be detected by both official salaries and the collection of commercial taxes.[23]

Indeed, early Ming monetary policies aimed to undermine the market expansion rather than to facilitate commercial exchanges. The court issued paper bills without restraint, which unsurprisingly resulted in a severe depreciation in the value of *baochao*. This further weakened the *baochao*'s status as a means of payment and even led to the rejection of using it at the marketplace. To facilitate the circulation of paper bills, the Ming court launched two campaigns. In 1404, Zhu Di ordered all households to pay a fixed amount of *baochao* annually for salt consumption, 12 *guan* for each adult and 6 *guan* for each child.[24] In 1409, he drastically increased the tax quotas assigned to the CTOs. About two decades later, Emperor Xuanzong (1426–1435) again launched a campaign to encourage the tax payment by paper bills. He not only expanded the number of urban-based taxes but also greatly increased the previous quota and announced the establishment of customs houses (*chaoguan* or *queguan*). These schemes could barely rescue the credibility of the *baochao*. Yet the unstable and often catastrophic financial management damaged the market mechanism. For our purposes here, the tax quota-fixing system makes it impossible to reconstruct the size of trade by extrapolating commercial tax data preserved in Ming gazetteers. Also, because of the ever-worsening depreciation of paper bills, which were regularly used in commercial tax payment after 1400, we do not have a clear idea of how the quotas were originally fixed, nor can we gauge the effects of later adjustments. Except for the early years of the Hongwu reign, Ming tax revenues from the CTOs can hardly offer any substantial information on the size of trade.

The quota-fixing policy along with the ever-threatening depreciation of paper bills eventually diminished the role of indirect taxes in Ming state revenues. Indirect taxes paid in paper bills increased from 4,076,000 *ding* in 1390 to 32,787,000 *ding* in 1429, an eightfold increase. Yet after factoring in the depreciation rate, indirect taxes collected in 1429 were equivalent to only 327, 870 tael of silver, just 8 percent of that collected in 1390.[25] The early Ming commercial tax data clearly demonstrates a worsening picture of domestic markets.

The 1381 tax figures allow us to reconstruct the size of the early Ming domestic market and to compare the 1381 economy with that of 1077. In the second section of chapter 3, I arrive at a gross size for the domestic market at 5.3 to 8.58 million taels of silver in contemporary prices. This estimated size of the domestic market was only 5 to10 percent of that in 1077. In the 1390s, households registered by the government totaled 10.6 million, which was two-thirds of the Song population in 1078 (with 16.6 million households). As measured in trade per capita, the sharp decline in the market economy is obvious.

Shrinking in Water Transports

Water transportation serves as the vehicle of trade in the preindustrial economy. After discussing important demographic and monetary changes, in this section I focus on my observations of the changes in Ming China's inland water transport. A decline in long-distance trade during the interim of the two economic booms was associated with the collapse of the Kaifeng-centered waterway network. At its worst moments, long-distance trade in Ming China relied solely on one water channel—the Grand Canal. For this reason, it is not surprising that quantitative information on Ming inland waterways is mostly confined to the Grand Canal.[26] All the other water channels were not reported for carrying goods over long distances until the domestic market regained importance toward the end of the sixteenth century. Wars and natural disasters, ecological deterioration and the dysfunction of the government in this unstable era all combined to bring about the collapse of the national waterway network.

The anti-market policy of the early Ming state was also responsible for the underdevelopment of water transportation. Not even the Grand Canal was conceived as a state project that aimed to develop a market economy. In the fifteenth century, the Grand Canal extended over 1,100 miles connecting Beijing, the political center of the Ming empire, with Jiangnan, the heart of the country's economy. It was originally conceived to deliver grain taxes from the Lower Yangtze, and from Jiangnan in particular, to Beijing where the Ming court and a large number of troops were located.[27] At its inception, only military vessels were permitted to deliver tribute grain, while private ships did not enjoy the same access. From 1470 onward, each tribute junk was allowed to load 10 *shi* of tax-free products as compensation for its sailors. Roughly a century later, the compensation increased to about 50 to 60 *shi*. In 1730, the Qing court dramatically increased the quota to 126 *shi*.[28] Owing to policy changes of the Qing government that favored long-distance trade, shipments of private goods by tribute junks along the Grand Canal increased sixty-six–fold in about three centuries.[29]

Because of its noncommercial-based transportation, the Ming administration did not attempt to tax shipments over the Grand Canal until private trade prevailed in the mid-fifteenth century. In 1429, the Ming court established seven customs houses (*chaoguan*) along the canal to collect transit taxes. This policy indicates the importance of the Grand Canal for the emergence of long-distance trade. From the 1480s to the 1770s, customs revenues collected from the Grand Canal increased sixteenfold (see table 5-7). Deflated by the index of prices, real growth was nearly sixfold. However, the share of national custom revenues collected from the Grand Canal declined to 41 percent by 1777. Given what we know about market growth during this period, the percentage of decline indicates rapid developments in long-distance trade along other major water transport routes.[30]

Table 5-7. Customs revenues collected along the Grand Canal
(taels of silver)

Year	Tax amount	Share of national customs revenue	Year	Tax amount	Share of national customs revenue
1480	120,000*	100%	1686	654,790	61%
1578	219,000	93%	1735	1,745,570	47%
1597	387,000	95%	1753	1,985,440	43%
1625	424,430	88%	1777	2,110,760	41%
1652	554,190	68%	1788	1,856,660	36%

*This includes all transit taxes collected by the Ming customs houses.
Source: Fan 1993, 130.

Revenues collected from Ming customs houses deserve further examination as they were transit taxes by nature and thus closely reflect developments in long-distance trade. We should note that in the mid-sixteenth century, all these tax stations were located along the Grand Canal, with only one exception—the customs house stationed at Jiujiang along the mid-Yangtze River. In table 5-8, I have given a brief report on the tax revenues generated by each customs house. By the end of the sixteenth century, the amount raised from all seven customs houses amounted to 334,000 taels, while the total amount of transit taxes was no more than 450,000 taels.[31] In nominal terms, this would be only 5.8 percent of the commercial tax revenues in 1077, or 2.2 percent of the tax revenues from commerce in the late nineteenth century.[32] From this comparison, even if we take perpetual deflation during the Ming period into consideration, the fact that the Ming state was an exclusively land-tax-based regime is self-evident.

We should not speculate that late Ming long-distance trade remained as unimportant as shown by this comparison. The small amount of commercial taxes only indicates the inefficiency of the Ming tax mechanism. It is impossible to recover the size of trade

Table 5-8. Increases in seven customs houses, 1530–1625

Tax stations	1530–1540	1597	1625
Hexiwu	46,000 taels	61,000	32,000
Linqing	83,000	108,000	63,800
Hushu	40,000	52,000	87,500
Jiujiang	15,000	20,000	57,500
Beixin	33,000	43,000	80,000
Yangzhou	13,000	18,000	25,600
Huai'an	22,000	32,000	45,600
Total	252,000	334,000	392,000

Source: Li Longqian 1994, 40.

in the sixteenth century by extrapolating tax figures.[33] It is noteworthy that Wu Cheng-ming, one of the leading scholars in the study of Chinese economic history and a main advocate of the sixteenth-century turning point paradigm, recognizes the lack of adequate quantitative evidence to support the argument of market expansion in the mid-sixteenth century.[34] Nonetheless, these figures can be used to measure the volume of goods conveyed along the Grand Canal. Since this unique water transport system played such an important role during much of the Ming period, it should reflect the development and changes the domestic market underwent during the last century of the late Ming. From 1530 to 1625, tax revenues from the seven customs houses, for instance, increased from 252,000 taels to 392,000 taels, an increase of 56 percent. Considering that prices rose 72 percent in one century, such slight increase in tax revenues is insignificant. In fact, while the amount of tax collected from tax stations located along the northern part of the Grand Canal, such as Hexiwu and Linqing, apparently dwindled, those collected from tax stations in the southern part increased without exception. In the mid-sixteenth century, Jiujiang only contributed 15,000 taels in taxes, the second lowest among the seven customs houses, but by 1625 they delivered 57,500 taels, an increase of 383 percent. From a broader perspective, the tax revenues submitted by Jiujiang constituted 14.7 percent of the national total, a drastic increase from a mere 5.2 percent. This change suggests the significant growth of long-distance trade along the Yangtze River by the end of the sixteenth century.

The tax data reported in table 5-8 indicates an enormous increase in customs revenues toward the end of the sixteenth century.[35] If we take 1578 as a benchmark year for observation, the amount of commercial taxes collected from the Grand Canal took almost a century (from 1480 to 1578) to double in the Ming, while it took half a century (from 1578 to 1652) during the Ming-Qing transition to achieve a 2.5-fold increase. Specifically, it took just a century (from 1578 to 1686) to triple the amount. Given the close relationship between the increase in customs revenues and the expansion in trade, one can immediately identify the only peak growth in trade during the two centuries from 1480 to 1686, and it occurred during the Ming-Qing transition. No other evidence than this indicates the premature nature of long-distance trade in the sixteenth century.

Grain transportation via the Grand Canal in the eleventh century was comparable to that of the Ming. On average, the Ming government annually shipped 4 million *shi* of grain through the Grand Canal. When compared with the grain transportation in the Song, this record sounds not surprising at all. The Song local administrations in the south were required to send 4 million Song *shi* of rice to Kaifeng every year through the Bian Canal. From 1007 to 1048, the annual amount of grain tribute from the south increased to 6 million Song *shi*.[36] The maximum grain shipment for the Bian Canal was about 8 million Song *shi* (5.4 million *shi*). Most of the increases in grain shipment were purchased at local markets in the south. In addition, 0.5 million Song *shi* of millet and 0.3 million Song *shi* of beans were shipped eastward along the Yellow River to Kaifeng. Finally, through the Guangji-Qing canals, the administrations in Shandong sent about 0.7 million Song *shi* of grain annually.

If the Ming Grand Canal was indeed a central artery rather than one of many waterways, it is clear that it failed to provide an integrated waterway network to encourage interregional trade in the north. Unlike Kaifeng in the eleventh century, a great national entrepôt did not exist in the north that may have played a major role in facilitating market integration. For this reason, neither Linqing nor Beijing could extend its influence into the western region of the grand plateau. No shipments from Linqing or Beijing, for instance, could reach Kaifeng, not to mention cities further west in Shanxi, Shaanxi, and Gansu. This led us to question why the construction of the Ming Grand Canal failed to create an integral waterway network to support trade in the north. The answer lies in the changing relationship between the Grand Canal and the course of the Yellow River.

Tan Qixiang proposed an important explanation by which the unpredictable relationship between the Grand Canal and the Yellow River in the grand plateau significantly contributed to the decline of water transportation in North China after the collapse of the Northern Song. Before the twelfth century, as Tan pointed out, the Grand Canal was one of the most important waterways that closely associated with other rivers and canals in the grand plateau of North China. Tan offered at least two reasons for this decline. First, shipping grain to Beijing across the sea was obviously much less expensive than transportation by inland waterways since the proximity of Beijing to the sea minimized technical difficulties in completing this transport. Had the early Ming rulers adopted sea transportation when they chose Beijing as the capital, they could have saved a great deal of money. This was, in fact, the policy adopted by the Mongols after they conquered the Southern Song. Nevertheless, the Ming grain tributes were carried by inland water transport for safety reasons.[37] Second, the construction of the Ming Grand Canal, though aiming to link the north to the south, meant a destructive end to the existence of an integrated inland waterway network in North China. The shipping route from Beijing to Hangzhou via Kaifeng resembled an arch in the eleventh century; however, from the fourteenth century onward, it became a straight line.[38] This change shortened the sailing distance by one-third, from 1,680 to 1,115 miles, a severe loss of navigation mileage for North China. Many cities in Henan and Hebei no longer had access to the distant market via waterways.

To elaborate on Tan's explanation, I turn to the contemporary writings produced by merchants and travelers between 1570 and 1644. These nonofficial writings offer firsthand accounts of water transportation at the turn of the century.[39] Modern researchers in the fields of historical geography and environmental history have also significantly contributed to our understanding of the waterways in North China in the post-Song eras. These will allow me to analyze why North China permanently lost most of its important waterways and measure the impact of that loss upon Ming domestic trade.

Published in 1570, Huang Bian's *Yitong lucheng tuji* was the most popular trade guide book written during the Ming period. It provided a complete list of the major water and land routes available to travelers, including two detailed sections on water routes entitled "waterways to the north of the Yangtze River" and "waterways to the south of the Yangtze River." In the first section, he recorded thirteen different water routes in the north. A careful examination, however, would suggest that some of these routes shared the same course. Almost all of them were branches to the Grand Canal. No river other than the Grand Canal formed an independent watercourse in water transportation in North China.[40] Six named routes (Routes 3, 4, 5, and 10, 11, 12), for instance, follow two important channels that linked the Grand Canal to various regions in eastern Henan. These routes, however, only became available after 1500. Besides these two channels, Huang listed no other river in the inland regions of North China that were available for navigation; even Kaifeng had lost its access to water transport.[41]

Huang's book vividly describes the lack of access in North China to water transport in inland regions west of the Grand Canal. As the canal shifted its course toward the seashore, only merchants from a few coastal regions (such as Shandong and Jiangsu) could take advantage of easy boat rides to the south. As Tan mentioned, a single, straight channel of the Grand Canal could hardly promote economic integration between the inland regions and the rest of the economy without providing an intensive waterway network. What happened to the Kaifeng hegemony that had flourished during eleventh-century China? By the sixteenth century, what forces had led to the widening gap between the insufficient water transport system in the north and the abundant network of the south?

In contrast, these primary resources portrayed a very different picture of the convenience of water transportation in the south. Both Huang and Cheng Chunyu, the compiler of another merchants' guidebook, the *Shishang leiyao*, produced detailed accounts of river navigation in the Lower Yangtze. Merchants and travelers enjoyed easy access provided by a reliable network of waterways to all of the major cities and entrepôts. The mature development of this southern water transit system is evident in Cheng's writing. In one instance, he was able to provide detailed tips for travelers heading to the depot of Hangzhou from Suzhou, including the exact type of boats (such as day-trip or night-trip) he would need to board, the location of boarding, the cost of the fare, and the price of food during the journey, just like what an ordinary passenger could expect from a standard travel guide.[42]

According to modern geographical studies, the worsening situation of the Yellow River in post-Song North China caused a permanent loss in the inland waterway network. Historically, the Yellow River had the tendency to shift course all over the grand plateau. After decades of heavy silting that raised the riverbed higher than the surrounding plain, and after a period of unusually heavy rainfall, the river would flood and break the dykes to open another course to the sea. From 602 BC to the present, the Yellow River had significantly changed course five times, and its levees have been breached more than 1,500 times. Yet, the frequency of floods had been much more uneven.[43] Studies of the Yellow River's history have highlighted irreversible changes to the geography of North China that were caused by catastrophic events. The most devastating episode marking the Yellow River's drastic change of course in 1194 AD was brought about by a man-made flood intended to defend the Song state against the Jurchen invasion. Floodwaters rushed south into the Huai River basin and took over its drainage system for the next seven hundred years. Meanwhile, the Yellow River swept back and forth across several hundred miles.[44] With each course change, the river would destroy the existing rivers and lakes, while loose silt in the stream turned farmlands into sandy wastelands.[45] Many tributary branches of the Huai River in eastern Henan, and western and central Anhui, such as the Sui, Wo, and Ying rivers, became much shallower or became completely unnavigable. The Juye Lake in Shandong, for instance, measuring a hundred miles in width, was once the biggest lake in North China and served as an important center of interregional trade in the grand plateau. Shipments from harbor cities such as Yunzhou, Xuzhou, Jizhou, and Yanggu, sailed through the lake and enjoyed easy access to the eastward-going Guangji-Qing canals and the southward-going Sishui Canal as well as a short distance land transfer to the lower Yellow River.[46] The southward shift of the Yellow River in 1194 left the lake nothing more than sandy deposition and marshes.

Consequently, the entire area became isolated from long-distance trade and, eventually, the poorest region in the grand plateau.

The deterioration of water transportation in North China varied from region to region. As one moved further north, the deterioration became more severe. Here, I want to use Huang's account of late sixteenth-century river navigation north of the Yangtze River to compare with Song water transportation. Huang reported a few short-distance water routes close to Huai'an, where the Yellow River met the Huai River in Jiangsu. All of these routes had once played a significant role in Song interregional trade. In the eleventh century, Chuzhou, Gaoyou, Haizhou (modern Qinhuangdao), Lianshui, and Baoying were all major city ports in northeast Jiangsu because of their importance in linking coastal trade routes with inland river transportation along the Bian Canal, the Sishui Canal, and the Huai River. These four interconnected city ports produced 198,483 strings of commercial taxes, which was 4.7 times that of Yangzhou.[47]

Among the cities along the Grand Canal, Chuzhou (Huai'an in the Ming period) was only second to Kaifeng in terms of collected commercial taxes during the eleventh century, which by far surpassed that of Yangzhou and Zhenzhou. Since the Huai River, the Bian Canal (the northern part of the Song Grand Canal), and the Sishui Canal all converged at Chuzhou, it is not surprising that it achieved such a central position in interregional trade.[48] Unfortunately, the Yellow River floods and the damage caused by the sediment destroyed or severely damaged this intricate canal-river network. In the fifteenth century, Huai'an, which was built near the Song city of Chuzhou, emerged as one of the largest entrepôts along the Grand Canal. However, since navigation along the Yellow River was often dangerous, Huai'an gradually lost its position as an inviting destination for seagoing vessels. According to Huang's account, although a water route did exist from Haizhou and Andongwei to Huai'an via Yuntiguan, the mouth of the Yellow River, merchants would rather take the land route because navigation via Yuntiguan was extremely difficult.[49]

Similarly, the prosperous history of Song coastal cities such as Lianshui, Haizhou, and Taizhou further underscored the sad state of coastal trade in late sixteenth-century Jiangsu. Sediment from the Yellow River not only greatly reduced the navigability of the Huai River but also hindered coastal transportation in Jiangsu.[50] Thus, a comparison of Huai'an in the late Ming with Chuzhou in the Song demonstrates a significant loss in the complexity of the water transport structure and a decline in the total mileage of navigable waters. An intensive waterway network that once existed in the eleventh century southeast of the Grand Canal had diminished to a few remaining tributary branches that could hardly support long-distance trade and seagoing shipments as in the eleventh century.

The fate of waterways west of the Grand Canal presented an altogether different picture. The routes reported by Huang consisted of two waterways that linked the Grand Canal and river-port cities in Henan either through the Huai River or the Yellow River. In the eleventh century, the Huai River basin was, in fact, the most important navigation area because of its intermediate location between the Yellow River and the Yangtze River. The flooding of the Yellow River combined with subsequent changes in its course ended any meaningful navigation along the Huai River or any other rivers and canals in eastern Henan and western Anhui over time.[51] A complete loss of water transportation occurred most frequently among cities located on the northern and middle parts of the plateau. Examples also include northeast Henan, central and southeast Hebei, and western Shandong, which were all regions west of the Ming Grand Canal. In these regions, the flooded Yellow River often buried cities, filled up lakes and riverbeds, and destroyed the water transportation network. The old Song capital, for example, was buried deeply beneath modern Kaifeng.[52] According to one study, the city's urban population "had been reduced to 90,000 from a previous high of nearly ten times of that."[53]

Other cities that were also adversely impacted include Puyang, Daming, Chaocheng, Enzhou, Huaiyang, Juye, and Dingtao.[54] Commercial taxes collected from these seven cities in 1077 amounted to 97,449 strings, which exceeded that of Hangzhou (82,173 strings). For most of the eleventh century, the Yongji Canal, Futuo River, Fuyangshui River, and, to some extent, the Yellow River formed an intraregional waterway network on the Hebei plateau.[55] The fifteen cities along the Yongji Canal also produced a combined total of 105,926 strings. If one includes the Guangji-Qing canals and the lower Yellow River, the commercial taxes collected in Hebei and Shandong would surpass those of the Lower Yangtze. However, sediment from floods eventually buried the Yongji Canal and many other Song cities.[56] The loss of this famous and longest inland canal, which had existed for over five hundred years, again signaled a great reduction in navigable mileage in North China and an end to its prosperous commerce.

Limit of Sixteenth-Century Trade

Contrary to the argument of an unprecedented late Ming trade boom, my examination suggests that Ming water transportation remained underdeveloped as late as the end of the sixteenth century. Since no fragmented water transportation system could have supported vibrant long-distance trade, the very late development in the Ming domestic market challenges the optimistic view of a blooming market economy in sixteenth-century China. Long-distance trade was narrowly confined to only three arteries: the Grand Canal, the Lower Yangtze, and the Gan River.[57] The waterways of South China, especially those south of the Yangtze River, were the least damaged during the post-Song periods. In fact, Jiangnan, Jiangxi, and Guangdong could have hardly been more fortunate. In contrast, water transportation in the upper Yangtze River and Sichuan declined dramatically. The Chengdu plain had been one of the most densely populated areas and rivaled the north and the Lower Yangtze in trade and industry. In 1077, commercial taxes from Sichuan contributed to 10.8 percent of the national total.[58] However, the Mongol invasions brought a destructive end to its success. The number of households in Sichuan, Guizhou, and Yunnan totaled 215,719 in 1393, which was merely 8 percent of Sichuan's population in 1173.[59] One can hardly imagine how inter- and intraregional trade in Sichuan could have survived such a heavy blow. It was not until the eighteenth century that another trade boom finally returned to the area between the Sichuan river basin and the mid-Yangtze River.[60]

Leaving aside these two extreme cases, that is, Jiangnan and the Sichuan basin, how did water transportation develop in other areas of South China? Did these places enjoy the benefits of rapid growth in water transport in the sixteenth century? Presuming South China did not gain from the losses of North China, is there any evidence that the south developed to such an extent that it balanced the loss in the north? The publication of the ZSYC, a multivolume series of monographs on waterways and ports in Chinese history, has allowed us to view the changes in water transportation at a regional level in China. The compilers of the ZSYC have provided rich documentary records on almost every aspect of water transportation throughout Chinese history, from antiquity to the twentieth century.[61] In this section, I focus on water transports in Jiangxi and Hubei, the two most important provinces in the mid-Yangtze.

In early Ming, Jiangxi ranked among the top provinces in terms of grain tax revenues and was second in provincial population.[62] Proponents of the late Ming trade boom regard the Gan and Yangtze Rivers served as the main transportation route for goods that made a significant contribution to the formation of a national trade network.[63] The volume of shipped goods on the Gan River in the late Ming period might have outmatched that of Song trade because, one may speculate, the ban by the Ming state on maritime trade made inland navigation of the Gan River almost the only connection between Guangdong and the outer regions in the late fifteenth and sixteenth centuries.

Much of the Jiangxi waterway structure had been created in the eleventh century as shown in the 1077 tax data. The mid-Yangtze River and its tributaries, such as the Gan River, Fu River (*rushui-wuyangjian*), and Xin Jiang, run across its territory and formed an intraregional waterway network. Meanwhile, important interregional trade routes included the following: those that linked Jiangxi to Hunan, Hubei, Anhui, and Jiangsu through the Yangtze River; Guangdong and Guangxi through the Gan River; Zhejiang through the Xin and Qiantang rivers; and Fujian through the branches of the Gan and Min rivers.[64] Jiangxi imported mining materials (copper and iron) and handicraft goods (porcelain, paper, lacquer ware, etc.).[65] The thirty-four port cities in Jiangxi contributed 267,274 strings of commercial taxes to the Song state. Qianzhou (modern Ganzhou), which was the entrepôt of north-to-south trade between Jiangxi and Guangdong along the Gan River, even exceeded Hongzhou (modern Nanchang), which was the provincial capital, on the amount of commercial tax contributions. Other port cities including Raozhou, Xinzhou, Fuzhou, Guangdejun, Nankangjun, Jianchangjun, and Nan'anjun are worth mentioning because their commercial tax quotas in 1077 were all above 10,000 strings.[66] All this testifies to the existence of a developed waterway and communication network in the eleventh century.

The tax data from the Jiujiang customs house indicates that prior to 1600 mid-Yangtze transportation played a minor role in trade. The Jiujiang customs house taxed ships that went through the Yangtze River between Jiujiang and Anqing, namely, all ships going upstream and downstream along the mid-Yangtze River as well as boats traveling between the Jiangxi inland waterways and the Yangtze River. Therefore, changes in Jiujiang transit taxes indicate precise increases in trade along this waterway.[67] Over three hundred years, the tax revenues collected from Jiujiang increased from 15,000 taels to 539,300 taels, an increase of thirty-six–fold (see table 5-9). If one makes allowance for inflation, the increase in real terms is still about ten times, or an annual rate of 0.7 percent over three hundred years. The gradual increase does not support a sixteenth-century trade boom. Instead, tax evidence suggests long-distance trade along the mid-Yangtze did not take off until the seventeenth century.

If Jiangxi failed to show much progress in water transportation based on transit tax data, then waterway trade in Hubei represented a much bigger failure. Transportation along the Han River suffered a most striking decline. The Han River basin was severely

Table 5-9. Commercial taxes from Jiujiang, 1493–1804 (000 taels)

Year	Value	Index of prices[1]	Year	Value	Index of prices
1493	15	100	1656	99.8	201
1580	10.9	88.3	1682	120.9	144
1597	25	113	1685	141	144
1621	37.5	163	1706	172.3	161
1625	57.5	163	1730s	354.2	167
1629	66.4	163	1799	520.1	289
1630	79.9	163	1804	539.3	363

Sources: Tables 3-2-1 and 3-2-2 in JX-ZSYC, 80, 82.

1. Index of prices: 1493 = 100.

wracked by wars after 1125, especially by the Mongol campaigns in the thirteenth century. In 1391, the number of households in Xiangyang prefecture was 16,272, less than one-tenth of the Song population that had settled in similar areas in 1102.[68] As no political and economic center existed in the Yellow River basin after 1300 and long-distance trade to the north diminished, the Han River soon lost its significance and regressed as a local waterway after the fourteenth century as it became much less navigable in post-Song times.[69] Changes in the river course and flooding worsened the situation for the basin and subsequently gave rise to Wuhan (Hankou) as the sole water transportation center in Hubei. In the seventeenth century, Wuhan became the most prosperous commercial city in inland China.[70]

The Han River was one of the most important trade routes during the centuries after the Rebellion not only because it was the only water route flowing north and south through central China, but also because it ran across several regions rich with very different resource endowments. Diversified branches of the Han River stretched westward and northwestward into the steppe areas and provided access to an external market for Song commodities. The tea-horse trade with Tibetans and Tanguts, for instance, was one of the most important foreign markets in the eleventh century. Besides tea and silk, many manufactured goods sold at the border were also shipped along the branches of the Han River. As Xiangyang and the Han River lost their significance in long-distance trade in the fourteenth and fifteenth centuries, these external markets were forced to be closed.[71]

Since the upper-Han River basin became the least populated area, the Jialing and Dan rivers only became navigable again after 1550 but were soon wracked by riots and wars. These connection points did not reassume their role as linkages for Hubei and Shaanxi until the mid-seventeenth century.[72] The navigation of the Jialing River began at the same time, making the navigable mileage from Baishuijiangzhen to Guangyuan roughly 578 li long.[73] In the Ming-Qing period, the Wei River ran only from Xianyang to Sanhekou, where it connected to the Yellow River and was about 400 li.[74] In all instances, the revival of these rivers as trade routes points to a commercial recovery date no earlier than the sixteenth century, and this revival was primarily confined to shipping goods to local markets.[75]

Conclusion

The comparison of the market performance in the Song and Ming eras is to compare two different kinds of economic mechanism, a market-based one and a command-based one, that ever worked in preindustrial China. Presumably, the economy in the former performs much better, say, more efficiently, in allocation of production resources than in a command system. The comparison, which is based on a series of economic data, does show the substantial difference in the performance of the market economy between the two eras. In almost all respects, such as population growth, money supply, water transportation, urbanization and trade, what the early Ming command economy could achieve was far behind the Song market-based system. Following the comparison that is already conducted in preceding chapters, in this chapter I continue to provide a comprehensive assessment of long-term and structural changes in the Chinese economy after 1200. The major conclusion drawn from this assessment, that of unprecedented economic (market) disintegration, is obviously consistent with what I have observed from other perspectives, either from a monetary perspective, or from a water transportation view, or from an institutional context, that market performance was worse in a command economy.

The Song-Ming comparison also tells a story of the Chinese political economy in historical contexts. The shift from a market-based system to a command economy is, as we turn to a historical view, far more complicated than modern economic theory can tell us. The dramatic changes in the organizational mechanism underneath the Chinese economy must be first triggered by a major external shock—the Mongol conquest. The Mongol conquest terminated the Song fiscal state and built a Sino-nomadic empire centered in Beijing. The formation of this giant empire exceeded the vision and supporting capacity of a Chinese state like the Song dynasty while failing to create an alternative administration to organize regional integration and foster economic growth.[76]

This period highlights how Chinese empires experienced strong tension between territorial expansion and economic integration. The decline in North China trade after 1125 was primarily associated with the collapse of its water transportation capacity. The permanent loss of inland waterway networks was caused by ecological changes, warfare, and dysfunctional governments. Kaifeng suffered the severest blow: All the Kaifeng-linked canals were buried deep underground with this capital city. This destructive change in river transportation hampered any hopes for trade recovery in North China before 1600. Consequently, the percentage of long-distance trade in North China within a national framework declined most precipitously.

The rise of Beijing-centered political power was a major legacy of the interim era. As the succeeding Ming state retained Beijing as the capital, it was haunted by this structural weakness and had to rely even more heavily on the wealth of the south. The reconstruction of the Grand Canal to divert water to Beijing testifies to the urgent needs to revive a water transport system in the north and the court's efforts to draw strength from the Lower Yangtze region. However, this imperial effort often obstructed rather than facilitated the integration of the market economy, because strengthening the frontier and the capital, which is too far from the center of the economy, means that little resources would be invested in the vast hinterland areas.

The survey of long-term changes in inland water transportation raised serious doubts of a sixteenth-century economic boom. Recalling the vital role water transport played in supporting the Song's market economy discussed in chapter 4, the development of a market economy from 1500 to 1800 described by the Ming-Qing transformation paradigm could hardly have occurred without adequate water transport networks. Until the turn of the seventeenth century, important trade routes were confined to three inland waterways: the Grand Canal, the Gan River in Jiangxi, and the Yangtze River.[77] In spite of the revival of trade and markets in the Lower Yangtze region, water transportation in the late Ming must have been at a preliminary stage. Thus, the backwardness in water transport is indicative of the slow growth in long-distance trade prior to 1600 in Ming China.

Chapter 6

Prices, Real Wages, and National Incomes

In the preceding three chapters the discussion is chiefly devoted to the expansion and contraction of the market economy in Song and Ming eras. It is evident that during the Tang-Song transformation, especially in the years from 960 to 1127, the Chinese market economy expanded enormously due to rapid growth in population, water transportation, and monetization. The survey also demonstrates the contraction of the market after the Mongol conquest. It clearly identifies the rise of a command economy in the early Ming period as the major cause for the economic recession that lasted through the fifteenth century. In the following chapters, I examine the subsequent impact on the economy caused by the radical shift from a market-based mechanism to a command system during the interim.

Scholars have put forward the market-driven theory to explain preindustrial growth in Chinese history.[1] Presumably, the expansion and contraction of the market would produce corresponding effects on changes in living standards. If economic growth occurred in Song China, following this theory, one can expect to find evidence of an increase in per capita real income during that period. Similarly, the operation of a command economy would have greatly constrained the role of the market in allocation of production resources and impede economic growth.

The contesting theory, however, views long-term changes in living standards as chiefly a result of demographic changes, especially the man to land ratio. The prevailing explanations of the early Ming economy are generally positive, and they are formed largely based on two presumptions. The first can be characterized as a political economy explanation—the economic recovery narrative addressed before. Although Zhu Yuanzhang's attitudes toward the elite, such as merchants, landlords, and literati, were negative, his policies were aimed at strengthening rural communities and protecting the interests of ordinary farmers. Therefore, many researchers cast a positive light on early Ming policies as they are believed to push economic recovery.[2] The Malthusian theory provides the second and prevailing one. As the fourteenth century marked the lowest man to land ratio in late imperial China, early Ming farmers would easily acquire a relatively bigger farm lot. As land prices declined due to the plentiful supply, real wages would necessarily increase as well.[3]

In macroeconomics, real income is a useful economic measure of national wealth often used to measure the performance of the economic system. This chapter compares real income between the Song and Ming eras in three important aspects: real wages, inequality or the distribution of wealth in a preindustrial economy, and long-term changes in nominal and real national incomes. Real wages are an important indicator of well-being. The real wages of nonskilled laborers, including payment in kind, can be viewed as an alternative standard representing the livelihood of the majority. In this chapter, I first provide an income comparison based on real wages. I focus on military wages to set up an index for comparison as this area provides the richest collection of data. Second, I examine the inequality issue associated with the market expansion during the eleventh and twelfth centuries based on Song official documents on household classification. Finally, I use the rough estimates of per capita real income to build up a series of Chinese historical national incomes. This series can be further used to compare the share of state revenues in national incomes of late imperial China. As important quantitative evidence, the extremely high share of state revenues in national incomes in coexistence with a much lower standard of living around 1400 significantly demonstrates the despotic nature of the early Ming command economy.

Real Wages in the Song and Ming Eras

As the market-driven theory argues that early Ming policies had a negative impact on the fifteenth-century economy, the Malthusian theory, which is supported by the economic recovery narrative, rather predicts a better-off life for common being. If one were to assume the nonexistence of the early Ming regime, and thus no constraints from a command economy, one can analyze what might have happened had the other variables (loss of population, decline in prices, etc.) continued to exercise their influence on the early Ming economy. To demonstrate this point, I introduce the normal pattern of a post-plague economy. Such an economy caused by a radical decline of population would, as M. M. Postan argues in his study of fourteenth- and fifteenth-century England, result in a rise of living standards for commoners, wages in particular, in response to the decline in population, since laborers became scarce while land remained relatively abundant. Real wages would increase to a higher level until the supply of laborers once again surpassed the labor demand, an indication of the end of the economic recovery.[4] In the following, I assemble real income data to test this line of Malthusian explanation.

The demographic change did result in a sharp decline in the man to land ratio on average. The reduction of the Chinese population to only two-thirds of its previous level must have played a significant role in causing the fourteenth-century crisis. Yet this single factor did not have the same impact across the Ming empire. In 1393, nearly three-fourths of the Ming population lived in southern China.[5] Such a degree of population concentration reveals how severely northern China was ravaged, with only 15.5 million residents in comparison to the 32 million in the same region in 1102. If one takes into account all the people in the north in the eleventh century, including the Kitans and Tanguts, the population in northern China declined more than 50 percent over three centuries.[6] Here depopulation was associated with the devastation of waterways and urban networks. Without the supportive infrastructure and sufficient investments of capital, one can hardly assume that the farmers were better-off only because the average sizes of their farms were much larger than that of their predecessors.

The Malthusian explanation often fails to recognize the role that the market played to increase welfare in a preindustrial economy. To avoid this bias, demographic changes should be examined in relation to changes in the market structure. The Chinese economy in the centuries from 1368 to 1450 suffered a shocking decline in the average prices of commodities. The price of rice, for instance, dropped to the lowest point in the last millennium of Chinese history. This decline soon turned into a century-long deflation. Around 1600 the price of rice only reached the levels found in the mid-eleventh century.

When measured in bronze coins, the gap between Song and Ming price levels might be at least three times as much as that measured in silver. The coin-based price of rice in the 1430s, for instance, was only one-tenth of that in the early thirteenth century. Bronze coins were one of the major currencies in imperial China and were necessary for small-sum transactions at local markets.[7] Because the Ming court made little effort to maintain the money supply, most bronze coins circulated in the Ming dynasty were still the old coins made by the Song imperial mints centuries before.[8] Moreover, a large amount of Song coins had been either hoarded or recast into utensils during the Song-Yuan-Ming transition. Therefore, the purchase power of bronze coins was much higher than that of silver in the Ming era.

As a striking fact, nominal wages plummeted in the century after 1368. In 1480, more than a century after the founding of the Ming dynasty, the daily wage of a non-skilled laborer in the capital of Beijing was 20 to 30 *wen* (*wen* is the minimum monetary unit for Chinese bronze coins). This wage-earner was reported to support a family of five to seven members. Meanwhile, a fortune teller in Suzhou earned only 1 *wen* from each customer. In contrast, an ordinary worker employed at the irrigation projects in Jiangnan in 1158 received 100 *wen* plus 0.03 Song *shi* of rice, about 145 *wen* per day.

The drop in prices of basic necessities and the fall in nominal wages between the Song and Ming eras indicate an overall decline in prices. Yet we have little knowledge of what happened to the economic performance as a whole and to real incomes in particular. To fill this gap, one needs to rely as much as possible on circumstantial evidence, regardless of how scanty or fragmentary it is. The data collection ranges from investments, real wages, household incomes and consumptions, and, most important, agricultural productivity. While real wages of nonskilled laborers are particularly important in testing the Malthusian-based hypothesis, the debate on the political economy of early Ming China also calls our attention to the other important aspects of the national economy such as investments and state-administered production such as military farms.

The dramatic changes in prices and nominal incomes imply prolonged economic stagnation, if not total decline, in the Ming era. Considering all of these political, institutional, and economic factors, one would expect a decline in living standards (especially in real wages) in the early Ming period. However, it is very difficult to prove this hypothesis since the usual data that economists use to measure living standards are not available. Zhu Yuanzhang's anti-market regulations have made it tremendously difficult for modern researchers to study income and consumption in the early Ming economy. Except for the salaries of soldiers, there are no other sources that document employment and wages due to the dominance of the command economy. Workers, soldiers, and criminals performed their obligatory duties in the construction of public projects, and the state certainly did not need to pay them anything.[9]

Price data, which are as important as wage data in describing the declining economic trend from 1400 to 1450, are also seriously flawed for the same reason. Zhu standardized the prices of grain and textiles when he began to issue paper notes in 1375. One *guan* of *baochao* could, according to Zhu's edict, purchase 1 *shi* of rice, or 1 tael of silver, or 2.5 bolts of linen.[10] In spite of this, private transactions must have followed market prices that varied from the regulated price, nor was the government always able to prohibit people from using silver.[11] The occurrence of hyperinflation of paper notes from 1430 to 1450, in fact, even pushed people to turn to a barter economy. Largely due to the conflict between monetary policy and private trade, little was recorded on events in the market. However, if one assumes that the regulated price did somewhat track changes in market prices even if it often lagged behind, then even though the overissuance of paper notes caused hyperinflation in paper currency, the trend in real prices of goods (indicated by silver and bronze coins) was declining.[12]

This proposed real wage study is also likely flawed by a comparison of payment in kind in a command economy with the salaries of laborers in a free market. To avoid such a flaw, I used the real wages of soldiers instead of choosing real wages of unskilled laborers.[13] I converted the soldiers' real wage data (SRW hereafter) into an index of real wages for comparison (see appendix E).

The index of the SRW clearly indicates a higher standard of living in the eleventh century. During the first hundred years of the Song dynasty, the real wages of soldiers came to a peak and then declined to a monthly payment of less than 300 liters per head. Severe inflation in the Southern Song (1127–1279) caused a decline in the real wages of soldiers. In a period of one hundred years beginning in the 1150s, wages were even lower and ranged between 100 and 200 liters per head. In comparison, Song soldiers prior to 1125 received payment 1 to 2.5 times higher than their counterparts in the Ming period. After 1125, their salaries were still 50 to 80 percent higher than that of early Ming soldiers. Yet, soldiers were better paid in the mid-sixteenth century than Song soldiers of the late twelfth century.

The wages of Song soldiers, according to Wang Zengyu, depended on their rank and skills. Their wages were usually comprised of three parts: cash, rice, and a clothing allowance for the spring and winter. The first two were paid monthly, and the latter was often converted into cash and paid biannually. A mid-rank soldier who served in the central armies was paid 2.5 Song *shi* (125.6 kg) in rice and 500 to 700 *wen* in cash each month, together with an annual compensation of 6 bolts of silk, 0.5 kg of cotton, and 3,000 *wen* of bronze coins.[14] The clothing allowance (about 6,000 *wen* of bronze coins in total, which was a greater amount than that of Ming soldiers[15]) is disregarded for a convenient comparison. The wage can be converted into 176 to 186 kg or 235 to 248 liters of threshed rice.[16] The preceding estimate is for a soldier stationed in Kaifeng, the Song capital. At the beginning of the eleventh century, the Song central armies (*jinjun*) had 660,000 soldiers, and about 3.5 percent were stationed in the capital. A soldier who served in other regions enjoyed as much as 6 to 15 percent more grain owing to the lower price of rice in relation to the monetary part of his payment. Soldiers in local troops (*xiangjun*) received monthly payments of 2 Song *shi* of rice, 100 *wen* in cash, an annual clothing allowance of 4 bolts of silk, plus 2,000 *wen* in cash.[17] For a soldier living in North China, this would be converted into 143 kg or 191 liters of rice.

Soldiers in the Southern Song, especially in the thirteenth century, suffered a moderate loss of real wages from inflation. After the Song central government moved to the south in 1127, the salaries of soldiers were adjusted accordingly. The cash part of the salaries increased proportionately: A soldier in the central armies would be paid 3,000 to 9,000 *wen* in cash and 0.9 to 1.5 Song *shi* of rice every month, with or without a clothing allowance.[18] If the clothing allowance is disregarded, a soldier in the central armies stationed in the Lower Yangtze delta in the mid-twelfth century would have been paid, in real wages, about 105.5 to 256.3 kg, or 141 to 342 liters of rice. In general, the armies in the Southern Song still maintained real wages at an average level of 120 to 150 liters of rice. This standard is lower than that of the eleventh century, which was about 200 to 240 liters of rice.[19]

This observation of long-term changes in real wages indicates both the expansion of the economy and the increase in per capita real income in the Song. In contrast to the high-level wages in the eleventh century, those in the Ming period remained astonishingly low and stagnant until the mid-sixteenth century. The wage level then bounced back to above 100 liters per head. This prosperity, as supported by the data on wages, perfectly fits the framework of the silver century as well as the Ming-Qing transformation paradigm that is favored by many socioeconomic historians.[20]

The low wages of soldiers in the Ming period from the 1360s to 1550s are striking. In a 1379 edict, Zhu Yuanzhang ordered that a soldier with a family should be paid 1 *shi* of rice per month, and a single soldier 0.60 *shi*. This rule continued throughout the Ming period. Therefore, 1 *shi* has been taken as the standard monthly payment of soldiers in Ming armies, a figure that can be converted into 75 kg, or 100 liters, of rice. Although many scholars have chosen this standard, I must emphasize that it should be viewed as the *ideal* standard according to the policy and not the real wage in general. From a financial perspective, the Ming military system was basically self-sustaining, as over half of the soldiers were sent to farm in order to procure enough food. The early Ming armies probably had 2.76 million soldiers at full strength; if 70 percent were engaged in farming, they would be equal to 1.93 million agricultural laborers.[21]

Many contemporary descriptions show that the soldiers were underpaid in the late fourteenth and fifteenth centuries. The de facto decline in their wages became noticeable in the early fifteenth century, especially in the Yongle reign under Emperor Zhu Di. After Zhu Di usurped the throne, he moved the capital from Nanjing to Beijing, which had been a major military base on the northern frontier and was located hundreds of miles away from the central regions of the Ming economy. A sharp increase in long-distance transportation costs worsened the problem of grain supplies. As recorded in the data, the soldiers and artisans who were enlisted to build the palaces and infrastructure in Beijing were paid 0.4 to 0.6 *shi* (40–60 liters) of rice per month.[22] In succeeding reigns, such as Hongxi (1425), Xuande (1426–1435), and Zhengtong (1436–1449), wages were often adjusted in many regions but remained lower than 1 *shi*.

The decrease in the pay of Ming soldiers is not immediately obvious from the official records. From the government's perspective, wages were not declining at all due to the adoption of the wage-compensation method (WCM hereafter). From high-ranking officials in the central government down to soldiers and artisans, wages were normally measured in rice units. However, to deal with the insufficiency of the grain supply, Zhu Di ordered on several occasions that all the salaries should be partly (sometimes as much as 50 percent) compensated with cinnamon and tropical wood, which were brought back by Zheng He's voyages to Southeast Asia and the Indian Ocean in 1405–1433. Since then, compensation with other kinds of goods instead of full payment in rice dominated the pay system until the end of the Ming dynasty.[23]

Salaries could include clothing, millet, or other goods, and a soldier would usually receive paper bills in the WCM. Inflation hit the paper currency hard, with the real value of *baochao* soon debased to 1/30 of its nominal value, 1/100 in the Zhengtong reign,

1/500 in the Jingtai reign (1450–1456), eventually falling as low as 1/1,000 of the face value. Disregarding this severe inflation, the Ming government insisted that compensation should be paid with *baochao* at its nominal value. Thus, the income of soldiers in fact depended on the exchange value of *baochao*. In other words, a Ming soldier's actual salary before the sixteenth century must have been below 1 *shi* of rice per month, less than the ideal established by the first Ming emperor.

The salary of Ming soldiers in the first century of the dynasty sheds light on the idea of a standard wage in a command economy. In pursuit of security, the early Ming government diminished the influence of the market economy and relied upon direct control of the population and resources. Hence, wages in the command economy were *planned*—they were not determined by labor supply and demand but by state policy. Modern surveys of prices and wages in the early Ming, including the present study, depend heavily on government-regulated prices and wage data found in official documents, which were recorded only when policies changed. Thus, the data on both grain prices and wages of soldiers show a very stable and even stationary trend for over a century.

The officials and troops stationed in Suzhou and Songjiang, for instance, were reported to have involvement in illegal businesses, such as salt smuggling and the sale of military equipment. Outbursts of the so-called Japanese pirates along coastal areas of southern China in the mid-sixteenth century were initially attributed to long-standing sea smuggling, which eventually dislodged the official prohibition of foreign trade that had been in place for over two hundred years. Although such shady income undoubtedly boosted the soldiers' livelihood, it is impossible to ascertain the amount so as to reach a reliable estimate of their total income.[24]

Following the Single Whip reform (*yitiao bianfa*), the Ming government permitted people to pay silver in lieu of labor service.[25] Even the army recruits from local communities were paid monthly in silver, and the percentage of these recruits may have been as high as 70 percent in some armies of the Lower Yangtze delta.[26] By the end of the sixteenth century, the Ming court had to send 3,800,000 taels (i.e., 140.6 tons) of silver to cover the salaries of the troops stationed at the northern frontier, which exhausted all of the state reserves.[27]

The SRW data show that soldiers benefited from this pay reform, especially in the Jiajing reign (1522–1566), but not to the extent of raising their pay to a level comparable with that of the eleventh century. The payment at that time for a soldier was 0.6 to 0.8 tael of silver per month. Given that the price of rice swung between 0.5 and 0.94 tael of silver per *shi* of rice, the real wage in the sixteenth century could have hardly exceeded 1 *shi* of rice.[28] Monthly salaries of more than 1 tael were generally paid only to those along the northern frontier, especially to those elite soldiers of the Nine Guards (*jiubian*). In the mid-seventeenth century, the salary of a soldier stationed on the border of Manchuria had risen to 2 taels per month.[29] However, the northern frontier in the Ming period was a line that divided the nomads and agricultural settlements and was surrounded by mountains, deserts, and barren land. Food and material had to be conveyed from great distances at a very high cost. According to Chuan, the grain price on the northern frontier increased ninefold in the years between 1450 and 1644.[30] This price inflation far exceeded the increase in the wages of soldiers. There are records of soldiers selling weapons, clothes, and even their children and wives in order to stay alive. The origin of the rebellions at the dawn of the seventeenth century was the failure of the

Ming fiscal system to support its troops along the northern frontier, which caused mobs of suffering soldiers to turn against the government.

Inequality in the Market Economy

Economic growth is feasible in a traditional society such as eleventh-century China, but the variation and uncertainty found in primary sources make it difficult to gain a clear image of how this progress happened over the course of the century. In contrast, the market expansion during the Tang-Song transformation, which is viewed as the major cause for preindustrial growth achieved in Song China, is quite conceivable. The market expansion also produced dynamics to social stratification by accelerating the accumulation of wealth in a variety of ways. Inequality became evident after the Rebellion, and contemporary people were under pressure to have a decent life and complained about the difficulty of maintaining their social status in the face of competition. As we focus on the distribution of wealth in a growing economy, it is necessary to know whether the majority could benefit from this growth.

The Song household property registration (HPR hereafter) data is particularly important to study the changes in inequality with regard to the living standard and inequality. The HPR is a survey conducted by the local administration for taxation and public purchasing purposes. Both urban residents and rural farmers are required to report their landholdings, movable property (capital, yearly earnings, and profits), real estate (houses, storage units, and inns), vehicles, and boats once every three years. The households are henceforth classified by their property and income into five ranks in the countryside and ten ranks in the cities. However, given regional variances in wealth and inequality there was no universal measurement in the Song dynasty. The fifth-rank farmers, for instance, were usually the poorest landowners in the villages. However, a fifth-rank farmer in the capital district could probably own property much more valuable than that of his counterpart in a remote mountain village. The HPR thus provides firsthand information on the social stratification in each county of Song China. Had all of these reports been preserved well, modern researchers should have no difficulties in the reconstruction of a national account of the eleventh-century economy.

The HPR data demonstrate diversified sources of income a farmers' household could earn in the twelfth and thirteenth centuries. In 1169, Li Dazheng, a local official in Zhejiang, complained to the court about the problems in the HPR administration. While examining local government assessments of different types of household income in the records, such as fishing, peddling, craftsmanship, and seasonal employment, Li found that most households involved in these activities were poor and earned only a small sum of money. Therefore, the government could hardly levy property taxes on such assets for fear of popular resistance. Li thus proposed that the assessment of non-land–produced income should be confined to the ownership of storage units, shops, inns, pawnshops, and leasing of transportation vehicles and draft animal power.[31]

For our concern about sources of household income, the HPR data revealed that a substantial share of local wealth was produced outside the farming sector. In fact, this was named "movable property and monetary income" (*fucai wuli*), which was independent of "land property" (*shiye wuli*). Most officials admitted the assessment of "movable property and monetary income" was more difficult because the circulation of capital was substantially more flexible. For modern researchers, this distinction provides invaluable information about the structure and social distribution of local wealth. An important example came from an assessment made in Lishui county during the Shaoxing reign (1131–1162). The total amount of assessed properties came to 1,001,000 strings of cash, among which land property was assessed at 868,500 strings and movable property at 142,000 strings. Lishui was located in the mountain areas of East Zhejiang and remained underdeveloped. The 6:1 ratio of land to capital (movable property) reflected a substantial share of the nonagricultural sectors such as mining, commerce, transportation, and other services in the local economy. This weight should be below average in the Lower Yangtze.

The HPR data also revealed that developments in the market economy, especially in urbanization, were accompanied by a high degree of inequality. Nonetheless, from a national perspective, inequality varied from place to place, and the relationship between inequality and the market economy is very complex.

The HPR data produced in the 1080s best reveals nationwide inequality. For the entire country, landless households or tenants amounted to 5.65 million, about one-third of the aggregate population. Nonetheless, the market was not the sole reason for the concentration of land. At a first glance, it appears that geography played a large role. Most regions with a high percentage of landless households were located in the south. Yet the Lower Yangtze (Liangzhe and Jiangnandong in the Song period), which was the fast-developing region in the south, showed the lowest percentage. Most of the north showed a low percentage of landless households.[32] This distribution, in fact, vividly indicates that the economic gravity shifted to the south during the Tang-Song transformation. The Chengdu plain in Sichuan and the Lower Yangtze occupied an important position in the national economy. In contrast to them, many inland regions in the south remained relatively backward. As demonstrated in table 6-1, among the top ten regions with the highest percentages of landless households are Kuizhou, Jinghubei, Jingxinan, Zhizhou, Jingxibei, Jinghunan, Fujian, Lizhou, Huainanxi, and Jingdongdong. They were either underdeveloped areas or isolated mountain valleys. Except for Fujian, the population density of all the other regions was pretty low. One can even find from contemporary writings that a substantial number of non-Chinese ethnic groups lived in the upper and mid-Yangtze valleys. There, the landlords were described as exercising certain direct control over the tenants and their families.[33] The high percentage of landless households in Kuizhou, Zhizhou, Lizhou, Jinghubei, Jinghunan, and Huainanxi matches this point.

In the case of the Lower Yangtze, the evidence is strong enough to support a negative relationship between the development of the market and the concentration of land by big landlords. The average share of landless households in this macro region was 20 percent, which is much lower than that of the nation. Similarly, a dividing line can be drawn within the Lower Yangtze. When a line is drawn for the 20 percent who were landless, it will include most of the mountain and hilly areas. For the prefectures, which experienced rapid population growth and economic developments such as Xiuzhou, Shaoxing (Yuezhou), Jinhua (Wuzhou), Huzhou, and Suzhou, most farmers tilled the land that they owned.

Miyazawa estimated that most farmers in the *liangzhelu* (mostly the Lower Yangtze) in 1077 owned their landholdings, and the average size was about 22.7 *mu* per household. The landless households consisted of 0.36 million, which accounted for only 10 percent of the rural population. When the aggregate households increased to 2.12 million in

Table 6-1. Shares of landless households in China, 1080s

Rank	Region (lu)	Landless households	Total households	Percentage of landless in total	Acreage (km²)	Percentage of acreage in total
1	Kuizhou	178,908	254,340	70.3	127.2	0.2
2	Jinghubei	377,533	657,533	57.4	18,793.5	14.8
3	Jingxinan	166,709	314,580	52.9	12046.5[1]	6.3
4	Zhizhou	229,690	478,171	48	—	—
5	Jingxibei	233,031	486,385	47.9	12046.5[1]	6.3
6	Jinghunan	395,537	871,214	45.4	14,709.5	10.8
7	Fujian	464,099	1,044,225	44.4	6,278.1	5.2
8	Lizhou	147,115	336,248	43.7	729.1	1
9	Huainanxi	318,746	738,499	43.1	55,104.1[2]	28.5
10	Jingdongdong	292,364	696,456	41.9	15,123.2[3]	10.4
11	Guangnandong	223,267	579,253	38.5	1,780.4	1.1
12	Jiangnanxi	451,870	1,287,136	35.1	25,596.3	20
13	Huainandong	202,681	612,565	33	55,104.1[2]	28.5
14	Jingdongxi	186,328	571,876	32.5	15,123.2[3]	10.4
15	Qingfeng	164,627	509,799	32.2	—	—
16	Hebeidong	154,531	526,028	29.3	15,795.2[4]	13.2
17	Chengdufu	243,880	864,403	28.2	12,232.8	16.3
18	Hebeixi	146,904	564,762	26.0	15,795.2[4]	13.2
19	Yongxingjun	219,993	846,405	25.9	25,306.1	9.8
20	Guangnanxi	63,238	258,382	24.4	31.2[5]	0.01
21	Liangzhe	360,259	1,778,941	20.2	20,570.8	16.2
22	Hedong	110,757	574,175	19.2	6,322.6	4.9
23	Jiangnandong	201,086	1,127,311	17.8	24,306.8	27.3
	Total	5,652,745	16,472,920	34.3	261,297.2	11

Sources: Yanagida 1986, 250; Shiba 2001a, 151.

Table 6-2. Shares of landless households in the Lower Yangtze, 1080

Rank	Area (prefect)	Landless households	Land-owning households	Total households	Percentage of landless in total
1	Xiuzhou	—	139,137	139,137	0.0
2	Yuezhou	337	152,585	152,992	0.2
3	Jinhua	8,346	129,751	137,097	6
4	Huzhou	10,509	134,612	145,121	7.2
5	Suzhou	15,202	158,767	173,969	8.7
6	Muzhou	9,836	66,915	76,751	12.8
7	Taizhou	25,232	120,481	145,713	17.3
8	Hangzhou	38,501	164,293	202,794	18.9
9	Quzhou	17,552	17,552	86,797	20.2
10	Changzhou	45,508	90,852	136,360	33.3
11	Wenzhou	41,427	80,489	121,916	33.9
12	Runzhou	21,483	33,318	54,798	39.1
13	Mingzhou	57,334	57,874	115,208	49.7
14	Chuzhou	68,995	20,363	89,358	77.2
Total		360,259	1,418,682	1,778,941	20.2

Sources: Yanagida 1986, 250.

1132, the number of landless households consequently dropped to 0.31 million.[34] The HPR data indicated a long-run decline of the landless in the share of aggregate rural households. Although the cause of this trend that occurred on a national basis is not clear, it is obvious that in the Lower Yangtze, as revealed in table 6-3, the relative decline in the poorest population was associated with the development of the market economy.

The decline in the share of the landless might be partially attributed to mid-century reform. The Wang administration (1069–1085) initially aimed to take part in an active role in the market economy and launched certain important policies such as the Equitable Transport and Price Equalization Policy (*junshu fa*), Green Shoots Policy (*qingmiao fa*),

Table 6-3. Share of landless households in the Lower Yangtze, 976–1222

Region		Landless households in early eleventh century	Percentage of landless in aggregate households	Landless households in twelfth century	Percentage of landless in aggregate households
Suzhou	L	7,306 (976–984)	20.8%	15,202 (1078)	8.7%
Kunshan, Suzhou	L	3,272 (1008–1016)	20%	3,700 (1195–1200)	9.5%
Changzhou	L	27,481 (976–984)	49.5%	45,508 (1078)	33.4%
Jiangyin	L	6,906 (976–984)	47.5%	17,064 (1008–1016)	58.2%
Xiuzhou	L			0 (1078)	0%
Mingzhou	L	16,803 (976–984)	60.7%	31,347 (1168)	23%
Huzhou	L	10,840 (1008–1016)	7.4%	3,988 (1182)	1.9%
Wucheng, Huzhou	L	3,496 (1008–1016)	13.3%	2,337 (1131–1162)	5.6%
Guian, Huzhou	L	2,956 (1008–1016)	11%	1,772 (1131–1162)	3.5%
Yunzhou	M	15,900 (976–984)	59.9%	21,480 (1078)	39.2%
Hangzhou	H	8,857 (976–984)	12.6%	38,513 (1078)	19%
Taizhou	H	14,422 (976–984)	45.2%	76,294 (1222)	30.6%

Source: Miyazawa 1984, 34–44.

Hired Service Policy (*Mianyi fa*), and Regulation on Agriculture and Water Conservancy (*Nongtian shuili fa*) to control the annexation of land. The Green Shoots Policy promised to provide short-term loans to farmers who needed urgent help to avoid bankruptcies during harvest failures. The Regulation on Agriculture and Water Conservancy required local officials to provide money and materials in assisting farmers to construct irrigation projects.

From the national scope, a positive relationship between the decline of poorest households and market development was also evident. As the aggregate households increased from 5.9 million in the 980s to 20 million in 1099, the share of the landless population declined nearly 10 percent (see table 6-4). The decline in the last four decades was so obvious that one can reasonably project that Wang's reform should have helped reduce the concentration of land.

If the developments in the market economy helped to reduce the inequality in the countryside, nonetheless, they had an opposite effect in the cities. The urban poor made their living on meager daily wages and accounted for the majority of the urban

Table 6-4. Changes in Song aggregate households and landless population, 980s–1099

Year	Landless households	Aggregate households	Percentage of landless in total
980s	2,415,708	5,859,551	41.2
1021	2,638,346	8,677,677	30.4
1023	3,753,138	9,898,121	37.9
1029	4,552,793	10,562,689	43.1
1031	3,402,742	9,380,807	36.3
1034	4,228,982	10,296,565	41.1
1037	4,438,274	10,663,027	41.6
1039	3,708,994	10,179,989	36.4
1042	3,636,248	10,307,640	35.3
1045	3,820,058	10,682,947	35.8
1048	3,829,868	10,723,695	35.7
1050	3,834,957	10,747,954	35.7
1053	3,855,325	10,792,705	35.7
1058	3,877,110	10,825,580	35.8
1061	3,881,531	11,091,112	35.0
1067	4,382,139	9,799,346	30.9
1072	4,592,691	15,091,560	30.4
1075	5,001,754	15684129	31.9
1078	5,497,498	16,492,631	33.3
1080	5,485,903	16,730,504	32.8
1083	5,832,539	17,211,713	33.9
1086	6,053,424	17,957,092	33.7
1088	6,154,652	18,289,375	33.7
1091	6,227,982	18,655,093	33.4
1097	6,366,829	19,435,570	32.8
1099	6,439,114	19,715,555	32.7

Source: Chen Lesu 1984, 77–98.

population. In Song official documents, the landless in the rural areas or urban poor were registered in the category of *kehu*. As demonstrated in table 6-5, the former represented a much greater share in the city than the latter in the countryside.

For either Fuzhou in Jiangxi, or Dingzhou in Fujian, the share of the poor in the registered urban populations was above 40 percent, indicating the worsening of inequality at the urban level. In comparison, Huizhou in the Lower Yangtze reported both the share of the urban poor (20.4%) and the share of landless agricultural laborers (7.2%) in moderate degree. Yet, the former was still three times as high as the latter.

The core question is whether the expansion of a market economy during the Tang-Song transformation would bring the same impact upon different social classes. The proportion of the poorest in the countryside, thus the landless households, seemed to decline during the Song era. If we extend our observation beyond the poorest, we will see that there is an obvious concentration of wealth in twelfth- and thirteenth-century China.

All extant records point to the existence of a huge majority of peasants who owned only small farms while the landholdings owned by the upper class, who were the richest landlords and account for a tiny percentage of rural households, reached one-fourth and above of the cultivated land. According to the HPR policies, all landowners, thus taxpayers in the countryside, were classified into five ranks in correspondence to the size and quality of their farms. Almost all Song statesmen and intellectuals indicated the fact that an overwhelming majority of the rural taxpayers were at the lower end of the social spectrum.

Shushu jiuzhang (Mathematical Treatise in Nine Sections), a mathematics textbook issued in 1247, introduced the application of property tax with regard to inequality across the landowners. As indicated in table 6-6, the way to distribute a surtax of 88,337.6 *liang* of silk between 11,033 landowning households in a county is posed by the author as a mathematical question. The rate of the property (land) tax applied for each rank is half of the preceding one. Thus a fifth-rank household paid just 5 percent of the tax rate of a first-rank household. However, the amount of the assigned surtax assigned to them accounted for nearly half of the total. About 90 percent of the landowners were identified as the fourth and fifth rank. Thus the overwhelming majority of the county farmers only owned a small farm. In contrast, the upper class, thus the landowners, ranked as the top three levels in household registration and occupied a significant share of the land property: 563 out of 11,033 households occupied 24 percent of the total land.

Table 6-5. Shares of urban poor and countryside landless households in thirteenth-century Lower Yangtze and Fujian

Areas	Year	Share of urban poor	Share of countryside landless
Huizhoiu	1227	20.4%	7.2%
Fuzhou	1208–1224	42.76%	29.2%
Dingzhou	1127	45%	31.4%
Dingzhou	1250s	54.9%	37.5%

Sources: Liang Keng-yao 2006, 23; W. G. Liu 2008, 274.

Table 6-6. Property tax rates in a county, thirteenth century

Rank	Number of households	Percentage	Tax burden per household	Index of tax rates	Tax amounts for each rank	Percentage of tax amounts for each rank
1	12	0.1	124	100	1,488	1.7
2	.87	0.8	62	50	5,394	6.1
3	464	4.2	31	25	14,384	16.3
4	2,035	18.4	12.4	10	25,234	28.6
5	8,435	76.5	4.96	5	41,837.6	47.4
Total	11,033	100.0	8	Nil	88,337.6	100.0

Source: Shushu jiuzhang, 369–73.

Although this is an example taken from a mathematical textbook, it is representative of the common notion that small landowners or the fourth- and fifth-rank households comprised the majority of rural landowning households.

The Share of State Revenue in National Income

Real income refers to the income of individuals or nations. Although per capita real income is essential in measuring the efficiency of an economic system, the notion of national income is useful in economic history. As the measurement of national income is used to estimate total economic activity, either total outputs or total income, it provides a chance for incorporating different variables such as population growth, prices, and wages into a framework. This observation of macroeconomic changes allows us to explore certain important features a national economy would possess such as the extent of monetization and the role of state finance.

The gap between nominal national income and real national income best reveals the extent of monetization in an economy in different periods. The expansion in national income is largely driven by population growth and the rise in the living standard as reflected in real wages or per capita GDP. The real wage of nonskilled laborers can be approximately viewed as GDP per capita. Using the index of the SRW and other relevant information such as aggregate populations and state tax revenues, I have estimated both the nominal and real national incomes in the Song and Ming eras for comparison (see table 6-7).[35]

The huge gap in nominal income between the Song and Ming is solid evidence for the low degree of monetization in the Ming economy. As shown in the preceding table, the estimated nominal income in 1400 was 81 million taels of silver, only 12 percent of that in 1080. Even the national income of Ming China in 1580 was still much lower than Song China's 673 million taels of silver. Long-term changes in the nominal state tax revenues follow a similar pattern. The total of Song state tax revenues reached 62.7 million taels, remaining a peak record until the Qing dynasty. As the tax revenues are reported from extant sources, the disparity among them provides strong support to the estimation of nominal incomes.

Table 6-7. Estimates of real incomes in China, 1080–1880

Years	A1 Real income per capita (shi of rice)	A2 Real income per capita (silver taels)	B Population (millions)	C National income (in millions of taels)	D Tax revenues (in millions of taels)	E Share of tax revenues to national income D/C
Song (1080)	7.5	7.5	89.7[a]	673	62.7	9.3%
Ming (1400)	3.8	0.73–0.95	85	81	12	16%
Ming (1580)	4.8	2.88	150	432	22.4	5.2%
Qing (1880)	5.96	7.63	364.4	2781	88.2	3.2%

a. For the number of populations, see the notes to table F-5 in appendix F.

Source: Table F-5 in Appendix F.

Our major concern with regard to the changing role of the state in the market expansion can be examined from the national income perspective. The question about the early Ming regime is the extent to which the command economy could replace the market economy, especially in consideration of how much it had crowded out the resources that could have been used by private investment. The early Ming state had the largest number of military troops in Chinese history up to that time, owned a great amount of land concentrated in the Lower Yangtze delta and coastal areas, and operated state-owned industrial enterprises at an unprecedented scale. Yet when all of these are translated into a quantitative measurement of economics, will it prove the point that the early Ming state could exert a powerful influence on the economy?

The state's tax revenues as a share of national income can provide a more definite answer. The comparison immediately points to the dominance of early Ming state power over a weak economy. On the one hand, the low level of real income per capita in the early Ming was only half of that in the early twelfth century. On the other hand, the proportion of tax revenue derived from national income doubled over the same period. The early Ming state taxed nearly one-seventh of all aggregate output, collecting it mostly as payments in kind. This figure probably represents the highest share in late imperial Chinese history. Meanwhile, the early Ming state also employed a huge amount of corvée laborers in construction, industries, and public services that I do not take into account for technical difficulties. All the financial resources and manpower were secured by coercive means. The total amount meant an unbearable burden to an agrarian economy that was still recovering. The paradox between a strong state and its poor economic base can only be explained as a consequence of despotism in the first century of the Ming dynasty.

The large amount of revenue collected as tax during the Song period, especially in the form of monopoly taxes, is often viewed as marking the excessive exploitation of an immature market economy, hence demonstrating Chinese "feudalism" characterized by strong bureaucratic control over the market economy.[36] Yet, if tax revenue is viewed in proportion to the national income, the Song tax regime fell far behind the early Ming regime. It is very unlikely that we have exaggerated the command nature of the early Ming regime by either overestimating tax revenues (which were mostly collected in grain and maintained in stable quantities with over 30 million *shi* of rice in the fifteenth century) or by underestimating the national income, because we have something close to the correct figure for the aggregate population of the Ming in 1393 and, to a somewhat lesser degree of certainty, evidence of the lower living standards in question.[37]

The decline in the tax capacity of the state was obvious in the late Ming. However, the lack of data makes it difficult to estimate per capita real income in 1600. Greater consistency appears among the remaining estimates of the other years such as 1080, 1400, and 1880. The study of the market performance in the eleventh century points to an expansion that went along with a sizeable growth in population, and a rise in prices owing to increases in the money supply and number of transactions. One peculiar feature of this expansion is that, in terms of money supply and price level, it achieved almost the same level as the Qing economy in the 1770s with perhaps even higher living standards. This is an unusual success in the preindustrial world, and one could conclude that market expansion did transform eleventh-century China.

The comparison on both the amount of nominal incomes and the share of state revenues in national income between Song and Ming strongly supports my argument on the shift from a market-based system to a command system during the Song-Yuan-Ming transition. A market expansion must result in an enormous expansion in the nominal income of a nation; in contrast, the rise of a command economy would greatly decrease the monetary size of an economy. The transition from the former to the latter would produce a plunge of income in nominal terms much greater than in real terms. The prevailing explanations about the early Ming economy can hardly capture this point because they usually assume there were no such radical institutional changes as to cause dramatic ups and downs in the monetization of the economy. Similarly, they view the role of the Chinese state in the economy as remaining stable if not unchangeable over many centuries—however, quantitative evidence provides a different and persuasive answer.

It is worth noting that estimates of real income in the late Ming (ca. 1550) are much less strongly grounded than estimates for the earlier period. It is for this reason that I have introduced the recorded wages of soldiers and estimated per capita real income in the nineteenth century for comparison rather than figures for the late Ming. Aside from the SRW data and the estimates of national incomes, the work of other scholars who have investigated both the Song and Ming military systems and economic policies also provides support for my perspective on the changes that took place in real wages and real national income. Policies in the military recruitment and payment of soldiers are far less responsive to temporal and situational variance than are other forms of wage data. Nonetheless, they are able to reveal the financial basis of military expenses, especially the wages of soldiers, and the means that supported these expenses and salaries. Several factors may affect the accuracy of my estimates. First, insufficient information on demographic change in the sixteenth century is the weakest link in our chain of reasoning. Secondly, there are questions about the reliability of the quality of late Ming economic data. A state weak in the realm of finance and taxes such as the late Ming leaves very few records that would be helpful to discern changes in real demand. Is it possible that the variances in real income per capita shown in the comparison can be accounted for not only by real differences in the market economy but also by how the data were produced? Even if this be the case, however, it is well known that late sixteenth-century communities in the Lower Yangtze witnessed the building of magnificent gardens, villas, schools, and bridges and appreciated luxurious food and clothing. Were these local projects a sign of improvement in living standards? They may have been. To prove this, however, one would need to examine numerous events recorded by local communities and interpret them in a manner appropriate to quantitative analysis. In any case, the prosperity was probably regional—a typical case that occurred only in the Lower Yangtze and the coastal regions in Southeast China.[38]

Conclusion

In this chapter I use real income data to study long-term changes in preindustrial China's living standard. The result points to a much higher level of real wages in the Song era and a negative relationship between market expansion and the number of poorest rural households. In contrast, the real wage dropped substantially even as the average man to land ratio declined in the early Ming period.

This chapter rejects the optimistic view on the early Ming living standard put forward by the Malthusian explanation. The early Ming case contradicts a normal pattern of recovery from a post-plague economy because it only shows a radical decline in the economy but no sign of improvement in real wages. It is beyond any doubt that the long-term trends in prices and wages, population, and marketization indicate a radical decline from the 1360s to the 1450s. As the population diminished dramatically from around 100 million in the 1300s to 60 million in 1391, one can find few signs of living standard improvements in the succeeding period and only a stationary economy at best. It is true that the early Ming command economy was not the only cause of the decline that took place in the early part of the dynasty. One can also look to the centuries of disaster and war that brought northern China to the margins of devastation. Yet ample evidence indicates that the early Ming command economy held back the awaited recovery for over a century and prevented an increase in real wages from happening. The price and wage data from the early Ming show that a worsening trend was triggered when Zhu Di moved the capital to Beijing in the 1410s, when the substantial decline in soldiers' wages was paired with a dramatic fall in prices.

Students of Ming history, who are impressed by the emphasis of self-reliance in the early Ming policy, may recall that the founder Zhu Yuanzhang asserted that governance with a small body of bureaucracy and modest involvement from a market economy would diminish corruption and reduce societal burdens in his ideal order. He even boasted that the state could maintain a million soldiers without taking a single grain of millet from the farmers.[39] Yet my comparison indicates that the share of tax revenues in the national income in Zhu's regime far exceeded the other Chinese dynasties.

Needless to say, the conclusion drawn from the real wage study is necessarily tentative for two reasons. First, one has to consider the marginal role of the market in the command system. In early Ming China, a self-sufficient mode prevailed that marginalized the power of money and made transactions of goods less frequent. The data on prices and money supply thus cannot serve as decisive evidence to changes in living standards. Second, the core evidence on real wages in the early Ming is limited to the salary of soldiers. We are uncertain whether a similar decline occurred across the board to include, for instance, agricultural laborers.

The remaining issue is how to reach a verifiable comparison between the living standards of the Song and the Ming eras from a perspective different from the current wage comparison. One must inquire deeply into agriculture, the main sector of the traditional economy. The inquiry shall cover all relevant evidence, such as information on rural household incomes and expenditures, average farm yield per household, or changes in the consumption of farmers to include basic necessities like diet and clothing. In the next two chapters, I demonstrate how one can observe a similar decrease in the household income of farmers in Jiangnan. A sharp decline occurred in agricultural productivity in North and Central China due to a shift in farming practice toward extensive agriculture. Thus, although the data on prices, real wages, and money supply do not offer conclusive evidence on the decline in living standards, they do reflect a downward trend that is consistent with the data on other aspects of the agricultural sectors.

Part IV

Agriculture

Chapter 7

Agricultural Development of the Lower Yangtze

The study of the Lower Yangtze agriculture (including Jiangnan) provides important evidence for development in China during the Tang-Song transformation. In comparison to the north, the Lower Yangtze was far more backward before CE 750. Human habitation was sparse and rural communities remained largely self-sufficient. Only beginning in the mid-eighth century did both farming technology and its market economy advance significantly.[1] As the Song economy began to boom toward the end of the eleventh century, the Lower Yangtze, along with Sichuan and Henan, became one of the three most advanced regions in China.

The Mongol conquest and the subsequent Ming fiscal policy precipitated a prolonged crisis in China beginning in the thirteenth century. Most scholars have therefore depicted the fourteenth century as a dark age in Chinese history. The Lower Yangtze, especially Jiangnan, however, presents a more complicated picture. Not only did population gradually grow during the thirteenth and fourteenth centuries, but the region's agricultural productivity also increased.[2] However, as this study of rural Jiangnan household income will document, living standards did decline.

In this chapter, I first provide a critical review of the current study of agricultural productivity in the Lower Yangtze region. I trace the shift from extensive farming toward intensive farming during the Tang-Song transformation by examining the relationship between population density, investments of capital, and commercialization. Second, I use tax data to suggest that in spite of the persistence of economic inequality throughout this period, over the course of the eleventh-century, economic expansion and market development helped diminish the proportion of the highly impoverished. Third, after introducing the different aspects of the current debate on the changes in agricultural productivity of Jiangnan, I tentatively conclude that both the supply and the demand data indicate a sharp decline in the living standards in the years between 1368 and 1450.

Agricultural Development in the Lower Yangtze

Two different perspectives describe the agricultural development of the Lower Yangtze from 750 to 1750 AD. From a macro perspective, the rise of the Lower Yangtze was associated with greater migration, cheaper water transportation, and increased urbanization. From a micro perspective, technical changes in farming and sericulture improved grain yields and increased household income from family-based textile production. On the one hand, immigrants not only provided cheap labor but also brought technologies and capital from the north. Developments in water transportation made the supply of agricultural products possible for external markets. Urbanization and water transportation greatly encouraged commercialization in agriculture that had been backward and self-sufficient. On the other hand, agricultural production underwent a transition from extensive to intensive farming. The latter refers to improvements in farm yields by increases of capital and labor input in correspondence to the expansion of the marketed output.[3]

An agronomic study of Song treatises on technologies employed by Lower Yangtze farmers have pointed to major breakthroughs achieved over the Tang-Song transformation, which include:

1. Oxen plow

2. Double cropping (wheat plus rice)

3. Sericulture

4. Application of fertilizer

5. Farming implements and field management (weeding)

6. Irrigation and water control[4]

Modern researchers view these technologies as "a major break with the past."[5] In terms of the agricultural technologies responsible for high farm yields in traditional China until the twentieth century, one can hardly find any important innovation that was not addressed by Wang Zhen in his *Treatise on Agriculture*, which was officially published in 1313. By quoting rich but nonquantitative evidence from contemporary treatises, poems, and official reports, Mark Elvin summarized agricultural progress in the Lower Yangtze in the centuries between CE 750 and 1100 in four aspects: preparation of the soil, planting, and seeding; new seeds and multiple cropping; water control; and trade and specialization.[6] He further identified the transformation of agriculture with the agricultural revolution and assumed that a high-level equilibrium trap existed throughout the Ming and Qing periods.[7]

It is noteworthy that Elvin heavily borrowed from Japanese scholars' agronomic studies prior to 1970. Two important aspects are missing in this narrative: First, the linkage between the macro and the micro perspective; and second, quantitative evidence, especially those changes reflected in wages and household income. In the 1980s, one decade after Elvin published the monograph, a group of Japanese scholars openly questioned such traditional explanations and reconstructed an alternative delta model to demonstrate agricultural developments in the Lower Yangtze.[8] Following Boserup's theory, this group of revisionists recognized increases in population density as the foundation of technical innovations in rice farming. Furthermore, these scholars attributed the dynamics of agricultural developments to commercialization and urbanization in the Lower Yangtze (including Jiangnan). In other words, it was the increases in aggregate demands outside the agricultural sector that played a decisive role. For our purposes, the crucial point is to determine when agriculture in the Lower Yangtze shifted toward intensive farming. Although there are differences in opinion, most revisionists believe that intensive farming did not occur until the late twelfth century.[9] For instance, based on his comprehensive survey of agriculture in the Lower Yangtze, Shiba provided a developmental narrative that consisted of consecutive stages. He argued that the economy of the Lower Yangtze in the tenth century continued to remain in the frontier development stage for three reasons: the "utilization of swamp lowlands in the lower deltaic core was still sparse and extensive," the low rate of grain taxation "matched with qualitative evidence testifying to the fragile productivity of these areas," and the relatively low density of the population. Instead, he dated the rapid development in both agricultural productivity and population density to the twelfth and thirteenth centuries. In his view, Shiba believed that these developments only marked the beginning of intensive farming, and it was only after the Ming-Qing transformation that the agricultural economy in Jiangnan advanced to an even higher level.[10]

The revisionist paradigm has greatly changed our thinking. Contrary to the overpopulation thesis, it viewed population growth and commercialization as the driving forces for agricultural development. Although this new paradigm shares important assumptions with the traditional model, its explanatory power lies in two aspects where the traditional explanation had failed to identify. First, it attempts to link the macro and the micro perspectives to offer a comprehensive survey. Second, it allows the researcher to use quantitative data to identify the development achieved over the course of the last millennium. In other words, this two-dimensional image of agricultural developments in the Lower Yangtze should be quantitatively examined: investments in irrigation and water transportation made possible by urbanization and commercialization on the one hand, and an increase in farm yields due to technical improvements on the other hand. It is important to seek support from empirical data to see how these two aspects were closely interlinked over the course of the transition. The three most important criteria at the macro level—population density, commercialization and urbanization, and irrigation works—all point to a transformative change that occurred during the centuries after the Rebellion.

As the water supply is a crucial factor in growing wet rice, irrigation facilities are the foundation of raising rice yields.[11] The records of irrigation works in the Lower Yangtze (see table 7-1) indicate extreme underdevelopment prior to the Tang dynasty. Furthermore, most of the Tang irrigation works were built in the post-Rebellion period, and their growth was closely related to the developments in the Lower Yangtze's settlements and rice growing. An even more rapid development can be found in the Song period. Li, for instance, reported that 55 projects were completed in Jiangnan in the Tang dynasty, of which 82 percent were built after the Rebellion.[12] From a national perspective, an obvious change occurred in the distribution of irrigation projects in late Tang. Prior to

Table 7-1. Distribution of irrigation works in the Lower Yangtze, 221 BC–1271 AD

Period	Highland	Upper delta	Lower delta
221 BC–618 AD	8	13	5
618–907	26	27	15
907–1127	50	52	53

Source: Shiba 2001a, 178.

756, the projects completed in the Jiangnandao, an administrative unit that was larger than the Lower Yangtze, accounted for only 13 percent of the total number of projects. In the succeeding years, the ratio grew to 49 percent.[13] Without the irrigation facilities, we can imagine how primitive rice farming was prior to the Rebellion. Undoubtedly, the Tang-Song transformation marks the turning point in the irrigation history of the Lower Yangtze.

The massive construction of irrigation works continued throughout the eleventh century. In the south, irrigation works completed in the 1070s added up to 7,183 projects, which is about 82.7 percent of the total reported in the Xining period (1068–1077). In comparison, irrigation works completed in the Mid- and Lower Yangtze (Jiangnan, Liangzhe, and Jinghu in table 7-2) amounted to 5,193 projects, about half of the total (see table 7-2). It is noteworthy that most of the projects completed in this period were partially funded by the government or sponsored by landlords. According to Shiba's study, the average size of the irrigated land per project in the south was 3,006 *mu*. This rather small amount is an indicator of land reclamation driven by the interests of private landowners.[14]

Along with commercialization and urbanization, population density in the Lower Yangtze steadily increased over the course of the Tang-Song transformation. This is evident from the change in its share of the population in the aggregate population. The literal meaning of Jiangnan is "the land south of the Yangtze River," which is significantly different in terms of the actual size of its territory after the Rebellion. Prior to the Rebellion, Jiangnandao, for instance, included all the regions south of the Yangtze River except for Sichuan and Guangdong. Yet its aggregate households reached merely 1,824,004 in 752, just one-third of the population in the north.[15] This clearly indicates the underdevelopment of the south before 750 AD. Over the course of the Tang-Song

Table 7-2. China's irrigation works and acreages, 1070–1076

I. North

Capital	25	1,574,929	Jingxi	1,010	3,336,145
Hebei	45	5,966,060	Shanxi	114	471,981
Jingdong	177	2,594,114	Sha'anxi	132	3,762,392
Subtotal	1,503	17,705,621			
Average size of acreage per project:			11,780 Song *mu*		

II. South

Sichuan	315	467,162	Jiangnan *lu*	1,507	1,537,747
Huainan *lu*	177	7,481,161	Liangzhe *lu*	1980	10,484,842
Fujian	212	302,471	Jinghu *lu*	1706	988,444
Guangnan *lu*	1,286	333,662			
Subtotal	7,183	21,595,489			
Average size of acreage per project:			3,006 Song *mu*		

Total:	8686 (10,793 [Shiba])			6,117,888 (191,530 [Shiba])

Source: Shiba 2001a, 203.

transformation, population density in the south gradually grew to match and even significantly exceed the north. As the regional economies gained prominence, the size of Jiangnan dwindled to only include the Lower Yangtze, which is equivalent to the combined territories of modern Jiangsu, Zhejiang, Shanghai, and south Anhui.

Moreover, to apply the delta model in his research, Li Bozhong adopted an even narrower definition of Jiangnan to include only the Tai Lake and the delta regions close to the mouth of the Yangtze River. In this case, Jiangnan comprised seven prefectures: Suzhou (being the most important prefecture), Changshu, Songjiang (Shanghai), Nanjing, Zhenjiang, Huzhou, Jiaxing, and Hangzhou. As shown in table 7-3, these seven prefectures evolved from five prefectures in the Tang dynasty: Suzhou (ranking at 8), Changzhou (3), Runzhou (1), Huzhou (4), and Hangzhou (1). Defined in this way, Jiangnan accounted for only a small portion of the Lower Yangtze.

In the mid-eighth century, population density in Suzhou ranked eighth in the Lower Yangtze and the lowest among those five prefectures, being half of that in Hangzhou and Runzhou (see table 7-3). As early as the late tenth century, population density of Jiangnan (groups I-a and I-b in table 7-4) already surpassed other Lower Yangtze areas such as the highlands and peripheries of the Lower Yangtze. The rate of population growth was even more stunning. Although the population density of Suzhou remained quite low toward the end of the tenth century, it increased from 21 people/km^2 in 980 to 277 people/km^2 in 1290, a thirteen-fold increase in three centuries. This change was associated with the inflow of immigrants and capital, and with rapid developments in urbanization and water transportation. It was not accidental that Jiangnan became the grain storehouse for the entire country during the Song era.[16]

It is noteworthy that the 1290 census, which revisionist scholars view as representative of demographic changes under the Mongol rule, were conducted just about twenty years after the Mongol conquest of the Lower Yangtze. Rather, they should indicate demographic changes at the end of the Song period. In other words, this enormous increase by 1290 indicates a revolutionary change in the aggregate grain consumption of Jiangnan, and this most likely reflects changes in grain supply over the course of the Song dynasty. All these increases could not have been made by the extension of farmland alone. Increases in farm yield per acre must have made a substantial contribution.

Table 7-3. Changes in the population density of the Lower Yangtze, 639–742 (0/sq km)

	Prefecture	639 AD	742 AD		Prefecture	639 AD	742 AD
1	Hangzhou	18.97	72.31	7	Muzhou	7.13	46.15
2	Runzhou	16.06	83.67	8	Suzhou	3.94	45.80
3	Changzhou	13.17	81.52	9	Kuozhou	3.43	14.49
4	Huzhou	11.86	74.10	10	Xuanzhou	3.05	2.19
5	Jinhua	10.81	67.36	11	Taizhou	2.92	40.23
6	Shaoxing	8.36	57.51	12	Huizhou	2.19	22.14

Source: H. Zhang 2003, 32.

Table 7-4. Population density in the Lower Yangtze

			Group I-a: Low-Core Areas (0/sq km)					
	980	1080	1102	1199	1279	1290	1390s	1770
Suzhou (8404)	21	104	91	103	196	277	292	756
Jiaxing (7790)	15	89	79	—	—	294	(506)	733
Hangzhou (7494)	47	135	138	174	261	241	144	367
Huzhou (6191)	31	117	131	165	—	192	162	348
Songjiang (3581)	—	71	74	—	—	55	70 (292)	548

Source: Shiba 2001a, 146. The 1770 figures are estimated by Cao Shuji (Cao 2000b, 708–709). There is a difference on the density of prefectural populations in 1380 between Shiba's estimation and Cao's; the figures reported in parentheses are Cao's estimates (see Cao 2000a, 240–241).

			Group I-b: High-Core Areas (0/sq km)					
	980	1080	1102	1199	1279	1290	1390s	1770
Nanjing (7084)	41	119	—	85	—	83	160 (229)	507
Zhenjiang (3405)	39	81	94	94	159	146	128	383

Source: Shiba 2001a, 146. The 1770 figures are estimated by Cao Shuji (Cao 2000b, 708–709).

			Group II: Highlands (0/sq kl)					
	980	1080	1102	1199	1279	1290	1390s	1770
Mingzhou (7177)	20	81	82	96	—	—	147	314
Shaoxing (9975)	28	77	140	—	137	150	134	447
Taiping (3581)	21	71	74	—	—	55	70	371
Huizhou (14882)	4	36	36	41	42	53	44	188
Xuanzhou (8874)	27	81	83	—	—	56	70	231
Chizhou (2614)	19	76	78	—	—	21	41	220
Guangde (3341)	16	60	62	—	—	66	70	133

Source: Shiba 2001a, 146. The 1770 figures are estimated by Cao Shuji (Cao 2000b, 708–709).

Group III-a: Periphery, North of the Yangtze (0/sq km)								
	980	1080	1102	1199	1279	1290	1390s	1770
Taizhou (14855)	12	15	19	40	—	76	(41)	330
Tongzhou (6488)	8	25	21	—	—	—	13	358
Yangzhou (6468)	23	42	44	28	34	—	95*	330
Tuzhou (4058)	25	—	50	49	—	—	5	98
Hezhou (2614)	19	75	65	—	—	18	41	127
Shuzhou (13821)	12	46	46	—	—	20	70	301

Source: Shiba 2001a, 146. The 1770 figures are estimated by Cao Shuji (Cao 2000b, 708–709).

*This comparison is problematic because the prefecture of Yangzhou in 1393 comprised at least 7 counties and occupied an area much larger than that in the Song dynasty. This made the size of the Yangzhou prefecture much closer to that of the East Huainan *lu* in the eleventh century. If one considers choosing the same area in the mid-eleventh century, the total of the households might arrive at 240,000 households, far above that in the 1390s.

Group III-b: Periphery, South of the Yangtze (0/sq km)									
	980	1010	1080	1102	1199	1279	1290	1390s	1770
Wuzhou (9392)	18	—	73	71	82	—	115	132	206
Yanzhou (8544)	7	27	45	48	52	70	—	43	151
Quzhou (3797)	11	49	61	—	72	(62)	70	58	112

Source: Shiba 2001a, 146. The 1390s and 1770 figures are estimated by Cao Shuji (Cao 2000a, 240–241; Cao 2000b, 708–709).

The core problem with the revisionist explanation is the lack of a cohesive concept of intensive farming, especially the absence of a shared quantitative standard to measure the growth that occurred in a broad range of fields mentioned previously. The revisionist scholars attempt to follow the Boserup's theory by pointing to a shift from extensive farming to intensive farming based on increases in population density. If we focus on population growth—the central point in the Boserup theory to account for the shift toward intensive farming—it is evident that the growth between 1368 and 1820 is far slower than that in the Song-Yuan period.[17] The population in Suzhou, for instance, increased from 2.3 million in 1393 to 5.4 million in 1820, which is slightly more than twofold (see table 7-5). This is no comparison to the thirteen-fold increase achieved between the three centuries from 980 to 1290. However, the fact of rapid increases in population density during the Tang-Song transformation, likely the most rapid and fundamental one

Table 7-5. Population growth in Jiangnan, 1393–1820

Prefecture	A. 1393	B. 1820	A/B
Suzhou	2,355,030	5,473,348	2.3
Songjiang	1,219,937	2,631,590	2.2
Changzhou	775,513	3,895,772	5.0
Zhenjiang	522,383	2,194,654	4.2
Nanjing	1,193,620	1,874,018	1.6
Hangzhou	720,567	3,189,838	4.4
Jiaxing	1,112,121	2,805,120	2.5
Huzhou	810,244	2,566,137	3.2
Total	8,700,415	24,630,477	2.8

Source: Li Bozhong 1998c, 45; 2003a, 142.

in Jiangnan's history, has been largely ignored in the revisionist narrative. Although the revisionists did not deny the rapid changes that occurred in the Lower Yangtze during the five centuries after the Rebellion, they often indicated that a more advanced stage of commercialized agriculture in Jiangnan did not occur until the eighteenth century, which brought about an unprecedented increase in farm yield per acre.

This argument refers to the definition of the developmental cycle of the regional economy in discussion, one of the main issues that have led to diverse opinions among researchers. Here the revisionists integrated the Boserup theory and the delta model to account for the agricultural development in Jiangnan in the last millennium and focused their research on Suzhou and Songjiang, the core areas of Jiangnan, which is the most wealthy yet a very small part of the Lower Yangtze. But this integration in methodology created more trouble than what revisionist researchers expected. The delta model originally comes from Yoshikazu Takaya's well-known study of agricultural development in the Chao Phraya River delta. In comparison to this delta region, Jiangnan is geographically far more complicated: It is a combination of Tai Lake, the surrounding highland areas, the Yangtze mouth, and other deltas. As the core area of the Lower Yangtze, Jiangnan enjoys a longer history of settlement and rice farming. The city of Suzhou, the main focus of the revisionist research, is not located in the outer rim of the delta but the lowland area beside Tai Lake. It is thus uncertain whether it is appropriate to apply this model to analyze the establishment of intensive farming in Jiangnan.[18]

The delta model rather depicts a linear pattern of rice farming in a delta basin presented in three stages: rice growing started from high lands, then moved to the upper land of the delta, and, finally, pushed by migration and commercialization, to the lower end. This process points to three factors that work together to reach the final stage of development: rapid growth in population largely due to migrants rushing in, increased investments of capitals such as irrigation projects and farming tools, and the opening of a market for harvested rice.[19] However, when applying this model to Jiangnan, empirical challenges make it difficult for researchers to uphold the same principle in defining the formation of intensive farming. This lack of consensus on such key issues leads to controversy among the revisionist researchers on the rise of intensive farming in Jiangnan. For instance, Takaya, who first proposed this delta model, argued a dividing line of land utilization in the tenth century based on the relationship between settlements, farm practice, and irrigation works.[20] Shiba viewed the thirteenth century as the turning point for intensive farming. In contrast, Li denied that intensive farming existed in Jiangnan until the eighteenth century.

If we are to choose from the two transformative periods of agricultural development in Jiangnan, the Tang-Song transformation, especially the eleventh century, is the right choice, for what happened during this period looks closer to what the delta model depicted about intensive farming. In the original Thai delta model, the outburst of intensive rice farming was associated with an extraordinary inflow of migrants and a wave of massive construction projects in irrigation and canal transportation. A similar pattern can be identified in the development of Jiangnan during the Tang-Song transformation. Rapid population growth, for instance, did occur in the Song and Yuan eras but slowed down thereafter. Undoubtedly one can find increase in capital investments during this period. Most of all, the peak of rice growing in Suzhou and Jiaxing took place in the Song era, and the shipment along the Grand Canal facilitated the rice export, for which Suzhou gained the reputation of state granary in the mid-eleventh century. Such export of rice disappeared in the Ming, and Jiangnan needed food imports to feed its people.[21] The eighteenth-century economic boom in Jiangnan did not really resemble that of the young delta of the Chao Phraya basin. The population in Suzhou grew even more slowly in the eighteenth and nineteenth centuries than that in the periphery, such as Hangzhou and Zhenjiang. Consequently, Suzhou and Songjiang's share of the Jiangnan population declined from 41 percent in 1393 to 33 percent in 1820.[22] What characterizes agricultural development in the eighteenth century, as Li's research has demonstrated, is a shift from rice growing to mulberry planting and handicraft industries.[23]

The revisionist argument is also flawed by inconsistencies between their narratives of agricultural development and commercialization. Although the latter commercialization is viewed as the major driving force for the rural economy, the revisionists hardly follow this line of thought to capture the cycle of the market economy in the last millennium of imperial China. This oversight casts doubts on the explanatory power of their linear explanation of Jiangnan's agricultural development. Shiba, for instance, viewed the thirteenth and the first half of the fourteenth centuries as a period of economic crises and agricultural stagnation in Jiangnan, while viewing the years of the early Ming as a period of recovery and development.[24] Yet, based on macroeconomic data on the money supply, water transportation, and long-distance trade, the market economy was expanding in the Lower Yangtze from the late eighth century to the end of the thirteenth century. Furthermore, I have shown in chapter 3 that it was in the early Ming period that the economy was demonetized. Following this line of thought, we must question how a demonetized economy could experience growth as Shiba suggested. Rather, the data from local societies in Jiangnan suggest a substantial decline in the first half of the fifteenth century in public projects including transportation, irrigation, and education.

Similarly, Li argues for a substantial increase in both farm yield per acre and household income took place exactly before and after the Song dynasty: the Tang and early Ming periods. At the same time, however, he viewed the Song as a period of slow changes. Li's finding contradicts what we can gather from primary sources. Prior to the Rebellion, the Tang economy was nothing more than a barter economy. The farmers in the Lower Yangtze had no incentive to produce any more than what was required for family consumption and taxation. Under no circumstances can one find evidence that the market played any role in agricultural developments. In terms of demographic changes, the early Tang saw the most rapid growth in population density of the Lower Yangtze. Most of the prefectural population grew more than five- to tenfold in a century. The population density in Suzhou, for instance, increased from 3.94 people/km^2 in 639 to 45.8 people/km^2 in 742, an eleven-fold increase in a century (see table 7-3). Whether such a high rate is questionable or not is beyond our concern, it is rather interesting to remind a reader that even after a rapid century-long increase in population, by the mid-eighth century the population density of Suzhou still remained half that of Jiangnan's highland areas such as Runzhou and Changzhou and ranked the lowest among the five prefectures that were known as Jiangnan in the Ming-Qing era. Given such low population density, development in pre-Rebellion Suzhou, the core area of Jiangnan, presents the model of extensive farming sought by the revisionist scholars. Hence, it will be rather interesting to examine how the density of population changed across this region in the centuries after the Rebellion. In the following century, Suzhou's registered households increased from 76,421 in 742 to 100, 808 in 813. It is the only recorded case of population growth in the Lower Yangtze, but this increase itself still looks moderate.[25] By 1080, Suzhou's population density increased to 104 people/km,^{2} just slightly lower than Hangzhou and Huzhou. By 1290, just two decades after the end of the Song dynasty, it reached 277 people/km,^{2} ahead of Hangzhou and Huzhou. This catch-up scenario best reveals Suzhou's leading role in Jiangnan's agricultural development during the Song and Yuan eras.

Variances in Estimation of Farm Yield per Acre in Jiangnan

Farm yield per acre and per household are the central criteria in measuring agricultural productivity. As Marxist historians emphasize that agricultural production is the foundation of economic development, discussion on long-term changes in imperial China's farm yields has attracted much attention. Unfortunately, many of their estimates, though empirical in nature, are poorly analyzed, as they lack comprehensive understanding of agricultural productivity in a preindustrial economy.[26] In contrast, Dwight Perkins's study has demonstrated an analytical framework based on the interdependent relationship between population growth, changes in agricultural outputs, and technological innovations, and underscores the important role that population growth played in rising farm yield per acre over the long run. In particular, he suggested a slow yet steady rise in rice yield per *mu* in Jiangsu, one of the major provinces in the Lower Yangtze. From 960 through 1900, the average yield increased from 326 *jin* of unhusked rice per *shi mu* in the Song period to 550 *jin* in the eighteenth century and declined to 501 *jin* in the nineteenth century.[27]

In his study, Perkins also reminded the reader about the issue of data quality. First, most of his samples were almost entirely taken from the Lower Yangtze. Second, he used a substantial amount of rent data from public land, particularly school land, and doubled the rent to reach an estimate of farm yields. Thus, whether school land could be ranked as average quality land is a key question to be resolved.[28] However, Perkins failed to address a third source leading to his bias: The land yield data is unevenly distributed throughout the different periods of time. In his 143 observations on Zhejiang, 115 (thus 80 percent) were from the Song records alone. For Jiangsu there were 171 observations

(Perkins mistakenly noted the number to be 169) with 143, 3, 11, 6, and 8 from the Song, Yuan, and Ming eighteenth- and nineteenth-century records, respectively. As the availability of school land data is limited to the Song period, the reconstruction of farm yields of the other periods relied only on treatises and a few case studies. This creates difficulties for a cross-dynastic comparison.

As the revisionist school advances a new paradigm of intensive farming based on a regional developmental cycle, their estimation of farm yields in Jiangnan can hardly avoid the same difficulties. The revised estimates soon led to a hot debate between the revisionists and their critics. In the following, I use the estimates made by Shiba and Li to demonstrate how widely the estimates diverged from each other and the very implications that one can draw from the debate.

To reconstruct the average per acre farm yield based on the most original sources that one can find, Shiba has collected 114 rent records preserved in the Changshu county of Suzhou in 1237 and doubled them to reach the rice yield per *mu*. The estimated average yield is as low as 0.65 Song *shi*. Nonetheless, Shiba acknowledged the wide gap between his estimation and those reported by contemporary writings. Hence he suggested 2 to 3 Song *shi* per *mu* for average farm yield in early thirteenth-century Suzhou and Songjiang.[29] This revision places Shiba in a close, though not exactly the same, position as other traditional researchers.[30]

Li, however, emphasized the value of Suzhou's rental data in his estimation to show low land productivity in the thirteenth century.[31] Based on the rental records of 51,310 *mu* public land in Changshu, Li arrived at an estimate of 1 to 1.36 Song *shi* per *mu*, which he believed was applicable to the entire Jiangnan region.[32] According to Li, farm-yield-per-*mu* increases in Jiangnan during the Tang and the early Ming eras are so impressive that one should dub these two periods the "agricultural revolution." In contrast, changes in the Song period were not only slow but also confined to merely "extensive growth" due to the lack of commercialization.[33]

In the eyes of Li's opponents, his estimate is also flawed with respect to data quality, especially for the three biases mentioned previously. They argued that the Song government often allowed public land to be rented at a 20 percent lower rate than that of private land.[34] For example, Liang Keng-yao discussed the lease samples of public land and recommended further clarification of their origins and management. He pointed out that the majority of the 51,310 *mu* of public land was donated by rural households for commutation of labor services and thus less fertile than average. In consequence, the

Table 7-6. Shiba's reconstruction of farm yields of school land, Changshu, 1237

Range of estimated rice yields	Number of plots	Percentage
0.45–0.62 Song *shi*	76	53%
0.63–1.20 Song *shi*	34	27%
1.21–2.25 Song *shi*	29	20%
Total observations	114*	100%
Average yield	0.65 (0.88) Song *shi**	

Sources: Shiba 2001a, 142–143; Fang Jian 2006, 511.

*Fang Jian pointed out the error in Shiba's calculation. He found 153 rather than 114 plots registered as Changshu's county school land in 1237 and determined 0.44 Song *shi* for average rent per *mu*, thus 0.88 Song *shi* average rice yield per *mu*.

land rent was low as well. Using the rent samples of donation-origin public land surely produces a bias in observation that lowers the estimated values of average farm yield per acre. To illustrate his point, Liang cited the average rent collected from another 800 *mu* of public land that reached 0.75 Song *shi* per *mu*, or an estimated farm yield of 1.5 Song *shi* per *mu*. Apparently, because the 800 *mu* of land was purchased by a magistrate with government funds, its productivity came close to the normal level of private landholdings.[35] Liang further cited the official report made in the early thirteenth century on land purchase and concluded that "nearly 50 percent of Suzhou's lands would produce 2 Song *shi* of rice per *mu*."[36] Although Liang and Shiba approach this issue with different evidence, their estimates of farm yields are close. However, Li's estimation was an extraordinary undertaking, for he attempted to measure increases in agricultural productivity over nearly two millennia. A reader would be surprised about the low farm yields in the thirteenth and the early twentieth century as indicated in table 1-1 of this book. I argue that such deviations exist because of the varying quality of primary sources: Only the reconstruction of farm yields in the thirteenth and early twentieth centuries can be supported by real data; estimates of other periods is largely based on nonquantitative sources, such as agricultural treatises, due to the lack of data. The qualitative samples drawn from these treatises often demonstrate the technically optimized production capacity of a farmer under certain circumstances regardless of how representative this sample is for ordinary peasants.

Li's estimate is closely related to his definition of the Jiangnan path toward intensive farming in the eighteenth century. In this regard, even if we accept all the estimates in table 1-1, a subtle but different interpretation can be gained from the Tang-Song transformation perspective. First, while Li suggested that there was rapid development in the Tang dynasty, almost all of his key evidence is drawn from the post-Rebellion period to indicate the changes in rice farming, irrigation, tea planting, and sericulture in Jiangnan. All of these technical advances were, more accurately speaking, achieved during the Tang-Song transformation. Second, contrary to Li's assumption that the economy was demonetized in the Song period, both money stock per capita and urbanization rates were unmatched in imperial China.[37] It was largely urbanization and commercialization that greatly helped agriculture to achieve such progress. Therefore, if one follows Li's definition of agricultural revolution, that is, a transition from extensive growth to Smithian growth, it is without doubt that such revolutionary changes occurred in the Lower Yangtze during the five centuries after the Rebellion.[38] Finally, Li and other revisionists ignored the impact of early Ming anti-market policies upon the Jiangnan economy. The last point could be easily proven if we make a comparison of real wages and income between 1200 and 1400. The latter was the lowest level indicating a recession caused by the early Ming command economy in 1368–1450.

According to Li's estimate, the shrinking in farm size per household caused no severe loss in grain output per family (see table 7-7). He suggests a positive relationship between them when measured in output per worker. Both Li and his opponents adopt a supply perspective to estimate the farm yields in Jiangnan. However, it is necessary to examine this debate from a demand perspective. Zhou Shengchun's reconstruction of farm yield per acre in Liangzhelu (the largest part of the Lower Yangtze) provides such an example. I have provided the results in table 7-8. Following Perkins's analytical framework, Zhou used demographic and food intake data to estimate how much rice was needed to feed the population of each prefecture in the Lower Yangtze. He then divided these figures

Table 7-7. Farm size and output in Jiangnan, Southern Song to early Ming

Period	Farm size (mu)	Yield shi/per mu	Output per family* (shi)	Farm income per family** (shi)
Late Song	40	1.0	40	39.2
Yuan	30	1.4	42	40.8–41.1
Early Ming	20	1.6	32	24

Source: Li Bozhong 2003a, 170.

*Li also used output per worker for comparison and assumed the decline in the family size in Songjiang from the Song through Ming: Each family had three adults in Southern Song and two in the Yuan and Ming. Therefore, output per worker was 13 *shi* in the Song, 14 *shi* in the Yuan, and 16 *shi* in the Ming. As most scholars assume that the average family size in this transitional period remained unchanged, Li is the first to address the shrinkage in family size in Jiangnan. Since this is an inconclusive observation, I turn to make a family-based comparison instead.

**I designed this column to compare the net grain income of a household after paying taxes to the government.

by acreages to reach an estimate of farm yield per *mu*. Twelfth- and thirteenth-century writers provide us with some idea of their daily consumption of food: An adult would consume 0.00974 Song *shi* (487 g) of husked rice; for a family of five members, the yearly consumption would amount to 26.77 Song *shi*. After one has determined the local populations, amounts of grain taxes and grain exports/imports, and the acreage, and then assumed the same consumption standard across villages and urban communities, an estimate of farm yield per acre may be derived. This demand perspective could apply to the study of the aggregate grain output and output per acre in China. Perkins did exactly so in his study of twentieth-century Chinese agriculture. This approach is also effective in tackling the variation and complexity demonstrated by the spatial structure of the Lower Yangtze agriculture.

His study reveals obvious regional variance in estimated farm yield per *mu* across the Lower Yangtze with a range between 1.188 and 2.750 Song *shi*. Noticeably lowland prefectures such as Suzhou and Huzhou ranked at the top. Estimated per *mu* farm yields in Suzhou reached 2.607 Song *shi* (266 *jin* per *mu*) in Suzhou and 2.705 (276 *jin* per *mu*) Song *shi* in Huzhou, only second to Taizhou by a slight gap. Following the developmental cycle of the delta model proposed by the revisionist scholars, one expects that higher farm yields per acre would concentrate on the highland and periphery areas as listed in table 7-4. However, there is no absolute gap between the highland prefectures such as Zhenjiang, Jiangyin, Changzhou, Mingzhou, and Taizhou on the one hand and lowland ones such as Jiaxing, Suzhou, and Huzhou on the other. Rather, lowland prefectures, which revisionist scholars defined as relatively backward, often but not always ranked higher than other prefectures in per acre farm yields. Given that per household farmland in Suzhou and Jiaxing was much larger than in the highland areas, this actually meant a lead in per capita farm yields as well. It thus signaled the rise of intensive farming in the core area of Jiangnan. Reconsidering Suzhou, it already met the three criteria required by the delta model: rapid growth in population density, the opening of the grain market by development in urbanization and water transportation, and the acceleration in investments and technical innovations. Now one can add the last and most important one: high farm yields measured both per acre and per head.

Table 7-8. Average rice yields per *mu* in Liangzhelu in the thirteenth century (Song shi)

Prefecture	(A) Households	(B) Grain tax	(C1) Alcohol Supply	(C2) Private & public purchase	(D) Cultivation acreage	(E) Aggregate output*	Output per mu
Zhenjiang	114218	192074	87429	0	23711448	2542430	1.573
Changzhou	209732	245822	110643	0	3431712	6478937	1.888
Jiangyin	64035	80000	36622	0	1253602	2035146	1.623
Suzhou	466158	882150	287384	1544684	6749000	11993733	2.607
Huzhou	255087	334122	136116	212413	3040147	5699976	2.750
Jiaxing & Songjiang	443017	602069	132890	151642	7280741	11096628	2.236
Jinhua	218673	173880	93427	0	2963876	4573593	2.264
Shaoxing	273343	332267	117092	0	3576925	8394049	2.347
Taizhou	266014		71147	0	2766546	7760194	2.805
Mingzhou	140349	144222	108596	0	2335953	4340203	1.858
	309071	119736			2608950	1.837	
Nanjing	117787	255242	139562	0	3269040	3882879	1.188
	220459	317852	139562		4474492	4833655	1.585

Source: Zhou Shengchun 2006, 270–271, 273–274.

*The aggregate output for each prefecture is its aggregate grain demand. Zhou suggested a formula to reach the estimate of the latter: (26.77 Song shi x A) + grain taxes (B) + alcohol supply (C1) – grain export/import (C2). Alcohol supply occupied an important part of grain consumption as the urban wine monopoly contributed significantly to the fiscal administration; for details see Sudo 1962a, 170–173, 239–242.

Zhou's demand-deducted research provides a different perspective to approach the current debate on Jiangnan's farm yields. This estimation is sound because it lies at the middle point of the varied estimates made from the supply perspective. Among the different estimates, Perkins and Li are located at the two ends of the spectrum. Zhou's estimates come close to that of Shiba and Liang Keng-yao (see table 7-9). Leaving aside Li's estimate about the Tang dynasty—which is too problematic as noted earlier—he also estimated 0.48 *shi* (72 *jin*)/*mu* for average farm yields in the century before 600 AD;[39] if we take this estimate as the typical output of extensive farming in Jiangnan, then in the six centuries farm yield per acre probably increased 2.7 times to reach 266 *jin/mu*. This nearly threefold increase, when compared with the later six centuries from 1250 to 1850, remains a record. Farm yields in 1800, according to Li's estimate, reached 255 to 375 *jin/mu*. Choosing Zhou's estimate (266 *jin/mu*) for the Southern Song era, one can find only a moderate increase in per acre farm yields in the next six centuries from 1200 to 1800. As the average family farm size shrank, per capita farm outputs were probably in decline. This speculation appears to be borne out by the fact that rice production was no longer able to support local consumption in the seventeenth and eighteenth centuries, even though growth in population was slow. Handicraft industries and other nonfarming activities would likely make a large contribution to household income. Nonetheless, if we choose Li's estimate for 1200, it will lead to a different story. A future exploration based on rich empirical evidence will undoubtedly cast light on this issue.

Debate on the Living Conditions in the Lower Yangtze

In the preceding discussion I have addressed the rise in farming productivity in the context of agricultural development in Jiangnan. Increase in farming output per acre or per head will lead to an increase in agricultural outputs if the inputs remain the same. However, how much a farmer is able to gain in economic development is also a political economy issue. It is more complicated than what took place in agricultural productivity because farmers did not necessarily benefit from productivity change. Meanwhile, one notices the shift from a market society to an egalitarian society caused by the rise of a command power in the late fourteenth century. We need to compare an ordinary farmer's

Table 7-9. Estimates of Suzhou's farm yields in the mid-thirteenth century (jin per mu)*

	Perkins	Shiba	Zhou	Liang	Li
Yield	300–450	204–306	266	204	78–100

Sources: Perkins estimated 2.0 to 3.0 *shi* husked rice *per mu* for Suzhou in the Song period, thus 300 to 450 *jin* per *mu* (Perkins 1969, table G. 4, 318). Shiba estimated 1 Song *shi* per *mu* for the late tenth century, and 2 to 3 Song *shi* toward the end of the Song dynasty (Shiba 2001a, 138, 140–141); Liang, 2001, 274; Zhou, 2006, 270; Li, see table 1-1 in the present volume.

*All yields reported here are for husked rice in *jin* per *mu*. 1 Song *shi* per Song *mu* = 102 *jin* per (*shi*) *mu* (Perkins 1969, 314).

living conditions in different contexts. Therefore, in this section I investigate changes in real income of rural households from Song to Ming in Jiangnan based on available information that I have collected from extant records.

This investigation provides important quantitative evidence on the role of the market in promoting welfare in a traditional economy, the central point in the debate, and brings out early Ming egalitarian society as a counterfactual model for testing. Although the revisionists tried to emphasize the extensive nature of eleventh-century agriculture in comparison to the very high level of labor and capital inputs in the eighteenth century, it is undeniable that the market economy (commercialization, urbanization, and water transportation) played a key role in the post-Rebellion agricultural developments. This would allow the farmer to adopt a flexible strategy in choosing either rice farming or cash crops, or a combination of both. It is evident that for rural households the return from investments into the latter is much higher than from rice farming alone. Chen Fu, for instance, calculated the profits earned by a rural family in Huzhou, an important area of Jiangnan, from sericulture. According to Chen Fu, just one month of hard work rearing silkworms and producing silk textiles by ten adults would produce 3.12 bolts of silk cloth, which was equivalent to 43.68 Song *shi* of rice. In other words, one month of work per head would produce 4.4 Song *shi* of rice, much higher than the rice yield per *mu*. For most farmers of the Lower Yangtze region in the eleventh century, sericulture was already one of the major sources of household income.[40] This market-oriented specialization must have impelled economic growth. When comparing the living standard in the Lower Yangtze in the long run, we need to keep in mind that farmers in the early Ming period earned very little besides minimal returns from tilling the land. The demonetized policy had largely deprived them of the opportunity to sell products to the market.

This viewpoint, however, is not widely accepted. Many Marxist researchers take a pessimistic view of the living conditions in the twelfth and thirteenth centuries and develop a landlordism argument. In their analytical framework, the landlord-tenancy relationship is the focal point through which one can define the major source for and stage of development in preindustrial China. The following outlines the debate between Marxist scholars and conservative historians, who likely view the market mechanism as a justified means in allocation of production outputs, on the nature of the Jiangnan economy and society during the Tang-Song transformation. On the one hand, in view of the rapid development in the agricultural economy associated with urbanization and monetization, Miyazaki argued for the emergence of the first "early modern" society in eleventh-century China. Entry to public service was open to members of the community via civil examination. Song farmers enjoyed free migration, private landownership, and free choice of career. Furthermore, he pointed out the connection between prevailing land transactions and commercialized agriculture, and asserted the dominant role of market mechanisms (such as tenancy and specialization in products and services).[41] On the other hand, Marxist historians such as Sudo Yoshiyuki viewed the tenant farmers as economically dependent on the lease and legally inferior to their landlords and dubbed the Song period a medieval society.[42] The Lower Yangtze, especially Suzhou, became the focus of the debate.

There is no standard answer to questions such as whether Jiangnan in the twelfth century is a medieval society or the first early modern market society; it all depends on the theoretical perspective that one follows.[43] What concerns us here is the question of the extent to which wealth was unequally distributed in a preindustrial market system. For instance, we are eager to know how large the share of estates owned by a big land-lord was in the total of cultivated land. Miyazawa is the first among Japanese scholars who has systematically exploited the HPR materials to study the social stratification in the Lower Yangtze. His study reveals the dominance of small landowners in the Lower Yangtze. Although Miyazawa follows the line of anti-landlordism to describe the Song economy as a *feudal* pattern, he admits that rapid economic development caused the decline of tenancy in eleventh-century Jiangnan. The following tables are based on Miyazawa's research and other primary sources. In the mid-eleventh century a proposal mentioned that the estimated rural households in Suzhou had reached no less than 150, 000, but those of the third-rank and above comprised only 5,000.[44]

Unlike what Miyazawa has claimed, the concentration of landholdings in Suzhou was rather moderate. The peasant class, who tilled all of their landholdings without employing laborers, occupied at least more than half of the total land acreage. The land supply in Suzhou in the eleventh century was flexible. If we adjust the upper end of their average farm sizes to 60 *mu*, it will raise their share to 80 percent or so. For the upper class, which included the top three ranks of rural households, the estimated share of land in the total acreage fell in the range of 17 to 45 percent (see table 7-10). The big landowners, who owned estates and were recognized with noble status, are really in a small number even among the upper class. The majority were third-rank households, who owned landholdings of 100 *mu* or so and partially relied on either tenancy or hired laborers.

It should be noted that Miyazawa probably overestimated the share of land owned by big landowners. He estimated that the average size of the landholdings owned by low-ranking households is between 10 and 30 *mu*, and hence the total owned by these households accounts for 14 to 42 percent of the acreage as shown in table F-1-a of appendix F. However, the low-bound value in his estimate is hardly acceptable. Suzhou was undergoing rapid development in the eleventh century, and a farmer would not have had any difficulty in securing a vacant lot. Li even suggested that up to the twelfth century the average size of a rural household in Suzhou was 40 *mu* (see table 7-7). It is unlikely the situation in the eleventh century was worsening.

Table 7-10. Land distribution in Suzhou, 1070s

Rank of households in total households	Percentage landholdings	Percentage of per household	Average landholdings
1–3 rank	3.0%	17–45%	1,246–1,835 *mu*
4–5 rank	88.3%	55–83%	40–60 *mu**
Landless	8.7%	0%	0
Total	100%	100%	64 *mu*

Source: Miyazawa 1984, 62.

*Miyazawa underestimated the percentage of land owned by ordinary farmers, and I thus make necessary adjustments. For Miyazawa's own estimation, see table F-1-a in appendix F).

The landless population data also cast doubts on the landlordism argument. The share of the landless declined from 20.8 percent in the 980s to 8.7 percent in 1078. Whether the distribution of landholdings was concentrated or not, the prevailing pattern of farming practice in late imperial China was the small farm run by a peasant family. Given this small share of tenancy in local population, if the upper class did grasp half the landholdings or even more in Suzhou as Miyazawa expects, then these big landlords would face questions such as to whom they were able to sublet these lands. Certainly they could not find enough laborers for hire. The tenants usually ran the smallest family farms, and the total land they could cultivate would not surpass the share of the fifth-rank households, the latter usually constituting the largest portion of the local population. But the fifth-rank households in the eleventh century were unlikely to rent a large amount of land because the land was rich in supply at Suzhou then, and also because they were able to accumulate certain capital to open new farmland for rice growing. At any rate, I accept the low-bound value of the estimation, thus 20 percent around, as the estimated share of the land owned by the upper class including large estates.

The concentration of wealth is nonetheless obvious in the highlands of the Lower Yangtze than that in the lowland areas. In Lanxi and Yongjia of Jinhua (Wuzhou), which are located at the periphery of the Lower Yangtze, the upper class were officially reported to own about 40 to 50 percent of the wealth.[45] One can roughly estimate the

Table 7-11-a. Share of landless households in Mingzhou, 976–1168

Year	Total households	Landless	Share of landless
976–984	27,681	16,803	60.7%
1078	115,208	57,334	49.8%
1116	123,692	29,118	23.5%
1168	136,072	31,347	23%

Source: Miyazawa 1984, 39.

Table 7-11-b. Share of landless households in Huzhou, 1008–1182

Year	Total households	Landless	Share of landless
1008–1016	129,540	10,840	8.4%
1078	145,121	10,509	7.2%
1131–62	159,885	9,143	5.7%
1182	204,594	3,988	1.9%

Source: Miyazawa 1984, 39.

Table 7-11-c. Share of landless households in Taizhou, 976–1222

Year	Total households	Landless	Share of landless
976–984	31,941	14,442	45.2%
1078	145,713	25,232	17.3%
1109	243,506	64,779	26.6%
1222	266,014	76,294	30.6%

Source: Miyazawa 1984, 43.

high-ranking households, which comprise less than 10 percent of the local population but owned nearly half of the landholdings and movable property.

However, everywhere in the Lower Yangtze the share of the landless in the local population declined substantially, a sign that contradicted landlordism. In the tenth century nearly two-thirds of the local population in Mingzhou was landless. Yet in 1168 it plunged to below one-fourth (see table 7-11-a). In the four centuries between 980 and 1390, the density of Mingzhou's population increased from 20 people/km² to 147 people/km²; while the commercial tax revenue increased from 26,947 strings in 1077 to 42,530 strings in 1225–1227. Commercial development played a significant role in reducing local poverty in Mingzhou. Mingzhou's commercial taxes increased from 26,947 strings in 1077 to 87,102 strings in 1225.[46] The extraordinary increase in Mingzhou (Ningbo)'s commercial tax in 1225 should be attributed to a boom in eleventh- and twelfth-century maritime trade in the Lower Yangtze. As a sea harbor city, it provided access to Guangzhou and the Pearl Delta on the one hand and to Korea and Japan on the other hand. Goods transported here from the sea could be further shipped via canal to Hangzhou.[47]

Economic development in Shaoxing and Huzhou shared the same story with Mingzhou (Ningbo) but in some different contexts of economic development.[48] Each of these three areas enjoyed easy access to water transportation. By the eleventh century, they became the most famous production sites for silk textiles. What Chen Fu recommended as an example for specialization in textile production is from Huzhou.[49] As shown in table 7-11-b, by the late twelfth century, the share of landless households dropped to 1.9 percent. In Shaoxing it already declined to 0.2 percent in 1080 (see table 6-2).

In contrast, Taizhou presents an example of underdevelopment opposite to the case of Mingzhou. In the ninth century the share of landless population in all highland prefectures was high enough to reveal the prevalence of tenancy dominated by landlordism. As trade gradually pushed the decline in the share of landless in Mingzhou and Shaoxing, commerce stagnated in inland hilly areas such as Yanzhou and Taizhou. In Yanzhou the commercial tax quota remained almost the same for more than a century.[50] Meanwhile, population in Taizhou grew slowly in the twelfth century and the share of landless households were pretty high.[51] It seems there were two contrasting patterns within the highland prefectures: the market expansion with the lower share of the poorest households such as Mingzhou and Shaoxing and the economic stagnation with the higher share of the poorest such as Yanzhou and Taizhou. Only for the second pattern is the anti-landlordism argument persuasive.

Although tenancy did exist in Jiangnan, it was not a severe social and economic problem as compared with other regions in the Lower Yangtze. Furthermore, the market mechanism played an important role in reducing the share of the poorest in local population. The living conditions of peasants in the Song era were better than what the anti-landlordism argument depicts. As Jiangnan evolved from a market society to an egalitarian society, surprisingly, the life of farmers became more difficult. After Zhu Yuanzhang controlled this region, he deliberately destroyed the landlord class and confiscated their landholdings.[52] *Guantian* or state-owned landholdings accounted for 44 percent of the acreage in Jiangnan (see table 7-12). In 1379, for instance, the *guantian* in Suzhou amounted to two-thirds of the land under cultivation. In Songjiang, the share was even higher with about 85 percent of the land under cultivation, and the share of private landholdings was merely 15 percent.[53] For this reason, the early Ming state became the sole and largest landlord in Jiangnan.

Table 7-12. *Guantian* and private land in Jiangnan

Prefecture	Official land (mu)	Private land (mu)	Percentage of official land in total land registration
Suzhou	6,500,300	3,469,700	65
Songjiang	3,985,600	730,028	85
Jiaxing	1,024000	2,793,800	27
Changzhou	904,115	5,273,619	15
Zhengjiang	1,036,771	2,236,306	33
Yingtian (Nanjing)	1,996,400	5,000,900	29
Total	15,447,186	19,504,353	44

Sources: Wu Dange, 1979, 140–1; Mori, 1988, 46. The registered land amounted to 34,951,539 *mu*, about 4,464,578 acres.

Such a dramatic reallocation of wealth remains unmatched in Chinese history even compared with the effects of the land reform that was launched by the Communist Party in the same region. After the Communist Party took power through the military victory in 1949, they enforced land policies by violent means that aimed to destroy the so-called *feudal* landlord class. According to the party report, in twenty-four out of the total twenty-seven counties in South Jiangsu, an area very close to the size of Jiangnan in the Ming era, 7,180,537 *shi mu* of land, was confiscated and reallocated to 1,519,472 peasants. The reallocated land accounted for 33 percent of the total arable area.[54] It is closely in line with the finding of an investigation of 1,436 *hsiang* in 18 South Kiangsu [Jiangsu] hsien [counties], which revealed that the proportion of land owned by landlords was 36.8 percent of the total.[55] The early Ming *guantian* program surprisingly achieved a much higher degree of land redistribution in the Yangtze delta. Under Mao's leadership, the land reform that took place in 1951–1952 in Jiangnan was only the first step toward the collectivization of agricultural production, namely, the total socialization of land, equipment, and livestock; the enforcement of the compulsory purchase of grain; and finally the establishment of approximately 1 million advanced cooperatives and communes.[56] By no means will the reader expect that the planned agriculture in the early Ming could be as effective as the collectivization of agriculture in Mao's China. Nonetheless, the reader needs to keep in mind that the *guantian* program is among many important pieces of evidence of Zhu's great efforts to reorganize Chinese people in a planned system, five centuries before the commune was established by the Communist Party. And it is a unique case that clearly indicates how successfully the first Ming emperor exerted power upon rural communities living in the heartland of China.

The confiscation campaign launched by Zhu Yuanzhang also targeted ordinary farmers and Buddhist monasteries. Recalling that in mid-eleventh-century Suzhou the estimated share of the land owned by the upper class was 17 to 45 percent with the low-bound value more likely (see table 7-10), the share of state-owned land far exceeded that low-bound value by 200 percent and the high-bound value by a substantial margin. Many ordinary families lost their lands because they failed to follow the orders of the early Ming court such as maintaining military service or submitting grain taxes on time.[57] Zhu's land policy benefited only the coercive power. In a comparison of the Song HPR data with the early Ming *guantian* data, one can clearly tell that Zhu's land policies exercised direct control on local resources and fundamentally changed social relationships in the Lower Yangtze.

From a national scope, the acreage of the early Ming *guantian* was about ten times the Song *guantian*.[58] While the Song *guantian* in the Lower Yangtze region accounted for only 0.27 percent of land under cultivation, the early Ming *guantian* expanded to 26.8 percent. It is beyond any doubt that such a concentration in land distribution enabled the Ming state to take an unprecedentedly high share of agricultural products from the Lower Yangtze.[59] Tax rates applied to the *guantian* in Jiangnan were usually five to ten times higher than those on private landholdings.[60]

Zhu's land polices immediately led to dramatic increases in tax revenues. Whereas the farmers paid land taxes at an average rate of about 10 percent or below of farming yields in the eleventh century,[61] they paid taxes in an amount as much as the land rent. As shown table 7-13, the entire grain taxes collected from Jiangnan in 1393 was nearly six times that in the twelfth century. In Songjiang, where the share of the *guantian* remained as high as 85 percent of the cultivated land, the amount of land taxes increased nearly seventeen times. In Suzhou, which was second to Songjiang in the share of state-owned land, the amount of was about fourteen times that of the twelfth century. Yet these were not the most dramatic increases—in Huzhou, the early Ming court collected about 101,545 kl of rice, about twenty-one times that of the Song era.

From this point of view, one can explain why the changes in distribution of wealth rather than improvements in agricultural productivity were responsible for the unprecedentedly high ratios of land taxes in the early Ming period. It should be noted that Shiba took for granted that this explosive increase in land taxes indicates a substantial

Table 7-13. Increases in the land taxes from Song to Ming in Jiangnan (rice kl)

Prefecture	A. early Ming (1393)	B. Song	A/B
Suzhou	466,988	33,114	14.1
Songjiang*	189,183	10,656	17.8
Jiaxing	92,802	28,464	3.26
Zhenjiang	41,336	10,972	3.77
Changzhou	90,100	32,259	2.79
Nanjing	54,505	19,708	2.77
Hangzhou	43,156	12,592	3.43
Huzhou	101,545	4,744	21.40
Huizhou	19,831	15,147	1.31
Jinhua	29,557	12,639	2.34
Shaoxing	19,538	23,745	0.82
Total	1,148,541	204,040	5.63

Sources: Shiba 2001a, 72, 154–155.

1 kl=5.88 Ming *shi*=10.54 Song *shi*. The land taxes of the Songjiang prefecture are from *ZDSJ*.

development over the course of the Song-Yuan-Ming transition. Without using data to support his argument, Shiba asserted that the average farm yield in the late fourteenth century reached 2 Ming *shi* per *mu*, thus 3.4 Song *shi* per *mu*.[62] However, nowhere can one find strong evidence for rapid developments in irrigation, water transportation, and farming technologies at that time. This misunderstanding of the relationship between taxation and agricultural outputs even led him to make low estimates of the farm yield in the Song dynasty. As discussed in chapter 2, the Song tax regime was largely based on indirect taxes. The court adopted a rather low ratio of land taxes regardless of changes in agricultural productivity. Unlike the market-based tax mechanism in the Song period, the early Ming government adopted nonmonetary ways to maintain its governance. The extremely high ratios of land taxes were a result of direct control of production resources by violent means. The economic system was run in early Ming Jiangnan at the deadly cost of rural community rights.

Shiba's view, however, exaggerates the role agricultural productivity played and misses the real determinant of the tax mechanism in Song and Ming eras. One can look further into the latter periods to examine the complicated relationship between state power, land taxes, and agricultural productivity. In the post-Song periods, the shift toward a land-tax-based regime was an important change in late imperial China's financial system. This tax structure is shared by both the Ming and Qing dynasties, which makes a cross-dynastic comparison of tax ratios plausible. The ratios of land taxes in the early Ming still remained the highest, much higher than the tax rates in the eighteenth century. From 1450 through 1850, land tax ratios considerably declined in the Lower Yangtze over the long run.[63] If this is a genuine indicator of farm yields, then it can be concluded that agricultural productivity steadily declined over the course of the Ming and Qing eras. Needless to say, this conclusion undoubtedly goes against the revisionist interpretation of the eighteenth-century agricultural development.

The land taxes enforced by the early Ming court thus greatly change our common wisdom about an egalitarian society; this egalitarian society in the early Ming was placed in a command economy, and its members had to pay a very large percentage of their farm output to the state. This point will lead us to review Li's comparison of household income between Song and Ming as presented in table 7-7. After assuming the average farm size and grain yields per acre, Li took the estimated grain yields per family as the real income. He thus failed to distinguish changes in agricultural productivity from the changes in a farmer's income by missing the heavy tax burden a farmer had to face in the late fourteenth century. The early Ming regime owned the majority of land in Suzhou and Songjiang, and on average, collected grain taxes as much as 0.4 *shi* per *mu*. This would be about ten times that in the twelfth century. In other words, the land tax under early Ming rule took away 25 percent of the farm yields (see the last column in table 7-7). Consequently, a farmer's grain income would be only two-thirds of that prior to 1386. It should be noted that Li's estimate takes an optimistic view of the early Ming economy. Yet one can find in his estimate a substantial decline in the real income of Jiangnan's rural households.

The ordinary people of early Ming Jiangnan must have lived a miserable life. Taking Huzhou as an example, in the twelfth century the land tenancy was a minor issue, as the share of the landless declined to 1.9 percent. The rural residents also took a large amount of real income from silk textile industries. When it came to 1393, they paid land taxes in an amount more than 20 times that of the Song era. Meanwhile, Zhu Yuanzhang's anti-market policies gave a deadly blow to rural household industries. While real wages of nonskilled laborers are particularly important in testing the Malthusian-based hypothesis, the debate on the political economy of early Ming China also calls our attention to the other important aspects of the national economy such as investments in Jiangnan's agriculture. In macroeconomics, investment is necessary for future production and important for measuring national income and output.[64] The century-long deflation reflects a sluggish economy and an obvious decline in urban consumption. Under such circumstances, it is still possible that despite the fact that they consumed less food, bought fewer clothes, and enjoyed less entertainment, local communities in Jiangnan invested a lot to push the economy to recovery as soon as possible. Some Ming historians like to point out that Zhu Yuanzhang's policies, though harsh toward merchants and literati, were aimed to revive the plagued economy by encouraging agricultural development.[65] Zhu Yuanzhang did often issue edicts that cautioned farmers to work hard and promote irrigation projects. However, in economic analysis one cannot assume such agrarian policies would necessarily lead to substantial investments in agriculture. The researcher must look carefully into every important aspect of agricultural production to verify this connection. The lack of reliable and complete data is a major problem one has to face in the study of investments in preindustrial China. For traditional economies, fixed investments were usually concentrated in three areas: agriculture, such as irrigation projects, housing, and drafting power; mining and handicraft industries; and the public sector, such as canal construction and school building. In extant documents one can find little useful information about production consumption and investment of rural households. Nonetheless, there are some records preserved in gazetteers and the *Mingshilu*, such as agricultural production in military farms and local public projects that speak to our concerns.

For investments in local projects (such as bridges, temples, and schools) in Jiangnan,[66] I observe a declining trend from the beginning of the Ming dynasty. Local communities continued to invest in local projects on a smaller yet reliable scale for several decades until they came to a halt in the 1430s, about seventy years after Zhu Yuanzhang ascended the throne. This trend is evidence of the worsening situation of the Songjiang economy and society over the first half of the fifteenth century. Bol also reports a similar pattern of change in construction projects in Jinhua, an inland region in Zhejiang. The seventy-year lag between the founding of the Ming (hence the end of an era of civil wars and natural disasters) and the vanishing of local projects contradicts the early Ming economic revival argument. Zhu's coercive policies against local society, rather than the civil wars that immediately preceded the founding of the Ming empire, should be responsible for this decrease in local investment. Because the early Ming economy was a command economy, and because the economic slump drove most farmers out of agricultural commercialization, such concrete data as figures for investment in local projects in the Lower Yangtze are greatly valued for providing a firsthand report of the local economy and society. If further investigation of construction projects in other early Ming rural communities across China also reveals a similar trend, this will strengthen my argument of a substantial decline in the real economy.[67]

The military farm system was the cornerstone of the early Ming command economy, and the whole system was operated against the market mechanism. The farming soldiers were de facto serfs of the state. They were assigned to a locality without choice. Not only the landholdings under cultivation but also the seeds and plow oxen belonged to the state.[68] A radical decline in grain output represents the collapse of the military farming system and by extension the crisis of the command economy. The decline in the military farm outputs came to its lowest point in 1434. It is not a coincidence that Zheng He's voyages ended in 1433. When Zhu Di died in 1424, his successor immediately gave up military expeditions into Mongolia, Burma, and Vietnam, and even planned to move the capital back to Nanjing in order to reduce state expenses on the northern frontier.[69] The Ming state finance was already in such a hopeless position that it could no longer afford the expense necessary to maintain the existing state machinery.

This crisis in the command economy and in state finance did not necessarily lead to an improvement in the private sector in the early Ming economy. Although there could have been opportunities for the private sector if the deterioration in the military farming system had resulted in the release of a large number of laborers and/or amounts of capital in its favor, the span from 1430 to 1450 was a period during which the government still made the utmost effort to strengthen the already-crisis-ridden command economy. In all of the policies on military household registration, promotion of military farms, prohibition of private mining and foreign trade, and adoption of tax captains, there appears to have been no loss of control. In terms of monetary policy, the court in 1425–1426 continued the prohibition of the use of silver in the marketplace in order to force the use of paper notes in transactions, even though the value of the notes had already dropped to as little as 1/50 or 1/100 of their face value.[70] Therefore, it is reasonable to conclude that the 1430–1450 crisis not only damaged the command economy but also worsened the private sector.

Conclusion

In the preceding chapters, I have argued that there was a substantial decline in the living standards in the early Ming period caused by both an economic crisis and anti-market policies. This argument is largely drawn from a quantitative study of real wages. However, due to the huge variances across imperial China, it is still necessary to test a specific macro region. Hence, I have conducted this study of the long-term changes in the Lower Yangtze's economy and living standards.

I argue in this chapter that the course of agricultural development in the Lower Yangtze might be more complicated than that presented by the revisionists. Progress undoubtedly was achieved during the Tang-Song transformation. Not only did the aggregate supply of grain increase in correspondence to population growth, but farm yield per acre probably also substantially increased. It is very likely that if the same was argued for the development during the Ming-Qing transformation, especially the eighteenth-century economic boom, the results would be even more impressive, but strong quantitative evidence would be required as proof.

The revisionists also ignored important changes in the institutional framework, which is the basis for the development of the market economy. The unusually high ratio of land taxes in the early Ming period, for instance, is interpreted by revisionist researchers as direct evidence for increases in agricultural productivity. However, even when one adopts this optimistic estimate, a critical examination of the evidence provided by the revisionists instead suggests a substantial decline in the farmer's household income in the early Ming. The government collected a much larger share of agricultural output from the majority of Jiangnan farmers via land taxes. Hence, the early Ming command economy should be credited as the major factor in causing a decline in living standards.

The Lower Yangtze played a leading role in the fourteenth-century economy; its population comprised some 20 percent of the entire Ming population and about 85 percent of the southern population. Had the early Ming court refrained from adopting anti-market policies, commercialization and urbanization could have been unparalleled in this area due to easy access to markets via water transportation. Yet my comparison based on a combination of recorded data and estimates clearly shows that the living standard declined along with a severe deterioration of the market economy in radical decline. I can find no reason other than the policies of early Ming despotism for this substantial decline in living standards.

Chapter 8

Changes in Agricultural Productivity, 1000–1600

Agriculture formed the main sector of Chinese preindustrial economy and remained largely distant from commercialization. Although in the previous chapters I have explored long-term changes in the market economy, it is still doubtful whether the cycle of market development and changes in living standards I have described were applicable to the agricultural sector and thus had any impact on the livelihoods of the majority of the population. Since the expansion of the Song economy in the eleventh century, as my research has shown, was chiefly driven by both rapid population growth and wide market development, this question should be discussed at two different levels. First, one should make certain whether such rapid growth in the Chinese population caused a decline in living standards. Second, if the living standards were maintained at a rather higher level during population growth, what would account for this increase in per capita income?

In this chapter, I rely on quantitative evidence to demonstrate two main types of agricultural changes in China from 1000 to 1500. The first change was a gradual shift toward intensive farming from 1000 onward, which not only made it possible for great expansion in the Song population but also laid the foundation for improving living standards. The second change refers to the retreat to extensive agriculture in the three centuries after the Mongol conquest, which caused a prolonged period of relatively low living standards among the majority of Chinese farmers until 1550.

Agricultural productivity can be directly measured by the comparison of a couple of key criteria: the ratio between seeds and harvested outputs, the return and capital investments, the increase in per capita farm outputs and in per labor unit farm outputs. For the same token, the shift away from intensive farming would cause a decline in agricultural productivity. Given scanty information devoted to agriculture, unfortunately none of these assessments can be achieved here. I focus instead on the different patterns of farming practice to account for the rise and decline in agricultural productivity. For instance, the introduction of intensive farming increased agricultural outputs at both the national and per capita level. The increasing food demand from population growth was largely met by both increases in the acreage of cultivated land and improvements in farm yields per acre. Commercialization in agriculture achieved an unprecedented level of success toward the end of the eleventh century. A large amount of grain output was provided for urban consumption via the market. The rising trend in grain prices encouraged farmers to improve agricultural productivity by widely exploiting new farming methods and increasing labor and capital inputs.

From the mid-thirteenth century, agricultural advancement ceased along with severe depopulation and deurbanization that occurred in many areas of China. In addition to the damage caused by military conflicts, strong evidence indicates that forced migration, the military farm system, and a self-sufficient mode that the early Ming court promoted all contributed to the wholesale retreat to extensive farming in the north. They further led to a prolonged period of relatively low living standards among the majority of Chinese farmers until 1580.

Rising Grain Production in per Capita and a Boom in Total Households from 980 to 1195

In the century from 980 to 1195, registered Chinese aggregate households increased from 6,418,500 to 19,526,273.[1] The entire Chinese population probably numbered between 98 and 117 million. This threefold increase achieved within a century was probably one of the fastest growth rates on record, if not the only one, in the last millennium of imperial China.[2] This extraordinary phenomenon begs one to explore the dynamic relationship between this rapid population growth and the grain production pattern.

As noted earlier, the possibilities of increasing grain production come from two sources: the expansion of land acreage under cultivation and the increase of farm yields per acre. To test the first possibility, we only need to collect available acreage data and examine their reliability. For the second, one has to know improvements in farm yield per acre is largely based on a shift in farming practice that requires substantial increases in labor and capital inputs per acre. This kind of measurement is, however, difficult to conduct because the lack of statistical evidence forces a researcher to rely on piecemeal temporary observations and scanty rent records. Yet, the fact that per acre farm yields and farm inputs varied greatly in a traditional economy makes any general estimation of farm yields per acre uncertain. Besides direct observations, economists have observed an interdependent relationship between population growth, acreage and farm yields. If one assumes, as Perkins does, a stable level for per capita grain output over a period, then an average yield figure can be readily obtained from the following formula: yield = (per capita grain output) x population/ cultivated acreage in grain.

For the aggregate population growth achieved in the first century of the Song dynasty, to maintain the same level of grain consumption or achieve an even higher level over the course of the century, aggregate grain outputs must keep abreast with or surpass that of population growth. Table 8-1a and 8-1b provide important information that one can use to reach estimate reach estimates of farm yields per acre during the eleventh century. Assuming that per capita grain consumption remains constant, my calculation suggests that about two-thirds of the increased grain outputs was made possible by the expanded acreage of cultivated farmland, and the remaining one-third was due to the increase in farm yields per acre.

Although Perkins already persuasively explained the enormous increase in Chinese population in the six centuries from 1368 to 1968 based on such an assumption, applying this approach to the study of the major trend in long-term changes of grain yields in both the Song and Ming eras is a completely different task. Furthermore, it is necessary

Table 8-1a. Reported aggregate population and acreage, 976–1109 (Song *mu*)

Year	Households*	Index (997 = 100)	Acreage	Index (997 = 100)
976	3,090,504	—	295,332,060	—
997	6,418,500	100	312,525,215	100
1021	8,677,677	135	524,758,432	170
1051	—	—	228,000,000	73
1066	12,917,221	(418) 312 201	440,000,000	142
1083	17,211,713	268	461,455,000	149
1109	20,882,258	325	660,000,000**	190–223

Source: Qi 1987, 58. Qi extracted the data mostly from *Wen Xian Tong Kao.*

*It should be noted that the figures for 976 AD are not appropriate for the comparison because they were made before the reunification in 979, during which certain large areas such as Fujian, Zhejiang, and Shanxi were beyond the jurisdiction of the Song court. The index becomes applicable from the year of 997 AD. In the first report covering the entire population created after the reunification, the registered aggregate households already reached 6,418,500 in 980 AD, among whom 3,625,366 (about 56.5 percent of the total) belonged to the landowning class. But the number of the households soon dropped to 4,132,576 in 997. Cheng Minsheng attributed this unusual decline to the change in policy: for the year 997, the court decided to rank the level of administrative units such as prefectures and counties based on the number of their registered landowning households. Therefore, the total number of the reported 4,132,576 households referred to the landowning households only. For this reason, I use the 980 figure (6,418,500 households) for more accurate comparison.

**Many scholars such as Chao, Hua, and Qi estimated 660 million *shi mu*, thus nearly 800 million Song *mu*, for the acreage at the turn of the century. Nonetheless, this estimate is too large. It is fairly safe to estimate 760 million Song *mu* for the up-bound value of the total acreage, and 560 million Song *mu* for the low-bound value. I, therefore, choose the medium value of 660 million Song *mu* (561 million *mu*) for calculation. For a discussion on the Song acreage estimation, see appendix D.

Table 8-1b. Average per household landholdings, 976–1109 (Song *mu*)

Year	Households	Acreage	Per household landholding	Index (997 = 100)
976	3,090,504	295,332,060	96	—
997	6,418,500	312,525,215	49	100
1021	8,677,677	524,758,432	60	122
1051	—	228,000,000	—	—
1066	12,917,221	440,000,000	34	69
1083	17,211,713	461,455,000	27	55
1109	20,882,258	660,000,000	32	65

Source: See Table 8-1a.

to consider the possibility of changes in per capita consumption/income as we conduct a cross-dynastic comparison. In the following, I propose a plausible steady rise in grain yields during the two centuries prior to the Mongol conquest and relate this rise to estimated grain yields per acre in the Ming dynasty. For convenience, I assume five people as the average size of Chinese families in the Song period.[3] Although the Ming land acreage and population data are better preserved, their availability is confined to the early Ming period. Both the population and the land acreage figures in the sixteenth century are estimated without direct evidence and are highly speculative. In comparison to the early Ming population data, the land data is more problematic. The reported acreage of land under cultivation nationwide, for instance, totaled 850 million Ming *mu* in 1393 and 622 million Ming *mu* in 1502. Both err on the side of overestimation. I follow Perkins and Chao to estimate 370, 730,000 *shi mu*, thus 425 million Ming *mu* or 436 million Song *mu*, for land acreage estimates in 1393.[4]

Given many important changes in population density, money stocks, and urbanization as revealed in preceding chapters, the assumption of a stable per capita grain consumption, though convenient for scholars to reach an estimate of average per acre farm outputs, certainly sounds unrealistic. Here I put to the test two hypotheses of long-term changes in per capita grain consumption in Song and Ming eras. Hypothesis A is drawn from Perkins's previous studies that suggests a stable level in per capita grain output in China over many centuries and chooses 570 *jin* (thus 5.67 Song *shi* or 286 kg) of husked grain for that level.[5] Hypothesis B is the assumption drawn from my calculation of GDP that per capita consumption/income was not always stable but changed substantially during the six centuries from 997 to 1581.

Following the per capita grain output, thus 570 *jin*, provided by Hypothesis A, and given the available information presented in Table 8-1, one may arrive at an estimate of the yields per cultivated acre over the century through the following calculation:

997   570 x 5 x 6,418,500/312,525,215 Song *mu* = 59 *jin* per *shi mu*
Or 0.58 Song *shi* per Song *mu*

1021   570 x 5x 8,677,677/524,758,432 Song *mu* = 48 *jin* per *shi mu*
0.47 Song *shi* per Song *mu*

1066   570 x 5 x 12,917,221/440,000,000 Song *mu* = 85 *jin* per *shi mu*
Or 0.83 Song *shi* per Song *mu*

1083   570 x 5 x 17,211,713/461,455,000 Song *mu* = 108 *jin* per *shi mu*
Or 1.06 Song *shi* per Song *mu*

1109   570 x 5 x 20,882,258/660,000,000 Song *mu* = 92 *jin* per *shi mu*
Or 0.9 Song *shi* per Song *mu*

1393   570 x 60,545,812/370,730,000 *shi mu* = 93 *jin* per *shi mu*
Or 0.91 Song *shi* per Song *mu*

1581   570 x 150,000,000/740,000,000 *shi mu* = 116 *jin* per *shi mu*
Or 1.13 Song *shi* per Song *mu*

Hypothesis A refers to a slow yet stable increase in per acre yield in the eleventh century. As the aggregate households increased from 6,418,500 to 20,882,258 in roughly a century, to maintain the same level of per capita grain consumption, total farm yields must grow at the same pace. This would mean farm yields per acre must increase from

59 catties/*jin* per *shi mu*, or 0.58 Song *shi* per Song *mu*, to 92 *jin* per *shi mu*, or 0.9 Song *shi* per Song *mu*. This calculation indicates that, given the rather elastic supply of land up to the mid-eleventh century, rapid growth in population could hardly cause a severe decline in living standards even if per acre farm yields only increased slowly.

The estimation on per acre farm yields in 1393 calculated here also shows a substantial difference with Perkins's estimation of the early Ming. In Perkins's approximations on grain yields in 1400, one can also find low estimates across all provinces in the north. Yet his national average estimate reaches 139 *jin* per *shi* mu, far above this estimate. There are a couple of reasons that lead to this variance. I should explain why despite following Perkins's approach in my first estimate I reached a different approximation of 93 *jin* per *shi mu*. First, based on his estimation of China's population falling somewhere between 65 to 80 million in 1400, he chooses 72 million as the middle value in his calculation. Unlike Perkins, who selected 1400 as his benchmark, I chose 1393, a year for which there was a recorded population figure of 60,545,812. Although there are only seven years between the benchmark dates, the population gap is not insignificant. Second, Perkins assumes invariably that grain outputs accounted for 80 percent of the gross value of national income. Although this assumption can be accepted in general, it is inapplicable to the early Ming since a self-sufficient mode of farming prevailed across the country during this unprecedented experiment of a command economy. These two factors together account for the existing variance between Perkins's own estimate and the adjusted estimate. Yet either of them is adequate when we further take into account the decline in per capita grain consumption that took place in the early Ming era.

Unlike Perkins, I have in the preceding chapters suggested that real incomes changed significantly during the centuries from 1000 to 1500. Applying Hypothesis B to the information presented in table 8-1, we find that per capita real income reached a peak in the Song era and then declined dramatically in the fourteenth and fifteenth centuries. In the sixteenth century, living standards in the Lower Yangtze and some coastal areas in Southeast China bounced back to a high level. Although the reconstruction of eleventh-century China's GDP is based on the quantitative measurement of the market economy, which indicates a higher level in per capita real income, the market was only a small portion of the entire economy. The question still remains whether economic growth did occur in the agricultural sector as reflected in the increase of both aggregate and per capita agricultural outputs during the Song era.

To answer this question, however, I must devise a means to measure average farm yields per acre to match the per capita real income I proposed. In chapter 6 of this book, I arrived at a tentative conclusion that per capita real income in late eleventh century was 7.5 *shi* (about 7.5 x 150 = 1,125 catties/*jin*). Since per capita real income (A) is derived from the outcome of GDP divided by the entire population, therefore, it must exceed per capita agricultural outputs (B), not to mention per capita grain outputs (C). My calculation roughly suggests a formula of C = 0.75A, which if applied to the Song case would come to C = 844 catties/*jin*, or a per capita grain output estimated at about 844 catties/*jin*.[6]

Taking this figure into calculation, per acre farm yield should have increased to 1.21 Song *shi*/Song *mu*, in 1066 AD and about 1.30 Song *shi*/Song *mu*, in 1109 AD. By the same token, per acre farm yield in 1581 AD should increase to 1.68 Song *shi*/Song *mu* to match the up-bound value of the eleventh-century standard:

1066	124 catties/*jin* per *shi mu* or about 1.21 Song *shi*/Song *mu*
1109	133 catties/*jin* per *shi mu* or about 1.30 Song *shi*/Song *mu*
1393	138 catties/*jin* per *shi mu* or 1.35 Song *shi* per Song *mu*
1581	171 catties/*jin* per *shi mu* or about 1.68 Song *shi*/Song *mu*

The results stress the plausibility of a higher living standard that could be achieved in the traditional Chinese economy. These averages are potentially realistic estimates when compared with the farm output records of the late nineteenth and twentieth centuries. The national average rice yields in 1958, for instance, reached 463 *jin* per *shi mu* and the average wheat yields 359 *jin* per *shi mu*, about two to three times that of the estimated per acre farm outputs in 1109.[7] The modern reader is reminded that traditional practices, including farming technologies and private ownership of landholdings, remained stable though not static from the eleventh century on.[8] Therefore, the estimate of 133 catties/*jin* per *shi mu* in 1109 falls within the safe range of agricultural productivity that traditional technology could have supported. One should not, however, take for granted the estimate for the year 1393, which was 138 catties/*jin* per *shi mu*, a figure surpassing that in 1109. Given the huge decline in the Chinese population and the devastation in many areas, such a high level of farm yields per acre was unlikely.

Few technical or institutional obstacles existed in the Song eras to hinder this growth rate in agricultural productivity. By the eleventh and twelfth centuries, most of the premechanized technological innovations and farming equipment were already available, and the cultivation of small private farms became the dominant practice in rural China. The incentives from increases in aggregate demands significantly contributed to the growth in farm outputs beyond the subsistent level of agriculture. Rapid developments in monetization, water transportation, urbanization, and consumption pushed up Song grain prices, which quadrupled in one and a half centuries. Therefore, peasants must have strived to maximize farm outputs by increasing labor and capital investments to meet rising market demands and enjoy the revenue gained from the sales of grain.[9]

Yet the plausibility should be also tested in the temporal and regional contexts before turning to a full examination of the shift toward intensive farming. Data from table 8-2 indicates that the share of landholdings in North, East, and Central China amounted to 81.4 percent of the total reported acreage in 1081. Therefore, improvements in living standards that occurred in these regions should have profoundly altered the path of agricultural history—even a moderate increase in per acre farm outputs across these

Table 8-2. Distribution of cultivated land in China, 1081–1957 (1,000 *shi mu*)

Year	NW	N	E	C	SE	SW	Total
1081	38,000	83,630	117,890	88,750	12,150	19,680	360,170
	10.6%	24.1%	32.7%	24.6%	3.4%	5.5%	100%
1400	22,680	128,800	111,570	56,510	41,790	9,380	370,730
	6.1%	34.7%	30.1%	15.2%	11.3%	2.5%	100%
1957	157,000	468,000	214,000	165,000	118,000	116,000	1,238,000
	12.7%	37.8%	37.8%	13.3%	1.5%	9.4%	100%

Source: Perkins 1969, table B.8. in appendix B.

regions would significantly boost the nation's total outputs. The remaining question is whether one can find sufficient quantitative evidence to prove this point.

The acreage and households data in 1080 support the possibility of a higher living standard based on rapid agricultural development in major farming areas. In North China, except for Hedonglu (modern Shanxi), the approximate average farm size per landowning household reached at least 30 *mu*. In Kaifeng and its western neighboring area, the number went beyond 60 *mu*. It should be noted that the average family-owned farm size in Jingdonglu (modern Shandong) was surprisingly low, about 19 *mu*. This abnormally low average is most likely due to underreporting as opposed to other unusual causes. To illustrate this point, let us compare the figures between the Northern Song and early Ming. The total acreage of cultivated land in the early Ming is estimated at a minimum of 5.5 million *mu*, more than double the size recorded in 1080.[10] Yet, there were only 720, 282 registered households in Shandong in 1391, just less than half of the 1,370,800 registered households in the Northern Song. The low land average in 1080 was obviously the result of underreporting. It seems that at least a half was concealed from the land registration.[11] Instead, I suggest 35 to 45 *mu* for the average family-owned farm size in Shandong in the 1080s.

In this section, I demonstrated how eleventh-century agriculture could have plausibly developed to such a level that per capita grain outputs would match the estimated real income I proposed in chapter 6 of this book. In the next section, I will explore how urbanization, population growth, and improvements in transportation during the

Table 8-3. Regional populations and acreages, 1077–1080 (Song *mu*)

Region	Households	Landowning households	Acreage	Per household landholding	Per landowning household landholding
N. Kaifeng	256,504	171,324	11,333,167	44.2	66.2
N. Jingdonglu	1,370,800	817,983	25,828,460	18.8	31.6
N. Jingxilu	651,742	383,226	25,562,638	39.2	66.7
N. Hebeilu	984,195	765,130	26,956,008	27.4	35.2
NW. Shaanxi	962,318	697,967	44,529,838	46.3	63.8
N. Hedonglu	450,869	383,148	10,226,730	22.7	26.7
E. Huainanlu	1,079,054	723,784	96,868,420	89.8	133.8
E. Liangzhelu	1,830,096	1,446,406	36,247,756	19.8	25.1
E. Jiangnanlu	1,073,760	902,261	42,160,447	39.3	46.7
C.W. Jiangnanlu	1,365,533	871,720	45,046,689	33	51.7
C.S. Jinghulu	811,057	456,431	32,426,796	40	71
C.N. Jinghulu	589,302	350,593	25,898,129	43.9	73.9
SE. Fujianlu	992,087	645,267	11,091,453	11.2	17.2
SW. Chengdufulu	771,533	574,630	21,606,258	28	37.6
SW. Zhizhoulu	?	261,585	—	—	—
SW. Lizhoulu	301,991	179,835	1,178,105	3.9	6.6
Kuizhoulu	320,847	68,375	224,497	0.7	3.3
SE. Guangnanlu	565,534	347,459	3,118,518	5.5	9
SE.-W. Guangnanlu	242,109	163,418	12,452	0.05	0.08

Source: Zhongshu beidui jiyi jiaozhu, juan 2, 58–65.

Tang-Song transformation gave rise to the commercialization of agriculture, which in turn drove the Chinese peasantry to move toward intensive farming. If my previously estimated middle-size farm ranging between 30 to 50 Song *mu* was largely achieved, then the stage was set for Chinese farmers to maximize their interests by producing surplus food for an expanding market. However, this progress could not have happened until there was a shift in agricultural practice from extensive farming to intensive farming.

The Path toward Intensive Farming

Intensive farming refers to an increase in labor and capital inputs invested per acre of landholdings that would significantly improve farm outputs. It includes two types of measures: The first is closely related to improved seeds, changing cropping patterns, and new crops; the second is capital formation such as farming implements, water control, and fertilizer. There are plenty of primary sources that demonstrate progress in every aspect that led to the spread of intensive farming in the five centuries after the Rebellion. Since most of these records are qualitative and are distributed unevenly in time and space, it is thus impossible to reconstruct a chain of causative steps that traces the progression from a certain point of origin. Scholars have made various arguments that focus on the development in a specific period or location, but none of these were accepted by the majority. Fortunately my task here is much simpler.

To support my hypothesis that a higher living standard was achieved in the agricultural sector, I only venture to clearly demonstrate how intensive farming was likely practiced by many mid-eleventh-century farmers. In the following pages, I draw evidence from a variety of primary sources such as treatises, historical data, and institutional background to portray an image of North China's agricultural development in the eleventh century. Japanese and Chinese agronomists have already made respectable studies on agricultural development in Tang and Song eras, and I will rely on their work to outline the major innovations achieved century by century.

The increase in grain production can be achieved by introducing improved seeds, changing cropping patterns, and new crops. Wheat and rice, in comparison to other staple crops, were most capable of producing higher per acre outputs. But they were also more dependent on existing irrigation techniques and the variety of seeds available at the time. Early studies demonstrate the introduction of a large number of improved seeds in the Southern Song period that were studied and catalogued according to the appropriate topography of the land, type of soil, and climate.[12] Yet Ho's study emphasizes the extensive dissemination of early-ripening rice at the opening of the eleventh century, which he credits as "the first long-range revolution in land utilization and food production in China during the last millennium." The well-known events highlighting this revolution were the Song administration's first import of this rice seed from Champa to Fujian, and then in 1012, 30,000 bushels were sent to farmers in the Lower Yangtze and the Huai River regions.[13]

Contrary to Ho's rapid dissemination theory, later research supports a rather gradual adoption of the application of improved seeds that was first described by Sudo. An important consideration in estimating the impact improved seeds had on the rate of growth in productivity is the pace at which new varieties were discovered and adopted.[14] As shown by table 8-4, new evidence found in local gazetteers supports this more complicated story in the Lower Yangtze.

Table 8-4. New varieties of rice recorded in gazetteers, 1174–1274

Regions	Variety	New variety	Region	Variety	New variety
Changshu	35	35	Hangzhou	10	8
Kunshan	34	21	Shaoxing	56	46
Wuxian	2	0	Mingzhou (Ningbo)	25	19
Wuxing	9	0	Dinghai	25	0
Haiyan	9	0	Taizhou	33	23
She county	32	29	Fuzhou	31	26
Total	301	212			

Source: You 1999a, 199.

What underlay the spread of the early ripening seeds and played a key role in driving up total grain outputs was the domination of wheat and rice as the most essential staple crops in the centuries after the Rebellion.[15] From earlier periods, although both rice and wheat were planted in China, millet was the main crop that claimed the largest share of grain consumption. Even though the productivity of rice and wheat per acre was much higher than millet, they could not have exerted much impact until enough labor and capital could be invested. The availability of the latter factors was the signal that intensive farming could finally take root. As the majority of the Chinese population was concentrated in the north during the early Song, the demand for grain in the south was not so great as to require intensive farming, and rice was still grown in an extensive way.

Before the introduction of intensive farming, millet was undoubtedly the preferred staple crop over wheat and rice. Millet required less rainfall during the growing season and could maintain low but stable yields regardless of drought and sterile land. The dominant position of millet was clearly documented in the Tang regulations on the *zu-yong-diao* taxation and grain storage. In fact, the word *zu* literally means a 2 *shi* millet tax duty levied on each male adult per year. Even up to the eve of the Rebellion, millet was considered the standard payment among grain taxes.[16] In 628 AD, the court decided to establish the benevolent granaries (*yicang*) across the country as a relief effort in times of drought and famine. This policy required farmers to pay millet at the rate of 0.02 *shi* per *mu*. Only in the south was rice admitted as a substitution.[17] In 749, the court estimated that there were about 0.2 billion *shi* of grain preserved in this type of government store.[18] All the imperial granaries near Chang'an and Luoyang, the two capital cities, also preserved a huge amount of millet. In the winter of 798, the court ordered the imperial granary to lend 0.42 million *shi* of millet to the local administration for famine relief.[19]

However, after the Rebellion, especially toward the eleventh century, pushed by population growth and market development, farmers overwhelmingly changed to wheat and rice cultivation that proved to exceed millet output by a large margin.[20] This cropping pattern favored double cropping and the extension of high-yield staple crops. Double cropping of rice in the south is difficult to manage for a farmer. In the north, this term actually refers to a two-year, three-crop rotation on the same plot of land: Wheat or barley was grown in the winter, followed in the summer by millet, rapeseed, or beans. However, it is unlikely that the contribution of double cropping to grain outputs in late eleventh- and twelfth-century China was significant.[21] Extension of high-yield staple crops meant both the extension of rice growing further northward and the extension of wheat planting into the south. The predominance of wheat and rice cultivation can be seen in government directives. The Song administration, for instance, encouraged farmers south of the Huai River to grow wheat in the land inappropriate for rice growing. Meanwhile, rice was not only intensively grown in the south, it was also planted throughout the north wherever the water supply was sufficient.[22]

Besides improved seeds and new crops, the formation of a moderate-size farm is the cornerstone of improving agricultural productivity. This development was directly related to the new practice of using ox plows that perfectly served the needs of a family-owned farm. The origin of intensive farming can be traced back to the Western Han dynasty (206 BC–9 AD). The Han emperor promoted agricultural farming with great enthusiasm. He sent officials to advertise the benefits of using ox plows and forming small landholdings to enhance farm yields per acre. This kind of plow required two oxen to draft and three people to manage in order to efficiently cultivate a farm of 500 mu. Yet an ordinary family could hardly afford such an ox plow team.[23] Irrigation projects were also carried out across the Han empire but were concentrated around the capital district and the vicinity of large cities.[24] Thus, despite imperial effort, agriculture in the Han dynasty generally remained extensive. After the collapse of the Han empire in 220 CE, the nomadic conquest of North China left many areas severely depopulated during the subsequent centuries. Although the plow underwent monumental development in the fourth and fifth centuries, intensive farming was undoubtedly an impractical option as land supply was rich while labor became scanty.[25]

As briefly demonstrated in table 8-5, it was during the Tang-Song transformation that various conditions were realized to make ox plow farming techniques more suitable for family-owned farms. The Northern Song figures approximate the ideal ratio between ox, labor, and farm size that set the stage for intensive farming. The advancement of the ox plow is no less important than the making of the iron plow in improving farm yields per acre; however, the former largely depended on whether and how the social

Table 8-5. Evolution plow-farming in China, 51 BC–1000 AD

Dynasty	Number of oxen	Number of laborers	Cultivated land per team
Han (51 BC–220 AD)	2	3 (4–6)	500 mu available for seed plow only
Northern Wei (386–534)	2	6	120 mu
High Tang (737)	2 (A)	5	240–300 mu
Late Tang (880)	1 (B) 1	1–2 1	120–150 mu 75 mu
Northern Song (1000)	1	1–2	30–50 mu

Sources: Osawa 1996, 94–99; Li Bozhong 1990, 231–233; Yang 2001a.

and economic conditions favored a single family farm in the rural economy. In addition to improved seeds and better farming techniques and equipment, the success of intensive farming involved other factors, such as the recognition and protection of private land-holding rights, adequate population density, the rising trend in grain prices, bigger profits from increased grain outputs based on market demand, and most importantly, the number of family-owned cattle.[26] Both the wide application of the ox plow that was compatible with moderate-size farms and an increase in the number of draft animals per capita, or even per unit of cultivated area, contributed significantly to rising farm yields. Assuming the marginal product of labor power was higher than the capital outlay on draft animals, an increase in the average number of animals per capita would presumably have raised per capita grain output.

Rural capital formation also played a role more crucial than improved seeds and the cropping pattern in advancing intensive farming.[27] The factors discussed here are farm implements and draft animals, water control construction, and natural fertilizers. As I have discussed in chapter 7, irrigation projects, such as the water control construction in the south, were essential for rice growing in certain regions. Likewise, wheat planting in the north relied heavily on irrigation projects as the uneven distribution of rainfall concentrated in the summer.[28] Nishijima's study reveals the rise of wheat planting in North China after the Rebellion, a development that course was probably more uneven than he expected due to insufficient irrigation projects until the mid-eleventh century.[29] Shortage in water supply rather than low temperature was the main obstacle to the spread of rice growing in the north.[30] Nonetheless, the data on irrigation projects seems to be better preserved in historical records compared to any other rural capital formation and hence is more useful in a comparative study of agricultural development in traditional China.

Various national surveys conducted by some scholars clearly point to the unprecedented development during the Song era (see table 8-6). From 50,000 projects listed in various gazetteers, Perkins has collected about 5,000 with clearly indicated dates of construction.[31] The number of irrigation projects completed in the eleventh and twelfth centuries was about two and half times that of the total built before 800 AD. It is worth noting that this rate of development could be a gross underestimation, since nearly 85 percent of the irrigation projects recorded in the Song era were concentrated in Southeast and East China. This indicates a bias in documenting similar projects implemented in

Table 8-6. Number of water-control projects in imperial China

Region	pre-9th	10th–12th	13th	14th	15th	16th	17th	18th	19th
Northwest	6	12	1	2	9	28	6	78	92
North	43	40	30	53	65	200	84	186	32
East	168	315	93	448	157	314	291	128	9
Central	50	62	21	52	91	361	85	116	131
Southeast	27	353	43	106	101	88	53	115	34
Southwest	19	10	6	5	31	83	61	195	96
Total	313	792	194	666	454	1,074	580	818	394

Source: Perkins 1969, 61.

North and Central China.[32] The preserved Song gazetteers account for only a small fraction of Song gazetteers with known titles, and most of them are from Jiangnan, Zhejiang, and Fujian. In comparison, the number of sixteenth-century irrigation projects in regions other than East and Southeast China amounted to 672, about five and half times that in the Song era. Therefore, an adjustment can be made to the Song records based on the number of water-control projects recorded in the sixteenth century for that in the Song era (except for East and Southeast China). This amounts to 1,340 in total across all regions under the Song, a peak record in Perkins's survey.

Despite inadequate records documenting all construction in every region period by period, the evidence still support the thesis of robust eleventh-century agricultural development. As Perkins points out,

> [F]rom the tenth century through the thirteenth centuries, most of this construction was confined to five provinces of east and southeast China. This concentration is not surprising, since these provinces contained nearly half of China's population in the Sung [Song] period and most other rice-growing areas, except possibly Szechwan (SW), were only sparsely settled at that time.[33]

The introduction of fertilizer is one of the most important factors among rural capital formation. It became widely used in growing staple crops in the north during the centuries after the Rebellion, which marked the transition toward intensive farming.[34] The most important textual evidence comes from a supplementary note (zashuo) to Qimin yaoshu. This introduction advocates for intensive farming without reservation:

> Whenever one manages his farm, he should consider the limit of what he can do. It is better to cultivate a small lot rather than one that is too big. . . . If a lot of landholding was sterile, the farmer should immediately add fertilizer to the lot.[35]

The introduction addresses an important method that had prevailed for many centuries in North China for the making of domestic fertilizer:

> After a farmer harvests the crops in the autumn, he should collect all the grain husks and crop stems and store them in a place. Every day, the farmer should distribute a certain amount of these resources underneath the cattle, about three inches thick. After a night kept under the cattle, this can be recollected in the morning and piled up in a place.
>
> Following this approach day by day, one can expect about thirty wagons of domestic-made fertilizer made available out of a couple of oxen over the course of the season. He, then, can use them at the dawn of the new year. It is estimated each mu of land costs five wagons of fertilizer. The total amount of domestic-made fertilizer can cover 6 mu altogether.[36]

Qimin yaoshu is a classical text in Chinese agronomy. The extant version of Qimin yaoshu was published in the eleventh century, and the spread of the domestic-fertilizer-making method in North China should be no later than this publication date. *Qimin yaoshu* is a classical text in Chinese agronomy. Jia Sixie, the author of *Qimin yaoshu*, who was a well-known scholar in the Northern Wei (386–543), made scanty reference to using fertilizer in growing staple crops in his book. This omission implies the dominance of extensive farming such as fallow and the raising of cattle and sheep in his time.[37] Based on textual study, most scholars believe the *zashuo* that addresses the fertilizer method was written much later and was subsequently added to the original text.[38] In 1020, about five centuries after Jia wrote his book, the Song emperor Zhenzong ordered the imperial library to print this famous treatise to promote agriculture across the country. Although it is difficult to tell when exactly this method was invented or promulgated, there is little doubt that by the mid-eleventh century this method of making domestic fertilizer was already widely adopted.

Agricultural Decline in North China

The Mongol conquest of China marked a turning point in Chinese population history. The man to land ratio should have been greatly improved in the succeeding two centuries as the number of registered households fell to a very low point. Yet the expansion of the average family farm did not lead to an increase in rural household income. In chapter 6 I have proposed a substantial decline in the living standard caused by the real crisis in the early Ming economy. Per capita real income in 1420 is estimated to be 3.8 *shi* of rice, about half of that in 1121. The crisis itself was complicated and had diversified sources: ecological deterioration, deserted villages and cultivated lands caused by military conflicts, plagues and depopulation, and the rise of a command economy. Such a severe decline in the real income should be closely associated with the decline in farm outputs at both aggregate and per capita levels. I follow Perkins's approach to arrive at an estimate of 93 *jin* per *shi mu*, or 0.91 Song *shi* per Song *mu*, for per acre farm yields in 1393.[39] As noted earlier, Perkins probably underestimated the early Ming acreage due to a misunderstanding of the institutional change and the consequent deterioration in farming practice. He already recognized that the prevailing pattern of private landownership, farming technology, and capital inputs in late imperial China owed its origin to the Tang-Song transformation and assumed it had remained stable in the late fourteenth century. Meanwhile, his assumption on constant per capita consumption might not apply to the early Ming.[40] Meanwhile, his assumption on constant per capita consumption might not apply to the early Ming.

In this section, I test my per capita real income hypothesis on the early Ming grain output per acre and per household. First, given that the self-sufficient mode of farming dominated the early Ming economy, it is reasonable to assume that grain production accounted for 90 percent of the total national income. Second, if we follow Perkins's suggestion of 500 to 600 *jin* (250–300 kg) in his calculation of per capita farm outputs, a minimum level of subsistence output should be set at 400 *jin*.[41] Now comparing what I estimated for the early Ming—3.8 *shi* of rice per capita, about 5.7 Song *shi* or 513 *jin* of grain—with Perkins's estimate, I find my estimate still falls within the narrow range of what Perkins suggests and clearly above the level of minimum subsistence. Further, we can adopt the adjusted estimate of land acreage to reach per acre grain outputs and compare it with that based on Perkins's land estimate. Using Perkins's land estimate, the early Ming grain outputs per acre can be calculated through the following formula:

1393   513 x 60,545,812/370,730,000 = 84 *jin* per *shi mu* = 0.56 *shi* per *shi mu*
Or 0.82 Song *shi* per Song *mu*

The estimated 84 *jin* per *shi mu* was the lowest among all the estimated per acre farm yields after 1066 but still higher than that of the tenth century. If we adopt 444,876,000 *shi mu*, the adjusted estimate, the result will be 70 *jin* per *shi mu*, equivalent of 0.47 *shi* per *shi mu* or 0.68 Song *shi* per Song *mu*. This can be used as the low-bound value of per acre grain output in 1393 and still higher than that in 1021 calculated earlier in this chapter. Nonetheless, my estimate, 70–84 *jin* per *shi mu* is substantially lower than any available estimate. The 1393 grain output by my calculation clearly marked a decline when compared with agricultural development in the twelfth century. Further analysis is required to determine whether this low estimate of grain yield is a reasonable guess.

Here we face two different estimates of per acre grain yield: 93–139 *jin* per *shi mu* or 70–84 *jin* per *shi mu*. The first estimate comes from the assumption of stable per capita grain consumption during the Song-Yuan-Ming transition. The high-bound value of the first estimate, 139 *jin* per *shi mu*, is made by Perkins himself. As noted before, I follow Perkins's approach with minor revisions to reach 93 *jin* per *shi mu*, which can be taken as the low-bound value. Then I follow my own estimate, 70–84 *jin* per *shi mu* and the narrow range between the low-bound and up-bound value is chiefly related to different estimation of early Ming land acreage.

The real issue for my discussion is what happened to the economic status of the early Ming agricultural sector rather than the different assumptions on per capita grain consumption.[42] Therefore, my primary concern is to explore whether a severe decline in farm yields per acre actually took place across the country around 1400. In chapters 3 and 6, I have argued for a substantial decline in the living standards of the early Ming people at two levels: the decline in real wages, especially in soldiers' wages, and an even more radical decline in per capita estimated money stock. Supported by detailed documentation, I demonstrated in chapter 7 a severe decline in household income in Jiangnan immediately after the first Ming emperor enforced his land policies. The decline in rural household income is of extreme importance because the Lower Yangtze was not only the most agriculturally advanced area in thirteenth- and fourteenth-century China but was also the economic foundation for early Ming state power. As Perkins notes, during the first half century of the Ming dynasty, "about half of the total population of the entire empire was within 200 to 300 miles of the capital," which was then located in Jiangnan.[43] However, the decline in the living standard of Jiangnan did not necessarily mean a fall in farm outputs per acre. This decline was rather caused by a huge increase in land taxes that seriously overburdened local farmers. The average farm size in Suzhou and Songjiang, for instance, was mostly around 20 *mu*, and the estimated yields reach 1.5 to 2.0 Song *shi* per *mu*, which apparently was above that of 1100.

But the cultivated land in the Lower Yangtze, especially in Jiangnan, accounted for only less than one-tenth of the reported acreage in 1393.[44] The majority of the cultivated acreage in 1400 was concentrated in depopulated areas. People who tilled such land were either soldiers or forced migrants who had no economic incentives; neither farming tools nor draft animals were provided to meet the basic farming necessities. As most rural households were expected to cultivate nearly 100 *mu* with poor facilities, a meager return that barely supported the family was an unavoidable outcome. This dev-astating scenario not only haunted farmers in the north, as Perkins's estimates already reveal, but also struck farmers in many areas in Central and East China. Consequently, an unusually low national average in farm yields per acre was likely to have occurred as the early Ming economy generated a regression to extensive agriculture.

Therefore, the much higher recorded farm yields per *mu* in Jiangnan weigh little in forming the national average; it is rather the average farm yields in Central and North China and in other areas outside of Jiangnan that together totaled more than 70 percent of the acreage in 1400. It was the minimal influence of the unique Jiangnan condition against the overwhelming decline throughout the Ming empire that played a decisive role in dragging down the national average grain output. In table 8-7, I present the two sets of estimates made by Perkins and me. When my estimates differ from Perkins's I put them in parenthesis. To be more specific, the variances between Perkins's estimate and mine largely fall in certain areas of Central and East China, such as Hubei, Hunan, Anhui, and Shandong. Given the very low estimated farm output per *mu* in Jiangsu, Anhui, and Hubei (presented in parenthesis), even when I adopt the high record from Jiangnan, my estimated national average is still substantially below Perkins's estimate. In the following

Table 8-7. China's estimated farm yields per acre in 1400 (jin per *shi mu* of cultivated area)

Northwest			
Shaanxi	57–68		
North			
Hebei	45–55	Shanxi	48–57
Shandong	86–103 (40–80)	Henan	44–53
East			
Anhui	105–125 (50–60)	Jiangsu	105–125 (50–80)
Zhejiang	182–218		
Central			
Hubei	146–175 (70–85)	Hunan	146–175 (80–100)
Jiangxi	183–220		
Southeast			
Fujian	185–222	Guangdong	81–97
Guangxi	88–106		
Southwest			
Sichuan	98–117		
National average	139 (86–112)		

Source: Perkins 1969, 17, 19. The figures in parenthesis are the adjustments I made to reflect low yields per acre in theses depopulated areas. I also follow Perkins's approach to reach a national average at the end of the table. I obtain the total grain output by adding up all grains produced at the provinces since the provincial acreages are provided by Perkins already (see table B.8 in Perkins 1969, 229). Then, I derive the national average by dividing this total by the total acreage. This can only be an approximation as we have poor information on grain production in 1400. Nonetheless, my two estimates of 93 *jin* and 84 *jin* per *shi mu* are rather supported by the adjusted outcomes.

pages, I concentrate on population distribution, farming patterns, and low farm yields in support of my estimation of the low averages in these provinces during the early Ming.

The astonishing discrepancy between the distribution of population and that of cultivated land in the early Ming period immediately alerts one to the signs of a substantial retreat from intensive to extensive farming across the Chinese agricultural sector. In table 8-8 I present the most important preserved population and land data in the early Ming still available to modern researchers. While about one half of the total population was living around the capital of Nanjing, the land they cultivated accounted for only a small percentage of the total cultivated acreage recorded. In contrast, at least two-thirds of the cultivated land was located in sparsely populated areas such as North and Central China with the exception of Jiangxi. Therefore, one needs to look beyond the Lower Yangtze to capture a more representative image of early Ming agricultural economy. As Zhu Yuanzhang organized all farmers into the *li*, which in theory comprised of 110 households and functioned as the basic unit of administration and production, the distribution of the *li* across the country and their average size of the cultivated land are important for our understanding of rural settlements and patterns of agriculture. In table 8-8 I present together the different kinds of officially report information, provincial populations, the number of the *li*, and acreages to gain a macroview of the early Ming command system.

From this official perspective, one can clearly tell the existence of the two main patterns of rural settlements based on the different size of the land each *li* tilled. For many rural communities in North and Central China, each *li* had to till the land as large as 20,000 *mu*. In contrast, each *li* would cultivate the land of no more than 6,000 to 8,000 *mu* in the Lower Yangtze, Zhejiang, and Fujian. The dividing line is, in fact, drawn between the immigrant-receiving areas and migrant-exporting areas. Even within Central China, per *li* acreage in Jiangxi was 4,230 *mu*, just close to that of Fujian and Zhejiang, and Jiangxi was well known for outgoing migration of populations in the early Ming. The same story can be told about Shanxi in North China, whose per *li* acreage in Jiangxi was 9,749 *mu*, just double that of the migrant-exporting areas in the south but far smaller than that of the immigrant-receiving areas in the north. Both Henan and Hebei, which received a large number of involuntary migrants from Shanxi, reported per *li* acreage 20 to 50 times the latter. *Nanzhili*, literally, the province directly administered by the central government and comprising of the 24 prefectures across the Yangtze river, is complicated as it was a both immigrant-receiving and migrant-exporting case. Those prefectures located in the north of the Yangtze River such as Yangzhou, Fengyang, and Hui'an are particularly depopulated by wars and floods and became the destination for the forced migrants.

Many researchers are concerned about the enormous size of the early Ming land acreages. The reported national total in 1393 was as large as 850 million *mu*, and the average per household acreage thus reached 80 *mu*. This figure also doubled another reported total in 1391, which was 387 million *mu*. Fujii Hiroshi first attributed this problem to either the overreporting or the printing errors in the documents. The possibility of overreporting is related to certain institutional factors such as early Ming policies of encouraging reclamation, the conversion of different units in the land measurement, and the planned migration movements. As Zhu Yuanzhang eagerly organized the migrants at the national scale to settle at the depopulated areas, the local officials might include

Table 8-8. Distribution of early Ming population, *li* and unadjusted acreage

I. North and Northwest

	Households	No. of *li* (*mu*)	Acreage (*mu*)	Per *li* acreage (*mu*)
Beijing & Hebei	334,792	2,784	58,249,951	20,923
Shandong	753,894	5,618	72,403,562	12,888
Shanxi	595,444	4,294	41,864,248	9,749
Shaanxi	294,526	2,330	31,525,175	13,530
Henan	315,617	2,784	144,946,982	52,064
Subtotal	2,294,273	17,818	348,989,918	19,586

II. East China

	Households	No. of *li* (*mu*)	Acreage (*mu*)	Per *li* acreage (*mu*)
Nanzhili	1,912,833	12,854.5	126,927,452	9,874
Zhejiang	2,138,225	10,869	51,705,151	4,757
Subtotal	4,231,058	23,714.5	178,632,904	7,533

III. Central China

	Households	No. of *li* (*mu*)	Acreage (*mu*)	Per *li* acreage (*mu*)
Hubei & Hunan	775,851	3,072.5	220,217,575	71,674
Jiangxi	1,553,923	10,193	43,118,601	4,230
Subtotal	2,329,774	13,265.5	263,336,176	19,851

IV. Southeast China

	Households	No. of *li* (*mu*)	Acreage (*mu*)	Per *li* acreage (*mu*)
Fujian	815,527	3,537	14,625,969	4,135
Guangdong	675,599	3,409	23,734,056	6,962
Guangxi	211,263	1,138.5	10,240,390	8,995
Subtotal	1,702,389	8,084.5	48,600,415	6,012

V. Southwest China

	Households	No. of *li* (*mu*)	Acreage (*mu*)	Per *li* acreage (*mu*)
Sichuan	215,719	1,324	11,203,256	8,461
Yunnan	59,576	559	—	—
Subtotal	275,295	1,883	11,203,256	5,950
Total	10,652,789	64,854.5	850,762,368	13,118

Sources: Ho 1959, 10; Liang 1980, 208–46, 340–1, 354–55. Both the household numbers and the acreage were based on the records of 1393 and remain unadjusted. The number of *li* and the amounts of land taxes levied were recorded in *Daming yitongzhi*, which was compiled in 1461.

some or all cultivatable waste lands in their annual reports to satisfy the emperor. The risks they were going to face were not high because the court's policies usually waived the new settlers many years from the duty of land taxes. The printing error is used to explain why the numbers of land acreages in Henan and Huguang, the two biggest among many, shall be counted as one-third or even one-tenth of the original size so the adjusted total in 1393 will be much smaller and come close to 400 million *mu*.[45] Although no direct evidence has been found to support the truth of such an assertion, for technical reason many researchers accept the printing error explanation and a downward adjustment of the early Ming acreage becomes common.

However, one needs to pay attention to the historical context of the early Ming state and economy, especially the large-scale involuntary migration and military farms that prevailed in the Hongwu reign. It was this command system that produced such land and population reports. In the above I use the unadjusted figures to calculate average per *li* land acreage only because putting these figures together one can find an official perspective to understand historical contexts. By no means have I agreed on adopting the amount of 850 million *mu* as the real acreage. It would be dangerous to make adjustments without knowing important changes in farming practice caused by the early Ming policies. Chao, for instance, not only uses the adjusted figures but also adopts per capita acreage to reconstruct the different sizes of a family farm in many areas of the late fourteenth century (see table 8-9). I also recalculate certain per capita acreages when I find them inappropriate and put Chao's in parentheses. According to his estimation, if one leaves Hebei aside, per capita acreages varied in a narrow range of 7 to 14 *mu* across North, East, and Northwest China. One can hardly tell the difference between immigrant-receiving and migrant-exporting areas. Per capita acreage in Henan, for instance, was simply lowered to 14.3 *mu*, not much less than Shanxi (10.2 *mu*). Because Chao assumes 3 to 4 *mu* of per capita acreage as the normal pattern in the south, he estimates 7.7 *mu* for Hubei and Hunan of Central China, a figure even lower than Shanxi.

Chao's reconstruction fails to recognize the very difference between the depopulated areas and the densely populated areas in the average size of family landholdings. He makes this reconstruction first based on the average farm size. The registered aggregate households reached 10,654,362, or 59,873,305 individuals, and the reported acreage in 1391 was 366, 771, 549 *mu*. This ratio gives per capita acreage of 6.1 *mu* and average family farm size of about 35 *mu*, a moderate farm size that appealed to intensive farming practices on the surface. Chao thus feels confident to narrow down the variance of family farm size in his estimation. Unfortunately average family farm size calculated at the national level is a misleading economic indicator because it hides the tremendous regional variations during the early Ming era. Table 8-9 shows the acreage in these areas together amounted to 300 to 350 million *mu*, about 60 to 70 percent of the unadjusted national acreage.[46]

Because of the severe loss of population in these areas, a laborer could acquire a lot much larger than he or she could manage. Most of the newly cultivated land was wasteland and inaccessible to irrigation. Consequently, per household landholdings in regions north of the Yangtze River went far beyond a manageable size for a farming family. In Nanzhili, the capital district, one can find manageable farm size prevailing in core areas, such as Suzhou and Songjiang, whereas the average landholding per household reached nearly 200 *mu* in Jiangbei (see table 8-9), the prefectures immediately north of the Yangtze River including Fengyang, Huai'an and Yangzhou. The result was a most

Table 8-9. Variations in per capita acreage, 1393

Province	Cultivated acreage (million mu)	Population (000)	Per capita acreage (mu)
I. Jiangbei area (north of the Yangtze River) in East China			
Jiangbei	70.6 (20.7)	2,096	33.7 (9.9)
II. North and Northwest China			
Hebei	58.2	1,926	30.2
Shandong	72.4	5,255	13.7
Shanxi	41.8	4,072	10.2
Henan	44.9–144.9*	1,912	23–76 (14.3)
Shaanxi	31.5	2,316	13.6
Subtotal	248.8–348.8 (231.4)		
III. Central China			
Hubei & Hunan	220.2 (36.4)	4,702	46.8 (7.7)
Total	850.4 (502.5)		

Source: Chao 1986, 81–82. The numbers in parenthesis are adjustments made by Kang Chao. It should be noted here that Chao gives little explanation of why, for instance, the Jiangbei acreage should be adjusted to such a degree. For further discussion on this issue, see appendix H in this volume.

*The originally reported acreage of Henan in 1393 reaches 144.9 million mu, which is too big to be true. Modern researchers tend to view it as a printing error and adopt 44.9 million mu instead.

complicated administrative unit within which intensive and extensive farming coexisted. Assuming six people for the average family size in early Ming, one can conclude that in Henan and Hebei, the average family farm size was also above 100 *mu*. In Central China the average even reached 200 *mu*.

Although to what extent these unadjusted figures shall be downwardly adjusted still remains an issue, they at least demonstrate that the differences in per capita acreage was exactly caused by the overexpansion of family farm size. This is clearly an important sign of changes in the pattern of farming practice in the early Ming and deserves our attention. It is necessary to look into the institutional perspective as suggested by Fujii when one adjusts the reported acreage of 1393. This land acreage is obviously the outcome of overreporting, nonetheless the total and the provincial breakdowns reveal the way how the early Ming court managed the land cultivation. The government not only promoted the ideal of a self-sufficient economy but also planned grain production in many depopulated areas by arbitrary ways. Extensive farming, as shown in the following, became a dominant pattern in depopulated areas and there were a lot of fallow land that was to be sown by hand in the next year. Whenever the local officials and military commanders were chiefly responsible for land reclamation as exactly happened to the Hongwu reign, they tended to report the totals based on the prevailing examples of average family landholdings provided by the organized military and civilian farms. Under such cases, the official reports included not only the fallow land that was to sown by hand in the next year but also the wasteland that was planned for cultivation. Highlight from this institutional perspective, the overexpansion of family farm size at these new settlements rather implies that the dominant mode of farming practice retreated to extensive farming, which further resulted in the lowest per acre grain outputs since 1000 AD. In the following I use the military farm and other examples to illustrate the connection between involuntary migration, extensive agriculture and the low per acre grain outputs.

The retreat to extensive land cultivation could be traced back to the Jurchen rule in the late twelfth century and became the dominant mode of farming after the Mongol conquest of North China. The process was also closely related to the demonetization of the economy, especially the rise of a command economy. The rise of the military farm system best illustrates this process. In the late twelfth century, in order to maintain their economic and social status, the Jurchen Jin dynasty (1115–1234) energetically enforced military farming in the territory that they conquered in North China. The average farm size owned by each Jurchen household reached 275 *mu*, yet the number of ox plows in 1183 numbered no more than 390,141, roughly just one plows per two household-owned farms.[47] During the Mongol conquest, Kublai Khan exploited the military farm system as an effective means to secure military provision. Later, the success of this policy prompted the future Yuan dynasty ruler to spread it throughout the empire. According to an incomplete official record, in the years between 1262 and 1331, military farms were established in seventy-two prefectural-level administrative units across the country, comprising 227,201 households and 16,454,720 *mu*.[48] Both soldiers and civilian households were employed to farm the land under this system. Table 8-10 shows the regional differences among farm size per household under the Mongol Yuan military farm system, which shows an overall expansion in average farming size per household.

Although the average farm size varied significantly across regions, one can still tell that extensive agriculture prevailed in the severely depopulated areas. Considering 110 households comprised 1 *li* in the early Ming command system, there was a striking

Table 8-10. Average size of the military farms in depopulated areas, 1262–1331

Region	Households	Cultivated land	Average size per household
I. North China			
Hejian	3172	1,298,638 *mu*	409 *mu*
Datong	12,765	700,000 *mu*	55 *mu*
II. East China			
Huai'an	19,909	4,037,666 *mu*	203 *mu*
Yangzhou	1,305	168,815 *mu*	129 *mu*
Luzhou	2,608	337,630 *mu*	129 *mu*
III. Central China			
Nanyang	6,041	1,066,207 *mu*	176 *mu*
De'an	15,340	887,996 *mu*	58 *mu*
IV. Northwest China			
Fengyuan	4,534	468,272 *mu*	103 *mu*
Ganzhou	2,290	116,664 *mu*	51 *mu*
Ningxia	3,004	224,650 *mu*	75 *mu*

Source: Wang Ting 1983, 247–49.

Table 8-11. Distribution and shares of involuntary migrants in China, 1368–1398

Province	Total population	Local population	Percentage	Civilian migrants	Percentage	Military migrants	Percentage
Nanzhili	11,711	8,804	75.2	1,863	15.9	1,044	8.9
Hubei & Hunan	4,525	2,811	62.1	1,333	29.5	381	8.4
Sichuan	1,800	900	50.0	800	44.4	100	5.6
Shandong	5,943	3,870	65.1	1,869	31.5	204	3.4
Beijing & Hebei	2,763	1,659	60.0	848	30.7	256	9.3
Henan	2,859	1,670	58.4	934	32.7	255	8.9
Total	29,601	19,714	66.6	7,648	25.8	2,240	7.6

Source: Cao 1997, 472.

similarity between the average military farm size reported in table 8-10 and that of 1393 in table 8-8. Under the Yuan military system, the average family farm size in Huai'an and Yangzhou, two regions to the north of the river, reached 203 *mu* and 129 *mu*, respectively. In 1393, average family farm size in the same regions, such as Yangzhou, was reported to be 192 *mu*. This perpetuated overstretching of family farm size across centuries implies that the extensive farming mode, including the practice of fallowing land and cultivation by hand, prevailed in these regions from 1200 to 1500 due to the extremely low man to land ratio.

For the first century of the Ming history, there is little doubt that agriculture in North and Central China was steered by a command economy. Zhu Yuanzhang greatly promoted the military farm system and imposed forced migration on the national scale to support this system. According to Cao's recent research, the involuntary migrants, including both civilian migrants and military households, amounted to 7.65 million in the Hongwu reign alone (see table 8-11). For the national population in 1393, he estimates that for every 6.4 persons, one was an involuntary migrant.[49] This is surely an unprecedented massive planned migration throughout Chinese history. Moreover, the number of involuntary migrants could be much higher if we were to focus on the regional level. As the majority of these involuntary migrants were being sent to depopulated areas, especially in North and Central China, the portion of migrants could reach more than one-third of the total population of the migrant-receiving places. Table 8-12 serves as an example that in certain regions, such as the many prefectures and counties of Henan, migrant villages greatly outnumbered native villages in rural communities.

Forced migration was designed to reclaim land in areas devastated by wars and natural disasters. For military migrants including soldiers and their families, cultivating

Table 8-12. Numbers of immigrant villages in Henan's rural communities

Type of village	Weihui	Shangqiu	Nanyang	Xiping
Local villages	34	39	62	4
Immigrant villages	85	64	144	23
Total	119	103	206	27

Source: Cao 1997, 247, 253, 259, 262.

military farms was their major task. Forced civilian migrants were also organized into a kind of *lijia* system for land cultivation. The basic unit for both systems was known as *tun*, and the local conditions made extensive farming an unavoidable practice. Both military and civilian migrants had no economic incentives to cultivate land in these remote areas. There was no infrastructure to support rural settlements. Water transportation was devastated and could not support long-distance trade. Only a small number of rural markets existed, and these were as sparsely distributed as per county in many places.[50]

What further exacerbated these migrant farmers was that the government provided very little subsidy. In 1403, the second Ming emperor, Zhu Di, issued an order to organize exiled prisoners into the *lijia* system in the north. Under this order, each male adult would be given 300 *guan* of *baochao* and each *li* of residents were expected to share five oxen.[51] Although the edict permitted capable households to purchase additional oxen, one can hardly imagine that many migrant households had such luxury.[52] For many of them, it is more likely that all 110 households within the same *li* shared the five oxen. Given that each adult male was eligible for at least 50 *mu* of farmland without an upper limit and assuming an average of one and a half male adults per household, the land to ox ratio could reach one ox per 1,650 *mu*. Such a ratio renders the ox-plow farming technique completely meaningless under these circumstances.

The lack of ox plows apparently characterized extensive agriculture in fourteenth- and fifteenth-century China. A national survey based on direct evidence is reported in table 8-12. While Zhu Yuanzhang urgently promoted military farms, he was also concerned with the availability of farming tools and draft animals. In response, the military commanders at the local level were required to report to the court the exact number of draft animals. The national total of oxen recorded in the 1393 amounted to over 25 million. Yet when equally divided by the acreage of all military farms, the per ox average landholdings was as large as 93 *mu*. For Central China, Henan and Shaanxi, the average was much higher. It should be noted that the acreage quotas I report in table 8-13 came from official data that probably dated from the Hongzhi reign (1488–1505), when the military farm system was in decline. This total acreage was likely much smaller than that around 1400. Therefore, it is safe to estimate that per ox landholdings in the early Ming military farm system should be at least 100 *mu*. If the absence of ox plows did indeed last throughout half of the Ming dynasty, this would be another factor contributing to a general decline in agriculture.

Low farm yields were the inevitable outcome of extensive agriculture. To be more specific, in the nearly three centuries since the Mongol conquest, average per acre farm yields in North China declined substantially. This declining trend is already observed by modern researchers. As one can see from table 8-14, per acre farm yields in the north probably did not regain the high level of productivity achieved during the eleventh century until 1550. In contrast to Perkins's estimate of 139 *jin* per *shi mu*, I have estimated 84 to 93 *jin* per *shi mu* for farm yields at the national level in 1393. Yet these reported estimates in North China are just half of my estimated national average. Only when combined with high farm yields per acre in the south, especially in the Lower Yangtze, is such an average estimate as mine more likely to be possible at the national level. By proposing a national average estimate three times higher than per acre farm yields in many areas in China, Perkins is surely overoptimistic about agricultural production in the early Ming period.

Table 8-13. Distribution of plow oxen in the military farms

Region	No. of oxen	Acreage (mu)	Landholdings per ox (mu)
I. East China			
Nanzhili	71,450	3,640,983	51
Zhejiang	2,246	227,441	101
II. Manchuria			
	13,878	1,238,600	89
III. North China			
Beijing & Hebei	64,387	1,640,276	25
Shanxi	26,958	2,308,128	86
Shaanxi	27,467	4,245,672	155
Shandong	5,999	206,000	34
Henan	36,319	3,639,017	100
IV. Central China			
Jiangxi	499	562,341	1,126
Hubei & Hunan	4,667	1,131,525	242
V. Southeast China			
Fujian	—	538,137	—
Guangdong	482	7,233	15
Guangxi	950	51,340	54
VI. Southwest China			
Sichuan	8,190	659,000*	80
Yunnan	15,284	1,087,743	71
Guizhou	5,272	933,929	177
Total	255,664	24,024,460	93

Source: Wang Yuquan 1965, 103, 122–123. The number of oxen in 1393 was originally recorded in *MHD*. The recorded acreages of military farms should date from the Hongzhi reign. The total acreage in the 1390s was estimated to be at least 40 million *mu.*

*The original figure for Sichuan was 65,954,526 *mu*, which seems too large to be true. Wang Yuquan attributed it to a conversion error in traditional Chinese standard units, which enlarged the real acreage by one hundred times (1965, 103–106).

Nonetheless, given such extremely incomplete quantitative information, the afore-mentioned estimation is hardly decisive. The publication of agricultural treatises came to a peak in Yuan China, many of which were supported by government funds.[53] Was it possible that after peace returned to North China farmers were able to exploit the technologies that were advocated in the treatises and increase use of fertilizer and other tools?

Change in population density is an important factor that produced the different patterns in farming practice in North China. In table 8-15 I provide a general trend in long-term changes in North China's population density. The figures come from the censuses conducted by the Northern Song, Jurchen, Jin, and Ming administrations over

Table 8-14. Estimated per acre farm yields in North China, 1000–1400

Period	Region	Per mu *farm yields*	Per mu *farm yields* (jin)
11th century	Henan	1.0–1.5 Song *shi*	94–148 *jin*
12th century	Henan	0.8–1.5 Song *shi*	75–141 *jin*
Late 13th century	Shandong	0.1–0.5 Yuan *shi*	13–67 *jin*
15th century	North Hebei & Shanxi	0.3 Ming *shi*	42 *jin*
First half of 16th century	Shandong	0.35–0.7 Ming *shi*	49–98 *jin*
Second half of 16th century	Shandong	0.8 Ming *shi* & below	112 *jin*

Sources: For the Northern Song period, see Hua 1982, 4–5. For the twelfth century, the estimation is derived from a report in 1219 recorded in *Jin shi*, shihuo. Chen & Shi (2007) provide an estimate on North China in the thirteenth century (113). For the fifteenth century, Gao Shouxian reports two typical low farm yield examples, one is on Datong in Shanxi and the other is on North Hebei. Even for harvests years, farm yields did not exceed 0.5 *shi* per *mu* in each case (Gao 2006, 75–76). For per *mu* wheat yields in Puzhou, the most advanced area in Shandong in the sixteenth century, Li Lingfu estimates 100 *jin*, which can be converted into 0.7 *shi* at the rate of 1 *shi* wheat equivalent of 140 catties (*jin*), or 70 kg (Li Lingfu, 198–199). Therefore, after dividing it by half, I take it as the estimated farm yield for other regions in the north.

Table 8-15. Changes in North China's population density, 980–1578 (individuals per sq km)

Region	980s	1102	1207	1393	1578
Henan	36.9	63.9	105.6	19.2	54.0
West S*	32.2	77.8	109.5	23.1	63.3
North S*	36.6	82.6	139.1	35.4	51.7
Hebei	39.7	71.9	141.6	19.7	58.4
Tianjin	15.3	25.1	67.0	17.8	18.0
Beijing	35.3	36.3	146	11.9	42.5
North H**	23.2	42.5	27.4	17.2	32.8
South H**	23.0	55.9	24.8	41.1	35.7
Total	31.3	59.6	93.8	22.2	46.2

*West S indicates West Shandong, and North S indicates North Shandong.

**North H indicates the Anhui and Jiangsu areas north of the Huai River, and South H indicates south of the Huai River in these two provinces.

Sources: Wu 1993b, 256, 262–263; Cao 2000a, 240–246. For the five benchmark years, only the population density in 1393 is recalculated based on Cao Shuji's study of the distribution of population density. The figures for Beijing and Tianjin are those on Beiping and Hejian in Cao's table. For Shandong and the Huai River areas, I recalculate the density of population based on the information on population and geographical size provided in Cao's table.

centuries. As noted in chapters 1 and 2, the population data reported after 1400 were not reliable because the purpose of the report shifted from enumerating rural households to preserving the quota of taxation. This shift caused stagnation and even "decline" in the reported populations at local levels. But a few provinces in the north are an exception to this general rule. Aggregate recorded households of the five northern provinces, for instance, increased from roughly 15.5 million in 1393 to 26.7 million in 1542. Hence I also adopt the 1578 figure for comparison further on.[54] With few exceptions, the population density in 1393 was the lowest in six centuries. This lowest record is compatible with my argument regarding the prevalence of extensive agriculture in the north.

For the fourteenth century, an important document was provided by Hu Zhiyu (1227–1293), who had been appointed as a high local official in the Shandong area, among other local posts. In a treatise, Hu criticized the inefficiency of extensive farming that was prevailing in the north. A farmer, according to his description, was cultivating 200 to 300 *mu* with only one aged draft animal. What he harvested was no more than 0.2 Yuan *shi* (26 *jin*) of unhusked grain per *mu*.[55] Hu's criticism is a persuasive portrait of the deplorable conditions in late thirteenth-century agriculture.

Direct evidence found in the *Mingshilu* reveals that military farms were among those farming units that generated the lowest per acre farm yields. Fortunately for modern researchers, as military farms formed the cornerstone of the early Ming command economy, local military commanders were required to file reports three times a year after growing seeds concerning heading and flowering, ripening, and harvesting.[56] The extant farm output data collected from *Mingshilu* provide firsthand information on how much a soldier could produce. An order issued in 1403 established the rule for the appraisal of performance by commanders and soldiers on the farm. A farming soldier, according to this order, had to submit all his grain output to the official granary before he could be assigned a certain portion (usually a half) of the submitted grain. The 1403 order established 24 *shi* of grain as the production quota that a farming soldier should meet. This standard suggests a negative relationship between military farm size and farm yields per acre: As farm size increased, the return decreased (see table 8-16). As most soldiers in North and Central China cultivated farmland no smaller than 50 to 100 *mu*, it clearly implies a fairly low average farm yield per *mu*, likely 0.2 to 0.4 *shi* per *mu*.

The grain production by military farms during the Yongle reign has often been cited to prove the economic revival around 1400.[57] A series of data on aggregate grain output produced by military farms is already made available in Wang Yuquan's monographic

Table 8-16. Estimated per acre farm yields in relation to military farm size in 1403–1450

Farm size	Total grain outputs	Farm yield per mu
12	24	2.0
20	24	1.2
30	24	0.8
50	24	0.48
100	24	0.24

Source: Wang 1965, 130.

research. The grain output of military farms reached 23 million *shi* of rice in 1403 (see table 8-17), which was two-thirds the total amount of land taxes for that year. The two gains, the land taxes collected from civilian households and the grain contributed by military farms, added up to over 50 million *shi*. This marks the apex of Ming state revenue over nearly three hundred years. The output declined rapidly thereafter, dropping to one-fifth in only two decades. In the mid-fifteenth century, it dropped to only one-tenth of the 1403 level.

The peak of annual grain outputs in 1403 should be the result of an important change in the aforementioned policy. This high-quota policy of 24 *shi* of grain impoverished farming soldiers. In a new edict issued in 1422, the amount of state payment was reduced by half. Thus, a farming soldier was required to submit 18 *shi*. In 1437, the court finally decided a soldier only has to turn in state payment to the granary, thus 6 *shi*.[58] By then, a farming soldier would submit just one-third of what he had submitted forty years before. The adjustments in the quota policy were made in response to the falling capacity of farming soldiers in meeting the farming plan, but this measure still meant they fell behind the pace. In 1409, just seven years after Zhu Di issued the quota edict, the reported outputs already declined by half. Bad weather, the lack of farming tools and plow oxen, the involuntary status of soldiers, and the inefficiency in the military organization all contributed to the instability of grain production.

It was not surprising that the national average of grain output per acre from military farms was low. In 1403, about 22,467,700 *shi* of grain were reported as the total outputs of military farms, the second highest record throughout Ming history. Following the high-quota policy (thus 24 *shi* of grain per farming soldier), it should require 935,450 soldiers to provide such an output. The size of the military forces then was estimated to be 1,200,000 and above. Over 70 percent of these soldiers were assigned to military farms.[59] This would lead to an estimate of at least 0.85 million soldiers who routinely tilled the land. The required number of farming soldiers in 1403 matches this estimate; this fact indicates the military farming policy was enforced to all troops in the empire. If one follows Wang's estimate to assume 60 to 90 million *mu* for the total acreage of cultivated military farms, then per acre yields were 0.2 to 0.4 *shi* grain per *mu*.[60] This national average comes close to the lowest estimates of per acre farm yields in North China under the Mongol rule. Ming military farms simply followed the extensive farming practices that were prevailing in the fourteenth century.

Table 8-17. Annual grain output from military farms
(rice in *shi*)

Year	Output	Index	Year	Output	Index
1403	23,450,799	100	1434	1,776,141	8
1409	12,229,600	52	1439	2,792,146	12
1413	9,109,110	39	1444	2,762,777	12
1423	5,171,218	22	1450	2,660,673	11
1428	5,552,057	24			

Source: Wang 1965, 213–214.

The rise and fall of the military farm system can be used as an index to gauge the extent to which extensive agriculture was practiced in Ming China. The peak of military farm production occurred during the first seventy years of Ming history. Yet by the Zhengtong reign it had declined to around 2.7 million *shi*. The lowest record was in the Zhengde reign (1506–1520), when annual grain outputs plunged to merely 1 million *shi*, just less than 5 percent of that in 1403.[61] At the turn of the sixteenth century, the military farm system and the command economy had become obsolete, and many rural households were more and more connected to the market. Yet, the economy of sixteenth-century Ming China shows significant regional variances in market development. Although population growth in the north was obvious, trade was largely confined to the areas along the Grand Canal and exerted limited influence on the majority of the rural population. When the Single Whip reform, a movement that promoted a conversion of labor services into money payments, began to spread in the Lower Yangtze and the coastal areas in Fujian and Guangdong in the mid-sixteenth century, the local officials in the north had no desire to follow their southern peers. Even when the court decisively enforced the reform policies in the northern provinces in the 1580s, many local gentry still complained that this fiscal reform was impractical because most rural households had few opportunities to own money. Therefore, one should not overestimate economic development in North China during the sixteenth century, especially when comparing it with that of the eleventh and twelfth century.

The general trend in long-term changes of population density in North China demonstrates the above point. As shown in table 8-15, the substantial increase in North China's population from 1393 to 1578 is evident. Yet when compared with the difference between 980 to 1207, the density of population in the late sixteenth century still fell behind. One important factor was the depopulation in the early Ming period. With few exceptions, the population density in 1393 was the lowest in six centuries. This is compatible with my argument about the prevalence of extensive agriculture in the north. Based on this comparison, one can hardly expect intensive farming in 1580 would regain its pre–Mongol conquest position.

Economic development in Henan serves as an important example of the nature of the sixteenth-century economy in the north. Henan was one of the most depopulated provinces in China during the Jin-Yuan-Ming transition, and migrants constituted the majority of the provincial population in the first half of fifteenth century. Given the unlimited land supply, Henan's aggregate households increased from 373,454 in 1391 to 541,387 in 1482, and, after another century, aggregate households increased to 633,067 in 1578. In nearly two centuries, the provincial population almost doubled. Such rapid growth should be treated as a recovery rather than a transformation of farming practice into intensive farming. This point is suggested by demographic evidence: The population density in 1393 was 19.2 people per square kilometer. In comparison, population density in Zhejiang at the same time was 110.4 people per square kilometer.[62] Even after this century-long rapid growth, Henan's population was still less than that in 1102, which is estimated to be around 5 to 6 million.[63] The peak population density record before the Mongol conquest was 105.6 people per square km in 1207, much higher than the late Ming record, which was 54 people per square kilometer in 1578.

When one examines market development in Henan for the first two centuries of the Ming dynasty, progress looks much more uncertain in comparison to its past performance in the Song era. Its once well-developed water transport network was ruined entirely in the early Ming period with the exception of those to the north of the Ji River. In the years prior to 1580, one can hardly find any important commercial center within Henan as the Grand Canal shifted its course away from this province. The underdevelopment of markets and urbanization would have provided little chance for the commercialization in agriculture.

A careful examination of changes in the average family farm size over one and a half centuries also raises doubts about whether farming practice in Henan ever shifted from extensive agriculture into intensive farming by 1550. Just as Henan's households increased from 373,754 in 1391 to 621,653 in 1552, average family farm size actually expanded beyond 100 *mu* (table 8-18). This increasing trend in average family farm size, however, is largely a calculation error for two reasons: First, the large family size underrates population growth; and second, Ma's estimate of cultivated acreage in 1391 is incorrect as I have mentioned in the note to table 8-18. If one follows Ho's explanation, hence 449 million *mu* for Henan's acreage in the 1390s, then the trend in average family farm size would shrink slightly rather than expand substantially. Nonetheless, the extremely large average family farm size represented in Ho's estimate still reveals the dominance of extensive agriculture. Since fallow land should have accounted for one-third or one-half of the total farmland, the average per acre farm yield was probably even lower if fallow land was included. In this case, grain production was obviously below the level of the late eleventh century. Even if we assume that per acre grain yields doubled, say, from 0.3 to 0.4 *shi* to 0.6 to 0.8 *shi*, and average family farm size indeed declined substantially by 1550, the highest level of farm yields per acre was still in a range similar to that of the eleventh century.

Table 8-18. Changes in Henan's population and acreage, 1391–1608

Year (1,000 mu)	Acreage	Index	Population (household)	Index	Average family farm size (mu)	Index
1391	449,000	100	373,454	100	73 (126)	100
1412	27,708	101	382,499	102	72	57
1482	28,698	104	541,387	145	53	58
1502	41,629	151	—	—	—	—
1552	73,615	267	621,353	166	118	128
1578	74,158	269	633,067	170	117	127
1608	95,418	347	—	—	—	—

Source: Ma Xueqin 1997, 51, 66. For Henan's population in the Ming era, Cao Shuji notes that average family size continued to increase from 6.9 in 1393 to 8.9 in 1482. He attributes this to the errors made by the household survey after 1400 (2000, 203–204). Therefore, the household growth represented here was slower than that of total individuals. For Henan's acreage in the Hongwu reign, the original figure reported in the Ming official history was 144,947,000 *mu*, which seems too unbelievably high. Ho identifies it as a printing error and suggests 44,947,000 *mu* instead (Ho 1988, 101). The acreage of 27,351,000 *mu* reported in the table is estimated by Ma Xueqin based on a faulty assumption that per capita landholdings in the 1390s was 14.1 *mu*. Ma Xueqing estimates the acreage of 27,351,000 mu for 1391 (Ma 1997, 35–39). I follow Ho to revise it as 449,000,000 mu.

Conclusion

This chapter aims to test the impact of the expansion and contraction in the market on agriculture. The core point is whether the market could play an important role in improving agricultural productivity in late imperial China. The Malthusian theory predicts an increase in farming output per head and subsequently a rise in the living standard around 1400 due to the extremely low man to land ratio. Meanwhile, my observation suggests that the economy then was highly demonetized due to the anti-market policies implemented by the Ming court. A command system was established to replace the market mechanism right after the Ming dynasty was founded. Under such circumstances, one may wonder whether a sharp decline in the monetization of the economy could faithfully indicate and even cause a decline in agricultural productivity.

Focusing on the rural economy, I have measured changes in agricultural productivity in North China in this chapter. My assessment is chiefly based on the distinction between the two farming patterns and the ways in which important changes in population density and aggregate demands influenced the adoption of one pattern or the other. The comparison of farming pattern and household production capacity between Song and Ming eras provides a tentative yet persuasive conclusion that the market played a role no less important than technology in agricultural development. Technically speaking, per capita real income in the Song era, when converted into average farm yield per acre, is a sound and *realistic* estimate. To match the estimated per capita income standard, my calculation suggests that average per acre farm yields must be at least 133 *jin* per *shi mu* or 1.3 Song *shi* per Song *mu* in 1109. This result is not only significantly below the ideal per *mu* yields recorded in contemporary agricultural treatises but also far below what the "Song economic revolution" thesis suggests. There is apparently a gap between what the authors of these treatises recommended and how things were in reality. The writings of such treaties should be understood as good theories rather than depictions of reality. Therefore, agricultural development during the centuries between 1000 and 1200 did not actually reach the ceiling, a hypothetical point that some assume marked the limit of what traditional society could achieve due to inadequate technology and knowledge.

A political economy perspective highlights what is missing in the current debate on the living standard in Jiangnan. It reminds the reader that as the Beijing-centered political system was established after the Mongol conquest, China was much less integrated, and the gap between the Lower Yangtze and the north was much greater than ever before. The plagued economy in the north assumes equal weight when we consider whether the Chinese economy around 1400 was still gloomy or already set in motion to overcome the crisis. In this sense, the fact that agriculture in the early Ming retreated to extensive farming is even more revealing. Contrary to the Malthusian view, it was not the lack of land supply that hindered progress in agriculture in China prior to 1600. In 1393 the man to land ratio reached the lowest point in the last millennium of imperial China, and estimated per acre farm yields also fell to the lowest point.

The study of extensive agriculture in the early Ming provides a definitive answer to the comparison between the market-based system and the command economy system. No doubt most of the early Ming story in North China was about how the court managed to operate a command economy. Military farms and involuntary migration provided the majority of labor forces that were needed to reclaim the land. The reconstruction of the economy and rural communities in North, Northwest, and Central China followed the state's scheme, and the *lijia* was the basic unit in organizing forced migrants. In most cases the market disappeared from this state-planned reconstruction. Yet this whole scheme was proven a low efficiency program. Extensive agriculture led to low farm yields. Although the estimation varies from region to region, average per acre farm yields in North China declined substantially in the nearly three centuries after the Mongol conquest. The rise of a command economy in the early Ming is chiefly responsible for the sharp decline in the standard of living.

Conclusion

This book compares two unique economic phenomena that occurred during the last millennium in Chinese history: the Song market economy, which was arguably the largest in the eleventh-century world, and the Ming command economy, which was the grandest attempt of its kind in the fourteenth- and fifteenth-century world. The study of the history of the Chinese market economy challenges a researcher to comprehensively assess market performance based on quantitative evidence. Therefore, I have devoted much effort to collecting macroeconomic data to accomplish such a goal. In contrast to the current wisdom that only emphasizes either social changes or agricultural productivity, I have extended my survey to include a broad range of economic activities. The demand-based data (indirect taxes, wages, prices, money stocks, consumption, and so on), which is the major finding among my collected sources, can be collectively interpreted to indicate long-term trends and structural linkages in the Chinese preindustrial economy and further allow us to check the observation on economic changes seen from the supply side (mainly agriculture).

The shift from a market economy toward a command economy is the most drastic change that steered the course of events between 1000 and 1500. The comparison of the market in the Song and Ming eras is essentially an evaluation of preindustrial China's market economy. The market not only plays a determining role in economic development but also significantly benefits the majority of the population by sustaining a higher standard of living, such as real wages for laborers, the average income of farmers, and the local projects in transportation and education. During the market expansion in the century from 980 to 1080, the proportion of tenant farmers in rural households, for instance, declined noticeably. Demolishing the market, therefore, entails a great loss of freedom for commoners and triggers a substantial decline in their income.

Studying Chinese Historical National Incomes

The study of the important changes in the economy between the Song and Ming eras is by nature an inquiry into the past. The preindustrial economic and demographic data that a historian is able to obtain could hardly satisfy social scientists studying the modern world. There are many key gaps in the available materials and much of the information is not particularly reliable. Any conclusion drawn from this study is necessarily tentative. However, quantitative analysis helps to clarify historical assumptions and highlights certain data sources that may lead to the reinterpretation and reexamination of events in the past from a different perspective. I am able to derive consistent conclusions from each data source and among different sources, a major step toward establishing a persuasive explanation.

My research aims to provide an estimation of some key variables, such as the size of domestic markets, structures of taxes and per capita tax burden, farm yields per acre, real wages, and population growth, all of which were vital factors engineering changes in Chinese historical national incomes. These estimates could be subject to a considerable margin of error without affecting the basic conclusions reached here. Based on these estimates, I hope to establish a probable framework showing long-term changes in preindustrial China's market economy that invites scholars to further explore the dynamic experiences in Chinese history.

Within the framework that links data analysis with historical inquiry, I examine the performance of the market economy in the Song and Ming eras, focusing on five major aspects: agricultural productivity, population growth, GDP per capita and real wages, and the degree of commercialization. For each aspect, I discern the directions, trends, and patterns in economic terms as depicted by available data and present these findings against their appropriate institutional backgrounds as well as important events in each period.

Market Development in the Eleventh Century

Quantitative analysis clearly indicates that China was significantly transformed by market development during the eleventh century. Fortunately, the Song data in 1077–1080 is the richest and most reliable among all the extant data. Each data category from this period describes rapid development in a related but different economic aspect, and together they point to the rising tide in the overall economy. The population data in the Northern Song show a swift growth in the number of households across the country. The 1077 commercial tax data prove rapid progress achieved in the Song waterway system, one that should be understood in the context of the transformation of the economy and political power during the transitional period after the Rebellion. Water transport played a vital role for the development of the Song mercantile state. Other market-based data, such as the reconstruction of the size of the domestic market in 1077, the estimated money stock for the Northern Song period, and the estimated volumes of major commodities in eleventh-century trade, all demonstrate that the performance of the market economy in the eleventh century reached an unprecedentedly high level of success.

I further measured the performance of the economy in the Song and Ming eras in terms of living standards. My comparison indicates that Song low-ranking soldiers and manual laborers enjoyed a strikingly higher level of living standards in the eleventh century than their early Ming counterparts. In light of market developments in the eleventh century, I explored the plausibility that development in agriculture, the main sector of traditional Chinese economy, might have achieved a comparable high level to other sectors. In the century from 980 to 1109, China's population increased more than threefold, and the acreage of cultivated land expanded to roughly double its original size. To meet the increasing demands for foodstuff from population growth and urbanization, the estimated average farm yield per *mu* in 1109 must have reached 133 *jin* per *shi mu*, or about 1.30 Song *shi* per Song *mu*.

The rise of intensive farming laid a solid foundation for the increase of aggregate grain outputs in the eleventh century. Yet the development toward intensive farming must be viewed from both the supply perspective and the demand perspective. From the former, the expansion in the acreage of cultivated land and increases in per acre farm yields was achieved by technical innovations, migration, and rural capital formation. From the demand perspective, the development in urbanization, water transportation, as well as population growth, together fostered the improvement in agricultural productivity.

The Retreat to a Command Economy

This book portrays China's intriguing retreat from a prosperous market economy to a stifling command economy in the century between 1368 and 1450. As political and institutional historians clearly demonstrated, the early Ming economic system was characterized by the *lijia* system, involuntary migration, and military farms. The rich and reliable early Ming economic data allowed me to investigate thoroughly the operation of this command economy and accurately assess the enduring negative effects it had on the Ming economy.

The demonetization of the economy was the immediate result of the dominance of the command economy. The early Ming land tax data reveal the prevalence of payment in kind in public finance until the dawn of the sixteenth century. I also used the commercial tax in 1381 to reconstruct the size of the early Ming domestic market and compare it with that in 1077. The early Ming state registered only 10.6 million households, barely two-thirds of the Song population in 1078. The gap in the size of domestic markets between 1077 and 1381 was even greater than that of aggregate households. In monetary terms, trade volume per household in the mid-eleventh century was about seven to ten times that of the 1380s. The early Ming court implemented various policies—such as nonmonetary payments, forced migrations, mandatory duties, and the employment of corvée laborers in public projects—to remove the market mechanism that had played an active role in Chinese economy. The land contracts collected from Huizhou reveal that the economy of the Lower Yangtze, once the most advanced region, retreated to a barter economy at the dawn of the fifteenth century. Contrary to their predecessors, early Ming farmers lived in a world with little need for money.

As a counterfactual example to the Song market-based development, the early Ming command economy demonstrates the costly economic consequences of anti-market policies. I begin the inter-period comparison of living standards by reporting the long-term changes in soldiers' real wages. Data on wages indicate that Song soldiers were paid much more than Ming soldiers, who received consistently low wages for two-thirds of the Ming dynasty from the 1360s to 1550s. Based on the data on soldier wages, I make the estimates for national income and real income per capita in 1080, 1400, and 1580. The estimated real income per capita in 1400 was only a half of the year 1080. Meanwhile, the share of early Ming tax revenues in total national income doubled that of the eleventh century. In other words, a typical farmer, despite earning less income, was forced to pay much higher taxes or bear the burden of heavy corvée labor. This clearly illustrates the coercive nature of early Ming rule and the dire economic consequences that followed.

Evidence from agriculture also supports my observation on the low real wages in the early Ming. Although agricultural productivity in Jiangnan maintained a high level in the early Ming period, farmers were deprived the right to produce for the market, which necessarily reduced a large portion of their household income. Moreover, the early Ming court, by confiscating the landholdings of big landlords and merchants, acquired an overwhelmingly dominant share of the land in Jiangnan. Solid evidence points to a fact that this share of *guantian* in arable land was much higher than that of the land reform enforced by the Communist Party in the roughly same region in 1951–1952. The Ming government then increased the land taxes by eight to ten times higher than before. This policy adversely affected farmers' real income.

In regions other than the Lower Yangtze, especially in the depopulated areas in North and Central China, the early Ming court established a command economy chiefly based on military farms and involuntary migrations. Neither farming tools nor draft animals were provided to meet the basic farming necessities. Many rural households earned barely enough for subsistence since they were expected to cultivate nearly 100 *mu* with poor facilities. Consequently, as the national average in farm yields per acre reached an unusually low level, the early Ming economy generated a regression toward extensive agriculture.

China in the Sixteenth Century

The comparison between the Song market economy and the early Ming command economy strongly suggests that the market could play an important role in determining economic development. It also could significantly benefit the majority of the population by sustaining a higher standard of living. The demolishing of the market would mean a great loss of freedom for commoners and would trigger a substantial decline in their income.

My interpretation became more persuasive as I show how the collapse of the Ming command economy coincided with the recovery of prices and the reemergence of a vibrant market. The resurgence of the market economy in the sixteenth century is thus an important and welcoming turning point for the Ming state and the common people. But the central issue here is whether the appearance of this market economy is, as mainstream scholars in China and Japan would like to claim, an unprecedented development in imperial China. Although the extant data are insufficient to resolve this question definitively, my research suggests a possible alternative in understanding this resurgence not as a new development but as a recovery of a once vibrant market economy from the eleventh century. To name just a few examples, prior to 1580, long-distance trade was still confined to the Grand Canal, Gan River, and the Lower Yangtze region. Money stock per capita still remained at a low level. Deflation prevailed in many regions. In contrast, the eleventh- and eighteenth-century economies are more comparable: Both periods witnessed an economic expansion that went along with a sizeable growth in the population and a rise in prices owing to increases in money supply and business transactions. Therefore, in the context of the comparison between eleventh- and fifteenth-century economies, the progress in sixteenth-century China may be described as a delayed recovery of the market economy rather than a new phase toward proto-capitalism. The importance of the early Ming regime can never be stressed enough when we try to understand the background of the resurgence of the market economy in the sixteenth century.

A General Guide to Chinese Economic
Data Sources in the Song and Ming Eras

As a quantitative study of the Chinese market economy, this book endeavors to provide a wide array of empirical data in the Song and Ming eras. It includes eight appendices that cover all major economic fields at the macro level. I believe this collection of quantitative information not only provides a solid foundation for current research but will also benefit other researchers who are interested in Chinese economic history or general subjects, such as the role of the market in preindustrial society.

Organization of the Appendices

Most of the Chinese economic data are collected from government-compiled records. Organized thematically into three groups, each appendix addresses a single issue and is supported by Song and Ming economic data placed side by side.

The first group includes appendices A, C, and H, and focuses on the theme of agriculture. It starts with population data, the most important and richest among the data sources, followed by data on Chinese land and farm yields. The last appendix in this group contains data on involuntary migrations and military farms in the early Ming. Viewed together, these three appendices offer a comprehensive understanding of long-term changes that occurred in China's agriculture over six centuries.

The second group is comprised of appendices B, C, and G, which are focused on the market. It includes data concerning changes in prices and money supplies, water routes, and estimated values of major goods in domestic markets. Together they present a comprehensive view of the market economy while each offers detailed analysis of a different aspect. An important assumption behind the juxtaposition of these data is that the size of China's domestic markets should be estimated from different perspectives. When the estimates are comparable enough to provide supportive information, then the approximated outcome will be more acceptable.

The third group deals with preindustrial national income data, which are presented in appendices E and F. The real wage appendix comprises a series of data on a variety of professionals such as artisans, clerks, and students. The most important one is the military wage. In appendix F I present all relevant information and basic calculations for estimating Chinese historical incomes. The most important information is the national income in the nineteenth century estimated by Chang Chung-li. Song historians' studies on social stratification also provide relevant information.

Major Data Sources

The major data sources used in this study to support the comparison of the market economy in the Song and Ming eras concentrates on two periods: the eleventh century and the first hundred years of the Ming dynasty. Quantitative evidence is the foundation of economic analysis. There are certain data that cover a much longer period and even extend into the seventeenth century and provide quantitative information on a specific field. But official reports on population and acreage of land are unreliable after the fifteenth century, which makes it difficult for macroeconomic analysis.

A unique contribution made by this book is the rudimentary yet systematic treatment of Song economic data. The Song data will be presented together with data from the other dynasties and examined for internal consistency. However, it is necessary to first address the primary sources of Song data and their historical contexts as many modern researchers are still unfamiliar with them.

Although extant Song data is probably one-fifth or one-tenth of the amount of Ming data, the quality of the former surpasses the latter. Most of the Song data come from *Song huiyao jigao*, a most important collection of Song official documents and financial data. The *Wenxian tongkao* and *Xu zizhi tongjian changbian*, which were both written based on primary sources and official archives, are equally important to historians of the Song. The nature of the Song data is closely related to the capacity of the state to tax the market. As discussed in chapter 2, indirect taxation was the major source of state revenues. For this reason, household registration in the Song era allowed for free migration and imposed no direct tax burdens on a household through registration. This policy greatly reduced any incentive to avoid official population registration. Therefore, most of the extant records of Song aggregate households look like a normal pattern that was characterized by gradual yet steady growth over a long period. Such internal consistency proves Song population data trustworthy. The land data, on the other hand, were much more problematic because immediately upon registration of any land, the landowner would be taxed accordingly. That is why contemporary officials and literati were often critical of the unfair distribution of land taxes caused by underreporting. In comparison with the collection of land taxes in rural communities, the study of long-distance trade and the urban economy based on commercial taxes is much likely to present a more accurate picture since the indirect tax is a hidden tax collected directly from merchants, who in turn charged customers by including the tax amount in the price when selling goods to consumers. Resistance to paying taxes was much weaker here than that of paying direct taxes. This made it much easier for tax officers to collect taxes as they faced only a small number of merchants instead of millions of consumers. In the case of the commercial taxes in the eleventh century, modern researchers would rather focus on the distribution of the more than two thousand tax stations in China and how they functioned with regard to commercialization of the economy.

Early Ming data are relatively rich and largely preserved in the *Mingshilu* (Veritable Records of the Ming), the imperial annals that recorded the day-to-day events that were important for the Ming dynasty. Information provided in the *Mingshilu* and other primary sources, such as the *Zhusi zhizhang* and *MHD*, have now become invaluable evidence for studying the Chinese economy in the late fourteenth and early fifteenth centuries. We know from these data that during the first century of the Ming dynasty, the emperors turned the entire empire into a command economy. All the people, regardless of their circumstances were organized into a *lijia* system and needed to report to the government routinely.

The value of the early Ming data has already been widely recognized largely due to the important work carried out by Ho and Perkins. Ho's work (1959) indicates the high quality of the 1393 census but discredits all the population returns in the succeeding centuries because they reflected changes in fiscal units rather than reports on real population. Based on Ho's research, Perkins further examined the key economic data in the early Ming period. He exploited a wide range of primary and secondary sources and made great efforts to reconstruct the Ming acreage and population information at both national and provincial levels. Consequently, researchers can confidently argue that through their work, the economic data on the early Ming command economy are already proven to be reliable. By following this line of thought, I have contributed some new information on military farms, forced migration, and the barter economy during this period.

Perkins's systematic examination of early Ming data opens the door for the study of the Chinese economy prior to 1368 since, whenever possible, he also extended his examination to the preceding and succeeding periods to confirm the internal consistency of the data. For instance, he exploited both aggregate households and acreage in the eleventh century to examine the internal linkage between the Song and early Ming data. His observations reveal the enduring impact of the Mongol conquest on Sichuan and many areas in North and Central China. This perspective on the Song-Yuan-Ming transition also greatly helped me in developing a comprehensive understanding of the economy after 1200. Without this perspective, a Song-Ming comparison would have lacked historical contexts. Data on the sixteenth-century economy lack both quality and quantity with the exception of land tax data. Both Perkins and Ho remarked on the major deficiencies of post-1500 economic data. Ho, in particular, attributed this deterioration in data quality to the adoption of fixed quotas. Along with the decline of the command economy, the Ming government was no longer interested in economic administration. Fixed quotas were widely adopted in taxation and household registration, which rendered official data irrelevant to what really took place. Although the economy was vibrant in this century, rarely would one be able to find useful information in official documents on market development that date to this period.

The only exception is the monetization in land taxes, especially the conversion of labor services into cash payment in the latter half of the sixteenth century. In many gazetteers, modern researchers will find detailed reports on various conversion rates and a huge decline in payment-in-kind taxes. It can be assumed that farmers must have had easy access to the market; otherwise, one can hardly imagine how they could have paid taxes in cash. Although this meant a revolutionary change to the early Ming command economy, its innovativeness cannot be overestimated in the context of the entire history of imperial China. A monetized public finance system was already firmly established as early as the Tang-Song transformation. By the mid-eleventh century, the majority of state tax revenues came from indirect taxation. In contrast, the major source of late Ming tax revenues were land taxes. The awkward inefficiency of the Ming fiscal regime in collecting indirect taxes makes it difficult to study the sixteenth-century market economy in a quantitative way.

1077 Data and Their Original Source

The most important quantitative source for the study of the eleventh-century economy is the annual financial and administrative report prepared by the central fiscal administration. This report not only included information on aggregate households, land acreage, tax revenues, and state budgets but also reported the breakdowns at either the circuit (*lu*) or prefecture level. In most cases, this report dates back to the year of 1077, which greatly facilitates modern researchers in observing macro-economic changes at a specific point in time.

It is confirmed that the Song central administration would routinely prepare this kind of report. The report on the Song state annual budget, which was known as *kuaijilu* and first came into use at the dawn of the eleventh century, was a statement of annual revenues and expenditures supported by statistical figures.[1] None of the Song annual budget report is extant, but fortunately, for 1077, most of the categories and figures in public finance are preserved in the *Song huiyao jigao* and *Wenxian tongkao*, which allows us to gain firsthand information on the sources and structure of state revenues. Modern researchers have speculated that this uniqueness was largely due to the publication and circulation of a book titled *Zhongshu beidui*, which was a collection of the official documents and financial reports prepared by Bi Zhongyan in 1080.[2]

The extant records drawn from the *Zhongshu beidui* primarily covered seventeen subjects:

1. Aggregate households, including the number of landowners and landless people, and their breakdowns at the circuit level in 1080.

2. Acreage of cultivated land and their breakdowns at the circuit level in 1077.

3. The amount of land taxes, including summer and autumn taxes, and their breakdowns at the circuit level in 1077.

4. The amount of mining revenues paid in kind, such as with gold, silver, copper, iron, tin, aluminum, among other metals, and their breakdowns at the circuit level.

5. The amount of textile products, such as silk, silk textiles, and hemp, and their breakdowns at the circuit level.

6. The tributary gold and silver, and silk textiles, during important holidays and imperial ceremonies.

7. The budget for canal transportation, such as planned shipments of grains via the canals, the number of ships built each year, and the salaries paid to the boatmen.

9. The total amount of commercial taxes and the exact quota for all tax stations in the empire, which numbered over two thousand, in 1077. A list of the old quotas was also given to all the tax stations.

10. A short list of all the large and important prefectures and cities that annually contributed to commercial taxes in excess of 5,000 strings in 1077.

11. Liquor monopoly revenues, including revenues made from the four capital cities and those collected from all liquor-monopolized prefectures in 1077.

12. The old quota for the liquor monopoly at local places before 1077 arranged in descending order.

13. Salt monopoly revenues and their breakdowns at local levels in 1079.

14. The total amount of copper and iron coins produced by imperial mints in 1080 and the quota for each mint.

15. Customary taxes collected as payment in kind, such as spices.

16. The *changping* fund in 1076 for famine relief and public projects at the local level.

17. *Mianyi* money for conversion of labor services in 1076 and their breakdowns at the circuit level.

18. Revenues from tax farms across the country in 1076 and their breakdowns at the circuit level.

This single source, which concentrates on a short interval of two to three years, provides the rare chance for modern scholars to obtain a snapshot of the Chinese economy in the eleventh century. Furthermore, the data preservation is beyond expectations, because the data often covered all the prefectures in the empire. In the case of commercial tax collection, the range of the localities even goes down to the level of the township.

Table. Levels and number of fiscal-administrative units in China, 1080

The court and central administration	
Capital (4)	Circuits (*lu*) (23)
Counties (50)	Prefectures (293)
Towns* (38)	Counties (1,185)
	Towns* (682)

Source: *Yuanfeng jiuyuzhi.*

*The towns here are those with tax stations. Therefore, there are fewer of them than the total number of counties. According to the *Yuanfeng jiuyuzhi,* the total number of counties reached 1,235 in 1080. After deducting the number of counties in the districts of the four capitals, I arrived at a number of 1,185 as listed in the right column.

Approaches to Test the Quality of
Chinese Historical Economic Data

Since historical data are imperfect, a researcher needs to tell the useful and acceptable from those poor or unacceptable ones. I have discussed in chapter 2 the nature of Chinese economic data from an institutional perspective and related the data with changes in the tax administration in historical contexts. An examination of the institutional background that generated economic data is imperative before these data can be used to explain historical changes. However, there are other approaches to test the quality of Chinese historical data. A systematic exploration based on different approaches is thus necessary, and Perkins's research has been most important on this issue. In this book, I have adopted the following principles proposed by Perkins to examine the raw data:[3]

1. How much effort was made to complete the investigation, census, or survey? Was there evidence showing serious effort to record all the targeted objects (population, cultivated acreage) throughout the empire, such as setting up the institutions suitable for the task?

2. Are there known errors or biases in the data?

3. Are the published data consistent with known historical events and plausible demographic/economic trends? For estimates, are they consistent with data in other periods and compatible with what we know of Chinese history?

The first principle speaks to an inquiry into historical contexts, which I have earnestly conducted not only in chapter 2 but other chapters whenever necessary. The second and third are about the internal and external consistency check of the dataset, which I am using to validate primary sources in the appendices. In statistics, internal consistency is a measure used to test the reliability of a dataset by examining how the internal parts/items within the dataset can correlate with each other. External consistency check refers to an examination on the correlation between different kinds of relevant primary sources. Guided by these principles, I carefully examine all these data series. Although the examination proves the reliability of the data in discussion, it is evident that their quality varied considerably. The data on the commercial tax in 1077, for instance, is the best one I can find. I thus have used it to reconstruct the size of domestic markets in chapter 3 and the structure of water transportation in eleventh-century China in chapter 4. In comparison, the historical records on farm yields were scattered and mostly inconsistent owing to the unstable nature of agricultural production in preindustrial times. This variance in data quality reminds a researcher to draw conclusions with caution.

Appendix A

Chinese Population Data

Population data is the most important, and luckily, also the richest among the three groups of data.[1] From the Han to the Tang dynasty the government was mostly concerned with household registration. In contrast, land registration was supplementary and unimportant.[2] Yet, studies by Western scholars such as Bielenstein, Ho, and Rawski have raised serious doubts about the quality of Chinese population data in the two millenniums. Ho persuasively demonstrates that the underreporting of rural households prevailed in Ming China due to the tax evasion. From 1393 onward, population records are available for at least 137 years of the 251 years of the Ming period, but this recorded population data covered only part of the entire Ming population and became increasingly irrelevant to real changes. For instance, of all reports, only the populations reported in 1403 and 1506 are slightly larger than those in 1391. The only reliable population returns were those made during the Hongwu reign.[3]

Nor can modern researchers find a way to amend some of the errors in the Ming population data. In her study of the Ming population in Fujian, Evelyn Rawski clearly denies any possibility of "construct[ing] a method which could explain and predict differential success in underreporting."[4] While Rawski's research confirms Ho's argument on Ming populations, the remaining question is whether the Chinese population data of the preceding periods were reliable or not. In the face of the unreliability of the Chinese population data in the sixteenth and seventeenth centuries, Perkins compares changes and distribution of the Chinese population during the Song, Yuan, and early Ming eras to validate the household data prior to 1400.[5] This cross-dynastic study provides a solid foundation for my study of the Chinese economy at the macro level. Nonetheless, Perkins's interpretation can be improved substantially as research in recent decades has provided much more detailed studies on Chinese population data. In this appendix, I focus my investigation chiefly on the Song population data, which Perkins had identified as a main issue in future research.

1.

Perkins makes serious efforts to reconstruct the Chinese historical population prior to 1400. A few of the important question he raises on the data quality include:[6]

1. How difficult was it to count the number of people in China?

2. Were the institutions set up to register the population suitable for the task?

3. Are the published data consistent with known historical events and plausible demographic trends?

Following these three lines of inquiry into the past, one can surely make good sense of the Chinese historical population records. Prior to the establishment of the Ming dynasty in 1368, the Chinese government made serious efforts to register population. The published data are fairly consistent with known historical events such as the Mongol conquest, which caused a great decline in Chinese aggregate households. Furthermore, observed from the household perspective rather than from that of the total recorded "individuals," the trends in demographic changes demonstrated in the extant data are plausible. Because the extant data were made independently by three dynastic powers, the demonstrated consistency in these data strongly suggests the reliability of such population data in projecting the main trend in Chinese demographic changes in the three centuries from 1080 to 1393.[7]

Enumeration of households and individuals were required when Zhu Yuanzhang built up the *lijia* system. The assignment of head-based labor service in particular needed such information. However, enumerating all residents could not be a routine task for the local administration, because it not only incurred huge costs but also confrontation from members of rural communities, who made every effort to avoid the tax burden. In reality the completion of taxation and services at the local level thus followed traditional practice to accept, with certain minor technical adjustments, the formerly reported population figures as the legitimate taxation basis. It had nothing to do with demographic growth that must have taken place during the three centuries. Except for the earliest records, the extant Ming population figures are meaningful only in this fiscal practice.

In chapter 2 of this book, I have argued from the institutional perspective the Song population returns were most trustworthy because population reporting was independent from tax collection. The increase in reported households was not immediately or directly related to increases in taxes. Household growth was rather expected to be one of the most important tasks a local official should achieve during his tenure.[8] It is also clear that the Song court did not ask the local administration to report the total number of family members as there were no tax benefits for the Song administration to do so. These two observations help to explain the seemingly controversial nature in Song population data as demonstrated in table A-1.

For the 84 records of aggregate households in the Song dynasty reported in the table A-1, 48 were produced before the year of 1127 when the Jurchen invasion ended the Kaifeng-centered Northern Song dynasty. For the extant records, the SHY provides the richest information. Of the 48 records that cover the years from 1003 to 1110, 33 are found in the SHY.[9] Except for the SHY, one can also find some records in other official documents such as XZTC, *Song shi*, and *Wenxian tongkao*. The major trend in Northern Song population changes in the eleventh century is clearly indicated by a rise in aggregate households from 6.86 million in 1003 to 20.88 million in 1110 at an average annual growth rate of 1.05 percent. Except for the 1011 figure, which was obviously an error, all other figures show a gradual and smooth pace in population growth. A substantial decline occurred in 1021 as the registered households reduced by 1 million. This unusual change might be related to the weakening of the Song administration during the financial crisis that was caused by the war against the Tangut during the Renzong reign. Hyperinflation was evident in the preserved Song indirect taxation data as well.

Table A-1. Song aggregate households, 1003–1223

Year	Aggregate households	Total numbers	Numbers per household
1003	6,864,160	14,278,040	2.08
1006	7,417,570	16,280,254	2.19
1008	7,908,555	17,803,401	2.25
1009	8,402,537	—	—
1011	133,112* (8,535,649)	541,419 (–)	4.07 (–)
1014	9,055,729	21,996,965	2.43
1015	8,422,403	18,881,930	2.24
1019	8,545,276	19,471,566	2.28
1020	9,716,712	22,717,272	2.34
1021	8,677,677	19,930,230	2.30
1023	9,898,121	25,455,859	2.57
1029	10,162,689	26,054,238	2.56
1031	9,380,807	18,936,066	2.02
1034	10,296,565	26,205,441	2.55
1037	10,663,027	22,482,516	2.11
1038	10,104,290	—	—
1039	10,179,989	20,595,307	2.02
1042	10,307,640	22,926,101	2.22
1045	10,682,947	21,654,163	2.03
1048	10,723,695	21,836,004	2.04
1050	10,747,954	22,057,662	2.05
1053	10,792,705	22,292,861	2.07
1058	10,825,580	22,442,791	2.07
1061	11,091,112	22,683,112	2.05
1063	12,462,317	26,421,651	2.12
1064	12,489,481	28,823,252	2.31
1065	12,904,783	29,077,273	2.25
1066	12,917,221	29,092,185	2.25
1067	14,181,485	—	—
1069	14,414,043	23,068,230	1.6
1072	15,091,560	21,867,852	1.45
1075	15,684,529	23,807,165	1.52
1077	14,245,270	30,807,211	2.16
1078	16,402,631	24,326,123	1.48
1080	16,730,504	23,830,781	1.42
1083	17,211,713	24,969,300	1.45
1086	17,957,092	40,072,606	2.23
1088	18,289,375	32,163,012	1.76
1091	18,655,093	41,492,311	2.22
1094	19,120,921	42,566,243	2.23
1097	19,435,570	43,411,606	2.23
1099	19,715,555	44,364,949	2.25
1100	19,960,812	44,914,991	2.25
1102	20,264,307	45,324,154	2.24
1103	20,524,065	45,981,845	2.24

continued on next page

Table A-1. Continued.

Year	Aggregate households	Total numbers	Numbers per household
1108	20,648,238	46,173,891	2.24
1109	20,882,438	46,734,784	2.24
1110	20,882,258	46,734,784	2.24
1159	11,091,885	16,842,401	1.52
1160	11,575,733	19,229,008	1.66
1161	11,364,377	24,202,301	2.13
1162	11,139,854	23,112,327	2.07
1163	11,311,386	22,496,686	1.99
1164	11,243,977	22,998,854	2.05
1165	11,705,662	25,179,177	2.15
1166	12,335,450	25,378,648	2.06
1167	11,800,366	26,086,146	2.21
1168	11,683,511	25,395,502	2.17
1169	11,633,233	24,772,833	2.13
1170	11,847,385	25,971,870	2.19
1171	11,852,580	25,428,255	2.15
1172	11,730,699	25,955,359	2.21
1173	11,849,328	26,720,724	2.26
1174	12,094,874	27,375,586	2.26
1175	12,501,400	27,634,010	2.21
1176	12,132,202	27,619,019	2.28
1177	12,176,807	27,025,758	2.22
1178	12,976,123	28,558,940	2.20
1179	12,111,180	29,502,290	2.44
1180	12,130,901	27,020,689	2.23
1181	11,567,413	26,132,494	2.26
1182	11,432,813	26,209,544	2.29
1183	11,156,184	22,833,590	2.05
1184	12,398,309	24,530,188	1.98
1185	12,390,465	24,393,821	1.97
1186	12,369,881	24,341,447	1.96
1187	12,376,552	24,311,789	1.71
1188	11,876,373	24,306,252	2.14
1189	12,907,438	27,564,106	2.31
1190	12,355,800	28,500,258	2.26
1193	12,302,873	27,845,085	2.24
1218	12,669,684	28,377,441	2.24
1222	12,669,310	28,325,070	2.24
1223	12,670,801	28,320,085	2.24

Sources: Fang 2010, 234–237; Chen and Qiao, 25–27.

*The reported households in 1011 was too small to be true. According to Cheng Minsheng, this number should be an increase of the aggregate households, and the total is adjusted to 8,535,649 instead (Cheng 2003, 19).

The Song aggregate population data after 1110 comprises 36 records that cover the years from 1159 to 1223, almost one for two years. As shown in table A-1, a sharp decline in aggregate households can be seen in 1159, a population reported shortly after the end of the war with the Jurchen. In the preceding two decades, the Song administration lost half of its territory and a great number of populations. The Southern Song population records were less reliable than that of the Northern Song.[10] The major trend observed from table A-1 is a slow growth in aggregate households from 1159 to 1200, with a peak record of 12.9 million in 1178. In the years after 1178 the records show stagnation. It is difficult to explain the many irregular yearly changes, though the Song government's loss of an efficient population reporting mechanism in the twelfth century should be a major reason.

The consistency of Northern Song population records can be further tested at the prefectural level. Writings on geography, jurisdiction, transportation, and populations in the Northern Song dynasty provide firsthand information. The extant records provide a full report of all 234 prefectural-level households in three benchmark years, the 980s, 1080, and 1102. In no other periods of Chinese dynasties can one find such detailed resources. Furthermore, as the three geographical treatises, the three independent sources for prefectural populations, were made in different periods, the result drawn from the comparison is trustworthy.[11] Wu Songdi has already compiled all these records and presented them in his work on Song population. He admits that for sixty-three prefectures, about one-fourth of the total, reported figures were suspicious because of irregular changes in the number of adult males or households.[12] But one can discern clearly a shared trend of rapid growth in total households at the circuit level in a century. When this rising trend is contextualized against the development in urbanization and water transportation as revealed by the taxation data, the expansion in the Chinese market economy in the eleventh century is unmistakably evident.

Knowing the reliability of the numbers of aggregate households allows us not only to project the major trend in long-term demographic changes in Song China but also to estimate the size of aggregate population. In the last three decades most Song historians have come to believe that the average family size in the Song dynasty fell between 5 and 6 people.[13] The numbers per family, as shown in table A-1, which ranged between 1.42 and 2.57, were actually a report of either male adults or males and had nothing to do with female members. By insisting that Song household registration covered all male members, Wu Songdi estimates 5.4 individuals for the average family size in the Song era. He reaches this estimate from two different sources. First, population returns in North China conducted by the Jurchen Jin dynasty in 1187 suggested that average family size was 6.0 to 6.2. Second, Wu Songdi collects population records preserved in famine relief reports of twenty-eight prefectures in the Southern Song. Food rationing during the famine relief period required full accounting of all members of a family. Thus, most of the average family size reported in the twelfth and thirteenth centuries was between 5.2 and 5.4. Wu, therefore, adopts 5.4 for the average family size in the eleventh century.[14] Meanwhile, a few scholars such as He Zhongli and Fang Jian suggest these per family numbers rather indicate male adults only, and therefore they conclude that the average family size in the Song dynasty reached around 6 people.[15]

It should be noted that this difference between both sides is not substantial enough to cause a huge gap in the estimation. In fact, based on solid evidence on Northern

Song population data, both agree that by the early thirteenth century, Song population should have exceeded 100 million. For 1078, one of the chosen benchmark years in the comparison of the national incomes between Song and Ming, the estimated population is 89.7 million. The registered households in 1077 numbered 16,603,954. This is close to the number of aggregate households in 1080, which numbered 16,730,504 (see table A-1). The 1080 total figure is most often cited because we have the full report of the population at the prefectural level. Nonetheless, the real population toward the end of the eleventh century should have fallen to the range of 90 to 100 million.

2.

Establishing consistency of the thirteenth- and fourteenth-century figures also affects the economic study of the interim period. Fortunately, Perkins accomplished this task when he compared the Yuan population returns with the 1393 census and offered a historical context to explain the radical changes at the provincial level. In proving the reliability of the early Ming data, his work inevitably demonstrates the huge loss in Chinese population caused by the Mongol conquest, especially in North China, the Upper Yangtze, and Mid-Yangtze regions (see table A-2).[16] In provinces/macro-regions other than these war-afflicted regions, population continued to grow. This continuity is clearly proven by the population growth in Zhejiang. As shown in table A-2, Zhejiang's population increased from 1.8 millions in 1080 to 2.3 millions in 1173. Population continued to increase after the Mongol conquest but declined 10 percent during the Yuan-Ming transition.

The observed changes at the provincial level during the Song-Yuan-Ming transition can hardly be extended to the prefectural/local level due to the lack of demographic information. Nonetheless, one can testify to such a trend in Lower Yangtze, Zhejiang, and Fujian because historians find a lot of population records preserved in the gazetteers compiled in the thirteenth and fourteenth centuries. The trend in population changes in the Lower Yangtze is extremely important to my comparison of market development and living standards in Song and Ming eras. Population data on the Lower Yangtze produced in different dynastic periods prior to 1400 also prove the consistency of the Song and Yuan data. Although the population records preserved in extant gazetteers are far from sufficient, the data on the chosen nine prefectures in the Lower Yangtze as shown in table A-3 present a roughly similar pattern of population changes.

The density of population increased obviously in the three centuries after the Mongol conquest in all eight prefectures shown in table A-3. In Suzhou, for instance, it increased from 21 people per square kilometer in 980 to 196 in 1279. The Mongol conquest brought little damage to the local economy and population growth as it increased to 277 people per square kilometer in 1290. The similar story is evident in Nanjing, Shaoxing, and Huizhou. This population growth can thus further support the argument on Jiangnan's agricultural development in the thirteenth and fourteenth centuries. Meanwhile, except for Suzhou, one can observe a slight decline in the density of population for these prefectures in the years of the Yuan-Ming transition.

The extant Song population data form a rich mine to be explored in the future. As this book compares market development in the eleventh century with the early Ming command economy, it is necessary to identify the approximated Chinese population around 1077 and 1400. The research on early Ming population has provided trustworthy

Table A-2. Chinese population data by province, 1080–1393

Province	Song 1080	Song-Jin 1173	Yuan 1270–1290	Ming 1393
Hebei (N)	984,195	2,277,131	593,852	334,792
Shaanxi-Gansu (N)	962,318	—	92,651	294,526
Shanxi (N)	450,869	—	241,969	595,444
Shandong (N)	1,370,800	—	363,611	753,894
Henan (N)	823,066	—	162,962	315,617
Subtotal	4,591,248	6,987,000	1,455,045	2,294,273
Hubei (C)	589,302	267,000	527,518	775,851
Hunan (C)	811,057	1,005,134	1,819,145	537,614
Jiangxi (C)	1,365,533	1,862,614	676,115	1,553,923
Subtotal	2,765,892	3,134,748	1,602,281	2,867,388
Anhui (E)	2,152,814	1,161,339	162,962	537,614
Jiangsu (E)	*	*	1,602,281	1,375,320
Zhejiang (E)	1,830,096	2,295,863	2,384,274	2,138,225
Subtotal	3,982,910	3,457,202	4,149,517	4,051,159
Fujian (SE)	992,087	1,424,296	1,364,467	815,227
Guangdong (SE)	565,534	526,913	681,477	675,599
Guangxi (SE)	242,110	505,883	386,239	211,263
Subtotal	1,799,731	2,457,092	2,432,183	1,702,089
Sichuan	1,403,484	2,721,911	99,538	215,719
Total	14,543,265	18,757,953	13,644,388	10,593,314

Source: Perkins 1969, 195. In his calculation of subtotal populations, Perkins combined Hubei, Hunan, Jiangxi, Anhui, Jiangsu, Zhejiang, Jiangxi, and Fujian together to show a sharp decline in population in these regions. I divide them into Central China, East China, and Southeast China for comparison.

*Most areas of Anhui and Jiangsu in Song eras belong to Huainanlu, thus the provincial figure is not available. The reported 2,152,814 households in 1080 and 1,161,339 households in 1173 refer to the population of both provinces.

Table A-3. Population density in the Lower Yangtze (individual/km²)

Prefecture	980	1080	1102	1199	1279	1290	1390s	1770
Suzhou	21	104	91	103	196	277	292	756
Hangzhou	47	135	138	174	261	241	144	367
Huzhou	31	117	131	165	—	192	162	348
Nanjing	41	119	85	—	83	160	116	507
Zhenjiang	39	81	94	94	159	146	128	383
Shaoxing	28	77	140	—	137	150	134	447
Huizhou	4	36	36	41	42	53	44	188
Yangzhou	23	42	44	28	34	—	95	330

Source: Table 7-4.

estimations of Chinese population around 1400. As Perkins has tested the consistency in Chinese aggregate household records three centuries prior to 1393, this appendix aims to prove the reliability of the Northern Song population data with regard to the comparison with the early Ming. To show that the Song household data is consistent throughout the century, I examined the eleventh-century aggregate household data and address the general information on distribution of the aggregate population in three benchmark years.

It is fairly safe to suggest that by the early thirteenth century, the Song population should have exceeded 100 million while the real population toward the end of the eleventh century should have fallen within the range of 90 to 100 million. Therefore, the estimated population of 89.7 million in 1077 can be taken as a reasonable approximation.

Appendix B

Long-Term Changes in Prices and the Money Stock

Peng's Index of Rice Prices

Owing to their strategic significance, the price of grain, especially that of rice, was frequently reported to the government throughout imperial China. Although there are several published series of grain prices, only Peng's research attempted to cover all periods of imperial China. Although a few scholars have studied prices in specific dynasties, such as those of the Song (960–1279), Ming (1378–1644), or Qing (1644–1912) period, the only comprehensive study that covers all the periods of later imperial China is the work by Peng Xinwei, *A Monetary History of China.*[1] Peng, a well-known economic historian, assembled a roster of grain prices that attempted to cover the entire span from 900 to 1900. Unfortunately, the data series produced by Peng and others still cannot give us a detailed account of the short-term fluctuations (such as seasonal changes and regional variances) in grain prices because for every three to four years one will find only one record, which was often not at the same site but only in close proximity. Nonetheless, the general trend described by Peng's observations of long-term changes in prices (such as those of grain and textile goods) has been supported by all the other data series based on a specific dynasty.

Yet even Peng failed to make an explicit cross-dynastic comparison that would allow us to view changes at different price levels from the tenth to the twentieth century through a single index and, therefore, to link price changes to changes in the real economy.[2] In order to provide such an index, I have tabulated a series of Peng's indexes of rice prices into a single index—the Peng index—as follows.

In the Peng index (table B-1) the price of rice in 961–970 is set at 100 points, so it is apparent that the grain price in the Song period gradually increased to 200 points over a period of nearly one hundred years. By the beginning of the thirteenth century, grain prices had risen three and a half to four times of those in the early Song period. During the three centuries, the price of rice continuously rose four to five times over those in the pre-Song periods. However, the lengthy upward trend in prices came to an end in the late fourteenth century. During the Ming period, prices moved in the opposite direction. The Peng index demonstrates that, by early the Ming, prices had almost returned to the original amounts of the mid-tenth century at a much lower rate. Yet they did not hit the lowest point: Grain prices bottomed out in the first half of the fifteenth century. Not until the mid-sixteenth century did grain prices reach 250 points.

Table B-1. Peng's index of rice prices, 960–1910

Period	Index*	Price**
961–70	100	2.39
971–80	153	31.12
981–90	95	11.76
991–1000	119	14.73
1001–10	184	22.76
1011–20	95	11.79
1021–30	98	12.21
1031–40	159	19.67
1041–50	382	47.33
1051–60	136	16.81
1061–70	207	25.7
1071–80	444	55.1
1081–90	260	32.25
1091–1100	283	35.04
1101–10	481	59.61
1111–20	366	45.37
1121–30	2141	265.42
1131–40	1960	243
1141–50	243	30.18
1151–60	346	42.84
1161–70	355	44.05
1171–80	297	36.81
1181–90	359	44.5
1191–1200	510	63.19
1201–10	775	96.08
1211–20	367	45.56
1221–30	401	49.66
1231–40	306	37.9
1241–50	306	37.9
1251–60	305	37.83
1361–70	89.7	11.12
1371–80	280	34.73
1381–90	140	17.35
1391–1400	105	13.02
1401–10	85.4	10.59
1411–20	*	*
1421–30	104	12.87
1431–40	78	9.63
1441–50	84	10.41
1451–60	100	12.38
1461–70	122	15.07
1471–80	124	15.33
1481–90	148	18.39
1491–1500	180	22.31
1501–10	172	21.3
1511–20	144	17.83
1521–30	162	20.14
1531–40	172	21.3
1541–50	165	20.48

Period	Index*	Price**
1551–60	184	22.75
1561–70	182	22.6
1571–80	159	19.66
1581–90	203	25.18
1591–1600	203	25.22
1601–10	215	26.6
1611–20	182	22.57
1621–30	293	36.37
1631–40	271	33.57
1641–50	380	47.11
1651–60	361	44.81
1661–70	258	31.94
1671–80	196	24.31
1681–90	260	32.22
1691–1700	223	27.5
1701–10	290	36.01
1711–20	279	34.53
1721–30	265	32.84
1731–40	301	37.37
1741–50	344	42.69
1751–60	493	61.06
1761–70	518	64.22
1771–80	458	56.75
1781–90	484	60.01
1791–1800	591	73.28
1801–10	654	81.13
1811–20	647	80.19
1821–30	584	72.44
1831–40	728	90.19
1841–50	679	84.13
1851–60	514	63.72
1861–70	789	97.84
1871–80	523	64.88
1881–90	468	58.04
1891–1900	724	89.72
1901–10	1172	145.28

Source: Peng 1965, 498, 505, 705, 850.

*Index: 961–70 = 100.

**The price is rice per hectoliter in grams of silver in silver value. The rice prices in the Song period are reported by Peng in silver taels, and I converted them into silver grams at the rate of 1 tael of silver equals 37.68 g.

It was only in the second quarter of the eighteenth century that grain prices reached the maximum found during the Song era. The two peaks were five hundred years apart.

Estimates of the Amount of Song Coins and the Ming Money Supply before 1550

By using the Fisher equation, changes in prices are expected to be closely related to two other variables at the macro level: money supply and population. If changes in money supply vary, for instance, much greater than demographic changes, then much of the discrepancies between prices in the Song and early Ming periods should be defined as changes in nominal price and need to be adjusted for inflation. Meanwhile, a decline in aggregate population could be a consequence of a crisis in the real economy, which in turn, indicates a real decline in living standards and a shrinking of the market economy. Therefore, the emergence of the two price regimes, the Tang-Song and the Ming-Qing, should be further examined by highlighting changes in both money supply and population over the last millennium of imperial China.

In the following, I focus on changes in money supply over the Song-Ming transition.[3] A couple of questions concern estimations on money supply. First, one has to ensure that the means of exchange between the different periods must be comparable before making any comparison; second, the existence of disparities in the circulation of money between the Song and Ming periods needs to be determined. These issues therefore shift our focus from the amount of money supply to the circulation of money, which is certainly more indicative of the total volume of traded goods made in a specific period. If holders of money in the Song period, for instance, were likely to keep money, then the total volume of trade would be less than that anticipated. Under such a circumstance, aggregate demand would also tend to be constrained.

I can only attempt to tackle the first question here. There are several implications to the second question. In terms of money supply per capita, Song consumers had more money than their counterparts in the Ming-Qing period until the nineteenth century. Although contemporary opinions on eleventh-century consumption often criticize the scarcity of bronze coins and money shortage (*qianhuang*) was an issue in many local communities, it was then that the Song court produced the largest amount of coins ever in Chinese history.[4] Such a paradox between the Song money circulation and money supply implies the extraordinary size of the Song economy; thus, money demand must have been quite excessive. This would have in turn compelled Song money-holders to spend faster than what is anticipated for a preindustrial economy. However, I will assume at this moment that the velocity of money remained constant between the Song and Ming eras to make the comparison easier to conduct.

The first question points to a variety of means of exchanges during the Song-Ming period. The Song state can be viewed as a regime with an expansive monetary policy. Precious metals, such as gold and silver, and bronze coins produced by the imperial mints would account for the major body of money in circulation. In addition, bills of exchange (*feiqian* or *bianqian*) began to be widely used in the tenth century, and in the twelfth century the government initiated paper money. The Ming state continued to issue paper money (*baochao*), which only resulted in hyperinflation, eliminating the worth of the *bao-*

chao in transactions.[5] This gave rise to the usage of silver and bronze coins for exchange.

To conservatively estimate the Song money supply, I only include bronze coins produced by the imperial mints. This severely downplays the total amount of money for Song China, since I include both silver and bronze coins in my estimation of the amount of money in the Ming period. In fact, silver output in the Song period was much more than Ming China's domestic output.[6] However, this conservative estimation does not change the result. Even excluding silver for the estimation of the Song era, the conclusion drawn later from this comparison demonstrates that the total amount of money in the Song era far exceeded that of the Ming era.

Hino, a well-known economic historian, collected data on Song imperial coinage. There were nineteen Song imperial mints that produced bronze coins in the late eleventh century. The average amount of annually minted coins is shown in table B-2.

The production of the imperial mints in fact depended on a sufficient supply of metals, especially copper and tin. Hino also surveyed the yearly output of copper controlled by the Song state and found that there is a very small margin between the reported copper output and average amount of yearly minted coins.[7] Therefore, the imperial mints could maintain their production at full scale. Using Hino's estimates of average yearly minted coins, Gao multiplied them by years to obtain the amounts for different periods of time.

I also estimate the total amount of bronze coins produced by the Song imperial mints based on Peng's data. Peng collected sixteen figures for yearly imperial minting output in a time frame of fifteen reigns.[8] I multiply them by the years of each reign, and the sum is 193.4 million strings. This could be an underestimation, either because I have excluded iron coins, which were officially minted and circulated in several regions in the Song period, or because the years (ninety-four years from fifteen reigns) taken into account here comprise only 64 percent of the total years in the Song period prior to 1127. However, the figures show a significant increase in coin minting in the early twelfth century, which was the New Policy era; the mints produced 106.8 million strings of bronze coins.[9] This aggregate figure would exceed all of the Song coins previously minted. Peng estimated that the total amount of bronze coins produced by the Song imperial mints prior to 1127 was 140 to 150 million strings, and if privately minted coins and coins produced by previous dynasties were included, the size of the Song money supply would reach 250 to 260 million strings.[10]

However, neither of these two figures, that is, Gao's estimate and mine, can be taken as the real output of Song bronze coins. Rather, they indicate a spectrum of real output. In considering other means of exchange in circulation such as paper notes, sil-

Table B-2. Average amount of minted coins per year, 995–1119 (000,000 strings)

Year	Amount	Year	Amount	Year	Amount
995	0.8	1021	1.05	1077	3.73
1000	1.25	1030	1.00	1080	5.06
1007	1.83	1050	1.46	1105	2.89
1015	1.25	1065	1.70	1119	3.00

Source: Hino 1936–1937, in *HKTSR*, Vol. 6, 345.

Table B-3. Amount of minted bronze coins, 995–1119 (000,000 strings)

Period	Amount	Period	Amount
976–82	0.49	1016–48	33.0
983–96	4.20	1049–73	40.0
997–999	2.40	1074–85	54.0
1000–15	18.75	1086–1125	109.20
Total:	262.04		

Source: Gao 2000, 103.

ver and gold, and iron coins, the Song money supply would at least approximate Peng's estimates of 250 to 260 million strings.

Ming imperial minting went into a decline. It is usually thought to have produced only a small number of coins in the last millennium of Chinese history. The peak number of official coins annually produced in the early Ming period was about 0.22 million strings in 1372, which was only 4.3 percent of the Song annual production in the 1070s. It is estimated that for the first 174 years, the average annual output was less than 35,000 strings of coins.[11] As "monetary contraction" became so apparent, the Ming government made no serious attempt to resolve coin shortages in the economy. In the century after 1430, there was little, if any, official minting. When it came to the Jiajing reign, the circulation of coins had been dominated by counterfeiting and coins from previous dynasties. The court launched new attempts to regulate by establishing new mints in Beijing, Yunnan, and other provinces. This resulted in a minimal increase in coin output, and this would add up to 4 to 6 million strings in total for the aggregate output of Ming imperial minting from 1368 through to 1572, a figure that roughly matches the annual output of the Song state in the 1080s.

However, coins, including those from previous dynasties and even counterfeits, were admittedly used in small transactions by the imperial authority most of the time. Given the scarcity of coinage from the Ming imperial mints, the majority of coins in circulation were in fact Song coins that were preserved in the day. Ming hoards discovered today are without exception in possession of a large quantity of Song coins. A special report on the hoarding in Henan, for instance, exposed that there have been more than ten thousand kilograms of Song coins excavated in three thousand sites across the whole province.[12] In comparison, the excavation of Ming coins is much more limited. For the purpose here, we need to know how many Song coins were preserved and used again in the Ming period. This might be found by examining the proportional amount of Song coins in the excavation sites of Ming hoards. It is unfortunate that no research has been carried out on the entire quantity of Song coins from excavations in proportion to that of the Ming coins at the aggregate level. However, Japanese numismatists have investigated hoarding sites of Chinese coinage in late sixteenth-century Japan and found that the amount of Ming official coins is about ten times that of the Song coins.[13] Chinese coinage had been for a long time used in Japan as the common currency until the mid-seventeenth century. This rationale would provide a clear implication of how many Song coins were in circulation along with Ming official coins. By considering that the trade between Ming China and Japan was officially either retarded by the state monopoly or forbidden, most Chinese currency should have flowed through smuggling channels into Japan, and this probably reduced the potential inflow of Ming coins, which were usually issued by official occasions.[14] Thereafter, I lower the rate to be 8 to 1 as the normal pattern of Song and Ming official coins in circulation over the Ming period.[15]

In addition to coins in circulation, silver was used as a major currency during the centuries after 1436. Aggregate silver output from domestic mining then, according to optimistic views, would reach 25 million taels. On second thought, 15 to 25 million taels of silver appear to be more appropriate. Therefore, before significant imports of silver into China began in the late sixteenth century, the money supply from the domestic side can be estimated as 46.5 to 71.5 million strings of coins in total value: 15 to 25 million taels of silver plus 36 to 54 million strings of coins.[16] This figure is only half of the money supply of the Song state prior to 1043. In the succeeding decades of the New Policy era, the output of coinage exceeded all that which had ever been previously produced in the Song imperial mints.[17]

Appendix C

Waterway Networks in the Eleventh Century

In chapter 3 I depicted the twelve major water routes. The amount of commercial taxes collected from the twelve major water routes presented in table C-1 easily add up to one-sixth of land tax revenues. In the following, I report nine cases that are either long-distance water routes or intraregional waterway networks. To highlight the deterioration in waterway transportation, I carefully chose the waterways that were performing an important role in North and Central China during the Tang-Song transformation. In the succeeding centuries, most of them served for short-distance shipments or were abandoned due to irreversible ecological changes.

Both an expansion in urban consumption and the development of long-distance trade contributed to the increase in commercial taxes. As Perkins notes, the commercial tax data is perfect to study the market expansion because they exactly point to the two major sources for the growing importance of nonagricultural sectors in a traditional economy. However, as the current focus is on water transportation, we are also concerned how to distinguish the role of waterways in promoting trade from the role of urbanization. Although there is no perfect answer to this question, we can approach it by comparing a specific harbor city with other cities in a waterway network. The influence of long-distance trade can be easily felt on the harbor cities along the canal. For cities along the Bian and Sishui canals (table C-6), the most important long-distance water route trade in Song China, trade produced prosperity. Nine out of sixteen cities were able to contribute separately the commercial tax above 15,000 strings.

For other waterways, intra- and intertrade together with urbanization led to the increase in the amount of commercial taxes. The relationship between them was complicated. By experience one can tell the difference in the size of cities and the number of their urban residents, especially prefectural capitals, are in a moderate range.[1] In any given river-linked city group listed here, there are huge differences in the tax quotas of 1077 among them. Even between those at the same level of administration (such as between county seats or prefectural capitals) the difference is still obvious. The city with extraordinary amounts of commercial taxes in comparison with its peer cities must owe this to long-distance trade facilitated by water transportation. Taking the cities listed in table C-5, three cities were reported to contribute huge amounts of commercial taxes: Fujiaya (22,467 strings), Gaojiagang (17,080 strings), and Yunzhou (32,444). Officially, Fujiaya and Gaojiagang were townships. They were far below the level of prefectural capitals like Jinan (11,836 strings) and Caozhou (4,439 strings). Yet they could collect a great amount of taxes because they were the key harbors for shipments along the canal and sea-canal transportation.

Occasionally, the military would bolster urban consumption and in consequence contribute significantly to the amount of commercial taxes. The amounts of the commercial taxes contributed by cities in Hebei (table C-8) seemed to come close. The majority fell in a narrow range of 9,000 to 15,000 strings. The Song court stationed a large number of troops in this area, mostly around the city, for defense against the invasion of nomadic power. Consumptions by soldiers and other military expenditures created a boom in urban commerce. Zhending (39,590 strings), Dingzhou (19,738 strings), and Xiongzhou (11,552 strings) were particularly important for the logistic supply within this defense zone. It is noteworthy that Yanshan was one exceptional case to this military consumption pattern. It was a sea harbor city well known for salt production and fishing. In 1077, it contributed 37,438 strings, second to Zhending.

Table C-1. Intraregional waterway networks around Kaifeng, 1077*

1. Route northward to Daming:
    Daming (大名, 38,628)–Cizhou (磁州, 7,544)–Xiangzhou (相州, 12,222)–Liyang (黎陽, 6,462)–Weizhou (衛州, 5,718).

2. Route westward to Luoyang:
    Chaocheng (朝城, 7,517)–Neihuang (内黃, 3,432)–Qingfeng (清豐, 6,009)–Puyang (濮陽, 15,568)–Mengzhou (孟州, 8,549)–Luoyang (洛陽, 37,943).

3. Route to Yingtianfu:
    Heyin (河陰, 5,740)–Kaifeng-Chenliu (陳留, 6,768)–Yongqiu (雍丘, 13,527)–Xiangyi (襄邑, 7,815)–Yingtianfu (應天府, 27,886).

4. Route eastward to Jiyin and Yunzhou:
    Kaifeng (402,379)–Dongming (東明, 5,421)–Jiyin (濟陰, 7,658)–Yuanju (冤句, 4,505)–Dingtao (定陶, 3,760)–Juye (巨野, 6,305)–Yuncheng (鄆城, 3,234)–Yunzhou (鄆州, 32,444).

5. Route southeast to Bozhou:
    Xianping (咸平, 9,635)–Taikang (太康, 11,867)–Bozhou (博州, 4,377).

6. Route southward to Chenzhou:
    Kaifeng-Heliuzhen (合流鎮, 1,752)–Changshe (長社, 18,334)–Chenzhou (陳州, 19,533).

*Figures in parenthesis are commercial taxes measured in strings. All figures in this table and the following table, if not specified, are from the 1077 commercial tax data preserved in *SHY*. I owe many thanks to the CHGIS program at Harvard for financing my research on this data.

Table C-2. The population density of Song core regions, 1078
(households per square kilometer)

1. Kaifeng and the nearby densely populated regions in the north

Kaifeng	13.6	Luoyang	7.1	Caizhou	8.4
Daming	16.9	Kaide	19.4	Bozhou	25.3
Dezhou	18.6	Weizhou	13.2	Yingtianfu	14.2
Xingrenfu	21.7	Puzhou	17.5	Bozhou	10.8

2. Densely populated regions in the south
   a. The Chengdu plain

Chengdufu	57.5	Meizhou	31.1	Pengzhou	65.7

   b. The Lower Yangtze

Hangzhou	27.7	Zhenjiang	17.2	Suzhou	21.6
Changzhou	18.3	Xiuzhou	21.9	Huzhou	24.9
Mingzhou	24				

   c. Jiangxi

Hongzhou	13.7	Yuanzhou	15.8	Linjiangjun	18.4

Source: Wu Songdi, 2000, 398, 434–435, 474–475, 495–496, 540–542.

Table C-3. River-port cities along the Yongji (*yuqu*) Canal with commercial tax quotas, 1077

Weizhou 衛州	5,718	Yongjizhen 永濟鎮	2,338
Anle 安樂	1,893	Xinxiangzhen 新鄉鎮	2,877
Linqing 臨清	2,104	Yongjingjun 永濟軍	23,891
Liyang 黎陽	6,462	Zongcheng 宗城	1,416
Daming 大名	38,628	Neihuang 內黃	3,432
Enzhou 恩州	9,738	Huanshuizhen 洹水鎮	2,208
Wucheng 武城	1,842	Liguzhen 李固鎮	1,046
Liting 歷亭	2,333		
Total: 105,926 strings			

Table C-4. River-port cities along the Lower Yellow River with commercial tax quotas, 1077

Puyang 濮陽	15,567	Liaocheng 聊城	12,261
Puzhou 濮州	19,637	Gaotang 高唐	3,334
Fanxian 范具	2,147	Dezhou 德州	30,429
Chaoyang 朝陽	7,516	Linyi 臨邑	6,251
Yanggu 陽谷	6,596	Yanci 厌次	26,760
Anlezhen 安樂鎮	1,532	Binzhou 宾州	8,877
Total: 140, 907 strings			

Table C-5. River-port cities along the Guangji-Qing Canal with commercial tax quotas, 1077

Caozhou 曹州	4,439	Dong'a 東阿	3,527
Zouping 邹平	3,327	Dingtao 定陶	3,570
Jingdezhen 景德鎮	2,930	Gaoyuan 高苑	26,526
Hecaizhen 合蔡鎮	1,160	Beixinqiao 北新桥	1,259
Boxing 博興	2,569	Juye 巨野	6,305
Fujiaya 傅家崖	22,467	Qiancheng 千乘	3,219
Yuncheng 郓城	3,234	Huajiakou'an 滑家口鎮	3,173
Gaojiagang 高家港	17,080	Yunzhou 郓州	32,444
Jinan 濟南	11,836	Pingyin 平陰	3,554
Zhangqiu 章丘	6,615		
Total: 159, 234 strings			

Table C-6. River-port cities along the Bian and Sishui canals with commercial tax quotas, 1077

Bian Canal 汴渠		Sishui 泗水	
Kaifeng 開封	402,379	Huaiyin 淮陰	2,197
Yongqiu 雍丘	13,527	Chuzhou 楚州	67,881
Chenliu 陳留	6,768	Baoying 寶應	16,080
Xiangyi 襄邑	7,814	Lianshui 漣水	21,191
Yingtianfu 應天府	27,886	Yangzhou 揚州	41,849
Yongcheng 永城	7,569	Zhenzhou 真州	53,536
Suzhou 宿州	15,079		
Lingbi 零壁	2,156	Subtotal:	230,860
Hongxian 虹具	2,042		
Qingyangzhen 青陽鎮	1,532		
Sizhou 泗州	21,682		
Subtotal: 106,055 (excluding Kaifeng)			
Total: 336, 915 (excluding Kaifeng) strings			

Table C-7. River-port cities along the Huimin Canal and the Wo River with commercial tax quotas, 1077

1. The Huimin Canal 惠民河

Chenzhou 陳州	19,533	Xihua 西華	3,156
Xiangcheng 項城	3,871	Changshe 長社	18,334
Yancheng 郾城	4,438	Yingzhou 潁州	3,241
Yexian 葉具	7,393	Shouzhou 壽州	17,550
Ruyang 汝陽	12,016	Zhengyangzhen 正陽関	4,094
Subtotal: 93, 626			

2. The Wo River

Taikang 太康	11,867	Bozhou 亳州	4,377
Mengcheng 蒙城	2,785	Haozhou 濠州	8,265
Subtotal: 27,294			
Total: 120,920 strings			

Table C-8. River-port cities in the Haihe River basin with commercial tax quotas, 1077

Zhending 真定	39,590	Dingzhou 定州	19,738
Xiongzhou 雄州	11,552	Mozhou 莫州	9,615
Hejian 河間	19,167	Jizhou 冀州	10,331
Qizhou 祁州	8,267	Zhaozhou 趙州	11,209
Cangzhou 滄州	10,475	Mingzho 洺州	6,368
Cizhou 磁州	7,545	Yanshan 鹽山	37,438
Total: 191,295 strings			

Table C-9. Port-cities in the Han River basins with commercial tax quotas, 1077

a. The main channel:

Xichuan 淅川	1,782 strings	Jinzhou 金州	8,330 strings
Shunyang 顺陽	1,569 strings	Xiangyang 襄陽	55,467 strings
Dengzhou 鄧州	21,370 strings	Yingzhou 郢州	8,818 strings
Junzhou 均州	6,977 strings		

b. The branch in Sichuan:

Xiyuanfu 興元府	27,484 strings	Chenggu 城固	3,147 strings
Yangzhou 洋州	11,131 strings		

c. The branch in Shaanxi:

Shangzhou 商州	8,944 strings	Guochuanzhen 虢川鎮	3,380 strings
Wuxiuzhen 武休鎮	9,392 strings		

Total: 234,667 strings.

Appendix D

Chinese Acreage, 900–1600

The extant records of Chinese acreage are unsatisfactory in terms of both quantity and quality. Even after the number of land figures significantly increased after 750 AD, their quality is still inferior to that of Chinese historical population data. While the estimated Chinese population increased, for instance, from 65 million in 1398 to 430 million in 1850, the reported acreage expanded from 800 million *mu* to 1.2 billion *mu*. Underreporting seems to be even more prevalent in land surveys.

The deficiency in acreage data, especially underreporting, should be understood within historical contexts. As land taxes became one of the major state revenues after the Rebellion and at that time the only major source of state income during the Ming era, underreporting of landholdings was a prevalent means of tax evasion. Farmers had every incentive to hide their landholdings or at least part of them from the land registration to lower their tax obligation. A trustworthy report of cultivated land is thus not available until the administration made great efforts to launch a land survey campaign at the national level. This policy, however, was rarely enforced in reality because it went against the economic interests of local landlords and was met with forceful resistance.

Empirical research by Perkins on Chinese land data is an example of how a researcher should approach the data issue. To narrow down the investigation, he raised three specific questions that can test data quality in a plausible way:

1. Was a serious effort made to record all the cultivated acreage in the empire?

2. Are there known errors or biases in the data?

3. Are the estimates consistent with data in other periods and with what we know of Chinese history?[1]

Before estimating the increase in farm yields per acre in the eleventh century, I need to ensure whether the acreage of cultivated land reported in Song official documents are appropriate. In this appendix, I follow Perkins's method to examine the extant China land data in the centuries from 600 to 1600. In the first section, I start with a general survey of extant acreage figures and relate their distribution to specific financial administrations in historical context. The survey points to the uneven distribution of reliable Chinese land data in the centuries from 2 AD to 1626 AD. Most of them were concentrated in the years between 959 and 1393, thus the period this Song-Ming comparison focuses on. In the second section, I check the land data in the Song and Ming periods at the provincial level. This check is largely a reexamination of the current land data drawn from Perkins's and Ho's research. It rather proves the central point emphasized by Ho that no available land data existed after the Hongwu reign. In the third section, I check the extant Southern Song land data at the local level with the relevant information such as average household farm size. This external consistency check demonstrates the connection between the Southern Song and early Ming eras in land acreages reported at the prefectural levels. In terms of land registration, the Southern Song government is proven effective as much as the early Ming command system. At the conclusion, I suggest adopting 561 million *mu* for the estimated national acreage in the 1100s.

General Survey of Extant Acreage Figures

Liang Fangzhong's research in Chinese historical population, land acreage, and taxation is a major effort to obtain useful quantitative information from preserved records by the Chinese government in the past two millennia. Liang intended to link the rich documented numbers in important aspects of the traditional economy to the effective administration of the Chinese bureaucracy; in this grand survey, however, one finds many series of records either flawed or false. Even Liang recognizes that the land data were much more problematic than the population registration. The Ho puzzle becomes unavoidable in this collection of primary quantitative sources, even though Liang thought the Chinese government produced richer and more trustworthy data in the later periods.

The first question that one should ask is, when studying Chinese historical land data, how much information is available on total acreage? The answer must be an unsatisfactory one. Available information on cultivated land in imperial China is extremely scarce. In table D-1 I use the land acreage data collected by Liang Fangzhong (1989) to demonstrate how poor our knowledge was. For nearly two thousand years from 2 AD to 1911 AD, one finds that only fifty-eight of these years have reported acreage figures. For the first millennium prior to 960, there were reliable records for only six years: all were distributed in the second century. For the remaining centuries up to the end of the Qing dynasty in 1911, the Song acreage data are apparently reasonable because they can present a plausible trend of long-term changes in both populations and total acreages. As the registered households increased from 3,090,504 in 976 to 17,211,713 in 1083, the reported acreage also expanded from 295,332,060 Song *mu* to 461,655,600 Song *mu*. As one focuses on the changing relationship between population growth and the expansion of cultivated land, only the period from 959 AD to 1393 seems to offer average size. In other periods, the data tend to be highly controversial either because the population showed no signs of change in a century or land acreage stagnated, or there are unbelievably large amounts of acreage in official reports.

The earliest extant land acreage reports cover the period from 2 AD to 146 AD. For one and a half centuries, we obtain reported aggregate land information for only six years. Checking against the available aggregate population data, one may arrive at 67 to 80 *mu* for average farmland per household (see table D-1).[2] This average size rather indicates a farming mode close to extensive farming. It is interesting to know how many regions had an average size below this value and thus clearly showed a pattern of extensive farming. Nonetheless, there is no breakdown for the totals. This makes it impossible for a modern researcher to find out what was exactly the prevailing pattern of farming practice for most regions in the Han dynasty.

Table D-1. Chinese historical population, acreage, and per household landholdings

Year	No. of households	Acreage (mu)	Per household landholdings (mu)
2	12,233,062	69,594,978	67.61
105	9,237,112	732,017,080	79.25
125	9,647,838	694,289,213	71.96
144	9,946,919	689,627,156	69.33
145	9,937,680	695,767,620	70.01
146	9,348,227	693,012,338	74.13
609	8,907,546	5,585,404,000	627.04
726	8,914,709	1,430,386,213	160.45
959	2,309,812	108,583,400	47.01
976	3,090,504	295,332,060	95.56
996	4,574,257	312,525,125	68.32
1006	7,417,570	186,000,000	25.08
1021	8,677,677	524,758,432	60.47
1053	10,792,705	228,000,000	21.13
1066	12,917,221	440,000,000	34.06
1083	17,211,713	461,655,600	26.82
1381	10,654,362	366,771,549	34.42
1391	10,684,435	387,474,673	36.27
1393	10,652,870	850,769,368	79.86
1403	11,415,829	—	—
1413	9,684,916	—	—
1423	9,972,125	—	—
1435	9,702,495	427,017,200	44.01
1445	9,537,454	424,723,900	44.53
1455	9,405,390	426,733,900	45.37
1464	9,107,205	472,430,209	51.87
1474	9,120,195	477,899,000	52.81
1484	9,205,711	486,149,800	52.81
1490	9,503,890	423,805,800	44.59
1502	10,409,788	622,805,881	59.83
1510	9,144,095	469,723,300	45.41
1519	9,399,979	469,723,300	45.41
1532	9,433,229	428,828,400	45.41
1542	9,599,258	428,928,400	44.68
1552	9,609,305	428,035,800	44.54
1562	9,638,396	431,169,400	44.74
1571	10,008,805	467,775,000	46.74
1578	10,621,436	701,397,628	66.04
1602	10,030,241	1,161,894,800	115.84*
1620	9,835,426	743,931,900	75.64
1626	9,835,426	743,931,900	75.64

Source: Liang 1980, 4–13.

*The original figure is 11.53 mu per household, which is obviously an error.

In the succeeding nearly eight centuries until 959, the government did not conduct land surveys as the poll tax became the sole source of state revenue. Control over the population during wartimes was a difficult battle that the government often lost to the nobilities and warlords. Only after the rise of a strong central government could the population registration be conducted nationwide. But the same could not be said for land registration. For example, the reported amount of cultivated land around 610 AD reached 5,585,404,000 *mu*, and the number of registered households 8,907,536, which came to be about 500 *mu* per household. No sources can verify whether this report was based on a serious investigation. In the Tianbao reign (742–756) of the Tang dynasty, the reported acreage reached 1,430,386,213 *mu*, which computes to about 160 *mu* per household.[3]

It is reasonable to conclude that both were fabricated figures required by the *juntian* and *zu-yong-diao* systems, under which a farmer received a lot of land and paid taxes and services. In theory, the size of the land cultivated by a rural household should not exceed 100 *mu*. Fallow land was also common in some areas. Officials reached the total acreage by adding up all assigned quotas of land allotment to each registered household, which had nothing to do with the real distribution of landholdings.

In principle, reliable land data is a prerequisite to the collection of land taxes. After the two-tax system (*liangshui fa*) was established in 780 AD, land taxes were the major means of taxing agricultural outputs.[4] However, the reported acreage declined to below 2 million *mu* immediately after the adoption of the two-tax system. For the succeeding three centuries, no land returns were seriously carried out on a national scale. This may have compelled the court to tax long-distance trade and urban consumption. After the reunification in the late tenth century, the Song administration was also met with popular resistance whenever officials planned to conduct a land survey. To encourage the reclamation of spare land in devastated regions, the court soon abandoned the plan.

Cultivated acreage in the Song dynasty, especially in the eleventh century, might have been underreported. Financial officials, including the vice chancellor, admitted that there was a low rate of principle in land taxation. They speculated that about 70 percent of the cultivated land was not reported and paid no taxes to the state. Unaware of this bias in Song land data caused by underreporting, scholars might underestimate the Song acreage. In a reconstruction of the land data, Perkins estimated the Song acreage to be 423 million Song *mu*, which is even lower than that in 1400. Perkins simply adopted the 1082 figure without making any adjustments.[5] The early Ming population in 1393, for instance, was less than two-thirds of that in the 1080s, yet early Ming acreage was estimated to be 425,401, 000 *mu*, which is even larger than that of 1082.[6]

The land survey conducted in the mid-eleventh century provides an example of how severely land acreages were underreported. From 1072 to 1085, the Wang Anshi administration conducted a land survey, better known as the Square Field Law, to assess the size and quality of private lands in many areas of North China. Before this project was halted by strong objections from local officials, about 248,434,900 Song *mu* were reported in total, about 2.1 times that of the presurvey period. Nonetheless, we are not provided with such information at the national level due to the abortion of the land survey project. By using this comparison as a basis, a few modern researchers, such as Qi, estimated that underreported acreage might be close to that reported. In 1083, the reported acreage amounted to 461,455,000 Song *mu* (see table 8-1a). Qi, therefore, suggested 700 to 750 million *shi mu* (about 800 million Song *mu*) as the acreage of land under cultivation. Similarly, Chao estimated that acreage in 1072 reached 666 million *shi mu* or 770 million Song *mu*.[7]

However, their estimated share of unreported land is also likely an overestimation. If their adjustments can be accepted, the acreage increased from 312 million Song *mu* in 997 AD to 800 million Song *mu* in 1083 AD, a two- to threefold increase in a period of nearly ninety years. In this case, the national acreage is more than half of that in 1957.[8] At the same time, aggregate households increased from 6,418,500 to 17,211,713, an increase that is equivalent to that in land acreage. Farm yields per acre should be maintained at the same level. This also means that each household would cultivate 47 *mu* over the course of the Northern Song period. This is a highly optimistic interpretation of land reclamation in the eleventh century. In determining a weighted average to the best of my ability, I chose 660 million Song *mu* as my estimation of land acreage at the dawn of the twelfth century.

The macroeconomic data are highly untrustworthy after 1393. The Ho puzzle speaks directly to the faked population and land data reported in the years from 1403 to 1626 as shown in table D-1. Both aggregate population and land acreage changed slowly in the remaining two centuries. As an exception, the land acreages reported in 1502, 1578, and 1602 substantially rose up. For this reason, some researchers such as Perkins use these aggregate figures to amend the bias in the Ming population data; the land acreage reported in 1602 is even more important as it approaches the end of the Ming dynasty and thus provides invaluable information of long-term changes in the cultivation of land. But their efforts achieve only insignificant results because the breakdowns of the 1602 return were not preserved and the details about when and how this return was conducted are also controversial.

Land Data in the Song and Ming Periods on the Provincial Level

Studies on Ming land acreage have to focus on the early part of the Ming period, and overreporting becomes the major issue. The national acreage reported in 1393, as presented in table D-2, was 850,762,368 Ming *mu* (793 million *mu*). The troubling fact is that the population in 1393 was just one-tenth of that in 1957, yet the reported acreage reached nearly half that of the latter. As Perkins points out, while the major cultivated regions in 1393 should be concentrated in Central and East China, the total acreage there by 1957 was no more than 730 million *mu*. Therefore, the national total of 1393 must be unreliable.[9]

A convenient explanation, which Perkins was inclined to adopt, is to relate this figure to printing errors in official documents while maintaining confidence in the land return conducted in early Ming. In other words, one can pick up a few errors in the reported land acreage and amend the national total accordingly. Fujii Hiroshi, for instance, argued that the size of cultivated land in Huguang could have been increased tenfold due to misprints.[10] After investigating the internal consistency of the 1393 acreage data with that of 1502, Perkins found that with the exception of Henan and Huguang (Hubei and Hunan in Central China), the reported acreages in most provinces for the two dates were similar. Therefore, he accepted Fujii's explanation and, in turn, took the

Table D-2. Distribution of land acreage in Ming China, 1393–1578 (*mu*)

Province	1393	1502	1578
Beijing & Hebei	58,249,951	26,971,393	49,256,844
Nanzhili	126,927,452	81,018,040	77,394,672
Zhejiang	51,705,151	47,234,272	46,696,982
Jiangxi	43,118,601	40,235,247	40,115,127
Hubei and Hunan	220,217,575	223,612,847	221,619,940
Fujian	14,625,969	13,516,618	13,422,501
Shandong	72,403,562	54,292,938	61,749,900
Shanxi	41,864,248	39,080,934	36,803,927
Henan	144,946,982	41,609,969	74,157,952
Shaanxi	31,525,175	26,066,282	29,292,385
Sichuan	11,203,256	10,786,963	13,482,767
Guangdong	23,734,056	7,232,446	25,686,514
Guangxi	10,240,390	10,784,802	9,402,075
Yunnan	—	363,135	1,799,359
Guizhou	—	—	516,686
Total	850,762,368	622,805,881	701,397,628

Source: Liang 1980, 340–341.

1502 land data as the basis for his reconstruction. He estimated that Ming acreage in 1400 reached 425 million Ming *mu* (370 million *mu*). In my calculation of farm yields per acre in 1393, I also adopted this estimate.

As scholars continue to debate early Ming acreages, it is impossible to address all the doubts raised about the 1393 figures.[11] It is noteworthy that Perkins tried to ensure that the Ming land data are, in general, consistent. After removing some unusually large figures in the reported Ming acreages (see table D-2), the data roughly suggest an increasing trend in the two centuries. Acreage rose from about 420 million Ming *mu* in the early fifteenth century to nearly 500 million Ming *mu* in the 1570s, then jumped to 700 million Ming *mu* around 1580. This gradual increase supports our observation of agricultural development in the sixteenth-century economy. Nonetheless, the lack of qualified data on population growth at the same time makes it difficult to confirm long-term economic changes from a demographic perspective.

However, Perkins's explanation only partially solved the problem of the national total. If one looks into the provincial level, there are still many controversies remaining to be explained. Reported land acreages in Nanzhili, Zhejiang, Jiangxi, and Fujian, all in the south, for instance, declined more or less from 1393 to 1502 and again to 1578. In Hubei and Hunan, the land acreage remained almost changeless: Even when one excludes the 1393 figure as Perkins did, there is no important difference between the acreage reported in 1502 and that in 1578; the two differ slightly by a less than 1 percent.

This internal controversy becomes even more dramatic if we examine the land acreage data at the prefectural level. As shown in table D-3, in Zhejiang, the long-term changes in the acreage of the thirteen prefectures present a stable pattern in the centuries between 1553 and 1932. For most of them, the size of the cultivated acreage remained larger in 1553 and 1610 than that in 1735 and 1932. For Huzhou, the acreage reported

Table D-3. Zhejiang land data

Prefecture	1553	1610	1735	1932
Hangzhou fu	4,197,388	4,257,457	4,296,328	3,790,563
Jiaxing fu	2,910,722	4,323,299	4,356,223	3,943,211
Huzhou fu	6,846,523	6,122,873	6,136,078	4,251,817
Ningbo fu	4,047,156	4,099,180	3,900,593	4,154,450
Taizhou fu	4,110,403	4,195,994	3,492,271	3,561,371
Shaoxing fu	6,534,104	6,714,730	6,826,539	7,233,891
Jinhua fu	7,356,074	7,374,160	7,440,802	6,552,210
Chuzhou fu	2,987,214	3,068,821	2,847,134	2,656,020
Yanzhou fu	2,805,009	2,848,060	2,859,169	2,029,375
Wenzhou fu	2,609,118	2,608,692	2,133,308	2,345,891
Quzhou fu	1,237,096	2,250,913	1,740,804	1,871,175
Total:	45,640,807	47,864,179	46,029,249	42,389,974

Sources: Perkins 1969, 230, table B. 9. The data are extracted from *Zhejiang tongzhi* (1736), Vols. 67–70, 1304–1353.

in 1553 remained the largest for centuries. The same pattern can be applied to Nanzhili, though to a lesser degree (see table D-4). The reported subtotal acreage declined from 126,927,452 *mu* in 1393 to 81,018,040 *mu* in 1502 and further down to 77,394,672 *mu* in 1578. Suzhou and Songjiang, the most well-known regions for the market expansion in sixteenth-century China, shared the same declining or stagnating trend in the years from 1502 to 1578.

Perkins used land data from other periods to test the internal consistency of these records. Here, he had two choices for comparing the Ming land figures with those of other dynasties in the same region: He could choose either the pre-Ming or the post-Ming figures. Yet the comparison with the post-Ming data is disappointing because the preserved Qing land figures remained largely stagnant for many provinces. In taking Zhejiang as an example, the reported acreage varied slightly between 45.6 million *mu* in 1553 and 46 million *mu* in 1735 (see table D-3). Similarly the reported acreages in Nanzhili (see table D-4), and in particular, in Jiangnan, either increased minimally or substantially declined. Therefore, Perkins decided not to use the post-1600 data as the basis for his reconstruction of Ming acreage.[12]

The comparison with pre-Ming data proves to be far more productive. In all three major patterns of economic changes during the Song-Yuan-Ming transitional period, the change in reported land acreage is consistent. As shown in table D-5, changes at the provincial level during the years between 1082 and 1393 clearly demonstrate three different patterns: First, rapid growth occurred in Jiangxi, a province south of the Yangtze River, in the fourteenth century. The acreage extensively expanded to 64 million *mu* in 1393. Second, Henan in North China, a region well known for depopulation during the Mongol conquest, showed the opposite. The acreage declined from 133 million *mu* in 1082 to 78 million *mu* in 1393 due to a severe loss of population caused by military conflicts and natural disasters. Third, between the two extreme cases is Jiangzhe (including Zhejiang). It remained prosperous during this period, and its acreage was the most stable. Nonetheless, the peak record appeared in 1300, which indicates that the Mongol

Table D-4. Distribution of land acreages in Nanzhili, 1393–1578 (*mu*)

Province	1393	1502	1578
Nanjing	7,270,175	6,997,408	6,9405,14
Suzhou	9,850,671	15,524,998	9,295,951
Songjiang	5,132,290	4,715,662	4,247,703
Changzhou	7,973,188	6,177,776	6,425,595
Zhenjiang	3,845,270	3,272,235	3,381,714
Luzhou	1,622,399	2,543,046	6,838,911
Fengyang	41,749,390	6,126,267	6,019,197
Huai'an	19,333,025	10,107,373	13,082,637
Yangzhou	4,276,734	6,229,707	6,108,500
Huizhou	3,534,977	2,527,752	2,547,828
Ningguo	7,751,611	6,068,297	3,033,078
Chizhou	2,284,445	891,963	908,923
Taiping	3,621,179	1,624,383	1,287,053
Anqing	2,102,937	2,189,066	2,190,531
Guangdezhou	3,004,784	1,540,430	2,167,245
Xuzhou	2,834,154	3,001,223	2,016,716
Chuzhou	315,045	291,284	280,996
Hezhou	425,228	1,189,170	621,580
Total	126,927,452	81,018,040	77,394,672

Source: Liang 1980, 340–341.

Table D-5. Acreage data consistency check (Data in 1,000 *mu* unconverted)

Yuan area	Song 1082	Yuan 1300	Ming 1393
Jiangzhe (E)	90,437	99,508	97,500
Jiangxi (C)	48,369	47,469	64,000
Henan (N)	133,000	118,077	78,000

Sources: Perkins 1969, 227, table B. 6. The data are extracted from the *Wen xian tong kao.*

conquest of the Lower Yangtze was even less damaging than the civil wars in the late fourteenth century.

Following the Song-Yuan-Ming transitional line described previously, Perkins compared the land data at the provincial level (see table D-6). The result is rather satisfactory. For many of the provincial units, Perkins found that they are mutually supportive. The only problems came from the Song data rather than from the Ming data. For instance, the reported acreages in Shandong and Shanxi in 1082 were much fewer than those in 1400. This problem must have originated from the underreporting as discussed in the first section of this appendix. The other underreporting problem lies in the acreage in Guangdong and Guangxi; however, this resulted from an intended policy adopted by the court after it conquered these areas. Both are related, as one can expect, to underreporting. Per household landholdings in 1083 reached 23 *mu* only, the lowest recorded number for the Northern Song period. Therefore, this minor discrepancy only serves to support my

Table D-6. Song and Ming acreage data

	Song 1082		Ming 1400		1957
	1,000 Song mu	1,000 shi mu	1,000 Ming mu	1,000 shi mu	1,000 shi mu
NW					
Shaanxi-Gansu	44,710	38,000	26,066	22,680	157,000
N					
Hebei	27,906	23,720	26,971	23,470	132,000
Shandong	26,719	22,710	54,293	47,230	139,000
Shanxi	11,171	9,500	39,081	34,000	67,000
Henan	32,688	27,700	27,705	24,100	130,000
Subtotal:	98,484	83,630	148,770	128,800	468,000
E					
Zhejiang	36,344	30,890	47,234	41,090	33,000
Anhui	{102,358*}	{87,000*}	24,991	21,740	88,000
Jiangsu	102,358	87,000	56,026	48,740	93,000
Subtotal:	138,702	117,890	128,251	111,570	214,000
C					
Hubei	25,989	22,090	13,548	11,790	65,000
Hunan	33,204	28,220	10,428	9,720	58,000
Jiangxi	45,223	38,440	40,235	35,000	42,000
Subtotal:	104,416	88,750	64,211	56,510	165,000
SE					
Fujian	11,092	9,430	13,517	11,760	22,000
Guangdong	3,146	2,670	23,734	20,650	58,000
Guangxi	55	50	10,785	9,380	38,000
Subtotal	15,103	12,150	48,036	41,790	118,000
SW					
Sichuan	23,148	19,680	10,787	9,380	116,000
Total:	423,733	360,170	425,401	370,730	1,238,000

Source: Perkins 1969, 229, table B. 8.

*The estimated figures are for Anhui and Jiangsu together. No separate estimate is available in Perkins's table.

up-bound adjustment of the Song acreage in chapter 8. The internal consistency check performed by Perkins has laid a solid foundation to conduct historical analysis by relying on, though not conclusively, these Chinese land data from 1000 to 1500. In comparison to the eighteenth- and nineteenth-century land data, which is subject to major errors, the quality of the economic data of this period is surprisingly better than expected. In fact, to find another comparable group of national land data in post-Ming eras, Perkins had to adopt the land returns in the twentieth century. However, he does not explain why the pre-Ming land data rather than the seventeenth-century data seem to be more consistent with the early Ming land data, a question which is worthy of discussion. The answer must be related to how the land data was produced during the Song-Yuan-Ming transitional period.

Southern Song Land Data at the Local Level

The question as to why the pre-Ming land data rather than the sixteenth- and seventeenth-century data are reliable is counterintuitive. Data produced several hundred years later are usually richer in quantity and more trustworthy in quality. Moreover, the Song-Yuan-Ming transitional period is well known in Chinese history for its ample records of conflicts and disasters. Important changes occurred to both the territory and the political system more than once during these centuries. Official documents, if not lost, were preserved as fragments. In chapter 2 I have attempted to answer this question by emphasizing how the state institution played an important role yet in different ways to obtain useful information. In this section, based on Ho's collection of average farmland per household during the Song-Yuan-Ming transitional period, I further argue for a high degree of internal consistency with the historical land acreage and population data.

Long-term changes in average family landholdings are an important indicator of the quality of both population and land data. As revealed in table D-1, the Ming data show great inconsistency in this regard. For the years 1435 to 1626, average family landholdings continued to expand over the course of time. In comparison, the Song data suggest a plausible rising trend in farm yields per acre along with a declining trend in average per capita farm size.

Prevailing studies on average family farm size reveal consistency in the Southern Song land data. Based on the information preserved in extant Song and Yuan gazetteers, Liang Keng-yao calculated the average size of family farms for thirty-seven counties in the Lower Yangtze, Zhejiang, and Fujian. One can clearly tell that the amount of arable land for each household ranged from 10 to 45 *mu*. Regional variances were largely attributed to the elasticity of land supply. While farm size in the upland and hilly areas was below 20 *mu*, in general it reached 40 *mu* in Jiangnan. As the core area in the Lower Yangtze, Jiangnan was endowed with large areas of lowlands, swamps, and lakes that could be transformed into arable land. In either case, this variance can be further attributed to different developmental stage in the region's settlement history. For example, as shown in Table D-7, the average farm size in Huating was close to 50 *mu*, the largest among the thirty-seven counties. This reveals that Huating was a relatively new settlement in the Lower Yangtze and underwent rapid growth in the twelfth century. In contrast, the average farm size in Shaoxing, one of the earliest settlements in the Lower Yangtze, was less than 10 *mu*.

The changing relationship between the amount of land taxes and land registration can cast light on the discussed issue on the reliability of land acreage. Ho's classic study revealed the deteriorating quality of the population and land data in the post-Zhu Yuanzhang eras. "With the sole exception of 1602," he noted, "there was no increase in officially registered land between 1398 and 1867."[13] He attributed this puzzling fact to the prevailing practice of adopting fixed quotas in the collection of land taxes. Ho's

Table D-7. Average farm size per household in the Southern Song (*mu*)

I. Tai Lake area (3 counties)	Arable land	All-inclusive land*
Changshu county, Suzhou	45.40	51.39
Huating county, Jiaxing	48.45	—
Jiangyinjun	19.58	—

II. Coastal Zhejiang (4 counties)	Arable land	All-inclusive land
Shaoxing	9.43	
Sheng county, Shaoxing	11.32	
Yin county, Ningbo (Mingzhou)	17.93	43.18
Cixi county, Ningbo	23.46	
Dinghai county, Ningbo	18.66	

III. Zhedong (Eastern Zhejiang)	Arable land	All-inclusive land
Yueqing county, Wenzhou	18.71	
Taizhou (5 counties)	9.88	21.17
Ninghai county, Taizhou	10.86	
Linhai county, Taizhou	9.03	
Huangyan county, Taizhou	13.90	
Tiantai county, Taizhou	7.14	
Xianju county, Taizhou	9.12	

IV. Fuzhou in Fujian	Arable land	All-inclusive land
Fuzhou (12 counties)	13.27	32.75
Min county, Fuzhou	10.26	
Houguan county, Fuzhou	10.90	
Huai'an county, Fuzhou	11.30	
Fuqing county, Fuzhou	10.99	
Changxi county, Fuzhou	17.85	34.93
Gutian county, Fuzhou	25.78	
Lianjiang county, Fuzhou	13.70	
Changle county, Fuzhou	15.11	
Yongfu county, Fuzhou	14.40	
Minqing county, Fuzhou	15.18	
Luoyuan county, Fuzhou	13.65	
Ningde county, Fuzhou	14.07	42.56

V. Nanjing (5 counties)	Arable land	All-inclusive land
Nanjing	37.34	52.71
Shangyuan county, Nanjing	41.37	68.21*
Jiangning county, Nanjing	38.46	43.86*
Suyang county, Nanjing	27.96	27.90*
Gourong county, Nanjing	39.96	36.85*
Sushui county, Nanjing	11.96	32.21

continued on next page

Table D-7. *Continued.*

VI. *Huizhou (7 counties)*	*Arable land*
Huizhou	23.93
She county, Huizhou	17.60
Xiuning county, Huizhou	15.53
Qimen county, Huizhou	46.19
Wuyuan county, Huizhou	18.57
Jixi county, Huizhou	36.89
Yi county, Huizhou	43.05

Sources: Ho 1988, 51–55; Liang 2006, 74–77.

*This includes not only arable land but also all kinds of economically useful soil, ponds, and hills.

observation points to the changing relationship between the amount of land taxes and land registration right after the collapse of the early Ming command economy.

Ho's study also revealed a connection between the early Ming and pre-Ming land data. In his forty-seven carefully chosen local cases, he found that in the reported acreages for eighteen prefectures and counties, about one-third of the total number were simply copied from Southern Song and Yuan records with minor adjustments.[14] Based on this comparison and a few other sources, Ho argued that the land survey ordered by Zhu Yuanzhang was confined to Zhejiang and Jiangnan. The quality of the early Ming land data is thus far less reliable than that of the population data because the population returns were firmly backed by the *lijia* system.[15]

Ho's argument on the reliance of the early Ming land registration on the pre-Ming land data, whether fully or partially accepted, at least helps to demonstrate the consistency in the land data during the centuries from 1200 to 1400. Ho, in particular, traced the origin of high-quality land returns to the Southern Song administration.[16] As shown in table D-5, some of the early Ming land figures appear to have a close connection with those of the Southern Song and Yuan eras. Yet the evidence is still insufficient to reveal a pattern that would cover the territory once subjected to the Southern Song dynasty. Needless to say, there is little direct information on the north. Nonetheless, Ho's finding also gives us confidence that at least for some localities during the Song-Yuan-Ming transitional period, the administration collected and reported land data through serious efforts.

The best case to demonstrate how seriously the local administration carried out the land surveys over the two centuries from 1140 to 1315 is Huizhou. The land return in the 1140s doubled the acreage by reporting 3 million *mu* of land. This figure remained the record even up to the twentieth century (see table D-10). It is also obvious that land acreages remained above 2.5 million *mu* during the three and half centuries prior to 1500.

Conclusion

The land data is the most lacking among Chinese economic data sources. It is common knowledge that land registration during the Hongwu reign produced the most reliable

Table D-8. Local land data in the Song, Yuan, and Ming eras

I. Tai Lake area	Southern Song	Yuan	Ming
Shanghai county, Songjiang	—	2,139,073	2,206,204
Chongming county, Songjiang	—	75,736	724,600
Changshu county, Suzhou	2,321,563	1,172,502	1,242,500
Wuxi	—	1,824,046	869,023
Wucheng, Huzhou			
Jiangyin	1,253,602	—	991,130
Yixing	—	2,249,569	1,551,354
Zhenjiang	—	3,661,127	3,845,270

II. Coastal Zhejiang	Southern Song	Yuan	Ming
Shaoxing	2,000,000 (6,122,952)*	6,257,740	6,517,155
Sheng county, Shaoxing	375,738	382,468	411,692
Yin county, Ningbo	746,029		
Cixi county, Ningbo	469,100		
Dinghai county, Ningbo	356,790		

*The figure in parenthesis indicates only arable land.

III. Zhedong (Eastern Zhejiang)	Southern Song	Yuan	Ming
Yueqing county, Wenzhou	460,000	417,662	428,932
Taizhou	2,628,283	2,634,292	2,554,586
Ninghai county, Taizhou	385,718		
Linhai county, Taizhou	668,383		
Huangyan county, Taizhou	957,974		
Tiantai county, Taizhou	313,122		
Xianju county, Taizhou	310,126		

IV. Fujian	Southern Song	Yuan	Ming
Fuzhou	4,263,318		
Min county, Fuzhou	335,825		
Houguan county, Fuzhou	293,451		
Huai'an county, Fuzhou	263,451		
Fuqing county, Fuzhou	533,078		
Changxi county, Fuzhou	826,834		
Gutian county, Fuzhou	609,041		
Lianjiang county, Fuzhou	255,756		
Changle county, Fuzhou	200,411		
Yongfu county, Fuzhou	282,735		
Minqing county, Fuzhou	231,015		
Luoyuan county, Fuzhou	169,175		
Ningde county, Fuzhou	284,891		

continued on next page

Table D-8. Continued.

V. Nanjing	Southern Song	Yuan	Ming
Nanjing	4,397,633		
Shangyuan county, Nanjing	775,431		
Jiangning county, Nanjing	523,426		
Suyang county, Nanjing	1,788,955	1,770,956	1,185,537
Gourong county, Nanjing	1,013,683		
Sushui county, Nanjing	296,139		
Yizheng	420,724	—	109,046
Gaoyou	1,153,296	—	526,319
Xuancheng	1,400,284	—	972,030

VI. Huizhou	Southern Song	Yuan	Ming
Huizhou	2,919,553	33,529,278	2,427,049
She county, Huizhou	458,156	468,890	550,408
Xiuning county, Huizhou	303,964	463,711	516,879
Qimen county, Huizhou	717,636	59,163	158,457
Wuyuan county, Huizhou	795,787	327,852	519,279
Jixi county, Huizhou	309,566	322,494	340,382
Yi county, Huizhou	334,440	358,866	341,642

Sources: Ho 1988, 51–55; Liang 2006, 74–77.

Table D-9. Huizhou land data

I. Song land data	
Pre-1140	1,516,201
1140s	3,000,000
1208–44	2,919,553

II. Yuan and Ming land data			
1315	2,984,553	1482	2,527,676
1365	2,000,979	1492	2,527,676
1391	2,427,049	1640s	2,056,466

III. Qing-Republic eras	
1640s	2,056,466
1699	2,053,457
1827	2,056,576
1877	2,055,973
1923	2,055,747

Source: Ho 1988, 64.

Table D-10. Breakdown of Huizhou land data

Huizhou—Song*	Pre-1140s	1140s	1200
Huizhou	1,516,200	3,000,000	2,919,553
She county	252,984	460,000	276,120
Xiuning	177,271	303,960	304,433
Wuyuan	679,707	790,000	795,787
Qimen	199,563	750,000	717,636
Yi county	92,125	334,430	104,648
Jixi	104,538	296,000	309,546

*However, the total acreage of Huizhou is slightly larger than when all the county acreages have been totaled. For instance, the acreages of the six counties in the 1140s add up to 2,934,390 *mu*.

Huizhou—Yuan/Ming Region	1315	1360	1365	1391
Huizhou	3,348,654	2,000,979	2,000,979	2,417,049
She county	466,974	468,890	468,956	550,408
Xiuning	463,711	463,711	463,648	516,879
Wuyuan	1,007,615	327,852	341,602	519,279
Qimen	729,737	59,163	130,339	158,457
Yi county	358,866	358,866	332,672	341,642
Jixi	322,494	322,494	322,385	340,382

Primary source: Hongzhi Huizhou fuzhi, juan 2.

land data in late imperial China. After that, the quality of the Chinese land data deteriorated so severely that one cannot use them without major adjustments. Yet, even for the most reliable data such as the 1393 land returns, one cannot accept the reported acreage without making necessary adjustments. For most of the land data, underreporting is the major reason for the data bias. As already demonstrated in chapter 2, after the establishment of the two-tax system in 780 AD, reporting of household landholdings is a prerequisite for the collection of land taxes. Therefore, farmers had strong incentives to hide at least part of their farmed lands from the registration.

Of primary concern is the reliability of the Song land data. I argue that the Song land acreage reported in the first two centuries was undoubtedly underreported. When one compares the 1080 land returns with the early Ming land data, the gap is obviously due to underreporting on the Song side. By 1110, the Chinese population should have already reached over 100 million people. Therefore, based on our knowledge about average family farm size in the Northern Song era, I am confident that an estimate of 660 million Song *mu*, thus 561 million *mu*, can be made for the national acreage in the 1110s. Yet the Song acreage figures are still reasonable as compared with the post-1600 land data. When comparing the early Ming acreages with those of the Southern Song and Yuan, one can discern a close connection between them at the local level. This connection implies that the Song land returns were improving in the twelfth century.

Appendix E

Long-Term Changes in Real Wages

Per capita real income indicates the material standard of living in a country. It is generally assumed that per capita real income will rise when the economic growth rate exceeds the population growth rate. To provide an even tentative answer to the questions raised by the Song-Ming comparison, some basic ideas of long-term changes in per capita real income are indispensable for measuring the performance of the economy. However, for the period under discussion, the poor quality of the demographic data in particular makes it impossible to exactly measure the GDP. It is preferable to choose the real wages of unskilled laborers as an alternative to living standards.[1] This solution, however, is also problematic: There were few records available on the wages of unskilled laborers for most of the time during the seven centuries.

I decided to select a wide range of low-level wages with the primary focus on soldiers' salaries. The primary sources include official documents, literati works, genealogies, local gazetteers, and various treatises (the data sources are listed in table E-3). The data on wages are classified into three categories:

1. Wages for nonskilled, hired laborers in irrigation and other construction works.

2. Stipends and salaries for low-status professionals, such as students and government clerks.

3. The wages of the soldiers.

In addition, sources of relief for the poor reveal something about the living standards of paupers, their allowances, and the situation of pauperism and welfare institutions in general. The state of pauperism indicates the degree of inequality, the size and structure of welfare in relation to national income, and wealth of the local society. Due to the limited length of this study, I do not discuss this issue here while focusing on wage earners.

The quality of the wage data greatly varies. The data on the real wages of soldiers (SRW hereafter) are the best indicators of long-term trends. Since we assume that a day laborer spends all that he earns in buying food, clothing, and shelter, the day wage for nonskilled laborers is ideal to illustrate the elasticity of the labor supply in a market economy and to indicate the relative cost of meeting the physical needs of a person. The nonskilled, hired laborers in irrigation and other building work serve this purpose perfectly. However, this kind of data mostly appears in the anecdotes and gazetteers, making a comprehensive survey quite unreliable. In contrast to the scantly recorded wages, soldiers' wages were recorded in official documents that are relatively rich in both quantity and detail.

There are two reasons to choose soldiers' salary as the standard for comparison. First, it is the richest source of wage data available. The wage data for unskilled laborers consist of 312 records, starting from 1004 through 1805. I have broken them down into subcategories according to different professions. The soldier category has the largest number of records among them (table E-1). For the 113 records in this category, 38 fall in the Song dynasty with only 8 records dating from before 1127. The Ming dynasty had 67 records, plus 1 from shortly after the end of the Ming period. However, since some of these records appeared in the same unit in the same year, only varying according to rank, service, or marital status, I have combined them into a single entry with necessary weighting. Thus, they are reduced to 84 entries for the SRW.

One may surely question whether the 113 records can represent period-by-period changes in the real wages of soldiers over the seven centuries. However, for our purpose of examining long-term changes in wages, the SRW records are adequate. Unlike evidence found in anecdotes and literary writings, they are *real events* in which governments made payments to soldiers and thus can be examined directly in relation to contemporary contexts, such as soldiers' duties, working situations, and wage variances that correspond to rank and skill. Although short-term fluctuations (e.g., seasonal) in prices might influence the purchasing power of monetary wages, changes in soldiers' wages in the long term were particularly related to state policies, the central government's revenue, and long-term changes in prices. Fortunately, government documents give many details on military expenditures, including payments to soldiers. The Ming military administration, for instance, made payments at differential rates depending on a soldier's marital status. While a single soldier would be paid 0.30 *shi* of rice monthly, a married soldier with family members was paid 0.50 *shi*. Therefore, I calculated the average payment as 0.40 *shi*.

Second, soldiers' wages represent the pay of commoners and particularly help us to understand their living standards. In a study of early modern British history, a soldier is identified as being part of the mass commoners with lower status and living in poverty.[2] The same is true in both Song and Ming China.[3] A fundamental change in the organization of military staff occurred in the late eighth century, when the army ceased being a hereditary, land-based military group (*fubing*) and became, instead, a mercenary army. Song soldiers were without exception recruited from society.[4]

The Song dynasty used military recruitment in famine regions to defuse the tensions among starving people. Prisoners due to misdemeanors were often sent to the army to perform miscellaneous services, and their status was even lower than that of the soldiers enlisted through other means. The descendants of a soldier, if they liked, were also allowed to join the army. Thus, the major body of the Song armies came from the lower

Table E-1. Distribution of wage records

Profession	Soldier	Heavy laborer	Artisans	Students	Clerks	Total
Number of observations	113	73	65	13	29	312
Percentage	36	23	21	5	9	100

levels of society. Yet recruitment operated in an open and fair manner: At the time of their recruitment, candidates were only required to pass the qualification examination that mainly tested physical strength and military skills. To ensure successful enlistment, the government immediately dispensed a sum of money (usually the equivalent of two or three months' salary).[5] The wages of the soldiers in the Song armies usually comprised three parts: a monthly payment in cash, a monthly payment in rice, and compensation for clothing in spring and winter. These also varied depending on the soldier's capabilities in the military arts and types of service.[6] The differences in payments according to rank and skill resembled the wage differentiation in the labor market.

The Ming dynasty presented a different case. In the early Ming period, people were obliged to provide professional services, and, in theory, the Ming government did not need to pay anything for such services. Soldiers in the early Ming armies were also required to devote seven-tenths of their collective labor to agriculture and only three-tenths to military duty. This goal for military self-sufficiency under the *wei-suo* system removed the Ming military from the market. Certainly, in this case, their salaries did not reflect the changes in the demand of the labor market that would have otherwise decided the income of a laborer.

For our purposes, I have collected the monthly payments of soldiers who were on full duty and thus excused from farming. Farming soldiers, who were also known as *tuntian qijun*, received no pay and lived entirely on their land. Even so, they had to pay the required portion of harvest grain to the *wei-suo* before they could receive their own shares. Their living standards were usually lower than soldiers who were on duty and receiving regular salaries. More relevant information about the military farm system can be found in appendix H.

A soldier's standard of living represents the real income of the commoners within a command economy in the late fourteenth and fifteenth centuries. The fiscal system of the early Ming dynasty was entirely organized through the direct control of material and laborer supply and was anti-market to a great extent. The military was the largest professional service in Ming China: Soldiers and artisans who served in the armies, together with their families, constituted 13.1 percent of the Ming population.[7] Most of the early Ming armies were stationed in and around the capitals and in the less populated areas,[8] especially along the northern and northeastern frontiers, places where tracts of land were available for cultivation or the building of palaces and walls was feasible. Their living conditions were likely near subsistence level and therefore representative of the living standards of commoners in the early Ming. However, the early Ming policy lasted only one and a half centuries; in the early sixteenth century, the military farm system collapsed and the central government began to pay soldiers in silver.[9]

This shift gave rise to local markets for the exchange of food and clothing along the frontier.[10] Along with the payment reformation, the Ming government also tried to recruit military staff instead of solely depending on inherited services provided by military households. After the sixteenth century, the payment of Ming soldiers came close to that of a free labor market, although their salaries would display regional variance from the labor market in the Lower Yangtze delta, which was much more prosperous than the northern frontier and Beijing.

I have converted the SRW data into an index of real wages for comparison (see figures E-1–E-4). The index clearly indicates a continuous decline in wages over a period

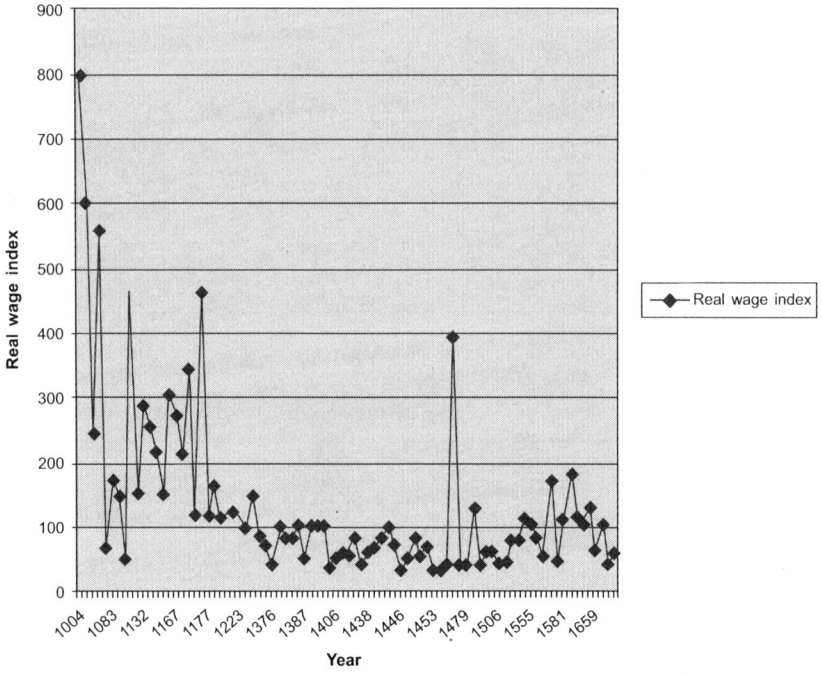

Figure E-1. Soldiers' real wages, 1004–1753

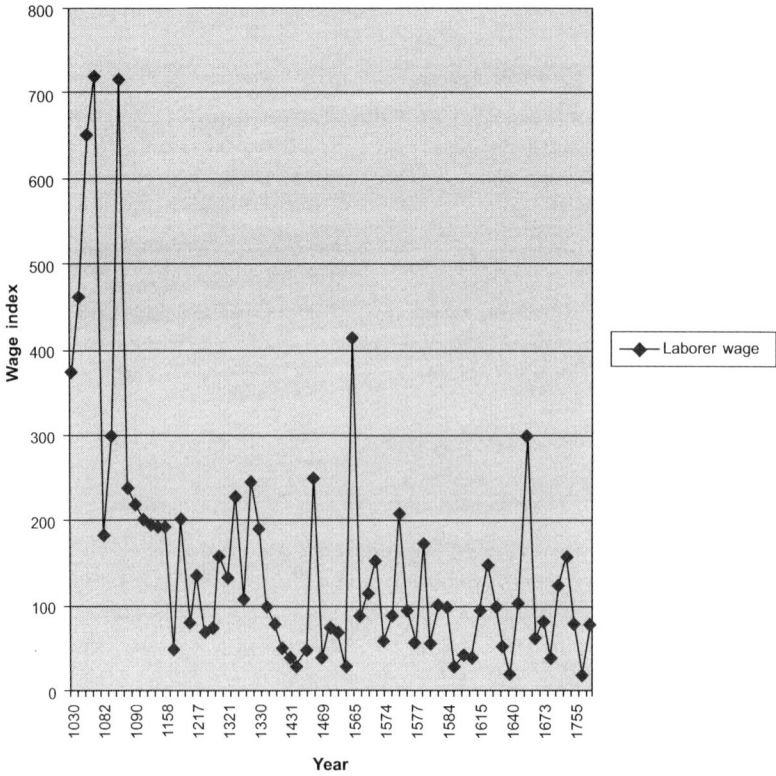

Figure E-2. Laborers' wages, 1030–1776

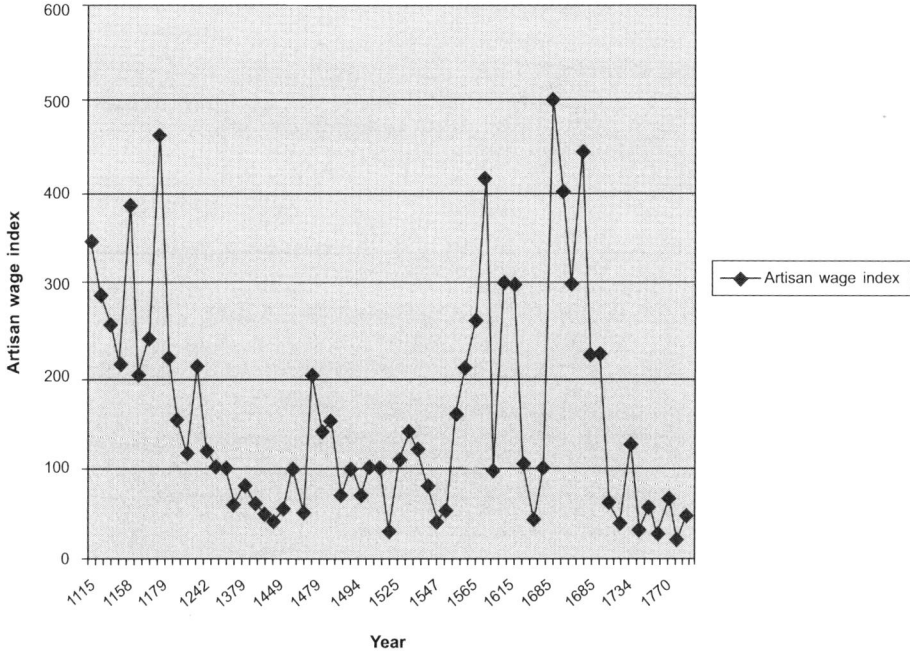

Figure E-3. Artisans' wages, 1116–1805

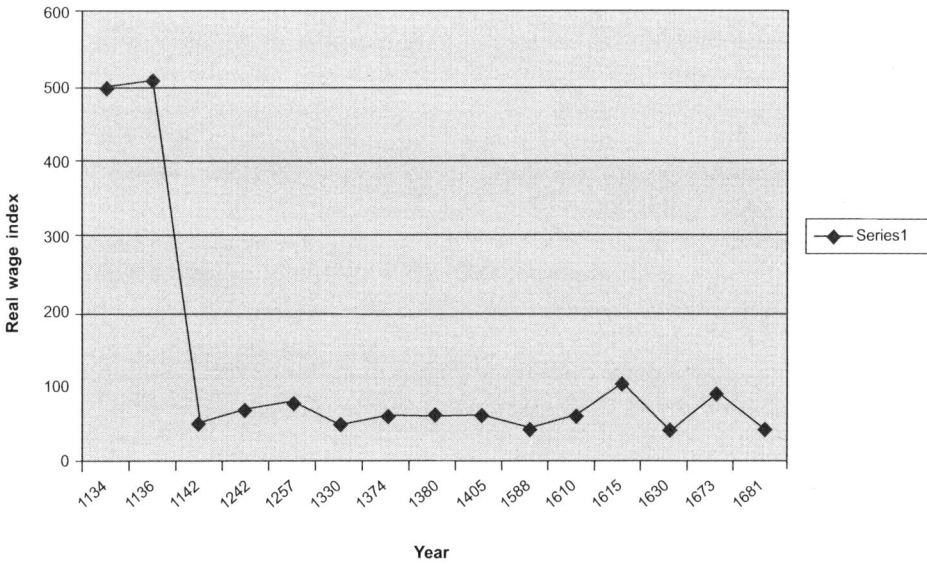

Figure E-4. Clerks' and runners' wages, 1134–1681

of seven and a half centuries. In other words, the soldiers in Song China were much better compensated than those in Ming China: The soldiers in the Song prior to 1127 received two to two and a half times higher payments than their counterparts in the Ming. In the Southern Song (Song China after 1127), due to severe inflation, payments to soldiers were just 50 to 80 percent higher than the early Ming soldiers—and probably no higher than those of the Ming soldiers when the latter were paid the highest salaries in the mid-sixteenth century. During the first hundred years of the Song dynasty, the wages of soldiers peaked and then declined to a monthly pay of less than 300 liters of rice per capita. In the century from 1150 onward, wages were even lower, ranging between 100 and 200 liters of rice per capita.

Besides this index and the SRW data, I have also found evidence to support my argument from three other sources. The first source is the research by other scholars on both Song and Ming military systems and policies. In the eleventh century, the Song central armies had over 0.4 million soldiers, while the local troops had over 0.2 million.[11] In accordance with studies by Wang, Koiwai, and Nagai, I arrive at an estimate of 200 to 240 liters of rice as the monthly pay for a Northern Song soldier and 120 to 150 liters for a Southern Song soldier. A soldier in the central armies stationed in the Lower Yangtze delta in the mid-twelfth century would have been paid about 141 to 342 liters of rice in real wages. At the same time, a soldier who was serving in a local troop in Jiangxi would have been paid a monthly amount of about 87 to 101 liters of rice in real wages in addition to a clothing allowance. If we take the payment for clothing into account, the real wages would be a little more: 92.8 to 113 liters of rice. These salaries remained as the standard in the Southern Song. However, due to inflation, the real wages of Southern Song soldiers would have been less than these figures suggested. Their real wages were probably maintained at an average level of 120 to 150 liters of rice.

This estimate basically matches what I have observed in the SRW data. Nonetheless, the SRW data also gives some higher recorded numbers that were mostly documented in the early eleventh century. As the Xining reign witnessed rising prices, a soldier's cash income from then onward would have constituted a smaller proportion of his real wages. The data also gives some lower recorded amounts: Not only soldiers in the formal troops but also those in civic guards and reserves were included in the data, and they were paid at a lower rate than soldiers.

The second source is from studies on real wages in preindustrial China. A few scholars have studied the long-term changes in prices and wages from the seventeenth century through the nineteenth century and pointed to an obvious decline in real wages over these centuries.[12] This case is clearly different from the eleventh century when real wages were maintained at a high level and the market economy sustained its expansion.

In the English literature, Chao's study is the only research on real wages in preindustrial China. His study of changes in eighteenth-century wages clearly proves the decline mentioned by other scholars. Furthermore, he attempted to trace this decline back to an earlier date and thus provided a long-term survey of real wages over a period of two thousand years (206 BC–1818 AD). Chao assumed that the increasing man to land ratio caused by the surplus population would invariably lead to the decline in "the marginal product of labor," in other words, a decline in real wages.[13] Chao argued that the turning point of such a decline occurred in the Southern Song dynasty, in which he found that the low levels of real wages for unskilled manual laborers were only one-fifth of those in the Northern Song.[14] However, Chao's wage data are very unevenly distributed; there were only twenty-seven observations prior to 1700, one for each period of seventy years. One can hardly accept the Southern Song turning point before ample evidence can be found.

The third source that supports the SRW-data-based argument is the wage data in other categories, such as artisans, clerks, and manual laborers. I have converted them into indices (see figures E-1–E-4). The long-term trends of real wages presented in these data clearly demonstrate a peak point in the eleventh century. This is especially true for the laborer wage data. In contrast, the artisan wage data show a more complicated pattern with some unusual fluctuations in the second half of the sixteenth century. There are probably two reasons that account for the obvious variances in their real wages. On the one hand, the artisan category includes many professions such as winemakers, ironsmiths, weavers, sailors, and carpenters, which would require different skills and hence had different pay standards. Therefore, certain observations of high levels of salaries in the late Ming period were biased—there happens to be other professions with higher pay.[15] On the other hand, these observations recorded salaries in the Lower Yangtze delta and Fujian in the late sixteenth century. This geographical concentration of higher wages for artisans may have been the result of the prosperity in these regions. Much uncertainty still remains here, and I expect a future study can solve this problem by providing better quantitative and qualitative evidence.

These data series also demonstrate the complexities in the Southern Song, when salaries reached both high and low points. The Southern Song economy was much more monetized, and paper notes became the normal means of daily financial transactions, even for commoners. Wage earners, including soldiers, received an increasing amount of paper notes as their salaries. Therefore, their income was more susceptible to inflation. Although real wages showed a substantial decline in comparison to those of the Northern Song prior to the Jurchen invasion, the Southern Song manual laborers, artisans, and clerks were well paid until the 1230s. Chao's thesis on the Southern Song turning point cannot be applied to the entire Southern Song. In the 1230s, a failed military campaign aiming to recover the lost territory in the north caused a severe crisis to the state's budget, which in turn led to debasements by the over-issuing of paper currency.

To prove this point, I have found an example from Song-Yuan publishing workshops. Some preserved Song-Yuan books provide information about the costs of publishing a book including the pay given to wooden block inscribers. The nominal wages in the late Southern Song, according to costs reported by these books, rose rapidly. The standard pay for inscribing one hundred characters onto a wooden block, for instance, rose from 750 *wen* in 1233 to 1,000 *wen* in 1238 and eventually reached 50,000 *wen* in 1253.[16] This increase can only be explained by the severe debasement of paper notes. However, if one chooses the pre-debasement period for a comparison with the Yuan-Ming pay standards, the 1230s still saw the highest salaries (see table E-2).

Table E-2. Wages of wooden block inscribers

Year	Pay standard wen per 100 characters	Monthly pay strings of cash	Real wages per month shi of rice
1233	600–700	18–21	3.45–4.02
1344	1,350[1]	40	0.95
1554	0.06 tael	1.8 taels	3.00
1630s	0.03 tael	0.9 tael	0.90

Sources: Yang 1984; Ye 1999, 154.

1. The monetary unit is the *guan*, the Yuan paper money *zhongtong chao*. In 1346, about 40 *guans* of *zhongtong chao* can purchase 1 Yuan *shi* of rice.

Table E-3. Sources of the wage data

Year	Sources
1004	SHY, 食货 42
1030	SHY, 方域 14, 治河: "正月下旬入山砍斫, 寒節前畢, 官給口食,亦有一夫出錢三五千以上 . . ."
1034	程琳, 宋史.兵志
1042	姚文灏, 浙西水利书
1045	XZTC, *juan* 157
1047	张方平, 奏疏, *juan* 23
1064	蔡襄, 文集, *juan* 18
1064	Ibid.
1064	宋史, 食货志, *juan* 191
1077	XZTC, *juan* 285, 熙宁十年十一月乙卯: "诏河北京东西淮南等路, 出夫赴河役者, 去役所七百里外, 愿纳免夫钱者听便, 每夫止三百五百."
1079	SHY, 2976
1080	SHY, 2976
1082	宋史, 食货志, *juan* 175
1083	SHY, 3488
1085	苏轼, 论役法差雇利害起请画一状, 苏轼文集, 1058
1086	XZTC, *juan* 376, 吕陶言 "每程只破二百文, 今若每程量添一百文 . . ."
1089	XZTC, *juan* 424, 李常言 . . .
1089	XZTC, *juan* 424, 李常言 . . .
1090	苏轼, 申三省起请开湖六条状, 东坡全集, *juan* 57
1092	苏轼, 祈罢宿州修城状, 苏轼文集, 1126
1104	SHY, 2979
1105	SHY, 6319
1108	杨龟山集, *juan* 2, 余杭所闻
1116	SHY, 4923
1120	SHY, 5398
1129	SHY, 6761
1132	SHY, 723–24
1132	SHY, 723–24
1132	SHY, 723–24
1132	建炎以来系年要录, *juan* 44
1132	SHY, 职官 57, 俸禄杂录

Year	Sources
1134	SHY, 5747
1134	SHY, 5747
1135	SHY, 职官 57, 俸禄杂录
1135	李纲,梁溪先生全集, juan 87
1136	SHY, 2969
1142	SHY, 3004
1142	SHY, 5747
1142	SHY, 5747
1144	SHY, 6324
1145	云间志, 卷下, 杨炬, "重开顾会浦记"
1158	SHY, 刑法二, 149
1158	浙西水利书
1158	SHY, 食货七, 水利三
1161	宋代蜀文辑存, juan 54, "双流昭烈庙记"
1162	Li Huarui, 1995, 179–78
1162	Li Huarui, 179–78
1164	洪适, "盤州文集," juan 42
1168	SHY, 6765
1168	SHY, 6767
1169	SHY, 6768
1169	SHY, 6768
1169	SHY, 6769
1169	范成大, 括苍金石志
1171	SHY, 5272
1177	朱熹, 朱子文集, juan 20
1179	淳熙三山志
1179	Ibid.
1179	Ibid.
1180	朱熹, 晦庵集, juan 20
1181	袁说友, "东塘集," juan 9
1192	SHY, 7053
1192	SHY, 7053
1192	SHY, 兵第三, 号兵, 光宗绍熙三年八月十八日
1216	叶适, 水心别集, 卷十六
1216	Ibid.
1216	Ibid.
1217	景定建康志
1217	勉斋先生黄文肃公文集,卷三十二, in BJGK, vol. 90, 657
1219	SHY, 3498
1222	嘉定赤城志, juan 18, 诸县寨兵
1223	Ibid, juan 18
1223	Ibid.
1241	四明它山水利备览
1241	四明它山水利备览, juan 1, 13–14
1241	Ibid., 13
1242	Ibid., 14
1242	Ibid.
1242	Ibid.
1242	Ibid.
1243	Ibid.

continued on next page

Table E-3. *Continued*

Year	Sources
1243	Ibid.
1250	永乐大典卷10950所引临川志
1250	Ibid.
1252	景定建康志.儒学, *juan* 29, 5.
1252	Ibid.
1252	Ibid.
1252	Ibid.
1252	Ibid.
1252	Ibid.
1257	景定建康志
1259	Ibid, *juan* 39
1287	通制条格, *juan* 13
1324	至顺镇江志
1324	浙西水利书
1327	元史, *juan* 64, 河渠志
1330	至顺镇江志
1351	徐一夔, 织工对, "始丰稿"
1370	MLAH, 349, 350
1374	MTZL, *juan* 91, 1597–98
1374	MTZL, *juan* 91, 1597–98
1374	MTZL, *juan* 91, 1597–98
1375	MTZL, *juan* 96, 1653
1376	MTZL, *juan* 96, 1653
1376	MTZL, *juan* 115, 1881
1377	MTZL, *juan* 115, 1882
1379	MTZL, *juan* 128, 2033
1379	MTZL, *juan* 128, 2033
1379	MLJJ, 90
1379	MLJJ, 90
1379	GTJ, 食货典, 国用部
1380	MTZL, *juan* 130, 2073
1380	MTZL, *juan* 130, 2074
1380	MTZL, *juan* 133, 2109
1382	MTZL, *juan* 144, 2264–65
1382	MTZL, *juan* 144, 2264–65
1383	MTZL, *juan* 154, 2401
1387	MTZL, *juan* 187, 2799
1388	MTZL, *juan* 187, 2799
1389	MTZL, *juan* 197, 2962
1392	WKL, *juan* 27, 943
1392	WKL, *juan* 27, 943
1404	MLJJ, 619
1405	MLJJ, *juan* 1, 218–19
1405	MLBJ, *juan* 1, 218–19
1405	MLBJ, *juan* 1, 218–19
1406	MLJJ, 768
1406	MLBJ, *juan* 1, 218–19
1406	MLBJ, *juan* 1, 218–19

Year	Sources
1406	*MLJJ*, 768; *MLBJ*, 216
1429	*WKL*, *juan* 37, 1192
1430	龚诩, 上巡抚周公书, 娄水文衡, *juan* 10
1430	Ibid.
1431	*MLZS*, 628
1437	明史, *juan* 91, 兵三
1438	*MHD*, 984
1438	*MHD*, 984
1438	*WKL*, *juan* 27, 943
1438	*WKL*, *juan* 27, 943
1438	*MLZS*, 1020
1438	*MLZS*, 1020
1438	*MLBJ*, *juan* 2, 62
1438	*MLBJ*, *juan* 2, 62
1439	*MLZS*, 765
1439	*MLZS*, 765
1439	*MLAH*, 329-30
1440	*MLBJ*, *juan* 2, 86
1442	*WKL*, *juan* 27, 943
1442	*WKL*, *juan* 27, 943
1443	*MLZS*, 768, 1026
1443	*MLZS*, 1026
1443	*MLAH*, 330
1443	*MLAH*, 330
1446	*MLAH*, 330–1
1449	*WKL*, *juan* 37, 1192
1449	*MLBJ*, *juan* 2, 205
1449	*MLBJ*, *juan* 2, 205
1450	*MLBJ*, *juan* 2, 223
1450	*MLJJ*, 95
1450	*MLJJ*, 95
1450	*MLZS*, 770
1450	*MLZS*, 770
1450	*MLZS*, 644
1451	*MLBJ*, *juan* 2, 264
1452	*MLZS*, 771
1452	*MLZS*, 771
1456	*MLBJ*, *juan* 2, 319
1457	*MLJJ*, 96
1457	*MLJJ*, 96
1462	*MLBJ*, *juan* 2, 382
1462	*MLBJ*, *juan* 2, 382
1463	*MLBJ*, *juan* 2, 385
1466	弘治興化府志, *juan* 30, 葉十四
1469	*HFSZ*, *juan* 33, 2
1472	王恕, 王端毅奏议, *juan* 2
1479	*MLBJ*, *juan* 2, 503/外卫京操官军口粮
1479	*HFSZ*, *juan* 1, 22–23
1479	*HFSZ*, *juan* 404–6
1481	*HFSZ*, *juan* 20, 521–22

continued on next page

Table E-3. *Continued*

Year	Sources
1485	MLJJ, 97
1487	胡世宁, 胡端敏奏议, *juan* 2
1488	WKL, *juan* 37, 1192
1488	WKL, *juan* 37, 1192
1494	明孝宗实录, *juan* 87
1495	马文升, 修饬武备疏, 御选明臣奏议, *juan* 8
1496	MLBJ, *juan* 2, 632
1497	WKL, *juan* 37, 1192
1498	MLBJ, *juan* 2, 648
1499	MLBJ, *juan* 2, 648
1502	杨一清, 关中奏议, *juan* 1
1503	MLJJ, 100
1504	明史. 志六十五.兵一
1506	杨一清, 关中奏议, *juan* 6
1506	Ibid.
1506	Ibid.
1507	Ibid.
1517	金山卫志, *juan* 3
1520	万历福州府志, *juan* 34, 时事 (又见载于王振忠, 1996).
1521	MLBJ, *juan* 3, 134
1524	MLAH, 842
1525	MLBJ, *juan* 3, 182–83
1529	MLJJ, 101
1530	MHD, 1112
1530	MHD, 1112
1530	MHD, 1105
1536	嘉靖事例, BJGK, 74
1536	Ibid., 82–83
1547	苏州织造局志, 卷三
1547	Ibid.
1553	郑若曾, "筹海图编" (*juan* 5, 398)
1555	MLAH, 850–1
1560	明史, *juan* 205, 李遂
1560	明史, *juan* 205, 李遂
1565	唐顺之, 武编. ZKJ, *juan* 5, 319
1565	Ibid.
1565	Ibid.
1565	Ibid.
1565	Ibid.
1569	海瑞, 备忘集, *juan* 1
1570	穆宗实录, *juan* 4, 引自梁方仲"明代的民兵," in Liang Fangzhong 1984, 174.
1571	潘季驯, "河防一缆," *juan* 16, 26
1574	万历和州志, 卷一
1574	Ibid.
1575	Ibid., *juan* 2.
1575	MLAH, 769
1576	Ibid, 896
1577	Ibid, 770
1580	潘季驯, "河防一缆," *juan* 7, 43–44

Year	Sources
1580	Ibid., 43–44
1581	*MLAH*, 868
1581	Ibid.
1581	Ibid.
1582	Ibid.
1583	Ibid.
1584	Ibid., 904
1587	Ibid., 341
1588	新修南昌府志, *juan* 8, 141
1591	王樵, 方麓集, *juan* 1
1602	盛万年"岭西水陆兵记," 卷上, in *BJGK*, vol. 51,652
1602	Ibid.
1602	Ibid., 656–57
1602	Ibid.

Appendix F

Estimates of National Incomes

There are multiple ways to estimate national income, and estimates derived from different methods may serve as a check on each other. In the following, I use a real-wage–based approach to make another assessment of the national incomes in the Song and Ming eras. This approach, which develops an index of change in real wages from the eleventh century to the eighteenth century, allows us to estimate the changes in real income per capita and to reconstruct the Song-Ming national incomes in connection to the estimated Chinese national income in the 1880s.

The widely accepted estimate of national income in preindustrial China is provided in Chang's study, which focused on the late nineteenth century. Chang chose the 1880s as the benchmark because it was the last phase of the Chinese preindustrial economy before it started to move toward industrialization, a long-term project not yet accomplished even today. Chang acknowledged that his estimates were only rough approximations but believed that they "at least show rough orders of magnitude that can be of general use."[1] Chang used the value-added or income-originating approach and totaled the contributions of the different sectors to the total products to generate his estimate. In doing so, he intensively explored the production data (data on the value or physical outputs of important agricultural and industrial products) through many contemporary sources, such as reports from customs and associations of merchants, surveys by foreign investigators and travelers, governmental publications, newspapers and local gazetteers, and genealogies. In Chang's calculations, the economy comprised agricultural and non-agricultural sectors, and the latter included mining, manufacturing (mostly the handicraft industry), construction, transportation, trade, finance, residential housing, governmental services, professions, the gentry, and other services.[2]

The Chinese economy in the 1880s was, according to Chang's estimates, still primarily agricultural (see tables F-2 and F-3). Two-thirds of the gross national product was from agriculture, in which grain output accounted for more than one-third of the GNP, and cash crops (tea, cotton, tobacco, produce, etc.) accounted for 18.6 percent. In contrast, the mining, manufacturing, construction, and transportation sectors together amounted to 8.2 percent.

Chang's research links both aggregate supply and demand in the economy. He arrived at his GDP estimate from the supply (production) side. While demonstrating how such goods and services were produced and consumed, he also referred to the demand side (income and consumption) to analyze the extremely unequal distribution of wealth (see table F-2).[3] The gentry class, for instance, gained a total income of 675,225,000 taels of silver in the 1880s, about 24 percent of the gross national product. The total number of gentry and their family members in the late nineteenth century was about 9,000,000, only 2 percent of the total population of 377,500,000 at the time.[4] In this way, Chang persuasively demonstrated how economic resources were controlled by a small number of the educated elite, who were not very interested in investing their wealth into trade and industry but rather endeavored to secure their income and social status through governmental and social services. The income from these kinds of professional services, according to Chang's estimate, comprised 52 percent of the gentry's income; this share was even greater than that from land rent (34 percent).[5]

Due to a lack of economic data, any attempts to explore the Song or Ming national income must take Chang's comprehensive analysis as the basis. The first step is to determine the real income per capita in the 1880s. GDP per capita in the 1880s, according to Chang, was 7.4 taels of silver. He reached this figure by dividing the national income in the 1880s (2,781,272,000 taels) by the aggregate population (377.5 million). Cao recently reported that the Qing population at the time was 364,389,000 people, and by following this, the GDP per capita can be adjusted to 7.63 taels of silver. The contemporary price of rice in Chang's calculation was 1.28 taels of silver per picul, and based on that, real income per capita in the 1880s was 5.96 *shi* (hectoliters) of rice.

The second step is to determine how one can use the real income per capita in 1880 as the basis to estimate Song real income per capita in the eleventh century. In the 1070s, a common soldier in the Song central armies would receive 2.35 to 2.48 *shi* of rice per month. A soldier in the local armies would receive 1.9 *shi* per month. This means 28.8 *shi* per year for the former and 22.9 *shi* per year for the latter. If such a ratio can be applied to real income per capita, Song real income per capita can be estimated from that of the 1880s. However, we need to consider the difference between an eleventh-century soldier's real wages and the 1880 real income per capita. The former was issued to pay for the daily life expenses of a soldier and his family. The latter is an arithmetic value of the average income per capita in correspondence to aggregate population; it includes, if accurate, both independent (especially male adults) and dependent populations (such as children, seniors, and semi-employed women). It is reasonable to consider that the wages of a soldier should be several times higher than the real income per capita, since not every person in his family would have to work, and the salary should be the major source of family income. Therefore, I have introduced a factor of 3.0 (to approximate a soldier and his dependents)[6] to divide the wages of Song soldiers that have been previously reported. This will lower their income per capita to 7.58 *shi* and 9.58 *shi* of rice, respectively.

Now, this estimate can be compared with Chang's GDP per capita data. Suppose that living standards in the Song era was either 30 percent or 50 percent higher than those during the Qing period; then, one can arrive at 7.75 *shi* (5.96 x 1.3) and 8.94 *shi* (5.96 x 1.5), respectively. Apparently, this result comes very close to the estimate of per capita real income in the Song era as mentioned previously. This also makes sense when the living conditions of Song soldiers are taken into consideration. Soldiers in Song local troops were not only paid less than their counterparts in the central troops but also had to conduct unskilled, heavy labor, such as building bridges and city walls. Their living standards represented the economic situations of the commoners in the Song period. To allow for a small range of overestimates in the wages of the Song soldiers, I am inclined to choose 7.5 *shi* instead of 9.0 *shi* as a rough estimate of real income per capita in 1077.

If my assumption about the family structure of Song soldiers is correct, it should also work for the Ming-Qing case. In terms of grain, the wages of a Qing soldier in the mid- and late eighteenth centuries was 0.92 to 1.25 *shi* of rice. Therefore, in dividing this number by a factor of 2.5, this results in 0.37 to 0.5 *shi*. This is even lower than the wages of the 1880s. However, the 1880s was a decade after the end of the Taiping Rebellion, the largest civil war in later imperial China, and the rice price was much lower than that in the 1770s. It must be the decline in grain prices that accounted for the increase in real wages, if it ever existed. I will choose 0.44 *shi* for the 1770s, and this means 5.28 *shi* per year.

The following discusses per capita real income in the Ming period. The performance of the Ming economies, both that of the early Ming regime and the sixteenth and seventeenth centuries, show significant variances with the Song and Qing eras. For the early Ming regime, evidence from official documentation shows that a soldier with a family was paid 0.6 to 0.8 *shi* per month. Real income per capita is calculated to be 2.9 to 3.8 *shi* (0.6–0.8/2.5 x 12). The late sixteenth-century case is more problematic. I tentatively decided to assume 0.6 taels of silver—the payment standard often officially documented in the 1580s—to be the standard monthly pay of a Ming soldier in the Lower Yangtze delta and obtain 3.95 *shi* for real income per capita according to the contemporary price (0.73 taels per *shi* of rice).

When these are put together and multiplied accordingly by the aggregate population, this will result in the size of the national income in real terms as displayed in table F-4. Tax revenues and tax burden per capita are introduced in columns D and F to show the tax capacity of the state in relation to the size of the economy and the tax burden of individual taxpayers.

These estimates may be better understood in an economic context as shares of sectoral economies and state revenues to the whole economy. Column C in table F-4 represents the Song, Ming, and Qing national incomes in terms of prices in the 1880s. They show a trend that is similar to that compared in relative terms. Columns D and E together reveal the changing pattern of tax revenues in later imperial China. As a share of the national income, the size of Song state tax revenues was second to that of the early Ming regime. The early Ming regime controlled around one-fifth of the gross national product. Although I have discussed at length the direct control of the early Ming state over society, this figure still appears to be unusually high for a government in preindustrial times. This is probably because I have overly relied on early Ming official documents and thus underestimated the size of the underground economy that was certainly beyond the control of the Ming court. On the other hand, the time frame that I have chosen for my estimate is in the 1420s, a period in which we can clearly see the worsening of living conditions caused by both aggressive imperial policies and the increase in natural disasters.

Leaving aside the exceptionally high share of tax revenues to national income, the other figures are consistent with my previous depiction of the state capacity in taxing the economy. The Song state extracted 8 to 9 percent of the gross national product, which appears to be very high in comparison with most early modern European countries. In fact, the share of taxes to national income in eighteenth-century Britain was not much more than this number until 1815. From 1665 through to 1805, the share of British national income appropriated as taxation, according to O'Brien, expanded from 3.4 to

12.9 percent, which was not far from the Song case.[7] The British government spent 60 to 70 percent of its total expenditures in waging war, the "fiscal-military state" as Brewer puts it.[8] Similarly, military defense surely consumed two-thirds of the Song state budget, and one can expect that after the Jurchen invasion of the 1120s, the share of Song taxes to national income would go up as the government sought to tax as much as possible to sustain a large number of soldiers on the battlefield. A smaller proportion of tax revenue to national income in the late Ming and Qing demonstrates the failure of the traditional Chinese state in taxing the market economy. This is especially the case for the Qing state prior to the Taiping Rebellion, which still held land taxes as the major source of taxes, though the market economy was expanding rapidly. In the 1770s, the estimated share of tax revenue to national income was merely 1.4 percent.

My estimates of the Song-Ming national incomes are largely based on Chang's estimates of those in the 1880s, and the explanatory power of the former should be secondary to the latter. What does this mean? Deliberation on the eighteenth-century case based on empirical studies of income and consumption will resolve many remaining uncertainties and improve our understanding of the Song and late Ming cases. For the Song case alone, I expect that an interested researcher can collect a few records of local censuses, which are preserved in gazetteers, to review my estimates. In current scholarship, studies of income and consumption concentrate on the family. My estimate of Song real income per capita can be converted into an annual income of 37 to 50 taels of silver per household (about 5.5 people), or in terms of grain, 37 to 50 *shi* of rice. For the late Ming, it is 15 taels, and for the Qing period in the 1770s, 30 taels.

The annual income of Song households still ranks first; that of the late Ming was only about half of the income of the Qing period in the 1770s. These rough estimates are averaged values by arithmetic calculation and do not represent regional and social variances. Yet they do indicate a general trend that accords with anecdotal evidence of real events. A tenant living in the thirteenth-century Lower Yangtze delta, according to Fang Hui, a contemporary, would rent for 30 *mu* and harvest 60 Song *shi* of rice. After returning 30 *shi* to the landlord as rent, he could use the other half for his five-member family.[9] In Fang's record, the 30 Song *shi* of rice can be converted into 20 *shi*. Fang's observation of the grain income of a peasant family seems to be lower than my calculations (37 to 50 *shi*). Nonetheless, this is a case of a tenant farmer who had no land to his name and who belonged, according to the Song household registration, to *kefu*, those categorized as the poorest and free from taxation. A farmer with similar resources and who cultivated a similar amount of land under his ownership would harvest 60 Song *shi* (40 *shi*) for his family, which exactly matches my estimate. The social groups with an average annual income of 40 to 60 *shi* were tenants (*kefu*) and poor farmers.

Although the Song government carried out nationwide classification of household property, the measurement standard varied across regions, and we are left with scant information. Qi made a social table of Song wealth and income distribution among the social classes. Qi put the Song official categories of household registration, which comprised five classes among rural households and seven to ten classes among urban residents, into a Marxist pattern of landowners versus peasants. The social classes below the annual income of 60 Song *shi* were more likely formed by tenants and poor farmers, which accounted for, according to Qi's estimate, over half of the Song households. While Qi's approach is not without flaws, it is strong in its observations of the low-income population. This merit must be attributed to the Song official statistics. It is the first time in Chinese history that we have knowledge of the number of the Song rural population who were landless in comparison to the land-owning class, thanks to the censuses conducted by the Song administration. Such information about land distribution across the country, especially the percentage of landless households, would not be provided in government records for almost another nine hundred years. In order to include more social groups other than the land-based ones, I have made some changes and presented instead a new form as table F-1. The Song classes still appear as a pyramid in which a few individuals controlled the largest share of the wealth and the majority lived in poverty. Nonetheless, my adjustments give credit to the poor who were not in the agricultural sectors, such as soldiers, laborers, among others. I have also added professionals (5 percent) for the large number of Song people who worked as clerks, brokers, doctors, and teachers as well as fortune tellers, students, monks, and nuns.

Similarly, without reliable information about the percentage of each population group and their respective wealth and incomes, neither Qi's nor my own adjusted table can be taken as the final estimate of Song national income. The large percentage of the Song poorer classes does not necessarily exclude the possibility that there was a higher standard in average family incomes.[10] However, it is possible to deduce a higher

Table F-1. A social table of Song household income and landholding distribution

Class	Total households (percentage)	Size of landholdings (mu)	Annual income (shi of rice)
Large landowners		>400	
Middle-class landowners	7–8	150–400	
Lower-class Landowners		100–150	>100
Professionals	5		—
Military[b]	2–3		37–50
Craftsmen & small shop owners	8–9		—
Laborers[c]	10		
Ordinary peasants	21.5	30–50<X<100	>50
Poor peasants	20	<30	—
Cottagers	25	0	—
Total	100		37–50

a. This includes clerks, doctors, fortune tellers, students, among others.

b. The total number of Song soldiers varied from 8 to 12 million. Suppose that the average family size is three; this means an aggregate value of 2.4 to 3.6 million, just 2.6 to 3.9 percent of the Song population then. I have lowered this value to 2 to 3 percent to compensate for nonmarried soldiers.

c. This includes hired laborers in both agricultural and nonagricultural sectors. In the Song household registration, they would be classified as *kefu* as well. I have distinguished here those who make a living by farming on rented land as tenants and those who do not own farms or businesses but are hired on a daily basis for a short or long period of time.

percentage of nonagricultural populations. If we count all peasants and cottagers and two-thirds of all laborers as the agricultural population, then it will be 73.2 percent of the total Song population, which is much higher than that of Britain in 1688. However, for the remaining almost one-third, if we allow a ratio of two-thirds who are living in towns and cities, we can arrive at 17 to 18 percent as the rate of urbanization.[11] This estimate will undoubtedly give the Song period the highest percentage of urbanization in Chinese history.

In the current literature, studies on Song urban population concentrate on the early thirteenth century, when records of urban households become available in local gazetteers. The share of urban population (at county seats and above) to the total population usually varied from 8 to 25 percent in the Lower Yangtze delta, Jiangxi, and Fujian.[12] Taking into account the population at the town level, I think that a moderate estimate would set the share of urban population in the eleventh century at 12 to 18 percent. The extraordinary size of trade as reflected in the Song commercial taxes in contrast to the relatively small percentage of agricultural taxes, and a noticeable expansion in mining, transportation, and handicraft industries, will support the proposition of a high degree of urbanization with a large share of nonagricultural population.

For the cases of the Ming and Qing, it is even more difficult to relate national incomes to the distribution of wealth and income. To put the estimates to a simple test, one can evaluate the degree to which they converged with the annual income of an ordinary peasant family in the Ming-Qing periods. For the late Ming, He's description of Songjiang farms is often cited by modern scholars. A mid-sixteenth-century household could plant 25 *mu* of rice and harvest 2.5 *shi/mu* for a total of 62.5 *shi* of rice.[13] In the late Ming period, Songjiang was already a region with a very high degree of land tenancy. It is reasonable to assume that a large number of farmers provided 50 percent of the rice output to landlords as rent. This would reduce a farmer's annual income to around 30 *shi*, just like the Song tenants in the Yangtze delta previously mentioned. The rice price in the mid-sixteenth century was about 0.5 to 0.7 taels per *shi*,[14] and 30 *shi* of rice would be sold for 15 to 21 taels of silver. The lower end of mid-sixteenth-century Songjiang farm income tallies exactly with what I have estimated for that of the later Ming period. Huizhou local documents are most illustrative of Ming rural society. A peasant family in Huizhou in the late Ming period earned about 10 to 15 taels of silver each year.[15] In Huizhou genealogies compiled by merchants, quite a few cases indicate the start of business ventures after attaining savings that amount to around 10 taels over several years.[16] A social historian of eighteenth-century China informs us that a hired laborer would earn 3,000 to 4,000 *wen* of coins per year, which is about 3.3 to 5.0 taels of silver. Marriage required the preparation of a betrothal gift in the amount of 20,000 *wen* in cash, which was about 22 to 25 taels of silver. Moreover, a middle-class peasant in north China with a landholding of 15 to 20 *mu* would harvest 30 to 40 *shi* of rice, which could be converted into an annual income of about 30 to 40 taels of silver.[17]

Table F-2. Gross national product of China in the 1880s (in 0,000 taels)

Sector	Amount	Percentage
Agricultural	1,672,456,000[a]	60.1
Grain	1,369,607	44.3
Living stock, fishery, etc.	142,945	4.6
Tea	84,000	4.5
Cotton	59,843	3.2
Other crops[b]	201,890	10.9
Nonagricultural	1,108,816	39.9
Mining	<u>47,800</u>	1.7
Coal	13,000	
Gold & silver	3,200	
Copper	200	
Iron	5,800	
Salt	20,000	
Others	5,600	
Manufacturing	<u>125,800</u>	4.5
Textile[c]	92,900	
Foodstuff	15,000	
Pottery & chinaware	3,000	
Instruments of Transportation	4,900	
Others	10,000	
Construction & transportation	<u>60,000</u>	2.0
Trade & finance	<u>294,645</u>	10.6
Residential housing	<u>164,000</u>	6.0
Government services	<u>164,000</u>	6.0
Gentry services	<u>241,313</u>	8.7
Total	2,781,272	100.00

Source: Chang 1962, 296, 303. I have combined several subcategories for convenience.

a. The original figure is 1,858,285,000 taels. Then, Chang deducted 10 percent for the costs. The percentage in column 3 uses the original figure as the aggregate value for calculation.

b. This includes tobacco, produce, and silk.

c. It can be further broken down as follows: 21,300,000 taels for cotton spinning, 51,300,000 taels for cotton weaving, and 18,600,000 taels for silk weaving.

Table F-3. Proportion of gentry income to gross national product according to different sectors of the economy

Sector of economy	GNP (in 0,000 taels)	Gentry income (in 0,000 taels)	Proportion of gentry income to GDP
Agriculture	1,672,456	220,000	13
Mining & manufacture	173,600	—	—
Construction & transportation	60,000	*	*
Trade & finance	294,645	113,600	38
Residential housing	164,000	30,000	18
Governmental services	164,000	121,000	74
Professional services	241,313	190,625	79
International transactions	11,258		
Total	2,781,272	675,225	24

Table F-4. Estimate of national income and the share of tax revenues, 1080–1880

	Song (1080)	Ming (1420s)	Ming (1580s)	Qing (1880s)
A1	7.5	2.9–3.8	3.95	5.96
A2	7.5	0.73–0.95	2.88	7.63
B	89.7	85	120–200	364.4
C1	673	247–323	474–790	2173
C2	673	62–81	346–576	2781
C3	861	316–413	607–1011	2781
D	62.7	48*	22.4	88.2
E	9.3%	15–19%	3.9–6.5%	3.2%
F	0.70	0.3–0.34	0.13	0.24

A1: Real income per capita in *shi* of rice.

A2: Real income per capita in taels of silver.

B: Population in millions. Registered total households in 1078 were 16,603,954. Wu Songdi suggests that the average size of a Song family is 5.4 (Wu Songdi 2000, 122–37, 162, 352). The official record in *Mingshilu* reports 51.4 million for 1420, a figure even lower than that in 1403 (about 66.6 million). Some scholars also estimate the population in 1400 had already reached 85 million, assuming it was 60 million in 1381 and increased at an annual rate of 0.4 to 0.5 percent (Heijdra 1998, 440). For a discussion on estimates of aggregates populations in the Ming era, see Cao 2000a, 281, 430. I follow Perkins and assume that the size of the late Ming population is 120 to 200 million.

C1: National income in millions of *shi* of rice.

C2: National income in millions of taels of silver.

C3: National income in terms of the 1880s, millions of taels of silver.

D: Tax revenues in millions of taels of silver.

E: D/C2.

F: Tax burden per capita in taels of silver.

*Taxes in grain (million *shi*).

Appendix G

Major Commodities in the Domestic Market

This appendix continues to explore the changes in long-distance trade between the Song and Ming periods. Here, I am particularly interested in several questions related to the composition of trade: What were the major goods that circulated in Song-Ming long-distance markets, and how much of each of these goods contributed to the aggregate value of trade? As original information in the extant sources on specific amounts of merchandise traded or consumed before the 1880s is unsatisfactory, there is the need to estimate as deemed necessary.

To conduct a Song-Ming comparison, we first need to identify the number of major commodities that were circulated at the time. It is well accepted that major commodities in a preindustrial economy were salt, tea, textile goods, grain, wood, sugar, paper, metals, porcelain, lacquer ware, among others.[1] In the tenth century, Song society was already able to consume these goods so extensively that one can probably call it "a revolution in mass consumption."[2] Production of paper, for instance, was concentrated in forty-seven prefectures, most of which were in Zhejiang, Fujian, Anhui, Jiangxi, Hunan, and Sichuan.[3] Yet we are hardly able to find quantitative information for paper production.

Quantitative information of Song commodity production concentrates on a few goods, such as grain, textile goods, tea, liquor, salt, and mining products (gold, iron, copper, etc.). The first source for such information is governmental provisioning. The Song administration normally bought a large amount of grain and silk cloth every year and thus left behind many records on the prices and amounts of the government purchases. It is without doubt that the quotas of government purchases are real trade data. Some evidence for government purchases in the grain markets (discussed later) suggests that the purchases were usually made in a competitive market.

The second source is state monopolies. During the Song period, the state launched projects to monopolize certain strategic resources that could either secure large revenues or supply military needs. Some metals, such as iron, silver, and copper, for instance, which were used to make weapons and mint coins, came under the supervision or even direct control of the state. Therefore, Song official reports preserved certain invaluable details about industrial investments. Hartwell amazingly used them as the basis to estimate iron outputs in the eleventh century, key evidence for his "early industrial revolution" thesis.[4] In addition to mining, monopolies of liquor, tea, and salt were the largest sources of cash income for the Song state.

Such evidence allows a researcher to explore long-term changes of trade at a more solid empirical basis. To identify the circulation of some important commodities in the sixteenth-century market, for instance, researchers used to reconstruct their estimates solely based on late nineteenth-century data. In their projections, they often assumed constancy of certain important criteria (such as living standards, consumption, or productivity per capita) over the course of three or even five centuries, which appears to be implausible to most economic historians. In the following, I make my own estimates on major commodities in Song long-distance trade and compare them with some widely accepted estimates of the size of trade in the Ming-Qing periods.

Estimates of Tea Production and Trade in China

The tea monopoly is an example illustrative of the binding relationship between the Song administration and long-distance trade. After 750 AD, the tea industry showed tremendous growth (see table G-1). In the mid-eighth century, the tea-producing regions were confined to fifty-two counties, which were only 3.31 percent of the total counties. In the succeeding three hundred years, tea production spread all over the country with a concentration in the south. For instance, in the Liangzhe Circuit, which included modern Zhejiang and southern Jiangsu, and the East Jiangnan Circuit, which included southern Anhui, Jiangsu, and eastern Jiangxi, 135 out of 176 counties were listed for tea production, which accounted for 48 percent of the total tea-producing counties in Song China.[5]

Long-distance tea trade rose from the coexistence of a concentration of tea production in the south and a large external market in the north. Tea was carried over hundreds of miles to consumers in North and Northwest China. This, in turn, allowed the Chinese state to intervene in the tea markets.

The Song state assumed monopoly over tea trade in several steps. First, tea was classified as "international trade" before the Song state, a Kaifeng-based military power, conquered the south. Merchants shipped tea from the kingdoms of the south to the border and sold it to the agencies of the Song state, which would resell the purchased tea through state-operated shops in Kaifeng. This "international trade" pattern was soon met with challenges when the Song state conquered the south. After gaining immediate access to the tea supply, the Song administration found that it was beyond their capacity to purchase all of the tea that was grown there. The markets in Kaifeng and other cities in the north could not absorb them. Meanwhile, the court rejected the idea of free trade, which meant allowing the merchants to go wherever they wanted and simply paying transit taxes at current rates, as this would have significantly reduced the profits previously secured through the "international trade" pattern. Instead, the Song state incorporated tea trade into an internal trade framework to keep a large share of the profits. The monopoly administration usually adopted three major strategies, though not always simultaneously:

Table G-1. The spread of tea planting, 742–1120

Year	Number of tea-producing counties	Index (742=100)
742	52	100
900–970	80	154
1120	277	533

Source: Sun 2001, 64–65, 69.

1. The official agency was entitled to the exclusive right to contract with farmers and tea plants in tea-producing areas for all tea products.

2. Merchants could buy tea only from official agencies.

3. Only with government permits (*chayin*, certificates for tea trade) could merchants sell tea at specifically assigned areas (one or a few prefectures in most cases) for a fixed period of time.

The state agencies were established and firmly controlled by the State Financial Commission. Their existence attested to the power of Song mercantilism in the market. Nonetheless, the mercantile pursuit had to adjust its pace in accordance to changes in the market. From the tenth century onward, the tea monopoly administration shifted their policies from strategies 1 and 2 to 3. The Song state was forced to relax its control on tea trade to reduce risks that would necessarily involve a strictly enforced monopoly system in the market. The exclusive right of an official agency in the tea purchase was designed to exclude private merchants from the competition, but it also brought market risks and increased supervision costs that would have undermined the prospect of profits. To secure a higher yield of tea, official agencies provided farmers with a large number of short-term loans to buy tools and fertilizer, which were repaid with tea at harvest seasons. However, tea growers might fail to submit tea to official agencies as scheduled due to the unpredictability of tea production. Furthermore, merchants might speculate in the tea market and were reluctant to buy tea from official agencies at current prices. Therefore, market instability often resulted in a large amount of surplus inventory and caused a great deal of loss to the official agencies.

In 1112, a reform led by Cai Jing, then the chief councilor, put an end to official purchases. Cai's policy allowed free trade between merchants and tea growers under official supervision. Merchants purchased licenses that specified the sale regions and dates of the purchased tea. Violators would be severely fined. These changes in the tea monopoly successfully encouraged more merchants to participate in the tea trade, on the one hand, and reduced the risk to the state monopoly, on the other hand. With Cai's reform, the Song government succeeded in reaping as much as 2.5 million strings per year in extra profits, and annual tea sales increased to 12,815,600 catties. The reform policies continued through the end of the Song dynasty with only minor modifications.

I have demonstrated that the tea monopoly aimed to control tea trade between the south, the main tea-producing region, and the north, the largest external tea market. Prior to the Cai Jing Reform in 1112, official agencies established in the major tea-producing areas served as privileged intermediaries: They purchased tea products from local tea plants and resold them to merchants, who then took the tea over to the markets in the north. It is not surprising that there is a large amount of official data on both tea output and the amount of tea purchases. An often-cited record of tea purchases by official agencies is presented in table G-2. The total amounts to 54.1 million Song *jin*, about 84.5 million *jin*, or 42.25 million kilograms.

Not counting the tea purchased from Sichuan, the remaining total amount is 24.1 million Song *jin*.[6] This figure has been often viewed as the tea output of South China (with the exception of Sichuan) in the tenth and eleventh centuries. However, it is wrong to equate the amount of official purchase with aggregate tea demand. All of these

Table G-2. Tea purchased by Song official agencies (000s Song jin)

Tea-purchasing sites	Sichuan	Huainan lu	Liangzhe lu	Jiangnan lu	Jinghu lu	Fujian lu	Total[b]
Amount	30,000	8,700	1,300	10,200	3,500[a]	400	54,100

Sources: Quoted from Jia and Chen 38–39; Liu 2000, 50–51. Originally recorded in the *SHY* and *Jingde ji.*

a. The original figure was 2,272,014 Song *jin*. This figure should be adjusted because of the great variance between the standard of local weight units, which were used in Jinghu's tea purchases, and the Song national standards (Fang 1993, 75–76; Liu 2000, 51).

b. In official records, tea from Sichuan was separately counted, because tea from all the other regions had been united into a national network for the tea monopoly, which was called "southeast tea (monopoly)."

figures came from the reports of official agencies that were established in the south. These official agencies were the only assigned suppliers for long-distance trade with the north, but could they sell all tea products to the north and leave local communities in the south without tea? Recently, C. Liu has persuasively argued that these figures indicate the amount of tea that Song official agencies purchased from local growers and sold to merchants of long-distance trade. Thus, 24.1 million Song *jin* of tea were exported to the north,[7] and this reported amount did not include local demand in the south.

Another way to test C. Liu's conclusion is to check whether she overestimated the amount of long-distance tea trade. As I noted earlier, tea trade contributed 0.57 million strings of commercial taxes in 1034. If the average tax rate is assumed to be 5 to 10 percent, this figure means a gross value of tea at 5.7 to 11.4 million strings. However, since the recorded wholesale prices of tea (from 30 to 900 *wen* per unit) greatly varied depending on quality and brand,[8] it is impossible to determine the average price without information on the amount of different kinds of tea. Nonetheless, I will use a record from 1058 to arrive at an approximate average price: In 1058, official agencies reported that 10.5 million Song *jin* of tea were sold with a total value of 2,254,047 strings. This calculation certainly includes tea sales at multiple prices, and, thus, I obtain an average value of 220,000 strings for 1 million *jin*. Dividing the estimated gross value of the tea trade (5.7 to 11.4 million strings) by this average price will result in 26 to 52 million Song *jin* of tea exported in long-distance trade (with the exception of Sichuan). The bottom value of this estimate comes very close to the reported amount of tea purchases in the south, which is 29 million.[9]

When centralized agencies were focusing on long-distance trade with the north, the tea markets for local consumption were regulated in a different way. The local administration established official retail shops in the prefectural cities of South China. However, these could hardly compete with private businesses, which operated as a semi-black or even openly black market, because local communities in the south had easy access to the tea supply. In 1058, for instance, local official shops sold 7.4 million Song *jin* of tea with a total value of 340,000 strings. Meanwhile, official agencies sold 10.5 million Song *jin* of tea with a value of 2,254,047 strings at a wholesale price.[10] The amount of tea officially retailed in the south was even less than that exported to the north. This contrast illustrates the prosperity of underground tea trade in local economies, for which contemporary opinions usually estimate sales to be several times those of official agencies. By paying a small sum of money as retail tax, private tea trade in local venues was even often publicly allowed by local administrations. Only the "across-border" (*yuejie*) trade, in which merchants smuggled tea across mountains and rivers to a distant market, was penalized by tea agencies and the government because it directly threatened long-distance trade under the monopoly.

One may wonder, given the challenges from the private tea business, why the local administration insisted on making retail sales. Unlike official agencies that aimed to control the market to ensure the quality of tea products, the local government purchased a great amount of crudely processed, low-quality tea (*chaoca*). These were usually sold at much lower prices to local consumers. Moreover, in the collection of land taxes, the local administration often allowed farmers to pay with tea or other cash crops instead of grain. Tea from all of these sources had to find an outlet through the official retail shops in the south. Although the retail amount came close to that exported to the north (a ratio of 1:1.4), the income from tea that was retailed in the south was only 15 percent of the wholesale income from long-distance trade. The much-lower prices were chiefly responsible for the low profits of retail tea.

This discussion of the tea monopoly highlights the relationship between the Song monopolies and long-distance trade. Though official agencies held much more regulatory power in the trade of tea than other goods, when faced with multiple buyers and sellers, the state was still unable to control the pricing in the long term but had to share profits with both tea growers and merchants. Private participants, either growers or merchants, could leave the market when they felt inclined to do so. Such decisions were not always made without difficulties, but the state also took risks. The negative effects caused by the monopoly were most likely transferred to the consumers.

I have provided an estimate of the size of the Song tea trade in table G-3. I assumed that the purchases made by official agencies were the only source of the long-distance

Table G-3. Estimates of tea trade in Song China (000s Song jin)

Region	Sichuan	The mid- and lower Yangtze River basins	Fujian	Total
Long-distance trade	8,000[a]	28,606[b]	394[c]	37,000
Marketed amount	22,000	26,600	2,806	53–63,000
Total amount	30,000	56,800–66,800	3,200	90–100,000

Sources: Jia and Chen, 38, 84; Liu 2000, 55–56.

a. The amount of tea that was sent to the Xihe region for tea-horse trade alone was 4 million Song *jin*. Therefore, I doubled this figure to include tea consumed in other regions of Shaanxi. No records about local consumption can be found. I deducted long-distance trade from the total amount, which had been estimated by local officials to be 30 million *jin*. This leaves 22 million *jin* for local consumption. In 1078, there were 478,171 households registered in Sichuan by the Song administration thus comprising 23,000,000 individuals. This would imply, if my estimate about local consumption is correct, 0.96 Song *jin* per capita for tea consumption.

b. The amount of tea purchased from the south (with the exception of Sichuan) was 24,100,000 Song *jin* (see table G-2). The tea purchased in Fujian is reported to be 400,000 *jin*; therefore, I deducted this figure to arrive at an estimate of long-distance tea trade in the mid- and lower Yangtze River basins. I also ignored those of Guangdong and Guangxi, which should not be significantly large enough to change the estimate.

c. The number 394,000 was cited by a Song official in 1084, which is quite close to the 400,000 presented in table G-2.

tea trade. This may result in an underestimate of the magnitude of long-distance trade because it does not take smuggling into account.

The size of the local markets in the south remains to be determined. Adding it to the size of long-distance trade as shown in table G-2 will give us an estimate of total marketed tea production in the eleventh century. Since contemporary accounts often assert that private tea sales in the local markets were several times greater than those in the official shops, C. Liu assumed that the former was two times greater.[11] The retail tea in the official shops came to 7.4 million Song *jin*, and so Liu estimated 22 million for private sales in the south. The total amount of sales from the tea trade in the south thus adds up to 60 to 70 million Song *jin*.[12] A ratio of 1:3 that is premised in C. Liu's approach still appears to be a modest figure. Nonetheless, it provides a figure for the reconstruction of the aggregate volume of trade based on governmental purchases.

In table G-3, 37 million Song *jin* of tea were exported from the south, about 40 percent of the tea output. This percentage may have underestimated the amount of tea that was privately traded in the mid- and lower Yangtze River basins. In Fujian, for instance, long-distance trade only accounted for 12 percent of the tea output.[13] Therefore, it would not be unreasonable to double the estimated amount of local tea consumption in the south. However, I have adopted C. Liu's figures, 90 to 100 million Song *jin* (about 115 to 128 million *jin*) as a modest estimation of aggregate tea output in the eleventh century.[14]

A comparison of tea production and consumption per capita over time is given in table G-4. Many of the centuries are missing between the eleventh and mid-nineteenth centuries because no such estimates were available prior to 1800. In terms of per capita tea consumption, the Song was not rivaled until the late nineteenth century. It seems that over the seven centuries, China's tea output grew too slowly to parallel the pace of the population growth.[15]

Table G-4. Tea consumption per capita and long-distance trade, 1000–1880s

Period	Tea output (000s jin)	Long-distance trade (000s jin)	Tea consumption per capita[1] (jin)	Share of long-distance trade to output (percentage)
11th century	115,200–128,000	47,360	1.28–1.42	37–41
1840	302,180	—	0.58	—
1880s	638,000	348,000[2]	1.5	55

Sources: For estimates around the 1880s, see Chang 1962, 303–4; for 1840, see Xu & Wu 2003, 335; for the eleventh century, see table G-3. The units of weight have been converted into the modern units of *jin* (500 g) at the rates of: 1 Song *jin* = 1.28 *jin*, 1 Qing *jin* = 1.16 *jin*.

1. Chang estimated 0.95 *jin* per head for domestic consumption and, when adding exports, 1.5 *jin* per head for tea output in the 1880s. Wu Chengming estimated 0.5 Qing *jin* per head for consumption prior to 1840. The Song population in 1078 was 90 million (2000, 348) thus 1.28–1.42 *jin* per head for consumption in the eleventh century.

2. Chang reported 200 million Qing *jin* for tea export in the 1880s and estimated 350 million Qing *jin* for domestic consumption. In the 350 million, I estimate that 100 million were exported in long-distance trade. Thus, 300 million *jin* would be the total volume of long-distance trade. For 1840, Xu and Wu estimated 60.5 million *jin* for the amount of exported tea and 200 million *jin* for the domestic consumption. Similarly I assume 57.1 million *jin* would be the total volume of long-distance trade.

Estimates of Textile Trade in China

Before cotton cloth became the major textile in the sixteenth century, silk cloth and linen were the traditional textiles consumed by commoners.[16] In the Song period, silk cloth was widely used, and the silk industry developed in the cities and the countryside. The silk industry was one of the most important handicraft industries in the Song era.[17] During the Song-Ming transition, cotton cloth gradually replaced silk as the favored textile by families and caused a radical decline in silk production.[18] With the rise of the cotton textile industry in Ming-Qing China, the opportunities that cotton planting and the weaving of cotton cloth provided for rural families to increase cash income, and hence raise agricultural productivity by absorbing surplus laborers within the family, are often emphasized in a microeconomic framework.[19] Yet scholars often ignore how this shift influenced the entire textile industry in the economy. Therefore, a comparison of textiles between the Song and Ming eras, including silk, linen, and cotton, will help to illustrate whether the development of the rural cotton industry could have resulted in an overall expansion in the aggregate value of textile production, and whether one can find strong evidence for an expansion in aggregate demand for textile goods over the course of the eight centuries. I will first examine the supply and demand of silk in the Song and Ming periods before I turn to cotton. A general comparison presented in table G-12 suggests that despite the huge production potential of the family-based rural cotton industry, only a very small amount of cotton cloth was exported in long-distance trade.[20] Furthermore, since cotton cloth is a low-value good, the gross value of cotton cloth in the late Ming long-distance trade was much lower than that of silk cloth in the Song period.

A survey of Song silk cloth will start with an examination on the supply side. In addition to a great number of rural families involved in sericulture and silk-cloth weaving, there were also many urban-based weavers and apprentices who specialized in raw-silk processing and silk-cloth weaving.[21] According to Qi's estimate, about 100,000 artisan households (jihu) worked in the silk textile industry in the cities.[22] The output of silk cloth, estimated from the production capacity, could have reached 20 to 36 million bolts of silk cloth, or about 24 to 43 million taels of silver in the late eleventh century.

Despite the development of the silk industry in the urban areas, the greater part of Song textiles are thought to have been produced by farmers. In consideration of the fact that the artisan class alone produced 20 to 36 million bolts of silk cloth, the aggregate output could therefore have been over 100 million bolts. The major base of the rural silk industry was shifting toward the Lower Yangtze delta, a region that generated two-thirds of the silk cloth taxes in the eleventh century. Traditional bases, such as the North China plateau and the Sichuan basin, still made significant contributions (see table G-5). Although an agro-industry, silk production techniques encouraged processing specialization, and this gave rise to employment in different fields of sericulture. In the rural silk industry, a division of labor emerged in mulberry cultivation and silkworm handling.[23] Under such circumstances, a rural family in Huzhou who specialized in silk and silk cloth could produce as much as 15 bolts of silk cloth a year, or the equivalent of 21.8 Song shi of rice.[24]

Table G-5. Regional distribution of Song silk revenues[a]

Region	Tax quota (bolts)	Contribution quota (bolts)	Total (bolts)	Percentage
The mid- and lower Yellow River	1,242,933	865,862	2,108,975	31.7
The mid- and lower Yangtze River	1,611,530	2,456,874	4,068,404	61.1
Sichuan	456,187	23,273	479,460	7.2
Total	3,310,650	3,346,009	6,656,839	100

Source: The figures are extracted from SHY, shihuo 64, 6100–7.

a. This includes tax quota (silk cloths from the land taxes) and contribution quota (tributary goods sent from local administrations to the court). The latter were mostly purchased from the market.

An analysis of the aggregate demand with respect to fiscal policies and government purchases supports the argument on the development of the Song textile industry. In the Song period, demand for silk cloth was also enhanced by tax policies in which the state encouraged farmers to pay their taxes in textiles. In the eleventh century, the share of silk textiles in Song land taxes was about twice that of cotton cloth in the late Ming land taxes.[25]

The Song government succeeded exactly where the Ming government failed. By the end of the sixteenth century, the Ming court collected 2.2 million bolts of cotton cloth from land taxes (see table G-6). This is already an obvious increase in comparison to the early sixteenth century.[26] Together, Shandong and the Lower Yangtze delta (Nanzhili) accounted for over half of the total amount in the sixteenth century. Such a high degree of output reveals the rapid development of cotton textile production driven by commercialization in these two regions.[27] However, in contrast to the large share of

Table G-6. Amount of cotton cloth and cotton in Ming taxes

Region	Cotton cloth quota in 1502 (bolts)	Cotton cloth quota in 1578 (bolts)	Cotton quota in 1502 (jin)
Shanxi	128,770	128,792	17,172
Shaanxi	291,000	291,000	102,500
North Zhili	5,700	27,878	103,739
Shandong	296,418	601,937	139,000
Henan	81,837	260,850	130,342
Sichuan	0	150,308	72,851
Huguang	0	200,000	
Jiangxi	100,000		
South Zhili	415,000	605,000	
Fujian	0	0	0
Guangdong	0	0	0
Total	1,318,725	2,265,765	565,604

Source: Nishijima 1948, vol. 1.

silk textiles that contributed to the Song land taxes, the contribution of cotton to the land taxes in the late Ming period seems insignificant. The Song government encouraged substitution of textiles and cash for grain in collecting land taxes. In the eleventh century, Song land taxes comprised 12 to 13.4 million *shi* (18 to 20 million Song *shi*) of grain, 2.5 to 3.5 million bolts of silk cloth, and 5 to 7 million strings of cash.[28] In the early twelfth century, the aggregate value of silk textile and cash income had already surpassed grain income.

In addition to tax substitution, the Song government also purchased a large amount of silk cloth from private markets and farmers for public use. In 1016, the Song state purchased 20 million bolts of silk cloth from the West Jingdong Circuit (Jingdongxi *lu*). The price was set at 1,000 *wen* per bolt, about 20 percent higher than the market price as the court claimed that this purchase was an attempt to reinvigorate the sluggish economy.[29] This was probably the largest governmental purchase of textiles in China prior to 1700. The average amount of annual purchases in the eleventh century had reached about 3 million bolts, which is close to the maximum amount of taxes received in silk cloth.[30]

The transition in Song land taxes from a grain-based pattern to a textile/cash-based pattern in the eleventh century provided incentives for farmers to grow cash crops and work at textile handicrafts. Meanwhile, a large amount of textile purchases also increased effective demand. The amount of silk cloth in lieu of grain for land taxes and the amount of government purchases indicate the immensity of marketed textile goods in Song China. Hino's comprehensive survey on Song government purchases provides very useful estimates of Song textile aggregate demand.[31] Aggregate demand for silk textile, according to Hino, probably reached over 100 million bolts in the eleventh century (see table G-7). This figure matches with my estimate from the supply side.

Despite the potential of preindustrial production for food and textiles, effective demand should play a central role in accelerating the entire industry by reducing production costs. The enormous demand from the private and public sectors should have had a huge impact on the development of the Song silk textile industry. Although there is no direct evidence of changes in the production costs of Song silk textiles, the prices, which were measured in silver, showed an obvious decline from the mid-tenth century to the early twelfth century (see table G-8). There was an even steeper decline in relative prices compared to the long-term trends in grain prices. The index of the relative prices between silk cloth and grain fell from 100 in the 960s down to 20 to 30 in the period of 1070 to 1110. If one variable is assumed to remain a constant, such a decline

Table G-7. Estimated demand for silk cloth in the Song period (bolts)

Region	Northern China	Sichuan	The Mid- and Lower Yangtze delta	Total
Estimated amount	Over 30 million	Several tens of million	Several tens of million	Over 100 million

Source: Hino 1952b, *HKTSR*, vol. 10, 466–68.

Table G-8. Relative prices between silk textile and grain, 961–1600

Year	Average price per bolt in silver	Index of silk textile price (961–970 = 100)	Silk textile per bolt measured in shi of rice	Index of relative prices between textile and rice (961–970 = 100)
961–970	1.2	100	3.65	100
971–980	1.25	104	2.48	68
981–990	—	—	—	—
991–1000	1.28	107	3.27	90
1001–1010	—	—	—	—
1011–1020	0.65	54	2.08	57
1021–1030	0.85	71	2.62	72
1031–1040	—	—	—	—
1041–1050	1	83	0.796	22
1051–1060	1.3	108	2.91	80
1061–1070	1.44	120	2.11	58
1071–1080	1.3	108	0.89	24
1081–1090	1.1	91	1.29	35
1091–1100	1	83	1.08	30
1101–1110	—	—	—	—
1111–1120	—	—	—	—
1121–1130	0.81	68	0.11	3
1131–1140	2.35	196	0.36	10
1141–1150	3.2	267	4	110
1151–1160	1.71	143	1.5	41
1161–1170	1.48	123	1.27	35
1171–1180	1.51	126	1.55	42
1181–1190	1.51	126	1.28	35
1191–1200	1.56	130	0.93	25
1211–1220	1.21	101	1	27
1368–1400	0.5	42	1.08	30
1401–1450	0.44	37	1.5	41
1451–1500	0.63	53	1.42	39
1501–1550	0.7	58	1.28	35
1551–1600	0.7	58	1.12	31

Source: Peng 1965, 505–7, 711.

in relative prices of silk and grain, each as a major representative commodity in the industrial and agricultural sectors respectively, demonstrates the growth in the productivity of the textile industry.

The relative prices between silk textile and grain remained stable in the Ming period, and the general trend even shows a curve with higher prices in the fifteenth century. Though the technological capacity of the Ming silk industry maintained a status quo, this stability in relative prices, especially the up-trend of the curve, indicates the stagnation of silk textile production owing to an obvious decline in aggregate demand.[32]

In the sixteenth century, the Ming land-tax mechanism experienced a similar transition at a much lower pace. Three prefectures, Songjiang, Suzhou, and Changzhou, contributed in total 0.6 million bolts of cotton cloth every year to the Ming court to substitute grain for land taxes. In contrast, the annual purchase of silk cloth by the Song government in the Lower Yangtze (Liangzhe lu) was about 1.1 million bolts along with 0.78 million bolts collected as substitution for land taxes. Although the cotton textile industry in Ming China is viewed as the largest industrial sector, it was, in fact, confined to Shandong, Zhejiang, and the Lower Yangtze delta. Wu, for instance, used cotton cloth from Songjiang as the only evidence to analyze the late Ming long-distance trade. This somewhat uneven distribution of textile production should be attributed to a narrow demand pattern.[33]

For most of the time in Ming history, there is no obvious decline in the relative prices between cotton cloth and grain. As shown in table G-9, the price of cotton cloth is the lowest in the 1610s. If we take into account this very late decline in the relative price, the two indices of the relative prices show a similar trend for the Ming period. This similarity may partly support my previous suggestion: The decline in the Ming aggregate demand for textiles (including silk and cotton cloth) probably hindered the development of the textile industry.

Nonetheless, it is of particular interest to determine the amount of these textile products that entered into long-distance trade. Since textile goods were under free trade, government purchases, for which we have preserved data, were merely a minor portion of the interregional traded textile. Hence, first, I will determine the average amount of government silk cloth purchases during normal times, since during famines or wars the government might use its reserves to purchase a greater amount of silk cloth, as in the case of the year 1066. Then, I will pin down the ratio between the size of long-distance trade and government purchases.

The government should purchase a large amount of silk cloth during normal times as there was an obvious gap between the amount of silk textiles expended and distributed by the court and what it could receive from the tax and the tributary. In 1021 the state distributed about 42.7 million bolts of all kinds of textile cloth.[34] As shown in table G-5,

Table G-9. Index of relative prices between Ming cotton textile and rice, 1368–1643

Year	Cotton textile per bolt measured in shi of rice	Index (1368 = 100)
1368	0.4–0.8	100
1407	0.83–1.0	153
1429	1	167
1457	0.75	125
1469	1	166
1499	1.2	200
1511	1	166
1610s	0.2	33
1643	0.087	15

Source: Peng 1965, 712.

the annual amount of the textiles the court received was 6.7 million, and the contribution quota accounted for half. Most of the contribution quota was in fact purchased from the market. An example of a normal government textile purchase is reported by Fan Zhongyan in 1042, in which about 20,000 bolts were purchased every year in Yuezhou (modern Shaoxing).[35] Zhang Fangping, a formal high official at the Ministry of Revenues, also wrote that the state annually purchased 3 million bolts of silk cloth from the Lower Yangtze and other regions in the south.[36] Thus, I will use 3 million bolts of silk cloth as the average amount of government purchases in the south. In my own estimation, the Song state purchased no more than 1 million bolts every year from the north and Sichuan. Therefore, the Song state is estimated to have steadily purchased an annual 4 million bolts. Considering that the Northern Song silk industry in the urban areas is estimated to have produced 20 to 36 million bolts of silk cloth, and that the aggregate output of Song silk textiles, according to Hino, reached 100 million bolts, the estimated 4 million bolts of government-purchased silk represents only a small percentage of the silk cloth trade. Therefore, I believe that the amount of silk cloth in long-distance trade should come close to the annual output from the Song silk industry in the urban areas and be estimated as 15 to 20 million bolts.

In addition to silk cloth, textile goods also include linen fabrics produced in the Song period. Although linen fabrics, such as ramie and hemp cloth, had been the main raw materials for clothing in ancient China, their dominant position was largely replaced by other textile goods by the Song period.[37] The surviving data on Song tax revenues demonstrate that linen fabrics were still widely used in some regions. In the eleventh century, the Song state collected nearly 3.2 million bolts of linen cloth from land taxes. This implies a much larger volume of linen fabrics in circulation. In 1030, a high official in Jiangxi noted that 50,000 bolts of linen cloth were purchased from Fujian to clothe the soldiers in Jiangxi.[38] Sichuan was probably the largest supplier of linen fabrics in Song China, and the trading of linen fabrics contributed to the commercial taxes collected there.[39] In the 1020s, the court began to purchase linen cloth in six prefectures

Table G-10. Linen fabrics in Song taxes, the eleventh century (bolts)

North China: 528,681	East China: 23,503
Hebei: 253,035	Zhejiang: 3,372
Shandong: 196,525	Huainandong: 11,214
Henan: 79,121	Huangnanxi: 3,870
Shanxi: 150,990	Jiangnanxi: 5,047
Northwest China: 2,164	Southwest China: 569,589
Shaanxi: 2,164	Sichuan: 569,589
Central China: 124,232	Southeast China: 181,248
Hubei: 17,223	Fujian: 995
Hunan: 101,962	Guangdong: 462
Jiangxi: 5,047	Guangxi: 179,791
Total: 3,192,765 bolts	

Source: Sudo 1962a, 334–35.

of Sichuan.[40] Until 1078, the court bought 700,000 bolts of linen cloth every year at the price of 400 to 450 *wen* per bolt. If we assume that the Song state purchased no less than 500,000 bolts of linen cloth,[41] which is a moderate estimate, and also that government purchase was one-fifth of the volume of long-distance trade, similar to the case of silk cloth, the total volume of the linen cloth trade can be estimated at 2.5 million bolts.

To make a comprehensive comparison of the textile goods between the Song and the Ming periods, we have to include Ming silk textile output. Wu estimated that about 30,000 bolts of silk cloth were exported from Jiangnan to long-distance markets, a gross value of 30,000 taels of silver. By the mid-nineteenth century, the amount of silk cloth in the domestic market was 4.16 million bolts. Even then, 80 percent of the total production came from Jiangnan, and the involved labor force was estimated to be 50,000. The tenfold increase of silk cloth production in the nineteenth century in Jiangnan strongly suggests the underdevelopment of the late Ming silk textile industry and, moreover, the poor demand for silk textile goods in the late sixteenth century.

A comparison is presented in table G-11. Due to the very conservative estimate of the Song long-distance trade, the total volume of textile goods shows little variance between the eleventh and late sixteenth centuries. However, nearly 90 percent of Song textile goods were silk cloth, while silk represented a very small percentage of textile goods in the Ming and Qing eras. This implies that the Song textile goods in long-distance trade had a very high value, since the price of silk cloth was usually several times that of cotton cloth. In Wu's estimates of textile goods in the late Ming market, for instance, silk cloth was sold at 0.70 to 1.00 taels of silver per bolt, but cotton cloth at only 0.16 taels per bolt.[42] Such a huge price variance demonstrates that the Song silk textile industry outweighed the Ming cotton industry in terms of the share of national income.

Table G-11. Volume of estimated textile goods in the Song, Ming, and Qing eras (000,000 bolts)

Period	Silk cloth	Silk cloth in long-distance trade	Linen or cotton cloth	Linen or cotton cloth in long-distance trade[a]
Song (11th century)	100	15–20	—	2.5
Ming (late 16th century)	0.3	0.3	—	15–20
Qing (1840)	4.16	4.16	314	45

Source: For estimates of textile goods in the Ming-Qing periods of time, see Wu Chengming 2001, 131, 134, 150, 161.

a. The Song figure concerns linen cloth, and the Ming-Qing figures concern cotton cloth.

Estimates of Grain Trade

Grain markets in China were highly competitive during the Song-Ming periods.[43] The rise of the Song grain trade can be attributed to "the great advances in agricultural productivity achieved since the middle of the Tang dynasty."[44] Great regional disparities in agricultural practices gave rise to specific grain exporting and importing regions. The Lower Yangtze, for instance, was one of the most important rice-exporting regions in the later twelfth century. Large landowners often received rice rent in thousands or tens of thousands of piculs, most of which would flow back into the market.[45] In addition to the Lower Yangtze, provinces in Central China such as Jiangxi, Hebei, and Hunan also came to be known as rice-exporting regions in the late twelfth century. In contrast, the coastal areas in Zhejiang and Fujian, such as Wenzhou, Taizhou, Ningbo (Mingzhou), Fuzhou, and Quanzhou, were rice-importing regions that relied on rice shipped from Guangdong and Guangxi to ease food shortages.[46] In addition to the interregional pattern, the grain inflow from the countryside into the cities along the lower Yangtze River had a significant share of the grain trade as well.[47]

There was also a noteworthy amount of state-managed grain transportation. Song soldiers were among the few social groups with a livelihood outside the agricultural sector. A large part of their salaries was still distributed in grain. Although there was only a slight gap between the amount of the grain that the state could secure from land taxes and the quantity that the state had to provide for soldiers and administrative staff, the concentration of the military in northern China made the supplying of grain a difficult task.[48] The capital Kaifeng and neighboring areas, for instance, needed 6 million Song *shi* of grain yearly to feed about 100,000 soldiers and a large number of official staff.[49] Therefore, over 6 million Song *shi* of rice was shipped to Kaifeng along the Bian Canal from the south. Among them, about 2 to 3 million *shi* was purchased by the official agencies.[50] The grain supply to the troops stationed along the northern frontier was also an urgent concern for the Song court. The troops stationed in Hebei, Shanxi, and Shaanxi numbered from 700,000 to 800,000 soldiers at their peak.[51] Local supplies of grain constituted a small share of the total consumption for the soldiers and their families. Grain supply for troops in Hebei in 1034, for instance, was 10.2 million Song *shi*; meanwhile, local farm output could barely support 30 percent of their food consumption.

To solve the problem of deficiency in grain supply, the Song court set up local grain-purchasing official agencies in Hebei.[52] In 1070, the court approved an annual budget of 2 to 3 million strings for official agencies to spend on food provision.[54] For other frontier regions, the Song administration in Shanxi usually purchased over 0.8 million Song *shi* of grain. During the war with the Tanguts in 1044, the troops in Shaanxi consumed about 15 million Song *shi* of grain and fodder, about half of the supplies from local farm output.[54]

Aside from cash, the Song state also used other commodities to purchase grain. Silk textile, for instance, was a popular means of exchange in grain purchases. Table G-12 shows that in the eleventh century, the Song administration occasionally purchased as much as 1 million Song *shi* grain with silk cloth. This demonstrates the large demand for food from nonagricultural sectors but not necessarily from the silk cloth market, since a large percentage of silk cloth paid in grain–silk cloth exchanges might have come from taxes.

Some portion of the officially purchased grain also entered the market. In order to estimate the size of long-distance trade in grain, it is necessary to determine if the amount of official purchases outweighed the amount that the private markets provided. The amount of official purchases must have accounted for only a small percentage of the marketed grain, or even a minimal share of farm output. Grain output per capita during the Song period, according to Wu's estimates, was higher than that of the Ming and Qing periods. This provides the basis of the supply for grain consumption in non-agricultural sectors.[55]

The real problem behind government purchase was not whether changes in per capita grain output would upset the market but rather the technical difficulties in buying grain at specific locations and dates, and transferring purchased grain to venues for consumption. An integrated waterway network would allow agencies to send staff to or even set temporary branches in areas with surplus grain. These agencies were thus able to purchase a larger amount during harvesting seasons.

Would such practices give rise to a monopolized trade pattern in which the official agency, as the largest purchaser, could manipulate pricing at the expense of other participants? I only have a partial answer to this difficult question. In the case of grain purchases in Hebei, an official agent would often come to compete with other officials

Table G-12. Song government purchase of grain in silk cloth, 1031–1061

Year	Place	Amount in silk (million bolts)	Amount in grain (million Song shi)
1031	All	6	10.8
1034	Hebei	3	5.4
1035	All	10	18
1036	Hebei	2	3.6
1037	Hebei	3	5.4
1037	Hebei, Shaanxi	5	9
1038	Shaanxi	10	18
1040	All	10	18
1040	All	10	18
1042	All	20	36
1043	All	30	54
1050	Hebei	10	18
1050	Hebei	6	10.8
1052	All	1	1.8
1052	Hebei	1	1.8
1053	Hebei	3	5.4
1054	Hebei	5	9
1055	Hebei	3	5.4
1056	Hebei	2	3.6
1058	Hebei	1	1.8
1061	Hebei	2	3.6

Source: Hino 1935b, in HKTSR, vol. 11, 355–56.

Table G-13. The size of the grain markets in the Song, Ming, and Qing periods

Year	Grain output (million jin)	Grain output per mu (jin)	Grain output per capita[b] (jin)	Grain supply to nonagricultural sectors (million jin)	Share of marketed grain to aggregate output
Song (1064–67)	151,864	325.8	1,518	25,417	17%
Late Ming (1550s)	134,200	346	895	21,687	12.8%
Qing (1770s)	310,890	385	1,085	53,660	17.3%

Source: H. Wu, 1998.

a. Guo estimated 171,601 million *jin* for late Ming and 286,152 million *jin* for the 1770s (2001, table 7, 389).

b. Wu used a figure of 125 million as the late Song population and 100 million for the 1550s. Both are obviously inadequate. I have adjusted them to 100 million and 150 million, respectively, and recalculated grain output per capita as such.

and private agents in the market by raising the purchasing price a little higher. In 1098, an official agency accused other official agencies administered by the local authority of giving a larger discount (only 4 percent higher, in fact, according to his complaint) to attract more rural grain brokers.[56]

My estimate of long-distance trade of grain in the eleventh century will start from the amount of grain that official agencies had steadily purchased in the market. Table G-14 illustrates that in Hebei, the average amount of grain purchase should have been at least 2 million Song *shi* of grain with a gross value of 2 million strings.

For the other two frontier regions, Shanxi and Shaanxi, I allow for 0.8 to 1 million Song *shi* of grain as the average annual amount of government purchase, which is lower than that purchased during times of war.[57] The amount of grain purchased in the south to supply Kaifeng also amounted to approximately 2 million. Thus, trade totaled over 5 million Song *shi*.

It is difficult to determine the exact percentage of government purchase in the total volume of grain in long-distance trade because there is no quantitative evidence on the latter. According to Wu, the volume of grain in long-distance trade in the late Ming should be less than 10 million *shi*, about 8.5 million taels of silver in contemporary prices.[58] Wu probably underestimated the volume of the grain trade. I have doubled this figure as the up-bound estimate. The volume of the eleventh-century grain trade is unlikely to be any less than that of the late Ming period. In the very beginning, Song militarization was already quite commercialized. The Song troops had over 1 million soldiers in the mid-eleventh century, and this probably meant that 3 million people were living on their salaries.[59] Meanwhile, the Song urban population in the mid-eleventh century is estimated to be 38 million, which indicates that the aggregate size of grain consumption was ten times that of the soldiers and their families. In consideration of the small percentage of the Song urban population who secured food provision through

Table G-14. Government grain purchases in Hebei in the eleventh century

I. Amount of grain purchases reported in official documents (million Song *shi*)

1041	0.85	1044	4	1055	1.6
1042	0.45	1052	3–4	1069	3.83
1043	1.04	1054	6		

II. Cost of grain purchases reported in official documents (million strings)

1052	4–5	1070	2–3	1083	2	1120	2
1055	5	1077	3	1094	2		

Source: Hino 1935c, in *HKTSR*, vol. 11, 381.

rental of land or rural markets, I suggest that 20 million *shi*, and thus over 30 million Song *shi*, was the size of long-distance grain trade in the eleventh century. Consequently, the ratio between government purchase of grain for military staff and the amount of urban grain consumption depending on interregional grain trade would be 1:5 or 1:7.

Table G-15 gives a comparison of long-distance trade in grain and shows that the Song period was surpassed only by eighteenth-century China. The Song population in 1078 was over 90 million, less than one-fourth of the Qing population in 1840. When converting these aggregate estimates into per capita grain in long-distance trade, Song China reached the peak. This implies that the urbanization rate in the Song period was probably much higher than in later times.[60]

Conclusion

In this book I propose a sharp decline in trade in the early Ming period based on the Song-Ming comparison. I focus this comparison chiefly on long-term changes in the money stock and water transportation. As the reconstruction of trade in the Song and Ming periods is based on a variety of partial evidence, it is not surprising that scholars vary considerably in their estimates of major goods in the Chinese market. In this appendix I provide a preliminary survey on interregional trade of tea, textiles, and grain and make

Table G-15. Estimates of the long-distance trade in grain, 1000–1840 (million shi)

Year	Song (1000–1100)	Ming (1550–1610)	Qing (1770–1840)
Amount	20	10–20	30–50

Sources: For estimates of long-distance trade in grain in the late Ming and Qing periods, see Wu Chengming 1983a, 1983b, and 2001, 123–26, 153–57.

rough estimations of the values and shares of these goods based on partial quantitative evidence. The results I report here invariably support the argument of the trade boom in the Song dynasty and that of the decline in the Ming period. It is generally agreed that there is no reliable way to estimate trade at a rural market; however, a rough estimate made by Perkins indicates that about 30 to 40 percent of the agricultural production was sold in the late nineteenth century.[61] The share of marketed agricultural goods was even smaller before the late nineteenth century. Meanwhile, Perkins estimated only about 7 or 8 percent of all farm output were exported for long-distance trade.[62]

Other scholars' quantitative research also supports my estimates. Wu's research focused on long-distance transportation and the marketing of staples during the late Ming and Qing periods. His estimates of major staple goods, such as grain, cotton cloth, and silk fabrics, are included in my comparisons. They clearly point to the underdevelopment of trade in the centuries between 1400 and 1600, and a rapid increase in the volume of long-distance staple commodities in the eighteenth and nineteenth centuries.[63] My estimates of long-distance trade support their estimates. For all the major commodities such as tea, grain, and textile goods, my estimates suggest that the size of long-distance trade in the Song period exceeded that of the late Ming.

The ratios of long-distance trade to national income also varied over the Song-Ming-Qing periods (table G-16). If my estimate is acceptable, it is quite obvious that the high ratio in Song China was unrivaled until the late nineteenth century. However, the calculations are not made from real data and are subject to revision if new evidence is found. A high ratio at best will indicate the emergence of a national market in eleventh-century China. As noted before, progress in water transportation laid a solid foundation for this well-integrated market. The development in long-distance trade at the time was far beyond the preliminary stage.

Table G-16. Long-distance trade and its share in national incomes, 1100–1880s (000,000 taels)

Year	I. Marketed goods long-distance	II. Amount of trade	III. National income	IV. II/III
Song (1100s)	—	100	662	15.1
Ming (1600s)	—	24.2–32.7[a]	252–760	3.2–9.6
Qing (1770s)	500	189.3	2,009	9.4
Qing (1880s)	—	420–500	2,780–3,338	12.6–17.8

Source: For Qing (1880–1889), see estimates made by Perkins (table I.8 in Perkins 1969, 355) and Chang Chung-li (cited in table F-2 in the present volume; for Qing (1770), see Wu Chengming 1983a and 1983b.

a. No estimate of late Ming China's long-distance trade is available. Wu estimated 12.1 million taels of silver for grain and textile goods in the 1550s. Since in estimates for Qing China (the 1770s), these three items account for 52 percent of long-distance trade, I doubled the late Ming figure to come up with an approximate solution.

Appendix H

Military Farms, Involuntary Migrations, and Extensive Agriculture

Both military farms and involuntary migrations were necessary means to reclaim land in sparsely populated areas. Soldiers and farmers had to farm a large amount of land in a remote site far away from the market. Infrastructure, such as roads and bridges, irrigation facilities, schools and temples, did not exist. While there was no limit in the supply of deserted land, and the average size of a lot for a family usually was 100 *mu*, farming soldiers and migrants were equipped with little money and tools. For some, even the plows were made by hand due to the lack of drafting animals. This further gave rise to extensive agriculture. The data on military farms and involuntary migration can, therefore, be used to depict a general image for the command economy in early Ming China. The migrant-receiving regions were usually associated with the very low density of population and the prevalence of extensive agriculture. One can determine the consistency of related data to test the central argument that the decline in agricultural productivity and living standards that were caused by the rise of a command economy.

Two important questions are to be solved before one can use the forced population movement to measure the control of the population by the early Ming court and its impacts on agricultural production: To what extent can one quantify the size and structure of military and civilian migrants at the macro level? Can we find important evidence from rural settlements to support the argument of the massive migratory movement across the empire around 1400? For the first question, we need to identify the major immigrant-receiving areas along with migrant-exporting areas at the provincial level. It is not difficult to make such an investigation because over the past half century modern researchers have accomplished many excellent empirical studies on this subject based on important information preserved in *Mingshilu*.[1] The second question, however, cannot be easily answered as one has to conduct field research and exploit unofficial documents such as genealogies and the collection of village names. Fortunately, more and more Ming dynasty studies are focusing on the detailed social and family history and greatly help to link the micro-level evidence to the macro-level population movement. In the following of this appendix, I provide a general survey that combines the important results obtained from these two sources.

Military Farms and Involuntary Migrations in the Frontier and North China

The *wei-suo* system in the early Ming was comprised of a large number of soldiers and their families, who were expected to till land to support a command economy. Soldiers

285

and the military households were administered by the Ministry of War through the military units such as the *wei* (guard) and *suo*. The extant records show the prevalence of military farms within the Ming empire. Moreover, military farm units were mostly distributed close to the farm units of involuntary civilian migrants, which were controlled by the civilian administration. Yet in the frontier regions, the *wei-suo* system was the only official administration. Involuntary migrants, without exception, received orders from the military commanders, which effectively consolidated self-sufficiency in a locality.[2]

Cao's research is the most systematic study on early Ming involuntary migration. He attempted to reconstruct migration movements at the turn of 1400 based on official records and genealogical sources. For the military population at the frontier, Cao used the *Mingshilu* to locate the numbers of military units, such as *wei* and *suo* and their distribution. Then, by assuming that the number of soldiers in these units reached the required quotas, or 5,600 soldiers per *wei*, he estimated the total number of *wei-suo* soldiers. After making certain adjustments based on relevant documents, he assumed the number of military family members to be two to three times that of soldiers.

Involuntary migrants constituted the overwhelming majority at the frontier, including Liaodong and Yunnan. As presented in table H-1, the estimated military population at the frontier (soldiers and their family members) amounted to 2.2 million individuals. He

Table H-1. Estimated military migrants at the frontier, 1368–1398 (1,000 individuals)

Area	Total population	Military population			Military migrants	Natives
		Soldiers	Families	Subtotal		
NE						
Liaodongdusi	500	130	270	400	200	100
N						
Shanxidusi						
Xuanfu	325	100	200	300	150	25
Datong	278	84	168	252	126	26
Subtotal	603	184	368	552	276	51
NW						
Shaanxidusi						
Yansui	66	22	44	66	33	0
Ningxia	87	23	46	69	69	18
Other areas	62	17	34	51	25	12
Shaanxi Xingdusi	258	69	139	208	104	50
Subtotal	473	131	263	394	231	80
SW						
Sichuan	134	31	62	93	93	41
Yunnan	705	120	240	360	360	96
Guizhou	510	140	280	420	420	90
Subtotal	1,349	291	582	873	873	227
Total	2,925	736	1,483	2,219	1,580	458

Source: Cao 1997, 320.

further estimated about 1.58 million of them had migrated to the frontier. The number of native civilians who were subject to military administration reached 0.46 million, a minority of the population at the frontier in 1400.

Military farms were established across the empire. Yet the acreage of the soldier-tilled land in official records was not accurate. The earliest extant record of Ming military farmland was in 1487, which was recorded at 891,041,194 *mu*.[3] Wang Yuquan found the reported total of 63,000,000 *mu* (9 million acres) in 1585, the second largest figure available in preserved documents. He suggested that the total acreage of military farms in the early Ming should be at least the same as that in 1585.[4] I assume that there were approximately 1.2 to 2 million soldiers in the early Ming period, and 70 percent of them were assigned to farmland. Each soldier acquired a lot of 50 *mu*. Therefore, my estimate lies between 42 and 70 million *mu* of land (6 to 10 million acres).

By examining the example of the Dezhou *wei* in Shandong (table H-2), an idea of how the military farm system worked can be obtained. This *wei* was located in west Shandong, an area depopulated by civil wars and natural disasters. All farming soldiers were organized into local units known as *tun*. The 111 local units were distributed across 14 counties. It should be noted that west Shandong was also a major area for receiving civilian migrants, who were also organized into *tun*. According to local gazetteers, in all of the 168 rural settlements in Dongchangfu of west Shandong, the number of *tun* reached 130, more than three times the number of native villages (table H-3).

The dominance of involuntary migrants and farming soldiers in the population of west Shandong are also evident in extant genealogies. In Liangshan county, for instance, a modern survey finds that among 167 surveyed villages, 106 have migrant backgrounds. All of these migrant-origin villages date back to the early Ming period. This is an important

Table H-2. The composition of military farms in West Shandong

Regions	Guard of Dezhou	Left Guard of Dezhou	Total
Dezhou	42	12	54
Enxian	5	13	18
Xiajin	7	0	7
Linqing	2	2	4
Wucheng	0	10	10
Gaotang	0	2	2
Qingping	0	4	4
Tangyi	0	1	1
Qinghe	0	1	1
Deping	0	2	2
Lingxian	0	2	2
Yucheng	0	2	2
Pingyuan	0	3	3
Yueling	0	1	1
Total	56	55	111

Source: Cao 1997, 365. The original source is extracted from the Qing gazetteer *Dezhou zhi, juan* 4, territory.

Table H-3. The distribution of rural settlements in Dongchang, 1368–1398

County	Tun	Native village	County	Tun	Native village
Guancheng	5	5	Xinxian	8	6
Wucheng	18	3	Boping	18	6
Renping	27	9	Xiajin	27	3
Linqing	27	6			
Total	130	38			

Source: Cao 1997, 166.

example that reveals that in the early Ming, the reconstruction of rural communities in many areas of west and central Shandong was based on involuntary migration.

In chapter 8, I revised Perkins's estimation of farm yields in early Ming Shandong based on the assumption that the farmland cultivated by involuntary migrants and farming soldiers should constitute an overwhelmingly large share of Shandong's land acreage in 1393. Information from tables H-2, H-3, and H-4 clearly support this assumption. A similar situation also took place in many places in Central and East China. In the following, I will present evidence to demonstrate the dominant presence of involuntary migrants in the rural populations of these areas.

Involuntary Migrations in Central and East China

In the early Ming command economy, extensive agriculture was associated with military farms and involuntary migration. Therefore, studies on migrant-receiving areas and the percentage of migrants in local populations clearly provide a social background for our understanding of the changes in farming practices and, in turn, the declining trend in early Ming agricultural productivity levels.

Table H-5 provides an estimation of involuntary migration, including both civilians and military individuals in inland provinces. One should take these estimates as a rough reflection of the major trends and directions of massive flows in early Ming population movement. It is obvious that involuntary migrants including both civilian and military

Table H-4. The origins of local settlements in Liangshan county, Shandong

Period	Native	East Shandong	Other provinces	Total
Pre-Yuan	5	—	—	5
Late Yuan	9	—	—	9
1368–1398	37	2	87	126
1403–1424	7	1	19	27
Total	58	3	106	167

Source: Cao 1997, 174.

Table H-5. Distribution of inland involuntary migrants during the Hongwu reign (1,000 individuals)

Province	Total	Native	Percentage	Civilian	Percentage	Military	Percentage
Nanzhili							
Jiangsu	8,349	6,641	79.5	902	10.8	806	9.7
Anhui	3,362	2,163	64.3	961	28.6	238	7.1
Huguang							
Hunan	2,787	2,056	73.8	539	19.3	192	6.9
Hubei	1,738	755	43.4	794	45.7	189	10.9
Sichuan	1,800	900	50.0	800	44.4	100	5.6
Shandong	5,943	3,870	65.1	1,869	31.5	204	3.4
Beijing	2,763	1,659	60.0	848	30.7	256	9.3
Henan	2,859	1,670	58.4	934	32.7	255	8.9
Total	29,601	19,714	66.6	7,648	25.8	2,240	7.6

Source: Cao 1997, 472.

constituted a murch larger share of local populations in Sichuan, Hubei, Henan, and Anhui than in other inland provinces. Such a pattern undoubtedly supports my argument of the overall decline in average grain yields per acre in the early Ming period, because the farmland in these migrant-receiving areas accounted for the largest share of officially reported land acreage in 1393. Local officials tended to include uncultivated land in their reports and the return of the crops was poor.

Because Nanzhili, where the early Ming capital Nanjing was located, was the core of the early Ming political system and the command economy, official records preserved rich details on the number and backgrounds of these involuntary migrants. This allowed Cao to come up with a more accurate estimate than for other provinces (see table H-6).

Table H-6. Distribution of migrants in Nanzhili during the Hongwu reign (1,000 individuals)

Prefect	Total	Native	Percentage	Civilian	Percentage	Military	Percentage
Nanjing	995	100	10.1	189	19.0	706	70.9
Yangzhou	790	263	33.3	477	60.4	50	6.3
Huai'an	666	433	65.0	200	30.0	33	5.0
Xuzhou	198	145	73.3	36	18.2	17	8.6
Fengyang	628	140	22.3	300	47.8	188	29.9
Anqing	418	92	22.0	309	73.9	17	4.0
Chizhou	219	134	61.2	68	31.0	17	7.8
Luzhou	367	110	30.0	257	70.0	0	0
H&T*	108	64	5	9.3	27	25.0	17 15.7
Total:	4,389	1,481	33.8	1,863	42.4	1,045	23.8

Source: Cao 1997, 78.

*H&T is the abbreviation for Hezhou and Tuzhou.

For the populations of the ten chosen prefectures in Nanzhili, the migrants comprised a large share—two-thirds—of the total population. Some migrant-receiving areas such as Yangzhou, Fengyang, and Luzhou, which are all located north of the Yangtze River, are exactly the same regions distinguished in chapter 8 as dominated by practices of extensive agriculture.

As one moves to Central China, involuntary migration also played an important role in land cultivation. Cao estimated that more than one-third of the local population in Huguang were migrants (see table H-5). As demonstrated in table H-7, for nearly six centuries in the Hanshou county in Hunan, migrating lineages were distributed very unevenly in time. Fifty-eight lineages moved to Hanshou during 1368 to 1400, which accounted for 74 percent of the total migrating lineages.

The share of migrants in Hubei was more than half of the local population, while that of the native population went as low as 16.8 percent, as it was the case in De'an. This example illustrates that the Mongol conquest and civil wars during the Yuan-Ming transition severely depopulated Hubei, and that the lost numbers were replenished by involuntary migration.

Table H-7. Distribution of migrating lineages in Hanshou, Hunan (1,000 individuals)

Period	Imi-Hunan*	Imi-Jiangxi*	Imi-Jiangxu*	Other provinces	Total
1127–1275	—	1	—	—	1
1300–1367	—	3	—	—	3
1368–1399	—	20	2	2	24
1400	—	29	2	3	34
Post-1500	1	6	—	1	8
Pre-1700	1	—	—	7	8
Total	2	59	4	13	78

Source: Cao 1997, 111.

*Imi-Hunan indicates that the received migrants were from Hunan, Imi-Jiangxi indicates those from Jiangxi, and Imi-Jiangsu indicates those from Jiangsu.

Table H-8. Migrants in Hubei in the late fourteenth century

Area	Total	Native	Percentage	Civilian migrants	Percentage	Military	Percentage
Huangzhou	626	288	46.0	304	48.6	34	5.4
Wuchang	294	138	46.9	122	41.5	34	11.6
De'an	113	19	16.8	91	80.5	3	2.7
Hanyang	50	20	40.0	30	60.0	0	0
Mianyang	88	35	39.8	36	40.9	17	17.5
Anlu	97	39	40.0	41	42.5	17	17.5
Jingzhou	334	130	38.9	160	47.8	44	13.2
Xiangyang	130	86	66.2	10	7.7	34	26.2
Shizhou	6 0	0	0	0	6	1	00
Total	1,738	755	43.4	794	45.7	18.9	10.9

Source: Cao 1997, 147.

In short, the study on involuntary migration reveals important contexts of the early Ming command economy. The reconstruction of the size and structure of migration movements in the early Ming by population historians provides strong evidence on the retreat to extensive agriculture at a national scale around 1400.

Notes

Introduction

1. Modern France (mainland) is 551,550 square kilometers. For the estimated territory size of the Song dynasty in 1111 AD, see Song 1994.

2. Recently scholars read the word *shanghe* in the title of the painting as "upper-river shipments" other than "along the river." See Cao 2011, 122–23.

3. Keith Bradsher, "China's Mona Lisa Makes a Rare Appearance in Hong Kong," *New York Times*, July 3, 2007.

4. Ihara 2001, 137.

5. For the recent discussion on estimation of the populations living at Kaifeng in the eleventh century, see Kubota, 2000. For the role of the Bian Canal in the eleventh century, see Aoyama 1963, 344, 351–53.

6. See table C-6 in appendix C; also see Guo Zhengzhong 1997a, 169.

7. Ihara 2001, 140–45.

8. Fan and Jin, 105–7, 114.

9. *Yingya shenglan*. Also see Zheng 1985, 48–56.

10. Dong Gu, *Xu Ganshui zhi*, juan 1.

11. Scholars usually trace the intellectual origin of anti-market policies to the Legalist doctrine presented in *The Book of Lord Shang*. By advocating rigid control of manpower and resources for military purposes, the author recognizes only two professions, farmers and soldiers, and resolutely proclaims weakening the capacity and autonomy of rural society as the founding principle, because "[a] weak people means a strong state and vice versa" (see Zhao 1986, 105–7). Hou Jiaju exploits the contrast between the Confucian liberal market economy versus the Legalist command economy as a basic theory to interpret the evolution of Chinese economy in the three millennia (Hou 1985a, 1985b, 2005).

12. The concept of a command economy is chiefly used to describe the central planning economic system that was in existence in the Soviet Union (Grossman 1962, 1963). For the study of the operation of such a system in twentieth-century China, see Perkins 1966.

13. Richard E. Ericson, "The Command Economy," in *The New Palgrave: A Dictionary of Economics*, second edition, ed. Steven N. Durlauf and Lawrence E. Blume (Basingstoke: Palgrave Macmillan, 2008).

Chapter 1. Issues and Approaches

1. See Persson 1988; Epstein 1994 and 2000; Hoffman 1996.

2. Pomeranz 2000; Allen, Bengtsson, and Dribe 2005.

3. Allen, Bengtsson, and Dribe 2005, 7.

4. Ibid., 111.

5. Ibid.

6. In the twelfth century, China's national income was about three times that of Europe; by the 1700s, however, the size of her national income was only 20 percent larger than Europe. This share is derived from the distribution of the world population reported by Maddison (1988, 20). Maddison also estimated the GDP per capita for Europe and China from AD 50 to 1700, which shows only small differences between the two regions (1988, 25). Thus, I assume that there were no significant differences in the GDP per capita in the preindustrial world and take the proportion of the Chinese population in the world population as the share of her national income in the total global products. For Europe, the estimated GDP per capita was $500 in 1280 and $870 in 1700 (1988, 25). The European population reached 380 million in 1280 and came to 592 million around 1700. The Chinese population was 100 million in 1280, 138 million in 1700, and 381 million in 1820 (1988, 20). However, Maddison's estimate of the 1700 population is too low to be true. The official census in 1775 shows an aggregate population of 310 million. If the 1700 figure estimated by Maddison could be accepted, the Chinese population must have increased 2.8 times in less than eighty years. Instead, I choose 200 million as an approximate estimate for China's aggregate population in 1700. This adjusted figure also shows China may have surpassed India (whose population was estimated at 153 million in 1700) in the size of aggregate population.

7. Elvin 1973, 113–99.

8. Kato Shigeru's pioneering 1926 research identified the Tang-Song transformation (750–1127) as the crucial period of the initial expansion in the market economy. In the three decades after the Second World War, scholars in China, Japan, the United States, and Taiwan published numerous monographs on diversified aspects of the Chinese market economy from CE 750 to 1800. The market-centered studies contend that the market is the principal source that shapes the nature and process of the economic evolution in China, as manifested in the increase of marketplaces, urbanization (such as the growth of the nonagricultural population and the size and structure of towns and markets), and commercialization (the increasing share of agricultural products sold at the markets, the spreading of payments in cash, etc.). See Kato 1926, 1933a, 1933b; Shiba 1968; Fu Yiling 1956, 1957, and 1989; Liu Shiji 1987; Fu Zongwen 1989; Fan Shuzhi 1990; Chen Xuewen 1993; Skinner 1964 and 1977; and D. Twitchett 1968.

9. In their efforts to seek evidence for commercialization and urban development in China after 1500, many scholars share the common assumption that economic growth was manifested by the concurrence of markets, urban areas (towns and cities), and the rise of merchant groups in Ming and Qing eras. Their research elaborated on Fu's scheme; hence, we can name the period from the 1980s to the present as the Fu Yiling era.

10. Skinner 1977, 276–81.

11. The concepts of "core" and "periphery" derived from the central place theory. For a demonstration of cores and peripheries in Skinner's analysis, see Skinner 1977, table 1, 287.

12. In 1984, a group of Chinese economic historians at an international conference in Italy launched an attempt to advance research along this line. Continuity and change, as argued by the papers presented at the conference, must be explored through the view of the Chinese economy and society in preindustrial times as "an aggregate entity of economies of a set of subordinate physiographic macro-regions, each constituting systems in which activities of many kinds are functionally differentiated and interdependent" (see *International Conference on Spatial and Temporal Trends and Cycles in Chinese Economic History, 980–1980* [Bellagio, Italy: 1984]).

13. Sands and Myers, 729–31; Wang Qingcheng 2004.

14. Skinner 1977, 27–28.

15. The estimated urbanization rate even in the Lower Yangtze, the most urbanized region in the 1840s, was below 8 percent (Skinner 1977, 28).

16. Skinner noticed this paradox and attributed it to the declining trend in technical innovations and the fiscal capacity of the state in the Qing era (Skinner 1977, 29).

17. I propose this differentiation based on the survey of Chinese domestic markets in 1077 AD (see chapter 4 of this book). Perkins differentiates two patterns of trade in preindustrial China: "trade that takes place between distant points" versus "trade within a given rural market-town area." He also views urban commerce, the third kind of trade, as having much in common with long-distance trade, except that the goods are transported over only short hauls (Perkins 1969, 112). For the market hierarchy in early modern Europe, see Braudel 1986, 111.

18. Xu 1997, table 3, 24.

19. Shiba 2002, 14. In 1076, registered marketplaces including ferries, according to Bi Zhongyan's report, amounted to 27,607. In the beginning of the twelfth century, marketplaces excluding ferries increased to 31,000 (Li Huarui 1995, 202). All these figures were cited by officials who reported the sources of farming-out revenues, such as ferries, wine shops, bridges, and temples, which were built by private money or managed by local elite in return for the franchise during a fixed period of time (often three years). These projects made profit for local investors and, viewed from a modern standard, were fairly close to the construction of rural markets. Sudo explicitly made this point in his analysis of the Song rural markets (*dian, shi, bu*) in relation to *maipu* and commercial taxes (Sudo 1965a, 803, 807–12, 821–23, 843–62). Also see Hino, *HKTSR*, vol. 12, 405–13.

20. As Perkins pointed out, there is no linear relationship between the number of rural markets and the frequency of a farmer going to the marketplace, on the one hand, and the amount or value of traded goods in those markets, on the other hand (Perkins 1969, 115).

21. Perkins 1969, 114–15.

22. Hartwell 1982.

23. While Hartwell promised to investigate interregional flows of goods, technologies, and capital in China, he basically accepted Skinner's assumption of the cycles of the Chinese macro-regional economies. Since Skinner assumes developmental cycles of these macro-regional economies were wholly unsynchronized due to high costs in (land) transportation, interregional exchanges were severely constrained. This interpretation implies that it is meaningless for researchers to study the traditional Chinese market economy as a whole (Skinner 1985, 280–81).

24. Hartwell particularly identifies four stages for a pattern of regional development in imperial China: frontiers, rapid development, systematic decline, and equilibrium. Meanwhile, his description and explanation of the macro-regional cycles are entirely based on demographic changes (1982, 373–5, 378).

25. Bengtsson 2004; Bengtsson et al. 2004.

26. While this question was implicit in many earlier studies, it was not formally addressed until Dwight Perkins offered a basic economic framework that laid down the foundation for later economic scholars, such as Mark Elvin, Philip Huang, or the so-called California School. See Perkins 1969; Elvin 1972, 1973; Philip Huang 1985; Lavely and Wong 1998; Lee and Wang 1999, Li Bozhong 1998d; and Pomeranz 2000.

27. Perkins 1969, 14–18.

28. For Ester Boserup's important study of the relationship between agricultural production and population growth, see *The Conditions of Agricultural Growth: The Economics of Agrarian Change under Population Pressure* (Chicago: Aldine, 1965).

29. Philip Huang, 1985; Li Bozhong, 1998, 1999.

30. Meng Wentong divided the three millennia into four periods based on secular increases in farm yields per acre and their impact on society, tax, and politics. The four periods are: the Warring States and the Han empire (401 BC–AD 220), the Wei, Jin, and Six dynasties (AD 221–589), the Tang and Song (618–1279), and the Ming and Qing (1368–1912). In Meng's

index, average farm yield per acre in the first period is set up as 100 points. It rose to 120 points in the second period, 200 points in the third period, and 300 points in the fourth period (Meng 1957, 27, 28–32).

31. Indeed, many estimates of aggregate grain supply and rural family incomes made from scanty records of crop yields have failed to capture the important changes underneath the general trend in farm output patterns. See Chen Hengli 1958; Min Zongdian 1984; Chao 1986; Wu 1985, 1998; and Guo 1994, 2001.

32. This recovery policy interpretation has become a prevailing narrative in China after 1950. In the biographic monograph on Zhu Yuanzhang published in 1949, Wu Han described the emperor as a despot who governed China by violence and horror. In the 1955 edition, he proposed Zhu was a great leader of the peasant rebellion and added a section to Zhu's policies for economic recovery. It noteworthy that Wu Han followed the comments from Mao Zedong, the chairman of the CCCP, to make such changes (see the preface to the biography of Zhu Yuanzhang). For the similar interpretations that prevailed in textbooks and monographs, see section 1 of chapter 8 in Jian 1979; Wei 1961, 79–87; Wei 1985; Han 1991, 1–19; Wang, Liu, and Zhang, 322–43, 382–86.

33. Elvin 1973, 113–30.

34. Ibid., 204–15, 306–15.

35. Chao 1986, 216, 220.

36. Ibid., 5–7, 221–27.

37. Ibid., 2–3.

38. Perkins 1969, 216, 240.

39. Ibid., 33. See also Jones's comment on Chao's population and land data (Jones 1990, 12–16).

40. This record depicts the salary of a tea picker in Fujian, which was, in fact, a description rather than a genuine event. For the entire two millennia prior to 1700, there are twenty records in total.

41. Correspondingly, agricultural fundamentalism holds that farm outputs per capita or per acre would be the precondition of structural change in the economy. However, there is the problem of endogeneity in the sense that increase in productivity resulted from rather than stimulated development of the market economy. Demographic changes in either the short or long term, for instance, might be independent of changes in per capita farm output. In their study of eighteenth-century Chinese demographic changes, James Lee and Wang Feng suggested the autonomous nature of demographic dynamism (Lee and Wang 1999). Peter H. Lindert also discussed the complexity of the interacting relationships among population, prices, and real wages, in which he suggested a correlated linkage of these trends (Lindert 1985).

42. For a detailed discussion on the delta model, see Takaya 1982; Watabe and Sakurai 1984.

43. The trinity model includes "one year double cropping," "a man works ten *mu*," and "man plows and woman weaves" (Li Bozhong 1998d, 153–54).

44. Ibid., 155.

45. Ibid., 47.

46. Ibid., 51.

47. Ibid., 51, 53, 72.

48. An examination of the supply side certainly agrees with this point. Many technical innovations in farming, cotton planting, and mulberry raising can be traced back to the Song era, but it was only in the eighteenth century that they were applied on a large scale. Markets rather than technology made changes available.

49. Li Bozhong, 1997, 1998a, 1998b, and 1998c.

50. In a series of his articles published in the journal ZGNS, Li calls for a careful investigation of historical records and modern research, and argued that many of the hydraulic projects and planting of early-ripening rice seeds appeared in the eastern part of the Lower Yangtze delta much

later than what modern researchers expected, and therefore it was impossible for local farmers to significantly increase harvests in the Song period. See Li Bozhong, 2000b.

51. See Ge and Gu 2000 and Li Genpan 2002.

52. On how to exploit the national income concept such as aggregate demand and supply in analysis of a preindustrial economy, see Cipolla 1993, 22–94.

53. Among the theories often cited by students of Ming-Qing history, the "industrious revolution" before the Industrial Revolution as originally proposed by Akira and De Vries, as well as "Smithian growth," point to the increasing share of agricultural output caused by an expansion of the market economy. For the "industrious revolution," see Hayami 1989; De Vries, 1994.

54. He also argued that the Song economic revolution would have hardly been possible because there was no substantial increase in average farm yield per *mu* at the same time in the Lower Yangtze (Li Bozhong 2000b, 178).

55. W. G. Liu 2013.

56. Skinner first divided nineteenth-century China into nine macro regions: North China, Northwest China, Upper Yangtze, Middle Yangtze, Lower Yangtze, Southeast Coast, Lingnan, Yun-Kwei, and Manchuria (1977, 212–13). Later, he detached Jiangxi from Middle Yangtze and named it Gan Yangtze for the tenth macro region (1985b, 273).

57. Although scholars usually admitted that there was a continuous uptrend in commerce and overseas trade in the Lower Yangtze and Fujian, there is no consensus on the Chinese economy under Mongol rule due to the scarcity of evidence.

58. Wang Zengyu 1983, 207–8, 228–35.

59. Skinner 1977; Hartwell 1982.

60. Dardess, 111.

61. Schurmann 1967, 2–12.

62. Yu 1987 and 2010.

63. Peng 1965, 493.

64. *MLJJ*, 67.

65. The unreliability of Ming demographic data is attributed by Ho to the fiscal function of the household registration; the administration was interested in only the male adults in a family who were liable to labor services or labor-service payment and thus came to be fixed like a quasi-quota. Nonetheless, Ho himself clearly admits that it was not the case for the early Ming censuses. The 1393 census covered "the entire population and respectable registrations were undoubtedly carried out in a large number of localities" (Ho 1959, 23). Recently, Luan made this point undisputedly in his study of the Ming Yellow Register (1998).

66. For the military pacifications against private mining in Zhejiang, Fujian, Sichuan, and Yunnan, see *MLJJ*, 122–25. The two rebellions in mid-fifteenth-century China were also closely related to migrants: One is the revolt in the western mountain and highland areas in Hubei, which involved about 1 million illegal migrants (see the report by the Ming governor, excerpted in *MLJJ*, 81); the other is the Deng Maoqi Rebellion (1448–1449) in the center of Fujian, a case of miner bandits as recorded in contemporary writings (Brook 1999, 81–85).

67. For the rebellion in Hubei and the pacification, see the report by the Ming governor, excerpted in *MLJJ*, 81; for the rebellion in Fujian, see Brook 1999, 81–85.

Chapter 2. The Nature of Song and Ming Economic Data

1. For the origin and distribution of Chinese dynastic economic data, see Liang Fangzhong, "Introduction," in Liang 1980.

2. For a recent study of the military meritocracy in the Warring States period, see Zhu 2008, 27–38.

3. *The Book of Lord Shang, juan* 4, *quqiang* 97 (Shang 2006).

4. Archaeological evidence, such as wood and paper scripts discovered in the inland regions and the frontier of China, provides firsthand information of the official reports of a rural household based on such formats in Han and Tang dynasties. For an introductory study to the household registration, see Ikeda 2007.

5. Bielenstein 1947, 156.

6. Ibid., 157.

7. The Chinese population reached 59,594,578 in AD 2 and 48,909, 800 in 742. Only considerable regional variations have occurred (Bielenstein 1947, 126, 157).

8. Cao Shuji 2000, 46.

9. Perkins 1969, 222–26. Also see Gao Shouxian, 3–25.

10. Ho 1959, 101.

11. Ho 1959, 4.

12. Cao 2000a, 704.

13. Gernet 1982, 252–59.

14. Li Jinxiu 2001, 9–10.

15. Bielenstein 1947, 156.

16. Yan 1986.

17. Dong 2002, 299.

18. Ho 1959, 1–23.

19. Chen Zhiping 2004, 3–21.

20. Yanagida 1995, 304–5; Liang 2006, 16.

21. For the rates of land taxes and their application in twelfth- and thirteenth-century Liangzhou, see W. G. Liu 2008, 236–54. Also see W. G. Liu 2012.

22. Du 1990, 2–10. Ge Jianxiong believes that the routine conduction of population census that covered all the people and contained exact information on their gender, ages, and heights was formed in the Qin kingdom and that this institutional innovation was made possible largely due to the influence of the Legalists (Ge 2002, 214–30).

23. The population census was conducted at the county level every year. The county magistrate and his staff were chiefly responsible for enumerating rural people (Ge 2002, 230–44). For a recent study of the household registration during the Han dynasty based on archeological evidence, see Zhang 2010, 80–88.

24. Du 1990, 24, 49–50, 93–96.

25. For the registered Han population data, see Durand 1960, 216. Ma Daying suggests the share of the population aged between seven and fourteen in the total was 17 percent, and the share of the population aged between fifteen and fifty-six in the total was 67 percent. Therefore, the taxable population accounted for 84 percent of the total. Based upon this assumption, the poll taxes would be 3.8 billion coins when the aggregate population reached 50 million and 4.5 billion coins when the aggregate population reached 60 million (Ma 1983, 63–64).

26. See Nishijima 1986, 588, 600–1.

27. Durand 1960, 216.

28. Ge 1986, 100–1.

29. For the reported totals, see appendix A.

30. Ge 2002, 399–408.

31. Few records were kept about grain prices in this period. According to the official rate of the salary, 1 Han *shi* was equal to 150 coins.

32. Miyazaki 1966, 251.

33. Twitchett 1970, 25–26.

34. Ikeda 2007, 84–86, 88–98.

35. *Tongdian, juan* 7.

36. Li Jinxiu 2001, 9–10.

37. *Tongdian, juan* 2. There were 8.9 million registered households in 755. Since the regulation suggested 160 Tang *mu* for the typical size of farmland cultivated by a household, the author reached the total of 1,430,386,213 Tang *mu*. This figure is even higher than the Chinese acreage in the 1950s.

38. In another place I have provided a definition for the tax state in Chinese history. A tax state should be capable in the following areas: state revenues must be highly monetized; indirect taxes (excises, customs, and mineral products) should take a dominant share in the structure of tax revenues; negotiable instruments begin to play an important role in public borrowing; high levels of centralization and professionalization are pervasive in the fiscal administration; public expenditures are large enough so that the direct impact of state policies on the market (such as inflation, investments, and real wages) becomes obvious.

39. Strictly speaking, the household tax was a mixed kind between the poll tax and the property tax. It was originally a miscellaneous tax charged against male adults but later on developed into a formal tax charged on each household. The household paid the tax with varying rates not only based on the number of male adults but also on the amount of real estate, servants, maids, and cattle it owned. For a discussion on the household tax and its role in the evolution of Tang taxation, see Li Jinxiu 1995, 468–500.

40. The yearly salt revenues reached 4 million in the mid-ninth century. In contrast, the income from the alcohol monopoly was less than a sixth of the net profit from the salt monopoly, and the total annual income from the tea monopoly was 12 percent (Twitchett 1970, 58, 62–63).

41. Wang Shengduo 1995, table 7, 709–17.

42. Jia and Chen, 38, 84; C. Liu 2000, 55–56; W. G. Liu 2005, 316, 318.

43. Guo Zhengzhong 1997b, 285. As reflected in the salt monopoly, increases in monopoly revenues far outpaced increases in salt production, but when one includes the influence of inflation, this gap almost disappears.

44. Bao 2001, 318.

45. Twitchett 1970, 111.

46. Ibid., 39–40.

47. "Yang Yan's Memorial to the Throne." For the English translation, see Twitchett 1970, 157–58.

48. Miyazaki 1952, 1971; Takahashi 2002, 3–38; Liang Taiji 1998, 82–96.

49. *Jiu Tangshu, juan* 14.

50. Chen Lesu 1947, 74–76; Cheng Minsheng 2003, 14–17.

51. Liang Taiji 1998, 44,

52. This problem can be traced back to the early years of the two-tax reform. The Tang court already adopted a tax quota system and allowed tax rates varying from one locality to another (Twitchett 1970, 41–46).

53. For further discussion of the role of textile payments in land taxes, see appendix G.

54. Shimasue, 231–39; Yanagida 1986, 102–24. The edict clearly mentioned that the number of adult males should be a factor for considering the rank of the landowning households; but as Yanagida points out, in local practice one could find few examples about the importance of this factor (the number of adult males).

55. Qi 1987, 442–44.

56. The acreage reported in 1078 was 461,655, 557 *mu*. The landowning households reached 10,995,133 and the total household 16,492,631(Liang 1980, 180, 399).

57. Cao 1997, 472–73. Also see appendix H in this volume.

58. Wang Yuquan, 1991.

59. The maximum estimate was made by Wu Han, who estimated 2.8 million Ming soldiers in the early Ming by citing a high official's report in 1501 (Wu Han 1937, 101). The number of

soldiers in 1392 was 1,198,434. Wu Han also estimated 2.8 million soldiers for the Ming army in the Yongle reign (Wu Han 1937, in 1955, 101). Cao Shuji reports three aggregate figures of the soldiers in the Hongwu and Yongle reigns: 1.91 million, 2.06 million, and 2.19 million. He estimates the total number of military households in the Yongle reign reached 2.19 million (Cao Shuji 2000a, 379).

60. Wang Yuquan 1965, 209.

61. The study of the Ming military system, especially the military farm, is a fruitful research field. I can refer to a few important works such as Wang Yuquan 1965; Terada 1972; Gu Cheng 1989a and 1989b; and Yu Zhijia 1987 and 2010.

62. Yu Zhijia 1987, 47–76; Hucker 1998, 62–65.

63. The state after 1500 was inactive due to diminished revenue. This situation remained unchanged even up to the twentieth century. According to Rawski, during this period taxes and public spending remained below 10 percent of GDP. With such a low share of state revenue, only two countries in the postwar world, Afghanistan and Ethiopia, could stay alive (Rawski 1989, 25–26). For a discussion of the very limited role of the state in Ming-Qing China, see Eastman 1988, 103–7, 130–4.

64. Wang Yumin argues that there a great numbers of households including depending labours controlled by the aristocratic families, state-controlled farmers, military households, and minorities, which were not reported to local administrations. He then suggests 6.80 million households and 38 million individuals for the population of the Three Kingdom period. Ge chooses 30 million as the low-bound value of the estimated populations (Ge 2002, 441–47).

65. Deng and Qi; He Zhongli, 1999.

66. *Xu zizhi tongjian changbian, juan* 4. For a study of Song household registration in the English literature, see So 1985.

67. For the institutional aspect of Song household registration, see So 1982 and Wu Songdi 2000, chapter 2.

68. Qi 1987, 329.

69. For the property classification in household registration, see Liang Taiji 1998, 19–36, 37–68; Wang Zengyu 1996, 8–27. For the household registration in rural areas, see Yanagida 1986, 102–31.

70. See Yanagida on the rural *kehu* households (Yanagida 1986, 240–83, 284–23). It is undeniable that a large number of urban *kehu* households lived in Song cities, but due to scanty documentation, scholars still debate whether the ten-level urban household registration should include the urban *kehu* households (Yanagida 1995, 198).

71. Fuzhou's population reached 247,000 households (*hu*), including 17,000 urban households and 15,300 rural households (Wang Zengyu 1996, 13–14).

72. The mainstream in the study of the sixteenth-century domestic market has largely adopted a social history approach. This is particularly true for the Fu era. Only a few attempted to quantify the market expansion in late Ming, but the results were disappointing. Wu Chengming, for instance, openly admits that it is unlikely to reconstruct the size of domestic markets in the Ming era based on the amount of commercial taxes because most of the taxes were quotas and fluctuated unreasonably over decades (1995, 164–67).

Chapter 3. How Large Was the Money Economy?

1. Elvin 1973, 203–4; Hartwell 1982, 405.

2. ZGRK-3, 261. For further discussion, see chapter 5.

3. Although the quality of the census varied over time, the population data can be internally tested through a comparison. The best evidence comes from population growth in the Lower Yangtze. Even though the censuses were conducted by different governments, a comparison

indicates gradual changes in the population of the Lower Yangtze over the centuries. This is an important sign of the high quality of the data because in terms of a general trend, there is no conflict among the sources that were independently acquired.

4. For the calculation, see table 5-1.

5. Perkins 1969, 195, 199.

6. Wu Songdi reports the aggregate households in Hunan increased from 205,583 in 980 to 2,075,422 in 1290 (2000, table 14-3, 635).

7. Both Peng and Chuan pointed out that the purchasing power of silver in the Ming was higher than that in the Song (Peng 1965, 706–22; Chuan 1967a). For instance, 1 *shi* of rice could be purchased at 0.29 to 0.60 taels of silver in the sixteenth century; yet in the twelfth century it ranged between 1.2 and 2.3 taels (Peng 1965, 506, 703).

8. Ikeda On compares the price level between Han (206 BC–220 AD) and Tang (618–907) China and concludes that prices remained at a relatively low level in ancient China until the eighth century. Acknowledging that the rise of prices had begun in the late eighth century and risen twice in Song China, he attributes this phenomenon to the transition in social-economic structure in Tang-Song China. See Ikeda On 1968.

9. Hartwell reported 14,724,000 households for the year 1391 and 18,839,000 households for 1542 (Hartwell 1982, table 1, 369).

10. Monetarists assume that the velocity of money is exogenous and unaffected by monetary policy (at least in the long run), and the real value of output is determined in the long run by the productive capacity of the economy. Under these assumptions, the primary cause of the change in the average price level is changes in the money stock. With exogenous velocity, the money supply determines the value of nominal output in the short run.

11. The early Ming court prohibited the circulation of gold and silver at the market upon the issuance of *baochao* in 1375. It was in the year 1488 that the court allowed the tax stations to accept bronze coins and silver as payments (*Ming shi, juan* 81, shihuo).

12. Chuan, 1967b.

13. Unlike Song and the Yuan, the Ming government prepared no reserve to back up the *baochao* but blindly commanded that the *baochao* was the only currency in the market. Neither coins nor silver could be used. This policy was disregarded by common people, who preferred coins and silver.

14. Danjo 1980.

15. Huang 1974, 69–70.

16. Peng 1965, 490–1.

17. Von Glahn 1996, 100.

18. The cause of the divergence between the Song and Ming price regimes, especially the great deflation in the period between 1400 and 1550, was not a simple combination of a shrinking money supply and a sharp decline in aggregate population. The insufficient money supply contributed to the price deflation in the Ming period only after the domestic market began to revive in 1550.

19. Goldstone's interpretation of the British price revolution highlights the fact that urbanization and rising population were agents that promoted a rise in V. The latter grows as the square of the rate of population growth when commercialization is spreading (Goldstone 1984).

20. Li Ruoyu reported about 1,062 Huizhou contracts collected in the Anhui History Museum, which date from 1368 to 1644. For the first century in Ming history (1368–1457), 226 cases are found, among which 72 payments were made in kind with cloth and grain, which comprised about 32 percent of the total contracts (Li Ruoyu, 1988, 40–41).

21. *Ming-Qing Huizhou shehuijingji ziliao congbian*, vol. 1, 10–11; vol. 2, 20–21.

22. In the contracts of the early Ming period, such as those of the Wang brothers, most transactions dealt with tracts of land less than one acre in size. The high price of Huizhou land in the Qianlong reign is paralleled by Suzhou (see the contracts of land sales collected in *Mingqing*

Suzhou nongcun jingje ziliao, 87–177). For a long-term survey of changes in land prices over the five centuries (1400–1900), see Chao, 130; Kishimoto 1990, 755.

23. *Doushangong jiayi jiaozhu*.

24. MTZL, vol. 230; MHD, vol. 189, Ministry of Works.

25. Although the development of markets and business networks showed continuity in China from the sixteenth century through the twentieth century, in Xu Tan's view, it was during the Qing that long-distance trade truly took off when trade expanded to coastal areas and to the Yangtze River system in addition to the trade volume already achieved along the Grand Canal in the mid-Ming (Xu Tan 2000).

26. Fu Chonglan provides a helpful survey of cities and industries along the Grand Canal in late Ming and Qing and traces their origins to the early Ming with regard to their administrative and military functions (Fu 1985).

27. Zhou Chen, "Yu xingzaihubuzhugongshu," in Hong 1988, 30–33.

28. Fan 1993, 139–140.

29. For North China, see Yamane 1995; for the Pearl River delta, see Ye Xian'en and Tan Lihua 1984; for Fujian, see Chen Keng 1986; for Shandong, see Xu Tan 1995. For the Lower Yangtze delta, see Fan Shuzhi and Liu Shiji. Xu Tan recently attempted to theorize these regional investigations on the basis of Skinner's framework. She gives a comprehensive analysis of the development of local markets and towns both chronologically and geographically (Xu Tan 1997, 1999, 2000). The early Ming economy only achieved the primary stage of the rural market development after the long-lasting civil wars that had destroyed the local economy and society.

30. In early Ming contracts, such as those of the Wang brothers, most transactions dealt with tracts of land less than one acre in size. The price, if paid in grain, often doubled the annual rent of the land. Although in terms of *baochao*, the land value inflated much in the Yongle reign, the prices of Huizhou land in the early Ming period remained as low as less than 1 tael of silver per *mu* (1 *mu* = 0.16441 acre) until the 1440s. It then jumped to about 10 taels in the Hongzhi reign and was lowered somewhat in late sixteenth and mid-seventeenth centuries. In the late seventeenth and the first decade of the eighteenth century, it rose slowly at first but then gained momentum in the second decade and finally came to a peak in the Qianlong reign (1736–1795), with the average price about 20 taels per *mu*. The high price in land markets in the Qianlong reign can find a parallel in Suzhou (see the contracts of land sales collected by Hong 1988, 87–177). For a long-term survey of changes in land prices over the five centuries (1400–1900), see Chao 1986, 130; Kishimoto 1990, 755.

31. The *lijin* tax in 1880–1889, for instance, amounted to 16,867,000 taels of silver. This figure does not include Chili, Yunnan, and Guizhou (464–720,000 taels) and Manchuria (15,104,000 taels). See Perkins 1969, table I.4, 350. This sum, along with the part from Manchuria and Chili, can lead to an estimate of interprovince trade in domestically produced goods of 420 million taels. The estimated value of goods is derived from the general rate of 1/20, therefore, the amount of 16,809,000 taels can be converted into 336,180,000 taels of silver. For taxes from Manchuria, the conversion rate is 1.5 percent, and for Chili, among other places, 1.25 percent (ibid., table I.5, 351).

32. This only represents domestically produced goods. The inclusion of foreign imports raises the total to over 1 billion teals (ibid., 349–57).

33. See table G-17 in appendix G. This percentage is fairly close to Perkins's estimated share of long-distance trade (not including imports from abroad) to farm output, which was about 12 to 14 percent at the turn of the century (Perkins 1969, 119).

34. Ibid., 117. The tax revenues in Sichuan were paid by iron coins; therefore, scholars in the early decades of the twentieth century often left the Sichuan figure outside the aggregate revenues of the Song commercial taxes. The Sichuan taxes can, however, be converted into bronze-coin-based calculations by assuming the exchange rate being 1:2 among them (Guo Zhengzhong 1997a, 219–23).

35. In 1077, 1 string of cash was equivalent to 1 tael of silver. I follow Balazs and Perkins to adopt a general tax rate of 5 to 10 percent. The calculation is conducted as follow: 7.7 million/ (5–10%) = 770 million. The reality is more complicated as each kind of commodity might be taxed with a different rate. For discussion on the same problems in the *lijin* revenues, see Perkins 1969, 345–49.

36. The local administrations for the collection of commercial taxes were known as *shukesi* and *shuikeju*. The commercial tax was only one major part of *kecheng*. Being a mixed nature, *kecheng* was comprised of payments in kinds and payments in *baochao*. On many occasions the former included direct taxes that were submitted by salt producers and tea planters in kind. As presented in *Mingshilu*, these taxes were levied directly from producers. So was the case for taxes against mining and fishing. Only seasonal failures or traffic problems forced the Ming government to accept the conversion in money. Some other sources for *baochao* were from sale of alcohol and vinegar, certification of contracts, and redemption of legal punishments.

37. In the late 1380s, Xie Jin, a literary and editorial aide to the emperor, mentioned in his memorial that the quota of the commercial taxes in the prefectures and counties were fixed regardless of the rise and decline in trade. See *Ming shi, juan* 147.

38. Peng 1965, 111.

39. Some other sources for *baochao* were from the sale of alcohol and vinegar, certification of contracts, and redemption of legal punishments. They accounted for a minor portion of the tax revenues collected in *baochao*.

40. Zhu Yuanzhang ordered in 1380 to close up 364 CTO stations because their annual tax income was below 500 *shi* of rice. For further information see chapter 5.

41. Mark Elvin first used this term to describe progress in the financial market of Song China, see Elvin 1973, 146-63. For important works on this subject, also see Miyazaki 1943; Hino 1983.

42. Chuan 1948b, 1967a; Gernet, 1962, 78. For a discussion of how silver functioned as the medium of exchange in the Song, see Wang Wencheng 2001.

43. Atwell 1990 and 1998; Von Glahn 1996, 113–41; Miyazawa 1998.

44. Von Glahn doubts if the existence of a unified monetary system can be applied as a standard to judge the development of the Chinese money economy and acknowledges that "the manifold currencies of late imperial China reflected the increasing diversity of market demand for monetary media as the range of money-use broadened." Tokugawa, Japan, even reversed from coins to rice as the standard for its payment; yet, this "regression" was uniquely applicable to economic growth occurring then in Japan (1996, 8–9, 11; Yamamura 1988). Sweden is another example of a country using low-value metal coins to introduce paper banknotes. Stockholms Banco (Bank of Sweden) issued the first paper money in Europe in 1661. To sustain a steady growth in money supply and to resolve the problems of making large payments with the *daler*, a currency minted by copper that required the transferring of a large amount of metal by horse and cart, Sweden resorted to issuing paper banknotes.

45. Chuan 1967a and 1967b.

46. See table 2.3.

47. Unlike the Song and the Yuan, the Ming government prepared no reserve to back up the *baochao* but blindly commanded that the *baochao* was the only currency in the market. Neither coins nor silver could be used. This policy was disregarded by common people, who preferred coins and silver.

48. For the sources on imperial minting production, see appendix B.

49. Gao 2000, 103. Miyazawa suggests the money stock was about 300 million strings over the Song prior to 1127 (Miyazawa 1993, 204).

50. Peng 1965, 111.

51. For the estimate of the coins produced by the Ming imperial mints, see appendix B.

52. Peng 1965, 646.

53. Suzuki 1999, 59–61.

54. For how I reach such a ratio, see appendix B.

55. Chuan 1967b. Chuan also notes that the silver collected in the Song was the tax part of mining output, while in the Ming, owing to the strict monopoly policy, mining households submitted 40 to 50 percent silver outputs to the court, which was much larger than in the Song. Chuan's explanation implies a greater variance in silver output between the Song and the Ming. See Chuan 1967b, 613–15. For a comprehensive view of mining policies in Song China, see Wang Lingling 1988 and 1998; Qi 1988, 576–97.

56. Chuan 1967b, tables 1 and 2, 602–8. For the period from 1487 through 1520 the mining revenues added gold and silver together; thus, the silver revenue would be a little lower than the records indicate. Also see *Cambridge History of China*, vol. 8, 386.

57. Wang gives optimistic estimates about the silver outputs during the two peak periods: For the years between 1537 and 1566, he chooses 481,710 taels of silver, the highest annual mining output record one can find for the Jiajing reign (1522–1566), as the normal average and reaches 1,448,100 taels as the total for these twenty-nine years; for the years between 1596 and 1620, he similarly chooses 333,300 taels as the average and reaches 7,992,000 taels (Wang Yuxun 2001, 19–20). They together added up to 9,440,100 taels, amounting to 68 percent of the estimated total of the later period (1520–1664). Given the unstable outputs in preindustrial mining industry, Wang's estimates are somewhat too idealistic.

58. I estimate 1 tael of silver to equal 0.7 strings of coins according to the contemporary price of coins in silver.

59. He further attributes this mid-fifteenth-century economic downturn chiefly to two factors: a decline in agricultural outputs caused by dramatic climatic changes and a sharp contraction in the international supply of precious metals (Atwell 2002, 92–96, 98).

60. He argues that during the Yongle reign "a relatively prosperous and vigorous Ming dynasty had tried to lead the rest of Eurasian out of the serious economic difficulties" (ibid., 98).

61. For what the Chinese received from foreign markets at this time, Atwell reports all kinds of goods other than precious metals: jade, coral, ivory, fragrant woods, pepper, spices, cobalt, timber, cotton goods, hides, and horses (ibid., 90).

62. Ibid., 97. For the prevalence of counterfeiting in sixteenth-century China, see Von Glahn 1996, 86–88, 97–99, 104–12.

63. W. G. Liu 2005, 111.

64. Von Glahn 1996, 140–41. Wu Chengming also suggests the silver import before the eighteenth century would triple the Ming silver stock (Wu Chengming 2002, 173, 249).

65. I suppose the contemporary rate between silver and bronze coins is 1 tael of silver = 0.7 string of coins.

66. Braudel 1974, 28.

67. For the recent theories of the market economy in the Lower Yangtze delta, see Li Bozhong, 1998.

68. The Single Whip reform, for instance, was first launched in Jiangxi in the 1560s. This reform allowed farmers to pay money in place of labor services and consequently increased the demand for silver. Scholars usually agree that the Single Whip reform extended nationwide no later than 1592; some favor an earlier date such as 1581 (Kuroki 1993, 599). Both dates are close to the year of 1600.

69. According to Braudel and Spooner, the total amount of metal money in circulation in Europe and the Mediterranean before the discovery of America was an approximate total of 5,000 tons of gold and 60,000 tons of silver. The arrival of bullion from America during the century and a half between 1500 and 1650 amounts to 1,600 tons of silver and 180 of gold (Braudel 1974, 28). The amount of silver imported into Europe in the sixteenth century now looks less significant than it used to. In contrast, the late Ming's silver imports would be an extremely unusual case indicated by the dominant size of silver imports over the domestic stock of money.

70. The year 1600 is currently recognized as the peak of Ming population. However, there is no reliable data on mid- and late Ming population. The estimates of the aggregate population then vary between 120 and 200 million. A few examples are: 150 million (Ho 1959, 264), 120 to 200 million (Perkins 1969, 216), 120 million (Xu and Wu, 39), 200 million in 1590 (Cao 2000a, 201).

71. Peng attempts to quantify the money supply over the course of Chinese history. His comparison sets up an example for later researchers, without whom the present research might be impossible. However, in Peng's estimates the money supply of the Ming in both total value and per capita are overestimated. Peng underestimates the aggregate population of the Ming as only 60 million and fails to identify the specific year on which he is focusing (Peng 1965, 781).

72. Despite the fact that most of China's socioeconomic historians, especially those engaged in the study of the Lower Yangtze delta and southeast coastal areas, often acknowledge the late Ming and early Qing as an integral part of economic development, the study of economic performance in preindustrial China represents two different cases in regard to aggregate data.

73. The term "unilateral payments" is borrowed from the study of medieval European economy, which is used to indicate revenues due to landlords that were settled in kind or in labor (Cipolla 1956, 7–8). I use it in the Chinese case to indicate the early Ming state extracted revenues from local societies almost exclusively in kind or in labor. Not until the mid-sixteenth century did local governments gradually convert those "unilateral payments" into cash income. And this became a national accomplishment as late as in the mid-eighteenth century.

74. Yang Guoqing estimates the size of corvée labor used in the construction of Nanjing's city wall. He points out that the potential human sources for building works included 200,000 soldiers, approximately 200,000 artisans, 1 million peasants, and several hundred thousand prisoners. The total work required 7 million individual workdays (Yang 2002, 37–44).

75. The Song government's total silver holdings in the 1120s, for instance, reached the sum of approximately 40 million taels (Shiba 1983, 92).

Chapter 4. Trade and Water Transport in the Eleventh Century

1. A recent study of pre–World War II transport in China reveals that waterway transport still represented 81 percent of the total estimated volume of freight transport (Rawski 1989, table 4.10, 200).

2. Elvin 1973, 131.

3. Miyazaki Ichisada 1950, reprinted in *Miyazaki Ichisada zenshu*, vol. 2, 157–59.

4. For technical inventions and shipping craft in early and medieval China, see Needham 1971. Needham focused on the design and invention of stern and hull, oars, the axial rudder, anchors, and the sailing raft before the third century.

5. Needham 1971, 54–55.

6. Hartwell 1982, 367–68, 385.

7. Elvin 1973, 136. For the original Chinese text, see the biography of Cui Rong in *Jiu-Tangshu, juan* 98.

8. Tan 1955, 276–77; Miyazaki 1950, reprinted in 1991, vol. 2, 157–59.

9. Xin 1989a and 1989b.

10. Chuan 1995, 16–24.

11. Xin 1996, 9.

12. Ever since Japanese scholar Kato Shigeru published his seminal article on Song commercial taxes in 1934, experts in China and Japan continued to debate every aspect of Song tax data. Some examples include the apparent discrepancy between these figures, what these figures reveal about the nature of Song trade patterns, the content of articles, and the regional variance in trade. However, most scholars are overwhelmingly concerned with bureaucratic control and tax

resistance rather than with the state's tax capacity (see Kato 1952; Song Xi 1947, 1948, 1953; Sogabe, 390–404; Guo 1997a, 123–233, 234–77; Miyazawa, 45–70). Laurence Ma's monographic publication has for decades remained the only and most important one in the English literature regarding the 1077 commercial tax data. Shiba also exploited a minor portion of the 1077 data in his study of urbanization and commerce in the Lower Yangtze (Shiba 1975). Meanwhile, Balazs and Perkins use them to measure the size of the market in preindustrial China.

13. Ikeda 1939, 144.

14. In my survey, I have omitted the trading ports and cities in the Lower Yangtze because it is well known that the economy of this region had easy access to raw materials and markets since the Tang-Song transformation through its intensified waterway networks (Zheng Xuemeng 2003, 127–38). This case supports my argument that preindustrial Chinese trade depended heavily on inland waterway transport.

15. Commercial taxes from Liangzhe *lu* and eastern Jiangnan *lu* totaled 1.22 million strings. Considering the double-counting of the port cities along the mainstream of the lower Yangtze River and a small number of cities independent of water transport, I multiply this figure by 0.8 to obtain 1 million strings.

16. Modern China has over 50,000 rivers with drainage areas (often referred to as river basins in this study) upward of 100 sq. km (Ren, Yang, and Bao, 80). There were a smaller number of rivers in the Song dynasty because the geographical size of China in the eleventh century was much smaller than the present.

17. Shipping along the main course of the Yangtze River in the Southern Song period was somewhat dangerous and often went through supplementary channels (*jiajiang*) parallel to the mainstream of the Yangtze River (Luo 1991, 222–23).

18. For construction and maintenance of these canalized water routes in Song times, the *Changjiang hangyunshi* (*gudai bufen*) (Luo Chuandong 1991) provides useful information: the Bian Canal, *Henan hangyunshi*, 128–33;the Guangji Canal, *Henan hangyun shi*, 138–40; the Yongji Canal (Wang and Xiao, 32–34); the Wei River, *Huanghe shui shi shuyao*; the Jiangnan and Zhedong Canal (Tong, 66–73); the Min River, *Fuzhou gangshi*, 19–20; the Gan River (Shen and Yang), 50–52; the Han River, *Henan hangyun shi*, 140–42; Wang and Xiao, 62.

19. Luo Chuandong 1991, 223–25.

20. Wang and Xiao, 9–10, 62, 92–94; An, 44–50. For the construction of canals in North China plain before 960, see Shi 1988.

21. Chuan 1995; Shi 1988, 153, 175, 189, 216–19; An, 659–77, 692–712.

22. Ren, Yang, and Bao, 87.

23. For China's climatic changes from the tenth to the twentieth century, it is generally argued that in the Song-Yuan period, the weather tended to be warmer and more humid in the Yellow River basin, and from 1300 to the twentieth century it became colder, a pattern usually identified as a "little ace age." However, during the period between 1300 and 1900, the eighteenth century was also a period of warm weather (Zou 1997, 28–47). Whether or not it is a coincidence, the two economic booms in the eleventh and eighteenth centuries witnessed two periods of warm weather.

24. If the pattern of domestic trade in preindustrial China had been determined by low transportation costs alone, making it even more reliant on the geographical features of rivers, long-distance trade should have been orientated from west to east. Under such a circumstance, the Yangtze River, the longest river in China, might have been critical to long-distance trade. This assumption is simply not supported by evidence. According to the 1077 data, commercial taxes collected along the main body of the Yangtze River from Kuizhou downward to the sea accounted for only 4.7 percent of Song commercial taxes (see table 4-1).

25. The key determinants of the trade routes and the volume of goods, as Perkins mentioned, were transportation costs, income distribution, and variance of climatic and soil conditions (Perkins 1969, 120).

26. Zheng 1996; 201-62; Zhang Jianguang, 2003. For a recent survey on the market expansion in t rural China, particularly the circulation of tea, textile and grain and the prevalence of cash payments in the south, during the Tang-Song transformation, see Liang 2013.

27. For a general view on this subject, see Hartwell 1982.

28. The total number of households in 1078 was 5,664,066 in the north and 10,939,908 in the south. The average size of a Song household is estimated at 5.5 members (Wu Songdi 2000, 122–35, 156). For the estimated population of Europe (excluding Russia), see Durand 1974, table 2, 259.

29. W. Liu 2013, 216–17.

30. In 1077, the commercial taxes collected in bronze coins reached 6,868,288 strings and those paid in iron coins 1,667,647 strings. Assuming 1:2 for the exchange rate between bronze and iron coins, Guo Zhenzghong suggests 7,702,112 strings for the total (Guo 1997a, 211).

31. The exchange of goods between the north and the south caused a larger trade deficit for the north. Thus, the state, according to Toru, initiated bills of exchange to solve this problem (Toru, 1993). These instrumental credit innovations gave rise to the emergence of a capital market in Kaifeng.

32. Chen and Wu, 123.

33. Xie 1995, 30.

34. Huang Shengzhang 1957. For shipments of grain from the Yangtze valley upstream along the Jialing River in the twelfth century, see Von Glahn 2003, 189–90.

35. Xingzhou, Sanquan, and Lizhou belonged to the Lizhou *lu* where the currency was iron coins. I converted their commercial taxes into bronze coin-based units at the exchange rate of 1 bronze coin to 2 iron coins.

36. The length of the Jialing River is close to 700 miles, and that of the Han River 950 miles.

37. Xiangyang ranked first among all the cities in the Yangtze River basin in terms of commercial taxes (see table 4-2).

38. Song 1962, 23–29.

39. Zou 2005, 138–49.

40. To secure a tea supply from the regions between the Huai and the Yangtze rivers, the Song court in the first half of the eleventh century set up thirteen Trade Commission of Tea agencies at Qizhou, Huangzhou, Luzhou, Shouzhou, and Guangzhou and six Monopoly Trade Bureaus (*quehuowu*) at Zhenzhou, Hanyangjun (modern Hanko), Qizhou, Jiangling, Haizhou, and Wuweijun, all of which were located on the northern side of the lower Yangtze River (Zhu Chongsheng 1985, 261–65; C. Liu 2000, 46–56).

41. It takes the combined commercial taxes of Hukou, Jiangzhou, and Xingzi, all three of which were major harbor cities in the northern part of the Boyang Lake, to surpass those of Ganzhou. In 1077, their combined tax quotas amounted to 55,870 strings. This case and that of the Changsha-Yueyang in the Dongting Lake case demonstrate that branches and lake districts made significant contributions to water transportation in the Yangtze River basin.

42. Miyazaki 1950, in *MTZS*, vol. 2, 157–59. Elvin believed that breakthroughs in "transport and communications were almost as important as agriculture in promoting the *medieval* economic revolution" (Elvin 1973, 131).

43. For a comprehensive account of Song transportation, see Shiba 1968, 49–132, and Shiba 1970, 4–44.

44. Shiba 1968, 56–70, 72–106, 109–29, and Wang Shigang, 1993, 66–85.

45. Shiba1968, 51–129; 1970, 4–44.

46. Needham 1971, 460–1; Elvin 1973, 137.

47. In the late thirteenth century, nearly twenty thousand privately owned ships were registered in Mingzhou, Wenzhou, and Taizhou, three major sea harbors in Zhejiang, 3,833 of which were vessels. A seagoing vessel could carry 5,000 piculs of cargo and/or 500 to 600 passengers (Shiba 1968, 102–3; 1970, 7).

48. Elvin 1973, 136.

49. In the eighth century, it would have cost 4,975 *wen* to ship 1 ton of goods upstream across 100 km and 1,658 *wen* downstream. In the Song era the same journey would cost only 995 *wen* and 332 *wen*, respectively. Given that grain prices rose dramatically between these two periods, the reduction in transportation costs in the Song era could have been even greater.

50. *XZTC, juan* 297. Assuming 1.1 string of cash could buy 1 *shi* of rice in 1079 (see Peng's index), the freight rate was 0.008 *shi* per 100 Song *jin*/100 *li*.

51. Peng 1965, 362, 457.

52. Kiyokoba 1996, 348.

53. Because the price level in the 1160s was close to that in the late eleventh and early twelfth century, one might take this case as evidence supporting the Song freight rate reported in table C-5. Inflation might have been a factor in the decrease in Song water transport costs in real terms, as we know that over the two and a half centuries of the Song dynasty, the grain price raised three to fourfold; meanwhile, freight rates remained at a similar level.

54. Chuan and Kraus, 1975.

55. The first century of the Ming price regime was predominantly characterized by a command economy, while grain prices varied greatly in different regions after 1500 (Chuan 1967d).

56. *XZTC, juan* 367, 8826

57. Before the 1060s the troops stationed in Shaanxi accounted for 37.5 percent of all Song troops; after the 1060s this ratio increased to 43.2 percent (Qin 1997, 173).

58. Hartwell has put forward a groundbreaking argument on the role of the Song state in rapid industrial development in eleventh-century China. This achievement, according to Hartwell, is particularly related to the demand for iron products from the Northern Song (960–1127) state, and the distribution of iron-producing centers was partially determined by its transportation costs in delivering products to Kaifeng (Hartwell 1962, 155–56; Hartwell 1966, 36)

59. The Song state collected 18 to 22 million Song *shi* of grain annually; if the substitution of cash and textiles is included, the total should be no more than 29 million Song *shi* (Bao 2001, 316–18). In contrast, the early Ming regime controlled a grain tribute of as many as 30 to 40 million *shi*; however, land taxes declined in the succeeding periods. For the late Ming, the total of the land taxes in 1531 is estimated to be 22 million *shi* (Tang 1991, 54, 188).

60. *Hino* 1980, in *HKTSR* vol. 11, 355–56.

61. Shiba 1974, 129.

62. Su Shi, *juan* 9, "zaiqi fayubshi yingfu zheximi zuang."

63. Hartwell 1966, 36; Kracke 1975, 50–51.

64. Hartwell 1967, 151; Skinner 1977, 16.

65. Hartwell 1966, 36.

66. Zheng Xuemeng, for instance, argues that it was toward the end of the Northern Song period that the Lower Yangtze gained a central position in China's economy (2003, 19). If this is true, the entire eleventh century can be viewed as a transitional period.

67. There were about sixty-two households per square kilometer in the Chengdu plain in 1102, about three times the figure for Hangzhou. It took another century and a half for the latter to catch Chengdu (Wu Songdi 2000, 465–56, 474–75, 540–42).

68. Wu Songdi 2000, 434–35, 474–75.

69. Cheng 1992, 321–25.

70. Kaifeng had no natural defenses to protect her from attack. In choosing Kaifeng as its capital, the Song state showed that economic concerns outweighed military or political concerns (Shi 1988, 215–19; Wang Xinyi 2001, 511–27).

71. Huang 1958.

72. For the history of Daming and its importance in the north after the Rebellion, see Shi 1994, 1–33. For the fate of the Yongji Canal after 1127 and how the city of Daming was buried underground by the floods around 1400, see Chen Qiaoyi 2008, 84–87, 100–1.

73. Chen Qiaoyi 2008, 80–84; *Huanghe shuilishi shuyao*, 178–96.

74. The commercial tax collected from the Shandong peninsula totaled about 740,033 strings (including East and West Jingdong *lu* in the 1077 data).

75. In addition to the lower Yellow River, twelve river-port cities in the Hutuo River basin produced nearly 200,000 strings of commercial taxes in 1077 (see table C-8 in appendix C) and nineteen cities in the Ji River basin accounted for about 159,000 strings (see table C-5 in appendix C).

76. Kracke 1975, 2–5.

77. McNeil 1987.

78. For the shares and amounts of Song state revenues attributable to various products, see Bao 2001, 318. For monopolies in salt and tea and the transportation issue, see Guo Zhengzhong 1997b and Huang Chunyan 2002. For further discussion, see W. G. Liu, 2005.

Chapter 5. China after 1200: Crisis and Disintegration

1. Although Skinner apparently downplayed the significance of Song trade, he noted the "devolutionary trend of the centuries from 1200 to 1500" and thus chose 1465 as a benchmark year for the beginning of what he named the late imperial cycle of urbanization and commercialization (Skinner 1977, 27).

2. Wu Songdi 2000, 352; Cao Shuji 2000, 199.

3. Xu and Wu, 111. Also see Wang, Liu and Zhang, 858–873.

4. "The establishment of the Henan Province in 1291 was aimed to connect Southern China to Beijing and thus comprised a broad range of areas, including many important cities north of the mid- and lower-Yangtze River such as Jiangling, An'qing and Yangzhou (see Li Zhi'an 2011, 183–184). In fact, for the total thirty stations listed under Henan Province, there were twenty-two tax stations from Anhui (17) and Hubei (5). In contrast, there were only seven stations from modern Henan.

5. Guo Zhengzhong 1997a, table 3-16, 211.

6. Wu 2000, Table 14-3, 635.

7. For instance, Fujian's trade came to prosperity under the Mongol rule (So 2000, 117–22).

8. For a discussion on how Kublai Khan, the founder of the Yuan dynasty, promoted trade and accorded merchants high status, see Rossabi 1988, 122–27.

9. For Kublai's efforts to improve the system of transport, especially the building of roads and the establishment of 1,400 postal stations, see Rossabi 1988,124. Eastman remarked that the Yuan "was seemingly the last of the dynasties to devote any persistent attention to the road . . ." (1988, 105).

10. Chen Gaohua 1997, 14.

11. Otagi 1973; Miyazawa 1998, 232–46.

12. The figures reported here are in the *zhongtong* bill; 1 *ding* = 50 *guan* (Chen and Shi, 511). The contemporary price of rice was about 40 strings (thus 0.8 *ding*) of the *zhongtong* bill per Yuan *shi* of rice (Peng 1965, 441–42).

13. Chen and Shi, 279, 283.

14. After the 1270s, the overprinting of paper currencies already triggered severe inflation. The price of rice, for instance, rose from 10 *guan* per Yuan *shi* to 30 *guan* in 1306, and in 1311, jumped to 35 *guan* (Li Gan 1985, 421; Chen and Shi, 277, 283; Peng 1965, 435).

15. Chen Gaohua 1997, 11.

16. The price of salt tickets (*yanyin*) increased from 14 *guan* per *yin* in 1281 to 150 *guan* in 1314 (Chen and Shi, 425). During the period between 1295 and 1342, the local administration often assigned quotas to rural households and forced them to pay (Chen Gaohua 1991, 76).

17. Commercial tax was only one major part of *kecheng* (the indirect taxes). For *kecheng* in the early Ming period, salt and tea were, as presented in the *Mingshilu*, basically levied as payment in kind. This was also the case for taxes on mining and finishing. Only seasonal failures or traffic problems forced the Ming government to accept money. Some other sources were from the sale of alcohol and vinegar, certification of contracts, and redemption of legal punishments. For further discussion, see appendix E.

18. A broader classification of the Ming commercial tax revenues, according to Sakuma, consisted of four sources: commercial tax offices, which included commercial taxes and license fees; customs houses; and offices of product levies (*choufen zhumuju*) on forestry products. Among them, the first and the third were the most important for the early Ming commercial tax revenues. See Sakuma, 1965, 53–58.

19. Li Longqian 1997, 101.

20. In 1380, Zhu Yuanzhang dispatched eunuchs and students from the Imperial Academy to check the collected revenues against the tax quota and cancelled 364 CTO stations that had submitted tax revenues below 500 *shi* of rice per year (*MLJJ*, 168).

21. Chen and Lin 1999, 403.

22. Another piece of information about the establishment of tax stations in a town located in the Lower Yangtze region also refers to the measurement and collection of commercial taxes in rice. A town known as Taiping collected close to 900 *shi* of rice from merchants, thus the local official in 1377 asked Zhu Yuanzhang to set up a tax station there. See *MLJJ*, 168.

23. For salaries officials and soldiers received from the government, see Zhang Jinkui, 111.

24. Fujii 1943b.

25. 1 *guan* of *baochao* (1/5 ding) equaled 0.2 tael of silver in 1390. In 1452, it equaled only 0.002 taels (Peng 1965, 494–93). For the figures of early Ming tax revenues reported in *baochao*, see table 3-2 in chapter 3.

26. The existing scholarship on Ming water transportation provides nothing beyond the Grand Canal and Jiangnan (Huang 1974, 53–55; Brook, 597–608; Ayao, 1969). Although the publication of ZSYC by Chinese scholars has significantly improved our knowledge of water transportation in preindustrial China, the lack of discussion on water transport in the Ming dynasty is still obvious. This is due to, as mentioned earlier in this chapter, lack of information: One can hardly find resources available in the Ming official documents on long-distance shipments along waterways other than the Grand Canal.

27. The major course of the Ming Grand Canal was initially constructed in the 1280s when the Mongols conquered South China. They felt that it was necessary to open a waterway for shipping grain tribute from the Lower Yangtze delta to Beijing, the Yuan capital. For the construction, maintenance, and utilization of the Grand Canal in Ming China, see Jihua 1961; Hoshi, 1963 and 1971; Shi 1988, 309–32.

28. Fan 1993, 139–41.

29. While about 1,775 tribute junks were exploited in mid-Ming period, 10,455 junks were used in the early eighteenth century, among which 9,362 junks were from the Yangtze valley (Fan 1993, 141).

30. Aoyama 1963, 352–53; Chuan 1944b, 105.

31. The Gan River was a famous trade route in the late Ming. The local administrations also set up tax stations in Ganzhou to tax goods carried across the border between Guangdong and Jiangxi, which came to over 40,000 taels of silver every year. In addition, Yuegang, the only port for maritime trade with foreigners in the late sixteenth century, also contributed 40,000 taels of silver (ibid., 396, 401, 405).

32. Before 1900, the revenues from commerce amounted to 20,300,000 taels of silver (ibid., 408).

33. Wu Chengming made the same point in his survey of commercial expansion in sixteenth- and seventeenth-century China (Wu 1995, 167).

34. Ibid; also see Xu and Wu, 84.

35. There were no nationwide standard of transition tax rates. Most of the Qing customs houses followed the late Ming practices with necessary modifications. In 1775, a comprehensive collection of regulations and precedents was officially published after most modifications were accomplished. Nonetheless, the tax rates in the first one and a half centuries of the Qing dynasty remained stable (Qi Meiqin, 213). Therefore, the amounts of taxes collected from each inland custom house over the Ming-Qing transitional period were highly comparable.

36. Aoyama 1963, 352–53; Chuan 1944b, 105.

37. Huang 2005, 111; Fan 2009, 111. For Tan's thesis, see Tan 1955.

38. Tan 1955, 277.

39. For a recent study of late Ming commercial manuals and travel guidebooks, see Chen Xuewen 1997.

40. Routes 1 and 2 constitute the Grand Canal. Routes 6, 8, and 13 link the Grand Canal to the ports and salt-making sites along the seashore. Route 7 links the Grand Canal and Qizhou, an inland city in the Shandong peninsular. Route 9 was a short passage that connected the Chao Lake and the Yangtze River.

41. As Huang noted, goods shipped from the south to the northern frontier and inland provinces must first be unloaded at the ports along the Grand Canal and then delivered by carts to their destination (*Yitong lucheng tuji*, 184).

42. *Shishang leiyao*, in *Yitong lucheng tuji*, 253–55.

43. After the famous water-control project led by Wang Jing in 69 AD, the Yellow River remained stable for over eight hundred years. This fact no doubt contributed to the long period of economic prosperity in North China. From the eleventh century onward, however, the Yellow River began to shift its course onto the Hebei plain without causing severe damage to the economy and ecology (Tan 1986, 72–75).

44. Tan 1986, 97.

45. From 1272 to 1493, the course of the Yellow River swung out into three independent branches and caused a great deal of floods in many areas. Between 1272 and 1363, the floods caused by dyke breaks occurred almost annually or every other year (Zou 1986, 96, 232–35).

46. For the related water routes, see *Zhongguo lishi ditu ji*, vol. 8, 14–15.

47. Hangzhou's commercial tax quota was 11,669 strings. For the tax quotas of Yangzhou and four other cities, see table A-6.

48. Song 1948.

49. *Yitong lucheng tuji*, 184.

50. Zou 2005, 191–207; Zhou Kuiyi, 77–79.

51. One example is the Huimin Canal. When the Song court first constructed the Huimin Canal in the tenth century, it served as intraregional transportation between Kaifeng and central Henan. This canal soon became an important waterway that linked Kaifeng and central Henan to the cities in the mid–Huai River basin. It was such a conspicuous success that contemporaries named the entire waterway network the Huimin Canal (Zou 2005a, 141).

52. Shi 1981, 64–66.

53. Skinner 1972, 16.

54. Shi 1981, 63–69.

55. In addition to the Yongji Canal and the Yellow, Futuo, Zhang, and Shanggan rivers, the Shanggan River formed the major part of the Haihe River in modern China, which constituted another major waterway network in Hebei. It expanded broadly into the Hebei plateau east to Taihang Mountain and formed a fan-shape structure. In comparison to the Yongji Canal, its multiple branches and tributaries linked many more cities in Hebei than any other waterway. One can name a dozen cities as important entrepôts for goods shipped along the Futuo River (see table A-8 in appendix A). They produced 185,282 strings of commercial taxes, about 2.3 times that of Hangzhou.

56. Li Xiaocong 1993.

57. Wu Chengming 1983; Fan I-chun 128.

58. Guo 1997a, 211.

59. Perkins 1969, 195.

60. During the Song and Qing trade booms, significant improvements were achieved in river navigation, such as building ports and dams, erecting navigation marks, river piloting, and removing submerged rocks, to protect sailing along the main body of the Yangtze River, especially the upper part, which was still a precarious endeavor for wooden boats (*CJH-ZSYC*, 78–84, 95–106). In contrast, we can hardly find any significant improvements in river navigation in the first century of the Ming regime.

61. Unfortunately, except for a few volumes, most authors in the ZSYC have adopted the Ming-Qing transformation paradigm to guide their surveys. As a consequence, the cases of the Qing water transport are often misused to prove the development in the Ming period.

62. Wu Chengming 2001, 206–7. Wu suggested a relative decline in the economy of Jiangxi from 1393 to 1767.

63. ZX-ZSYC, 56, 69–78.

64. ZX-ZSYC, 56, 36–38. Most of these water routes are used to transfer goods on land over a short distance.

65. Ikeda 1939, 65–73.

66. One can find the 1077 commercial tax quotas of the port cities in modern Jiangxi in *Shangshui zalu*, SHY.

67. Xu Tan 1999, 86–87.

68. Cao Shuji 2000, 125; Wu Songdi 2000, 130. The Song population is calculated by adding the populations of Xiangzhou, Guanghuajun, Junzhou, Fangzhou, and Suizhou together.

69. The Jianghan Canal was destroyed by the Song troops in the mid-thirteenth century to defend against the invasion of the Mongols (*HB-ZSYC*, 62).

70. *HB-ZSYC*, 155–59. For the rise of Wuhan as a commercial center, see also Rowe 1984 and Liu Shengjia 1992. The construction of the Yuan Dam in 1635 marked the very beginning of rapid development in Hankou for the succeeding two centuries (Liu Shengjia, 125)

71. For Song tea and horse trades, see Smith 1991.

72. Huang Shengzhang 1982, 214–17; SX-ZSYC, 191–93.

73. SX-ZSYC, 193–94.

74. Ibid., 199–202.

75. Huang Shengzhang believed that water transportation from the Wei River to the Yellow River was no longer available after the mid-eleventh century; however, archaeologists have recently found pathways that were constructed by Song artisans in the 1120s on a gorge cliff close to Shanzhou, a center for the Wei and Yellow River shipments. These pathways, which were obviously used by manual laborers to facilitate river-shipping across the gorges, indicate that this water route was still in use in the early twelfth century (*Huanghe Xiaolangdi*, 65–78).

76. Gernet notes the substantial difference between the central administration of the Song and Ming and attributes "the autocratic character of the new Ming empire" to the influence of the Mongol empire (Gernet 1982, 387, 396).

77. Xu and Wu, 111. Also see Wang, Liu and Zhang, 858-873.

Chapter 6. Prices, Real Wages, and National Incomes

1. Wong 1990; Wong 1997, 17–22. See also Pomeranz 2000, 69–107.

2. Wu Han 1965, 229–62; Wei 1961, 79–87; Wei 1985; Atwell 2002; Shiba 2001a, 91, 153, 252.

3. Chao, 111; Perkins, 111.

4. Postan 1972.

5. See table 2.2. in chapter 2. The demographic data indicated a great loss (about a third) of the Chinese population caused by civil wars and disasters during the Yuan-Ming transition (see chapter 2). However, for the population in the Lower Yangtze delta, the decline was much less severe (about quarter at most) from the late thirteenth century to the late fourteenth century. Li Bozhong provided a more optimistic estimate of the population in the Lower Yangtze delta in 1368 and suggested that it was only one-tenth smaller than that of 1298 (Li Bozhong 2003, 28–34).

6. The Southern Song population reached 80 million in 1223, and the population in North China under Jurchen rule reached 43.8 million. Thus, the aggregate population living in China proper would come to be about 124 million (Wu Songdi 2000, 366).

7. Peng 1965, 646; Von Glahn 1996, 98–102.

8. Liu 2011b.

9. Iwami 1986, 7–25; Tang Wenji 1991, 93 108; Iwai 2004, 318–26.

10. Ichiko 1977, 81, 106.

11. Danjo 1995, 129–30; Brook 1998, 68–69.

12. Real prices in silver can be deducted from the fixed conversion rates of different goods by the administration. In 1376, 1 *guan* of *baochao* could purchase 1 *shi* of rice or 1 tael of silver; therefore, one can assume 1 *shi* of rice can be exchanged for 1 tael of silver at that time. In 1407, according to the conversion rates, it took 30 *guan* of *baochao* to purchase 1 *shi* of rice and 80 *guan* to purchase 1 tael of silver. This change in the conversion rates indicates that 1 *shi* of rice could be exchanged for 0.375 tael of silver (Peng 1965, 703; Ichiko 1977, 75).

13. For a discussion of adopting the wage of unskilled laborers as an alternative standard for real income per capita and why the wages of soldiers can be used in particular, see appendix B.

14. Wang Zengyu 1983, 216–19.

15. For the clothing allowance of Ming soldiers, see appendix E.

16. I have adopted the prices in Kaifeng during the Xining reign (1068–1077). Typically, 1 bolt of silk equaled 1,000 *wen* bronze coins, or 1 Song *shi* of rice, or 1,000 *wen* of cash. In other regions, 1 Song *shi* of rice ranged from 500 to 700 *wen*, lower than in the capital. One Song *shi* equaled 0.67 Ming *shi*. One *shi* of rice weighs 150 catties (*jin*) or 75 kilograms.

17. *Song History*, *juan* 194, military section.

18. Wang Zengyu 1983, 220–24.

19. For a detailed discussion, see appendix E.

20. For a general reference on the silver century, see Von Glahn 1996, chapter 4.

21. According to the military section in *Ming History*, military guards (*wei*) in the late fourteenth century were increased by as many as 493. Each guard had 5,600 soldiers at its full strength. Supposing that all the guards were at full strength, which is quite possible at the beginning of the Ming system, there would have been 2.76 million soldiers in the Ming troops. Although this is a large number, it only includes the soldiers, not all the people involved in or regulated by the military institutions, including relatives, households registered as military professions, and the reserves. Cao Shuji estimated the population in the military system to have been about 6.2 million, about 8.5 percent of the total population in the early Ming (2000a, 247).

22. According to Hucker, the base pay of a Ming soldier in a guard was one bushel, thus 36.4 liters, of grain per month. Hucker also believed all clothing, weapons, and equipment were provided by the government, which I doubt was the case (1998, 67).

23. A combination of cash and grain in paying soldiers and officials was the practice as early as 1376 (Sun Zhengyong, 271). The central government only gave 50 to 70 percent of the pay in rice with the remaining part paid in coins or paper notes. However, we have little idea of how often such cases occurred or what pressures this put on soldiers in the Hongwu reign.

24. A similar challenge comes from the study of the average incomes in communist China until the beginning of the reform era in the late 1980s. Except for the fixed salary and

housing regulated at a national standard, which were decided by high officials in Beijing, one can hardly estimate how much a person could make for himself by exploiting the government resources.

25. Liang 1952; Iwami 1986, 107–34; Tang Wenji 1991, 228–65, 285–316.

26. Fan Zhongyi 1998, 130.

27. Chuan 1967d; Terada 1972, 57.

28. Huang Miantang reports that the average price of rice in the Lower Yangtze in the mid-sixteenth century was 0.5 tael per *shi* of rice, while Chuan estimates an average of 0.94 tael for the entire sixteenth century (1985a in 1985b, 355). Wu Chengming also uses 0.85 as the average price for the Jiajing reign (Xu and Wu, 130).

29. Liang Miaotai 1997, 46.

30. Chuan 1967d, 678.

31. *SHY*, 65/97.

32. Qi 1987a, 197–218, 349–50.

33. Jingxinan and Jingxibei, the most depopulated region in the north, had a high percentage.

34. Miyazawa 1984, 53–54.

35. For details about the estimates, see appendix F.

36. Miyazawa 1998, 53–54, 505–7; Bao 2001, 306.

37. Perkins had given his tentative estimate of the grain taxes as the share of farm outputs and national income in the early Ming (1420), and his estimates set the early Ming national income higher than mine; thus the grain taxes as a share of farm output and national income are consequently smaller. The variance between his figures and mine can be attributed to the estimate of aggregate population (he estimates 80 million in 1400, and my estimate, following contemporary official records, is 66.6 million) and the estimate of grain output per capita (where he estimates 3 to 4.0 *shi*, and I, supposing living standards to be much lower in the early fifteenth century than in later times, estimate 2.9 *shi* per head). Even so, his estimates also show that the share of tax revenue to farm output in 1400 was exceptionally high (about 10 percent) in contrast to that in the mid-eighteenth century, which is estimated to have been only 5 to 6 percent of aggregate grain output (Perkins 1969, 176).

38. For information on the economy and society in the Lower Yangtze delta after 1400, see Fujii 1953–1954; Fu 1956 and 1957; Fan Shuzhi 1990; Chen Xuewen 1993; Li Bozhong 1998 and 2000.

39. *Yanshan waiji, juan* 34, *tongyilu.*

Chapter 7. Agricultural Development of the Lower Yangtze

1. Elvin 1973, 113–14, 129–30.

2. Li Bozhong (2003) has recently raised serious doubts about the Dark Ages image of the fourteenth century with his reconstruction of a series of estimates of farm yields in Jiangnan over the millennium. As Li had focused his observations on Jiangnan, a small but central part of the Lower Yangtze, his revisionist argument reminds us of the huge variances in agricultural development even within the same macro region.

3. Shiba 2001a, 160–61.

4. Amano 1962; Deng 1993.

5. Myers 1966.

6. Elvin 1973, 118–29.

7. Elvin stressed that late traditional Chinese farming already worked "near the limit of what was possible by pre-modern means," and that "it was the expansion of population which produced that combination of high-level farming and transportation technology with a low per capita income" (1973, 118, 298).

8. For a critical review on traditional explanations by the revisionists, see Osawa 1985 and Osawa 1996, 235–52.

9. Osawa 1993; Shiba 2001a, 160–61; Li Bozhong 2000b.

10. Shiba 2001a, English abstract, 5, 13.

11. For a brief introduction on this issue, see Bray 1984, 106–23. For further discussion, see Watabe and Sakurai, 1–22; You and Zeng, 284–96.

12. Li Bozhong 2009, 59–64.

13. Zou 2005, 73–77.

14. Sudo 1962a, 363–432; Nagase, 1974; Qi 1987a, 89–96. Also see Yanagida's analysis on the interdependent relationship between irrigation projects, the rise of landlords, and the formation of rural communities (1995, 394–404).

15. Dong 2002, 198–99.

16. Chuan 1942b, 403–404.

17. Due to the poor quality of the Ming population data, only data that are nearly five centuries after the 1390s are available for examination. Therefore, it is difficult to obtain a full picture of the rural population increases in the Ming dynasty.

18. The latest important development in Jiangnan's commercialized agriculture is the planting of cotton in highland areas such as Songjiang and Shanghai, far away from the central area of the lowlands (Watabe and Sakurai, 239–63).

19. In the history of land development in the Chao Phraya basin in Thailand, changes in land use, especially the rise of intensive farming, in the low and swamp areas of the delta, were accompanied by the inflow of a large number of immigrants and the transformation of the delta through irrigation and drainage. This caused the location of the economic core region to move downstream along the river, from Nan in the upper reaches to Ayuthaya in the old delta and finally to Bangkok in the young delta toward the end of the nineteenth century. In approximately two centuries, Bangkok had transformed from a fort originally built on the west bank of a river into a capital city with 0.4 million residents around 1850. From then to the mid-twentieth century, the pattern of land use in the young delta gradually evolved from a predominance of woods, garden crops, and sugarcane to rice farming (Takaya 1987, 179–214, 251–33).

20. Watabe and Sakurai, 79–88. Shiba viewed the thirteenth century as the turning point for intensive farming. In contrast, Li Bozhong denied that intensive farming existed in Jiangnan until the eighteenth century.

21. Iwami 1962.

22. For the population of Suzhou, Songjiang, and Jiangnan, see table 9-5.

23. See discussion on the trinity model in the second section of chapter 1.

24. Shiba 2001a, 82.

25. Chen Yong, 346.

26. Chinese Marxist historians have tended to stress the decisive role of technology in agriculture regardless of changes in population growth and aggregate demands. They have not seriously considered regional variances in their estimates. Therefore, these Marxist scholars have often made their estimates based on a single example for all of China over the centuries.

27. Perkins 1969, table G. 2, 315. He also estimates 2.5 to 3 shi per mu for Zhejiang's farm yields in the Song period (Perkins 1969, table G. 3, 316).

28. Perkins had raised this question and admitted that "[a] downward bias from this source would not be serious if school-land data were distributed fairly evenly among periods of a particular province." After all, he had the tendency to believe that "school land may well be worse than the best land, but not worse than average quality land" (Perkins 1969, 312).

29. Shiba also collected a variety of Song primary sources (memorials, gazetteers, stone inscriptions, and official records) other than the rent data reported earlier (see table 1, 140–41, Shiba 2001a). However, most of these sources pointed to much higher farm yields than the rents of public lands predicted.

30. Li Bozhong noticed the ambiguity in Shiba's estimation; see Li Bozhong 2000b, 180.

31. For all other kinds of primary sources that indicated high farm yields in the Song period, Li followed Osawa's argument that they were either made for the purpose of advocating rice planting, and thus false information, or that the descriptions of the advanced technologies were exploited in the high land areas rather than Songjaing and Suzhou, the core areas of Jiangnan.

32. Li Bozhong 2000b, 182–83.

33. Also see table 1-1 in chapter 1. Nonetheless, Li argued that only the development of the late Ming period can be designated as an economic revolution because it is really a transition from extensive growth to Smithian growth (intensive growth) in preindustrial China caused by commercialization (Li Bozhong 2001, 173–75).

34. Ge and Gu, 80; Liang Keng-yao 2001, 267.

35. Liang Keng-yao 2001, 267.

36. Ibid., 274.

37. Li uses the "natural economy" term to describe the demonetized nature of the Jiangnan society in the Song period (Li Bozhong 2001, 182).

38. Li defines the transition in two aspects: first, new dynamics in agricultural developments; second, specialization and division of labor caused by commercialization (Li Bozhong 2001, 172–75).

39. See table 1-1 in chapter 1.

40. Matsui 1991, 26–56.

41. Miyazaki 1952; Miyazaki 1971.

42. Sudo 1950; Sudo 1980; 603–726.

43. For a recent review of this debate, see Takahashi 1978.

44. *Wu junzhi, juan* 19.

45. Miyazawa, 1984, 67–68.

46. Song 1948, Vol. 2, 78-79. Song reported 42,530 strings for the amount of Ningbo's commercial taxes. According to Lu's study, it had already reached 87,102 strings in 1225 (Lu 2007, 289).

47. Chen & Wu, 109–13; Huang Chunyan, 222–23.

48. For study on Mingzhou and Shaoxing in the Song era, see Shiba 2001a, 453–78, 551–73. Also see Lu 2007.

49. Shiba 2001a, 380–86.

50. The amount of Yanzhou's commercial was 35,556 strings in 1077 and 38,275 strings in 1275 (Song 1948, Vol. 2, 78–79).

51. The annual growth rate of population was 0.006 percent for Taizhou from 1109 to 1222 and 0.039 percent for Yanzhou from 11860 to 1262. The growth rate of Taizhou was the lowest in the Southern Song Lower Yangtze (see Wu Songdi 2008, 206).

52. Masao 1988, 111–19.

53. Wu Dange 1979, 142. Many local elite in Songjiang were involved in the rebellion shortly after the Ming government conquered the Lower Yangtze. After the defeat, they were exiled to the military posts in the frontier; this may help explain why the share of Songjiang's guantian ranked at the top in the Lower Yangtze.

54. Ash 1976, 521.

55. Ibid.

56. For details, see Perkins 1966.

57. Masao 1988, 111–19.

58. The acreage of the Ming guantian was 598,456 *qing*, about 9 times the Song *guantian* (see Table 4.3 & 4.4). Taking into account the military farms, the Ming state-owned landholdings were 340,941 *qing*, 14 times the Song *guantian*.

59. Wu Dange, 1979; Wei 1985, 27–29; Masao 1988, 119.

60. Land tax rates of private landholdings ranged between 0.03–0.005 *shi* per *mu*, while for the confiscated landholdings (*chaomutian*) the rates were usually 0.2 to 0.4 *shi* per *mu* (Masao 1988, 151).

61. Shiba 2001a, 153, 156.

62. Shiba 2001a, 139.

63. Huang, 1974; Yeh-chien Wang, 1973

64. For a general description of investment (capital formation) in preindustrial economies, see Cipolla 1993, 80–91.

65. Gernet 1982, 390–92; Brook 1998, 18–19.

66. See appendix F in Liu 2005 for a detailed analysis of local projects in Songjiang prefecture.

67. Bol also reports a similar pattern of change in construction projects in Jinhua, an inland region in Zhejiang (Bol 2003, table 1, table 3, 16–17).

67. Wang Yuquan 1965, 223–65; Zhang Jinkui 2007, 233–35.

69. Aramiya 1993, 75–79.

70. Peng 1965, 670.

Chapter 8. Changes in Agricultural Productivity, 1000–1600

1. Durand 1960, 226, 228–29.

2. In the Qing records, the aggregate population grew from 17,094,637 in 1680 to 102,750,000 in 1753, a nearly sixfold increase in less than a century. Yet for most modern researchers, this growth rate was an exaggeration because the 1680 figure was severely underreported for two reasons. First, it was conducted during the civil war period. Second, both the 1680 and the 1753 figures did not cover the entire population. Second and most important of all, the Qing local administration followed the Ming practice to report the "population" as a fiscal measurement of taxes, which had little to do with the real population (Ho 1959).

3. For discussion on average family size in Song China, see the fifth section in chapter 2.

4. For the estimation on land acreage in the early Ming, see Perkins 1969, 222–26.

5. For discussion on choosing this as a stable standard for per capita grain output, see Perkins 1969, 14–15.

6. According to Perkins (1969, 289), gross value of grain (rice, wheat, millet, barley, etc.) accounted for 75 percent of total farm output in the 1910s. Cash crop accounted for 17 percent, among which, cotton and soybean ranked first, totaling about 6.8 percent. All animals including sheep, horses, and hogs accounted for 8.4 percent, the latter (hogs) alone 6.5 percent. Therefore, the share of grain production in national products in the 1910s was estimated at about 60 percent. It is surely inappropriate to use this figure for the share of grain outputs in the eleventh century. I thus suggest 75 percent for two reasons: First, the estimated share of urban households reached 15 percent in the mid-eleventh century, which roughly indicates the size of the urban economy; second, the non-grain outputs, especially mulberry plantation and textiles, also made a significant contribution to agricultural development.

7. Perkins 1969, 35, 302.

8. Ibid., 56–58; Amano 1979.

9. See table B-1 in appendix B.

10. Li Lingfu 2000, 83–84.

11. When the Song administration conducted a land survey in the 1080s, known as *fangtian junshui fa*, the surveyed data on North China suggest more than half of the acreage of cultivated land was concealed. Therefore, one can double the land acreage of Shandong in 1080 as an approximation of the real acreage, which will finally lead to 40 *mu* for the average family-owned farm. I adopt 35 to 45 *mu* to allow the variance. For further discussion, see appendix E.

12. Fujii 1943a; Perkins 1969.

13. Ho 1959, 170–71; Perkins 1969, 38–39.

14. Perkins 1969, 39.

15. Nishijima 1966, 12–19.

16. In ancient Chinese mathematical texts, the origins of weight and volume are both from the measurement of millet. The standard rates for grain conversion among millet, wheat, and rice was solely based on millet. For this conversion during the Tang dynasty, see *Sunzi suanjing* written by Li Chunfeng (602–70).

17. It was Dai Zhou who recommended the benevolent granary. In his memorial, Dai viewed millet as the principle choice (*Jiu Tangshu, juan* 70, [Biography of Dai Zhou]).

18. *Tongdian, juan* 26.

19. Two major imperial granaries were asked to lend millet for disaster relief: 120,000 *shi* from the Hanjia granary and 300,000 *shi* from the Tai granary. For the details, see Kiyokoba 1997, 552–53.

20. That wheat became the major crop during the Tang-Song transition is a prevailing argument among scholars, see Nishijima 1966, 235–77; Liang Jiamian, 336–68; Dong and Fan, 387; Li Genpan 1997, 238–40.

21. Perkins notes that "prior to the twentieth century, however, increased planting of wheat as a second crop made a significant contribution to rising yields per *mou* [*mu*]" (1969, 46–47).

22. Liang 1989, 389–90.

23. Ibid., 206–8.

24. The rare records on intensive farming in the Han dynasty were largely preserved in the treatise known as *The Treatise by Fan Shengzhi* (*Fan shenzhishu*). Fan, the author of the book, was once a county official at the capital district and taught farming technology there (see Liang 1989, 209–12).

25. According to Bary, "Chinese ploughs from Han times on fulfill all these conditions of efficiency nicely" (*SCCH*, vol. 6, part 2, 178–79). Most Chinese agronomists tend to believe it was not until the Northern Wei dynasty that the plow-centered farming technology in the north became fully developed. For a full discussion, see Liang Jiamian, 265–70; Min 1992, 140–42; Dong and Fan, 278–85. The view of developed Han agriculture has been also challenged; see Yang 2001a.

26. Li Genpan, for instance, thinks that most ordinary farmers in Tang and Song times owned an ox per household so that use of the ox plow could spread across the country (2005).

27. About half of the rise in yields between 700 and 1200 cannot readily be explained by new seeds, new crops, or changing cropping patterns; it must be further recognized that many of the new cropping patterns could not have been introduced except in conjunction with other complementary factors.

28. Zhu Kezhen 1964, 458–59, 463.

29. Nishijima 1966, 167–99.

30. Perkins 1969, 43.

31. To estimate the rate of growth in capital inputs of this type, information is required on the size of the various projects and their date of construction. For many others, Perkins explains, "dates are given when major repairs were undertaken, but these are of little use in determining net capital formation" [[AU: please cite page for quote from Perkins]].

32. Perkins also notices this downward bias due to the lack of historical records: "the pre-Ming records available to compilers of gazetteers for these provinces were probably very incomplete and hence the small number of projects recorded for Tang and Sung may be misleading" (1969, 62–63).

33. Ibid., 62.

34. You 1999a.

35. *Qimin yaoshu,* "zashuo."

36. *Qimin yaoshu,* "zashuo."

37. You Xiuling thinks that *Qimin yaoshu* was written to recover from the devastated economy in the Northern Wei. Thus extensive agriculture dominated in the north (1994).

38. Dong and Fan, 230.

39. Perkins already estimates 139 *jin* per *mu* for early Ming grain production at 1400, which looks too high in comparison to that of the eleventh century. Meanwhile, Perkins's assumption on constant per capita consumption might not apply to the early Ming (1969, 17).

40. See Perkins's definition and further discussion on China's traditional agricultural technology in chapters 2 and 3 and his generalization of land tenancy in chapter 5 (Perkins 1969).

41. Ibid., 14–15.

42. This low-bound estimate is still within a reasonable range. In a primary calculation, Perkins, for instance, points out that 3.8 *shi* of unhusked rice (thus 500 *jin*/catties) of per capita annual income for a laborer of the Ming dynasty can be taken as the average per capita grain consumption (ibid., 298).

43. Ibid., 178.

44. For the official report of land acreage in 1393, see table 8-8. This national total of 850 million *mu* is too big and often adjusted to a much lower value.

45. Fujii 1943a; see also Liang 1980, 335–38.

46. Here I adopt Chao's adjusted figure for Chinese acreage in 1393, which is 338 to 359 million *mu*. The original figure was around 640 million *mu* (Chao, 81). Perkins estimates 425.4 million Ming *mu* for the year 1400 (Perkins 1969, 229).

47. This type of military farm under the Jin was an ethnic-group-based organization known as *meng'an mouke*. In addition to their own members, these farms also exploited a large number of slaves and bondsmen. Based on *Jinshi*, Liang reports 171,008,792 *mu* of land were controlled by 621,379 Jurchen households (Liang 1980, 165).

48. See the military in *Yuan history, juan* 100. Also see Liang 1980, 322–28; Wang Ting 1983.

49. Cao Shuji 1997, 472–73.

50. Yamane 1995, 4.

51. *Mingtaizong shilu, juan* 22.

52. The market value of *baochao* declined radically in the early Ming period. In 1400 the court ordered that 1 *shi* of rice equals 30 *guan* of *baochao*, almost one thirtieth of its original value in 1376. Therefore, the market value of 300 *guan* amounted to only 10 *shi* of rice.

53. Deng 1993, 111.

54. According to Ho's research, this increasing trend documented by the local officials was likely close to what really happened to the Ming population. The rural residents in these areas had less incentive to underreport their family members because they were assigned with slight quotas of taxes when they emigrated here to reclaim the wasteland (Ho 1959, 263).

55. Hu Zhiyu, *Zishan daquanji, juan* 22.

56. This edict was issued by Zhu Yuanzhang in 1388 (Wang Yuquan 1965, 203).

57. Jiang and Lin, 111; Atwell 2002, 85–86.

58. Wang Yuquan 1965, 130–32.

59. Ibid., 39–48. Also see the discussion in appendix H.

60. The highest record was 23,450,799 *shi* reported in 1401. Wang Yuquan estimates 60 to 90 million *mu* for the total military farm size (1965, 219, 227).

61. For a yearly record of the grain outputs contributed by military farms, see Wang Yuquan (1965, 219–23).

62. Cao 2000a, 240–46.

63. In 1102, there were 261,117 households living in the Kaifeng district, 549,744 households in Jingxilu, and 204,079 households in the prefectures of South Jingxilu that were confined to the north of the Huai River. All these add up to 1,014,940 households. Assuming five to six members for the average family size, the total population would be 5 to 6 million.

A General Guide on Chinese Economic Data Sources in the Song and Ming Eras

1. According to *Song History*, Ding Wei, the vice chancellor and the head of the central fiscal administration, prepared such a report in the Jingde period (1004–1007).

2. This book comprised four volumes and each volume two to three *juans*. Therefore, there were 10 *juans* in total that covered 125 subjects (*men*).

3. Perkins 1969, 192–93, 218.

Appendix A. Chinese Population Data

1. Liang is the first among Chinese scholars who argues persuasively that the Chinese historical economic data were made available by the official administration. He also argues that from the Han to the Tang dynasty the government was mostly concern with household registration. In contrast, land registration was supplementary and unimportant (Liang 1980, preface).

2. Liang 1980, preface.

3. Ho 1959, 3–23.

4. E. Rawski, 181.

5. Perkins 1969, 195.

6. Ibid., 192–93.

7. Ibid., 196–201.

8. Cheng 2003, 11–12.

9. For the sources of population data in the Northern Song period, see Wu 2000, 348–49, 354–55; Cheng 2003, 17–19.

10. For a discussion on the distribution and quality of population figures in the Southern Song, see Wu Songdi 2000, 138–54.

11. The three sources are: *Taiping huanyu ji* (Records of the Universal Realms in the Taiping era) accomplished in the 980s, *Yuanfeng jiuyu zhi* (Treatise on the Nine Territories in the Yuanfeng era) accomplished in 1080, and the 1102 household data reported in the geographical treatise of *Song shi*.

12. Wu 2000, 119–21.

13. For a brief review, see He 1999, 338–45.

14. Wu 2001, 155–62.

15. He 1999, 363–64; Fang 2010, 231–77.

16. Perkins estimates 126 millions people for the aggregate population in 1124 (Wu 2001, 352). He suggests that the population reached 104–125 millions in 1109 (He 1999, 364).

Appendix B. Long-Term Changes in Prices and the Money Stock

1. For studies on prices in the Song period, see Wang 1987, Miyazawa 1998, and Long 1993; for the prices in the Ming period, see Quan 1967, Atwell 1990 and 1998, and Huang 1985; and for the Qing period, see Von Glahn 1996 and Kishimoto 1997.

2. Peng certainly acknowledged in some parts of his book the rising trend in grain prices in the eleventh century and the extraordinarily low grain prices in the fourteenth and fifteenth centuries.

3. The central point made with regard to demographic changes is that there was an overall decline in demographics during the Song-Ming transition. It is widely accepted that the early Ming suffered a huge loss in population due to wars and natural disasters.

4. In terms of money shortage, see Hino 1935, 1936, reprinted in 1983, 367–77, 443–47; Gao 2000, 333–44.

5. For the circulation of *baochao*, see chapter 3.

6. Chuan 1971, in *Zhongguo jingji shi lucong*, 365.

7. Hino 1936, in *HKTSR*, vol. 6, 357–666.

8. Peng 1965, 451.

9. The annual minting output during the New Policy period is given by Peng (ibid., 401–2, 416).

10. Ibid., 451.

11. Wang 2001, 3.

12. *Xinyang Zhumadian qianbi faxian yu yanjiu*, 10.

13. Ichiko, 55–61; *Xinyang Zhumadian qianbi faxian yu yanjiu*, 10.

14. For the official contacts between Ming China and Ashikaga shogunate Japan, see Kimiya 1965, 521–86.

15. For this estimated ratio, see W. G. Liu 2011a.

16. I estimated 1 tael of silver as being equal to 0.7 strings of coins according to the contemporary price of coins in silver.

17. I have dismissed the preservation of silver from previous dynasties into Ming circulation. Certainly, the Ming economy inherited certain precious metals from previous dynasties, but contrary to the case of Song coins, precious metals such as gold and silver, because of their high value in relatively small volumes, were more likely to have been transferred outside China or disappeared over nearly three centuries of wars before the establishment of the Ming state. To make the estimate convenient, I also dismissed silver from the Song money supply and further dismissed the potential inheritance of silver by the Ming dynasty. These will more severely underestimate the Song money supply as opposed to that of the Ming.

Appendix C. Waterway Networks in the Eleventh Century

1. Shiba 2001b.

Appendix D. Chinese Acreage, 900–1600

1. Perkins 1969, 218.

2. According to Perkins's calculation, the average size of a family farm in China was around 50 *mus* in the second century (1969, 228).

3. *Wenxian tongkao, juan* 3. The reported total was actually the result of the standard land allotments, thus 160 Tang mu per household, times by the number of registered households (Wang 1962a, 196ab).

4. Twitchett 1970, 38–43.

5. Perkins 1969, 229.

6. Ibid., 225.

7. Chao 1986, 80, 87.

8. The national acreage in 1957 was 1,238 million *shi mu*, about 1,457 million Song *mu*.

9. Perkins 1969, 222.

10. Ibid., 224.

11. For a summary of the recent debate, see Gao 2006, 3–12.

12. Perkins clearly acknowledged that "Qing acreage data are subject to major errors" (1969, 231).

13. Ho 1959, 116.

14. Ho 1988, 50.

15. Ho 1988, 38–47, 58–59.

16. Ho argued that the land survey led by Li Chunnian during the years between 1142 and 1149 was the first and only attempt made by the Song central administration at the national level in the twelfth century. Unfortunately, no total acreage figures are available. Only in a few extant gazetteers will one find certain evidence on a few prefectures. A glimpse into these local cases will prove the high quality of the land data that were recorded in the 1140s (1988, 24–25).

Appendix E. Long-Term Changes in Real Wages

1. Adopting the wages of unskilled laborers as the standard for real income per capita is widely applied in the study of the living standards in pre- and early industrial economies. The best-known example is the Brown and Hopkins index of English building wages. For a recent case, one can refer to Lindert 1980; Lindert and Williamson 1982; Williamson and O'Rourke 1999; Allen 1988; Allen, Bengtsson, and Dribe.

2. In King's estimate of the population and wealth in England and Wales in 1688, a common soldier earned £14 yearly, identified as higher only to cottagers and paupers, which were the lowest in the pyramid of the status and wealth in seventeenth-century Britain. This account was supported by other political arithmeticians, such as Massie and Colquhoun. In both accounts, the wages of common soldiers were close to those of agricultural laborers. Their estimates are accepted with necessary modifications by modern scholars in the construction of wage indexes and national income. See King 1936 Coleman 1977, 5–7; Mathias 1979, 171–189; Lindert 1980; and Lindert and Williamson 1982.

3. Wang compared the incomes of soldiers and wage-laborers in Song China. In the eleventh century, the annual income of a male laborer in salt processing was about 21 strings of cash. An agricultural laborer in Fujian earned 17 to 22 strings, and a laborer in irrigation in Hangzhou earned 26 strings. In comparison, a Song soldier in a local troop was paid annually at around 20 strings of cash. Ihara adopted the soldier salary as the major reference for the commoner wage in the Southern Song dynasty. See Wang Shengduo 1991, 446–49; Ihara 2001.

4. The author of *Song History* declares that "the troops might be organized in a diversified way: by recruiting natives into the civic guard; by recruiting a man's family members who would like to succeed him in the service; by recruiting people near starvation; by taking the prisoners into the military campus. The strong are sent to the central armies; the weak to the local troops" (*Song shi, juan* 9).

5. Wang Zengyu 1983, 207–15, 35–42.

6. Ibid., 215–28.

7. Cao 2000a, 379–80.

8. In the early Ming, three cities, Nanjing, Beijing, and Fengyang, served as the imperial capitals or the auxiliary capitals. Except for Nanjing, which was located in the Lower Yangtze delta, the other two belonged to the underdeveloped northern China. For a discussion on choosing the capital in relation to the highly concentrated nature of political power of the early Ming, see Farmer 1976, 173–82.

9. The Ming court in Beijing began to transfer silver to troops stationed at the northern frontier in the Zhengtong reign, but in small amounts. It was not until the Jiajing reign that silver became the major source of funds in the military supply at the frontier region (Terada 1972, 21–27, 45–59; Liang Miaotai 1996).

10. Terada 1972, 120–32.

11. Wang Zengyu 1983, 154.

12. Peng 1957, Wu 1983, Huang 1992, Song 1997, and Hu 2000. This decline was caused by the rising trends in prices and the stability of nominal wages. Song provided a comprehensive survey of the decline in real wages (1997). See also Chao's research (1986, 218–19).

13. Chao 1986, 6–8.

14. Ibid., 219–20; Chao 1983, 53.

15. Five observations from Tang Shunzhi's proposal for coastal defense give weight to the wage level in the 1560s.

16. Yang 1984, 51.

Appendix F. Estimates of National Incomes

1. Chang 1962, 292.

2. Ibid., 292–93.

3. Owing to the lack of a reliable survey of income distribution among social groups, he adopted the two-dimensional division (the gentry and the commoners) in his demand study, which failed to capture many aspects of the complex social structure. For the eighteenth and nineteenth centuries we are left with detailed archives about household income, professions, and consumption, and one can expect that the future research will improve in this field.

4. Ibid., 326–27.

5. Ibid., 329.

6. The family size of a Song soldier was smaller than that of an ordinary family. Song armies were scheduled to shift garrison duties every few years. New garrison sites might be over a hundred miles away from the old ones. Soldiers were not allowed to bring their wife and children with them during the shift. Lengthy separation of a soldier from his family should have played a role in constraining birth rates. One can also find in documents that many urban residents at Kaifeng bought grain from soldiers because they were able to have a surplus of grain (originally distributed to them as a part of their wages) owing to a smaller family size. Kubota estimated that the average size of a soldier's family was three, including the soldier, his wife, and their child (Kubota 2000, 12).

7. O'Brien 1988, 3.

8. Brewer 1988, 40.

9. *Xu gujinkao*, vol. 18.

10. The social table of Britain in 1688 created by Lindert and Williamson also shows a very high percentage of poor social classes in the social structure. Soldiers, laborers, agriculture workers (freeholders and farmers), cottagers, paupers, and vagrants together consisted 67.9 percent of the total population but only 37.9 percent of the national income (see Lindert and Williamson 1982).

11. This urbanization rate is still close to the estimate by Chao (19.2 percent). See Chao 1986, 56.

12. Liang Keng-yao estimates the rate of Song urbanization in the thirteenth century was 3 to 14 percent for different regions (Liang 2006, 5–7); other scholars suggest 12 percent (Wu Songdi 2000, 619) and 15 percent (Long 2003, 49). Chao estimates 20.1 percent for the Song period in the eleventh century and 22.4 percent for the thirteenth century (Chao 1986, 56).

13. *Siyouzhai congshuo*. Also see Li Bozhong 1998, 139–40.

14. For Peng's index, the price of rice in the sixteenth century remained stable at 0.58 to 0.63 taels of silver. Wu reported 0.49 to 0.57 taels for nominal years and 0.96 to 1.09 taels as the average price in consideration of the famine years (Wu Chengming 1995).

15. *Fuchuji*.

16. In the *Mingqing huishang ziliao xuanbian*, I could find several related cases (the numbers in parenthesis are the page numbers in the source): Wang Yanshou (58) 5 taels; Li Kui (60) 10 taels; Pan (64–65) 10 taels; Cheng Shenbao (69) 30 taels; and Cheng Zhai (86) over 10 taels.

17. Wang 2000, 177–78.

Appendix G. Major Commodities in the Domestic Market

1. A comprehensive but nonquantitative survey of major commodities in the Song domestic market is provided by Shiba (1968, 132–305).

2. For a variety of consumption patterns in Song urban and rural communities, see ibid., 467–95.

3. Ibid., 258–61.

4. Hartwell 1962 and 1966. For recently completed work in this regard, see Wang Lingling 2005b.

5. Sun 2001, 70. I have calculated the aggregate and percentage values.

6. Sichuan was separated from the other regions by the tea monopoly. Sichuan alone enjoyed free trade in tea until 1074. Then, in order to support the colonial expansion in the northwest, the court developed an enormous international tea market and took it under its strict control. Since Sichuan was the major supplier of this international tea market, the majority of its tea was exclusively purchased by the tea agencies of the state.

7. C. Liu 2000.

8. Sun 2001, 139–50, tables 2–3.

9. Sichuan tea was excluded in the monopoly then and should not be included here.

10. Sun 2001, 53.

11. C. Liu 2000.

12. Ibid., 54.

13. In 1084, a high official who was in charge of the tea monopoly in Fujian suggested to the court that it should exclusively purchase the tea produced there. The tea output of Fujian, according to his estimate, amounted to 3 million Song *jin*, and the official agencies then purchased only 0.39 million (ibid.).

14. The other estimates of Song tea output ranged between 84 and 150 million *jin* (Fang Jian 1993, 76; Sun 2001, 81).

15. Changes in Sichuan tea output demonstrate a declining trend between the late thirteenth and the eighteenth centuries, but no such aggregate figure is available for tea production in the south.

16. For consumption of silk cloth in the Tang dynasty, see Lu 1995, 154–75.

17. The silk industry was one of the most important handicraft industries in the Song era, see Zhao (1972, 1976), Matsui (1976, 1990–92), Qi 1987a, 632–62.

18. Zou 2005, 460–67.

19. For the early studies, Nishijima's research on the rural cotton textile industry in sixteenth-century Songjiang is most important and helps to develop a theoretical framework (see Nishijima 1944).

20. According to Cong's survey, cotton cloth production in the Ming period in most of the northern provinces (Shanxi and Henan in particular), Huguang, Jiangxi, and Southwest China was rarely reported due to the underdevelopment of the cotton textile industry (Cong 1981, 65–69).

21. For an introduction on specialization and technology in the Song silk industry, see Zhu Xinyu 1992, 207–33.

22. Qi 1988, 644. Qi also reported the amount of silk cloth collected by the Song government through taxes and purchases amounted to 24.45 million bolts in 1086, which is about triple the estimate that I have made further on. However, he gives no reference for the sources of information (ibid., 627).

23. Fu Zongwen 1989, 261, 264–65. For the rise in the specialized markets for mulberry plants, leaves, and silkworms, see Perkins 1968, 286–88.

24. According to the treatise, this is assumed to be a large family with ten members in Huzhou, the heart of the silk industry in the Lower Yangtze (Perkins 1968, 289–90).

25. Bao 2001, 318.

26. A few times, Zhu Yuanzhang distributed 1 to 2 million bolts of cotton cloth to soldiers at the frontier. However, how these large amounts were collected is still not clear. Nishijima attributed this to the conversion of land taxes during harvest failures (Nishijima 1948, in Nishijima 2002, vol. 1).

27. Nishijima is the first to point out the significance of the development of the cotton textile handcraft industry in Songjiang in relation to the commercialization of the peasant economy (1944, 268, 277–78).

28. Bao 2001, 318.

29. Hino 1952b, *HKTSR*, vol. 10, 466–68.

30. Zhao 1973, 83–84.

31. Hino 1952b, *HKTSR*, vol. 10. Also see Appendix E. The examples Hino has addressed include: Several times in 952 the state bought 3,500 bolts in Qingzhou; twenty prefectures in the Eastern Jingdong lu in the mid-ninth century contributed several to ten million bolts; Songzhou in the Jingxi lu in 953 sold over 0.1 million bolts. For examples from the south, the administration in 1042 purchased 30,000 bolts from Yuezhou in Zhejiang. In 1028, Hangzhou alone sold 20,000 to 30,000 bolts.

32. A lot of evidence is still needed to fully prove this point. Xu and Wu observe a similar trend for long-term changes in the relative prices between silk textile and rice for both Song and Ming eras (2003, 130). Yet they have drawn an opposite conclusion that the average relative price was even lower in the Ming than in the Song. There are two major flaws in their analysis. First, their average prices for Song and Ming cover three centuries each and thus miss decade-based change. Secondly and most important, Xu and Wu select 0.85 tael of silver for 1 Ming *shi* of rice in the Jiajing reign, which is too high to represent the average grain prices for mid-sixteenth-century Jiangnan.

33. Xu and Wu, 98.

34. Matsui 1990, 2.

35. *Xuzizhitongjian changbian, juan* 135.

36. Hino 1952b, *HKTSR*, vol. 10, 465.

37. For a study of linen fabrics in Song China, see Sudo 1962a, 321–62.

38. They were purchased from Fujian coastal areas at a price of over 300 *wen* per bolt (ibid., 341).

39. Ibid., 349.

40. Local communities welcomed this policy, but later on, they found that the local administration tended to pay less than market prices in purchasing linen cloth. Lu Tao, a famous opponent of the New Policy administration, accused his colleague of paying only two-thirds of the price for cloth since 1078 (ibid., 346–47).

41. Another case of linen cloth purchase was in Guangxi and related to Chen Yaosou, who during his official term in Guangxi purchased cloth at a higher price in order to promote the production of linen cloth (ibid., 350–51).

42. Wu Chengming 2001, 131, 134.

43. For studies on the grain trade in Song China, see Chuan 1936; Perkins 1969, 142–84, Qi 1987, 982–83. For grain trade in late Ming China, see Wu Chengming 1983a and Terada 1972 on grain markets at the northern frontier (1972, 120–79).

44. Shiba 1970, 50.

45. Ibid., 51–52.

46. Ibid., 61–62.

47. Because Shiba focused on grain trade from the twelfth century onward, he did not note the starting date of this interregional grain trade.

48. The grain from the land taxes in the mid-eleventh century was about 18 million Song *shi*, and the Song state had grain incomes from other sources such as state-owned lands, which would increase the total to 26.9 million. The annual amount distributed to soldiers alone was 23 million (Shiba 1974, 128).

49. Aoyama 1963, 352–53; Chuan 1944b, 105.

50. Shiba 1974, 128.

51. Ibid., 130.

52. Ibid., 130–31; Li Xiao 2004, 81–86.

53. Hino 1935c, in *HKTSR*, 380.

54. Ibid., 134.

55. Chao argued that "obviously there was a rising trend of per capita grain output between" the first and the eleventh centuries, although he also overestimated the Song population to be 121 million in 1109. This overestimation certainly lowers per capita grain output in his calculation (1986, 89, 216).

56. Li Xiao 2004, 92.

57. Grain purchases in Shaanxi amounted to over 3 million Song *shi* of grain during times of war.

58. In Wu's estimate, the grain-import areas in the 1530s were none other than the Lower Yangtze, Huizhou, and Fujian (1983b). He did not consider the rapid development of the market after 1580. He also excluded the increasing volume of grain exported to the northern frontier toward the end of the sixteenth century. The troops stationed at the nine major military bases increased from 0.37 million in 1531 to 0.65 million in 1582; meanwhile, the salaries of soldiers shifted from grain to cash. Their annual consumption of food and fodder amounted to 1 to 3 million *shi* (Lai 2008, 275–76, 279). It is very likely the demands from the military defense in the frontier reached about 1 million *shi* of grain at the turn of the century.

59. The average size of a soldier's family is assumed to be three members.

60. Perkins pointed out that grain marketing problems influenced the size and location of Chinese cities, and these cities in turn set the amount and direction of long-distance internal commerce (1969, 139).

61. Perkins 1969, 114.

62. Ibid., 115.

63. Wu Chengming refused to compare trade between the Song and Ming periods because he followed a Marxist line of thought that condemned the intervention of the Song state in the economy. He even viewed this Song state pattern as "feudalistic" (2000, 6–7). Despite this terminological difference, his estimates rarely conflict with my observations.

Appendix H. Military Farms, Involuntary Migrations, and Extensive Agriculture

1. For example, Xu Hong (1982) and Yu Zhijia (2010).

2. Gu Cheng 1989a; Cao 1997, 267.

3. In *MHD*, one can find the reported amounts of the farmland from local military administrations. According to Wang Yuquan, these reported figures were recorded in the Hongzhi reign. The aggregate size is arrived by adding them up (see Wang Yuquan 1965, 107–8, 113).

4. Wang Yuquan 1965, 113.

Bibliography

The following abbreviations are used in the notes and bibliography:

Chinese Sources

BJGK	*Beijing Tushuguan Gujizhenben Congkan* "北京图书馆古籍珍本丛刊"
CSJB	*Congshu Jicheng Chubian* "丛书集成初编"
CZSJ	*Chongzhen Songjiang fuzhi* "崇禎松江府志"
DZLL	*Zhongguo Difangzhi Lianhemulu* "中国地方志联合目录"
GTJ	*Gujin Tushu Jicheng* "古今图书集成"
HFSZ	*Huangming Tiaofa Shileizhuan* "皇明条法事类纂"
MHD	*Ming Huidian* "明会典"
MLAH	*Mingshilu leizuan: Anhui shiliaojuan* "明实录类纂安徽史料卷"
MLBJ	*Mingshilu Beijing shiliao* "明实录北京史料"
MLFT	*Mingshilu Fujian Tanwan Shiliaojuan* "明实录类纂福建台湾史料卷"
MLJJ	*Mingshilu leizuan: jingji shiliaojuan* "明实录类纂经济史料卷"
MLZS	*Mingshiluleizuan: Zhejiang Shanghaishiliaojuan* "明实录类纂浙江上海史料卷"
MTZL	*Mingshilu: Taizu shilu* "明实录, 太祖实录"
QHDZ	*Qinding Daqing Huidian Zeli* "钦定大清会典则例" (SKQS)
RZDC	*Riben cang Zhongguo hanjian difangzhi congkan* 日本藏中國罕見地方志叢刊
SHY	*Song Huiyao Jigao* "宋會要輯稿"
SKCM	*Siku Quanshu Cunmu Congshu* "四庫全書存目叢書"
SKJK	*Siku Weishoushu Jikan* "四庫未收書輯刊"
SKQS	*Wenyuange Siku Quanshu* "文淵閣四庫全書"
SYDF	*Songyuan Difangzhi Congshu* "宋元地方志叢書"
WKL	*Wangli Kuaijilu* "萬曆會計錄" (BJGK)
ZDJJ	*Zhongguo Difangzhi Jicheng, Jangxuifuxianzhi Ji* "中國地方志集成.江苏府縣"
ZDJS	*Zhongguo Difangzhi Jicheng, Shanghaifuxianzhi Ji* "中國地方志集成.上海府縣志輯"
ZDJX	*Zhongguo Difangzhi Jicheng, Xiangzhenzhi Zhuanji* "中國地方志集成. 鄉鎮志專輯"
ZDSJ	*Zhengde Songjiang Fuzhi* "正德松江府志"
ZHFL	*Essays in Chinese Martime History* 中國海洋發展史論文集. Taipei, Sun Yat-sen Institute for Social Sciences and Philosophy, Academia Sinica.
ZSYC	*Zhongguo shuiyunshi congshu* "中国水运史丛书," including:

I. Waterways:

AH-ZSYC	*Anhui hangyunshi* 安徽航运史

329

CJ-ZSYC	*Changjiang hangyunshi* 长江航运史
GH-ZSYC	*Guangdong hangyunshi, the pre-industrial time* 广东航运史 (古代部分)
GX-ZSYC	*Guangxi hangyunshi* 广西航运史
HB-ZSYC	*Hebeisheng hangyunshi* 河北省航运史
HN-ZSYC	*Henan hangyunshi* 河南航运史
HU-ZSYC	*Hubei hangyunshi* 湖北航运史
JS-ZSYC	*Jiangsu hangyunshi, the pre-industrial time* 江苏航运史 (古代部分)
JX-ZSYC	*Jiangxi neihe hangyunshi* 江西内河航运史 (古近代部分)
SX-ZSYC	*Shaanxi hangyunshi* 陕西航运史
ZJ-ZSYC	*Zhejiang hangyunshi* 浙江航运史 (古近代部分)

II. Ports

FZ-ZSYC	*Fuzhou gangshi* 福州港史
JJ-ZSYC	*Jiujiang gangshi* 九江港史
SH-ZSYC	*Shanghai gangshi* 上海港史 (古近代部分)
WH-ZSYC	*Wuhan gangshi* 武汉港史

Chinese Academic Journals

LSYJ	*Lishi Yanjiu* 历史研究. Beijing, CASS.
LSDL	*Lishi Dil* 历史地理. Shanghai, Fudan University.
MSYL	*Mingshi Yanjiu Luncong* 明史研究论丛. Beijing, Zhongguo shehuikexueyuan.
ZGNS	*Zhongguo Nongshi* 中国农史
ZGSK	*Zhongguo Shehuikexue* 中国社会科学. Beijing, CASS.
ZGSY	*Zhongguoshi Yanjiu* 中国史研究. Beijing, CASS.
ZHWL	*Zhonghua Wenshi Luncong* 中华文史论丛
ZJYJ	*Zhongguo Jingjishi Yanjiu* 中国经济史研究. Beijing, CASS.
ZSYJ	*Zhongguo Shehui Jingjishi Yanjiu* 中国社会经济史研究. Fujian, Xiamen.

Japanese Literature

HKTSR	*Hino Kaisaburo toyo shigaku ronshu* 日野開三郎東洋史学論集
MIZS	*Miyazaki Ichisada zenshū* 宮崎市定全集
THGK	*Toho Gakuho* 東方學報
TOKK	*Toyoshi kenkyu* 東洋史研究
TYGH	*Toyo Gakuho* 東洋学報
SGZH	*Shigaku zasshi* 史學雜志

English Literature

EEH	*Explorations in Economic History*
EHR	*Economic History Review*
JAS	*Journal of Asian Studies*
JEH	*Journal of Economic History*
HJAS	*Harvard Journal of Asiatic Studies*
SCCH	*Science and Civilisation in China*

Primary Resources

Anhui shengbowuguan 安徽省博物馆. 1988. *Ming-Qing Huizhou shehui jingji ziliao congbian* 明清徽州社会经济资料丛编, Vol. 1. Beijing: Zhongguo shehuikexue.

Cao Jiaju 曹家驹. *Shuomeng* 說夢. In *SKJK*.

Chen Shunyu 陈舜俞. *Duguan Ji* 都官集. In *SKQS*.

Cheng Yizhong 程毅中. 2000. *Song-Yuan Xiaoshaojia Huabenji* 宋元小说家话本集. Jinan: Qilu shushe.

Chongxiu Fenjing xiaozhi 重修楓涇小志. In *ZDJX*.

Jinze xiaozhi 金澤小志. In *ZDJX*.

(*Kangxi*) *Chongming Xianzhi* 康熙崇明县志

Da Yuan haiyun ji 大元海運記.

Daoguang Kunxin Liangxian Zhi 道光昆新两县志

Dong Wei 董煒. *Jiuhuang Huominshu* 救荒活民書. In *CSJB*.

Du You 杜佑. *Tongdian* 通典.

He Liangjun 何良俊. 1959. *Siyouzai congshuo* 四友齋叢說. Shanghai: Zhonghua shuju.

Hong Huanchun 洪煥椿. 1988. *Mingqing Suzhou nongcun jingji ziliao* 明清蘇州農村經濟資料. Nanjing: Jingsu Guji.

Hu Zhiyu 胡祇遹. *Zishan daquanji* 紫山大全集. In *SKQS*.

Huang Zhangjian 黃彰健. 1979. *Mingdai Lyuli huibian* 明代律例彙編. Taipei: Zhongyang yanjiuyuan lishiyuyan yanjiusuo.

Jiading chicheng zhi 嘉定赤城志. In *SYDF*.

Jia Sixie 賈思勰. 1982. *Qimin yaoshu jiaoshi* 齊民要朮校釋. Miu Qiyu 繆啓愉, ed. Beijing: Nongye.

Jingding yanzhou xushi 景定嚴州續志. In *SYDF*.

Li Chunfeng 李淳風. *Sunzi suanjing* 孫子算經.

Li Guoxiang 李國祥. 1995. *Mingshilu leizuan, Zhejiang shanghai juan* 明實錄類纂. 浙江上海卷. Hubei: Wuhan.

Li Heng 李衡. *Lean yulu* 樂庵語錄. In *SKQS*.

Li Tao 李焘. *Xu Zizhi Tongjian Changbian (XZTC)* 續資治通鑒長編.

Liang Kejia 梁克家. *Chunxi Sanshan zhi* 淳熙三山志.

Liu Xu 劉昫. *Jiu Tangshu* 舊唐書.

Lu Shen 陸深. *Yanshan waij i* 儼山外集.

Ma Huan 馬歡. *Yingya shenglan* 瀛涯勝覽.

Qin Jiushao 秦九韶. 1992. *Shushu jiuzhang xinshi* 数书九章新释. Wang Shouyi 王守义, ed. Hefei: Anhui kexuejishu.

Schurmann, Herbert Franz. 1967. *Economic Structure of the Yuan Dynasty*. Translation of chapters 93 and 94 of the *Yuan Shih* 元史. Cambridge, MA: Harvard University Press.

Shang, Yang. 2006. *The Book of Lord Shang*. Translated into English by J. J. L. Duyvendak; translated into modern Chinese by Gao Heng. Beijing: Shangwu yinshuguan.

Shao Hengzhen 邵亨貞. *Yechu ji* 野處集. In *SKQS*.

Sun Pei 孫佩. *Hushu Guanzhi* 滸墅關志.

Tao Zongyi 陶宗儀. 1959. *Nancun Cuogen Lu* 南村輟耕錄. Shanghai: Zhonghua shuju.

Tuotuo 脫脫. *Song shi* 宋史.

Wang Anshi 王安石. 1999. *Wang Anshi quanji* 王安石全集. Shanghai: Shanghai guji.

Wang Heming 王鶴鳴. 2000. 上海圖書館藏家譜提要. Shanghai: Shanghai guji.

Wang Qi 王圻. *Xu wenxian tongkao* 續文獻通攷.

Weijing 衛涇. *Houle ji* 後樂集. In *SKQS*.

Wu Lyuzhen 吳履震. *Wurong Zhiyi Suibi* 五茸志逸随笔. In *SKJK*.

Xiao Lu 肖鲁 and Cao Qinghua 曹清华. 2003. *Song Zhao Qingxian gong nianpu* 宋趙清獻公年譜. In *Songren nianpu congkan* 宋人年谱丛刊, 1293–1330. Chengdu: Sichuandaxue.

Xie Guozhen 謝國楨. *Mingdai Shehui Jingji Shiliao Xuanbian* 明代社會經濟史料選編 Vols. 1, 2, 3. Fujian: 1980. (*MSJS*)

Xie Yingfang 謝應芳. *Guichao gao* 龜巢稿. In *SKQS*.

Xu Guangqi 徐光啟. 1979. *Nongzhen quanshu* 農政全書. Shanghai: Shanghai Guji.

Xuxiu Fengjing Xiaozhi 續修楓涇小志. In *ZDSJ*.

Yang Weizhen 楊維楨. 1995. *Yang Weizhen ji* 楊維楨集, 傳世藏書版. Haikou: Hainan Guoji Xinwen Chuban Zhongxin.

Yanzhou tujing 嚴州圖經. In *SYDF*.

Wanli fuzhou fuzhi 萬曆福州府志. Pan Yilong 潘頤龍等修, 1579. In *Mingdai guben fangzhi zhuanji* 明代孤本方志专辑.

Wanli Xuxiu Yanzhou fuzhi 萬曆續修嚴州府志. In *RZDC*.

Wanli Yanzhou fuzhi 萬曆嚴州府志. In *RZDC*.

Yunjian zhi 雲間志. In *SYDF*.

Zhang Haipeng 张海鹏 and Wang Tingyuan 王廷元. 1985. *Ming-Qing huishang ziliaoxuanbian* 明清徽商资料汇编. Hefei: Huangshan shushe.

Zhang Zhihan 張之翰. *Xiyan ji* 西巖集. In *SKQS*.

Zhang Tingyu 張廷玉. *Ming shi* 明史.

Zhao, Shiyan 趙世延 and Jie, Xisi 揭傒斯, eds. 2002. *Da Yuan haiyun ji* 大元海運記. Shanghai: Shangahi guji.

Zheng Yuanyou 鄭元祐. *Qiaowu ji* 僑吳集. In *SKQS*.

Zhiyuan jiahe zhi 至元嘉禾志. In *SYDF*.

Zhengde jinshan weizhi 正德金山衛志.

Zhongguo shehuikexueyuan lishiyanjiusuo 中国社会科学院历史研究所. 1990. *Ming-Qing Huizhou shehuijing ziliaocongbian* 明清徽州社会经济资料丛编, Vol. 2 Beijing: Zhongguo shehuikexue.

Zhou Shaoquan 周绍泉. 1993. *Doushangong jiayi jiaozhu* 竇山公家议校注. Hefei: Huangshan shushe.

Zhu Yuanzhang 朱元璋. 申明佛教榜册 *Shenming fojiao bangce*.

All Other Works

Abu Lughod, Janet L. 1988. *Before European Hegemony: The World System AD 1250–1350*. New York: Oxford University Press.

Allen, Robert C. 1988. "On the Road Again with Arthur Young: English, Irish, and French Agriculture during the Industrial Revolution." *JEH* 48 (38): 117–25.

———. 1992. *Enclosure and the Yeoman: The Agricultural Development of the South Midlands, 1450–1850*. New York: Oxford University Press.

———, Bengtsson, Tommy, and Dribe, Martin, eds. 2005. *Living Standards in the Past: New Perspectives on Well-Being in Asia and Europe*. Oxford: Oxford University Press

Amano, Motonosuke 天野元之助. 1979. *Chugoku nogyoshi kenkyu* 中国農業史研究. Tokyo: Ochanomizu Shobo.

Aoyama Hakushi Koki Kinen Sodai Shi Ronso Kankokai 青山博士古稀紀念宋代史論叢刊行会. 1974. *Aoyama Hakushi Koki Kinen Sodai Shi Ronso* 青山博士古稀紀念宋代史論叢. Tokyo: Seishin Shobo.

Aoyama, Sadao 青山定雄. 1963. *To-So jidai no kotsu to chishi chitu no kenkyu* 唐宋時代の交通と地誌地圖の研究 (Study of the communication systems of the Tang and Sung China and the development of their topographies and maps). Tokyo: Yoshikawa Kobunkan.

Aramiya, Manabu 新宮學. 1993. Nankin kanto 南京還都." In *Wada Hironori Kyōju koki kinen, Minshin jidai no ho to shakai* 和田博德教授古稀記念・明清时代法と社会 (Tōkyō: Kyūko Shoin, 1993), 59–90.

Ash, Robert. 1976. "Economic Aspects of Land Reform in Kiangsu [Jiangsu], 1949–52." In *The China Quarterly* 66 (67): 262–92, 519–45.

Atwell, William S. 1990. "A Seventeenth-Century 'General Crisis' in East Asia?" *Modern Asian Studies* 24 (4): 68–90.

———. 1998. "Ming China and the Emerging World Economy, c. 1470–1650." In *The Cambridge History of China, Vol. 8, The Ming Dynasty, 1368–1644, Part 2*, 376–417. New York: Cambridge University Press.

———. 2002. "Time, Money, and the Weather: Ming China and the 'Great Depression' of the Mid-Fifteenth Century." *JAS* 61 (1): 83–113.

Bai, Shouyi 白寿彝. 1957. "Mingdai kuangye de fazhan 明代矿业的发展." In *Zhongguo zibenzhuyi mengya wenti taolunji* 中国资本主义萌芽问题讨论集, 947–93. Reprinted in 1994, *Bai Shouyi shixue lunji* 白寿彝史学论集, 84–124.

Balazs, Etienne. 1960. "The Birth of Capitalism in China." *Journal of Economic and Social History of the Orient* 4(3): 196–216. Reprinted in *Chinese Civilization and Bureaucracy*, 34–54.

———. 1964. *Chinese Civilization and Bureaucracy: Variations on a Theme*. Trans. H. M. Wright. New Haven: Yale University Press.

Bao, Weimin 包伟民. 1986. Songdai minjiang chagu zhidu shulue 宋代民匠差催制度述略, *Songshi yanjiu jikan* 宋史研究集刊, 43–86. Hangzhou: Zhejiang guji. Later reprinted in *Chuantong gujia yu shehui* 傳統國家與社會, 960–1279 年, 166–209, Beijing: Shangwu.

———. 2001. *Songdai difang caizhengshi yanjiu* 宋代地方财政史研究. Shanghai: Shanghai guji.

Bao, Yanbang 鲍彦邦. 1992. "Mingdai caoliang zhezheng de xingshi ji yuanyin 明代漕粮折征 的 形式及原因." *Mingshi Yanjiu* 明史研究 2 (14): 73–82.

———. 1995. *Mingdai caoyun yanjiu* 明代漕运研究. Guangzhou: Jinan daxue.

Bengtsson, Tommy. 2004. "Living Standards and Economic Stress." In *Life under Pressure: Mortality and Living Standards in Europe and Asia*, ed. Bengtsson, Campbell, and Lee, 27–59.

Bengtsson, Tommy, Cameron Campbell, and James Z. Lee, eds. 2004. *Life under Pressure: Mortality and Living Standards in Europe and Asia*. Cambridge, MA: MIT.

Bielenstein, Hans. 1947. "The Census of China during the Period of 2742 A.D." *Bulletin of the Museum of Far Eastern Antiquities* (19): 125–163.

Blake, Robert P. 1937. "The Circulation of Silver in the Moslem East Down to the Mongol Epoch." *HJAS* 2 (3/4): 291–328.

Bol, P. K. 1993. "Government, Society, and State: On the Political Visions of Ssu-ma Kuang and Wang An-shihh." In *Ordering the World: Approaches to State and Society in Sung Dynasty China*, ed. Hymes and Schirokauer, 128–92.

———. 2003. "The 'Localist Turn' and 'Local Identity' in Later Imperial China." *Late Imperial China* 24 (2): 1–50.

Braudel, Fernand. 1974. "The Mediterranean Economy in the Sixteenth Century." In Earle, 1–44.

———. 1977. *Afterthoughts on Material Civilization and Capitalism*. Baltimore: Johns Hopkins University Press.

———. 1986. *The Perspective of the World*, Vol. 3. In *Civilization and Capitalism, 15th–18th Century*. New York: Harper and Row. English translation.

Bray, Francesca. 1984. *Science and Civilisation in China*, Vol. 6, *Biology and Biological Technology, Part II: Agriculture*. Cambridge: Cambridge University Press.

———. 1997. *Technology and Gender: Fabrics of Power in Late Imperial China*. Berkeley: University of California Press.

Brewer, John. 1988. *The Sinews of Power: War, Money, and the English State, 1688–1783*. Cambridge, MA: Harvard University Press.

Brook, Timothy. 1998. "Communication and Commerce." In *Cambridge History of China*, Vol. 8, 579–707. New York: Cambridge University Press.

Brown, Roxanna M. 2005. "Ming ban-Ming gap: Southeast Asian Shipwreck Evidence for Shortage of Chinese Trade Ceramics." In *Shier zhi shiwu shiji zhongguo waixiaoci yu haiwai maoyi guojiyantaohui wenji* 十二至十五世紀中國外銷瓷與海外貿易國際研討會論文集, ed. Pei-kai Cheng, 78–104.

Cao, Shuji 曹树基. 1997. *Zhongguo Yiminshi* 中国移民史, Vol. 5, *Ming shiqi* 明时期. Fuzhou: Fujian renmin.

———. 2000a. *Zhongguo Renkoushi* 中国人口史, Vol., 4, *Ming shiqi* 明时期. Shanghai: Fudan Daxue.

———. 2000b. *Zhongguo Renkoushi* 中国人口史, Vol. 5, *Qing shiqi* 清时期. Shanghai: Fudan Daxue.

———, and Li, Yushang 李玉尚. 2006. *Shuyi: zhanzheng yu heping: zhongguo de huanjing yu shehui bianqian* 鼠疫: 战争与和平: 中国的环境与社会变迁 (1230–1960年). Jinan: Shandong huabao chubanshe.

Cao, Songye 曹松叶. 1929–1930. "Song-Yuan-Ming-Qing shuyuan gaikuang 宋元明书院概况." *Guoli Zhongshandaxue yuyanlishixue yanjiusuo zhoukan* 国立中山大学语言历史学研究所周刊 10 (111): 4425–53; 10 (112): 4479–97; 10 (113): 4505–31; 10 (114): 4541–62; 10 (115): 4576–89.

Cao, Xingyuan 曹星原. 2011. *Tongzhou gongji: Qingming shanghe tu yu Beisong shehui de chongtu tuxie* 同舟共濟: 清明上河圖與北宋社會的衝突與妥協. Taipei: Shitou.

Cao, Yonghe 曹永和. 1984. "Shilun Ming Taizu de haiyang jiaotong zhengce 試論明太祖的海洋交通政策." *ZHFL* 1 (1): 41–70.

———. 1988. "Ming Hongwuchao zhongde zhongliu guanxi 明洪武朝中的中琉关系." *ZHFL* 5(3): 83–312.

Carus-Wilson, E. M. 1962. *Essays in Economic History, Reprints edited for The Economic History Society.* 3 vols. London: E. Arnold.

Chaffee, John W. 1995. *The Thorny Gates of Learning in Sung China: A Social History of Examinations.* New ed. Albany: State University of New York Press.

Chang Chung-li 张仲礼. 1955. *The Chinese Gentry: Studies on Their Role in Nineteenth-Century Chinese Society.* Seattle: University of Washington Press. First paperback ed., 1967.

———. 1962. *The Income of the Chinese Gentry.* Seattle: University of Washington Press.

Chao, Kang, also see Zhao, Gang (趙岡). 1986. *Man and Land in Chinese History: An Economic Analysis.* Stanford: Stanford University Press.

Chen, Chaoyong 陈朝勇. 2003. "Qianglongchao 'Wuliao jiazhi zheli' zhongde wujia yu gongjia 乾隆朝 '物料价值则例' 中的物价与工价." Paper presented at the Third International Symposium on Ancient Chinese Books and Records of Science and Technology. Germany: The Eberhard Karls University of Tuebingen.

Chen, Feng 陈锋, ed. 2006. *Ming-Qing yilai changjiangliuyu shehuifazhan shilun* 明清以来长江流域社会发展史论. Wuhan: Wuhandaxue.

Chen, Gaohua 陈高华. 1991. *Yuanshi yanjiu lungao* 元史研究論稿. Beijing: Zhonghua shuju.

———. 1997. "Yuandai shangshui chutan 元代商税初探." *Zhongguo shehuikexueyuan yanjiushengyuan xuebao* 中国社会科学院研究生院学报 97 (1): 8–16.

———. 2005. *Yuanshi yanjiu xinlun* 元史研究新论. Shangahi: Shanghai shehuikexue.

———, and Shi, Weimin 史衛民. 2007. *Zhongguo jingji tongshi* 中國經濟通史, *Yuandai jingji juan* 元代經濟卷. Beijing: Zhongguo shehuikexue.

———, and Wu, Tai 吳泰. 1981. *Song Yuan shiqi de haiwai maoyi* 宋元時期的海外貿易. Tianjin: Tianjin renmin.

Chen, Guodong 陈国栋. 1991a. "Qingdai zhongye xiamen de haishang maoyi 清代中葉廈門的海上貿易, 1727–1833." *ZHFL* 8 (4): 61–100.

———. 1991b. "1780–1800, Zhongxi maoyi de guanjian niandai 中西貿易的關鍵年代." *ZHFL* 8 (4): 61–100.

Chen, Guocan 陈国灿, and Xi, Jianhua 奚建华. 2000. *Zhejiang Gudai Chengzhenshi Yanjiu* 浙江古代城镇史研究. Hefei: Anhui daxue.

Chen, Hengli 陳恒力. 1958. *Bu nongshu yanjiu* 補農書研究. Beijing: Zhonghua shuju.

Chen, Keng 陈铿. 1986. "Ming-Qing Fujian nongcun shichang shitan 明清福建农村市场试探." *ZSYJ* 5 (4): 52–60.

Chen, Lesu 陈乐素. 1947. "Zhukehu duicheng yu beisong hubu de hukou tongji 主客户对称与北宋户部的户口统计." *Zhejiang Xuebao* 1(2). Later reprinted in *Qiushi ji*, 68–99.

———. 1984. *Qiushi ji* 求是集. Vol. II. Guangzhou: Guangdong renmin.

Chen, Qiaoyi 陳橋驛. 2008. *Zhongguo yunhe kaifa shi* 中国运河开发史. Beijing: Zhonghua shuju.

Chen, Shiqi 陈诗启. 1958. *Mingdai guanshougongye de yanjiu* 明代官手工业的研究. Wuhan: Hubei renmin.

Chen, Wenhua 陳文華. 1991. *Zhongguo gudai nongye kejishi tupu* 中國古代農業科技史圖譜. Beijing: Nongye.

Chen, Xuewen 陈学文. 1993. *Mingqing shiqi hangjiahu shizhenshi yanjiu* 明清时期杭嘉湖市镇史研究. Beijing: Qunyan.

———. 2000. *Mingqing shiqi Taihu liuyu shangpinjingji yushichangwangluo* 明清时期太湖流域的商品经济与市场网络. Hangzhou: Zhejiang renmin.

Chen, Yong 陳勇. 2006. *Tangdai changjiang xiayou jingjifazhan yanjiu* 唐代长江下游经济发展研究. Shanghai: Shanghai renmin.

Chen, Zhichao 陈智超. 1987. "Beisong shangshui e buque 北宋商税额补缺." *ZGSY* 36 (4): 114.

Chen, Zhiping 陈支平. 2004. *Ming-Qing wenshu yu minjian fuyishi yanjiu* 民間文書與明清賦役史研究. Hefei: Huangshan shushe.

———, and Lin, Feng 林枫. 1999. "Mingdai wanli qianqi de shangye shuizhi yu shuie 明代万历前期的商业税制与税额." *Ming-Qing Luncong* 明清论丛 1 (12): 396–413.

Cheng, Minsheng 程民生. 1987. "Songdai beifang jingji jiqi diwei xintan 宋代北方经济及其地位新探." *ZJYJ* 7 (3): 17–24.

———. 1992. *Songdai diyu jingji* 宋代地域经济. Kaifeng: Henan daxue.

———. 2003. "Songdai hushu tanyan 宋代戶數探研." *Journal of Henan University (Social Science)* 河南大學學報 (社會科學版) 43 (6): 11–19.

Cheng, Nianqi 念念祺. 2005. "Zhongguo gudai jingjishi zhongde niugeng 中國古代經濟史中的牛耕." *Shilin* 88 (6): 1–15.

Cheng, Pei-kai. 2005. *Proceedings of the International Conference: Chinese Export Ceramics and Maritime Trade, 12th–15th Centuries*. Hong Kong: Zhonghua.

Chien, Cecilia Lee-fang. 2004. *Salt and State: An Annotated Translation of the Songshi Salt Monopoly Treatise*. Ann Arbor: Center for Chinese Studies, University of Michigan.

Ch'u T'ung-tsu. 1961. *Law and Society in Traditional China*. Paris: Mouton.

Chuan, Han-sheng (also see Quan Hansheng) 全漢昇. 1936. "Nansong Hangzhou de xiaofei yu waidi shangpin zhi shuru 南宋杭州的消費與外地商品之輸入." *Zhongyang Yanjiuyuan Lishiyuyan Yanjiusuo Jikan* 中央研究院歷史語言研究所集刊 9 (7): 91–119.

———. 1939. "Bei-Song Bianliang de shuchuru maoyi 北宋汴梁的輸出入貿易." *Zhongyang Yanjiuyuan Lishiyuyan Yanjiusuo Jikan* 12 (8). Later reprinted in *Zhongguo jingji shi luncong* 中国经济史论丛, 87–200. Beijing: Sanlian.

———. 1942a. "Zhonggu ziran jingji 中古自然經濟." *Zhongyang Yanjiuyuan Lishiyuyan Yanjiusuo Jikan* 中央研究院歷史語言研究所集刊 10: 75–176.

———. 1942b. "Nan-Song daomi de shengchan yu yunxiao 南宋稻米的生產與運銷." *Zhongyang Yanjiuyuan Lishiyuyan Yanjiusuo Jikan* 中央研究院歷史語言研究所集刊 10: 403–31.

———. 1944a. "Tang-Song wujia de biandong 唐宋物價的變動." *Zhongyang Yanjiuyuan Lishiyuyan Yanjiusuo Jikan* 17 (11). Later reprinted in *Zhongguo jingji shi luncong*, 29–86.

———. 1944b. *Tang-Song diguo yu yunhe* 唐宋帝国与运河. Chongqing: Shang wu yin shu guan. Reprinted in *Zhongguo jingjishi yanjiu*, vol. 1, 265–395.

———. 1948a. "Songmo de tonghuopengzhang jiqi duiyu wujia de yingxiang 宋末的通貨膨脹及其對於物價的影響." *Zhongyang Yanjiuyuan Lishiyuyan Yanjiusuo Jikan* 中央研究院历史语言研究所集刊 21 (10). Later reprinted in *Zhongguo jingji shi luncong*, 325–54.

———. 1948b. "Tang-Song zhengfu suiru yu huobi jingji de guanxi 唐宋政府岁入与货币经济的关系." *Zhongyang yanjiuyuan Lishiyuyan Yanjiusuo jikan* 21(20). Reprinted in *Zhongguo jingjishi yanjiu*, vol. 1: 209–55.

———. 1957. "Meizhou baiyin yu shiba shiji zhongguo wujia geming de guanxi 美洲白銀與十八世紀中國物價革命的關係." *Zhongyang yanjiuyuan Lishiyuyan Yanjiusuo jikan* 28: 517–50.

———. 1967a. "Song-Ming jian baiyin goumaili de biandong jiqi yuanyin 宋明间白银购买力的变动及其原因." *Xinya xuebao* 新亚学报8 (1). Reprinted in *Zhongguo jingjishi yanjiu* 中国经济史研究, vol. 2, 179–208.

———. 1967b. "Mingdai de yinke yu yinchan e 明代的银课与银产额." *Xinya shuyuan xueshu niankan* 新亚书院学术年刊 9. Reprinted in *Zhongguo jingjishi yanjiu*, vol. 2, 209–32.

———. 1967c. "Ming-Qing jian meizhou baiyin de shuru zhongguo 明清间美洲白银的输入中国." *Zhongguo Wenhua Yanjiusuo Xuebao* 中国文化研究所学报 1: 27–49. Later reprinted in *Zhongguo jingji shi luncong*, 435–50.

———. 1967d. "Mingdai beibian miliang jiage de biandong 明代北边米粮价格的变动." *Xinya xuebao* 新亚学报 9 (2): 49–96. Reprinted in *Zhongguo jingjishi yanjiu*, 261–308.

———. 1971. "Zi Song zhi Ming zhengfu suiruzhong qianyin bili de biandong 自宋至明政府歲入錢銀比例的變動." *Zhongyang yanjiuyuan Lishiyuyan Yanjiusuo jikan* 42 (3): 391–403, later reprinted in *Zhongguo jingji shi luncong*, 1996 (Taiwan: Daohe), 355–68.

———. 1972. *Zhongguo jingji shi luncong* 中國經濟史論叢, Vol. 1–2. Hong Kong: Xinya. 1996. Reprinted in Taiwan: Daohe.

———. 1974. "Ming-Qing shidai yunnan de yinke yu yinchan e 明清时代云南的银课与银产额." *Xinya xuebao* 新亚学报20 (11): 61–88.

———. 1975. "The Chinese Silk Trade with Spanish America from the Late Ming to the Mid-Ch'ing Period." In *Studia Asiatica: Essays in Asian Studies in Felicitation of the 75th Birthday of Professor Ch'en Shou-yi*, ed. Laurence G. Thompson, 99–117. San Francisco: Chinese Materials Center.

———. 1976. *Zhongguo jingjishi yanjiu* 中国经济史研究, Vols. 1, 2, 3. Hong Kong: Xinya yanjiusuo.

———. 1984. "Ming zhongye hou zhongri jian de siyin maoyi 明中葉后中日間的絲銀貿易." *Zhongyang Yanjiuyuan Lishiyuyan Yanjiusuo Jikan* 中央研究院歷史語言研究所集刊 55 (4): 635–49.

———. 1993. "Luelun xinhanglu faxianhou de zhongguo haiwai maoyi 略論新航路發現后的中國海外貿易." *ZHFL* 10 (5): 1–16.

———, and Richard A. Kraus. 1975. *Mid-Ch'ing Rice Markets and Trade: An Essay in Price History*. Cambridge: Harvard University Press.

———, and Li Longhua 李龍华. 1972. "Ming zhongye hou taicang suiru yiliang de yanjiu 明中叶后太仓岁入银两的研究." *Zhongguo Wenhua Yanjiusuo Xuebao* 中国文化研究所学报 5 (1):169–244.

Cipolla, Carlo M. 1956. *Money: Prices and Civilization in the Mediterranean World, Fifth to Seventeenth Centuries*. Princeton: Princeton University Press.

———. 1993. *Before the Industrial Revolution: European Society and Economy, 1000–1700*. London: Routledge, 1993.

Coleman, D. C. 1977. *The Economy of England, 1450–1750*. Oxford: Oxford University Press.

Conference on Spatial and Temporal Trends and Cycles in Chinese Economic History, 980–1980. *Papers from the Conference on Spatial and Temporal Trends and Cycles in Chinese Economic History, 980–1980*. Bellagio, Italy.

Cong, Hanxiang 丛瀚香. 1981. "Shilun Mingdai mian he mian fangzhiye de fazhan 试论明代棉和棉纺织业的发展." *ZGSY* 9 (1): 61–78.

Crafts, N. F. R. 1985. *British Economic Growth during the Industrial Revolution*. New York: Oxford University Press.

Dai, Jianguo 戴建国. "Songdai jizhang zhidu tanxi, yi hukoutongji wei zhongxin 宋代籍帐制度探析—以户口统计为中心." *LSYJ* 3 (2007): 33–73.

Danjo, Hiroshi 檀上宽. 1980. "Shoki Min cho no tsuka seisaku 初期明王朝の通货政策." *TOKK* 39 (3): 527–56. Reprinted in *Min cho sensei shihai no shiteki kozo*, 115–50.

———. 1995. *Min cho sensei shihai no shiteki kozo* 明朝専制支配の史的構造. Tokyo: Kyuko Shoin.

Dardess, John W. 1983. *Confucianism and Autocracy: Professional Elites in the Founding of the Ming Dynasty*. Berkeley: University of California Press.

Davies, Glyn. 2002. *A History of Money: From Ancient Times to the Present Day*. 3rd ed. Cardiff: University of Wales Press.

De Vries, Jan. 1994. "The Industrial Revolution and the Industrious Revolution." *JEH* 54 (2): 249–70.

Deng, Gang. 1993. *Development versus Stagnation: Technological Continuity and Agricultural Progress in Pre-Modern China*. Westport: Greenwood Press.

Deng, Guangming 邓广铭. 1980. "Beisong de mubingzhidu jiqi yu dangshi jiruo jipin he nongye shengchan de guanxi 北宋募兵制度及其与当时积弱积贫和农业生产的关系." *ZGSY* 2 (4): 61–77.

———, and Li, Jiaju 郦家驹, ed. 1984. *Songshi yanjiu lunwenji: 1982 nian nianhui biankan* 宋史研究论文集: 1982 年年会编刊. Zhengzhou: Henan renmin.

———, and Qi, Xia 漆侠. 1984. *Liangsong zhengzhi jingji wenti* 兩宋政治经济问题. Shanghai: Zhishi chubanshe.

Deng, Yibing 邓亦兵. 1996. "Qingdai qianqi yanhai yunshuye de xingsheng 清代前期沿海运输业的兴盛." *ZSYJ* 15 (3): 40–52.

———. 2008. *Qingdai qianqi guanshui zhidu yanjiu* 清代前期关税制度研究. Beijing: Beijing Yanshan.

———. 2009. *Qingdai qianqi shangpin liutong yanjiu* 清代前期商品流通研究. Tianjin: Tianjin guji.

Di Cosmo, Nicola, ed. 2002a. *Warfare in Inner Asian History, 500–1800*. Boston: Brill.

———. 2002b. "Introduction: Inner Asian Ways of Warfare in Historical Perspective." In *Warfare in Inner Asian History, 500–1800*, 1–29. Boston: Brill.

Dong, Kaichen 董恺忱. 2007. *Dongya yu xiou nongfa bijiaoyanjiu* 東亞與西歐農法比較研究. Beijing: Zhongguo nongye.

———, and Fan, Chuyu 范楚玉, eds. 2000. *Zhongguo kexue jishushi, Nongxue juan* 中国科学技术史.农学卷. Beijing: Kexue.

Dong, Guodong 凍國棟. 2002. *Zhongguo Renkoushi* 中国人口史, Vol. 3, *Sui Tang Shiqi* 隋唐时期. Shanghai: Fudan daxue.

Dreyer, Edward L. 1982. *Early Ming China: A Political History, 1355–1435*. Stanford: Stanford University Press.

Du, Wenyu 杜文玉. 1998. "Tang-Song jingji shili bijiao 唐宋经济实力比较研究." *ZJYJ* 52 (4): 37–52.

Du, Jiaji 杜家骥. 1999. "Qing zhongqi yiqian de zhuqianliang wenti 清中期以前的铸钱量问题." *Shixue jikan* 史学集刊 44 (1): 27–31.

Durand, John D. 1960. "The Population Statistics of China, A.D. 2–1953." *Population Studies* 13 (3): 209–256.

———. 1974. "Historical Estimates of World Population: An Evaluation." *Population and Development Review* 3 (3): 253–96.

Earle, Peter, ed. 1974. *Essays in European Economic History, 1500–1800*. Oxford: Clarendon Press.

Eastman, Lloyd E. 1988. *Family, Fields, and Ancestors: Constancy and Change in China's Social and Economic History, 1550–1949*. New York: Oxford University Press.

Elvin, Mark. 1973. *The Pattern of the Chinese Past*. Stanford: Stanford University Press.

———. 1984. "Why China Failed to Create an Endogenous Industrial Capitalism." *Theory and Society* 13: 7–46.

Endicott-West, Elizabeth. 1989. *Mongolian Rule in China: Local Administration in the Yuan Dynasty*. Cambridge, MA: Harvard University Press.

Epstein, S. R. 1994. "Regional Fairs, Institutional Innovation, and Economic Growth in Late Medieval Europe." *The Economic History Review*, New Series 4 (3): 459–82.

———. 2000. *Freedom and Growth: The Rise of States and Markets in Europe, 1300–1750*. London: Routledge.

Fan, Hua 樊铧. 2009. *Zhengzhi juece yu Mingdai haiyun* 政治决策与明代海运. Beijing: Shehuikexue wenxian chubanshe.

Fan, I-chun 范毅军. 1998. "The Study of Ming-Ch'ing market Towns in the Lower Yangtze Delta: A Review 明清江南市场聚落史研究的回顾舆展望." *New History* 新史學 9 (3). Taipei: "Xin shi xue" za zhi she bian ji wei yuan hui.

———. 1993. Long-distance Trade and Market Integration in the Ming-Ch'ing Period, 1400–1850. Stanford University PhD dissertation."

Fan, Jinmin 范金民, and Jin, Wen 金文. 1993. *Jiangnan Sichoushi Yanjiu* 江南丝绸史研究. Beijing: Nongye.

———, and Xia, Weizhong 夏維中. 1993. *Suzhou diqu shehui jingjishi Mingqingjuan* 苏州地区社会经济史 (明清卷). Nanjing: Nanjing daxue.

Fan, Shuzhi 樊树志. 1988. *Zhongguo fengjian tudi guanxi fazhanshi* 中国封建土地关系发展史. Beijing: Renmin.

———. 1990. *Mingqing jiangnan shizhen taiwei* 明清江南市镇探微. Shanghai: Fudan daxue.

Fan, Zhongyi 范中义. 1998. "Lun Mingchao junzhi de yanbian 论明朝军制的演变." ZGSY 78 (2): 129–39.

Fang, Jian 方健. 1993. "Tang-Song cha chandi he chanliang kao 唐宋茶产地和产量考." ZJYJ 30 (20): 71–85.

———. 2006. "Guanyu Songdai Jiangnan nongye shengchanli fazhanshuiping de ruogan wenti yanjiu 关于宋代江南农业生产力发展水平的若干问题研究." In *Jiangnan shehuijingji yanjiu* 江南社會經濟研究 (Beijing: Zhongguo nongye), ed. Jinmin Fan, 506–95.

———. 2010. *Nan-Song nongye shi* 南宋農業史. Beijing: Renmin.

Fang Xing 方行. 1996. "Qingdai nongminjingji kuodazaishengchan de xingshi 清代农民经济扩大再生产的形式." ZJYJ 41 (1): 32–46.

———. 1996. "Qingdai jiangnan nongmin de xiaofei 清代江南农民的消费." ZJYJ 43 (3): 91–98.

———. 2004. *Zhongguo fengjian jingji lungao* 中国封建经济论稿. Beijing: Shangwu.

Farmer, Edward L. 1976. *Early Ming Government: The Evolution of Dual Capitals*. Cambridge, MA: Harvard University Press.

Feng, Xianming 冯先铭, An, Zhimin 安志敏, An, Jinhuai 安金槐, Zhu, Boqian 朱伯谦, and Wang, Qingzheng 汪庆正. 1982. *Zhongguo taoci shi* 中国陶瓷史. Beijing: Wenwu.

Feuerwerker, Albert. 1980. "Economic Trends in the Late Ch'ing Empire, 1870–1911." In *The Cambridge History of China, Vol. 11, Late Ch'ing, 1800–1911*, ed. J. K. Fairbank and Kwang-Ching Liu. New York: Cambridge University Press.

———. 1984. "The State and the Economy in Late Imperial China." *Theory and Society* 13 (3): 297–326.

———. 1995. *The Chinese Economy, 1870–1949*. Ann Arbor: Center for Chinese Studies.

Fu, Chonglan 傅崇兰. 1985. *Zhongguo yunhe chengshi fazhanshi* 中国运河城市发展史. Sichuan: Sichuan renmin.

Fu, Yiling 傅衣凌. 1956. *Mingqing shidai shangren ji shangye ziben* 明清时代商人及商业资本. Beijing: Zhonghua shuju.

———. 1957. *Mingdai jiangnan shimin jingji shitan* 明代江南市民经济试探. Shanghai: Shanghai renmin.

———. 1989. *Mingqing shehui jingji bianqian lun* 明清社会经济变迁论. Beijing: Renmin.

Fu, Zongwen 傅宗文. 1989. *Songdai caoshizhen yanjiu* 宋代草市镇研究. Fuzhou: Fujian renmin.

Fujii, Hiroshi 藤井宏. 1943a. "A Critical Examination of Cultivated Acreage Statistics in the Ming Dynasty 明代田土統計に關するの一考察." *TYGH* 30 (3–4); 31 (1), Aug., 1943; Aug., 1944; and Feb., 1947.

———. 1943b. "Mindai hukou shokuenhou ni tsuite 明代戶口食鹽法に就いて." In *SGZH* 13 (3): 213–42.

Funakoshi, Taiji 船越泰次. 1996. *A Study of Liang-shui-fa in the Tang Dynasty* 唐代兩税法研究. Tokyo: Sanichi Shobo.

Gao, Congming 高聡明. 2000. *Songdai Huobi yu Huobi Liutong Yanjiu* 宋代货币与货币流通研究. Baoding: Hebei daxue.

Gao, Shouxian 高壽仙. 2006. *Mingdai nongyejingji yu nongcunshehui* 明代農業經濟與農村社會. Hefei: Huang shan shu she.

Ge, Jianxiong 葛剑雄, Cao, Shuji 曹树基, and Wu, Songdi 吴松弟. *Jianming Zhongguo Yiminshi* 简明中国移民史. Fuzhou: Fujian renmin.

Ge, Jinfang 葛金芳, and Gu Rong 顾蓉. 2000. "Songdai jiangnan diqu de liangshi muchan jiqi gusuan fangfa bianxi 宋代江南地区的粮食亩产及其估算方法辨析." *Hubei daxue xuebao* 湖北大学学报 3 (5): 78–83.

Gernet, Jacques. 1962. *Daily Life in China: On the Eve of the Mongol Invasion, 1250–1276*. Trans. H. M. Wright. New York: Macmillan.

———. 1982. *A History of Chinese Civilization*. Trans. J. R. Foster. Cambridge: Cambridge University Press.

Gerschenkron, Alexander. 1962. *Economic Backwardness in Historical Perspective*. Cambridge, MA: Belknap Press of Harvard University Press.

———. 1968. "On the Concept of Continuity in History." In *Continuity in History and Other Essays*. Cambridge, MA: Belknap Press of Harvard University Press.

Gibbs, Jack, and Walter T. Martin. 1962. "Urbanization, Technology and the Division of Labor: International Patterns." *American Sociological Review* 27: 667–77.

Gilboy, E. W. 1934. *Wages in Eighteenth-Century England*. Cambridge, MA: Harvard University Press.

Golas, Peter J. 1977. The Sung Wine Monopoly. Harvard University PhD dissertation.

———. 1988. "The Sung Economy: How Big?" *Bulletin of Sung Yuan Studies* 19: 90–94.

———. 1995. "A Copper Production Breakthrough in the Song: The copper Precipitation Process." *Journal of Sung Yuan Studies* 26: 154–68.

Goldsmith, Raymond W. 1987. *Premodern Financial System: A Historical Comparative Study*. Cambridge: Cambridge University Press.

Goldstone, Jack A. 1984. "Urbanization and Inflation: Lessons from the English Price Revolution of the Sixteenth and Seventeenth Centuries." *American Journal of Sociology* 89 (5): 1103–42.

Goetzmann, William N., and K. Geert Rouwenhorst, eds. 2005. *The Origins of Value: The Financial Innovations That Created Modern Capital Markets*. Oxford: Oxford University Press.

Grossman, Gregory. 1962. "The Structure and Organization of the Soviet Economy." *Slavic Review* 21 (2): 237–40.

———. 1963. "Notes for a Theory of the Command Economy." *Soviet lavic Review* 21 (2): 237–40.

Gu, Cheng 顾诚. 1988. "Weisuo zhidu zai Qingdai de biange 卫所制度在清代的变革." *Beijing Shifandaxue Xuebao* 北京师范大学学报 33 (2): 15–22.

———. 1989a. "Ming diguo de jiangtu guanli tizhi 明帝国的疆土管理体制." *LSYJ* 36 (3): 135–50.

———. 1989b. "Tan Mingdai de weiji 谈明代的卫籍." *Beijing Shifan Daxue Xuebao* 北京师范大学学报 95 (5): 56–65.

———. 1999. "Shen Wansan jiqi jiazu shiji kao 沈万三及其家族事迹考." *LSYJ* 46 (1): 66–85.

Gunn, Geoffrey G. 1999. *Nagasaki in the Asian Bullion Trade Networks*. Nagasaki: Nagasaki Daigaku Keizaigakubu Tonan Ajia Kenkyujo.

Guo, Daoyang 郭道扬. 1982, 1988. *Zhongguo kuaiji shigao* 中国会计史稿(上，下), Vols. 1 and 2. Beijing: Zhongguo caijing.

Guo, Songyi 郭松义. 1994. "Qing qianqi nanfang daozuo diqu de liangshi shengchan 清前期南方稻作地区的粮食生产." *ZJYJ* 33 (1): 1–30.

———. 2001. "Mingqing shiqi de liangshishengchan yu nongmin shenghuoshuiping 明清时期的粮食生产与农民生活水平." *Zhongguo Shehuikexueyaun Lishiyanjiusuo Xuekan* 中国社会科学院历史研究所学刊1 (10): 373–96.

Guo, Zhengzhong 郭正忠. 1982. "Nan-Song haiwai maoyi shouru jiqi zai caizhengshuifu zhong de bilu 南宋海外贸易收入极其在财政税赋中的比率." *ZHWL* 21 (1): 255–69.

———. 1990a. *Songdai Yanye Jingjishi* 宋代盐业经济史. Beijing: Renmin, 1990.

———. 1990b. *Songyan guankui* 宋盐管窥. Taiyuan: Shanxi jingji.

———. 1997a. *Liangsong chengxiang shangpin huobi jingji kaolue* 两宋城乡商品货币经济考略. Beijing: Jing ji guan li.

———. 1997b. *Zhongguo yanyeshi, gudaibian* 中国盐业史. Beijing: Renmin.

Haeger, J. Winthrop, ed. 1975. *Crisis and Prosperity in Sung China*. Tucson: University of Arizona Press.

Hamashima, Atsutoshi 濱島敦俊. 1982. *Mindai Konan noson shakai no kenkyu* 明代江南農村社會の研究. Tokyo: Tokyo Daigaku.

Han, Dacheng 韩大成. 1991. *Mingdai chengshishi* 明代城市史. Beijing: Renmin daxue.

Han, Maoli 韩茂莉. 1993. *Songdai nongye dili* 宋代农业地理. Taiyuan: Shanxi guji.

———. 1999. *Liao-Jin nongye dili* 遼金农业地理. Beijing: Shehuikexue wenxian.

Han, Rulin 韩儒林. 1986. *Yuanchao shi* 元朝史. Beijing: Renmin.

Hartwell, Robert M. 1962. "A Revolution in the Chinese Iron and Coal Industries during the Northern Sung, 960–1126 AD." *JAS* 21 (2): 153–62.

———. 1966. "Markets, Technology, and the Structure of Enterprise in the Development of the Eleventh-Century Chinese Iron and Steel Industries." *JEH* 26 (1): 29–58.

———. 1982. "Demographic, Political and Social Transformation of China, 750–1550." *HJAS* 42 (2): 539–93.

———. 1984. "Government Finance and the Regional Economics of China, 750–1250." In *Papers from the Conference on Spatial and Temporal Trends and Cycles in Chinese Economic History, 980–1980*. Bellagio, Italy.

Hayami, Akira 速水融. 1973. *Nihon ni Okeru Keizai Shakai no Tenkai* 日本における経済社会の展開. Tokyo: Keio Tsushin.

———. 1988. *Keizai shakai no seiritsu, 17–18-seiki* 経済社会の成立, 17–18 世紀日本経済史 1.Tokyo: Iwanami Shoten.

———. 1989. "Kinsei Nihon no keizai hatten to Industrious Revolution." In *Tokugawa Shakai Kara no Tenbo: Hatten, Kozo, Kokusai Kankei* (A Perspective from the Tokugawa Society: Development, Structure, International Relations). Tokyo: Dobunkan.

He, Pingli 何平立. 2005. "Zheng He xiaxiyang yu Mingdai xiangliao maoyi 鄭和下西洋與明代香料貿易." In *Zheng He xiaxiyang yanjiu wenxuan*, ed. Zhen He xia Xi yang 600 zhou nian ji nian huo dong chou bei ling dao xiao zu 鄭和下西洋600周年紀念活動籌備領導小組, 369–75. Beijing: Hai yang.

He, Weizhi 何伟帜. 2002. *Mingchu de huanguan zhengzhi* 明初的宦官政治. 2nd ed. Hong Kong: Wen xing tu shu you xian gong si.

He, Zhongli 何忠禮. 1999. "Songdai hubu renkou tongji kaocha 宋代戶部人口統計考察." *LSYJ* 46 (4): 83–98. Later reprinted in *Keju yu Songdai shehui*, 338–64.

———. 2006. *Keju yu Songdai shehui* 科舉與宋代社會. Beijing: Shangwu.

He, Ziquan 何兹全. 1991. *Zhongguo gudai shehui* 中国古代社会. Zhengzhou: Henan renmin.

Heijdra, Martin. 1998. "The Socio-Economic Development of Rural China during the Ming." In *The Cambridge History of China*, Vol. 8, 417–578. New York: Cambridge University Press.

Hicks, John. 1969. *A Theory of Economic History*. Oxford: Oxford University Press.

Hino, Kaisaburo 日野開三郎. 1935a. "Hoku-So jidai ni okeru dotetsusen no chuzogaku ni tsuite 北宋時代における銅鐵の铸造額に就いて." *SGZH* 46 (1): 46–105.

———. 1935b. Hokuso jidai no hakuteki ni tsuite 北宋時代の博糴に就いて. In 歷史學研究, Vols. 4 and 3. In *HKTSR* 11: 333–63.

———. 1935c. Sodai no binteki ni tsuite 宋代の便糴に就いて." *TYGH* 23 (1). In *HKTSR* 11: 365–417.

———. 1936–1937. "Hoku-So jidai ni okeru dotetsusen no jukyu ni tsuite 北宋時代に おける銅鐵錢の需給に就いて." *Rekisjigaku kenkyu* 歷史學研究 6 (5–7): 482–510, 663–85, 791–98.

———. 1952a. "五代.北宋の歲幣. 歲賜と財政—五代.北宋歲幣. 歲賜考第二章."東洋史學 6 (12). In *HKTSR* 10: 415–440.

———. 1952b. "銀絹の需給上見た五代.北宋の歲幣. 歲賜." *TYGH* 35(1–2). 東洋史學6 (12). In *HKTSR* 10: 441–500.

———. 1982. *To-Gudai no kahei to kinyu* 唐五代の貨幣と金融. In *HKTSR* 5.

———. 1983. *Sodai no kahei to kinyu* 宋代の貨幣と金融. In *HKTSR* 6 and 7.

———. 1989. *Gyousei to zaisei* 行政と財政. In *HKTSR* 12.

Ho, Ping-ti (also He, Bingdi 何炳棣). 1959. *Studies on the Population of China, 1368–1953.* Cambridge: Harvard University Press.

———. 1970. "An Estimate of the Total Population of Sung-Chin China." *Études Song* 1 (1): 33–53.

———. 1988. *Zhongguo gujin tudishuzi de kaoshi he pingjia* 中國古今土地數字的攷釋和評價. Beijing: Zhongguo shehuikexue.

Hoffman, Philip T. 1996. *Growth in a Traditional Society: The French Countryside, 1450–1815.* Princeton: Princeton University Press.

Hoshi, Ayao 星斌夫. 1963. *Mindai soun no kenkyu* 明代漕運の研究. Tokyo: Nihon Gakujustu Shinkokai.

———. 1971. *A Study on the History of the Traffic System during the Ming and Ching Periods* 明清時代交通史の研究. Tokyo: Yamakawa Shuppansha.

———. 1985. *Chugoku shakai fukushi seisakushi no kenkyu: Shindai no shinsaiso o chushin ni* 中国社会福祉政策史の研究：清代の賑済倉を中心に. Tokyo: Kokusho Kankokai.

Hosono, Koji 細野浩二. 1977. 耆宿制から里老人制へ—太祖の『方巾御史』創出をめぐって. In 中山八郎教授頌寿記念明清史論叢, 27–58.

Hou, Jiaju 侯家駒. 1985a. *Xiaqin rujia ziyou jingji sixiang* 先秦儒家自由經濟思想. Taipei: Liangjing.

———. 1985b. *Xiaqin fajia tongzhi jingji sixiang* 先秦法家統制經濟思想. Taipei: Liangjing.

———. 2005. *Zhongguo jingji shi*中國經濟史, Vols. 1 and 2. Taipei: Liangjing.

Hua, Shan 華山. 1982a. *Songshi lunji* 宋史論集. Jinan: Qilu shushe.

———. 1982b. "Guanyu Songdai nongyeshengchan de jige wenti 關於宋代農業生產的幾個問題." In *Songshi lunji*, 1–29.

Huang, Jianhui 黃鑒暉. 1992. *Shanxi piaohuao shi* 山西票号史. Taiyuan: Shanxi jingji.

Huang, Lisheng 黃丽生. 1986. *Huaihe liuyu de shuili shiye* 淮河流域的水利事业. Taipei: Guoli Taiwan shifan daxue lishi yanjiusuo.

Huang, Miantang 黃冕堂. 1985a. *Mingshi Guanjian* 明史管见. Jinan: Qilu shushe.

———. 1985b. "Mingdai wujia kaolue 明代物价考略." In *Mingshi Guanjian* 明史管见, 346–72.

———. 1992. "Qingdai nongcun changgong zonghengtan 清代农村长工工价纵横探." *ZJYJ* 27 (3): 71–78.

Huang, Minzhi 黃敏枝. 1989. *Songdai fojiao shehui jingjishi lunji* 宋代佛教社会经济史论集. Taipei: Taiwan xue sheng shuju.

Huang, Philip C. 1985. *The Peasant Economy and Social Change in North China.* Stanford: Stanford University Press.

———. 1990. *The Peasant Family and Rural Development in the Yangzi Delta, 1350–1988.* Stanford: Stanford University Press.

———. 2002. "Development or Involution in Eighteenth-Century Britain and China? A review of Kenneth Pomeranz's *The Great Divergence: China, Europe, and the Making of the Modern World Economy.*" *JAS* 61 (2): 501–38.

Huang, Qichen 黄启臣. 1989. *Shisi—shiqi shiji zhongguo gangtie shengchanshi* 十四—十七世纪中国钢铁生产史. Zhengzhou: Zhongzhou guji.

Huang, Ray. 1974. *Taxation and Governmental Finance in Sixteenth-Century Ming China.* Cambridge: Cambridge University Press, 1974.

Huang, Shengzhang 黄盛璋. 1957. "Chuan-Shan jiaotong de lishi fazhan 川陕交通的历史发展." *Dili xueba* 地理学报 11, later reprinted in Huang, *Lishi dili lunji* (Beijing: Renmin, 1982), 201–26.

Hucker, Charles O. 1998. "Ming Government." In *The Cambridge History of China*, Vol. 8, 9–105. New York: Cambridge University Press.

Hymes, Robert. 1986. *Statesmen and Gentlemen: The Elite of Fu-chou, Chiang-his, in Northern and Southern Sung.* Cambridge: Cambridge University Press.

———, and Conrad Schirokauer. 1993. *Ordering the World: Approaches to State and Society in Sung Dynasty China.* Berkeley: University of California Press.

Ichiko, Shozo 市古尚三. 1977. *Mindai Kahei Shiko* 明代貨幣史. Tokyo: Otori Shobo.

Ihara Hiroshi 伊原弘. 2001. "The Qingming shanghe tu by Zhang Zeduan, and Its Relation to Northern Song Society." *Journal of Song-Yuan Studies* 31: 135–56.

Ikeda, On 池田温. 1968. 中國古代物價の一考察(1) (2)—天寶元年交河郡市估案斷片お中心として. *SGZH* 77 (1–2): 1–64.

———. 2007. *Chugoku kodai sekicho kenkyu (Zhongguo gudai jizhang yanjiu)* 中国古代籍帳研究. Chinese translation by Gong Zexian. Beijing: Zhonghua shuju.

Ikeda, Shizuo 池田靜夫. 1939. "北宋に於ける水運の發達." *Toa keizai kenkyu* 東亞經濟研究 23 (2–6): 1–40, 41–60, 48–61, 70–89, 61–74; 1940 24 (1): 45–70.

Iwai, Shigeki 岩井茂樹. 2004. *Chugoku kinsei zaiseishi no kenkyu* 中国近世財政史の研究. Kyoto: Kyoto Daigaku Gakujutsu.

Iwami, Hiroshi 岩見宏. 1962. "湖廣熟天下足." *TOKK* 20 (4): 527–27.

———. 1986. "Studies on the Statute Labor System in the Ming Dynasty (Mindai yoekiseido no kenkyu) 明代徭役制度の研究." *Oriental Research Series* 39. Kyoto: Dohosha.

Iwao, Seiichi. 1953. "Kinsei nisshi boeki ni kansuru suryoteki kosatsu 近世日支貿易に關する數量的考察." *SGZH* 62 (11): 981–1019.

———. 1976. "Japanese Foreign Trade in the Sixteenth and Seventeenth Centuries." *Acta-Asiatica: Bulletin of the Institute of Eastern Culture* 30: 1–18.

Jia, Daquan 贾大泉, and Chen, Yishi 陈一石. 1988. *Sichuan Chayeshi* 四川茶叶史. Chengdu: Bashu shushe.

Jian, Bozan 翦伯赞, ed. 1979. *Zhongguo shi gangyao* 中国史纲要. Beijing: Renmin.

Jiang, Shoupeng 姜守鹏. 1996. *Ming-Qing beifang shichang yanjiu* 明清北方市场研究. Changchun: Dongbei shifandaxue.

———, and Lin, Qian 林乾. 1998. *Ming Yongxuan shengshi* 明永宣盛世. Zhengzhou: Henan renmin.

Jiang, Xidong 姜锡东. 1993. *Songdai Shangye Xinyong Yanjiu* 宋代商业信用研究. Shijiazhuang: Hebei jiaoyu.

———. 2002. *Songdai shangye xinyong yanjiu* 宋代商业信用研究. Beijing: Zhonghua.

Johnson, Linda Cooke. 1993. *Cities of Jiangnan in Late Imperial China.* Albany: State University of New York Press.

———. 1995. *Shanghai: From Market Town to Treaty Port, 1074–1858.* Stanford: Stanford University Press.

Jones, Eric L. 1987. *The European Miracle: Environments, Economies, and Geopolitics in the History of Europe and Asia.* 2nd ed. Cambridge: Cambridge University Press.

———. 1988. *Growth Recurring: Economic Change in World History.* Oxford: Clarendon.

———. 1990. "The Real Question about China: Why Was the Song Economic Achievement Not Repeated." *Australian Economic History Review* 30 (2): 5–22.

Kanazawa, Yo 金沢陽. 1990. "明代景德鎮民窯製品の販路について." In *Yamane Yukio kyoju taikyu kinen Mindaishi ronso*, 885–902. Tokyo: Kyuko Shoin.

Kato, Shigeru 加藤繁. 1926. "To So no kusaichi ni tsuite 唐宋の草市に就いて." *SGZH* 37:1, later reprinted in S. Kato *Shina keizaishi kosho* 支那経済史考證, 380–86.

———. 1933a. "To So jidai no kusaichi oyobi sono hatten 唐宋時代の草市及び其の發展." *Ichimura Hakushi koki kinen toyoshi ronso* 市村博士古稀紀念東洋史論叢 (Tokyo: Fuzanbo), later reprinted in S. Kato, *Shina keizaishi kosho* 支那経済史考證, 387–421.

———. 1933b. *To So jidai no ichi* 唐宋時代の市, *Fukuda Tokuzo Hakushi tsuiioku ronbunshuu keizaigaku kenkyu* 福田德三博士追憶論文集経済學研究 (Tokyo: shinsan), later reprinted in S. Kato, *Shina keizaishi kosho* 支那経済史考證, 347–79.

———. 1953. *Shina Keizaishi kosho* 支那経済史考證. Tokyo: Toyo Bunko. Chinese trans. Wu Jie 吴杰. Beijing: Zhonghua shuju.

Kawagoe, Yasuhiro 川越泰博. 2001. *Mindai chugoku no gunsei to seiji* 明代中国の軍制と政治. Tokyo: Kokusho Kankokai.

Kawakatsu, Mamoru 川勝守, ed. 1993. *Higashi Ajia ni okeru seisan to ryutsu no rekishi shakaigakuteki kenkyu* 東アジアにおける生産と流通の歴史社会学的研究. Fukuoka: Chugoku Shoten.

———. 1999. *Social History of Market Towns in the Lower Yangtze Delta during the Ming and Qing Periods: Historical Sciences Based on Space and the Social Foundation* 明清江南市鎮社会史研究. Tokyo: Kyuko Shoin.

———. 2004. *Chugoku jokaku toshi shakaishi kenkyu* 中国城郭都市社会史研究. Tokyo: Kyuko Shoin.

Kennedy, Paul M. 1989. *The Rise and Fall of the Great Powers: Economic Change and Military Conflict from 1500 to 2000.* New York: Vintage Books.

King, Frank H. H. 1965. *Money and Monetary Policy in China, 1845–1895.* Cambridge, MA: Harvard University Press.

King, Gregory. 1936. *Natural and Political Observations and Conclusions upon the State and Condition of England.* In *Two Tracts*, edited with an introduction by George E. Barnett. Baltimore: Johns Hopkins University Press.

Kinugawa, Tsuyoshi 衣川強. 1970. "宋代の俸給について—文臣官僚お中心として." *THGK* 41: 415–66.

———. 1971. "Kanryo to hokyu 官僚と俸給." *THGK* 42: 177–208.

———. 1977. *Songdai wenguan fengji zhidu* 宋代文官俸给制度. Taipei: Taiwan shang wu yin shu guan.

Kishimoto, Mio 岸本美緒. 1990. "明末の田土市場に関する一考察." In *Yamane Yukio kyoju taikyu kinen Mindaishi ronso*, 751–70. Tokyo: Kyuko Shoin.

———. 1997. *Shindai chugoku no bukka to keizai hendo* 清代中國の物價と経済變動. Tokyo: Kenbun.

———. 1999. *The Ming-Qing Transition in Jiangnan: the Problem of Social Order in Seventeenth-Century China* 明清交替と江南社會. Tokyo: Tokyo Daigaku.

Kiyokoba, Azuma 清木場東. 1992. "唐代の水陸運賃について—脚法お中心として." *TOKK* 50 (3): 58–74. Later reprinted in *Todai zaiseishi kenkyu: Unyu hen*, 305–54.

———. 1996. *Todai zaiseishi kenkyu: Unyu hen* 唐代財政史研究.運輸編. Fukuoka: Kyushu Daigaku.

———. 2005. *Hokuso no shogyo katsudo* 北宋の商業活動. Fukuoka-shi: Chugoku Shoten.

Koiwai Hiromitsu 小岩井弘光. 1977. "南宋大軍兵士の給與錢米について—生券.熟券問題と關連して." *TOKK* 35 (4): 87–117.

———. 1998. *Sodai heiseishi no kenkyu* 宋代兵制史の研究. Tokyo: Kyukoshoin.

Koizumi, Teizo. 1972. "The Operation of Chinese Junks." In *Michigan Abstracts of Chinese and Japanese Works on Chinese History*, trans. Watson, 1–14.

Kubota Katsuo 久保田和男. 2000. "宋都開封の人口数についての一試論." *TYGH* 82 (2): 163–94.

———. 2010. *Songdai Kaifeng yanjiu* 宋代開封研究. Chinese translation by Wanping Guo. Shanghai: Shanghai guji.

Kuroki, Kuniyasu 黑木國泰. 1993. "一条鞭法研究の課題と展望." In *Minshin jidai no ho to shakai* 明清时代法と社会, 593–608. Tokyo: Kyuko Shoin.

Kuhn, Philip, A. 2002. *Origins of the Modern Chinese State*. Stanford: Stanford University Press.

Kuznets, Simon. 1973. "Modern Economic Growth: Findings and Reflections." *The American Economic Review* 63 (3): 247–58.

Lai Huimin 賴惠敏. 1983. *Mingdai nanzhili fuyi zhidu de yanjiu* 明代南直隸賦役制度的研究. Taipei: Taiwan daxue.

Lai, Jiancheng 賴建誠. 2008. *Bianzhen liangxiang: Mingdai nanzhili fuyi zhidu de yanjiu* 邊鎮糧餉：明代中後期的邊防經費與國家財政危機. Taipei: Lianjing.

Latimore, Owen. 1988. *Inner Asian Frontiers of China*. Hong Kong: Oxford University Press.

Lee, James, and Wang, Feng. 1999. *One Quarter of Humanity: Malthusian Mythology and Chinese Realities*. Cambridge, MA: Harvard University Press.

Lee, Thomas, H. C. (also see Li Hongqi 李弘祺). 1985. *Government Education and Examinations in Sung China*. Hong Kong: Chinese University Press.

Levathes, Louise. 1994. *When China Ruled the Seas: The Treasure Fleet of the Dragon Throne 1405–1433*. New York: Simon & Schuster.

Li, Bozhong 李伯重. 1990. *Tangdai Jiangnan nongye de fazhan* 唐代江南农业的发展. Beijing: Nonye.

———. 1997. "Songmo zhi Mingchu Jiangnan renkou yu gengdi de bianhua, shisan-shisi shiji Jiangnan nongye bianhua tantao zhiyi 宋末至明初江南人口与耕地的变化：十三世纪、十四世纪江南农业变化探讨之一." *ZGNS* 16 (3): 18–32.

———. 1998a. "Songmo zhi Mingchu Jiangnan nongye jishu de bianhua, shisan-shisi shiji Jiangnan nongye bianhua tantao zhi'er 宋末至明初江南农业技术的变化：十三世纪、十四世纪江南农业变化探讨之二." *ZGNS* 17 (1): 16–24.

———. 1998b. "Songmo zhi Mingchu Jiangnan nongmin jiyingfangshi de bianhua, shisan-shisi shiji Jiangnan nongye bianhua tantao zhisan 宋末至明初江南农民经营方式的变化：十三世纪、十四世纪江南农业变化探讨之三." *ZGNS* 17 (2): 30–38.

———. 1998c. "Songmo zhi Mingchu Jiangnan nongye bianhua de tedian yu lishi diwei, shisan-shisi shiji Jiangnan nongye bianhua tantao zhisi 宋末至明初江南农业变化的特点和历史地位：十三世纪、十四世纪江南农业变化探讨之四." *ZGNS* 17 (3): 39–46.

———. 1998d. *Agricultural Development in Jiangnan, 1620–1850*. New York: St. Martin's Press.

———. 1999. "Zhongguo quanguo shichang de xingcheng 中国全国市场的形成, 1500–1840." *Qinghua daxu xuebao* 14 (4): 48–54.

———. 2000a. *Jiangnan de zaoqi gongyehua* 江南的早期工业化, 1550–1850. Beijing: Shehuikexue wenxian.

———. 2000b. "Xuanjing, jicui yu Songdai jiangnan nongye geming '选精'、'集萃'与'宋代江南农业革命.'" *ZGSK* 127 (1): 177–92.

———. 2002. *Fazhan yu zhiyue, Ming Qing Jiangnan shengchan li yanjiu* 发展与制约,明清江南生产力研究. Taipei: Lian jing chu ban shi ye gu fen you xian gong si.

———. 2003a. "Was there a 'fourteenth-century turning point'? Population, Land, Technology, and Farm Management." In *The Song-Yuan-Ming Transition in Chinese History*, ed. Paul J. Smith and Richard von Glahn, 135–75. Cambridge, MA: Harvard University Press

Li, Gan 李幹. 1985. *Yuandai shehuijingji shigao* 元代社会经济史稿. Wuhan: Hubei renmin.

Li, Genpan 李根蟠. 1997. *Zhongguo nongye shi* 中國農業史. Taipei: Wenjin.

———. 2002. "Changjiang xiayou daomaifuzhongzhi de xingcheng he fazhan 长江下游稻麦复种制的形成和发展." *LSYJ* 49 (5): 3–28.

———. 2003. "Lun Mingqing shiqi nongyejingji de fazhan yu zhiyue 论明清时期农业经济的发展与制约." *Hebei Academic Journal* 河北学刊 23 (2): 155–61.

———. 2005. "Zhongguo jinggengxizuo de lianzhong leixing he niugeng shiyong de bianhua 中国精耕细作的两种类型和牛耕使用的变化." *Shiyuan* 史苑 8 (1): 20–27.

Li, Guoxiang 李國祥, and Yang, Chang 楊昶. 1993. *Mingshilu leizuan: jingji shiluojuan* 明實錄類纂：經濟史料卷. Wuhan: Wuhan.

Li, Huarui 李华瑞. 1995. *Songdai jiu di shengchan he zhengque* 宋代酒的生产和征榷. Baoding: Hebei daxue.

Li, Jinming 李金明. 1990. *Mingdai haiwai maoyi shi* 明代海外贸易史. Beijing: Zhongguo shehuikexue.

Li, Jinxiu 李锦秀. 1995. *Tangdai Caizheng Shigao*, Vol. I 唐代财政史稿 (上卷). Beijing: Beijing daxue.

———. 2001. *Tangdai Caizheng Shigao*, Vol. II 唐代财政史稿 (下卷). Beijing: Beijing daxue.

Li, Lingfu 李令福. 2000. *Ming-Qing Shandong nongyedili* 明清山東農業地理. Taipei: Wunantushu.

Li, Longqian 李龙潜. 1994. "Mingdai chaoguan zhidu shuping 明代钞关制度述评." *Mingshi Yanjiu* 明史研究 4: 25–43.

———. 1997. "Mingdai shuikesi, ju he shangshui de zhengshou 明代税课司, 局和商税的征收." *ZJYJ* 48 (4): 95–118.

Li, Longsheng 李隆生. 2005. "Mingmo baiyin cunliang de guji 明末白银存量的估计." *China Numismatics* 中国钱币 22 (1): 3–8.

Li, Qing 李卿. 2002. "Lun Songdai huabei pingyuan de sangcan sizhiye 论宋代华北平原的桑蚕丝织业." *Xiamen Daxue Xuebao* 厦门大学学报 149 (1): 80–87.

Li, Ruoyu 李若愚. 1988. "Cong Mingdai de qiyue kan Mingdai de bizhi 从明代的契约看明代的币制." *ZJYJ* 12 (3): 39–43.

Li, Wenzhi 李文治, and Jiang, Taixin 江太新. 1995. *Qingdai de caoyun* 清代的漕运. Beijing: Zhonghua.

Li, Xiao 李晓. 2000. *Songdai gongshangye jingji yu zhengfu ganyu yanjiu* 宋代工商业经济与政府干预. Beijing: Zhongguo qingnian.

———. 2002. "Sondchao de zhengfu goumai zhidu 宋朝的政府购买制度." *Wenshizhe* 文史哲 270 (3): 139–44.

———. 2004. "Beisong de hebei dibiansi 北宋的河北籴便司." *LSYJ* 51 (2): 77–92.

Li, Xiaocong 李孝聪. 1990. "Gongyuan shi zhi shier shiji huabei pingyuan beibuyaqu jiaotong yu chengshi dili de yanjiu 公元十至十二世纪华北平原北部亚区交通与城市地理的研究." *LSDL* 10 (9): 239–63.

Li, Yan 李埏, and Lin, Wenxun 林文勋. 1996. *Song Jin chubishi xinian* 宋金楮币史系年. Kunming: Yunnan minzhu.

Li, Zhi'an 李治安. 2011. *Yuandai Xingsheng Zhidu* 元代行省制度研究. Beijing: Zhonghua shuju.

Liang, Fangzhong 梁方仲. 1952. "Mingdai yitiao bianfa nianbiao 明代一条鞭法年表." *Lingnan Xuebao* 岭南学报 12 (1): 15–49.

———. 1957. *Mingdai liangzhang zhidu* 明代粮长制度. Shanghai: Shanghai renmin. Reprinted in 2001.

———. 1980. *Zhongguo lidai hukou tiandi tifu tongji* 中国历代户口、田地、田赋统计. Shanghai: Shanghai renmin.

Liang, Jiamian 梁家勉, ed. 1989. *Zhongguo nongye kexuejishu shigao* 中國農業科學技術史稿. Beijing: Nongye.

Liang, Keng-yao 梁庚堯. 1998. *Songdai shehui jingji shi lunji* 宋代社會經濟史論集 (上、下), Vols. 1 and 2. Taipei: Yun chen wen hua shi ye gu fen you xian gong si.

———. 2001. "Songdai Taihu pingyuan nongyeshengchan wenti de zaitantao 宋代太湖平原農業生產問題的再檢討." *Humanitas Taiwanica* 臺大文史哲學報 54 (4): 261–303.

———. 2006. *Nan-Song de nongcun jingji* 南宋的農村經濟. Beijing: Xinxing.

———. 2013. "Zi zhonggu ru jinshi 自中古入近世: 唐宋鄉村商業活動的擴大." In *Papers from the Fourth International Conference on Sinology, Change and Continuity in Early Modern China* 第四屆國際漢學會議論文集, 近世中國的變與不變, ed., Liu Liyan 柳立言, 261–303. Taipei: Academia Sinica.

Liang, Miaotai 梁森泰. 1991. *Ming-Qing Jingdezhen chengshi jingji yanjiu* 明清景德镇城市经济研究. Nanchang: Jiangxi renmin.

———. 1994. "Mingdai jiubian de xiangshu bing guyin 明代"九边"的饷数并估银." *ZSYJ* 13 (4): 46–56.

———. 1996. "Mingdai jiubian xiangzhong de zheyin yu liangcao shichang 明代"九边"饷中的折银与粮草市场." *ZSYJ* 15 (3): 27–39.

Liang, Taiji 梁太济. 1998. *Liangsong jieji guanxi de ruogan wenti* 兩宋阶级关系的若干问题. Hebei: Hebei Daxue.

Lin, Liping 林立平. 1988. "Tang-Song shiqi chengshi shuishou de fazhan 唐宋时期城市税收的发展." *ZJYJ* 3 (4): 22–38.

Lin, Man-hung 林滿紅. 1990. "Shijie jingji yu jindai zhongguo nongyeshi 世界經濟與近代中國農業." In *Jindai Zhongguo nongcun jingji shi lunwenji* 近代中國農村經濟史論文集, 291–325. Taipei: Zhongyang Yanjiuyuan Jindaishi Yanjiusuo.

———. 1991. "Zhongguo de bayin wanliu yu shijie de jinyin jianchan 中國的白銀外流與世界的金銀減產." *ZHFL* 8 (7): 1–44.

Lindert, Peter H. 1980. "English Occupations, 1670–1811." *JEH* 40 (4): 685–712.

———. 1985. "English Population, Wages, and Prices: 1541–1913." *Journal of Interdisciplinary History* 15: 609–34.

———, and Jeffrey G. Williamson. 1982. "Revising England's Social Tables, 1688–1812." *EEH* 19 (4): 385–408; 1983 20 (1): 94–109.

Liu, Chunyan 刘春燕. 2000. "Dui Bei-Song dongnan chaye chanliang de chongxin tuice 对北宋东南茶叶产量的重新推测." *ZSYJ* 19 (3): 46–56.

———. 2001. "Shi Songdai 'maichae' he 'chanchae' 释宋代买茶额和产茶额." *Academic Journal of Zhengzhou* 中州学刊 122 (2): 158–61.

Liu, Dazhong 刘瑞中. 1987. "Shiba shiji zhongguo renjun guomin shouru guji jiqi yu yingguo de bijiao 十八世紀中国人均国民收入估计及其与英国的比较." *ZJYJ* 7 (3): 105–20.

Liu, William Guanglin (also Liu, Guanglin 刘光临). 2005. *Wrestling for Power: The Changing Relationship between the State and the Economy in Late Imperial China, 1000–1770*. Harvard University PhD dissertation.

———. 2008. "Shichang, zhanzheng he ciahzengguojia 市場、戰爭和財政國家: dui Nan-Song fushui wenti de zai sikao 對南宋財政問題的再思考." *Historical Inquiry* 臺大歷史學報 42: 221–85.

———. 2011a. "Mingdai tonghuo wenti yanjiu 明代通货问题研究—对明代货币经济规模和结构的初步估计." *ZJYJ* 1 (March 15): 72–83.

———. 2011b. "Yinjin qiantui yu mingdai huobi liutong tizhi 银进钱退与明代货币流通体制." *Journal of Hebei University, Philosophy & Social Sciences* 河北大学学学报人文社会科学版 36 (2): 24–32.

———. 2012. "Lingnan zhoufu Song-Yuan-Ming zhiji liangshui zhengshou de bijiaoyanjiu 嶺南州府宋元明之際兩稅徵收的比較研究—以連州、廣州、潮州、惠州為例." In *Clio at Beida* 北大史學 17, 68–105. Beijing: Beijing daxue chubanshe.

———. 2013. "Chuantong zhongguo ruhe dui liutongshangpin zhengshui 傳統中國如何對流通商品徵稅—關於宋代和晚清商稅徵收的比較研究." *Historical Inquiry* 臺大歷史學報 52: 145–249.

Liu Hongyou 刘宏友, and Xu Cheng 徐诚. 1995. *Hubei hangyunshi* 湖北航运史. Beijing: Renmin jiaotong (ZSYC).

Liu, James T. C. 1959. *Reform in Sung China: Wang An-shih (1021–1086) and His New Policies*. Cambridge, MA: Harvard University Press.

———. 1962. "An Administrative Cycle in Chinese History." *JAS* 21 (2): 137–62.

———. 1978. "Liu Tsai (1165–1238): His Philanthropy and Neo-Confucian Limitations." *Oriens Extremus* 25: 1–29.

———. 1988. *China Turning Inward: Intellectual-Political Changes in the Early Twelfth Century*. Cambridge, MA: Harvard University Press.

Liu, Kaiguo 劉開國, et al. 2001. *Xinyang Zhumadian qianbi faxian yu yanjiu* 信陽駐馬店錢幣發現與研究. Beijing: Zhonghua shuju.

Liu, Miao 刘淼. 1996. *Mingdai yanye jingji yanjiu* 明代盐业经济研究. Shandou: Shandou daxue.

———. 2012. "Mingdai qianqi haijin zhengce xiade ciqi shuchu 明代前期海禁政策下的瓷器输出," in *Kaogu* 考古 48 (4): 84–91.

Liu, Qiugen 刘秋根. 1995. *Zhongguo diandang zhidushi* 中国典当制度史. Shanghai: Shanghai guji.

Liu Sen 刘森. 1993. "Songdai de tieqian yu tie chanliang 宋代的铁钱与铁产量." ZJYJ 30 (2): 86–90.

Liu, Shiji 刘石吉. 1977. *Mingqing jiangnan shizhen yanjiu* 明清时代江南市镇研究. Beijing: Zhongguo Shehuikexue.

Liu, Xinyuan 刘新园. 1983. "Jiang Qi Taoji zhuzuo shidai kaobian (1), (2)—Jianlun Jingdezhen Nan-Song yu Yuandai ciqi gongyi, shichang ji shuizhi deng fangmian de chayi 蒋祈《陶记》著作时代考辩—兼记景德镇南宋与元代瓷器工艺、市场及税制等方面的差异." *Wenshi* 文史 18: 111–30; 19: 97–107.

Liu, Xufeng 劉序楓. 1999. "Qing Kangxi-Qianlong jiannian yangtong de jinkou yu liutong wenti 清康熙-乾隆年間洋銅的進口與流通問題." ZHFL 16 (7): Part 1: 93–144.

Liu, Zhiwei 刘志伟. 1997. *Zai guojia yu shehui zhijian, Ming-Qing Guangdong lijia fuyi zhidu yanjiu* 在国家与社会之间, 明清广东里甲赋役制度研究. Guangzhou: Zhongshan University Press.

Long Denggao 龙登高. 1993. "Songdai liangjia fenxi 宋代粮价分析." ZJYJ 29 (1): 152–60.

———. 1997. *Zhongguo chuantong shichang fazhanshi* 中国传统市场发展史. Beijing: Renmin.

———. 2003. *Jiang nan shi chang shi: shi yi zhi shi jiu shi ji de bian qian / Long Denggao zhu.* 江南市场史: 十一至十九世纪的变迁. Beijing: Qing hua daxue.

Lu, Huayu 卢华语. 1995. *Tangdai cansang sichou yanjiu* 唐代蚕桑丝绸研究. Beijing: Shoudu shifan daxue.

Lu, Minzhen 陸敏珍. 2007. *Tang-Song shiqi mingzhou quyu shehuijingji yanjiu* 唐宋明州區域社會經濟研究. Shanghai: Shanghai guji.

Luan, Chengxian 栾成显. 1998. *Mingdai huangce yanjiu* 明代黄册研究. Beijing: Zhongguo shehuikexue.

———. 2007. "Mingdai renkoutongji yu huangcezhidu de jige wenti 明代人口统计与黄册制度的几个问题." In MSYL 明史研究论丛, Vol. 7, 25–40. Beijing: Zhongguo shehuike xueyuan lishi yanjiusuo mingshiyanjiushi.

Luo, Chuandong 罗传栋. 1991. *Changjiang hangyunshi (gudai bufen)* 长江航运史(古代部分). Beijing: Renmin jiaotong.

Luo, Ergang 罗尔纲. 1939. *Xiangjun xinzhi.* Changsha: Shang wu yin shu guan. Reprinted in *Minguo congshu.* Shanghai: Shangai shudian, 1996.

———. 1945. *Lyuying bingzhi* 绿营兵志. Chongqing: Shangwu yinshuguan. Reprinted in *Minguo congshu.* Shanghai: Shangai shudian, 1996.

Luo, Lixin 罗丽馨. 1988. "Mingdai jiangjirenshu zhi kaocha 明代匠籍人数之考察." *Shihuo yuekan* 食貨月刊 17 (1–2): 1–20.

Luo, Tonghua 羅彤華. 2005. *Tangdai minjianjiedai zhi yanjiu* 唐代民間借貸之研究. Taipei: Taiwan shangwu.

Luo, Yudong 罗玉东. 1936. *Zhongguo lijin shi* 中国厘金史. 2 vols. Shanghai: Shangwu.

Lü, Zhuomin 呂卓民. 2000. *Mingdai xibei nongmuye dili* 明代西北農牧業地理. Taipei: Hongyewenhua.

Ma, Daying 馬大英. 1983. *Handai caizhengshi* 漢代財政史. Beijing: Zhongguo caizhengjingji.

Ma, Laurence J. C. 1971. *Commercial Development and Urban Change in Sung China (960–1279).* Michigan Geographical Publication, No. 6. Ann Arbor: Michigan University Press.

Ma Maotang 马茂堂, ed. 1991. *Anhui hangyunshi* 安徽航运史. Hefei: Anhuirenmin (ZSYC).

Ma, Xueqin 馬雪芹. 1995. "Mingdai Henan de tudikenzhi 明代河南的土地墾殖." *Zhongguo lishidili luncong* 中國歷史地理論叢 9 (1): 161–76.

———. 1997. *Ming-Qing Henan nongyedili* 明清河南農業地理. Taipei: Hong ye wen hua shi ye you xian gong si.

Ma, Yi 马依, and Shu, Ruiping 舒瑞萍. 1991. *Guangxi hangyunshi* 广西航运史. Beijing: Renminjiaotong (ZSYC).

Maddison, Angus. 1998. *Chinese Economic Performance in the Long Run.* Paris: OECD.

Maeda, Naonori 前田直典. 1973. "Gencho jidai ni okeru shihei no kachi hendo 元朝時代における紙幣の價値変動." In *Gencho shi no kenkyu* 元朝史の研究, 107–43. Tokyo: Toyo Daigaku.

Mann, Susan. 1987. *Local Merchants and the Chinese Bureaucracy, 1750–1950*. Stanford: Stanford University Press.

Mao, Boke 茅伯科. 1990. *Shanghai gangshi* 上海港史(古近代部分). Beijing: Renmin jiaotong (*SH-ZSYC*).

Mathias, Peter. 1959. *The Brewing Industry in England, 1700–1830*. Cambridge: Cambridge University Press.

———. 1979. *The Transformation of England: Essays in Economic and Social History*. London: Methuen.

———, and Patrick Karl O'Brien. 1976. "Taxation in Britain and France, 1715–1810: A Comparison of the Social and Economic Incidence of Taxes Collected for the Central Governments." *Journal of European Economic History* 5: 601–50.

Matsui, Shuichi 松井秀一. 1976. "Todai ni okeru sanso no chiikisei ni tsuite 唐代における蚕桑の地域性について: 律令制期の蚕桑関係史料を中心に." *Shigaku zasshi* 史學雜誌 85 (9): 1249–89.

———. 1981. "中国律令制期の蚕桑に関する若干の問題について: 栽桑の規模と夏蚕の飼養を中心に." *Shigaku zasshi* 史學雜誌 90 (1): 1–35.

———. 1991. "Sodai no sanso oyobi kinuhaku seisan kenkyu joron 宋代の蚕桑及び絹帛生産研究序論 (一、二、三): 地域性の考察を中心に." *Bulletin of Sapporo Otani Junior College* 札幌大谷短期大学紀要22 (A):1–58; 23 (A): 1–66; 1992. 25 (A): 1–64.

———, and Barbara Sands. 1986. "The Spatial Approach to Chinese History: A Test." *JAS* 45 (4): 721–43.

Mayhew, N. J. 1995. "Population, Money Supply and the Velocity of Circulation in England, 1300–1700." *EHR*, New Series, 48 (2): 238–57.

Mazundar, Sucheta. 1998. *Sugar and Society in China: Peasants, Techonology, and the World Market*. Cambridge, MA: Harvard University Asia Center.

McKnight, Brian E. 1971. *Village and Bureaucracy in Southern Song China*. Chicago: University of Chicago Press.

McNeill, William H. 1976. *Plagues and People*. New York: Anchor Press.

———. 1982. *The Pursuit of Power: Technology, Armed Force, and Society since AD 1000*. Chicago: University of Chicago Press.

———. 1987. "The Eccentricity of Wheels, or Eurasian Transportation in Historical Perspective." *The American Historical Review* 92 (5): 1111–26.

Meng, Wentong 蒙文通. 1957. "Zhongguo lidai nongchanliang de kuoda he fuyi zhidu ji xueshu sixiang de yanbian 中国历代农产量的扩大和赋役制度及学术思想的演变." *Sichuan daxue xuebao* 四川大学学报 5 (2): 27–106.

———. 1961. "Cong Songdai de shangshui he chengshi kan zhongguo fengjianshehui de ziranjingji 从宋代的商税和城市看中国封建社会的自然经济." *LSYJ* 8 (4): 45–52.

Miao, Shumei 苗书梅. 2000. "Songdai jiandangguan chutan 宋代监当官初探." In *Songshi Yanjiu Lunwenji*, ed. Qi Xia 漆侠 and Li Yan 李埏. Baoding: Hebei daxue.

Min-Shin shi ronso kankokai 明清史論叢刊行會. 1977. *Nakayama Hachiro kyoju shoju kinen Min-Shin shi ronso* 中山八郎教授頌壽記念明清史論叢. Tokyo: Ryogen shoten.

Min, Zongdian 闵宗殿. 1984. "Song-ming-qing shiqi shuidao muchanliang de tantao 宋明清时期水稻亩产量的探讨." *Zhongguo nongshi* 中国农史 10 (4): 37–52.

———. 1989. *Zhongguo nongshi xinian yaolu* 中國農史系年要錄. Beijing: Nongye.

———. 1992. *Zhongguo gudai nonggeng shilue* 中國古農耕史略. Shijiazhuang: Hebei kexuejishu.

Mindaishi Kenkyukai, Mindaishi Ronso Henshu Iinkai 明代史研究会, 明代史論叢編集委員会. 1990. *Yamane Yukio kyoju taikyu kinen Mindaishi ronso* 山根幸夫教授退休記念明代史論叢. Tokyo: Kyuko Shoin.

Miu, Quanji 繆全吉. 1969. *Mingdai xuli* 明代胥吏. Taipei: Jia xin shui ni gong si wen hua ji jin hui.

Miyazaki, Ichisada 宮崎市定. 1943. *Godai Sō sho no tsūka mondai* 五代宋初の通貨問題 Kyōto: Hoshino Shoten.

———. 1950. *Toyo no kinsei* 東洋の近世. Tokyo: Kyoiku taimusu sha. Later reprinted in *MIZS* 2.

———.1952. "Sodai igo no tochi shoyuu keitai 宋代以後の土地所有形体." *TOKK* 12 (2): 1–34.

———. 1953. "Songdai shuuken seido no yurai to sono tokushoku 宋代州県制度の由来とその特色." *Shirin* 史林 6 (2). Later reprinted in *MIZS* 10: 216–45.

———. 1954. "Mindai So-Sho chiho no shidaifu to minshu 明代蘇松地方の士大夫と民衆." *Shirin* 史林 37 (3): 1–33. Later reprinted in *MIZS* 13: 3–39.

———. 1966. "Todai fueki seido sinnkao 唐代賦役制度新攷." *TOKK* 14 (4): 249–72.

———. 1969. "洪武から永乐へ." *TOKK* 27 (4). Later reprinted in *MIZS* 13: 40–65.

———. 1971. "Bukyoku yori tendo e 部曲より佃戸へ—唐宋間社会変革の一面." *TOKK* 29 (4): 30–65; 30 (1): 1–32.

———. 1977–1978. *Chugokushi* 中國史, Vols. 1 and 2. Tokyo: Iwanami Shoten. Later reprinted in *MIZS*, Vol. 1.

———. 1991–1994. *Miyazaki Ichisada zenshū* 宮崎市定全集. Tokyo: Iwanami Shoten.

Miyazawa, Tomoyuki 宮澤知之. 1984. "Sodai senkin chitai no kaiso kosei 宋代先進地帯の階層構成." *Yorei shigaku* 鷹陵史学10: 25–82.

———. 1993. "唐より明にいたる貨幣経済の展開." In *Namamura Satoru, Higashi Ajia sensei kokka to shakai, keizai* 東アジア専制国家社会経済, 185–220. Tokyo: Aoki Shoten.

———. 1998. *Sodai Chugoku no kokka to keizai: zaisei, shijo, kahei* 宋代中国の国家と経済. Tokyo: Sobunsha.

———. 2007. *Chugoku dosen no sekai: senka kara keizaishi e* 中国銅銭の世界: 銭貨から経済史へ. Kyoto: Shibunkaku.

Mokyr, Joel. 1990. *The Lever of Riches: Technological Creativity and Economic Progress*. New York: Oxford University Press.

———, ed. 1993. *The British Industrial Revolution: An Economic Perspective*. Boulder: Westview Press.

Momose, Hiromu 百瀬弘. 1935a. "Mindai Chugoku gaikokuboueki 明代中国外国貿易." Reprinted in *Min Shin shakai keizaishi kenkyu* 明清社会経済史研究, 3–21. Tokyo: Tokyo Daigaku.

———. 1935b. "Mindai no gin ubu to gaikoku gin ni tsuite 明代の銀産と外国銀に就いて." Reprinted in *Min Shin shakai keizaishi kenkyu* 明清社会経済史研究, 22–70. Tokyo: Tokyo Daigaku.

Mori, Masao 森正夫. 1988. *Mindai Konan tochi seido no kenkyu* (A Study of the Land System in Jiangnan during the Ming Dynasty) 明代江南土地制度の研究. Oriental Research Series, No. 42. Kyoto: Dohosha.

———. 1992. *Local Towns in the Jiangnan Delta: Historical and Geographical Analysis* 江南デルタ市鎮研究. Nagoya-shi: Nagoya Daigaku.

Morihiro, Furubayashi 古林森廣. 1987. *Sodai sangyou keizaishi kenkyu* (A Study of Industrial Economics in the Sung Dynasty) 宋代産業経済史研究. Tokyo: Kokusho Kankokai.

Mote, Frederick W. 1961. "The Growth of Chinese Despotism." *Oriens Extremus* 8 (8): 1–41.

———, and Denis Twitchett. 1988. *The Cambridge History of China, Vol. 7, The Ming Dynasty, 1368–1644, Part 1*. New York: Cambridge University Press.

———. 1998. *The Cambridge History of China, Vol. 8, The Ming Dynasty, 1368–1644, Part 2*. New York: Cambridge University Press.

Myers, Ramon H. 1966. "Review on Amano, *Chugoku nogyoshi kenkyu*." *JAS* 25 (3): 509–10.

Nagai, Chiaki 長井千秋. 1993. "Nanso gunpei no kyuyo 南宋軍兵の給與—kyuyogaku to kyuyo hoshiki wo chushinni 給與額と給與方式お中心に." In *Chugoku kinse no hosei to shakai* 中國近世の法制と社會, ed. Umehara Kaoru 梅原郁, 249–92. Kyoto-shi: Kyoto Daigaku Jinbun Kagaku Kenkyujo.

Nagase, Mamoru 長瀬守. 1974. "Sodai konan ni okeru suiri kaihatsu 宋代江南における水利開發."In *Aoyama Hakushi Koki Kinen Sodai Shi Ronso*, 315–37.

———. 1983. *So-Gen suirishi kenkyu* 宋元水利史研究. Tokyo: Kokusho Kankokai.

Nakajima, Gakusho 中島楽章. 1994. "Mindai nochuuki roujinsei to xiangson saiban 明代"中期の老人制と郷村裁判." *Shiteki* 史滴 15 (1): 16–30.

Nakamura, Jihe 中村治兵衞. 1986. *Nakamura Jihe Sensei koki kinen Toyo shi ronso / Nakamura Jihe Sensei Koki Kinen Toyoshi Ronso Henshu Iinkai hen, [daihyo Shimada Johei]* 中村治兵衞先生古稀記念・東洋史論叢 / 中村治兵衞先生古稀記念東洋史論叢編集委員会編, [代表嶋田襄平]. Tokyo: Tosui Shobo.

Nakamura, Satoru 中村哲, ed. 1993. *Higashi Ajia sensei kokka to shakai, keizai* 東アジア専制国家社会経済. Tokyo: Aoki Shoten.

Nakamura, Tadashi 中村質. 1988. *The History of Foreign Trade in Nagasaki during the Premodern Period (Kinsei Nagasaki boekishi no kenkyu)* 近世長崎貿易史の研究. Tokyo: Yoshikawa Kobunkan.

Nara Shuichi 奈良修一. 1993. "Juushichi seiki chugoku ni okeru seishi seisan to nihon e no shunyuu 一七世紀中国における生絲生产と日本への輸入." In *Minshin jidai no ho to shakai* 明清时代法と社会, 469–90. Tokyo: Kyuko Shoin.

Neal, Larry. 1990. *The Rise of Financial Capitalism: International Capital Markets in the Age of Reason*. Cambridge: Cambridge University Press.

Needham, Joseph, ed. 1971. *Science and Civilisation in China*. Vol. 4, *Physics and Physical Technology*. Part 3, *Civil Engineering and Nautics*. Cambridge: Cambridge University Press (SCCH).

Nie Chongqi 聶崇岐. 1941. "Songdai fuzhoujunjian zhi fenxi 宋代府州军监之分析." *Yanjing Xuebao* 燕京学报, Vol. 29. Reprinted in *Songshi congkao*, Vol. 1, 70–126.

———. 1979. *Songshi congkao* 宋史丛考, Vols. 1 and 2. Beijing: Zhonghua shuju.

Nishijima, Sadao 西嶋定生. 1944. "Shokoufu ni okeru mengyou keisei katei 松江府における棉業形成過程について." *Shakai keizai shigaku* 社會經濟史學 13 (11–12). Reprinted in *Nishijima Sadao Higashi Ajiashi ronshu* 西島定生東アジア史論集, Vol. 1, 243–50.

———. 1948. "Mindai ni okeru momen no fukyu ni tsuite 明代における木棉の普及について." *SGZH*, Vols. 56 and 57. Reprinted in *Nishijima Sadao Higashi Ajiashi ronshu* 西島定生東アジア史論集, Vol. 1, 251–300.

———. 1966. *Chugoku keizaishi kenkyu* 中國経済史研究. Tokyo: Tokyo daigaku.

———. 1986. "The Economic and Social History of Former Han." In *The Cambridge History of China*. Vol. 1, *The Ch'in and Han Empire, 221 B. C.–A. D. 220*, ed. Denis Twitchett and John K. Fairbank, 551–607. New York: Cambridge University Press.

———. 2002. *Nishijima Sadao Higashi Ajiashi ronshu* 西嶋定生東アジア史論集, Vols. 1–5. Tokyo: Iwanami Shoten.

Nishioka, Hiroaki 西岡弘晃. 2004. *Chugoku kinsei no toshi to suiri* 中国近世の都市と水利. Fukuoka: Chugoku Shoten.

North, Douglas C. 1981. *Structure and Change in Economic History*. New York: W. W. Norton & Company.

———, and Robert Paul Thomas. 1973. *The Rise of the Western World*. Cambridge: Cambridge University Press.

Oberst, Zhihong Liang. 1996. Chinese Economic Statecraft and Economic Ideas in the Song Period (960–1279). Columbia University, PhD dissertation.

O'Brien, Patrick Karl. 1988. "The Political Economy of British Taxation, 1660–1815." *EHR*. 2nd ser. 41 (1).

———. 1991. *Power with Profit: The State and the Economy, 1688–1815*. London: University of London.

———. 1996. "Path Dependency, or Why Britain Became an Industrialized and Urbanized Economy Long before France" *EHR*, New Series, 49 (2): 213–49.

———, and Caglar Keyder. 1978. *Economic Growth in Britain and France, 1780–1914: Two Paths to the Twentieth Century*. London: George Allen & Unwin.

Okuyama, Norio 奥山憲夫. 1993. "Mingun no kyuuyo shikyuni tsuite 明軍の給与支給について—正統、景泰期お中心にいて." In *Wada Hironori Kyōju koki kinen, Minshin jidai no ho to shakai*和田博德教授古稀記念・明清時代法と社会, 133–53. Tokyo: Kyūko Shoin.

———. 2003. 明代軍政史研究. Tokyo: Kyuko Shoin.

Ormrod, W. M., Margaret Bonney, and Richard Bonney. 1999. *Crises, Revolutions and Self-Sustained Growth: Essays in European Fiscal History, 1130–1830*. Stamford: Shaun Tyas.

O'Rourke, Kevin H., and J. H. Williamson. 1999. *Globalization and History: The Evolution of a Nineteenth-Century Atlantic Economy*. Cambridge, MA: MIT Press.

Osawa, Masaaki 大沢正昭. 1985. "'So-Ko juku, tenkasoku 蘇湖熟，天下足'—'虚像' と'實像' のあいだ." In新しい歴史学のために, Vol. 179. Revised as chapter 7, "宋代'江南'の生産力評價をめぐて," in *To So henkakuki nogyo shakaishi kenkyu*, 235–52.

———. 1996. *To So henkakuki nogyo shakaishi kenkyu* 唐宋變革期農業社會史研究. Tokyo: Kyuko Shoin.

Otagi, Hajime 愛宕元. 1991. *Chugoku no jokaku toshi: In Shū kara in Min Shin made* 中国の城郭都市：殷周から明清まで. Tokyo: Chuo Koronsha.

Otagi, Matsuo 愛宕松男. 1953. "朱呉国と張呉国—初期明王朝の性格に関する一考察." 文化 17 (6): 597–621. 東北大学文学会. Reprinted in *Gencho shi* 元朝史, 431–55.

———. 1973. "Atsudatsusen to sono haikei: Jusan-seki Mongoru Gen-cho niokeru gin no doko 幹脱銭とその背景—13世紀モンゴル＝元朝における銀の動向." *Journal of Oriental Researches*東洋史研究 32 (1): 1–27; 32 (2): 23–61. Reprinted in *Tozai koshoshi*.

———. 1988. "*Gencho shi* 元朝史." In *Otagi Matsuo Toyo shigaku ronshu* 愛宕松男東洋史學論集, Vol. 4. Tokyo 東京: San'ichi Shobo 三一書房.

———. 1989. "*Tozai koshoshi* 東西交渉史." In *Otagi Matsuo Toyo shigaku ronshu* 愛宕松男東洋史學論集, Vol. 5. Tokyo 東京: San'ichi Shobo 三一書房.

Oyama, Masaaki 小山正明. 1992. *Min Shin shakai keizaishi kenkyu* 明清社会経済史研究. Tokyo: Tokyo Daigaku.

Peng, Xinwei 彭信威. 1965. *Zhongguo Huobi Shi* 中国货币史. 3rd, ed. Shanghai: 1965.

———. 1994. *A Monetary History of China (Zhongguo Huobi Shi)*. Vols. 1 and 2. Trans. Edward H. Kaplan. Bellingham: Western Washington University.

Peng, Zeyi 彭泽益. 1957. *Zhongguo Jindai Shougongyeshi Ziliao* 中国近代手工业史资料, 1840–1949. Beijing: Zhonghua shuju.

———. 1960. "Xu Yikui 'Zigongdui' jishi de niandai he zhiye wenti 徐一夔'织工对'记事的年代和织业问题." In *Zhongguo Zibenzhuyi Mengya Wenti Taolunji Xubian* 中国资本主义萌芽问题讨论集续编. Beijing: Sanlian.

———, and Wang Renyun 王仁运, eds. 1991. *Zhongguo yanyeshi guoji xueshu taolunhui lunwenji* 中国盐业史国际学术讨论会论文集. Sichuan: Sichuan renmin.

Perdue, Peter. 1987. *Exhausting the Earth: State and Peasant in Hunan, 1500–1850*. Cambridge, MA: Harvard University Press.

Perkins, Dwight H. 1966. *Market Control and Planning in Communist China*. Cambridge, MA: Harvard University Press.

———. 1967. "Government as an Obstacle to Industrialization: The Case of Eighteenth-Century China." *JEH* 27 (4): 478–92.

———. 1969. *Agricultural Development in China, 1368–1968*. Chicago: Aldine.

Persson, Karl Gunnar.1988. *Pre-industrial Economic Growth: Social Organization and Technological Progress in Europe*. Oxford: Blackwell.

Pomeranz, Kenneth. 2000. *The Great Divergence: China, Europe, and the Making of the Modern World Economy*. Princeton: Princeton University Press.

———. 2002. "Beyond the East-West Binary: Resituating Development Paths in an Eighteenth-Century World." *JAS* 61 (2): 539–90.

Postan, Michael M. 1972. *The Medieval Economy and Society: An Economic History of Britain in the Middle Ages.* London: Weidenfeld and Nicolson.

———. 1973. *Essays on Medieval Agriculture and General Problems of the Medieval Economy.* Cambridge: Cambridge University Press.

Qi, Meiqin 祁美琴. 2004. *Qingdai queguan zhidu yanjiu* 清代権关制度研究. Huhehaote: Neimenggu daxue.

Qi, Xia 漆侠. 1987. *Songdai Jingjishi* 宋代经济史. Shanghai: Shanghai renmin.

———, ed. 2000. *Songshi Yanjiu Luncong* 宋史研究论丛, Vol. 4. Baoding: Hebei daxue Songshi yanjiu zhongxin.

———, and Li, Yan 李埏., eds. 2000. *Songshi Yanjiu Lunwenji* 宋史研究论文集. Kunming: Yunnan minzu.

Qiu, Shusen 邱树森, ed. 1989. *Jiangsu Hangyunshi, the Pre-Industrial Time* 江苏航运史(古代部分). Beijing: Renminjiaotong (ZSYC).

Rawski, Evelyn S. 1972. *Agricultural Change and the Peasant Economy of South China.* Cambridge, MA: Harvard University Press.

Rawski, Thomas G. 1989. *Economic Growth in Prewar China.* Berkeley: University of California Press.

———, and Lillian M. Li.1992. *Chinese History in Economic Perspective.* Berkeley: University of California Press.

Ren, Fang 任放. 2001. "Ershi shiji mingqing shizhen jingji yanjiu 二十世纪明清市镇经济研究." *LSYJ* 48 (5): 168–82.

Ren, Mei'e, RenzhangYang, and Haosheng Bao. 1985. *An Outline of China's Physical Geography.* Trans. Zhang Tingquan and Hu Genkang. Beijing: Foreign Language Press.

Rossabi, Morris, ed. 1983. *China among Equals: The Middle Kingdom and Its Neighbors, 10th–14th Centuries.* Berkeley: University of California Press.

———. 1988. *Khubilai Khan: His Life and Times.* Berkeley: University of California Press.

Rowe, William T. 1984. *Hankow: Commerce and Society in a Changing Society.* Stanford: Stanford University Press.

———. 1985. "Approaches to Modern Chinese Social history." In *Reliving the Past: The Worlds of Social History*, ed. Oliver Kunz, 236–96. Chapel Hill: University of North Carolina Press.

Rozman, Gilbert. 1973. *Urban Networks in Ch'ing China and Tokugawa Japan.* Princeton: Princeton University Press.

———. 1982. *Population and Marketing Settlements in Ch'ing China.* New York: Cambridge University Press.

Russell, J. C. 1958. *Late Ancient and Medieval Population.* Transactions of the American Philosophical Society New Series, No. 48, Part 3. Philadelphia: The American Philosphical Society.

Sakuma, Shigeo 佐久間重男. 1943. "明代の商税制度." *Shakai keizai shigaku* 社會經濟史學 13 (3): 31–60.

———. 1962. "Mindai no shosei seido 明代景德鎮窯業の一考察." In *Shimizu hakushi tsuito kinnen Mindaishi ronso* 清水博士追悼記念明代論叢, ed. Shimizu Hakushi Tsuitō Kinen Mindaishi Ronsō Hensan Iinkai 清水博士追悼記念明代史論叢編纂委員會, 457–88. Tokyo: Daian.

———. 1965. "Mindai ni okeru shosei to zaisei to no kankei 明代における商税と財政との關係." *SGZH* 65 (1–2): 1–28, 46–65.

———. 1977. "Mindai no montansei to toshi shogyou to no kankei 明代." In *Nakayama Hachiro kyojukinen Min-Shin shi ronso* 中山八郎教授頌壽記念明清史論叢, ed. Min-Shin shi ronso kankokai, 271–301. Tokyo: Ryogen shoten.

Sakuma Shigeo kyoju taikyu kinen chugokushi tojishi ronshu henshu linkai 編集佐久間重男教授退休記念中国史.陶磁史論集編集委員会. 1983. *Chugokushi. Tojishi ronshu: Sakuma Shigeo-kyoju taikyu kinen* 中国史.陶磁史論集: 佐久間重男教授退休記念. Tokyo: Ryogen shoten.

Sands, Barbara, and Ramon H. Myers. 1986. "The Spatial Approach to Chinese History: A Test." *JAS* 45(4): 721–43.

Sasaki, Tatsuo 佐佐木達夫. 1985. *Gen-Min jidai yogyoshi kenkyu* (History of ceramics in the Yuan and Ming dynasty) 元明時代窯業史研究. Tokyo: Yoshikawa Kobunkan.

Satake, Yasuhiko 佐竹靖彦, ed. 1996. *So Gen jidaishi no kihong mondai* 宋元時代史の基本問. Tokyo: Kyuko Shoin.

Schumpeter, Joseph. 1954. "The Crisis of the Tax State." *International Economic Papers* 37(4): 5–38. Reprinted in 1991 in *The Economics and Sociology of Capitalism*, ed. Richard Swedberg and Joseph A. Schumpeter, 98–140. Princeton: Princeton University Press.

———. 1968. *The Theory of Economic Development: An Inquiry into Profits, Capital, Credit, Interest, and the Business Cycle*. Cambridge, MA: Harvard University Press.

Schurmann, Herbert Franz. 1956. "Mongolian Tributary Practices of the Thirteenth Century." *Harvard Journal of Asiatic Studies* 19(3/4): 304–89.

Scogin, Hugh. 1978. "Poor Relief in Northern Sung China." *Oriens Extremus* 25: 30–46.

Sen, Amartya. 1982. *Poverty and Famines: An Essay on Entitlement and Deprivation*. Oxford: Clarendon Press.

Shang, Chuan 商传. 1983. "Shilun Mingchu zhuanzhi zhuyi zhongyang jiquan de shehui jichu 试论明初专制主义中央集权的社会基础." *MSYL* 2: 114–32. Nanjing: Jiangsu renmin.

Shen, Xingjing 沈兴敬, and Yang Zhusen 杨竹森, eds. 1991. *Jiangxi neihe hangyunshi* 江西内河航运史(古今代部分). Beijing: Renminjiaotong (ZSYC).

Shi, Nianhai 史念海. 1986a. "Sanmenxia yu gudai caoyun 三门峡与古代漕运." In *Heshan ji*, Vol. 1, 232–52.

———. 1986b. "Huanghe liuyu sangcanshiye shengshuai de bianqian 黄河流域桑蚕事业盛衰的变迁." In *Heshan ji* 河山集 1: 232–52. Beijing: Sanlian shudian.

———. 1986c. "Huangtu gaoyuan zhuyao heliu liuliang de bianqian 黄土高原主要河流流量的变迁." In *Huanghe liuyu zhu heliu de yanbian yu zhili*. Shaanxi: Shaanxi renmin.

———. 1988. *Zhongguo de yunhe* 中国的运河. 2nd ed. Xi'an: Shanxi renmin.

———. 1994. "Shui-Tang shiqi yunhe he changjiang de shuishang jiaotong jiqi yan'an de duhui 隋唐时期运河和长江的水上交通及其沿岸的都会." *Zhongguo Lishidili Luncong* 中国历史地理论丛 8 (4): 1–33. Reprinted in *Tangdai lishidili yanjiu* 唐代历史地理研究, 313–46. Beijing: Zhongguo Shehuikexue.

———. 1999. *Huanghe liuyu zhu heliu de yanbian yu zhili* 黄河流域诸河流的演变与治理. Shaanxi: Shaanxi renmin.

Shiba, Yoshinobu 斯波義信. 1968. *Sodai Shoyoshi Kenkyu* 宋代商業史研究. Tokyo: Kazama Shobo.

———. 1970. *Commerce and Society in Sung China*. Trans. Mark Elvin. Ann Arbor: University of Michigan, Center for Chinese Studies.

———. 1974. "Sodai ichibai seido no enkaku 宋代市糴制度の沿革." In *Aoyama Hakushi Koki Kinen Sodai Shi Ronso* 青山博士古稀紀念宋代史論叢, 123–59. Tokyo: Seishin Shobo.

———. 1983. "Sung Foreign Trade: Its Scope and Organization." In *China among Equals*, ed. Morris Rossabi, 89–115. Berkeley: University of California Press.

———. 1986. "Sodai konan toki nae gaku kou 宋代江南秋苗額考." In 中村治兵衛先生古稀紀念東洋史論叢, ed. Nakamura Jihe Sensei Koki Kinen Toyoshi Ronso Henshu Iinkai hen 中村治兵衛先生古稀記念東洋史論叢編集委員会, 303–19. Tokyo: Tosui Shobo.

———. 1988. *Sodai konan keizaishi no kenkyu* 宋代江南経済史の 研究. Tokyo: Tokyo Daigaku Toyo Bunka Kenkyujo. The Chinese translation, 2001.

———. 1991. "Sodai no shoshi, seisansuijun shitan 宋代の消費.生産水準試探." *Chugoku Shigaku* 中國史學 1(10): 147–72.

———. 2001a. *Sodai konan keizaishi no kenkyu* 宋代江南経済史の 研究. 2nd ed. Tokyo: Kyuko Shoin.

———. 2001b. "宋代の都市化お考える." *Tohogaku* 東方學 102: 1–18.

Shimasue, Kazuyasu 島居一康. 1993. *A Study of the Tax Policy of the Song Dynasty* 宋代税政史研究. Tokyo: Kyuko Shoin.

Shimizu hakushi tsuito kinnen Mindaishi ronso hensan iinkai 清水博士追悼記念明代論叢編纂委员会, ed. 1962. *Shimizu hakushi tsuito kinnen Mindaishi ronso* 清水博士追悼記念明代論叢. Tokyo: Daian.

Shuilibu huanghe shuili weiyuanhui Huanghe shuilishi shuyao bianxiezu 水利部黄河水利委員會"黃河水利史述要"編寫組. 1982. *Huanghe shuilishi shuyao* 黃河水利史. Beijing: Shuili.

Skinner, G. William. 1964. "Marketing and Social Structure in Rural China, I–II." *JAS* 24 (4): 3–43; 25 (1): 195–228.

———, ed. 1977. *The City in Late Imperial China*. Stanford: Stanford University Press.

———. 1985a. "Rural Marketing in China: Repression and Revival." *China Quarterly* 103: 393–413.

———. 1985b. "Presidential Address: The Structure of Chinese History." *JAS* 44 (2): 271–92.

Smith, John Masson, Jr. "Mongol and Nomadic Taxation." *Harvard Journal of Asiatic Studies* 30: 46–85.

Smith, Paul J. 1991. *Taxing Heaven's Storehouse: Horses, Bureaucrats, and the Destruction of the Sichuan Tea Industry, 1074–1224*. Cambridge, MA: Harvard University Press.

———, and Richard Von Glahn, eds. 2003. *The Song-Yuan-Ming Transition in Chinese History*. Cambridge, MA: Harvard University Asia Center.

So, Billy K. L (苏启龙, also see Su Jilang 苏基朗). 1985. "The System for Registration of Households and Population in the Sung Dynasty: An Institutional Analysis." *Papers on Far Eastern History* 25 (3): 1–30.

———. 2000. *Prosperity, Region and Institutions in Maritime China: The South Fukien Pattern, 946–1368*. Cambridge, MA: Harvard University Press.

Sogabe, Shizuo 曾我部静雄. 1940. *Kaiho to Koshu* 開封と杭州. Tokyo: Fuzanbo.

———. 1974. *Sodai seikeishi no kenkyu* 宋代政経史の研究. Tokyo: Yoshikawa Kobunkan.

Song, Xi 宋晞. 1979. *Songshi yanjiu luncong* 宋史研究論叢. Taipei 台北: Zhongguo wenhua xueyuan chubanbu 中國文化學院出版部.

———. 1948. "Bei Song shangye zhongxin de kaoha 北宋商業中心的考察." *Zhongyang riba. Shihuo zhoukan* 中央日報.食貨周刊 83. Reprinted in *Songshi yanjiu luncong* 宋史研究論叢, 23–29.

Song, Xuwu 宋敍五. 1997. "Qingchu zhi Qianjiajian wujia ji gongzhi de biandong 清初至乾嘉間物價及工資的變動." *Xieya xuebao* 新亞學報 45 (18): 49–98.

Song, Yan 宋岩. 1994. "Zhongguo lishishang jige chaodai jiangyu mianji de gusuan 中國歷史上幾個朝代疆域面積的估算." *Shixue lilun yanjiu* 史學理論研究, Beijing, 03: 149–50.

Sudo, Yoshiyuki 周藤吉之. 1950. "Sodai no tendosei 宋代の佃戸制—奴隷耕作との関聯に於いて." In *Rekishigaku kenkyu* 歴史学研究 (143): 20–40. Later reprinted in *Chugoku tochi seidoshi kenkyu*, 107–72.

———. 1962a. *Sodai keizaishi kenkyu* 宋代経済史研究. Tokyo: Tokyo Daigaku.

———. 1962b. "Nansou no chomanuno seisan to so no ryutsu katei 南宋の苧麻布生産とその流通過程." In *Sodai keizaishi kenkyu*, 321–62.

———. 1962c. "宋代州県の職役胥吏の發展." In *Sodai keizaishi kenkyu*, 655–816.

———. 1965a. "宋代州県の職役胥吏の發展." In *Sodai keizaishi kenkyu*, 655–816.

———. 1965b. "宋代の郷村における店.市.歩の發展." In *To So shakai keizaishi kenkyu*, 782–866.

———. 1980. *Chugoku tochi seidoshi kenkyu* 中國土地制度史研究. Tokyo: Tokyo Daigaku.

Sun, Hongsheng 孙洪升. 2001. *Tang-Song Chaye Jingji* 唐宋茶叶经济. Beijing: Shehuikexue.

Suzuki, Kimio 鈴木公雄. 1999. *Shutsudo senka no kenkyu* 出土銭貨の研究. Tokyo: Tokyo daigaku shuppankai.

Takahashi, Yoshiro 高橋芳郎. 1978. "Sōdai tenant no mibun mendai 宋代佃户の身份问题" *TOKK* 37 (3): 390–417.

———. 2002. *Sōdai Chūgoku no hōsei to shakai* 宋代中国の法制と社会. Tokyo: Kyuko Shoin."

Takaya, Yoshikazu 高谷好一. 1982. *Nettai deruta no nogyo hatten* 熱帯デルタの農業發展: ソナム.デルタの研究. Tokyo: Sobunsha.

———. 1987. *Agricultural Development of a Tropical Delta*. Trans. Peter Hawkes. Honolulu: University of Hawaii Press.

Tamura hakushi taikan kinen jigyokai 田村博士退官記念事業会, ed. 1968. *Tamura hakushi shoju Toyoshi ronso* 田村博士頌壽東洋史論叢. Kyoto: Tamura Hakushi Taikan Kinen Jigyokai.

Tan, Qixiang 谭其骧. 1955. "Huanghe yu yunhe de bianqian 黄河与运河的变迁." *Dili zhishi* 地理知识 8–9: 243–78. Beijing: Zhongguo dili xuehui.

———. 1962. "Heyi Huanghe zai Dong-Han yihou hui chuxian yige changqi anliu de jumian 何以黄河在东汉以后会出现一个长期安流的局面." *Xueshu yukan* 学术月刊 6 (2). Reprinted in *Huangheshi luncong* 黄河史论丛, 72–101.

———, ed. 1986. *Huangheshi luncong* 黄河史论丛. Shanghai: Fudan daxue.

———, ed. 1982–1987. *Zhongguo lishi ditu ji* 中國歷史地圖集. Vols. 1–8. Shanghai: Ditu.

Tang, Changru 唐長儒. 1983. "Tang Zhenguan shisinian shoushizhong de shoutian zhidu he dingzhong wenti 唐貞觀十四年手實中的受田制度和丁中問題." In *Dunhuang Tulufan wenshu chutan* 敦煌吐魯番文書初探. Wuhan: Wuhan daxue. Reprinted in 2011, *Shanju cungao sanbian* 山居存稿三編, 71–94. Beijing: Zhonghua shuju.

———. 2011a. *Shanju cungao sanbian* 山居存稿三編. Beijing: Zhonghua shuju.

———. 2011b. *Wei-Jin-Nanbeichao Sui-Tang shilun* 魏晉南北朝隋唐史論. Beijing: Zhonghua shuju.

Tang, Wenji 唐文基. 1991. *Mingdai fuyi zhidushi* 明代賦役制度史. Beijing: Zhongguo shehuikexue.

Terada, Takanobu 寺田隆信. 1968. "Minmatsu ni okeru gin no ryutsuryo ni tsuite—aruiwa Sho Chin no choho ni tsuite 明末における銀の流通量について―あるいは蔣臣の鈔法." In *Tamura hakushi shoju Toyoshi ronso* 田村博士頌壽東洋史論叢, ed. Tamura hakushi taikan kinen jigyokai 田村博士退官記念事業会. Kyoto: Tamura Hakushi Taikan Kinen Jigyokai.

———. 1972. *Sansei shounin no kenkyu* (The Study of Shansi Merchants) 山西商人の研究：明代における商人および商業资本. Kyoto: Toyoshi Kenkyukai. Also see Chinese translation (Taiyuan: Shanxi renmin, 1986)

T'ien, Jukang (also known as Tian, Rukang 田汝康). 1981. "Chêng Ho's Voyages and the Distribution of Pepper in China." *Journal of the Royal Asiatic Society* 113 (2): 186–97.

Tilly, Charles, ed. 1990. *Coercion, Capital, and European States*. Oxford, UK: Cambridge University Press.

Tilly, Richard, ed. 1999. *The State, the Financial System and Economic Modernization*. Cambridge: Cambridge University Press.

Titow, J. Z. 1972. *Winchester Yields: A Study in Medieval Agricultural Productivity*. Cambridge: Cambridge University Press.

Tong, Longfu 童隆福, ed. 1993. *Zhejiang hangyunshi* 浙江航运史(古近代部分). Beijing: Renmin jiaotong (ZSYC).

Toru, Yuki 幸徹. 1960. "北宋の過税制度." *Shien* (Journal of History) 史淵 83 (12): 81–105.

———. 1964. "北宋時代の盛時における監當官の配置狀態について." *TOKK* 23: 52–76.

———. 1993. "唐宋時代における南北商業流通証券類についての諸問題." In Kawakatsu, 233–71.

Tracy, James D., ed. 1991. *The Political Economy of Merchant Empires*. New York: Cambridge University Press.

Twitchett, Denis C. 1962. Land Tenure and the Social Order in T'ang and Sung China, inaugural lecture, November 28, 1961, School of Oriental and African Studies (London).

———. 1966. "The Tang Market System." *Asia Major* 12 (2): 202–48.

———. 1968. "Merchant, Trade and Government in the Late Tang." *Asia Major* 14 (1): 63–95.

———. 1970. *Financial Administration under the T'ang Dynasty*. 2nd edition. Cambridge: Cambridge University Press.

———. 2003. *Imperial China, 900–1800*. Cambridge, MA: Harvard University Press.

Vermeer, Edward B., ed. 1990. *Development and Decline of Fukien Province in the 17th and 18th Centuries*. New York: Brill.

Von Glahn, Richard. 1996. *Fountain of Fortune: Money and Monetary Policy in China, 1000–1700*. Berkeley: University of California Press.

———. 2003. "Towns and Temple: Urban Growth and Decline in the Lower Yangtze Delta, 1100–1400." In Smith and Von Glahn, 176–211.

Wang, Chunyu 王春瑜, and Du, Wanyan 杜婉言. 1986. *Mingdai Huanguan yu Jingji Shiliao Chutan* 明代宦官与经济史料初探. Beijing: Zhongguo Shehuikexue.

Wang, Deyi 王德毅. 1970. *Songdai zaihuang di jiuji zhengce* 宋代灾荒的救济政策. Taipei: Zhongguo xue shu zhu zuo jiang zhu wei yuan hui.

Wang, Kai 王开, and Xin Deyong 辛德勇, eds. 1997. *Shaanxi hangyunshi* 陕西航运史. Beijing: Renminjiaotong (ZSYC).

Wang, Jianying 王剑英. 1992. *Ming Zhongdu* 明中都. Beijing: Zhonghua shuju.

Wang, Lingling 王菱菱. 1988. "Songdai kuangye jingying fangshi de biange he yanjin 宋代矿冶经营方式的变革和演进." *ZJYJ* 9 (1): 45–53.

———. 1998. "Songchao zhengfu de kuangyeye kaicai zhengche 宋朝政府的矿冶业开采政策." *Journal of Hebei University (Philosophy and Social Sciences)* 河北大学学报 23 (3): 17–23.

———. 2000. "Lun Songdai kuangchanpin de jinque yu tongshang 论宋代矿产品的禁榷与通商." In *Songshi Yanjiu Lunwenji* 宋史研究论文集, ed. Qi, Xia 漆侠 and Li, Yan 李埏. Baoding: Hebei daxue.

———. 2005a. "Mingdai Lu Rong shuyuan zaji suoyin Longquan xianzhi de zuozhe ji shidai, jianlun Songdai tongkuang de kaicai yelian jishu 明代陆容'菽园杂记'所引'龙泉县志'的作者及时代——兼论宋代铜矿的开采冶炼技术." *ZJYJ* 64 (4): 96–101.

———. 2005b. *Songdai kuangyeye yanjiu* 宋代矿冶业研究. Baoding Shi: Hebei daxue.

Wang, Qian 汪籛. 1962a. "Shijishang de Sui-Tang tianmushu fei shiji gengdi mianji 史籍上的隋唐田亩数非實際耕地面積." In *Guangmin ribao* 光明日報 (August 15), later reprinted in *Wang Qian Suitangshi lungao* 汪籛隋唐史論稿, 40–45.

———. 1962b. "Shijishang de Sui-Tang tianmushu shi yingshou tianshu 史籍上的隋唐田亩数是應受田數." In *Guangmin ribao* 光明日報 (August 29), later reprinted in *Wang Qian Suitangshi lungao* 汪籛隋唐史論稿, 46–55.

———. 1962c. "Tangdi shiji gengdi mianji 唐代實際耕地面積." In *Guangmin ribao* 光明日報 (October 24), later reprinted in *Wang Qian Suitangshi lungao* 汪籛隋唐史論稿, 56–69.

———. 1981. *Wang Qian Suitangshi lungao* 汪籛隋唐史論稿. Beijing: Zhongguo shehuikexue.

Wang, Qingcheng 王庆成. 2004. "Wangqing huabei de jishi he jishiquan 晚清华北的集市和集市圈." *Jindaishi yanjiu* 近代史研究 26 (4): 2–69.

Wang, Shengduo 汪圣铎. 1985a. "Nansong liangjia xibiao 南宋粮价细表." *ZSYJ* 4 (3): 38–52.

———. 1985b. "Nan-Song gejie huizi de qiqi, shu'e ji huijia. 南宋各界会子的起讫、数额及会价." *Wenshi* 文史 25: 129–44.

———. 1987. "Beinan Song wujia bijiao yanjiu 北南宋物价比较研究." In *Songshi yanjiu lunwenji* 宋史研究论文集, eds. Deng, Guangming, and Qi, Xia, 238–54. Shijiazhuang: Hebei jiaoyu.

———. 1991. "Guanyu Songdai tihu de jige wenti 关于宋代亭户的几个问题." In Peng, Zeyi and Wang, Renyun, 445–62.

———. 1995. *Liang-Song caizheng shi* 两宋财政史. Beijing: Zhonghua shuju.

———. 2003. *Liang-Song huobi shi* 两宋货币史, Vols. 1 and 2. Beijing: Shehuikexue.

———. 2004. *Liang-Song huobi shiluo huibian* 两宋货币史料汇编. Beijing: Zhonghua shuju.

Wang, Shigang 王轼刚. 1993. *Changjiang hangyunshi* 长江水运史. Beijing: Renminjiaotong (ZSYC).

Wang, Shucai 王树才, and Xiao, Mingxue 肖明学, ed. 1988. *Hebeisheng hangyunshi* 河北省航运史. Beijing: Renminjiaotong (ZSYC).

Wang, Ting 王頲. 1983. "Yuandai tuntian kao 元代屯田攷." *Zhonghua wenshi luncong* 中華文史論叢 22 (4): 222–50.

Wang, Weiping 王卫平. 1999. *Mingqing shiqi jiangnan chengshishi yanjiu: yi shuzhou wei zhongxin* 明清時期江南城市史研究: 以苏州为中心. Beijing: Qun yan.

Wang, Wencheng 王文成. 2001. *Songdai Baiyin Huobihua Yanjiu* 宋代白银货币化研究. Kunming: Yunnan University Press.

Wang, Xiaoyan 王晓燕. 2004. *Guanying chama maoyi yanjiu* 官营茶马贸易研究. Beijing: Minzhu.

Wang, Xingya 王兴亚. 1999. "Ming-Qing shiqi beifang wusheng mianfangzhiye de xingqing yu fazhan 明清时期北方五省棉纺织业的兴起与发展." *Journal of Zhengzhou University* 郑州大学学报 32 (1): 78–85.

Wang, Xinyi 王鑫义. 2001. *Huaihe liuyu jingjikaifa shi* 淮河流域经济开发史. Hefei: Huangshan shushe.

Wang, Yeh-chien. 1973. *The Land Taxation in Imperial China, 1750–911*. Cambridge, MA: Harvard University Press.

Wang, Yongxing 王永興. 1987. *Sui-Tang Wudai jingji shiliao huibian jiaozhu* 隋唐五代經濟史料彙編校註, Volume 1, Parts 1 and 2. Beijing: Zhonghua shuju.

———. 1994. *Dunhuang jingji wenshu daolun* 敦煌經濟文書導論. Taibei: Xin wen feng chu ban gu fen you xian gong si.

Wang, Yuesheng 王跃生. 2000. *Shiba shiji zhongguo hunyin yu jiating yanjiu* 十八世纪中国婚姻与家庭研究. Beijing: Fa lü.

Wang, Yuquan 王毓铨. 1965. *Mingdai de juntun* 明代的军屯. Beijing: Zhonghua shuju.

———. 1991. "Mingchao de peihudangchai zhi 明朝的配户当差制." *ZGSY* 49 (1): 24–43.

———, Liu, Chongri 刘重日, and Zhang, Xianqing 张显清, eds. 2000. *Zhongguo jingji tongshi, Ming part* 中国经济通史明代卷, Vols. 1 and 2. Beijing: Zhongguo shehuikexue.

Wang, Yuxun 王裕巽. 1998. "Mingdai baiyin guonei kaicai yu guowai liuru shu'e shikao 明代白银 国内开采与国外流入数额试考." *China Numismatics* 中国钱币 62 (3): 18–25.

———. 2001. "Shilun Ming Zhong-hou qi de shizhu yu wujia 试论明中、后期的 私铸与物价." *China Numismatics* 中国钱币 74 (3): 18–25.

Wang, Zengyu 王曾瑜. 1983. *Songchao Bingzhi Chutan* 宋朝兵制初探. Beijing: Zhonghua shuju.

———. 1996. *Songchao Jieji Jiegou* 宋朝阶级结构. Shijiazhuang: Hebei jiao yu.

Wang, Zhenzhong 王振忠. 1996. *Jin 600 nianlai ziranzaihai yu Fuzhou shehui*. 近600年来自然灾害与福州社会. Fuzhou: Fujianrenmin.

Watabe, Tadayo 渡部忠世, and Sakurai, Yumio 櫻井由躬雄. 1984. *Chugoku Konan no inasaku bunka: sono gakusaiteki kenkyu* 中國江南の稲作文化:その學際的研究. Tokyo: Nihon Hoso Shuppan Kyokai.

Watson, Andrew, trans. 1972. "Transport in Transition: The Evolution of Traditional Shipping in China." In *Michigan Abstracts of Chinese and Japanese Works on Chinese History*, No. 3. Ann Arbor: Center for Chinese Studies, University of Michigan.

Wei, Qingyuan 韦庆远. 1961. *Mingdai huangce zhidu* 明代黄册制度. Beijing: Zhonghua shuju.

———. 1985. "Lun mingchu dui jiangnan diqu de jingji zhengce 论明初对江南地区的经济政策." *MSYL* 4 (3): 23–44.

Will, Pierre-Etienne, trans. 1990. *Bureaucracy and Famine in Eighteeth-Century China*. Stanford: Stanford University Press.

———, R. Bin Wong, James Lee, contributions by Jean Oi and Peter Perdue. 1991. *Nourish the People: The State Civilian Granary System in China, 1650–1850*. Ann Arbor: Center for Chinese Studies, University of Michigan.

Williamson, H. Raymond. 1935–1937. *Wang An Shih, a Chinese Statesman and Educationalist of the Sung Dynasty*. London: A. Probsthain.

Williamson, Jeffrey G., and Kevin H. O'Rourke. 1999. *Globalization and History: The Evolution of a Nineteenth-Century Atlantic Economy*. Cambridge, MA: MIT Press.

Wong, R. Bin. 1990. "The Development of China's Peasant Economy: A New Formulation of Old Problems." *Peasant Studies* 18 (1): 5–26.

———. 1997. *China Transformed: Historical Change and the Limits of European Experience*. Ithaca: Cornell University Press.

———, and Pierre-Etienne Will. 1991. *Nourish the People: The State Civilian Granary System in China, 1650–1850.* Ann Arbor: Center for Chinese Studies, University of Michigan.

———, and Jean-Laurent Rosenthal. 2011. *Before and Beyond Divergence: The Politics of Economic Change in China and Europe.* Cambridge, MA: Harvard University Press.

Wu, Chengming 吳承明. 1983a. "Lun Qingdai qianqi woguo guoneishichang 论清代前期我国国内市场." *LSYJ* 30(1): 96–106. Reprinted with revisons in *Zhongguo de xiandaihua* 中国的现代化, 144–66. Beijing: Sanlian shudian.

———.1983b. "Lun Mingdai guonei shichang he shangrenziben 论明代国内市场和商人资本." In *Zhongguo shehuikexueyuan jingjiyanjiusuo jikan* 中国社会科学院经济研究所集刊, Vol. 5. Reprinted with revisions in *Zhongguo de xiandaihua, shechang yu shehui* 中国的现代化：市场与社会, 111–43. Beijing: Sanlian shudian.

———. 1988. "Xiandaihua yu zhongguo shiliu,shiqi shiji de xiandaihua yinsu 现代化與中國十六，十七世紀的現代化因素." *ZJYJ* 52 (4): 3–15.

———. 1995. "Shiliu yu shiqi shiji de zhongguo shichang16 与17世纪的中国市场." In *Huozhi: Shangye yu shichangyanjiu* 货殖：商业与市场研究, Vol. 1, ed. Zhongguo shangyeshi xuehui 中国商业史学会. Beijing: Zhongguo caizheng jingji. Reprinted in *Wu Chengming Ji*, 140–76.

———. 1999. "Shiba yu shijiu shiji shangbanye de zhongguo shichang18 与19世纪上半叶的中国市场." In *Huozhi: Shangye yu shichangyanjiu* 货殖：商业与市场研究, Vol. 3, ed. Zhongguo shangyeshi xuehui 中国商业史学会. Beijing: Zhongguo caizheng jingji. Reprinted in *Wu Chengming Ji*, 177–228.

———. 2001. *Zhongguo de xiandaihua, shichangyushehui* 中国的现代化：市场与社会. Beijing: Sanlian shudian.

———. 2002. *Wu Chengming Ji* 吳承明集. Beijing: Zhongguo shehuikexue.

Wu, Dange 伍丹戈. 1979. "Mingdai de guantian he mintian 明代的官田和民田." *ZHWL* 9 (1): 119–63.

———. 1982. *Mingdai tudi zhidu he fuyi zhidu de fazhan* 明代土地制度和赋役制度的发展. Fuzhou: Fujian renmin.

———. 1995. "Mingdai Zhouchen fuyi gaige de zuoyong he yingxiang 明代周忱赋役改革的作用和影响." *MSYL* 4 (3): 1–22.

Wu, Han 吳晗. 1937. "Mingdai de junbing 明代的军兵." *Zhongguo shehui jingjishi jikan* 中國社會經濟史集刊 2 (2). Reprinted in *Dushi zhaji* 读史札记, 92–141. Beijing: Sanlian shudian.

———. 1949. *Zhu Yuanzhang zhuan* 朱元璋传. 2nd edition. Beijing: Zhonghua shuju.

———. 1956. *Dushi zhaji* 读史札记. Beijing: Sanlian shudian.

———. 1965. *Zhu Yuanzhang zhuan* 朱元璋传. Beijing: Sanlian shudian.

Wu, Hongqi 吳宏岐. 1997. *Yuandai nongyedili* 元代農業地理. Xi'an: Xi'an ditu.

Wu, Hui 吳慧. 1985. *Zhongguo lidai liangshi muchan yanjiu* 中国历代粮食亩产研究. Beijing: Nongye.

———. 1990. "Mingqing(qianqi) caizheng jiegouxing bianhua de jiliang fenxi 明清(前期) 财政結構性變化的計量分析." *ZSYJ* 9 (3): 39–56.

———. 1998. "Lishishang liangshi shangpinlyu shangpinliang chegu: yi Song, Ming, Qing weili, 歷史上糧食商品率商品量測估：以宋明清为例." *ZJYJ* 52 (4): 16–36.

Wu, Jianguo 武建國. 1992. *Juntianzhi yanjiu* 均田制研究. Kunming: Yunnan renmin.

Wu, Jihua 吳緝華. 1961. *Mingdai haiyun ji yunhe de yanjiu* 明代海运及运河的研究. Taipei: Zhongyang Yanjiuyuan Lishi Yuyan Yanjiusuo.

Wu, Liangkai 吳量愷. 1983. "Qing qianqi nongye gugong de gongjia 清前期农业雇工的工价." *ZSYJ* 2 (5): 17–30.

Wu, Renan 吳仁安. 1997. *Mingqing Shiqi Shanghai Diqu de Zhuxingwangzu* 明清时期上海地区的著姓望族. Shanghai: Shanghai renmin.

Wu, Songdi 吳松弟. 1993a. *Beifang yimin yu nansong shehui bianqian* 北方移民與南宋社會變遷. Taipei: Wen jin.

———. 1993b. "Huang-Huai-Hai diqu lishishiqi renkou fenbu de chubu yanjiu 黄淮海平原历史时期人口分布的初步研究." *LSDL* 13 (11): 155–168.

———. 2000. *Zhongguo Renkoushi* 中国人口史. v.4, *Liao Song Jin Yuan Shiqi* 辽宋金元时期. Shanghai: Fudan daxue.

———. 2008. *Nan-Song renkou shi* 南宋人口史. Shanghai: Shanghai guji.

Wuhan shuili dianli xueyuan Zhongguo shuili shigao 武漢水利電力學院 "中國水利史稿" 編寫組. 1979–89. *Zhongguo shuili shigao* 中國水利史稿. 3 vols. Beijing: Shuili dianli.

Xi, Longfei 席龙飞. 2000. *Zhongguo Zhaochuan Shi* 中国造船史. Wuhan: Hubei jiaoyu.

———, Yang Xi 杨熺, and Tang Xiren 唐锡仁. 2004. *Zhongguo Kexue Jishu Shi Jiaotongjuan* 中国科学技术史.交通卷. Beijing: Kexue.

Xia, Xiangrong 夏湘蓉, Li Zhongjun 李仲均, and Wang Genyuan 王根元. 1980. *Zhongguo Gudai Kuangye Kaifashi* 中国古代矿业开发史. Beijing: Dizhi.

Xiao, Lijun 肖立军. 2001. *Mingdai zhonghouqi jiubian bingzhi yanjiu* 明代中后期九边兵制研究. Changchun: Jilin renmin.

Xie, Yuanlu 谢元鲁. 1995. "Changjiangliuyu jiaotong yu jingjigeju de lishibianqian 长江流域交通与经济格局的历史变迁". In Zhongguo lishidili luncong 中国历史地理论丛, No. 1, 27–44.

Xin, Deyong 辛德勇. 1989a. "Han-Tang qijian Chang'an fujunde shuilu jiaotong 汉唐期间长安附近的水路交通." *Zhongguo lishidili luncong* 中国历史地理论丛 3 (1). Reprinted in 1996, *Gudai jiaotong yu dili wenxianyanjiu* 古代交通与地理文献研究, 166–76. Beijing: Zhonghua shuju.

———. 1989b. "Chang'ancheng xiqi yu fazhan de jiaotong jichu 长安城兴起与发展的交通基础." *Zhongguo lishidili luncong* 中国历史地理论丛 3 (2). Reprinted in 1996, *Gudai jiaotong yu dili wenxianyanjiu* 古代交通与地理文献研究, 177–85. Beijing: Zhonghua shuju.

———. 1996. *Gudai jiaotong yu dili wenxian yanjiu* 古代交通与地理文献研究. Beijing: Zhonghua shuju.

Xu, Dixin 许涤新, and Wu, Chengming 吴承明, ed. 1985. *Zhongguo Zibenzhuyi de Mengya, Zhongguo Zibenzhuyi Fazhanshi* 中国资本主义的萌芽—中国资本主义发展史. Beijing: Renmin.

———. 2000. *Chinese Capitalism, 1522–1840*. Houndmills, Basingstoke, Hampshire: Macmillan Press; New York: St. Martin's.

Xu, Hong 徐泓. 1982. "Ming Hongwu niande renkou yixi 明洪武年间的人口移徙." In *Lishi yu Zhongguo shehuibianqian yantaohui lunwenji* 历史与中国社会变迁研讨会论文集. Taipei: Zhongyang Yanjiuyuan Sanminzhuyi Yanjiusuo, 235–94.

Xu, Tan 许檀. 1992. "Ming-Qing shiqi yunhe de shangpin liutong 明清时期运河的商品流." *Lishi dang'an* 历史档案 12 (1): 80–85.

———. 1997. "Ming-Qing shiqi nongchun jishi de fazhan 明清时期农村集市的发展." *ZJYJ* 45 (2): 21–41.

———. 1998a. *Ming-Qing shiqi Shangdon Shangpin Jingji de Fazhan* 明清时期山东商品经济的发展. Beijing: Zhongguo Shehuikexue.

———. 1998b. "Ming-Qing shiqi jiangxi de shangye chengzhen 明清时期江西的商业城镇." *ZJYJ* 26 (3): 106–20.

———. 1999a. "Qingdai qianqi liutong geju de bianhua 清代前期流通格局的变化." *Qingshi Yanjiu* 清史研究 9 (3): 1–13.

———. 1999b. "Qingdai qianqi de jiujiangguan jiqi shangpin liutong 清代前期的九江关及其商品流通." *Lishi dang'an* 历史档案 73 (1): 86–91.

———. 2000. "Ming-Qing shiqi chengxiang shichang wangluo tixi de xingcheng ji yiyi 明清时期城乡网络体系的形成及意义." *ZGSK* 3 (3): 191–202.

———. 2002. "Ming-Qing shiqi zhongguo jingji fazhan guiji tantao 明清时期中国经济发展轨迹探讨." *Tianjin Shifan Daxue Xuebao* 天津师范大学学报 161 (2): 43–47.

———. 2004. "Qingdai qianzhongqi dongbei de yanhaimaoyi yu yingkou de xingqi 清代前中期东北的沿海贸易与营口的兴起." *Fujian shifan daxue xuebao* 福建师范大学学报 124 (1): 6–11.

Xu, Xinwu 徐新吾. 1992. *Jiangnan Tubushi* 江南土布史. Shanghai: Shanghai shehuikexuyuan.

Yabuuchi, Kiyoshi 藪内清, ed. 1967. *So-Gen jidai no kagaku gijutsushi* 宋元時代の科学技術史論集. Kyoto: Kyoto Daigaku Jinbun Kagaku Kenkyujo.

———, and Yoshida Mitsukuni 吉田光邦, eds. 1970. *Minshi jidai no kagaku gijutsushi* 明清時代の科学技術史論集. Kyoto: Kyoto Daigaku Jinbun Kagaku Kenkyujo.

Yamada, Katsuyoshi 山田勝芳. 1993. *Shin-Kan zaisei shunyu no kenkyu* 秦漢財政収入の研究. Tokyo: Kyuko Shoin.

Yamamura, Kozo. 1998. "From Coins to Rice: Hypothesis on the Kandaka and Kokudaka Systems." *Journal of Japanese Studies* 14 (2): 341–67.

———, and Kamiki, Tetsuo. 1983. "Silver Mines and Sung Coins: A Monetary History of Medieval and Modern Japan in International Perspective." In *Precious Metals in the Late Medieval and Early Modern Worlds*, ed. J. F. Richards, 329–62. Durham, NC: Carolina Academic Press.

Yamane, Yukio 山根幸夫. 1960. "Min-shin jidai Kahoku ni okeru teiki-ichi 明清時代華北における定期市." *Tokyo joshi daigaku shiron* 東京女子大學史論 8 (11): 493–504.

———. "Min-shi sho no Kahoku no shishu to shinshi, gomin 明.清初の華北の市集と紳士.豪民." In *Nakayama Hachiro kyojukinen Min-Shin shi ronso* 中山八郎教授頌壽記念明清史論叢, ed. Min-Shin shi ronso kankokai, 303–32. Tokyo: Ryogen shoten.

———. 1995. *Min Shi Kahoku teikishi no kenkyu* 明清華北定期市の研究. Tokyo: Kyuko Shoin.

Yamawaki, Teijiro 山脇悌二郎. 1964. *Nagasaki no Tojin Boeki* 長崎の唐人貿易. Tokyo.

Yan, Gengwang 嚴耕望. 1996. "*Yuanhezhi huji yu shiji hushu zhi bikan* 《元和志》戶籍與實際戶數之比勘." *Zhongyang Yanjiuyuan Lishiyuyan Yanjiusuo Jikan* 中央研究院歷史語言研究所集刊 67 (1): 1–42.

Yanagida, Setsuko 柳田節子. 1986. *So-Gen Shakai Keizaishi Kenkyu* 宋元社會経済史研究. Tokyo: Sobunsha.

———. 1995. *So Gen Gosonsei no Kenkyu* 宋元鄉村制の研究. Tokyo: Sobunsha.

Yang, Guoqing 杨国庆. 2002. "Ming Nanjing chengqiang zhucheng renyuan goucheng ji yonggongliang chutan 明南京城墙筑城人员及用工量初探." *Dongnan Wenhua* 东南文化 153 (1): 37–44.

Yang, Jiping 楊際平. 1996. "Tangdai chibu muzhi muchan xiaoyi 唐代尺步畝制畝產小議." *ZSYJ* 15 (2): 32–44.

———. 1998. "Cong Donghaijun jibu kan Handai de muzhi muchan yu Han-Wei tianzue 從東海郡集簿看漢代的畝制漢魏田租額." *ZJYJ* 17 (2): 74–80.

———. 2000. "Zaitan Handai de muzhi muchan 再談漢代的畝制畝產." *LSYJ* 19 (2): 39–47.

———2001a. "Qin-Han nongye: jinggeng xizuo yihuo cufang gengzuo 秦漢農業：精耕細作抑或粗放耕作." *ZSYJ* 272 (4): 22–32.

———. 2001b. "Shilun Qin-Han tienongju de tuiguang chengdu 試論秦漢鉄農具的推廣程度." *ZSYJ* 20 (2): 69–77.

Yang, Jiping 楊際平. 2003. *Beichao Sui-Tang juntianzhi xintan* 北朝隋唐均田制新探. Changsha: Yuelu shushe.

Yang, Lien-sheng. 1952. *Money and Credit in China: A Short History*. Cambridge: Harvard University Press.

Yang, Shengxin 杨绳信. 1984. "Cong Jishazang keyin kan Song-Yuan yinshua gongren de jige wenti 从《碛砂藏》刻印看宋元印刷工人的几个問題." *ZHWL* 29 (1): 41–58.

Yang, Zhengtai 杨正泰. 1994. *Mingdai yizhan kao* 明代驿站考. Shanghai: Shanghai guji.

Ye, Dehui 叶德辉. 1999. *Shulin qinghua, shulin yuhua* 书林清话,书林余话. Changsha: Yuelu shushe.

Ye, Tan 叶坦. 1991. *Fuguo fumin lun: lizuyu songdai de kaocha* 富国富民论:立足于宋代的考察. Beijing: Beijing.

Ye, Xian'en 叶显恩, ed. 1989. *Guangdong hangyun shi, the pre-industrial time* 广东航运史(古代部分). Beijing: ZSYCRenminjiaotong.

———, and Tan, Lihua 谭棣华. 1984. "Ming-Qing Zhujiang sanjiaozhou nongye shangyehua yu xushi de fazhan 明清珠江三角洲农业商业化与墟市的发展." *Guangdong shehui kexue* 广东社会科学 1 (2): 73–91.

Ye, Xiaoxin 叶孝信, ed. 1993. *Zhongguo minfa shi* 中国民法史. Shanghai: Shanghai renmin.

———. 2002. *Zhongguo fazhishi* 中国法制史. Shanghai: Fudan daxue.

Yin, Junke 尹钧科. 1993. "Mingdai Beijing jiaoqu cunluo de fazhan 明代北京郊区村落的发展." *LSDL* 13 (11): 233–45.

Yin, Lingling 尹玲玲. 2008. *Ming-Qing lianghupingyuan de huanjingbianqian yu shehuiyingdui* 明清两湖平原的环境变迁与社会应对. Shangahi: Shangahi renmin.

Yoshida, Mitsukuni 吉田光邦. 1966. "Sodai no tetsu ni tsuite 宋代の鐵について." *TOKK* 24 (4). Reprinted in *Chgoku kagaku gijutsushi ronshu*, 353–71.

———. 1972. "Sodai no gijutsu 宋代の技術." In *So-Gen jidai no kagaku gijutsushi*. Reprinted in *Chgoku kagaku gijutsushi ronshu*, 287–371.

———. 1970. "景德鎮の陶瓷生産と貿易." In *Minshi jidai no kagaku gijutsushi* 明清時代の科学技術史論集, ed. 藪內清 Yoshida and Mitsukuni 吉田光邦. Kyoto: Kyoto Daigaku Jinbun Kagaku Kenkyujo. Reprinted in *Chgoku kagaku gijutsushi ronshu*, 489–567.

———. 1972. *Chgoku kagaku gijutsushi ronshu* 中国科学技術史論集. Tokyo: NHK.

Yoshioka, Yoshinobu 吉岡義信. 1978. *Sodai Koga shi kenkyu* 宋代黄河史研究. Tokyo: Ochanomizu Shobo.

You, Xiuling 游修齡. 1999a. "Fangzhi zai nongye kexueshi shang de yiyi 方志在農業科學史上的意義." In *Nongshi yanjiu wenji* 农史研究文集, 197–208. Beijing: Zhongguo nongye.

———. 1999b. *Nongshi yanjiu wenji* 農史研究文集. Beijing: Zhongguo nongye.

———, and Zeng, Xiongsheng 曾雄生. 2010. *Zhongguo daozuo wenhuashi* 中國稻作文化. Shanghai: Shanghai renmin.

Yu, Yuezu 郁越祖. 1988. "Guanyu Songdai jianzhizhen de jige lishidili wenti 关于宋代建制镇的几个历史地理问题." *LSDL* 8 (6): 94–125.

Yu, Zhijia 于志嘉. 1987. *Mingdai jinhu shixi zhidu* 明代军户世袭制度. Taipei: Xuesheng shuju.

———. 2010. *Weisuo, junhu yu junyi* 衛所、軍戶與軍役——以明清江西地區為中心的研. Beijing: Beijingdaxue chubanshe.

Yuan, Liangyi 袁良义. 1995. *Qing Yitiao bianfa* 清一条鞭法. Beijing: Beijing University Press.

Zhang, Bincun 張彬村. 1984. "Shiliu shiji zhoushanqundao de zousi maoyi 十六世紀舟山群島的走私貿易." *ZHFL* 1 (1): 71–96.

Zhang, Dexin 张德信, and Lin Jinshu 林金树. 1987. "Mingchu juntun shue de lishi kaocha 明初军屯数额的历史考察." *ZGSK* 47 (5): 187–206.

Zhang, Fang 張芳. 2009. *Zhongguo gudai guangai gongcheng jishushi* 中國古代灌溉工程技術史. Taiyuan: Shanxi jiaoyu.

Zhang, Gong 張弓. 1986. *Tangchao cangbing zhidu chutan* 唐代倉廩制度初探. Beijing: Zhonghua shuju.

Zhang, Haiying 张海瀛. 1993. *Zhang Juzheng gai ge yu Shanxi Wanli qing zhang yan jiu* 张居正改革与山西万历清丈研究. Taiyuan: Shanxi renmin.

Zhang, Jianguang 张剑光. 2003. *Tang Wudai jiangnan gongshangye buju yanjiu* 唐五代江南工商業佈局研究. Nanjing: Jiangsu guji.

Zhang, Jinkui 張金奎. 2007. *Mingdai weisuo junhu yanjiu* 明代軍戶衛所研究. Beijing: Zhonghua shuju.

Zhang, Rongqiang 張榮強. 2010. *Han-Tang jizhang zhidu yanjiu* 漢唐籍帳制度研究. Beijing: Shangwu.

Zhang, Shengcheng 张圣城. 1989. *Henan hangyunshi* 河南航运史. Beijing: Renminjiaotong (ZSYC).

Zhang, Tingmao 张廷茂. 2004. "Guanyu shiliushiqi shiji chu huashang zai dongnanya huodong de xifang wenxian 关于十六十七世纪初华商在东南亚活动的西方文献." *ZGSY* 102 (2): 139–51.

Zhang, Wen 张文. 2001. *Songchao shehui jiuji yanjiu* 宋朝社会救济研究. Chongqing: Xinan shida.

Zhang, Youyi 章有义. 1984. *Ming-Qing Huizhou tudiguanxi yanjiu* 明清徽州土地关系研究. Beijing: Zhongguo Shehuikexue.

———. 1990. "Guanyu zhongguo jindai nongye shengchan jiliang yanjiu de jize gengju 关于中国近代农业生产计量研究的几则根据." *ZSYJ* 9 (2): 67–71.

Zhang, Zexian 張澤咸. 2003. *Han-Jin-Tang shiqi nongye* 漢晉唐時期農業. 2 vols. Beijing: Zhongguo shehuikexue.

———, and Guo, Songyi. 1997. *Zhongguo hangyun shi* 中國航運史. Taipei: Wenjin.

Zhao, Gang 趙岡 (also see Chao, Kang) and Chen, Zhongyi 陳鐘毅. 1982. *Zhongguo tudi zhidushi* 中國土地制度史. Taipei: Lianjing.

———. 1986. *Zhongguo jingji zhidu shilun* 中國經濟制度史論. Taipei: Lianjing.

———. 1989. *Zhongguo nongye jingjishi* 中國農業經濟史. Taipei: Youshi.

———, and Liu, Yongcheng 劉永成, Wu Hui, et al. 1995. *Qingdai liangshi muchanliang yanjiu* 清代糧食畝產量研究. Beijing: Zhongguo nongye.

Zhao, Jing 赵靖. 1986. *Zhongguo gudai jingji sixiang jianghua* 中國古代經濟思想講話. Beijing: Renmin.

Zhao, Yashu 趙雅書. 1972. "Songdai cansiye de dili fenbu 宋代蠶絲業的地理分佈." *Shiyuan* 史原 3: 65–94.

———. 1976. "Songdai nongjia jingying zi cansiye 宋代農家經營之蠶絲業." *Bulletin of the Department of History* 臺大歷史學報 3 (5): 119–29.

Zheng, Kecheng 郑克晟. 1988. *Mingdai zhengzheng tanyuan* 明代政争探源. Tianjin: Tianjin guji.

———. 2001. "Mingchu Jiangnan dizhu de shuailuo yu beifang dizhu de xingqi 明初江南地主的衰落与北方地主的兴起." *Beijing Shifandaxue Xubao* 北京师范大学学报 46 (5): 49–58.

Zheng He xiaxiyang 600 zhounian jinian huodong choubei lingdaoxiaozhu. 2005. *Zheng He xiaxiyang yanjiu wenxuan* 鄭和下西洋研究文選, 1905–2005. Beijing: Haiyang.

Zheng, Shaobin 郑少斌, ed. 1994. *Wuhan gangshi* 武汉港史. Beijing: Renmin jiaotong.

Zheng, Tianting 郑天挺. 1960. "Guanyu Xu Yikui 'Zhonggongdui' 关于徐一夔'织工对'." In *Zhongguo Zibenzhuyi Mengya Wenti Taolunji Xubian* 中国资本主义萌芽问题讨论集续编, 520–43. Beijing: Sanlian shudian.

Zheng, Xuemeng 郑学檬. 2003. *Zhongguo gudai jingji zhongxin nanyi he Tangsong jiangnan jingji yanjiu* 中国古代经济重心南移和唐宋江南经济研究. Changsha: Yuelu shushe.

Zheng, Yijun 鄭一鈞. 1985. *Lun Zheng He xia xiyang* 論鄭和下西洋. Beijing: Haiyang.

Zhongguo gudai meitan kaifashi bianxiezu "中国古代煤炭开发史" 编写组. 1986. *Zhongguo gudai meitan kaifashi* 中国古代煤炭开发史. Beijing: Meitan gongye.

Zhongguo guisuanyan xuehui zhubian 中国硅酸盐学会主编 (主编小组: 冯先铭, 安志敏, 安金槐, 朱伯谦, 汪庆正). 1982. *Zhongguo taocishi* 中国陶瓷史. Beijing: Wenwu.

Zhongyang Yanjiuyuan Lishi Yuyan Yanjiusuo 中央研究院歷史語言研究所. 1999. *Zhongguo jinshi jiazhu yu shehui xueshu yantaohui lunwenji* 中國近世家族與社會學術研討會論文集. Taipei: Zhongyang Yanjiuyuan Lishi Yuyan Yanjiusuo.

Zhou, Baozhu 周宝珠. 1999. *Songdai Dongjing yanjiu* 宋代东京研究. Kaifeng: Henan daxue.

Zhou, Liangxiao 周良霄. 1957. "Mingdai Susong diqu de guantian yu zhongfu wenti 明代苏松地区的官田与重赋问题." *LSYJ* 4 (10): 63–75.

———, and Gu, Juying 顾菊英. 2003. *Yuanshi* 元史. Shanghai: Shanghai renmin.

Zhou, Shengchun 周生春. 1995. "Shilun Songdai Jiangnan shuilitian de kaifa he dizhu suoyouzhi de tedian 試論宋代江南水利田的開發和地主所有制的特點." *ZGNS* 14 (3): 1–11.

———. 2006. "Song-Yuan jiangzhe zhujun daomi danchan shitan 宋元江浙諸郡稻米單產試探." *Zhongguo shehui jingjishi luncong* 中國社會經濟史論叢, 263–77. Beijing: Zhongguo shehuikexue.

Zhou, Yumin 周育民. 2000. *Wanqing caizheng yu shehui bianqian* 晚清财政与社会变迁. Shanghai: Shanghai renmin.

Zhu, Chongsheng 朱重聖. 1985. *Bei Song cha zhi shengchan yu jingying* 北宋茶之生產與經營. Taipei: Taiwan xuesheng shuju.

Zhu, Kezhen 竺可楨. 1964. "論我國氣候的幾個特點及其與糧食作物生產的關係." *Acta Geographica Sinica* 地理學報 1 (1): 1–13. Reprinted in *Zhu Kezhen wenji*, 455–65.

———. 1973. "中國近五千年來氣候變遷的初步研究." *Science in China* 中國科學 16 (2): 168–189. Reprinted in *Zhu Kezhen wenji*, 475–98.

———. 1979. *Zhu Kezhen wenji* 竺可楨文集. Beijing: Kexue.

Zhu, Shaohou 朱绍侯.2008. *Jungong juezhi kaolun* 军功爵制攷論. Beijing: Shangwu.

Zhu, Xinyu 朱新予, ed. 1992. *Zhongguo Sichoushi* 中国丝绸史. Beijing: Fang zhi gong ye.

Zou, Yilin 邹逸麟. 1978. "Lun Dingtao de xingshuai yu gudai zhongyuan shuiyun jiaotong de bianqian 论定陶的兴衰与古代中原水运交通的变迁." *ZHWL* 17 (8): 191–207.

———. 1981. "Shandong yunhe lishi dili wenti chutan 山东运河历史地理问题初探." *LSDL* 1: 80–98.

———. 1986. "Huanghe xiayou hedao bianqian jiqi yingxiang gaishu 黄河下游河道变迁及其影响概述." In *Huangheshi luncong* 黄河史论丛, ed. Tan, Qixiang 谭其骧, 221–42. Shanghai: Fudan daxue.

———. 1988. "Huaihe xiayou nanbei yunkou bianqian he chengzhen xingshuai 黄河下游南北运口变迁和城镇兴衰." *LSDL* 8 (6): 57–72.

———, ed. 1997. *Huang-Huai-Hai pingyuan lishidili* 黄淮海历史地理. Hefei: Anhui jiaoyu.

———. 2005. *Chunlu shidi lungao* 椿廬史地論稿. Tianjin: Tianjin guji.

Index